LORD ROBERTS' VALET

IN DECEMBER 2011, ABI AUSTEN ARRIVED IN KANDAHAR, AFGHANISTAN.

FOR THE NEXT 1000 DAYS, SHE ACTED AS A KEY ADVISOR TO THE GREATEST MILITARY ADVENTURE OF OUR GENERATION. THIS BOOK IS THE TRUE STORY OF THOSE YEARS.

WELCOME TO THE MADNESS.

'*Lord Roberts' Valet* is a no-bullshit description of modern-day soldiering. Most only ever dream of the moment—*Lord Roberts'* is the next best thing to being there.' — General Patrick Kidd

ALSO BY ABIGAIL AUSTEN

Sugar and Spice: A Memoir – coming 2016

LORD ROBERTS' VALET

AFGHANISTAN KANDAHAR WAR

THE TRUE STORY OF THREE YEARS IN THE SUCK

ABIGAIL AUSTEN

All text, except where credited, and images
Copyright © 2015 Abigail Austen

All rights reserved.

The right of Abigail Austen to be identified as the Author of this Work has been asserted by her in accordance with the Copyright, Designs and Patent Acts 1988.

ISBN (print): 1517204836
ISBN-13 (print): 978-1517204839

Cover photo: Abigail Austen

Print Formatting: By Your Side Self-Publishing
www.ByYourSideSelfPub.com

No part of this publication may be reproduced or transmitted in any means or by any means, electronically or mechanically, including photocopying, recording or any information storage or retrieval system, without the written permission in advance from the author.

DEDICATION

Without Debs, I would never have found the way back.

For all that was and is no longer.

TABLE OF CONTENTS

Foreword	1
Enter the Madhouse	2
What the Fuck?	4
Colly-Wobble Blues	8
Kabul Interlude	22
Girding the Loins	34
Bobbie and Burrows	45
Out of the Frying Pan	71
Coordinates; 31.30.26.0N 65.51.1.0E	78
FIDO	85
Boom-Bang-a-Bang	100
The Steenberger Generation	106
Veni, Vidi, Deus Vicit	118
The 325TH	124
Boardwalk Blues	131
Unravelling the Ball of String	137
Day Two: FIDO	174
An Afghan Family	178
Spinning Up the Wheels	187
Sex in the Shitty	195
Becoming Lord Roberts' Valet	207
Bales	209
Road to Nowhere	214
The Prism Changes	227
Air Afghan	231
On the Hamster Wheel	239
Contract Crazy	246
A New Future	255
Candy Stripe Madness	265
New Chapters	287
Soak	297
Inside Shooter	299
Three Becomes Four	307
Upping the Ante	311
Aiming for the Sun	321
The Class of 2012	326
PK and the Lion	333
Days of Wine and Roses	343
Anja	365

Last Post	368
Last Encore	372
Watching from Afar	377
Appendixes	385
Why I Love America	386
Joint Influence Operations Fusion Cell Pitch	394
Photos	399
Author's Note	407
About the Author	408

FOREWORD

Afghanistan. Kandahar. War.

This isn't a history book. It's too personal for that. In any case, I write 'fuck' far too many times for a teacher to ever approve.

This is a personal polemic, an external expression of an internal anger based on personal experience. I lived all of it. This is exactly how I remember the years.

Since the Twin Towers fell, I have spent over six years of my life overseas on combat operations, fighting this never-ending conflict. The most productive years of my working life have been spent at war.

Everything that is described here really happened. All the madness, every last drop. A few timelines are telescoped, some names and characters are amalgams, to help the narrative flow. All the generals and all the Afghans are real people and I use their real names.

So this isn't 'inspired by real events'.

It is all real.

And it was fucking crazy.

ENTER THE MADHOUSE

I had a home in Kandahar.

It wasn't much, just a room in a brick barrack block, shared with forty other soldiers. We had three showers, three wash hand basins and three toilets between us.

My home was on the first floor, up a communal flight of stairs, through a key-coded glass entrance, second door on the left. I had tinsel stencils of high-heeled shoes on the door, and a sign that read; 'ladies, keep your business quiet.' Inside, my home measured twelve feet by eight. I had a bed, a chair, a desk and two wardrobes. The beige walls were covered in old movie posters—of Bogart and Bacall, Burton and Taylor. I tacked fairy lights to the ceiling and had a flower-patterned throw on the bed.

It was my womb from the world outside. I had it all to myself. Outside, in the war, the noise and the bluster was just one big hurricane. Like Dorothy, you just clung on to the flotsam and let the wind take you off to Oz.

Most on my camp lived four to a room. Further forward, in more remote locations, as I had lived on earlier tours, folks slept on camp cots, or the ground.

I counted myself very lucky.

At night, I wore earplugs to deaden the noise of the fighter jets taking off just a couple of hundred feet away. I kept my body armour and helmet at the end of my bed, in case of attack.

I wore it often.

Kandahar was my home for three straight years. They were the happiest years of my life. 1,000 days that will never come again.

I loved it all, every second.

Kandahar was, for a time, the most dangerous place on earth. Kandahar was its own, special reality, a bubble of madness—the beating heart of the war. My home was slap-bang in the middle of it all. Nothing between me and the bad guys except a few strands of barbed wire and a load of armed and dangerous soldiers.

I lived there for four months at a time, working seven days a week, immersed in the craziness. Kandahar was like grabbing a big bag full of glue and inhaling. The rush just blew your mind.

I'd take two weeks off. Fourteen days of mad, drunken debauchery. I'd pick a place in the world I wanted to see, and just went there, first class. I'd find the best hotel, and drink the mini-bar dry.

I'd fly back to the maelstrom for four more months, plugged into the mains: 240 volts, mainlined into my nervous system. Sixteen weeks of living the warrior monk, then two weeks of anything I wanted. It didn't matter what it cost, when the clock was ticking to go back. That day might well be my last day. Enjoy it while you can. Fuck it, *carpe diem*, sister....

In Kandahar, I counted myself lucky to have a hot shower, and I lived in five star luxury hotels when I was not. I earned a queen's ransom for risking my life when I was in the suck—and spent like a queen when I was not. There was nothing to buy when I was there, and enough money in the bank to buy anything I wanted when I unplugged.

When I was in Kandahar, I dreamed of being back in the world. When I was in the world, I longed to be back in Kandahar.

One crazy ride.

My life was a rollercoaster of adrenalin, hooked onto an addict's drip of danger. I lived at the tip of the spear of the greatest and most diverse expeditionary adventure the world has seen in seventy years. What I did on a daily basis affected everything from international politics to my own personal survival. Stuff I did really mattered there, more than anything I had ever done in my life.

I was a true believer: in Afghanistan, in the mission, in my friends. There was nothing more important, anywhere. Back in the world, I smashed it because it was so fucking beige.

Every emotion registered in Afghanistan. Colours were more intense, smells more profound. I laughed more, cried more and loved more, with an unyielding and intense passion. I met people who came to know me better than my mother and father: as I did them. I grew closer to God than I have ever been, and I saw more evil than any human should ever see.

Now it is over, I think of it every day. I have become the war veteran who hates war but longs for its drumbeat.

I am fifty.

I doubt I will ever do anything as fulfilling ever again. It is depressing being back in the world. It is just so... boring.

I miss war.

WHAT THE FUCK?

My marvellous adventure was one of those co-incidences of fate. I've always been a creature of fancy. My life has been an orgasmatron of personal indulgence. I have no family, no children, nothing to hold me back from the maelstrom. Wherever I have wanted to go, I've found a way to go.

Afghanistan is my eighth war. I cannot forget any of them.

I'd been to the 'Stan before, in a previous incarnation as a journalist. I went to Pakistan and the border during the mujahideen days against the Soviets. In the '90's, I'd gone back for a madcap journey during the civil war. Hitching a lift in Peshawar, we'd driven up over the Khyber Pass, then a giddying, terrifying journey along the Kabul Pass, to witness a city destroying itself. We'd watched the tanks firing over open sights, the buildings crumble, the tracer fly, the desperate souls scramble.

We camped out in the deserted international terminal at the airport, surrounded by wrecked Soviet MiG fighters, watching the rounds hit TV hill, before catching a mercy flight with the UN, up to Mazar-E-Sharif. There, I had witnessed tens of thousands, the diaspora of war, living in huge, makeshift refugee camps, the tragedy of war, forgotten by the world.

Later, after the Twin Towers came down, I'd served multiple tours in Afghan with the British army, swanning about with big, bearded men who did bad things to bad people. We'd travelled the country in a blizzard of armoured limousines, huge jets and ass-kicking helicopters.

Afghanistan had always been a crazy ride. Lead me to the trough. Afghanistan was life.

In 2007, I'd been medevacked back to the UK from Kunduz, in the North, after one adventure too many. My army career was over, and I joined the Scottish police.

The cops meant well, I suppose, but police service is culturally inert. Advancement is earned through time served: not by talent, enthusiasm or imagination. Until you've clocked on, coppering is all about just chugging away, waiting your turn.

It's fucking boring.

At interview, the board told me they liked my history of command and leadership. They then warned me that the job might not be enough for me.

I didn't listen.

It didn't take long for me to figure out it would be six years, even doing well, to make sergeant, the lowest level of promotion, another six to make inspector, the second. At a push, I'd make chief inspector by the fifteen-year mark. I'd left the army in the equivalent rank.

I'd have to spend fifteen years, just to get back to where I had already been.

I was forty-four when I joined the service. Even doing well, I'd make the rank I had already held right before I'd be forced to quit. I'd already been on the journey they were offering. And that previous journey had been a lot more stimulating.

I actually enjoyed being a cop. There were days when I came in from walking my beat, knowing I had done some good. Bad folks were behind bars. I could sleep easy.

It just wasn't enough: not nearly enough.

I could mash the paperwork faster than anybody else I knew—and police paperwork is truly baffling. I had one of the highest arrest records in my station.

There was just no… buzz.

The two-year probation period oozed like thick molasses. Nothing ever changed. I mastered everything I was told as soon as I was told, but police work is all about repetition and confirmation. I had to fill in a weekly 'lessons learned' portfolio. After one full week, spent standing behind a police tape at a crime scene, I put down; 'I learned how to master boredom'. My sergeant told me that wasn't funny. I changed it to:

'Upon examination, I learned to recognise the right side of police crime-scene tape'.

After a year, they told me, as a treat, I could go on a bicycle assessment course. After that, if I passed, I could go on cycle patrols. I'd last sat a cycle test when I was six. Fuck me. Was this for real?

At eighteen months, I was sent on a driving course. I could now drive a police car at thirty miles an hour—what they called patrol speed. No blue lights, though. That would take more years of service to even be considered. Every time I asked for something different, I was told; 'consolidate your position'. Police speak for; 'get back in your box'.

Despite my spats, I really tried my best to fit in. It didn't work.

Matters came to a head on the day of the royal wedding, of Prince William to Catherine. Glasgow decided to hold an all-day rave, which turned into a drunken riot. My partner and I spent the day wrestling with idiots, locking up as many as we could. There were moments that day when it was all genuinely life-threatening. Afterwards, police counsellors came by, to talk to all of us. Many of my colleagues were in tears. Several went off sick.

A well-meaning therapist asked me how I felt. I told her it was fucking magic, truly the best day I had had on the force. I had loved it—it was like being back in a Belfast riot. I was asked to go and see my inspector. I hadn't been flagged for emotional stress, quite the opposite.

He asked me what I wanted to do in the police. At that time, I was quite keen on joining the firearms teams. He told me that the force was quite against former service-people joining firearms. The force believed that former military had been trained to shoot, whereas the police was all about not shooting anybody at all. More particularly, in my case, with my psych evaluation, as a fire-eating riot lover, it would be unlikely I would be let near anything with potential to go fatally violent.

That was it for me.

Stymied from promotion, stymied from my ambition, I resolved to find something else. The news was full of shaky footage of British soldiers, fighting in Helmand Province. Stuff was going on there, stuff I had loved. I needed the high, to walk the tightrope again. Back in the war, life had been worth living.

Being a cop was just an existence. So, the search began. And it proved to be a pretty easy hunt.

A quick web-search revealed that NATO was looking for a civilian staff member to run forward-based teams, across Afghanistan, producing what the military calls psychological operations. In simple-speak, they were looking for somebody to produce media stories to promote NATO to the Afghan people. Yeah, baby…

My CV might as well have been written for the job. I had years in the media, years in the military and years in Afghanistan behind me. This was the one. I wrote off, in great excitement, and packed my bags.

I didn't get the job.

It went to an American who had just finished a long stint in Kabul with NATO, doing psychological operations, six months earlier. He knew the board personally. On the other hand, I did my telephone interview at seven in the morning from inside a moving police squad car with a very noisy prisoner kicking off in the back.

It wasn't my finest hour.

In any case, I was out, and Eric, the American, was in. I went back to policing, and forgot all about NATO.

Money was pretty tight as a cop. For working a forty-hour week, I earned about fifty pounds a week more than if I had been claiming benefits. You do not get rich as a police officer. It was straight pay cheque to pay cheque stuff. In my three years on the force, I didn't take a single holiday. I couldn't afford to. When my car fell apart, I walked to work. I ate homemade sandwiches, and counted myself lucky to have twenty pounds in my purse at the end of the month. Money doesn't make you happy, but not having any is guaranteed to make you miserable.

Then, completely out of the blue, in late 2011, I got a call from Kabul. It was Eric. He'd had a sudden vacancy, in Kandahar:

'Would you like the job? No interview needed, nothing like that, you'll be fine. Just get yourself onto a plane and get over here. Everything will be sorted when you arrive. Don't worry about the work. You'll pick it up, on the job.

Just get here.'

Man, talk about a fastball. I was flattered, but divided. The police had been going a bit better. I'd been spotted, and given a mentor. I'd been told that I might, with a following wind, make sergeant within five years, something of a record for promotion in the Scottish Police.

Yet...

There was Afghanistan, laid out in front of me. That glittering prize that had always quickened my blood when I was there, and still had a niggling hold on the back of my cerebellum. The rush was so close I could smell it.

They were even going to throw in a medal for free. I might get killed, but I'd be able to afford a nicely decorated casket.

What to do? What to do? In truth, it wasn't even a debate.

On the one hand, the police wasn't the most exciting thing I'd ever done, but it was steady. It was a permanent job, and I couldn't be fired, thanks to the arcane legislation that governed being a British cop.

On the other, it was Afghanistan. I loved the place. It was an exciting job, tons of money, and I truly missed the military. Not the bullshit part, I have always been too much of an individual to knuckle down to the rank and uniform pressing BS.

I missed the camaraderie, the sense of doing something worthwhile.

Yet, this trip, I wouldn't be in the army anymore and it was a short-term contract. One year, no more than that guaranteed. Given Afghanistan, it also stood a decent chance of being permanently short-term.

Afghanistan was anything but steady.

I have always been a risk-taker. I think my mind had already been made up the second Eric called. Hey, the bell was ringing. Time to get on the horse one last time, take one for the team, do one for the Gipper.

It was just too damned... romantic, to miss.

I did try to make the decision more difficult. I went to see my chief inspector. I laid out the offer I had and asked him what the police would offer me, to make me consider staying. He thought for a moment, and said that in two more years, if I did well, he would consider sending me on an advanced driving course, so I could turn the blue lights on and legally drive very fast. Anything else was way too soon for me to consider.

'You're kidding,' I replied.

'Nope,' came his reply, before he added; 'whatever you may have been before you came here, in this job, you are just another walking yellow jacket.'

Fuck you very much. Thanks for the encouragement. The choice was there, all laid out in black and white:

Be a somebody or a nobody. I resigned the next day. I might get killed, but it would be fun. Let's do this.

Hey, what the fuck?

COLLY-WOBBLE BLUES

So I spent what little savings I could muster on getting jabbed for everything from tuberculosis to emphysema and bought a one-way ticket to Germany.

My joining instructions were delightfully vague. I was to get myself to Ramstein US Air Force base, near Munich, Germany, from where I was to jump aboard a flight for Kabul. I was sent a NATO travel order, my ticket for the plane from Ramstein to Afghanistan, and nothing else.

I was back in the game. No more going for tests before I could ride a bicycle. No more nannying. Just get yourself to Germany, bring what you think you'll need for a year away from home, and make it up from there.

It was adult movie time.

As I left, the news played footage of a massive car bomb in Kabul. It had killed dozens and destroyed a city block. Yes, I thought, this was going to be fun.

Most folks would have packed a rucksack and boots for Kandahar. I packed two Dianne Von Furstenberg gold monogrammed suitcases—and added a feather boa, for those dramatic moments. The only flat boots I had were my old police patrol boots. I decided they made my ass look fat and swapped them for a pair of high-heeled ankle boots. If I got shot, I was determined to be a well-dressed corpse. Told you I am an individual. I am not a number.

A friend drove me in the early hours of a dark, Scottish winter's morning to Glasgow International Airport. I had last minute colly-wobbles, and cried dramatically as he dropped me off. His last act was to shove a twenty-pound note for emergencies into my hand, before he drove off into the darkness.

Colly-wobbles or not, I had to go. I had no job, no money and no future, other than Kandahar. Talk about risk-taking. This wasn't just burning the boat, I'd burned the paddles and the life-vest too.

As I flew from Glasgow, down to London, and then on to Munich, the nerves left. I phoned all my chums, to tell them I was for the off again. I walked around Terminal 4, Heathrow, and window-shopped all the expensive handbags, watches, perfumes and sunglasses. I had just enough for coffee and a sandwich. Next time, though, I resolved, I'd be on my way back. It'd be different then—and it was too.

They nearly didn't let me into Ramstein. The American MPs told me my travel order didn't have the right stamps in the right places. They sent me to the German entry control gate. I shed a few real tears there. I didn't have the money to get home again—or even for a hotel room for the night. This was a one-way trip. The Germans took pity on me. They gave me a one-day pass, made me sit with them until the offending MP went off-duty, and sent me through with a wink and a nod.

I was in. And what a revelation Ramstein was. Sitting on the runway in that one base were more heavy-lift aircraft than the entire Royal Air Force possessed. The military passenger terminal was the same size as Glasgow airport. All this metal and muscle, flexing away there like a steroid Rambo. The adrenalin was back.

I was in my groove. I had come home.

Twenty years earlier, in another war, in another time and place, I had sat at the side of Al-Jubail runway, Saudi Arabia, and watched the US fly in an aircraft every six minutes, twenty four hours a day, seven days a week, a non-stop conveyor belt of jet fumes and metal. That time, we were liberating Kuwait.

Twenty years later, the United States was still an awesome force. The planes at Ramstein just kept on landing and taking off in one never-ending Duracell bunny marathon of military business. How could we possibly lose with all this stuff? Ramstein was rammed with hard metal. It was the main conduit for everybody heading 'down-range', as the Americans call going to the suck.

Troops milled everywhere, in a dizzying succession of badges, uniforms and camouflages. The terminal was filled with a cacophony of the sound of important people telling me to join one queue, then another, then to open my bags, then to close them, then to move to another queue, then back to the first queue I had been in. None of my papers seemed to be good enough. My passport was minutely examined, scanned, taken away, returned, then taken away again:

'Who are you? Where are you going? Why aren't you an American? What is this ISAF thing? You're in the wrong queue… over there. What are these cases? Where is your rucksack? Where are your orders? You're in the wrong queue… over there. Who are you again?'

The US Air Force prioritises its passengers—and my travel order put me at the bottom of the queue. I was what is known as 'space A'. Which is to say, the military equivalent of flying stand-by. Anybody and anything else with an urgent desire to go to Afghanistan would take precedence. I was road kill un-important.

I was cut: 'no flight today, ma'am.'

The next plane out was delayed by twenty-four hours. We were told to report back tomorrow. The tannoy announced that military personnel would be accommodated in a nearby hotel. I didn't have money for a hotel, and I couldn't stay in the terminal for twenty-four hours. I grabbed the nearest soldier, a US marine, and asked him to carry my cases. Being a good southern boy, he happily obliged. I joined the long line heading for the waiting buses and acted as if I belonged.

Blag it, baby. I had no choice. It was that or the gutter.

I spent the first night of my Afghan adventure in a very comfortable four-star hotel in Munich, quaffing pilsner alongside some deliciously handsome marines. Thank you, Uncle Sam.

Next day, our flight duly arrived. Most of the passengers, all military personnel, had already been travelling for days, criss-crossing the States, picking up passengers, before it had even hit the Atlantic. The plane, a 747, belonged to a charter. All the company did was fly US military to Afghanistan. The air-bridge operation was so vast that it employed entire airlines to keep it running.

Being 'space A', I just managed to squeeze into the last seat on the last row, way in the back.

As I entered the plane, the steady hubbub of conversation went quiet. The only civilian, and the only female, on the flight, I was a novelty. Men, particularly military men, placed on their own, quickly adopt a different

dynamic. It's as if the caveman bursts out of them. Put those men into uniform give them a gun, tell them they are going to war, and all restraint disappears.

The military is a boy's world. It's a place where Darwin is alive and well. Women are tolerated, if they play by men's rules: but only in supporting roles. The key combat arms are barred to females. No penis, no get in. Women exist to man the home front, rear children and to be protected from harm.

A feminine cotton wool: women just aren't as important. It is a medieval outlook, but one which military culture, with all its big dick sensibility, prizing aggression, physicality and dominance, actively encourages.

A lone female, in make up, heels and a tight sweater, was not only rare but near non-existent. In all my time there, I would refuse to compromise. It cost me dear, in terms of stares, salacious advances and inappropriate moments. As a woman, life was like walking past a building site in a mini-skirt, all day, every day. To survive, adopting one old army phrase, I had to grow a pair. Ignore to thrive and survive.

It's a dynamic I've endured before, but it was a long walk to the back of the plane, as three hundred pairs of eyes swivelled on stalks. Lock target, evaluate, engage, destroy. They mentally screwed me until their necks couldn't turn any further. I reminded them of home. They hadn't yet got the tour goggles, where the mere sight of a living, breathing woman evoked an instant supermodel. But they were on the way there.

The Americans were more restrained than the Brits. The US troops sat in respectful silence as the stewardesses ran through the evacuation procedures. The practical display of the life jacket, where the stewardess blew meaningfully into the top-up air nozzle, always elicited a howl of approval on a British flight.

At least the yanks didn't do rank-relative seating. On a Brit flight, the top knobs always get called first, which the boys always resent.

During the first Gulf War, our brigade had been commanded by a toffy, posh general called Christopher Hammerbeck. Before the brigade went in, he'd done a public school rabble-rouser for the boys, where he'd promised them all a beer when we got to Baghdad. Four months later, job done, the boy's plane home to Germany was held on the tarmac while Hammerbeck arrived late, disappearing straight into his carefully reserved seat. Getting into Germany, with the boy's families waiting on the tarmac, the troops were held up again, to allow Hammerbeck to take the official press welcome as the returning hero of the hour. Enough was enough. As the brigadier got to the door, a lone voice from the back yelled out:

'Hey, boss, where's our fucking beer then?'

Check out the footage sometime. He is livid coming down the stairs. Man, we laughed...

Our flight from Ramstein didn't take us into Afghanistan. We were destined for Manas, Kyrgyzstan. An old Soviet-era airbase from an old Soviet-era republic, the whole left-behind, crumbling mess had been leased by the Americans to be a feeder hub for troops entering and leaving Afghanistan. Manas was one of many such bases. In the past, I'd been flown by the Germans through Dushanbe, and by the Brits via the Mid-East, Romania and Turkey. Afghanistan was never an easy trip. It was a hell of a long way to go to fight a war.

One memorable flight into central Turkey, we'd landed at a regional commuter hub. While the aircrew went off and did strange aircrew things, we ended up taking coffee in the terminal amidst the morning rush hour. At least, the officers did. The boys headed straight for the bar and threw the local *reki* down their necks like men possessed. While we officers determinedly looked the other way, an equally determined sergeant major had clumped his big stick onto some hard heads to stop the rot. It wasn't pretty. Lord knows what the Turks thought of our finest.

Flying east over Europe, as we did, is instructional. At first, the ground below is a constant patchwork of lights, linking towns and cities. Further and further east, the clusters of lights get less and less. Until you hit the Urals, when they die out altogether. We left Kansas way behind. As we flew, we left our cosy western civilisation in our wake.

We arrived at Manas at the beginning of December, when daytime temperatures reach a balmy minus four degrees centigrade. At night, it was cold enough to freeze your eyeballs, mid-blink. Manas is a complete fucking dump, and a bloody glacial one too.

The camp itself was all about one thing: proximity to a runway big enough—and safe enough—to take wide-bodied jets, each filled with hundreds of troops. The rest of it consisted of several gently rusting hangers, a couple of unserviceable Soviet fighter jets and a collection of tents and containerised accommodation blocks, put up by the Americans. The whole mad Stalinist experiment had just stopped mid-1990, when the wall came down. Manas had just sat there since, for twenty years, gently going mouldy, until the Americans arrived to polish up a turd.

When I arrived in late 2011, the base had been in continuous use for ten years, yet we were still using porta-loos and drinking bottled water. The food was all air lifted in, direct from the United States. Nothing was permanent, despite the permanent nature of the war.

Manas was my first insight into one of the great conundrums of how the US fights. The US spent a fortune on contracts to fly in bottled water, when it could actually have built its own filtration plant and bottling facility, or just bought the stuff locally for a fraction of the cost. Buying the local H2O was off the menu. To the febrile conspiracy paranoid military, it could have been poisoned.

The military likes to think 'expeditionary'. As more than one senior officer told me, putting in proper plumbing and drinking facilities would make the troops soft. Carrying a gun and getting shot at is not enough. The military love the whole idea of living rough. They even have a name for it—combat camping.

In any case, budgeting for permanent facilities would have meant long-term planning, and one thing the entire Afghanistan experiment never had was any form of long-term planning. So we all risked dysentery to shit in plastic boxes full of blue liquid and littered the landscape with thousands of plastic bottles. We endured being made tougher and harder at the expense of our own personal morale. Manas was miserable.

Transit personnel were accommodated in vast tents, filled with cheap metal bunk beds, three tiers high. Because of the cold, we were issued with greasy Russian quilts and cotton sheets, all bought locally. We were grateful for them, even as we wondered how many sleeping bodies had used them in the past ten years.

Manas was a never-never land, where thousands of soldiers would mill around, neither in the war, nor out of it. In uniform, but not asked to do anything but wait, until their number co-incided with a seat on a plane to somewhere else. The whole place was dedicated to getting the fuck out of it. For some, it could take days. For others, such as poor, dumb schmucks like me, living on a tenuous 'space A' pass, I would dream that dream for eighteen straight, mind-numbing days of tedium before it was my turn to hotfoot it out of Dodge.

Everything was rudimentary. The camp had several unheated circus tents, with big screen TVs, internet access and temporary coffee shops. Meals were available twenty-four hours a day, as flights came and went all day and all night. One plus was it was all free, which was something, but even free long-life muffins and 'Gladiator' on constant repeat got pretty fucking old pretty fucking quickly. Why is it that soldiers waiting for wars only ever watch war movies? Isn't the imminent reality enough?

There were a few bars on site, where alcohol was served. That surprised me, as America is a prudish nation. The whole booze issue had been a running sore with the troops for years. Alcohol was served depending on which service you belonged to. Air force and navy were allowed two drinks each. Army could sometimes sneak one, depending on the mood of the person serving. Marine corps, definitely none: and their uniform, a different camouflage from everybody else's, conspired to make them easy to spot.

Uncomfortable evenings resulted. Folks being folks, those who wanted booze would get their teetotal buddies to buy their two drinks and hand them over to the needy. While most would stay just the right side of public drunkenness, the evening would descend into raucous groups of air force, being glowered at by muscled marines, who were both piously sober and jealous as hell at the same time.

The object of Manas, of course, was simple. Everybody just wanted to leave, as soon as possible. That is, apart from the poor souls whose rotation had come up with a posting to manage the constant flow of bodies and boxes. A tour in Manas must have been truly grim. It was a helluva lot safer than Afghanistan, but a year there must have been a military lobotomy.

Even for those of us with a reason and a ticket out of there, Manas could reach out with its sticky tentacles of confusion.

Military transport aviation is governed by a few simple rules.

Firstly, never transport anybody at a logical time. The generals hate to think that a soldier could be flying when a troop could be working. Therefore, all flights take off at night, when humans should be sleeping, so that you arrive shell-shocked and weary at your destination, but ready to do a full day's work. Military time is therefore not wasted, even if the human in green is.

Secondly, you must check in five minutes before the five minutes before. In the real world, the norm is check-in three hours before departure. In the military, because you must do the five minutes before the five minutes before, you must present six hours before a flight. The reason given at Manas was to 'palletise' the baggage, in other words to pack it for flying. Which we had to do for ourselves, in a muddy outdoor field littered with boxes and wooden crates.

In order to meet our pre-dawn flight, the criteria of rule one, I was required, by rule two to present for check-in at ten each night. Every night, in the dark, I would drag my by now rather dog-eared Diane Von Furstenberg designer luggage over to the muddy field and lump it onto a metal pallet. My precious cases would then be covered in piles of green canvas rucksacks.

Soldiers travel with an enormous amount of stuff. It's not just the obvious stuff, like a gun and a uniform. American soldiers plan for contingencies. Every soldier carried a full set of winter clothing, summer clothing and a large caseful of equipment for a possible chemical war. There had never been an incident requiring a gas mask in the entire Afghan war. Nonetheless the troops carried one, just in case.

The army didn't have enough gas masks to give one to everybody. They just issued an individual case of stuff, with strict orders never to open any of it. The soldiers would hump the case all over the country for a year and then return it, un-opened, to Manas stores on their way home: whereupon the un-opened gear would be re-cycled for the next rotation passing through Manas on their way to the war. Like unwanted Christmas presents, the troops added mounds and mounds of gas masks that would never be used onto my DVF cases. The pallets literally weighed tons. The issued body armour alone weighed over thirty pounds.

When I was a young soldier, we didn't have such a thing as body armour. We didn't have sleeping bags or wet weather clothing either. We did have a lot of woolen stuff that got ridiculously heavy when it was wet, which was often in Germany. Smelled pretty rank, too. I remember those days of the British Army of the Rhine as being uncomfortable, but not so unreasonable that we would have wanted—or needed—the mountain of stuff soldiers got for Afghanistan.

This world was, at one stroke, more dangerous and more safety-minded, all in one enormous military mindfuck.

My two suitcases would be buried under an avalanche of green stuff, most of which would never be used, but which had to be brought along: just in case, in a case, or, more correctly, several cases.

I would then have a fitful few hours sleep on a metal camp chair in the terminal. Before being told, at three in the morning, that there was no room in the inn for my 'space A' carcass. I would drag my dented bags out from the bottom of the pallet, and hasten back to my tent before my eyeballs froze, usually to find my recently vacated bunk had been filled by another snoring mass of transitory humanity.

I did the same cycle for eighteen straight days before my obvious signs of emotional distress convinced a sympathetic female flight sergeant to smuggle me onto a flight. There's a special place in Hell reserved for a female who doesn't help another sister in need. I was delighted to going somewhere, anywhere, but back to that stinky tent.

I had, however, forgotten rule three of military transport aviation. That is that the plane will be late and will never take you to where you want to go, only sideways or backwards. This is why the Royal Air Force is universally known as crab air.

The flight was duly six hours late, and it wasn't going to Kabul, where I needed to go, but to Bagram Airbase, north east of the capital. It was Afghanistan, just not the bit I needed to be in. Still, after nearly three weeks, I would be, at least, in the right country.

More importantly, I would be anywhere but fucking Manas.

Bagram had been the main Soviet airbase, during the occupation. I'd first seen it in '94, during the civil war, when the runway had been deserted, and you had to be extremely careful where you stood, as the entire place had been booby-trapped and mined. The mines just sat there in the mud. You could literally see them piled up.

Later in the campaign, in-coming soldiers had to go through a mocked-up mine lane, to identify the various types of hazard they may face. In the early days, you just looked over the barbed wire. Stuff that would kill you was everywhere.

After 9/11, Bagram was the first place I landed with the military. I had been struck then at how this little piece of Afghan soil had been quickly converted into a little piece of America. Even in those very early days, when US troops numbered only a few thousand, they had brought with them a mobile Burger King and Pizza Hut, conveniently trailer-ised into one air-portable lump of saturated fat.

We flew in to Bagram on an unimaginatively named but cavernous military transport plane, known as a C-17. I'd have called it the 'super-liner', or something with much more dramatic, romantic flair to make up for the spartan interior.

We sat on nylon webbing seats, arranged down the sides, with a cargo of rubber tyres along the middle of the plane. At least I didn't have to pee. Facilities consisted of a slot, built into a bulkhead, where the male troops inserted the obvious, in full view of all. Apart from lacking the physical equipment, there was no way I was showing my knickers to one and all. The crew did carry a sort of shower curtain that could be erected around the airborne *pissoir*, for the 'delicate' gender, but the length of time it would have taken to erect would have been uncomfortably embarrassing.

It was bad enough that, when we boarded, I had had to ask the crew chief to help me up the step onto the rear ramp.

The troops all shared the same carry-on: a gun. Everybody was armed. Weapons of all sizes, from pistols strapped to hips to assault rifles and machine guns. A few extremely large men in civilian clothes carried exotic-looking German rifles, notably different from ones the regular army boys carried. They wore wrap-around shades, back to front baseball caps, had outrageous facial hair and called each other 'dude' a lot. Afghanistan was full of exotic creatures. The regular soldiers studiously ignored them, while quietly wondering exactly who they were. The big, bearded men sat quietly, drinking in the hidden adulation, and smiled big, toothy, predatory smiles towards me.

On approach, the crew chief ostentatiously called the troops to prepare for landing. Everybody ferreted in their huge carry-on and extracted terribly heavy body armour and Kevlar helmet. Much was made of buttoning straps and tightening belts. As I didn't have any armour, I did up the buttons on my fur and wrapped my boa around my neck.

The big men with beards pretended to sleep, even after we hit the ground with a jolt.

By 2011, Bagram was vast. The Americans had built a second runway, and turned the place into a US-only establishment. NATO might have been an international concern, but wherever the US worked, it became American. The Americans were happy to accommodate a coalition: but only ever on American terms.

Field Marshal Lord Alan Brooke, Chief of the British Imperial Staff during the Second World War said that; 'the US does not defeat its enemies, it overwhelms them.' Allies, too, could quickly be subsumed.

When I landed, the Americans called the military police. I wasn't carrying any contraband, merely a NATO travel order. The Devil's own work was afoot. NATO paperwork meant *nada*. My NATO travel order wasn't American orders. Nor did I possess American ID. Probably also didn't help that I'd got dressed for travelling in long suede high heeled boots, a pink polo neck sweater and a leopard print fur coat, with my feather boa in reserve. I don't think Lisa Minnelli could have up-staged my Afghan arrival combo.

The MPs thought I was a spy. I spent an uncomfortable half hour, on a wooden bench in the jail, before they relented. To be fair, they apologised. One asked me; 'gee, Miss Austen (Americans are terribly formal), you *SURE* you belong here?'

The transit staff told me that my 'space A' curse would mean a layover of a few more days. Just as I resigned myself to another transit tent, another town, rule four of military transport aviation struck.

Which is to never believe anything you have previously been told.

A harassed clerk grabbed me to say that a helicopter was leaving in thirty minutes with the mail—and they had room for me. Off I went, as dusk fell, to join a sleek Blackhawk helicopter, all 'Apocalypse Now', whirring noisily, impatient to get flying. The crew were suitably surprised to have me on board with the postal round, but they were gentlemen and gallantly helped me, and my golden cases, on-board.

Then we were off, skimming over the mountains. I made my low-level, glorious entrance to Kabul with the sharp edge of a delivery box from Amazon digging into my ass.

I've always loved travelling in military helicopters. It's flying stripped to its bare essentials. They are draughty, uncomfortable and extremely noisy. There's nothing more exhilarating than sitting in the open doorway of one, flying at mega-mach, low-level, wind whipping across your face, nothing but air and the earth whipping beneath your feet. It's the way they just rise from the ground, then tip forward, as the world rushes beneath your feet, faster and faster.

Or the way they suddenly rear up, as they skid to a halt. In Afghanistan, a combat landing meant total dis-orientation, in a cloud of dirt and dust, a swirling vortex of stinging sand, senses momentarily confounded by the dirt flying, the madness of the noise. All those Hollywood movies, where they chat in the back of the helicopter, on the way to their mission? Impossible. All you can hear in those things is wind.

The United States makes particularly sexy helicopters. Europe makes some quite effective transport helicopters, but they all look like pregnant cows, fat in the belly, football shaped. The Blackhawk, on the other hand, is a lozenge-shaped, sports car of a helo. It's just one long penis of fuck-me desire.

The pilots sit up front, in an armoured cockpit, followed by the open passenger compartment. The crews all wear Judge Dredd helmets, with dark visors over their eyes, and tailored flight suits, with lots of pockets and pistol-filled holsters and pilot stuff. They look cool as fuck.

In Afghanistan, the helos always flew with two door gunners, one each side, armed with wicked 7.62mm machine guns. As you took off, the gunners would swing their machine-guns around, freeing them on their mounts, checking the guns were loaded and cocked. Depending on the location, they'd fire a burst, to zero them in. Often, they'd fire burning flares, which flew in graceful arcs to each side, like a peacock spreading its wings, when they thought there was a threat. If you were lucky, they'd give you a headset, to listen into the crew chatter—and Americans do crew chatter better than anybody:

'Tango three six oscar mike, in-bound your location, echo tango alpha figures fifteen mikes, confirm, over.'

There's a difference between radio chatter and man-sexy radio chatter, in a deep southern US drawl. Done properly, it's like going to church. Just listening to all that Top Gun mania could leave a damp patch on a girl's chair.

Doors open, nothing between you and the ground, skimming along a couple of hundred feet off the ground, hurtling into heart-crunching side-ways skids. Yep, it is just like all those Vietnam movies you have ever seen.

And the crew that day loved nothing more than showing off to the chick in the feather boa in the back. We flew fast and low into Kabul airport, and settled into a low hover, next to a brightly lit and suspiciously new brick building.

The original Kabul airport terminal looked like an up-turned shoebox. It had been a gift of the Soviet Empire, and had been built with all the subtlety of a Stalinist nursery rhyme. I'd camped out in its empty departure lounge nearly twenty years earlier, lived in it again when the west had invaded, and had used it as an office on a later tour of duty. It was stark, utilitarian and single-purpose effective.

In those early days, there hadn't been a single runway light. You just landed, and got off the back of the plane. The whole place had been run by what pilots call VFR—visual flight rules. In other words, if it looked clear, just go for it.

Now, though, in 2011, civilisation had caught up with Kabul. The runway was littered with daisy chains of fairy lights. A large, rotating radar stated that aviation civilisation had arrived. Half-a-dozen commercial jets, lights blinking, waited in an orderly queue to take off. Emblazoned in the livery of Pakistan and Turkish airlines, it was obvious Kabul had changed. It was all just too damn ordinary. Where was the war?

Next to the old Soviet terminal sat a shiny, new shoebox. This turned out to be a new international terminal, gifted by the Japanese. The old Soviet terminal now governed domestic departures only. The entire airport complex had, in my absence, been turned back to the Afghan nation and doubled in size. It seemed to be prospering very well indeed.

We were hovering on the other side of the runway, in front of the split new headquarters of the International Security and Assistance Force, the title the West had given to the force sent to police and develop Afghanistan. ISAF was my new employer. We'd handed back the old airport terminal and built ourselves some brand new digs on the other side of the runway. That new headquarters was home to the unit I was going to be working for.

The military love nothing more than military-speak. This basically involves taking quite simple ideas and name-places, and dressing them up into three-letter acronyms, which only make sense to the military. Indeed, sometimes not to the military either. Even the three-letter acronym has its own acronym: the TLA.

The TLA also covers the four, and even five-letter, acronym. The military likes to keep things simple. The military dislikes conundrums of more than three disparate elements. Potentially confusing for the men—and the army avoids confusion at all costs. Example? In the military, nature's miracle has been diluted to three types of trees: bushy-topped, pine and poplar. The bushy-topped variety was so designated to; 'stop you smarty-pants officers confusing the men.' As my Sandhurst colour sergeant had patiently explained to me. I had told him, on one exercise, that I thought the pretend bad guys were under a rather glorious spreading oak, beside a stand of sycamores. 'Too much fucking information', I was told.

A concept defined by another favourite military saying: KISS. Keep it simple, stupid. Which is a four-letter TLA. No idea how that one got past the TLA censor.

Try as the army might, TLAs made life rather hard. There was no handy reference guide for TLAs. I have spent what must be years in staff meetings. Erudite staff officers brief with a never-ending series of buzzwords and acronyms, while the audience duly nod wisely. Even as the speaker drones on, I know I am not the only one in the meeting to wonder what the heck it all means.

How many whispered conversations have been held afterwards, where one officer would ask another:

'Without being rude, old boy, what exactly is a FARP?'

That's a forward air re-fuelling point. At least, I think it is. It may very well be, depending on context, a complex intestinal disorder. See what I mean? It's all very confusing.

The Brigade of Guards has a tradition of banning TLAs, which is eminently sensible. Except that quite a few staff officers only know a piece of kit by its acronym. Which can lead to lots of confusion.

Like the wonderful time a chum of mine was describing the work of a CET, a combat engineer tractor. This is simply a large armoured vehicle with lots of implements bolted on, like a mechanical digger, to do important engineering stuff. It's a multi-tool on tracks. My friend, briefing the Guards, barred from using TLAs and therefore CET, had momentary amnesia, and was reduced to describing the pride of the Corps of Engineers' armoured capability as; 'the thing with a shovel on the front.'

In Afghanistan, life was no different. So, Kabul airport was known as KAIA; Kabul International Airport. Why four letters for a three-word name? Does that not defeat the principle of the TLA? I hear you ask. Simply to have called it KIA means something else in military speak—killed in action—so KAIA it became.

The bit I had just landed at, the new headquarters of the whole shooting match, was known as KAIA north, or KAIA-N. Imaginatively described thus because the camp had been built on the north side of the runway. KISS.

KAIA-N played host to the military headquarters of the international effort in Afghanistan, which was part of NATO, the North Atlantic Treaty Organisation, founded to defend Europe at the end of the Second World War. The NATO Afghan mission was known as ISAF—the International Security and Assistance Force. ISAF was the impressive cover-all for the 140,000 foreign soldiers in Afghanistan, all beavering away in the name of freedom.

KAIA-N, which housed some four thousand troops, enclosed the IJC, ISAF Joint Command: the top headquarters for the war. The IJC was the reason I was in Afghanistan.

A sub-unit of the IJC was the CJPOTF—the Combined Joint Psychological Operations Task Force—part of which contained the FMT Section—the Forward Media Team section. Ultimately, my new line management.

To précis my journey:

In Afghanistan, I had landed at BAF (Bagram airfield), my APOD (airport of disembarkation, as opposed to Manas, which had been my APOE (airport of embarkation), then flown rotary air (planes are known as fixed wing, helicopters are rotary air, even though they don't have wings and don't necessarily fly in circles, don't ask why), to KAIA –N (the camp I was hovering over), preparatory to JSROI (joint staging, reception and onward integration—basically, posh words for a welcome cocktail and chat) at IJC (ISAF Joint Command). Before going to work for CJPOTF/ FMTS (Combined Joint Psychological Operations Task Force/ Forward Media Teams).

I have a headache.

Got it? You may have to re-read that. Afterwards, you may feel as I did, as my Blackhawk settled on the runway. Rather worn-out and tattered. The army can be quite the secret society. You can't exist in the military without learning the private lingo. Without it, you're like the mason who doesn't know which trouser leg to roll up.

Nonetheless, I had arrived. Once again, my credentials proved to be sparse cover, as I negotiated my way past the security checkpoint. This time, I had to use hand signals and a smile to make my case, as the post was manned by a Mongolian soldier. Not a soldier who looked Mongolian—an actual Mongolian.

He was my first introduction to the patchwork quilt that made up ISAF. Over fifty nations contributed to the force, many of which were not in NATO at all. I'd never met a Mongolian before, but he looked smart enough, in his US camouflage uniform and American rifle. As I was to find out later, many of the smaller nations merely contributed the human bodies. America clothed, fed, armed, transported and paid for all the rest.

ISAF was not an alliance of equals. It was, however, a useful fig leaf for what was, essentially, a US-led and staffed operation to have so many nations involved. In return, Mongolia got to be friendly with the world's sole superpower: quite handy when you consider Mongolia's neighbours.

Once we had negotiated my new guardian's relative lack of English and my complete lack of Mongolian ('me British. Liverpool football club? Excellent!'), it was off to pick up my gold cases from the mud once more.

Eric was waiting for me in the terminal. We had never met, and I didn't spot anyone I thought might be him, in the excited melee that surrounded the arrival of the mail. But, as the only female in the place, and the only person in high heels and a feather boa, he took a punt.

Eric hailed from California. About six feet three, with a swimmers build and balding head, he looked good in his khaki chinos and boots. Afghan had a way of stripping any spare flesh. After a few months there, we all looked ripped. The heat just melted the weight off you like a solar microwave. Eric was in full flush.

Male contractors in Afghanistan all wore the 'combat collection by Gap'—khaki or green everything—which the men would adorn with unit badges, or a joke T-shirt, emblazoned with 'Taliban hunter road crew', or something similarly macho. It wasn't enough to just be a Westerner in Afghanistan, the men all played alpha male too. As consciously as they tried to disdain the military, they aped the dress etiquette.

Eric wasn't especially pleased to see me. My unexpected arrival had interrupted his evening. Contractors were allowed to wander on and off base. In 2011, the party was always happening in Kabul. He'd planned a night out drinking.

However, one of umpteen ISAF rules stipulated that, until you had an ISAF badge, you had to be escorted on base. As a new arrival, I hadn't had the badging experience, so Eric had had to put his night on hold to welcome me, hold my hand, and keep me from being accidentally shot. I don't think he was expecting me to arrive with such a large amount of luggage. The guys usually came with a rucksack, or duffel bag, hardy warriors all. It was part of the image.

I can say with some certainty, I had the only padded gold Diane Von Furstenberg cases in the country. Such are the male sensitivities of implied sexuality in a war zone that he only very sniffily agreed to carry one for me.

It was dark by the time we left the terminal, so I couldn't get much of a sense of the place. However, the old smell hit me as soon as I landed.

Kabul is a city of millions. It is also a city with no waste disposal or sewerage. Rubbish—including human-produced waste—is either abandoned or burned. The air is thick with the stink of it. Add to that fragrant *melange* the fact that the only reliable source of electricity comes from tens of thousands of diesel generators, which spew out tonnes of dirty soot. Mix it all together in a mad chemist's brew and you have *eau de Afghan*. Kabul is a toxic and odious mass of olfactory temptations.

Those tiny dots of human excrement and rubbish are carried in host clouds of dust, whipped up from the parched earth. It is dust that gets everywhere—and which is the only constant in all of Afghanistan. Wherever I went in Afghanistan, and no matter how long I stayed, I was always dirty.

Afghan dust is finely ground mica, almost invisible on its own, which insidiously permeates every surface. Even the most recently built, shiny, hermetically sealed, super secret squirrel headquarters would, in a matter of days, be covered in a fine mist of dirt. Every part of your body would be covered in it. Conjunctivitis and coughs went hand in hand with Afghan service.

After a while, you became inured to it. You could always spot a new arrival by the way they were scandalised by the dirty desks and chairs they were to occupy. There would follow a fortnight of frantic cleaning, like Canute holding back the tide, until the inevitable overwhelmed. In Afghanistan, you are always dirty.

Kabul sits in a mountain bowl. The air is thin, the city being at an elevation of around seven thousand feet. It is remarkably beautiful, to view from afar. Particularly in winter, as the jagged peaks that protect and surround the city are constantly covered in a thick dusting of icing sugar.

That night, a full moon, I could see the glint of ice-topped mountains in the distance. As I walked with Eric, to my new compound, I could sense I had come home.

Even as I breathed in the dirt and filth, it felt good to be back.

KABUL INTERLUDE

Eric was pleased to see me. He needed me to get down to Kandahar ASAP. Kandahar, for reasons I will explain, is the vital Afghan lodestone. Lose Kandahar, you will lose an Afghan war. So far, so good, but what exactly was I going to be doing there?

My unit, the ponderously named Combined Joint Psychological Operations Task Force, or CJPOTF, or just POTF when you got fed up with all the letters, had been without a presence in Kandahar for several months. My arrival into theatre was eagerly awaited.

The CJPOTF was a unique beast.

The army encompasses many disciplines, from intelligence to engineering. An army's purpose, though, is designed for the simple mission of closing with, and killing, the enemy. Armies exist to defend a country from that country's foes. Although armies can be, and frequently are, asked to do everything from covering fireman's strikes to peacekeeping, at its core, an army's business is killing folks and destroying stuff.

From the day a soldier or officer joins, training, exercises, indeed the entire ethos and life, is centred on fighting wars. However you dress it up, at some stage, an army's function is to get bloody and fuck up your day: permanently.

Everything else, what the army calls 'non-lethal functionality', will always sit uncomfortably in the arena of combat. Partly because it is not seen as core business, but also because quantifiable success in the army is statistic based: ground taken, tanks destroyed, bombs dropped, enemies killed.

What the POTF did had nothing to do with killing folks, nor could it be judged by any objective military measure of success. What it did do, or at least purported to do, was little understood, and even less well implemented by a military fixated with fighting.

Psychological operations are defined as military operations to alter or change attitudes and perceptions within the target audience. Previous generations would have known this as propaganda. In today's more sensitive climate, the term propaganda has been outlawed, even though everything the

POTF did would have been eminently recognisable to Josef Goebbels.

NATO recognised that, in a country as complex and traumatised as Afghanistan, tens of thousands of foreign military wandering around the place might need some explaining to the natives. So, the POTF was born. In later years, its functions had broadened, but, at its core, it remained a mission to help explain just what the international community was trying to do in Afghanistan. Hopefully explaining in a positive way, thus altering and changing attitudes and perceptions in the target audience. Which was, in this case, the Afghan population. POTF was unique to Afghanistan. NATO had never before attempted to run such an outfit.

The POTF had high ambitions.

It ran its own national newspaper, which at one time had been the only national publication in Afghanistan. That publication, with the nebulous title of *'Sada E Azadi'*, or *'Voice of Freedom'*, had a reported print run of some half million copies every month. In a country with an extremely low literacy rate, perhaps the most effective tool POTF ran was a national network of radio stations. This was backed by advertising billboards, and, as the media landscape developed, TV advertising. All of it was nominally designed to support NATO's ambitions in securing and re-shaping Afghanistan.

Aside from the physical production of product, POTF also ran a more improbable enterprise, attempting to divine attitudes and perceptions amongst the Afghan people, through focus groups and surveys. The end result, a vast quantity of bar graphs and pie charts, was scientific enough. The gathering process, of audience surveys and questionnaires, much less so.

What all the disparate functions of POTF had in common was the vast expense incurred in making any of it happen. POTF was not a cheap organisation. I was to come to deeply question the effectiveness of all of this effort.

The POTF was not the only game in town. Each of the major nations engaged in Afghanistan, notably the Americans, Germans, Italians and, to a lesser extent, the British, all ran their own psychological operations. In the vast spider's web of NATO command accountability, each of these national efforts nominally tied in their work with the POTF. The reality was that each nation effectively did its own thing—as did the POTF. The idea was that the POTF sat at a strategic level, with its work coordinating and supporting the different regional efforts. It rarely happened that way.

The POTF compound sat on the outskirts of KAIA-N. Most of the camp itself was, for once, a purpose-built complex. The POTF building was a second-hand removal job. It had originally been sited in the German national camp on the outskirts of Kabul, near the main Jalalabad road, in an old factory complex called Camp Warehouse. When that base had closed, in the never-ending game of ISAF base musical chairs, the entire complex had been lifted, lock, stock and barrel, to KAIA-N.

The buildings themselves were the usual Afghan war mix of pre-fabricated shipping containers and concrete walls. The perimeter of the camp was demarcated by what the military called 'T-walls'. Which were fifteen feet high concrete wall blocks, resting on a wide base forming an upside down letter 'T'.

Every major ISAF camp in Afghanistan had more than its fair share of T-walls. The outer perimeters were made of T-walls. The inner compound perimeters were made of T-walls. It was like living in a maze of grey concrete. At the end, they were too big to remove. In years to come, they will be the longest lasting contribution we have made to Afghanistan.

Inside the concrete walls, the containers themselves formed three two-story blocks. One housed the offices and studios, the other two, the accommodation and rest areas. The containers were laid lengthways, in two lines, with a central corridor between the two sides. In the work block, some interior walls were removed to create open-plan offices and conference rooms. In the accommodation buildings, civilians and military were carefully demarcated.

In general, the military, which controlled the compound, made sure they had a room to themselves, whilst the civilians were packed in two to a room. ISAF had a very real pecking order between the military, regardless of rank, and its civilian staff. If the military had had their way, I am sure they would have forced us in three or four to a room. However, our contracts stated that two was a maximum to a container. Even then, it could be very claustrophobic.

The rooms were about fifteen feet in length, by six feet in width. Each had a door at one end, a window at the other, with an air-conditioning unit mounted on the wall. Ablutions were shared, with a couple of showers and sinks for thirty people, at the end of each corridor. Bed spaces were allocated one by the window, with the other towards the door. The bed space by the window was hotly contested, as the occupant could then draw a curtain to divide their half of the room. The poor soul at the other end had to endure their roommate walking by every time they entered or left.

Privacy came very much a premium. Living and working in such close proximity hot-housed personal issues. It was not an easy environment.

Outside, the compound had a table-tennis table and a few battered plastic chairs. Various half-hearted attempts had been made to start a garden, but the evidence was mostly in the form of a few withered plants in plastic pots littering the courtyard.

From the accommodation block, it was mere yards to the studios and office complex. The ground floor hosted the radio and TV stations. Upstairs, the offices held the headquarters and planning units, which were accessed by a series of code accessed doors. CJPOTF staff never got away from each other. They lived and worked right on top of each other.

In total, the unit had about thirty military staff, the same again in civilian consultants, and a local staff of around seventy Afghan journalists and technical staff, who did the actual broadcasting, translation and technical maintenance of the facility.

Our poor Afghan staff was regarded with great suspicion by the military, and, despite many having worked for NATO for years, were daily subject to humiliating body searches. Afghans were not permitted to stay overnight in the base, so had to go through the entire rigmarole of entry and exit checks twice a day. Even in the CJPOTF compound, they were relegated to the ground floor areas only.

Although ISAF seemed, at first sight, to be a monolithic organisation, the reality was much more convoluted. To staff the overall mission, the IJC maintained a massive spread sheet, both of personnel and of physical terrain, and advertised it to the various nations. The whole operated like a massive job centre.

The contributing nations offered to fill functions and requirements by providing whole military units, such as New Zealand providing air logistics management. Or in geographic areas, such as operations in the North of the country being managed by Germany.

Big functions, which easily fitted the military matrix, were relatively easy to fill. Smaller units, or ISAF specific functions, such as IJC and POTF, were much harder. These were individual units, formed for the ISAF mission alone. No single national component had such a capability. Units such as the POTF called for individual nations to bid for individual slots. Much of which became a national battle for prestige and influence. The process could become rather bitchy, as countries swapped postings like poker cards.

As a NATO/ ISAF asset, not a national contribution, the CJPOTF was basically a quango, staffed by military folks from a rainbow of nations. Which each had different ways of doing their business. POTF was the sort of place where smaller nations could place a single staff officer. Which fulfilled a national political obligation to join the party, but at very little national cost.

A battalion of soldiers costs money, a single staff officer relatively little. The smaller nations could their bit, within their means. As a result, POTF attracted lots of eastern European and non-NATO military: very few of whom had any literacy at all in English, the de facto working language of NATO—and of POTF's entire range of product.

There were many frankly bizarre moments where simply introducing oneself took on a 'me Tarzan, you Jane' quality, as variable fluencies in English were probed. Instead of becoming a cohesive whole, the Turks would hang with the Turks in one corner, while the Romanians would sit in another. If for no other reason than they could actually communicate freely with each other. It made effective management a nightmare of mis-construed context and individual conversations. As time went on, the Anglo-American native tongue-speakers ended up taking on more and more of the work, just to get it done. Thus getting more and more pissed off at the majority who just shrugged their shoulders and said; *'non comprende.'*

Despite having an expensive and highly qualified civilian staff, every meaningful appointment in CJPOTF was filled by uniformed, military folks: the vast majority of whom had absolutely no experience at all in the media game. It was a little like employing a truck driver to fly a plane, simply because he was in the transport business.

For one desperate four-month period, I had nominally to seek approval from a US major whose entire military career to date had been spent as a watch-keeper overseeing inter-continental missile launches. That relationship ended in mutually assured destruction. Particularly when I told him I'd been, absolutely truthfully, as a teenager, a member of the British Campaign for Nuclear Disarmament. My American chum forever thereafter looked on me as a communist spy.

He'd only volunteered to come to Afghanistan as he needed a combat report to get promotion. With no discernable Afghan-applicable skill, nuclear weapons being unlikely to ever be deployed there, he'd been posted as the head of media production. I knew more about nuclear missiles than he knew about newspapers. Which is to say, nothing at all.

He was, however, cursed to be part of a generation that defined itself by war. If he wanted a career, he would require a combat posting to match his peers. Promotion was judged, after ten years of war, on combat tour reports. He needed to go to war to get on. Where he went and what he did was not important, as long as he went. The CJPOTF endured his presence until we could get rid of him.

Our mutual trouble was that he hated his posting. Like most military folks, he wanted to go and live in a slit trench and throw hand grenades. Life in a big headquarters, attempting to comprehend media planning modules just didn't float the boat. On the other hand, I loved doing just that. Trouble was, he was nominally in charge, as the military always trumped the civilians, no matter the relative levels of expertise. So what happened was cultural paralysis, as we glowered at each other over the top of our mutual slit trenches.

Every now and again, we'd get an enlightened officer, who was either interested in the subject, or was bright enough to see its importance—and clever enough to let us use our skills. That, however, was very rare.

As a NATO sinkhole for otherwise unemployable officers, CJPOTF was a human resources management dream and an operational nightmare. It was also one of those NATO units where it was possible to while away a six-month tour doing nothing, particularly if you didn't speak much English.

Nominally, everybody worked within the same rank structure. In practical terms, if, for example, a Bulgarian said he wouldn't take orders from an Australian, there wasn't much anybody could actually do about it. Everybody was generally very polite, but the amount of actual, discernable, effective work the place produced was marginal.

Given that the CJPOTF, for understandable reasons, cost an absolute fortune, and had no definable military impact, the unit's very existence was always in doubt.

Psychological operations was one of those subjects that generals always got excited about, but the POTF raised more questions than it answered.

In recognition of this dearth of experience, POTF employed, at great expense, a core cadre of civilian staffers like me, who actually made the material that was broadcast or printed.

Unlike the military, each and every one of us had undergone a rigorous selection process to confirm our media prowess. While not many of us could muster military service, all of us had, at least, worked in a newspaper or media environment. Skills that were actually relevant to what we were trying to achieve. In several cases, myself included, we had decades of both media and military experience, including years working in Afghanistan.

Despite our specialist knowledge, none of us were ever invited to fill even junior management positions.

Life between the two camps was never easy. Subjective journalistic creativity and objective military planning are not easy bedfellows. The military is deeply ingrained as a logical and sequential thinking organisation. Planning processes follow set templates. I've never, ever heard the military have a blue-sky session.

We civilians didn't wear a uniform, and had a habit of calling each other by our names, not our rank. Scandalous. Thus, the military side looked on the civilians as lazy, unkempt and over-paid. The civilians, in turn, looked on the military as arrogant, ignorant and priggish.

In the middle of this witches brew sat the forward media team section, where I was going to be working. In point of fact, had it been properly managed, it would have been the brightest and most effective concept that the CJPOTF ever had.

Across the country, ISAF was deployed in several regional commands. Each of those regional headquarters had its own military psychological warfare units, which deployed with each rotation of troops. Alongside those troops, the CJPOTF employed a forward media team, comprising a western civilian expert—my job in Kandahar—supported by a team of local Afghan journalists. The job was two-fold: to produce product for the CJPOTF, and to provide a vital link between the national resource, in the shape of the CJPOTF, and the regional command, coordinating all that national and regional work.

The forward media teams, despite being the biggest POTF section overall, had a very small management presence in Kabul. It consisted of Eric and his Macedonian deputy, a charming man called Luka. He had been a forward media team leader himself, but had quit the field for a more comfortable billet in headquarters.

If the CJPOTF was a strategic asset, sitting, as it did, with a countrywide brief, the forward media teams actually impacted at regional and local level, where most Afghan business is actually conducted. National government has always had only a limited remit in Afghanistan. While an Afghan may call himself an Afghan, loyalty and interest has always been directed first at the local level. It was there that the FMTs could, and did, have real impact.

At ISAF's height, there was a forward media team in every operational location.

Not just a staff officer co-located with a headquarters, a specialist media operator, backed up by a team of local journalists who lived and worked in the community. Even forgetting about the production value of such an organic newsgathering mechanism, FMTs were an invaluable source of objective metrics that operated largely outwith the chain of command.

Every senior commander's nightmare is to be out of touch with the battlefield. That observational task is a nightmare to execute and maintain: information and intelligence arriving at a higher headquarters has already been filtered by several layers of staff officers before it even gets there. Those filters instinctively want that information to be good news. The POTF, through the FMTs, nominally provided that extra context. The FMTs worked outside the loop.

An army does not like negativity. Bad news is not good news for an officer's career prospects. Sitting within the structure, but directly guided by Kabul, the regional teams should have provided objective regional reach that was unmatched by any other ISAF asset. The idea was great; the execution was not always as effective.

Operating essentially as a one-stop shop, the forward media team leaders needed to be not just skilled journalistic operators, but politicians and survival experts. Such a mix of qualities is rare. We operated completely on our own, with little direct contact with our home unit. In my three years in Kandahar, I had but one brief visitor from Kabul, and I visited the Kabul office precisely four times. An FMT leader had to be a complete self-starter.

While I nominally worked for a unit hundreds of miles from my location, I lived beside a regional unit—which had little interest in what I did either. As each nation executed its own psychological operations plan, the Kabul-based CJPOTF was essentially side-lined at the regional level, where the pedal met the metal. It was a little like being part of two independent train tracks, with the FMT leader as the piling trying to hold the two sides together.

Basically, an FMT leader was left to make up their own job spec. When it worked, the FMT section became a vital mission memory, product and information source for the command, where the constant churn of troops was a massive hindrance to strategic planning. Where it didn't, it was remarkably easy to goof off and do nothing.

The trouble with the CJPOTF was that, for all its mis-fires and stuttering progress, what it purported to do was actually *really* important. If we could persuade the Afghan population to support ISAF and the international community, to support their own government and security forces, then we would starve our enemy of their base of support, and therefore win the war without destroying the country in the process.

It was a no-brainer to me.

Eric and I didn't always see eye to eye, but I did come to respect his drive and ambition. When he had arrived to take over the forward media team section, filling the job I had failed to get, he had inherited a disparate group of individuals, most of whom had been in post for years.

The CJPOTF FMT man in Kandahar had been a former Canadian army officer, called Terry. He'd been there since 2007, arriving in the first great wave of NATO expansion into the South. Those were the days when we thought we could win in the South without firing a shot. Money was no object, and getting a job with ISAF required little more qualification than a glass eye and a swimming certificate. If you were upright and breathing, the latter being somewhat optional, you were in.

Terry had done an early stint, as a reserve officer with the Canadian army, in Kandahar. As soon as his service was over, he'd beetled back as a civilian, to run the newly minted Kandahar forward media team.

Somewhere, between then and my arrival, he'd lost the plot.

Late 2011, the Taliban rather cleverly tunnelled into Sarposa Prison, in Kandahar City, and held their very own great escape. Hundreds of suspected terrorists had managed to crawl their way out to freedom. CJPOTF had urgently been trying to fill the information vacuum with some sort of good news. Eric had called Terry, our man in Kandahar, to action a response.

In reply, Terry had been very vague, saying he was stuck in a special forces camp in Daikundi Province. Terry then failed to answer his phone at all, which he later claimed had fallen into a portaloo and been lost.

Eric, being a suspicious soul, mounted his own enquiry. It turned out that Terry had left Kandahar military base some time ago, sneaking out to the civilian airport and flying home to Canada. He'd been phoning it in from a different continent for months.

He'd have got away with it in perpetuity too, had the Sarposa break not wrong-footed him. In the bigger picture, it wasn't just that incident which was embarrassing. Pretty much everything that the CJPOTF had put out as gospel news in the previous year had only existed in Terry's febrile imagination. Evelyn Waugh could happily have nicked Terry for 'Scoop'.

Even armed with the passenger manifests, proving malfeasance on a pretty grand scale, Eric had struggled to get Terry removed. It was remarkably difficult to get rid of a civilian staff member. The POTF commanding officer had had to literally thump on Chief Human Resource's desk to get him removed.

Later, it turned out that Terry had cancer, which he had kept hidden from everybody. He was using his considerable salary to pay for chemo-therapy back in Canada. Desperate conditions action desperate acts. His ailment, though, proved terminal. Terry died in 2013.

Part of me admired his sheer balls, part of me was appalled, part of me felt sorry for him, but the larger part was selfishly grateful for Terry's actions, as it had occasioned the mad rush to get me into post. Mind you, the fact that nobody had even picked up on what he was up to pointed early on to some serious issues with command and control oversight.

Terry was the first time I'd come across the mass fraud and lunacy that characterised the ISAF mission. It would not be the last.

Having pushed the boat out to get rid of Terry, Eric was on something of a mission to shape up the rest of the section. Although Terry's omissions had been rather obvious, Eric had his eye on several others. By the time of Eric's arrival, inheriting the section, successive bad management had allowed the entire team to fall apart. Several of my colleagues were, at best, filing one story a week. Sometimes, even less.

The personal behaviour was even more off-the-wall. Our man in Helmand was eventually fired for downloading animal porn on his official work computer. When they cleared his room out, they found a drawer full of condoms, neatly tied up, with his semen carefully preserved inside. Afghanistan could be fucking weird.

The military didn't see it, they never stayed long enough to check into the weeds, but the FMT section was mis-firing. I was Eric's first hiring, and the pressure was on both of us to make it work.

As Eric and I walked to the CJPOTF compound, we sized each other up, and the realities hit of what I was about to undertake. Undoubtedly, facing down the Terry legacy, and building the team up from scratch would bring its own, special challenges. I couldn't help but be excited. I've always been best at start-ups, and running my own shop sounded right up my street.

Eric made it clear that while I was a welcome arrival, I was very much on trial. I was to serve a three-month probation before I could count my contract as safe. He'd pushed the boat out to get rid of Terry and bring me in. Both of us would be held responsible if Kandahar was another screw-up. In the tradition of the proverbial rolling downhill, I knew that Eric wasn't going to go under the bus for me if I cocked it up.

I had a lot expected of me. It would be easy to fail, but personal failure for me was not an option. I'd given up what life I had to come to Afghanistan. I had to make it work. I had nothing back home. There was no safety net. That initial chat was something of a throat swallowing moment.

I spent that first night in the CJPOTF 'transit' room. It stank of pee and sweat. FMT leaders tended to travel through Kabul on their way to leave. Last chance in-country motel for some fun.

Kabul was, and still is, a party town for ex-pats and contractors. Despite being a conservative Muslim country, another drink is only a taxi journey away. By 2011, the US, as the dominant partner in ISAF, was trying hard to tighten down on the carousing. While the military was now, grudgingly, a dry shop, for the civilian staff it was still game on. The transit room was barely sanitary. The stains and smells weren't worth too close an investigation.

By the next morning, after a sleepless night, a somewhat bedraggled Abster made her way up to the morning huddle.

The days started at POTF with a rather pointless group brief at 0830. In any media organisation I have worked for or managed, we began the day with a summary of the news, and what we would do to cover it. In the POTF, the news was never discussed. The group meet was basically administrivia, which was remarkably banal.

For reasons I never quite understood, everybody had to write down the camp password of the day and week—and would be tested on it afterwards. Most folks never left the compound, let alone the camp. In all the time I was there, I was never asked for any passwords, except in that meeting.

Unfortunately, the military staffer delegated to man the password barricades was a lowly Turkish sergeant, with very poor English. We would all listen stoically and cough politely as he mangled his words and spelled out the difficult ones phonetically. We'd also get an update on such pressing matters as the filthy state of the washing machines and who had left empty beer cans in the corridors. Such civilian laziness exercised the military greatly, much to our amusement. The more they moaned, the more untidy we were. It was such a game.

The meeting was basically a roll call to make sure everybody had turned up for work. Quite often, you'd see the civilians roll out of bed at 0820 and stagger up to the meeting with their hangovers, in whatever clothing came to hand. Journalists are not known for their timekeeping. That didn't impress the military either, who had to come to the party suited and booted.

After the meet, the various staff groups would break off to their own offices and digest the never-ending litany of e-mails. On a typical day, that would occupy the staff until the coffee shops opened at 1000, when all would make a beeline for a hot latte. Then, time for a little more work, then the gym and lunch, until mid-afternoon. Bit more work, then an early finish to 'work in the room', which translated as goofing off with a movie. The key thing was to avoid the military, just as they tended to avoid us.

If it all sounds a little childish, remember that was life day after day after bloody day. It never varied. And some of the staff had been doing this for years. After mere months, it was bone-crushingly, repetitively draining. I've never been in prison, but I imagine life would be remarkably similar, except in prison you are unlikely to get rocketed or shot.

The real conflict with the military came during the inevitable change in gear each rotation brought.

Every six months, a new team would arrive, all bright-eyed and bushy tailed, eager to win the war on their shift. They'd compliment the out-going crew, then rip up the playbook the day after they had left. The military on operations very much lived the 24/7 life-style. For the consultants, the never-ending succession of bright idea fairies meant a constant battle to preserve previous success and trying to stop the inevitable waste of energy on re-energising ideas that had already been proven to fail. Nobody, apart from us civilians, remembered, or even cared, what had happened during the last six-month rotation.

The problem was that each military contingent was convinced it was right. We learned not to put too much work into each new plan, as we all knew none of them would survive into the next rotation. Likewise, the military kept all the higher planning functions to themselves, so we never really understood the big picture. Indeed, we strongly suspected there was none.

The soldiers made just being there immensely tiring.

Eric was fond of saying Afghan was a marathon, not a sprint. The military saw Afghan as a sprint, not a marathon. After a year or two as a civilian, it was inevitable that one burned out. The pace was unsustainable. Nor was there any need for it. The issue was really in how the work was viewed.

The military came to each tour after six months training and planning. Each new rotation was just busting to get going. They saw what we did in simple, objective, concrete military terms.

For example, CJPOTF produced a newspaper. From the military's point of view, success was defined by physically printing a 44-page newspaper every two weeks. What the civilians defined as success was what content filled the 44 pages. We saw the same problem from opposite ends of the spectrum—and how we approached the problem fundamentally differed too.

Every military officer has on their desk an issued manual that shows

EXACTLY how everything from a letter to complicated written orders will be written. In turn, every military officer will interpret those orders in exactly the same way. It has to be that way—you can't have a tank attack the wrong hill just because the orders to do so were penned as a fluffy story, not factual instruction.

Writing those orders is not a particularly creatively tiring business. It's process, repetition and plagiarism of the last set of orders.

Then, there is the pressure to be available. Nobody wants to leave the office before the general does. The guys in uniform would sit fourteen fucking hours a day, at their computer, just in case. Just in case of what, I was never sure. They just felt they had to be there, trying to complete the internet and every YouTube video ever up-loaded.

Writing for a newspaper is creatively tiring. I am writing this book in three thousand word chunks. It's about as much as I can sustain before my brain gets fried. It takes me a few hours to put my thoughts into order before I write, a couple of hours at the computer to get it down. I then like to go for a walk, before coming back, with fresh eyes to sub-edit. I'll then let it stew overnight, before checking it and re-arranging it the next day. That process drives army officers NUTS.

We were never there when they thought they needed us, and when we were, we'd produce random thoughts, or half-written notes, not NATO formatted staff papers. The irony is that, to be effective, we had to take time off, just to think—but it was our work that kept the place afloat.

The Americans, in particular, were extremely Calvinist about taking time off. In the early days, ISAF had been a lot of fun, with a lot of successes too. As the war had ramped up, and the US had made its over-whelming resources more apparent, America had come to shape the entire coalition.

By 2011, fun was being gradually banned. Fine if you were on a six month tour, and quite easy to sustain. If you were a civilian, already treated worse then the lowest private, it quickly became very hard to put up with. Civilian staff stayed for years; working for ISAF wasn't just a posting, it was life itself. After a while, you could actually see the arc of progress. The military were so busy just keeping the hamster wheel spinning, they forgot to smell the roses.

After a year or two, going to work became a struggle. The work never ended, the living conditions were akin to a Siberian work camp. Unlike the military, which had a 'no return' date stamped on every serviceman's passport until a decent interval had passed between six month tours, civilians were expected to just keep on chugging or quit. A sensible employer would have recognised the strain and organised month-long furloughs every couple of years or so. That, however, would have required strategic thinking, and, as you are beginning to understand, ISAF rarely thought beyond the immediate rotation.

So civilians stayed on in post long after their effectiveness was finished, hanging on for the salary. The forward media teams had one member who lasted seven years. By the time she left, she was barely capable of doing much more than sleeping and waking up. I was joining a unit that was at war with itself. Not just between the military and the civilians, but between the civilians as well. Everybody was just frazzled.

GIRDING THE LOINS

After a couple of days of making a token attempt of remembering the password of the day, I was rather keen to be rid of Kabul, and on to Kandahar. NATO, however, had other plans. First, I had to complete the dreaded JRSOI—Joint Reception, Staging and Onward Integration—package.

On my first British army tour of Afghanistan, way back, at the beginning of the war, we had literally just got on the plane and gone to war. We didn't even have desert uniforms.

My only issued map resembled a sheet of sandpaper. Correction—the sandpaper would have had more detail. On the first plane over, I had re-read George McDonald Fraser's fictional novel 'Flashman', which takes place during the 1st Anglo-Afghan war. It was the only available book on Afghanistan we had.

By 2011, life was much more bureaucratic—a weeks worth of bureaucracy, to be precise.

Most important was getting the ISAF badge. This laminated three by two-inch card was your ID, passport and lifeline, all in one. That card dictated everything from what you were allowed to do to where you were allowed to do it and for how long. Required be displayed openly at all times by civilian staff, losing it was a cardinal offence. An entire military section was employed merely to issue it.

Eight soldiers, expensively and expansively trained and equipped to fight a war, spent their entire tour of duty sorting and issuing laminated badges for the IJC. And that was merely the badge section in KAIA-N. All over the country, dozens of other soldiers were occupied issuing badges.

That was just for an ISAF badge. Each headquarters, all over the country, also issued their own, supplementary, badges—with their own, supplementary badge issuing section of soldiers. An entire battalion of soldiers dedicated to badges and their issuing. Afghanistan was a badge conspiracy.

By the time I left, I had a deck of cards worth of various IDs, just to get into the various places my work required me to be.

The military is very similar to the Boy Scouts. Badges, whether they be rank, unit, qualification, nationality or identity, define who and what you are. the military is badge-crazy.

To the untrained eye, uniform is uniform, they all look the same. A practised eye will spot the differences. It's in the nuances. With a little experience, you can take all in the badge iconography with a mere glance. Your place in the rigid totem pole of military structure is easily discerned.

We civilians, with our long hair and disreputable clothing, confused matters considerably. We didn't conform. Therefore we had to have extra badges, and an imposed structure. Much as the Nazis issued different coloured badges for Jews, homosexuals, political prisoners etc., so ISAF employed a colour-coded system for anybody not in a uniform. Badgery, and all things badge-related, was a fulltime, and very serious industry to place our round pegs into the military's square holes.

ISAF had a very distinct, and very military, system for assigning badges. In the early days, ISAF had all been one big ship, and pretty much everybody had just rubbed along. As the war had progressed, as the United States had become more dominant, the 'in it together' ethos had dissipated, to be replaced with a very real paranoia over base access. By 2011, there was a distinct US-inspired class structure over status.

Military personnel were issued with yellow ID badges. This was the top tier, VIP, access all areas, bring me champagne and grapes of badges. It marked one out as chosen. Yellow badges got to do everything, everywhere, at any time. In truth, I don't think the military were ever aware, or stayed long enough to be aware, of the whole badging apparatus, or the hoops everybody else had to jump through. If you wore a uniform, the world was yours, simple as that—despite the fact that the various cadres of civilian staff outnumbered the military by a considerable factor. In most places, the military didn't bother even wearing their badges. The uniform was enough.

Next in the pecking order came NATO staff, known as ICCs—International Civilian Consultants, of which I was one. We were given green badges. To be an ICC, you had to have a national security clearance. So we were sort of trusted agents. More importantly, we were covered fully by the terms of the international Military Technical Agreement, which defined the terms of the military mission in Afghanistan. If we were shot, we would have the right to be admitted to ISAF hospitals—which was nice to know. Our badges were marked in same way as the military's, with the ISAF logo.

After us came general contractors. Their badges were not marked with the ISAF logo. Not having an ISAF badge indicated you were not officially part of the mission. The contractor population numbered tens of thousands and covered everything from the guys who repaired the helicopters to the man who managed the coffee shop. Critically, you could only be classed as a contractor if you came from a NATO country, or a contributing nation. Wrong place of birth, no contractor badge. Generally speaking, they could access the general base areas and their work place, but not military compounds.

Last of all in the badge apartheid came the human tragedy that was called Third Country Nationals—TCNs.

TCNs were defined as those poor souls who came from a country other than NATO members or ISAF coalition partners. This covered a vast underclass, several hundreds of thousands, who actually did all the crap jobs that kept the place running.

Most of these guys were economic migrants, travelling the world for a fast buck. Generally speaking, they had arrived via Dubai and the human trafficking industry. The TCN population was ISAF's guilty secret that nobody really ever talked about. Nobody knew how many there actually were in Afghanistan. Bangladeshi, Nepalese, Filipino, Kenyan, you name it. They did everything from sort the rubbish to emptying the portaloos. A TCN badge was the mark of Cain. They were barred from even having a mobile phone on ISAF bases.

Neither contractors nor TCNs had the right to be treated at ISAF hospitals, except in life-threatening conditions. It was never made clear what actually happened after the life-threatening moment had been dealt with, or what actually constituted a life-threatening moment. Contractors and TCNs were definitely below the salt.

Just having a badge wasn't the end of the appraisal. Different physical areas had different security classifications. To get access to what were known as Class 1 areas, designated the most secure, you had to have the relevant enhanced security clearances and the signature of a military officer above the rank of major. If you were then deemed important enough your badge would then gain a bold red border, which was special juju indeed.

As an ICC, I had Class 1 access, and I jealously protected it.

The badges defined where one could work—across Afghanistan, or on your own camp only. It proclaimed whether one could have access to the base shops and gyms, something most TCNs were routinely excluded from, which must have made their lives miserable indeed. They couldn't even buy a bag of crisps.

Getting 'badged' was quite a pivotal moment. Unless you had a badge, you couldn't get onto any base. Without a badge, you had no status whatsoever. The badging system was a very real, and very unfair, apartheid. Even getting the simplest and lowest classification required a ream of paper, signed off by base security officers and supporting national and company paperwork. It could, and did, take days of office calls to collate it all.

The military automatically qualified without any of that, just as long as they wore a uniform. They never stayed long enough to need more than one badge, nor understand the caste system they had enacted. We civilians, on the other hand, had to go through the same tortuous process of badge renewal every six months.

Given that we were in Afghanistan, you might expect that there would be considerable numbers of Afghans employed in the ISAF camps. After all, we had come to try and help the place. Giving folks jobs would have been a start.

Quite the opposite happened. There were remarkably few ISAF Afghans. Those that were generally ran in-camp Afghan concessions, which allowed limited, daylight hours of access. There could also be a few interpreters, or, in the case of the CJPOTF, a few specialist staff. However, for all the billions spent, ISAF was not the great employer of locals it might have been.

Afghans had their own, special badges, even further down the tree than TCNs. Afghans were not trusted.

I had a badge-holder that I wore round my neck. I never went anywhere without that bloody badge. It was just too much trouble to even think about. In civilian clothing, any military member could challenge you at any time to show that ID. We had no right to challenge them. Without a badge, you could get yourself shot. In contrast, the military rarely wore theirs. It was as if a set of camouflage put you automatically inside the circle of trust.

The ISAF class structure was rarely far away.

In general, the military are rather like the masons. Strange and mysterious to those outwith the club, to those inside, the paraphernalia and ritual are comforting tokens of status and place. In ISAF, that structure was amplified by the very nature of our status as invaders and occupiers of a foreign land that was less than convinced that it wanted us there in the first place. Deployed military very much saw themselves as a class of warrior monk.

Until I was badged, Eric had to escort me everywhere, and I wore an orange triangle, to designate me as an alien guest. Once I was photographed, fingerprinted and badged, Dave could safely leave me on my own, in the expectation that I was not about to commit grand espionage.

I was issued with a very uncomfortable set of body armour and helmet. As with all military clothing, which is euphemistically described as 'unisex', the reality is that it is made for men. Men do not generally do curves. The other half of the population, being very much in the minority in the military, has to make do. Particularly where lady bumps are prescribed. Nature blessed me in that regard. The body armour hung off my chest like a fucking ski-slope. I could have balanced a teacup on the front plate.

Nonetheless, I was sternly told I had to wear it when ordered, or when I left camp. It goddammed hurt. It made me look fat. I wanted to look like Boadicea. I looked like widow bloody Twanky.

I was also supposed to be issued with a first aid kit, a set of gloves and some eye goggles. In true military tradition, there were none available. I was shown a photograph of them, though, and told what they would have done to protect me, had any been available. My name went on a list, should any ever become available in the future. I kept the photo, to remind myself of what I was missing.

Luka issued me with a toughened laptop, monitor, phone, camera and a ton of wires and cables. Apart from the camera, which was genuinely useful, the rest of it spent three years gathering dust under my bed. He also gave me a brick-sized file of security and personnel instructions, which I didn't read, and a load of free gifts, such as pencil sets and exercise books, monogrammed with the CJPOTF logo, to give to any Afghan kids I came across.

I had so much extra stuff I had to buy another suitcase.

Outside of the CJPOTF compound, KAIA-N's main function was to act as the headquarters for ISAF's international joint command, known, in the inevitable military-speak, as the IJC. This was a relatively new organisation that had sprung up after the initial debacle of command that had followed the big expansion of ISAF into the South and East in 2006-07. I've written more about that later, so I won't spoil the fun. Suffice to say, you won't believe it happened the way that it did.

The trouble with the IJC was that it had turned out to be a lot bigger than anybody had planned for. By 2011, some fifty-odd nations contributed to ISAF, and all fifty-odd expected to have some sort of representation at the highest operational headquarters going.

On top of the staff officers who actually ran operations, each country had a national support element (inevitably called an NSE) of concerned officers to look out for their own national interests, and individual liaison officers tasked with making sure everybody knew about those national interests. It was duplication of effort on a massive scale, and a hugely over-complicated command and information flow. The IJC and its spider's web was 'The Blob'. It just consumed people, literally thousands of people, all generating internal memos and important-looking files.

Each country had what were known as national caveats, which defined what each country would, and would not, do. Before the IJC issued any order, each line had to be pored over by each of the involved parties, and, in most cases, sent back to the individual capitals for checking. Thus, the Germans would not go on patrol at night. The Bulgarians would only patrol in vehicles inside camps, not on foot or outside the perimeter. More than half the countries that sent troops employed national caveats. Remarkably few actually came to fight a war.

The Americans had one, un-spoken caveat; that they would not take orders from anybody but an American. American soldiers called ISAF 'I saw an American fight.'

Days at the IJC merely mirrored the CJPOTF on a grander scale. In essence, the IJC ran the war. There was another supreme headquarters, called HQ ISAF, which dealt mostly with the military-political direction of the war, but the day-to-day operational decisions all came from the IJC. It was commanded by an American three star general, as befitted the kingpin status of the nation that contributed the lion's share of pretty much everything in Afghanistan.

And the Americans liked to spend money. When the Americans sent a general to do a colonel's work, then everybody else sent a general too. Same over-promotion applied to whole departments, and buildings and vehicles and guns and planes and all the other stuff. Putting stuff in gave back bragging rights. It would have been easier to pass out measuring tapes and let them all measure their willies. There were a lot of high-powered folks in IJC doing middle-powered jobs.

Building anything in ISAF required years of planning. By the time the actual work passed the planning, authorisation, budget and actual construction stage, a very large proportion of what actually sprang out of the ground no longer fitted the original purpose. If the military had been a private company, it would have gone out of business years ago.

KAIA-N and the IJC was one of those compounds. In the beginning, the plans had been for a small, lean outfit that could really command the war. By the time it had been built, with all that US-inspired competitive tendering, the IJC staff and stuff was way too big for the original building it was supposed to fit into. Quarts do not fit into pint pots.

The only space all those Duracell bunny staff officers could now remotely physically occupy was the space originally been earmarked to be the gymnasium. It was the only room big enough for the extra bodies and the computers.

After years of assiduous planning, the headquarters for the biggest overseas intervention since Korea was shoehorned onto the laminated wood floor of a basketball court. Being a gym, there was no room for all the ancillary offices a big headquarters required. The whole complex was surrounded with plywood huts, tents and yet more containers, exactly the sort of Heath-Robinson moment the entire project had been designed to avoid.

Inside the nerve centre of the headquarters, endless rows of computers and desks were arrayed into a raised horseshoe, in front of several massive television screens. It was very much akin to launch control for a space mission. I kept waiting for the organ to rise out of the orchestra pit and play the five tones. Theoretically, the TV screens allowed the watching staff to monitor everything in-theatre, down to individual vehicles. In front of it all sat several soft sofas, for visiting VIPS and the generals in charge.

IJC must have been a miserable place to work. There wasn't a window in the place and the room was way too small for the amount of people and equipment. What had been formulated as a showpiece permanent facility resembled little more than a gypsy camp.

The sacrifice of the permanent gym was mitigated by a plastic tent replacement, with remarkably inefficient air-conditioning. Winter or summer, sweat would condense on the inside and drip down on the occupants like rain. It stank of body odour and rancid training shoes: nothing like going for a treadmill run and being soaked by somebody else's body fluids dripping down on you.

Going to war can be remarkably boring, particularly if one's job was in a headquarters. Soldiers have a very keen sense of themselves as warrior knights. Much was made of the gym, condensed sweat or not, which contained a huge weights room. The military being overwhelmingly male, the sound of grunting filled the air, as soldiers strove to turn themselves into Schwarzeneggers. Men are just as body-conscious as women.

The IJC staff might not fire any actual guns, but at least the boys would go home looking the part. The Brits called this Operation Get Massive. Physical exercise was the only legitimate reason a staff officer could use to leave the desk. Getting the body into shape was a full-time pre-occupation in Afghanistan. That whole muscle-mary scene was remarkably homoerotic, as big men helped spot each other's weights and mutually admired their bulging physiques. Getting the body-perfect, upside down V was much desired. The tailors did a roaring trade taking in uniform jackets as the boys outdid each other's Van Damme styling.

The gym sat next to another circus tent, which contained what the US military call MWR—morale and welfare. Despite the multi-national image of the coalition, yet again this was all American funded. Inside the tent, the Americans had built a wooden two-storey structure, with a small library, internet café and some hotly fought over computer games consoles.

And that, folks, was kinda it for the work part. Not much else went on in IJC-land: all of it contained in about a half-mile square of over-congested dirt. The place could drive you stir-crazy, bat-shit mad really fast.

The IJC had more permanent buildings than most of the camps in the country. Most of these were accommodation blocks, made of concrete, but rendered with brick-effect tiles. These actually had flushing toilets and built-in shower rooms, a real luxury in Afghanistan.

Beside the accommodation blocks were a small hospital and a large buffet-style refectory, which the Americans called a D-FAC, or dining facility. While the food here was reasonable enough, the place fed thousands. The cacophony of noise, and the constant, ever-changing rush of warm bodies exchanging squeaking chairs, made any form of convivial eating impossible. Food was purely fuel, to be ingested as quickly as possible. Soldiers eat faster than any other humans I've ever met. They are living hoovers. Just watching gave me indigestion.

The only other building of note was the military air terminal itself, where I had arrived. On the camp side, it faced out onto a large parking lot, with a circular patio in the middle, containing the myriad flags of all the nations that contributed to ISAF. During the day, the parking lot filled with a never-ending succession of armoured vehicles and limousines, set to transport VIPs to their ever-urgent meetings. It was a hoot to see the strutting close-protection teams, self-importantly checking magazines and sights, in what was really just an over-sized car park.

If the physical structure of KAIA-N was nothing remarkable it was easily outdone by the shopping and fine dining facilities. The IJC had a European heritage, going right back to its founding days. While America, and American puritanism, was gradually taking over, in 2011 there were still enough Europeans to ensure that fun hadn't totally evaporated.

It was a matter of national culture. The Americans always seemed to me, at least publicly, to be determined to make things as fucking miserable as possible for everybody, including themselves. The European outlook on fighting the war could be just as serious as the Americans. Europeans just believed that it didn't have to be all black sackcloth and ashes too.

Originally, booze was on-tap all over ISAF. I recall earlier tours, before the Americans took over ISAF, being quite the bacchanalian enterprise. In 2004, I well remember driving nightly around Kabul with the most senior British officer in-theatre, hunting for the next very drunken party. Pretty much every night, we were out on the lash.

Christmas parties at the British Embassy were quite legendary, with invited guests wearing black tie and ball gowns, dancing away like 'Downton Abbey'.

My own finest moment came at the weekly UN shindig, where I barely made it back to my staff car in an upright condition, after a champagne lunch that had started at eleven in the morning. The UN compound had a staircase from a Disney movie and a forty-foot dining table. I'm a bit fuzzy on the detail, but I do seem to remember the centrepiece, a whole roasted boar with an apple in its mouth, being fist-malleted by a very angry marine.

Suffice to say when the Americans took over they tried very hard to stamp out the drinking. It took a couple of years, but by 2011, ISAF was mostly a drink-free zone. Which included the IJC.

The bar, however, remained open, in the form of a poorly-lit and alcohol-free discotheque, which spewed out very loud Euro-pop every night. The nightclub sat next to a very pleasant Greek restaurant (the salad and chips were very tasty), which was itself very close to a large Thai restaurant, a Lebanese restaurant, two very good cafes, serving frothy lattes, and an excellent steak house.

In pride of place were the shopping malls. Perhaps hard to believe but there were two. One was an Afghan-only facility, of about a dozen quite large stores. Here, it was possible to buy everything from tailor-made suits to extremely big knives. Souvenir-hunting soldiers, who would never fight anything more dangerous than a crashing computer, would order up 'Taliban-killer' T-shirts by the dozen. One could also buy the latest movies, including a raging trade in porn, direct from China, literally days after their release in the West.

In the centre of camp was the Western mall, which was another two-story confection of shipping containers, bolted together. The Italians contributed a pizza and pasta bar, and a very well stocked supermarket. I much enjoyed the fresh mozzarella balls and pilchards. The Turks supported a store selling hubble- bubble pipes and strange-smelling cigarettes.

The German exchange offered a bizarre mix of military clothing and accessories. Considering each and every soldier had brought at least their own body weight in uniforms and gear, I was always surprised at the amount of stock they shifted here. The Germans did a roaring trade in Seal Team 6 copies of camouflage jackets, gun sights, more badges, rucksacks and torches. It was even possible to buy a chess set, one set of pieces being painted ISAF soldiers and the other a very piratical set of Afghan bandits. All yours for a very reasonable $700 US.

Very, very few of the tens of thousands who served in the IJC ever saw anything of Afghanistan other than the inside of the KAIA N compound. The IJC was an alternate reality, of shiny staff officers, rushing around with important-looking briefing documents under their arms.

The cafes were full of debonair and nonchalant uniformed military theorists, smoking thin cheroots, squinting knowingly while talking rapidly out of the sides of their mouths. Military TLAs were liberally espoused. Tactical operations were forensically examined alongside grand strategy. All prefaced by the basest scuttle-butt and sexual innuendo.

The merest sight of a woman walking past would cause a table-full of men to stop conversation, swivel and enjoy the view. Which got really old really quickly for the women, but a never-ending source of fun for the men.

IJC was a heady and colourful mix. While the Americans wore matching, and very drab, camouflage baseball caps, the Europeans affected a bewildering and dazzling array of coloured berets and caps, emblazoned with flashy gold eagles and feathers.

One finely turned out Spanish officer proudly told me his impressive tricorn contained a bullet, so that he always had one round left to shoot himself should the enemy ever overwhelm him. Given that he told me this over an agreeable latte and cake in the Lebanese coffee shop, I couldn't foresee any immediate need for such dramatic gestures.

The British were just as affected, sporting a wide variety of vivid multi-coloured, striped three-inch wide belts and a multitude of beret colours from bright red to a rather puce green.

Affixed to sleeves and chest, every uniform sported a variety of skulls, eagles, spears, lightning runes, flags, guns, planes, tanks, horses and parachutes, all woven into a kaleidoscope of coloured badges. There wasn't enough uniform velcro for it all. The place was a Lilliputian delight, straight from the panto dressing-up box. Soldiers just love accessorising, bless them.

Every country had its own, individual rank badges, and each service—navy, air force and army—had its own sub-variety. An American colonel wore an eagle badge, while a Polish colonel wore two stripes and three stars. A German captain wore three four-pointed stars, the same pattern as a Belgian major general, while an American brigadier general wore one five-pointed star, the same as a Dutch 2nd Lieutenant. Even the ranks themselves had different names in each country and service. A naval captain wasn't the same as a captain in the army, but a colonel, a rank called a group captain by most European air forces.

It was a logistical nightmare for the poor enlisted soldiers, who were universally expected to salute officers of any nation. Office walls held huge, poster-sized charts explaining just exactly what the mix of stars, bars, stripes and colours meant to each of the fifty countries. Officers were categorised as OF, followed by a number, according to their seniority, up to an OF-7, which is somebody very important. The troops were categorised as OR, or 'other ranks', which, given they were the ones who did the heavy lifting, always seemed remarkably pejorative to me.

The boys always got the sharp end of the stick. When I first joined the army, all-ranks dinner invites were addressed as:

'To officers and their ladies, non-commissioned officers and their wives, other ranks and their women.'

The whole get-up was a military uniform spotter's delight and completely and utterly worthy of Lewis Carroll in its insane glory.

I have no doubt that the lowly staff officers worked rather hard, but the IJC also contained a bewildering number of generals, all of whom had very impressive titles like C-MOC-A. I never found out what that was, but it was engraved on a very impressive brass doorplate.

My last IJC visit, to the accounts department, to do my singularly important payroll induction, took me down an entire corridor of generals. I knew I was in a corridor full of important people because it had a shiny floor and a row of flags. General's corridors are always shiny. They have people who make them shiny. This is why they are generals. If you were anybody in Afghanistan, you had to have at least one equally shiny flag on show. The military has always had something of the pompadour about it.

My final combat indicator of rarefied air indeed was the presence of a bored soldier at a desk, whose function in life was to stand up when a general passed and to inspect minutely the badges of those who were patently not.

Although I was the proud possessor of a red-fringed green ISAF badge, and therefore not immediately subject to arrest, I didn't have the extra badge that I needed to enter the general's corridor. Getting into places was always a matter of having another badge. I had failed in the contest. I did, however, need to at least transit said corridor, in order to get at the money, a task at which I was determined to succeed.

My interrogator was Italian, and therefore a tremendous flirt. He took a long glance at my silk scarf, conveniently knotted at chest level, told me he liked the material, and waved me through with a large and lascivious wink.

I wasn't sure of exactly where accounts were, so, not being a man, and therefore not regarding seeking help to be a traitorous act, I resolved to ask somebody in the first office I passed. Which turned out to be occupied by a Spanish general. He was terribly obliging, but didn't know where accounts were either. A general would have had somebody fetch the money for them, therefore no need to know.

So he asked his neighbour, a large German general. He was equally unsighted, so they both asked their mutual neighbour, an Italian general. He wasn't sure either, but was delighted to help a damsel in distress: *Tres gallant*. All three quickly disappeared to fetch their very colourful, elaborate, ostrich-feathered, be-jewelled berets and off we set.

My generals were a bit confused when I told them that I just loved their look. After a couple of false starts and much competitive door-opening for me, we made it. Their imposing arrival *en masse* at the cash office gave a startled clerk the *oomph* I needed that dealing with me promptly would be a good idea.

Once my protectors had disappeared in a flurry of heel-clicking and elaborate saluting, signing-on was promptly completed. While the multiple stamping and signing of papers carried on, I decided to press my luck a little. My arrival had been impressive enough to warrant a little risk. Over three weeks in to my Afghan adventure, the tiny stock of cash I had brought with me was exhausted. I was skint. I couldn't afford another latte. So I asked for an advance.

'Of course', came the immediate reply. 'How much would you like?" After a breathless pause, I nonchalantly replied; 'och, nothing much, how much can you afford to give me?' A couple of hundred quid would have been a lifesaver, but I was sharp enough to play this one out. The clerk thought for a second, before replying; 'I have the payroll this afternoon, I am afraid. There's not much left. Would three thousand be enough?' Three fucking thousand?? You kidding me??

That was two months graft in the police. I hadn't realised then, but ISAF in 2011 was awash with cash. I could have asked for ten thousand and got it. As it was, I feigned an exasperated shrug of the shoulders and thanked him for making an exception. I took the precious envelope back to my room, spread the money out on the bed and lay on it all, making angel shapes with my arms.

My, what a life: a mega job, excitement on every corner, generals in funny hats escorting me and folks giving me as much cash as I could carry. My car had been worth less than the money I was lying on. This was living....

It was also my first inkling on how to win at this military game of rank of rank and status. I might only be a civilian, lower, in the military's eyes, than the newest private, but I'd seen how to get stuff done. Find a general; three, if possible.

I'd got the money by just being seen with these guys. In the military, generals are rock gods. They are the Beatles and Led Zeppelin, all wrapped up into one Thor hammer-wielding force of nature. It's not for nothing that a general's rank badges are called 'stars'. The more stars, the more the gravitational pull. Stuff just happens around them. It's Jean-Luc Picard instructing: 'make it so'. And it just does.

The odds were considerably against me making a success of this gig. I'd be going to Kandahar, a rather dangerous place to be. I'd be taking on a poisoned chalice of a job last occupied by a fraudster, working for a unit based hundreds of miles away. I'd be entirely on my own, representing an organisation which held only a very tenuous respect outside the rarefied atmosphere of the IJC. Add to that my civilian status, and being very much a female in a very macho world. I didn't have so much as a flat pair of shoes.

I did, though, have a lot of ambition. And, if I modestly may state, quite a bit more knowledge of Afghanistan and my subject matter than the average ISAF staffer. Even at this very early stage, I was formulating a concept to change the way we prosecuted the information war. I was determined to be much more than just a writer of articles.

I would need friends. In the military, the friends you need are generals.

As it came to pass, I would become close friends, for what I hope will be life, with several. I would succeed in making my job into everything I hoped for, and came close to changing the very base concept on how ISAF conducted psychological operations. All on my own, I gravitated to the top.

Like Icarus, though, I would find myself flying too close to the sun. Trouble is, the air can get mighty thin at that altitude.

BOBBIE AND BURROWS

Before I could leave for Kandahar, I had one last obligation to fulfil; my last brief, the dreaded 'backgrounder'. It made sense that the hundreds of thousands of soldiers, contractors, diplomats and hangers-on who came to Afghanistan knew at least something about the country they were nominally there to save.

As one of the very few military folks who had actually been to Afghanistan before the invasion of 2001, you might have thought my knowledge would have been in demand.

Ten years earlier, I'd prepared a brief on Afghan history—a madcap half hour romp through the modern country's foundation in the 1740's, right up to the fall of the Taliban regime, for the invading British contingent. A very senior officer, to whom I showed the draft, told me to cut it down to no more than five minutes on immediately relevant military history.

The United States has a roughly similar time-line as a formed state. I was being asked to distil Afghan history into the equivalent of describing the complexities of American history as:

Independence war, civil war, Indian war, World War (times two), cold war. The End.

The West had invaded Afghanistan, and sought to re-shape a complex, Islamic, socially conservative society, traumatised by thirty years of constant war, into a modern European liberal democracy. You might have thought the soldiers assigned to forge that vision could have expected a little more information.

The cuts demanded by this very important person were ridiculously savage. The British Empire had bordered Afghanistan for two hundred of modern Afghanistan's two hundred and sixty year history. Great Britain and its colonial levies had already fought three wars in Afghanistan that had defined the very borders of the country. More than any other country on earth, Great Britain shaped the entire Afghan personality and sense memory of conquest and foreign intervention—right down to the composition of the national flag.

I was told to remove any mention of that colonial adventure, beyond a cursory sentence that:

'In the nineteenth century, Britain and other powers had engaged in a great game of influence over Afghanistan.'

The reason given was that Britain had suffered two of its greatest colonial defeats of arms in Afghanistan. As the senior officer concerned put it:

'Soldiers are like horses. Feed them and stable them, give them a run out every once in a while, but don't scare them before the race is run.'

That was fucking patronising nonsense.

Then, I'd had to do as I was ordered. By 2011, matters were little better. Apart from the few thoughtful scholars of military history that I encountered, very few soldiers I met could recount any Afghan history at all. The ignorance was dumbfounding, even down to where exactly Afghanistan was. Americans in particular seemed to conflate the conflict. I lost count of the numbers of soldiers I asked whether they had been in Afghanistan before, only to be given the name of a city in Iraq in reply.

What the troops did get plenty of was why they were being sent—to find and kill the perpetrators of the 9/11 tragedy and to re-build Afghanistan. Most could recall those two aims without difficulty. Even if re-building Afghanistan wasn't why we had invaded and was very much an after-thought. Where they got unstuck was trying to explain why so many Afghans resented them being there, why they were being shot at by Afghans, and why so many of their friends were dying.

America and its allies are the good guys. Why didn't the Afghans understand that? If they'd read a little Afghan history, they might have understood.

As British, Dutch, Danish, Australian and American troops died in droves fighting over Kandahar and Helmand, they didn't know that the very soil they were bleeding into was the lodestone of the greatest battle Afghanistan as a nation had ever fought and won.

That one event explains in microcosm why the Pashtun people will always fight an armed invader. That one event coalesces all of Afghanistan's conundrums into one, singular episode. That one event was only ever mentioned in passing, if they were lucky, to succeeding rotations of soldiers who were bright and able enough to understand its message. Had their commanders thought to deliver it.

What happened at the Battle of Maiwand shaped a fragile peace that still eats into the hearts of every Pashtun and every Afghan. It is a event so venerated that the winner of the 2014 Nobel prize for peace bears the name of that day's greatest heroine: Malalai.

Afghanistan is a country that attracts the extraordinary, perhaps more so than any other land. In this century, Afghanistan marks the longest military campaign the United States has ever fought. In the nineteenth, it was the turn of the British to wield the sword of martial ardour, across one hundred years of near-unbroken tribal warfare. There is surely no other country in the world that bears witness to the boot-marks of so many marching columns of British soldiers, over so many years, as Afghanistan.

Early in the morning of 27th July 1880, one of those soldiers, British horse gunner James Collis, struggled to corral his team into bridle and bit. He could little know that the day to come would be the defining moment of his life. His actions would become part of history. He is one of the flotsam and jetsam that litter Afghan history, whose intrepid valour sit as grammatical pauses in the florid prose of its incredible history.

Collis joined the British army in 1872, eight years before he found himself in Afghanistan, near the head of a dusty column of khaki uniformed British soldiers. Collis trained as a gunner, before joining the horse artillery. At a time when the sudden parry of warfare was judged by the speed of a canter, his regiment was charged with moving swiftly, alongside the cavalry, to provide deadly close support in battle.

He and his fellow horse soldiers used the Armstrong 9 pound muzzle-loading cannon, well respected for its ease of use and maximum range of 4,000 yards. Collis rode with a gun-team, riding at the front of the traces of his team of six horses, which towed a limber of ammunition and equipment, paired by the gun itself behind. It made for an ungainly procession of three moving parts that required great skill and strength to manoeuvre and manhandle into position.

James was not, by today's standard, a big man, but he was undoubtedly physically doughty. The 27th of July would see his physical endurance tested to the limit.

Collis was posted to India, where his unit, E battery of B brigade, Royal Horse Artillery, formed part of the British Empire's Indian army. After years of dreary and uneventful service, his moment in history would chime as part of one of those swells in public opinion that occur once in each generation. A 'something must be done' moment, where the resources of a great nation, borne along on a wave of righteous indignation, set into play chess pieces that cannot be recalled.

Then, as now, the world was divided into competing great powers. Just as the United States would claim the latter part of the 20th century as its own, so Great Britain claimed the latter part of the 19th. The British ruled an empire forged in trade and commerce, commanded and led by a remarkably small military, diplomatic and administrative cadre. No more so than in British India, which was effectively held in sway by coercion, bribery and ruthless application of *force majeure*.

British rule was, first and foremost, about exploitation of India's remarkable human and natural resources. Begun by the British East India Company, the Indian Army had been, in effect, a mercenary force, enlisted and paid for by the company, not the British government. The Indian mutiny of 1857 had seen the small cadre of British regulars re-inforced, and the Indian army had been forced to fall more in line with the dictates of London, but that sense of Indian independence and separate tradition still ran extremely strong.

It took months to reach India, by steamer, from London. Officers assigned to India would expect to serve their entire careers in India. British regiments posted to India could expect to spend decades in continental service. Likewise, government officials would spend years living in the same localities, dispensing justice under the shade of a jacaranda tree, quill and ink in one hand, the other firmly on the hasp of the money chest.

British rule was, in many senses, a two-edged sword for those charged with its implementation.

On a positive note, the British undoubtedly had a familiarity with the environment and culture they ruled. Colonial officers were required to study the local languages. Decisions on development would directly affect those officers, as they would have to live with the consequences—literally. The British-Indian ruling classes became as much a product of India as the playing fields of Sussex that had shaped their youth.

On the negative side of the ledger, such a system could breed a sense of in-bred superiority. It was as inconceivable for James Collis to doubt his own heritage as it is for today's American soldier to doubt his own belief in the righteousness of the cause of American democracy. Being top dog does not breed self-doubt.

Of course, such self-belief is inherently built upon a concept, an idea—the inherent right of the British to rule, simply because they were British and therefore better. The very epitome of 'manifest destiny.'

The British believed they were better educated, better bred and more advanced as a civilisation than their colonial vassals. When simply setting a better example to the natives didn't work, the British could fall back on the most advanced armed forces in the world to re-inforce the point.

Manifest destiny, as a concept, worked well for a prosperous nation, whose only wars were fought for possession of overseas territory. British society, despite its Dickensian class inequality, had systems, laws and governance that had all conspired to make Great Britain the greatest country in the world. Every British citizen felt part of the experiment, which enshrined the right to individual advancement through hard work and enterprise.

To this day, the inside leaf of a British citizen's passport contains the words:

'Her Britannic Majesty's Secretary of State requests and requires in the Name of Her Majesty all those to whom it may concern to allow the bearer to pass freely without let or hindrance, and to afford such assistance and protection as may be necessary.'

At the height of Empire, British prime ministers sent gunboats to enforce Britain's right to rule the world as it saw fit.

Not so in Afghanistan, which was for much of the nineteenth century wracked with civil war, poverty and destitution. All very well to debate the 'Rights of Man' when bellies are full and hearth fires are blazing. In Afghanistan, debate has always been motivated by the very essence of survival, of immediate gain, not the higher echelons of philosophical existence. Then, as now, the average Afghan saw little more ambition than the desire to wake alive the following morning.

In 1880, Afghanistan and Britain were radically different societies—and neither side chose to see the problem from the other's point of view. The British saw Afghanistan, or more precisely, the problem of Afghanistan, through the prism of their own existence. What the average Afghan wanted was immaterial. How could their aspirations be different from those of the greatest power on earth? Afghan and Briton effectively looked through the kaleidoscope of life from opposite ends—and never the twain would meet.

For Britain, Afghanistan was a never-ending problem. The porous Afghan/ Indian border, and the volatile hill tribes it sheltered, posed a constant threat to the sedate Indian hinterland. British India was the jewel of empire. Its economic importance—and the prestige possession gave—obsessed British society and government.

Great Britain remained greatly exercised by the manoeuvres of an avaricious Russian Empire. The ruinous Crimean war may have stymied Russian expansion into Europe and Asia Minor, but the Russian bear's ambitions across Persia and South Asia were very real. Afghanistan remained a pawn between two military and economic giants, eying each other across the boxing ring of global hegemony. Both Russia and Great Britain regarded Afghanistan as key terrain.

The British shared a sense of dis-belief that such a 'primitive' society as Afghanistan would not readily embrace the concepts of British rule, justice and governance as inherently better than the constant tribal bickering, warfare and medieval abuse that the Afghans seemed to espouse. Just as we, in our century, would attempt to re-mould Afghanistan into a wishful Asian Switzerland, so the British would regard Afghanistan as an unruly school child, just waiting to fall under the shadow of benevolent Victorian munificence.

That is not so say that the British did not recognise the enormous cost in operating within Afghanistan's forbidding frontiers. By 1880, Britain had tread the mountain passes of the Hindu Kush on more than one occasion.

James Collis' moment of glory came at the apex of Britain's second great foray into Afghanistan. A disastrous first expedition, in the winter snows of 1842, to place a surrogate friendly to British interests on the Afghan throne, had led to the destruction of the entire British invasion force. Surrounded and depleted by harassing Afghan tribesmen, the British had unwisely retreated from Kabul in the midst of winter. Attempting to reach the temperate plains of Jalalabad, through the snow-bound Kabul Pass, the entire column of 16,500 men and women had been butchered to the last soldier.

For forty years hence, the British had maintained an uneasy peace with their Afghan neighbours.

Vacillating between policies defined as 'forward first' and 'masterly inactivity', the British had alternately intervened, ignored and paid off a succession of ever more rapacious would-be Afghan Emirs. All the while, the British had suspiciously watched an expansionist Russian empire encroach further south, until it had come to touch the very western borders of Afghanistan itself. Vigorous U-turns in British policy were mirrored by the on-going debate taking place at the core of British domestic politics. The climatic struggle between those titans of 19th century British politics, Gladstone and Disraeli, would come to define Great Britain's role in the world.

As Disraeli and Gladstone fought for power, so that great debate would, almost by osmosis, twitch along the telegraph wires to Delhi. British success in

Africa would lead to a surge in domestic pride for British arms abroad. The 'forward first' proponents mounted punitive expeditions to land-grab more and more territory.

The campaign to seize the province of Sind, in 1843, which would buttress British India directly against the borders of Afghanistan, was justified by its commander, General Sir Charles Napier, with this muse on the nature of power:

'The best way to quiet a country is a good thrashing, followed by great kindness afterwards. Even the wildest chaps are thus tamed.'

The trouble was, of course, that by 1879 the British were not the only game in town. Great Britain found itself under threat from a series of usurpers. In Africa, Belgium and Germany succeeded in destroying Cecil Rhodes' dream of a British rail express from Cairo to the Cape. In Asia, the ambitions of the Russian bear, which had caused the disastrous Crimean War a mere 25 years earlier, had metamorphosed into a covert, but keenly fought, campaign for influence over the potentates and kingdoms of Asia and the mid-East.

Not for the first time in its history, Afghanistan found itself once again under the magnifying glass of international attention, as both the meat in the sandwich between two aggressive commercial and ambitious Empires and as a through-route for conquest.

On the one side, to the east and south, the fatted calf of British India, the heart-blood of empire, and the single biggest trading partner Great Britain possessed: itself a nation dependent for its very existence on trade and commerce with its docile dominions. On the other, to the north and west, a Russian empire and its surrogates, eager for territory, seeking, through geographic expansion, to extend its influence from the borders of Europe to shores of the Indian Ocean to the arctic wastes of Alaska.

In the middle, land-locked Afghanistan—a dichotomy of history, worthless to the world as a physical territory, but priceless as security for external interests. Not for the first time in its history, Afghanistan in the 1870s was convulsed by a complicated series of internecine struggles. By the end of the decade, that struggle between brothers and cousins had become a deadly reality, resulting in a conflict that would reverberate across continents.

To an eager outsider, regardless of the timeline of history, looking for an ally to cleave to a cause, the myriad intricacy of Afghan politics is impenetrable.

The British decided that thrashing the untameable Afghans was their only option to secure their own borders. What happened in 1879 was not an invasion of Afghanistan to stay, it was an attempt by an external power to produce a stable Afghanistan that would not be a threat to everybody else: mixed with a healthy dose of imperial hubris.

The great irony of Afghanistan is that it can produce ruthless and driven leaders by the barrel-load, yet remarkably few that have had the foresight, or ability, to harness both the Afghan people and manipulate external aggressors. The irony for Afghanistan's invaders is that, try as they might, the puppets they have chosen have rarely proven to be either supine or independently effective. Most have remained resolutely mediocre.

Does any of this sound familiar? It ought to.

Just as in 2001, 19th century Afghanistan found itself to be victim of international forces beyond its control or influences. The Afghanistan of 1879 was no player in the great game of world political and military domination, just as in 2001.

Both invasions were pre-meditated primarily by fear. In 1879, the root cause was British fear that Russia could attack British India through Afghanistan. In 2001, the root cause was that Al-Qaeda, another third party enemy, could mount further attacks on America through its bases in Afghanistan. In neither case was Afghanistan the author.

Granted, in 1879, there was no single 9/11 attack on the homeland, more a gradual chain of events over decades. Still, the eventual outcome was the same—an over-whelming feeling that 'something' should be done. In both cases, invasion was portrayed as pre-emptive defence of a way of life, whose values the average Afghan could not recognise, in either century. In both cases, the threat was exaggerated, but fear of the Afghan bogeyman would be enough.

The similarities continue:

In 1879, the Afghans had the mis-fortune to host a Russian delegation, much to the fury of the British, who ordered the Afghans to expel them. The Afghans refused. In 2001, the Afghans hosted Al-Qaeda, much to America's fury, which ordered the Afghans to expel them. The Afghans refused.

From the Afghan end of the telescope, expelling a guest was anathema, in terms of both Islamic and Afghan culture. In both cases, Afghanistan apologised politely, but insisted on not complying. Afghanistan has paid a high price for its stubborn independence of thought and action. More honest mis-understanding than wilful deceit, history, indeed, repeats itself throughout Afghanistan's long battles.

Something continually has to be done about Afghanistan. Which is a remarkable legacy for a land-locked, largely undeveloped South Asian country.

In 1879, Sher Ali Khan, the reigning Afghan amir, appeared favourable to Russian entreaties. Sher Ali was, by then, on his second stint on the throne. He had been amir in the 1860s, before losing power to an uprising led by one of his brothers. That brother had conveniently died three years later, to be replaced by another brother, who also died in quick succession. Sher Ali Khan once again regained the throne.

All terribly Afghan, but an inconsistency viewed with dismay by Afghanistan's British neighbours. The apparent chaos of an ever-changing ruling succession caused deep disquiet.

Now Sher Ali Khan had turned to Russia. Given the ups and downs of Sher Ali Khan's life, that entreaty may have been merely an act of personal insurance. It was, however, an act of deadly treachery for the British.

What mattered less was the future of Afghanistan itself. If Afghanistan played host to Russian troops, then British India itself would be deemed under threat. The British and Russians had only just concluded peace at the Congress of Berlin, following a disastrous series of wars, including that in the

Crimea. Fear of Russia, and the role Afghanistan was playing in encouraging Russian overtures, caused alarm in Delhi and in London.

Afghanistan was proving, yet again, to be an un-scratchable burr under the saddle.

The British in India decided to invade, to settle the matter once and for all. Proving once again the independence and primacy of India, Lord Lytton, the British viceroy of India, effectively decided imperial policy on his own. He would usurp Sher Ali Khan's rule and force his compliance, or ensure his replacement with an administration more pliant to its dominant neighbour.

Three columns of British troops were duly assembled. During the winter of 1878-9, they drove hard at Afghanistan's heart. Conquest was swift. By the late spring, the British found themselves in control of the key centres of Eastern Afghanistan.

Sher Ali Khan withdrew to Mazar E Sharif, in the North, where his pleas to the Russians for assistance were ignored. He died shortly afterwards. It must have been an ignominious end for the Amir, with most of his country under British occupation. He left his son, Mohammad Yacub Khan, a compromise leader, to sign a peace treaty with the British: the Treaty of Gandamak.

Gandamak marked the very spot where, forty years earlier, the first British army had been massacred in the deep snows of the Afghan winter. The British did not choose the place of signing accidentally.

Yacub Khan was faced with little choice. He had no loyal forces of his own, much his country was under British control, occupied by an invading force of some 40,000 troops. His right to rule was internally heavily disputed—his very life depended on signing. As price for his signature, the British agreed to provide him with an annual stipend, but, more importantly, their patronage. In return, he agreed to the most humiliating terms any Afghan leader has ever signed with a foreign power.

He signed away his country's right to act freely on the international stage, and condemned Afghanistan to be a mere vassal of the British Indian Empire:

'His Highness the Amir of Afghanistan and its dependencies agrees to conduct his relations with Foreign States in accordance with the advice and wishes of the British Government. His Highness the Amir will enter into no engagements with Foreign States, and will not take up arms against any Foreign State, except with the concurrence of the British Government. On these conditions the British Government will support the Amir against any foreign aggression with money, arms, or troops, to be employed in whatsoever manner the British Government may judge best for this purpose.'[1]

The British must have felt it was the end of the business. Afghanistan had agreed, through a formal treaty, not to act against British interests. Indeed, to only act in support of British interests—and only when the British said so.

For good measure, the British also insisted on Afghanistan ceding the territory around the Khyber, as well as Quetta. In a single stroke, they had

---

[1] Extract from Treaty of Gandamak

moved the boundary of British India several hundred miles to the west. In their delight at their sheer cleverness and bravery, the British failed to take note that the new border completely cleaved the homelands of Afghanistan's most numerous tribe, the Pashtun, in two.

On a topographical map, the terms made absolute sense. The British would gain the defence buffer of the Suleiman mountains, and the important regional centres of Peshawar and Quetta. Even if Afghanistan fell under Russian dominance, the new border would provide an ideal defensive barrier.

On a sociological map, the treaty was an absolute disaster. Half the Pashtun people would fall under British rule, half would remain free, under Afghan rule. The new border agreement was to be as controversial as the Berlin Wall.

In a spirit of triumph, the vast majority of the British force withdrew, across the mountains to the newly created North-West frontier.

In Afghanistan, resentment simmered dangerously, and quickly came to boiling point. For Afghans, to this day, the Treaty of Gandamak remains an act of mortal deceit.

The Afghan flag is a tri-colour of red, green and black. Red represents blood and sacrifice. Green represents hope and growth. The black is a permanent reminder of what was ceded by Afghanistan in the Treaty of Gandamak. The terms were so onerous that they are permanently commemorated as an event so dire that they should never again be repeated.

Above all, Afghans are a proud and independent nation. The Pashtun ruling classes define their very masculinity on their independence. What the British did certainly bought them time. It did not buy even the acquiescence of their neighbour, however much they may have felt they had forced Afghan consent.

In 2003, another invading army made much the same mistake. In the aftermath of the punishing Taliban regime, with the country in a shambles, a new composite Afghan administration was under much the same duress as Yacub Khan's. Compromise leader President Hamid Karzai depended completely on international support. But the terms of that support were just as qualified as the British Treaty of Gandamak had been. No matter that the international community was insistent it had not come to Afghanistan eighteen months earlier as invaders, the terms of their presence had an awful ring of history.

The new invaders called themselves ISAF –the International Security and Assistance Force. Its presence was mandated by the United Nations itself. At the time of signing, most Afghans welcomed the demise of the Taliban. As the years were to pass, that initial euphoria came to be questioned, as war continued to dog Afghanistan. The very terms of the military technical agreement that authorized the presence of international forces has come to hauntingly remind ordinary Afghans of the infamous treaty of Gandamak:

'The Interim Administration understands and agrees that the International Security and Assistance Force (ISAF) Commander will have the authority, without interference or permission, to do all that the Commander judges necessary and proper, including the

use of military force, to protect the ISAF and its Mission. The Interim Administration understands and agrees the ISAF will have complete and unimpeded freedom of movement throughout the territory and airspace of Afghanistan.'[2]

Placed next to the treaty of Gandamak, how those words, to an Afghan, must echo the same imperial spirit of conquest. In late 2013, as the ten year term of the original MTA ran out, the Americans sought to put in place a new agreement, allowing for the retention of a rump force of US soldiers to remain in Afghanistan. Despite convoluted and complex negotiations, President Karzai refused to sign. I well remember sitting with American generals and ambassadors, listening to their obvious frustration at what they saw as obduracy and dis-loyalty from the Afghan side.

How could the Afghans reject the overtures of the most powerful country in the world, to stay and conduct counter-terror missions, to train and advise Afghan soldiers?

Just as the British had failed generations before, now the Americans could not see the view from the other end of the kaleidoscope. They failed to comprehend how each and every Afghan generation since the time of Yacub Khan has seen the Treaty of Gandamak as a national humiliation. How closely the MTA resembled that document, and how President Karzai, to the last day he held power, would refuse to go down in history as the next Yacub Khan—a man seen as turncoat and traitor to his people.

Yacub Khan was not forgiven. Yacub Khan had been a reluctant ruler in the first place, telling Lytton that:

'I would rather work as your servant, cut grass and tend your garden than be the ruler of Afghanistan.'

In a country where pride is all, he had thrown his reputation away in a moment of grovelling self-survival. The British had got their man to sign to their terms, but at what price?

During the late summer of 1979, the British installed a delegation in Kabul, to oversee Afghan affairs, but foment quickly rose within the country, in opposition to British control. Another Afghan rebellion, this time led by Yacub Khan's brother, Mohammad Ayub Khan, a mere three months after the treaty signing, led to Yacub Khan swiftly abdicating.

Matters quickly spun out of control. The small and poorly protected British delegation in Kabul was slaughtered to a man by a rampaging mob. British imperial ambition, only months previously at its apogee, had, yet again, been snubbed by what was seen as a primitive and barbaric nation of mere tribal levies.

British indignation and a thirst for revenge were swift. This was an act of terror that must be avenged. Ample evidence appeared that suggested the British delegation had not just been killed by a violent mob, but that their bodies had been torn apart and mutilated.

---

[2] Extract from the Military Technical Agreement between ISAF and the interim government of Afghanistan

Just over twenty years earlier, during the Indian mutiny, the British had suffered much the same fate in a chilling pre-cursor. The generation of 1857 remembered well the depravity of the black hole of Calcutta, Cawnpore and Lucknow. That generation now led British India.

As with the horrific destruction of the Twin Towers, it wasn't just the physical act itself. It was the perception of violent repudiation of British values, of British imperial prowess, riches and power. How could such a people refuse to embrace British liberal democracy and protection? Coupled with abject fear that the entire institution of British imperial rule was itself under mortal threat. Thirty years later, with Britain still fighting pointless engagements over the same territory, Winston Churchill described the Afghans as:

'Degraded a race as any on the fringe of humanity: fierce as a tiger, but less cleanly: as dangerous, not so graceful.'[3]

In 1879, the fire of British imperialism and self-belief was at its apogee. British power had no match in the world. Afghanistan would be made to pay, and pay heavily.

As with so many actions in Afghan history, British actions were defined through the prism of individual perspective. The Indian viceroy, Lord Edward Lytton, again acted presumptively. He was a proud subject of the Queen Empress Victoria. Yet, in reality, he was almost a king in his own right. The first direct telegraphy link with London had not been established until 1870. Lytton controlled a landmass that covered not just modern-day India, but Pakistan, Bangladesh and Burma. At the time of the Treaty of Gandamak, he still ruled by proxy—and informed London afterwards.

For Lord Lytton, the murder of the British envoy in Kabul, Major Louis Cavagnari, and his entire delegation was as much an act of terrorism and a direct threat to an entire way of life as the Twin Towers are to our generation.

As viceroy, he controlled the British Indian army, an amalgam of native levies and British regulars. Lytton's outrage at Afghan duplicity, combined with his executive power, made him a formidable avenger.

The men that led his furious response were to become, perhaps, a more memorable group than Lytton himself. Names such as General Sam Browne, the one-armed general, who invented the cross belt still worn by officers the world over. And a small firecracker of a man, only 5'2", who was to become the highest decorated officer of his generation Field Marshal Lord Frederick Roberts of Kandahar.

As ever with generals, the thirst for engagement came naturally. Being a soldier is a little like being on the substitute's bench for the big game. Each longs for the opportunity to play. War being the game. British officers in India were no different. Long, hot and tortuous days on the parade grounds of Cowpur and Madras were made bearable by the romantic thought of adventure on the North West Frontier. Fighting in Afghanistan had the same

---

[3] 'The Story of the Malakand Field Force', Winston S. Churchill

romantic attachment to that generation of soldier as it does to today's.

It is a rare soldier that reflects on the causes of conflict when offered the opportunity to enter the field of battle. Soldiers act, they do not meditate. The British army of 1879 was no different.

Offered the chance of yet another foray into the Afghan interior, the army set off with a strong sense of righteous entitlement and a fire in its belly for action and revenge. They were cheered on by near-complete public approval for an act of revenge and settling of accounts.

Just as in 2001, the Afghans were unable to resist this new invasion force. Despite some heroic defensive actions, the British force, combined of both British regulars and Indian levies, used their advantages of superior training and equipment to good effect.

Major General Roberts quickly marched to take Kabul from the north, while a second column marched from Quetta to Kandahar, under Lieutenant General Donald Stewart. Gunner James Collis and the men of the Royal Horse Artillery marched with Stewart to Kandahar.

Roberts swiftly took the capital, despite heavy opposition, by skilful use of ground and well-drilled troops. He then ran into difficulty in subduing the provinces around Kabul, which showed the usual Afghan stubborn aggression to invading outsiders. Roberts needed extra troops to make good his success. Stewart left behind a garrison in Kandahar, including Collis' horse artillery, to make his way to Kabul to assist Roberts –winning a notable victory at Ahmed Khel on the way. Heavily outnumbered, his British and Indian troops won through by steady discipline, tactical leadership and a withering rate of fire.

The tide turned decisively in favour of British arms. Ayub Khan fled to Herat, in the West, while the British hunted down any and all accused of being involved in the massacre of the British legation. Roberts was to earn a dubious reputation as the sword of British justice by ordering the public hanging in Kabul of any captured ringleaders. By mid-summer, it looked as if the British were, once more, in charge.

Ayub Khan was made of sterner stuff than his brother. While the British contented themselves with control of the East, he gathered an army around him. The British, suddenly facing an organized foe, needed to find a replacement amir—and quickly. Realizing that returning Yacub Khan was wholly untenable, they instead chose to place another cousin, Abdul Rahman Khan, on the throne instead.

The hapless Yacub Khan, whose father had precipitated the entire chain of events by hosting the Russians in the first place, was quietly dispatched to Simla, in British India, where he would quietly live out his days on a British stipend. His reputation would forever be dust amongst his own people.

Ayub Khan and a large proportion of the Afghan people were outraged. First, the British had forced the removal of Sher Ali Khan, by act of invasion. The British had then propelled a weak puppet, Yacub Khan, to the throne, whom they had forced to sign over Afghan freedom of action and a huge swathe of territory in a humiliating act of submission. When the Afghan people had risen against this degradation, the British had forced an Afghan

Bonny Prince Charlie, Ayub Khan, from his throne, to replace him with yet another puppet.

The British had provided Ayub Khan with all the popular support he would need. By the summer of 1880, he was ready. He marched from Herat towards the key city of Kandahar, and his date with destiny.

The British garrison opposing him in Kandahar was to be poorly served by its commanders. The officer sent to oppose Khan was Brigadier George Burrows. A popular officer, he had, however, never commanded troops in the field: particularly one of a combined force of infantry, cavalry and artillery.

Burrows and Roberts had both been Indian army officers for decades. Both had risen through the quartermaster general's office. Yet, Burrows geniality and evident popularity with his troops was his downfall. While Roberts proved ruthless and decisive, Burrows proved incapable of making the incisive decisions required of frontier warfare.

Burrow's brigade, on paper, looked formidable—a mobile force of some 2,500 troops. Under the surface, although stiffened by a crack British regiment, the 66th of foot, most of his levies were completely untried in battle. Despite the rawness of his brigade, Burrows failed to hold rehearsals and exercise before his departure from Kandahar. His men were nowhere near combat ready.

Amongst their number were the guns of E battery of the Royal Horse Artillery. Gunner Collis found himself suddenly at the tip of the spear of British imperial intent. On the morning of 27th July 1880, as history beckoned, he placed harness on his horses, and prepared to ride west, in column of march, towards the forces of Ayub Khan.

James Collis was an invader, one of countless thousands who have come from foreign homes to 'change' Afghanistan. Like those countless thousands, he must have wondered at the futility of such a mission. What had begun as yet more garrison duty, guarding lines of communication through Kandahar, had suddenly acquired an urgency and fury he could not yet fully comprehend.

As ever, Afghanistan had proved to be a beguiling foe. What had begun as an act of revenge, founded on fear and misunderstanding, had suddenly mutated into a vicious civil war, which threatened to spill out of control.

What Collis and his fellow British soldiers would do that sultry summer day provides the circumstances for the single most defining event of Afghan history that carries resonance through to this day, just as if it had all happened only yesterday.

The two opposing forces, of Ayub Khan and George Burrows, were destined to crash together in a grinding of tectonic plates that represented not just a trial of martial ardour but a struggle between two completely different societies and cultures.

For an Afghan, the events of 27th of July 1880 would prove to be as much an epic of national pride and endurance as the resistance of three hundred Spartan hoplites at Thermopylae are to the liberal democracies of the west.

27th July 1880 is what Bannockburn is to a Scot, or Little Big Horn is to the plains Indian. It is both overwhelming martial achievement and pyrrhic victory. It is a legend learned at a mother's knee, and imprinted on the conscience of every Pashtun child.

What was to become known as the Battle of Maiwand embodies the very perversity of the Afghan spirit, their spirited independence, to the point of collective destruction, and their desire for self-reckoning and governance.

The climatic battle would happen on the border of what is now Helmand and Kandahar Provinces. As Ayub Khan marched south-east from Herat, Burrows came west from Kandahar. The two sides met in a border district still known as Maiwand, at a village called Khig. The village is still there, just as the monument to what happened is still there, at the end of a road called

'The Avenue Of Martyrs.'

That day, the cause of Afghan nationalism and pride was to induct its greatest legend, and its greatest call to arms against a foreign invader. Maiwand is the pivotal battle in Afghan history. This generation of British soldier, many the successors to the 66th of Foot, would fight over the same ground in the Helmand campaign of 2007-14. History can, indeed, provide its own ironies.

Brigadier Burrows thought he would be facing a force of between 10 and 15 thousand. Given the record of British forces, and their preponderance of modern munitions, the odds were not seen as over-whelming for his 2,500 troops. Precedents, such as Ahmad Khel, all favoured British superiority in battlefield technology and discipline. In any case, Burrow's orders were to blunt the Afghan force before it enveloped Kandahar itself, not to force mortal combat.

Burrows had left Kandahar filled with a sure conviction in his own leadership and his troop's capability against an unworthy foe. Operating in a land he had never before traversed, his troops travelled in slow-moving column of route. Despite having never worked or fought together, Burrows failed to commit to any reconnaissance, completely dismissing intelligence of a fast-moving horde headed in his direction.

Burrows had already suffered setback. In earlier skirmishes, the British-appointed Wali of Kandahar, an erstwhile ally, had deserted to Khan, taking many locally recruited troops with him. The Wali and his men had acted as Burrow's local scouts. The British were now effectively blind on the battlefield.

His Indian regiments, the bulk of Burrow's force, had never been tested or manoeuvred, under fire. Many of the Indian levies did not even know the names of their English officers.

Most critically, Burrows did not know that Ayub Khan had rallied thousands more to his banner. He moved against Burrows with a force not of 15,000: but of nearly 25,000. The British were outnumbered ten to one.

Burrows did not know the ground, the strength of his enemy, his foe's intent and was unsure of the morale and capability of his own forces. Like Custer, Burrows almost deliberately did not foresee the battle that was to follow, or the fate that was to befall him. It was a fatal act of hubris.

Ayub Khan's ranks were swollen with fanatical *ghazis*, sworn to jihad against the foreign invaders. They were by no means crudely armed. His force mustered the very same Armstrong guns, captured from the British, that Gunner Collis prided himself on. The Afghans knew how to use those guns; many rebel gunners had originally been trained by the British.

Burrows, contrary to his orders to delay, not fight Ayub Khan, inexplicably decided to offer battle. Burrow's Brigade was marching to disaster.

After a confusing, and tiring, night march, Burrows pulled off the main Helmand-Kandahar highway and drew his forces into a long extended line, facing roughly north to south. He placed his best force, the British 66th, to the south. While the levies, artillery and native cavalry stood in exposed terrain, surrounded by culverts and deep ditches, in a long and obvious line to their north. By the afternoon, their water was exhausted. In July, the daytime temperature in Maiwand can peak at nearly at nearly fifty degrees centigrade. It is an unremitting and relentless inferno. Under the glare of the mid-summer sun, troops collapsed from heat exhaustion.

The Afghan hordes surrounded the line, as a glove covers an outstretched hand. It began as a long-range snipe, followed by a cannonade. From three sides, the Afghans mounted a fierce artillery barrage. Using those hidden ravines, they squirreled closer and closer to the British lines, sniping at the officers, panicking the troops.

The British remained supine, taking casualties in the open, as their tactical mobility eroded, their leadership was killed and their positions became steadily untenable. Morale dissipated as the British watched the Afghans advance as surely as a raindrop will run down a windowpane. What had begun as a trickle became a torrent, as the sheer weight of Afghan numbers became more and more apparent.

Nonetheless, the British force continued to pour fire upon the Afghan masses, which charged heedlessly towards them, seeking to break the line. The guns of the Royal Horse Artillery, and Gunner James Collis, scampered from position to position, bolstering resolve, firing point-blank at ranges of less than 25 yards, into the enemy ranks. Afghan soldiers were torn limb from limb, as grapeshot and shrapnel tore into the frenzied ranks of charging *ghazi* warriors.

Collis' battery commander was killed, his own gun commander gravely wounded. The limbers ran out of ready ammunition, the seats of the carriages filled with wounded as they were used as makeshift ambulances.

James Collis had his moment with history. As his colleagues loaded more wounded onto the gun limbers, in the midst of the inferno, he ran out from his gun-line, in an act of suicidal bravery, drawing enemy fire towards him: a selfless gesture of personal bravery, allowing momentary respite for his wounded comrades to be driven to safety. Before Collis too was borne headlong in retreat before the screaming masses of the Afghan horde.

The Afghan ranks began to falter, their fighting spirit blunted by the ferocity of the British fire and the mounds of dead and dying across the field. Despite the odds, the British hung grimly to their positions. The guns regrouped, the deadly fire of the disciplined British Tommy regained its tempo to begin its steady beat—load, fire, re-load, fire. At the last, as hope withered, the British could, perhaps, win through.

Until a brave cry shook the Afghan lines, an act of near spiritual bravery, a call to arms that has resonated through the centuries. A young girl, posted in the Afghan ranks to tend succour to the wounded, removed her veil, to hold it aloft as a banner, and cried aloud:

'*Young love! If you do not fall in the battle of Maiwand,*
By God, someone is saving you as a symbol of shame!'[4]

Her name was Malalai. On what was to have been her wedding day, with her sweetheart and her father both in Ayub Khan's ranks, she had chosen to be with her menfolk. Her example stirred the Afghans to new ferocity. The wavering ranks of *ghazis* stilled. Warrior looked at warrior, Malalai's simple act of uncowed womanhood shaming their Afghan pride into action once more. They charged forward again, as Malalai called out:

'*With a drop of my sweetheart's blood,*
Shed in defence of the Motherland,
Will I put a beauty spot on my forehead,
Such as would put to shame the rose in the garden.'

As she spoke her last verse, her heart was torn asunder by a British bullet, and she fell as she had risen, on the field of Maiwand.

Her sacrifice provided an impetus that fatally shook the British ranks. After so much sacrifice, after so many lay dead upon the field of battle, a new Afghan battle-line rose as one, to press again upon the exhausted British regiments. As a tumbling pile of stones would spill, so the British northern flank began to turn in on itself.

The untried Indian levies had suffered hours in the open, exposed to endless cannonades and harassing fire. Their officers dead, ammunition exhausted, barrels fouled with cordite, this new Afghan charge would prove decisive. Burrows froze—no orders were issued. The British troops looked to their commander for direction. None came, as the Afghans charged ever closer. Surrounded on all sides, an attempt to form square proved too much for the unrehearsed and panicked troops. The Indian levies had given all they could. The decisive moment had come.

Burrow's brigade broke and ran.

The guns of the Royal Horse Artillery barely escaped in the pell-mell charge to the rear. Gunner Collis hung on to his horse's traces in grim self-survival as the gun carriages bucked their way south over the broken desert. In the centre, Burrows again froze, his uncertainty compounded by his unfamiliarity of command in battle. Shorn of their British officers and abandoned by their commander's hesitation, the brigade sought a chimera of shelter and safety, fleeing towards what remained of the British line. Morale collapsed. Surrounded on all sides by a baying Afghan mob, order was lost in a calamitous race to escape the carnage.

All that was left in the rout were the doughty fighters of the 66th, who

---

[4] Traditional Afghan folklore

grimly held to the southern flank. Yet one battalion could not hold against tens of thousands. Attempting to fall back in good order, sheer force of numbers disintegrated unified command. Companies became platoons. Dispersed platoons mere lone, battered khaki-clad soldiers, fighting for survival in vicious bayonet and sword combat. The battlefield descended into grim tableaus of destruction, as the Afghan *ghazis* sensed victory.

Colonel Galbraith, commanding officer of the 66th, ordered the regimental colours to be uncased. A last stand of the regiment formed around the sacred emblems. The Union Jack and the regimental standard briefly flew, before the young ensigns who held them aloft were shot down in a merciless tide of Afghan counter-fire.

Outside the village of Khig, the few survivors of the 66th formed ragged square and volley-fired into the Afghan horde, now baying in the certainty of complete victory. Amidst the ranks, a small dog yapped. Bobbie, a terrier, the 66th regimental mascot, still snarled defiance at his master's killers.

As the 66th stood, the desperate survivors, including Brigadier Burrows, fled east, back towards Kandahar. The 66th hung on for precious minutes to protect the retreat. Colonel Galbraith fell, mortally wounded, sword still drawn, exhorting his men, to the end commanding volley fire from the dwindling ranks. The regimental standards still flew, now held aloft by sergeants. No officers remained alive.

Then, one by one, the 66th perished. Bandoliers empty, the rifles fell silent. Ammunition exhausted, a last stand of eleven souls fixed bayonets, and, seeking no quarter, charging into the baying mob. Slaughtered to the last, the triumphant tribesmen brought Ayub Khan the bloodstained regimental colours of the 66th and laid them at his feet.

The British defeat was complete. Over the next two days, covered by Gunner Collis and the remnants of E Battery, the shattered remnants of Brigadier Burrow's command slunk back to Kandahar city. Amongst their number, Bobbie, the regimental dog of the 66th, wounded but still alive.

Burrows losses amounted to half his Brigade—over 1,000 killed and wounded. In some of the Indian regiments, losses came close to 90%. They had, though, inflicted cruel losses on their Afghan enemy, costing Ayub Khan over 2,500 killed, with thousands more wounded.

The scale of the British defeat could not just be measured in lives, grievous though the losses had been. The loss of the colours at Maiwand came hot on the heels of another disaster for British arms at Isandlwana. Where another British column had been completely routed and slaughtered by the Zulu nation. Two major defeats in succeeding years were an absolute disaster for British imperial pride. Yet again, British progress in Afghanistan had come to a stuttering halt. The entire invasion plan was now deeply in question. The future hung in the balance.

At the moment of victory, the Afghans froze. Ayub Khan's remaining troops bottled up the British in Kandahar, but inexplicably failed to exploit their victory further. Critically, Ayub Khan did not proclaim his win. No messengers were sent out across the land. The Afghans completely failed to follow through their advantage. Ayub Khan failed to carry public opinion and the country did not come over to his side.

The British, however, keenly understood that disaster loomed without prompt and firm action. The main British force in Kabul, some three hundred miles away, prepared to march to relief their comrades in the South. It was a tall order. The British did not hold the ground between Kabul and Kandahar.

Yet again, history provides a lesson on just how successful campaigning is achieved in Afghanistan.

The British chose Frederick Roberts to command the relief force. He had already shown his mettle in taking Kabul, and his ruthless side in hanging the ringleaders of the revolt that had murdered the British envoy and his party.

Roberts was no Afghan neophyte. He had already won the Victoria Cross, Britain's highest decoration for personal valour, during the Indian mutiny of 1857. He followed that with extensive service in Africa, putting down local revolts in the mountainous terrain of Abyssinia, before returning to a lengthy stint on the quartermaster general's staff in India. In 1878, he had been appointed to command the elite Kurram field force and had just concluded a year of field command, fighting on the Afghan border. All before he had even entered the country, in revenge for the killing of Major Cavagnari.

Roberts was highly experienced, a talented commander, with a superb eye for ground, and a charismatic leader, adored by his men. His men called him 'Bobs' Roberts. The phrase 'Bob's your uncle' is widely thought to have originated from his troop's affection. He was a completely driven and focused leader. He only had one eye, having lost the other as a child. He overcame that handicap by sheer force of will. During the march, he drove himself to the point of collapse. Roberts just never allowed his physical limitations to defeat him.

Robert's is not the only general to share those qualities. What made him by far the most successful British general to ever serve in Afghanistan, over the course of four wars, was his ability to see the conduct of warfare as more than just the movement of troops and the expending of bullets. He would not have called it such, but he firmly believed in non-lethal capability to protect the lives of his soldiers.

Most importantly, he personally communicated with local leaders before entering their territory. He did not provoke battle, but sought free passage, making sure the alternative, his heavily armed soldiers, were always in full view. He was quite happy to broker local deals and pay bribes to get his way—and to show absolute ruthlessness when he was betrayed or second-guessed. Roberts never lied to the Afghans. He always played with a very straight sword—and used Pashto-speaking British officers to translate his intent, avoiding any confusion.

Roberts never tried to conquer Afghanistan. His military actions were always closely in line with the over-riding political direction, but he was not afraid to show considerable discretion in how he achieved that goal. Once he had achieved his aim, he left the Afghans to run their own affairs.

He compromised, cajoled, persuaded, threatened, inspired and, at the last, killed, to achieve his aim. He was as close to an Afghan as any British commander ever came. As much as Roberts was feared, he was also very respected. In turn, he respected the Afghans.

His background on the quartermaster's staff heavily influenced his actions in the harsh physical environment of Afghanistan. He insisted troops each carry no more than thirty pounds in equipment—weapon, ammunition, bayonet, water and an immediate ration. Nothing more. Such a load kept his troops fresh and unencumbered enough to move swiftly and decisively when required.

While his men travelled with what they needed to fight an immediate battle, his columns were always accompanied by thousands of pack animals carrying enough equipment for a sustained campaign. He used terrain wisely: pushing his logistics train through the valleys, with his flanks protected by his lightly clad soldiers leapfrogging from mountain to mountain, in over-watch positions. He made sure he carried proper maps, and employed a large and talented group of scouts to reconnoitre the ground before he advanced.

Despite Robert's many qualities, what he achieved next was truly remarkable. He assembled a field force of 10,000 men and 8,000 camp followers in seven days and then marched them 300 miles from Kabul to Kandahar in just three weeks. The Battle of Maiwand took place on 27th July. Roberts and his entire force arrived at the gates of Kandahar just over four weeks later, on 31st August. Ayub Khan was still savouring the fruits of his victory.

Roberts took the Afghans completely by surprise.

Militarily, he was aided by his limitations on the amount of kit his men each carried and by their personal fitness. Roberts carefully husbanded their strength. His troops were all experienced veterans, who knew him as a commander and who had trained, rehearsed and fought beside him. His logistic tail eschewed heavy artillery, or anything that could not be carried on the back of a donkey, which took into account the appalling nature of the available roads. Roberts carefully chose a route that offered the least topographic obstacles. Not the direct route—the one most easily traversed.

Roberts realized the importance of carrying the population with him. Using psychological warfare techniques, he made sure his men paid for everything en route—accommodation, food, feed for the pack animals—and for any damage. Including publicly punishing his own troops if they insulted an Afghan.

Finally, he made sure the successor to Ayub Khan, Abdul Rahman Khan, was fully complicit in supporting his actions. Rahman Khan's envoys accompanied Roberts and secured local deals that ensured a smooth and conflict-free passage for Roberts and his column. Rahman Khan helped Roberts, but his involvement also ensured Rahman Khan fully bought into Robert's success. As the Americans would say, Roberts made sure Rahman Khan had 'skin in the game'. That allowed Roberts to portray his force as supporting ally to the one rightful ruler of Afghanistan, not a foreign invader.

None of his 1880 success would have been achievable had Roberts not had a lifetime of frontier service behind him. Roberts didn't pull a six-month tour and leave. He stayed for decades—and that tenure showed in the quality of his decision-making. It was that experience that turned a talented and driven man into a military hero.

Ayub Khan must have been truly shocked to see Robert's fresh, battle-hardened column approach. He panicked and withdrew his men from their desultory siege of Kandahar, north into the Arghandab valley.

Roberts immediately ordered a detailed reconnaissance and relentlessly pursued his quarry. The very next day, Roberts decided to offer battle.

Led by his best troops, two Scottish Highland regiments and the Gurkhas, he systematically forced the Afghans off the high ground surrounding the Arghandab, with a series of hard-fought bayonet charges. Shorn of the advantage of terrain, Ayub Khan's men were unable to enfilade the British, as they had at Maiwand.

It was Ayub Khan's turn to panic. By nightfall, his army broken, he had fled the battlefield. In a little over a month, Roberts and his men had reversed the cataclysmic defeat at Maiwand by marching the length of the country and defeating a hitherto victorious Afghan horde.

The British followed up the military coup with a diplomatic one, confirming Rahman Khan as Amir, and offering him considerable financial and military assistance to ensure he stayed on the throne. In return, Rahman Khan quietly ratified the Treaty of Gandamak. Although Rahman Khan was to use the treaty as a useful rallying call for the remainder of his reign, the British always had his silent agreement to keep their mountain buffer zone.

Roberts and the entire British contingent swiftly withdrew from Afghanistan. Battles won, diplomatic agreement completed, pliant allay on the throne, he did not tarry.

Rahman Khan went on to prove the most durable of Afghanistan's leaders. He remains Afghanistan's only leader to die of natural causes while still in office. He held onto power for another twenty years, continually fighting internal wars, including pursuing and killing Ayub Khan. He was a ruthless killer who is remembered as 'the iron emir'. For all the bloodletting, Afghanistan's problems remained internal ones. What happened in Afghanistan stayed in Afghanistan. Rahman Khan remained careful not to bite the hand that fed. He continually rebuffed Russian overtures, while the British were equally careful to keep the annual stipend, of money and guns, flowing.

With British India secure for a generation, the strategic outcome of the 2nd Anglo-Afghan war was, for the British, a near complete victory that kept a relative peace for a generation.

After a brief respite, Roberts returned to Great Britain and a hysterical welcome. Promoted to field marshal and ennobled, he returned to his family's native estates in Waterford, Ireland, as commander-in-chief of British forces in Ireland. At the turn of the century, he was once more called into imperial service, as commander-in-chief of British forces during the 2nd Boer War in South Africa. He once again showed his sensitivity to what is now known as counter-insurgency warfare, by his evolving the revolutionary tactics he had used in Afghanistan and the North-West Frontier.

To deny his Boer enemy a secure home base, Roberts gathered the local populations into protected hamlets, and secured his lines of communications with block houses. Robert's Boer War template was in turn borrowed by General Gerald Templar, commander of the successful Malayan campaign of the 1950's. A blueprint for success that still inspires today's counter-insurgency warfare planners. Including those who planned the present campaign in Afghanistan.

Roberts had six children, of whom four survived infancy. His only son joined the army: and died in battle. Frederick junior emulated his father's example in winning the Victoria Cross. An act of valour that cost him his life, one of only three father-son pairings joined in similar martial glory.

James Collis survived the battle and relief of Kandahar. In 1881, he was presented with his nation's highest decoration for valour, The Victoria Cross, at Poona racecourse, India by General Roberts himself. Both men now wore the same decoration. In 1885, Collis was stripped of his medal, following a conviction for bigamy. He was to die a pauper in 1918, and lay in an unmarked grave for eighty years, before his remains were exhumed and laid to rest under a headstone engraved with the Victoria Cross. His medal was never restored to his family.

The most remarkable story of all belongs to Bobbie, the regimental dog of the 66th. Bobbie survived the massacre, and was presented to her Majesty Queen Empress Victoria, alongside other survivors of the 66th. Less than a year later, he was run over by a London taxi and killed. His body was preserved and stuffed. To this day, Bobbie can be seen, with an Afghan campaign medal around his neck, at the Berkshire Regiment's museum in Salisbury, England.

Malalai's sacrifice remains the most permanent legacy of Maiwand and its aftermath. Her remarkable courage has come to represent the indomitable spirit of Afghanistan. Today's most famous Malalai, the victim of a Taliban bullet, has shown the same unconquerable spirit, going on to win the Nobel peace prize for her campaign against female persecution.

The original Malalai may not have actually spoken such eloquent verse, as she raised her tattered veil on the battlefield, but the words still speak volumes. An Afghan will never unwillingly allow an invader to conquer their lands. An invited guest is welcome. Those who fail to respect Afghanistan and its people are most definitely not. An Afghan understands 'don't tread on me' just as readily as an American.

The British like nothing more than leaving an empty plate. Having gobbled up their Afghan war aims, they then set to ratify the exact terms of the Gandamak Treaty, by physically surveying and defining the borders between the new, truncated Afghanistan and the Empire's newly acquired mountain provinces. The British appointed Sir Mortimer Durand, a senior diplomat, to work the issue. For his part, Rahman Khan negotiated adroitly, but his hands had been tied. Durand's military surveyors demarcated the border as they saw the land fit British desire for tactical defence, not as had been formally agreed.

In some places, the British moved the white border cairns as much as five miles from the agreed demarcation.

The result was a semblance of a border, one that both sides regarded merely as limits to 'zones of control'. It is a porous border that exists to this day—and one that Afghanistan still regards as immoral. The Durand Line, as it is still known, has never been ratified between Pakistan and Afghanistan. More importantly, it continues to cleave the Pashtun nation in two. Former Afghan President Karzai is himself the scion of a prominent Pashtun tribe, the Popolzai. He has often called the Durand line 'a wound between brothers.'

When ISAF looked to expand into the South in 2006, they consulted with doctor Ashraf Ghani, then a prominent Afghan economist, now President of Afghanistan. He told ISAF that they were mad. By sending large numbers of troops into Kandahar and Helmand, all they were doing was invoking the sense memory of Maiwand. Ghani understood. ISAF refused to listen.

In late 2013, then-President Karzai repeatedly refused to sign a military technical agreement with America, allowing US troops to remain in Afghanistan. He cited two reasons:

Firstly, concern over a US demand to continue to pursue special operations with impunity. Secondly, the lack of a firm US commitment to pursue peace negotiations with the Taliban sheltering within Pakistan. His refusal led to senior American generals repeatedly telling me they thought Karzai had gone mad. I was otherwise convinced. Karzai was not crazed. He just remembered Maiwand and the last time an Afghan had signed an agreement with an invading power.

Afghans never forget. They remember their history like it was yesterday. I once asked a member of the prominent Pashtun Sherzai family, leaders of the Barakzai tribe, why they had a feud with the Popolzai tribe and President Karzai. Sherzai thought for a second and replied:

'Well, I'd have to start with Dost Mohammad.'

Dost Mohammad was ruler of Afghanistan in 1830. The Sherzai's altercation with the Popolzai has lasted the best part of two hundred years—and the details just as keenly remembered. Afghan politics and its fall-out as are deeply embedded in the national psyche as Catholic and Protestant rivalry is in Ireland. To an outsider, it is just as unfathomable.

It took until the 1920's, and another war with the British, before Afghan independence was restored. No Afghan will ever willingly give that up again, in any form, even if it means the destruction of their own country. Nobody tells an Afghan what to do.

The public perception of Afghanistan is that it has never been conquered. It is certainly true that, as a country, it has been the death knell for generations of fighting men, and several different Empires. As to conquest, it depends on your perception of the word. For an Afghan, their very hearts are pierced by the notion that their country has been the victim of centuries of outside interference. The national flag, of black, red and green stripes is testament to that sense of injured national pride. The black is a signal warning, a national sense of mourning to recognise the time when the British controlled this country.

For all that superior military prowess has dictated tactical success on the battlefield, so every foreign power that has visited this glorious and rich country has never managed to extinguish the flame of cussed independence and freedom that burns brightly in the breast of every noble Afghan male.

It is a dichotomy that, in a country where tribe and family is the defining characteristic, where the subjugation of individual ambition to the will of the clan is first and foremost, the moral compass of the individual is held in the highest esteem. An Afghan male is respected for his ability to wear the cloak of warrior monk. The individual ability to thrive, independent of thought, material needs and outside interference is revered.

In that sense, each and every foreign invader has merely been a visitor. As much as we have felt we can change the Afghans, so they have bent like a reed in the wind, accepted our largesse, and quietly rejected our own form of governance and culture. When we have sensibly compromised to the Afghan will, we have been welcomed as honoured guests. When we have been obdurate in our demands, bringing guns, not butter, each and every aspiring conqueror has perished on the granite rock of Afghan stubbornness and national indomitability.

That rugged independence is, in part, a product Afghanistan's geography.

The country's external boundaries are physical features. To the north, the Oxus and the Amu Darya rivers. To the west, desert traverses. To the south and east, the Suleiman mountains. Afghanistan's size has waxed and waned through the ages, but geography has always defined the limits of accessibility and governance.

Afghanistan plays host to the tail of the mighty Himalayas, which peters westward from its lair in Tibet and Nepal, across the mass of Afghanistan. Still hugely impressive, it is the tail of a tiger that demarcates the country, piercing its heart, right across the middle, in an arc from north east to south west. Known as the Hindu Kush, its jagged peaks play host to the inhospitable interior of the country. Just as Afghanistan's external borders are physically constrained, nature has again shown its sense of humour by further bifurcating the country.

Afghanistan is, in essence, two donuts within each other. The outer ring is arable land that contains the great cities of Mazar-E-Sharif, Herat, Kandahar and Jalalabad. The inner, the Hindu Kush mountains. At its heart, the capital of Kabul and the hidden valleys of Bamyan.

Everything about Afghanistan dictates isolation. Its external-facing geography emphasises rugged individuality. Fed by mighty rivers that cascade with sparkling torrents from the interior, none drain into the ocean. Even the rivers end in the Afghan desert. Afghanistan is truly land-locked, bound by nature.

Its people are equally inward looking, never more content than when left alone. Afghanistan's historic problem has always been that its neighbours just cannot keep but interfering.

In that sense, Afghanistan is strategic only in its geographic positioning as a route to get to other places and people. Alexander the great sought to conquer it to reach the riches of India and China. The British desired it to create space against its bitter rival, the Russian empire. The Russians desired it as a land to traverse to conquer India, then feared it as an unstable neighbour to its irascible Asian vassal states. Since 2001, the west has become intractably engaged with Afghanistan not as a strategic state, but as home to world's most wanted terrorist.

None of Afghanistan's invading armies have sought Afghanistan for Afghanistan. All have merely travelled there to pass through or achieve something else. Afghanistan itself has never been the objective, merely control of Afghanistan. That sense of aggrieved second-place, perhaps more than anything, drives the Afghan imbued national sense of pride, sometimes to the point of self-destruction.

Afghans have the same sense of home, the same sense of belonging, of national destiny, as any nation. Yet they also sense that every nation that comes to Afghanistan has always had another purpose. They feel that Afghans themselves, despite all the rhetoric, have never truly come first. Afghanistan has always been prevented from being the great nation its people regard it is destined to be by the actions of outsiders. In that complex game of realpolitik, the Afghan nation has always come second-place.

As a Scot, I instinctively understand that. Just as Afghans are brought up to remember Malalai and Maiwand, so I was brought up in tales of plucky Scots fighting the English for independence of a conquered land. In what is essentially a peaceful and developed country, Scots resentment of England is still very much alive and well. In Afghanistan, a country shattered by wars predicated by outside interference, that tension is never far from boiling point.

Maiwand and its fallout is lesson 101 in understanding Afghanistan. For a military person, it's also lesson 101 in how to successfully fight there. Topography, logistics, the role of light infantry, equipment scales, language skills, information operations, coordination of political and military objectives, the list is endless.

In 2001, the British Army had not been interested. In 2011, nothing much had changed.

My in-country brief was delivered by an absolutely charming Italian lieutenant colonel. Who insisted on taking me for coffee to deliver it. I learned a lot about ISAF four stage expansion plans, provincial reconstruction teams, anaconda strategies and courageous restraint. Lots of buzzwords and information on ISAF: the supposed good guys. Very little on Afghanistan itself—and I did ask. My charming interlocutor shrugged in that very Italian, apologetic kind of way and replied he was unsighted on this issue at this time. Even NATO staff officers were talking in American management doublespeak.

To put his response into perspective: my brief was given by a relatively senior middle manager to another middle manager. This wasn't the nuts and bolts, 'here's the absolute basics you need to know', kind of brief the boys were getting. This was a brief designed for leaders and managers—and it contained nothing on Afghanistan's history, demographics or social make-up.

Maiwand, the British imperial involvement and its repercussions are absolutely fundamental to that understanding. That brief still didn't exist, ten years after we had invaded the place.

At the conclusion of coffee, I learned I was now formally qualified, suited, booted, tied and dyed, all tooled up to serve ISAF. I was shocked.

Later in 2011, I sat with a senior US army officer while we argued with a district governor over an issue of US military assistance to the governor's staff. In short, the governor felt the Americans were doing too much and stifling native creativity. I raised a point about the governor's staff being largely illiterate, therefore needing more initial support. The governor turned on me, angrily replying:

'If you British had left us alone, we wouldn't be in this mess. You started this country's problems.'

In Afghanistan, nobody forgets. Except, perhaps, ISAF. I say perhaps because most never learned in the first place.

I'll confess here that I have skin in the game. I really care about Afghanistan. It is part of my family blood. My grandfather served with the British Army, on the North-West Frontier, near Peshawar, in what is now Pakistan, for over a decade. I still have his diaries and pictures. The images are remarkably similar to those of today: dusty hill top forts, stunning sunsets, soldiers standing post on lonely crags.

He told me about Maiwand, how a Pashtun, or Pathan, as he called the tribesmen, had never forgotten the British-enforced border. Or the rumour that the British had lied about the contents of the Gandamak Treaty, presenting it to Yacub Khan in English, a language which he could not read.

He told me of the Afghans incredible generosity and their absolute ruthlessness. How crime and murder was a game, until it affected family or women, when it became a blood debt, to be settled in blood. To never trust them, even when they were smiling. Most of all, that they will welcome a guest, but never forgive an invader.

He also told me that British imperial military muscle was very sparingly used. Better, he said, for them to think of the hammer about to fall than to see it. Too much exposure to the British would let the Afghans realise the British were exactly the same as them—ordinary human beings. When troops were used, he said they arrived as a rapier and left as quickly. Otherwise, the safest course of action was to leave well alone.

My grandfather came to stay. He loved his ten years in Waziristan as the finest of his life. His regiment built permanent garrisons, even a light railway, up to the Durand Line, that runs to this day. I visited there, twenty years ago. His regiment's emblem, The Welch Regiment, is still hewn into the rock face outside his former regimental headquarters.

ISAF troops came and went like the wind. Just when they had been around long enough to know where the stationery cupboard was, they were gone. While they were there, precious few could stop themselves meddling. Yet remarkably few ISAF soldiers ever met an Afghan, let alone ever leaving their hermetically sealed camps. ISAF's main effort was focused on just being there, maintaining the massive industrial-military complex.

Unlike my grandfather, there was no collective memory, no desire to learn, no intuitive understanding of the people we came to help. How many times did I hear that the Afghans were lazy/ duplicitous/ corrupt/ incompetent? They aren't, they are just superficially different from us. But hardly anybody ever hung around long enough to find that out.

We didn't fight a fourteen-year war in Afghanistan, we fought fourteen one year rotations.

Why am I interrupting my narrative to tell you all of this? Well, because, as this story develops, there will be moments when you will wonder just what the heck happened there. Believe me, so did I when I lived through it. As those moments arrive, remember Maiwand.

I just wish we had taken the time to smell the coffee and read some books. A lot less money would have been wasted—and lot more folks would still be alive.

OUT OF THE FRYING PAN

To celebrate my imminent departure, Eric decided to round up a couple of the other civilians from the CJPOTF and go hit the town. Kabul has been overrun with nightclubs, restaurants and bars since the 2001 invasion. Finding a drink is not an issue.

The pleasure spots vary from five star hotels, complete with spas and swimming pools, to a French restaurant that would not be out of place on the Champs-Élysées. Kabul has always been a bit of a party town, if you know where to look. Even during the civil war, I had been able to find a few beers. Granted they were two year out of date Heinekens, which we drank by candlelight, punctuated by the staccato of tracer flying overhead, but it was alcohol. Kabul is not the strict Muslim city one might think.

The invasion didn't just bring hundreds of thousands of troops. The whole nation-building exercise had also brought a huge influx of charities, aid organisations and a whole host of strange hangers-on. I've been part of eight wars, but Kabul holds my personal record for the amount of folks who claimed to be a SEAL/ SAS/ CIA/ Delta Force/ GSG9 or just plain, 'agency'. The downtown scene was a playground for the deluded and deranged.

Perhaps the most notorious haunt of all was the Mustafa Hotel, which sported a basement bar. Gunfights regularly broke out here, to the extent that a journalist chum of mine, boarding in one of the rooms above, took to sleeping in the bathtub for protection.

Right outside KAIA-N is the Baron Hotel. Complete with swimming pool (and poolside table service), tennis courts, manicured lawns, supermarket and fully equipped gym, it hosts some 376 en-suite rooms. Baron's was the off-duty destination of choice for most of CJPOTF—including the military, when they could get away with it. One of the unit's US officers was inside when the hotel got hit by a truck bomb, and found himself cowering behind the bar with a loaded pistol, contemplating either the imminent end of his life, or a courts martial if ISAF found him there.

Baron's is also the in-country home for US AID departments. No fool they, the luxury rooms start at $275USD per night. Serving in Afghanistan wasn't a hardship posting for everybody. Staying in accommodation like the Baron certainly ate into the so-called Afghan development fund. Lots of people got very rich in Afghanistan, comparatively few of them Afghan.

Getting out of KAIA-N was maddeningly difficult, with the gate being a full mile and a half away from the main compound, round the airport perimeter. A regular bus service dropped off by an inner cordon, which was followed by a delicate meander around a muddy track, a large number of concrete chicanes, Afghan police check-points and ISAF control towers, manned by rather nervous Belgians.

The Afghans were pretty laid back about life, but the Belgians would aggressively point loaded weapons right at your chest. It was a good idea to put your hands up in the air when they were around. The Belgians were pretty much the only western soldiers in the whole of the IJC to have to deal with Afghanistan and Afghans on a daily basis, and they were extremely nervous about it.

Once outside the gate, it was a left turn into the Baron, through two large metal gates and a security point where an Afghan took an imprint of an ID and a credit card check. Too many foreigners had skipped town without paying their bill for the owners to take any chances.

Once inside, though, the Baron was a home from home. Unlike KAIA-N, with its tent cities and rudimentary containers, the Baron could have fit anywhere in the world as a four star hotel. The place had been built at the same time as the IJC: and by the same contracting construction company. The hotel showed what could have been done with a little planning and imagination.

Of most interest that night was the comfortable bar, complete with darts board and pool table. We sat on the leather sofas, ordered pizza and made a beer can mountain. Eric and I danced a little salsa disco, while the boys spent the night moaning about the military. Life in Kabul was could be kinda cool. No wonder there had been few takers for my job down in Kandahar.

Not that the military had always suffered. In 2004, Camp Warehouse, which housed ISAF operational headquarters at that time, also hosted over 25 bars. I know because I personally visited them all. Mostly hidden away in grimy tents, nights were punctuated by the constant throb of Euro-disco. You'd just follow the beat, throw open the flap, and be greeted by a slab of cigarette smoke and forty pairs of eyes staring back at you. Booze was everywhere.

Warehouse had no drink restrictions at all. During the day, soldiers quite openly bought a slab of beer, and carried it right through camp. At that time, CJPOTF ran a weekly barbeque and drinks bar, which was the toast of camp. Alcohol fuelled the entire enterprise. Not just beer, hard spirits too. My close protection team was sourced by Portuguese special forces, who began the day with a calvados sherry and an espresso. At the very civilised time of ten in the morning.

Even ISAF HQ itself, where the top generals lived, had its own circuit. Formerly the Afghan army officer's club, the building was more country house retreat than military headquarters. Inside was all mahogany panelled walls and curved staircases. I once had a very nice office, at the head of the main stairs, from which I would perambulate to meetings outside in the large rose garden, complete with neatly trimmed hedge alcoves and bowers.

In the very beginning, the main HQ bar had been contained in a circus tent, which came complete with an acrobat's swing, from which athletically inclined officers would perch. Later, when the Italians had assumed command, they turned it into a marble café/ restaurant complex, complete with squash courts. The Brits built a very nice bar, called the Blue Parrot, with real beer hand pumps.

The party had all come to a crashing end in October 2009. Up north, the Germans had called in an air strike against reported Taliban militants, who were deemed to be looting two civilian tankers. The Taliban turned out to be civilians and ISAF managed to kill over 90 innocents. Newly arrived ISAF commander, US general Stanley McChrystal, phoned Camp Warehouse to demand an explanation from the senior German commander. Unfortunately, he couldn't be found—as he was off his face in one of the bars at the time. Stanley—rightly—was not amused and the US began quietly putting pressure on the different nations to end the fun.

The US quickly changed the character of ISAF HQ too, which had always been a low-key, pleasant place to work. America always brings a ton of stuff and people. ISAF already had a plethora of staff officers, but the US is not the most collegiate of players and always brings its own, duplicate structures. The football pitch was quickly built over to accommodate the myriad new arrivals, and new street signs sprang up, such as 'Victory Highway'. The culture quickly changed, which was all rather depressing.

Although I did notice that the volleyball court was now occupied by a very high walled, private compound containing separate, and no doubt rather pleasant, accommodation for the American senior generals. The Europeans might have goofed off a little more, but at least we all lived together.

Rather ironically, ISAF Commanding General Stanley McChrystal was himself fired a year later, for getting rip-roaring drunk on a trip around Europe. During which he succeeded in repeatedly bad-mouthing President Obama to a visiting 'Rolling Stone' reporter. Maybe if he hadn't been so dashed puritanical about everybody else, he might not have been so tightly wound.

The ISAF part of Kabul in 2011 was a very different place from the fun times I remembered. I was quite happy to be moving on. However, getting a flight out to Kandahar posed the same problems as getting in to Kabul.

In the early days, the whole ISAF adventure had been a freewheeling adventure. You just picked a place to land a plane and parked it. There was no air traffic control, no radar—no rules at all.

On my first tour to Afghanistan with the military, the British had only two planes in the entire country. They were workhorse Hercules C-130 transport planes, a four-engined stalwart of military aviation. My job allowed me free access to them both. One was an ancient old C-130H variant, over twenty years old. It had a flight deck that Biggles or Doolittle would have recognised. The other was a fancy C-130J—an updated, computer controlled version. It flew a lot faster than the H, thanks to its six-bladed propellers, and mounted a literally dazzling array of counter-measures.

The Hercules has been around for decades and is a truly remarkable aircraft. The crew sit on an elevated platform, up a step-ladder from the cavernous cargo compartment, which fills the remainder of the four-engined airframe. At the back of the aircraft is a large retractable ramp, with a roller system on the floor. Most cargo was palletised on standardised platforms that were shaped and designed to match the floor rollers. That way, the Hercules flight crew could easily push parachute bundles out the back door. The interior could be organised for a variety of uses, with a Meccano set of webbed seats. It is utilitarian, uncomfortable and spartan, but remarkably effective. The Americans went so far as to mount a howitzer and a couple of mini-guns into one side, creating an orbiting gun platform. They used this in Afghanistan to terrifying effect.

The trouble with the modern C130J was that computers kept intervening. Afghanistan had hardly any paved runways. Most of the landings we needed to do were in far-flung areas, a likely strip being little more than a flat field. It was extreme flying, great fun, and more than a little dangerous. Taking a C-130J into those situations caused the computers to automatically over-ride the pilot—a sort of electronic; 'are you kidding me?' Which wasn't much use when you actually wanted to land.

We much preferred using the old H variant. Being steam-driven, and therefore more pliable, it could land anywhere. On one memorable descent, near a remote town called Maimana, we were rather startled to find one of the port side landing wheels suddenly appear through the floor, into the cargo compartment. It was rather a loud bang. We had hit a massive boulder on landing, which destroyed the entire landing gear assembly. It's a testament to that old bird that, after a few days hammering and tinkering, she flew herself right out of Dodge.

Hercules crews don't exactly have the sexiest jobs in the air force. They are the workhorse transporters of the fleet, moving personnel and equipment all over the world. What the Americans described as hauling ass and trash. In those days, before the Royal Air Force acquired fancy jet transports on lease from the Americans, a C-130 was also the only way to get to Afghanistan. As versatile as the Hercules is, it isn't the fastest thing in the skies. Getting to Afghanistan meant three days stuck in the back, sleeping on top of piles of crates and boxes. Glamorous it was not.

The RAF only flew one C-130 flight a week to Kabul. Half the flights never made it. The planes were so old and over-worked they were perennially breaking down. Working in ISAF then was truly expeditionary.

My job back then was to run a small team doing specialist work all over the country. We'd load two land cruisers into the back of the plane, pick a spot on the map, land, drive off down the ramp and just go do stuff. It was a heady time, the best experience I ever had in the military.

The flying was crazy too. With no air traffic to manage, the pilots would skim along at two hundred and fifty feet, flying nape of the earth. The crews we used then were the cream of the crop, specially trained to work in specialist missions. We'd often stop in to Kandahar in those days, on the way back from a mission.

Kandahar at that time had the biggest post-exchange in the country, and was the only ISAF base to offer a chilled café mocha, thanks to American largesse. The PX was filled with a plethora of T-shirts and other useless souvenirs, so we'd all buy special forces finger torches and Seal Team camouflage scarves, before heading off to slurp away at our sugared, frosted delights. It was a fun goof-off to visit Kandahar.

We loved the old H but she did show her age. As the team leader, I used to stand up on the flight deck with the crew, right behind the pilot, hanging on to the back of his seat. One time, flying out of Kandahar, each of us balancing a large vat of freshly brewed American coffee, our very debonair pilot interrupted the *craic* to calmly say; 'I think we'll have to pop back to Kandahar, boys, the port inner is on fire'. Looking out the window, I could see fifteen feet flames coming out of one of the engines. We were zooming along at scarcely five hundred feet. The return flight to Kandahar was what I would modestly call interesting.

In 2011, all the adventure had long gone. Afghan air space was as closely controlled as Europe's. It was a radar-controlled, closely monitored, internationally accredited country now. Afghanistan even had its own aviation ministry.

The IJC had its own permanent terminal. Even getting on a flight meant going to a booking office and entering your name onto a formal passenger manifest. This was controlled by an extremely bored military team, who felt they hadn't joined the air force just to book civilian females in feather boas onto flights. It wasn't a kick-ass job and they let everybody else know it. Their office only opened for two hours in the mornings, and their favourite word was 'no'. Taped to the wall outside their glass-fronted cubicle were a host of typed papers, covering timetables and flying rules. All were headed; 'Read this first before asking us a question.'

ISAF ran its own internal airline. Each country donated a number of aircraft to the mission, and each sequentially offered those aircraft to fly NATO missions. There was a daily schedule of routine passenger flights, which departed on a round robin to all the major ISAF operating bases— Jalalabad in the east, Mazar E Sharif in the north, Herat in the west, Camp Bastion, where the British had set up camp, in the south-west and Kandahar in the south. Booking a flight was no more exciting than visiting a travel agent. Later on, the whole process even became computerised nationally. It was all remarkably normal. Except these travel agents were all military personnel and the planes were all Hercules C-130s.

What ISAF air shared with every other military was the application of military transport aviation rules 1-4, which I had already experienced on my in-flight through Manas. Flights were very often cancelled—just as the planes would not always go where they were advertised to go. I learned to check with the crew chiefs as I got on that my ride was actually heading to my planned destination. Travelling in Afghanistan was always a moveable feast.

A lot depended on which nation was flying the mission. Each country had its own caveats. The British, for example, operated their own flights alongside the ISAF schedule. Called 'Thumper' flights—I never found out why—they would only allow military personnel and British contracted civilians on board. The British could be remarkably selfish at times. In the early days, British flights had been code-named 'Hilton', in a knowing wink to the accommodation the crews would use, while army pukes like me had to make do with a sleeping bag.

When the Australians flew ISAF missions, they insisted on no hand baggage at all. Exasperated staff officers, looking to catch up on a little writing during the flight, would be forced to hand over their laptops. Checked baggage was then slung onto a flat pallet, secured with webbing belts and levered onto the back ramp. More than one officer would worry if their delicate MacBooks would come back to them in one piece. The Australians also insisted that everybody wore body armour and helmets thorough-out the flight, which was ridiculously uncomfortable.

The Dutch would segregate civilians from the military, onto different sides of the plane. I never understood why. The Dutch, though, did give out free ear defenders, unlike many others. A C-130 is not blessed with noise dampening. No earplugs meant a memorable headache.

ISAF always insisted that every passenger had body armour, complete with ballistic plates, front and back, and a helmet before even allowing passengers on the plane. It's easier to wear than carry, so I'd put it on for the inspection, and take it off as soon as I got on the plane. Unless the Australians were running the flight, in which case I'd feel my boobs go ever more numb as my ski-slope front plate got heavier and heavier.

The military always gives you extra stuff to carry. Just as the military is never done checking you actually have the extra stuff they told you to carry.

The US Marine Corps, on the other hand, couldn't care less who got on, who carried what, or whether you wore body armour or not. I always liked the Marine Corps. Except their planes were truly ancient, many of them having flown in Vietnam. Bits kept falling off, which could be a bit worrying. The United Arab Emirates, on the other hand, had brand-new, sparkly aircraft, but they weren't used to flying females, so I would spend the entire flight being stared at, while the crew whispered comments to each other.

What every country had in common was no toilet facilities on board for women. The boys were fine, with two tubes being readily available. Girls just had to clench. Last thing I did before getting on any flight was go to the loo, just as my grandmother had taught me.

ISAF-76 was the call sign for the daily flight to Kandahar. As an extremely unimportant 'space A' passenger, it took me two days to get on a flight.

Finally, on the 17th of December 2011, my US Marine Corps C-130 laboured into the sky above Kabul. Inside, I sat on my orange webbed-nylon jump seat, my discarded body armour at my feet and steadily froze all the way south, as the thirty-year old heating system had broken down.

COORDINATES; 31.30.26.0N 65.51.1.0E

Fly there and you will find Kandahar Airfield, or KAF as the military called it.

KAF was home to ISAF's efforts in the south. On the edge of the Maruf desert, eight miles from the city of the same name, Kandahar airfield sits snug against the backdrop of a studded landscape of dragon's teeth peaks and flat, cultivated plains. KAF is south east of Kandahar, about a forty-minute drive away, and physically separated from it by a long ridgeline.

It has been here since the late 1950's, when a previous generation of generous Americans gifted its construction to an Afghan nation struggling to evolve and adapt to the demands of new century and an ambitious King.

Zahir Shah nominally ruled Afghanistan from 1933 to 1973. A time that marks the longest period of relative stability that Afghanistan has known. His reign is known as a golden period in Afghanistan today, before the communists took power in a coup.

The end of the Second World War saw inter-continental air travel develop in earnest. Yet the technology of the time used propeller driven aircraft with limited range. They needed to re-fuel. In the same way as Shannon airfield in Ireland was built to refuel trans-Atlantic flights, so King Zahir Shah hoped that Kandahar might become a hub for flights from Europe to the Far East. Such stopovers brought money, in landing fees and fuel costs, creating employment and a sense of togetherness with the technologically developed outside world.

With the British withdrawal from empire and the partition of British India in 1947, the main players in town became the Americans and the Soviet Union. The north, including Kabul, saw much Soviet assistance, such as the construction of strategic hydro-electric dams and Kabul airport. In the south and west, the Americans looked to consolidate a foothold, nearer their surrogate ally, the Pahlavi regime in Iran.

King Zahir Shah proved adept at using both world powers to benefit his country. The 1950's saw huge American aid projects blossom in the south. Invited as guests, with such security as was needed provided by the Afghans themselves, the Americans oversaw the construction of a major series of irrigation canals, in Helmand and Kandahar. They built Kajaki Dam, in northern Helmand, which provided the south with reliable hydro-electric power for the first time. Much of Lashkar Gah, provincial capital of Helmand, which was to become the hub of British Afghan efforts from late 2006, was built as a dormer town for resident American aid workers.

In Kandahar, the Americans also designed and built the airport and runway. While the Afghans saw it as a necessary economic lever, the Americans likely also saw it as a useful military base, should the Soviets ever force a nuclear conflict.

Kandahar airport is a confection of Eisenhower-era optimism. It shares the same soaring concrete sweeps as Dulles, in Washington DC, which was built at roughly the same time, albeit Kandahar is on a much smaller scale. The design reflects a woman's open fan. The ruffled edge is marked by a series of curved, concrete arches that gracefully sweep across the arrivals apron. Two elegant covered passenger walkways form the outer V edges of the fan, the terminal building itself, the base of the fan.

The 1950's were an age long before security checks and metal detectors. Architecture, not security, is the key requisite defining Kandahar airport's construction. It truly is a delight to walk through. Inside, the arches open up into a communal double height open lounge area, behind which sits a graceful fountain and a series of fragrant open gardens.

In the 1950's, the terminal complex was surrounded by groves of scented pine trees. A tarmacked lane led to whitewashed staff villas. A little ways off, a square, square arched building acted as maintenance and storage sheds, with a silver hanger next door.

The whole is a remarkably compact and very evocative emblem of American confidence and largesse. Walking through it always reminded me of Tracey Island, from 'The Thunderbirds'. Anywhere else in the world, the terminal would be a treasured, listed building.

Unfortunately for Afghan ambition, the arrival of long-range jet aircraft scuppered the dream of a regional transit hub. The airport sank into a long decline but which still assisted in producing a marked improvement in economic and social standards. I have a number of postcards from the era, showing mini-skirted women walking down the rear steps of a TriStar jet.

Remarkable images, when you compare them to today's austere and conservative Afghan society: a near exact copy of the mental images I remember from my youth, flying to Spain in the early 1970s. The King's reign was a very different time sociologically and culturally, before religion came to dominate Afghan life. King Zahir Shah was overthrown by Afghan Communists: and Afghanistan's future violently changed.

When the Soviets invaded, the airport was turned into a regional military base. The south-west end of the runway complex was filled with revetments for MiG fighter jets, while a large bomb storage facility was constructed to the north.

Which is exactly as I had first viewed KAF, not long after the invasion of

2001. In the days before ISAF moved to the south, it was a rather compact American base. The troops lived and worked in the old terminal building, with the more sensitive headquarters side being located in the sturdy maintenance sheds. In between the two, a distance of about 700 yards, lay a motley collection of tents and plywood huts. At most, there were a couple of thousand troops there. The perimeter was a single coil of barbed wire. Beside the famous coffee shop there was a small row of Afghan owned shops, selling mostly imported jewellery from Pakistan. One enterprising soul had opened a shop offering electric massage chairs for rent.

The place of most interest was the prison, from where many of Guantanamo Bay's future inmates would be processed. It was right beside the terminal, but the Americans would get very twitchy if we asked what it was and photography was strictly forbidden.

There were no metalled roads. To the west lay dozens of wrecked Soviet aircraft, in a maze of bunkers. We were warned not to indulge in any combat tourism, as the place was still heavily mined. Aircraft were pretty rare too. Tower control was exercised from a caravan, with a mobile truck-borne radar beside it. When we first requested permission to land in our C-130H, a cheerful American voice told us:

'Just mosey on in, fellas, the weather's fine.'

In those early days, not much happened in Kandahar. Until 2004, what did go on was an exclusively American enterprise, focussed on legacy counter-terrorism operations to find and kill Al-Qaeda. Then, the mission started to spread.

I often flew down to Kandahar to meet with the first RAF detachment to base itself in Kandahar. Flying the now near-defunct, but rather marvellous, British-made Harrier jump-jets, around 250 airmen and a couple of women found themselves guests of the American military. The RAF had based themselves at the far western end of the runway, which involved driving along a dirt track, past rusting Soviet aircraft, to a couple of tents and sunshades, containing Britain's sole public presence in southern Afghanistan. The whole operation was protected by a single strand of barbed wire and a couple of bored airmen, armed with five rounds of ammunition each.

For a while it was great sport to stand at the end of the runway, as the Harriers performed combat take-offs, literally feet above one's head. The pilot would put the whole thing into overdrive and zoom off across the desert at twenty-five feet, for about a mile past the runway, before shooting vertically up into the sky. It was terribly thrilling to be stood under, as the jet wash was powerful enough to knock you off your feet. Unfortunately, somebody stuck the video evidence on the newly invented YouTube and the powers that be in London stopped the fun with a couple of swift reprimands.

The civil terminal had then been closed off to all and headquarters were re-located inside the old maintenance building, which had been converted by a maze of plywood partition walls. This building had been the last holdout of the Taliban regime in 2001. Matters had been settled when the Americans dropped a couple of bombs on the roof, the percussion wave killing everybody inside. It was a matter of intense debate to the pilots who visited whether the bombs themselves had actually exploded or not. What was undeniable was that everybody inside had been killed.

The building itself, which sported four feet thick masonry walls, remained remarkably undamaged, save for a large hole in the roof. The space below the open impact crater had been converted into an open-air, al-fresco patio for yet another coffee bar, resplendent with tables and striped sun umbrellas. The military named the whole complex the TLS—the Taliban's Last Stand.

Much more sinister was the hanger next door to the TLS, covered in aluminium sheeting. We called it the silver blimp. When the Taliban took power, the women of Kandahar had protested at the draconian imposition of restrictions on their dress and freedom of life. The Taliban had rounded up fifty of the ringleaders and bussed them out to the blimp. Where they had hanged the women from the rafters for their impudence.

That was it, though, all remarkably simple and elementary. On one trip south, we had unloaded our Land Cruisers and gone for a drive into Kandahar: just six of us, in two cars, with nothing more overly threatening than a couple of rifles. No body armour, no helmets, no extra escort, driving white civilian vehicles. I had merely a pistol, with eight rounds of ammunition. Nothing happened. The locals waved at us, we waved back, and we had a fine time taking photographs and shaking hands.

In 2004, there was no insurgency in Kandahar. NATO had no presence and ISAF only patrolled Kabul and certain parts of the North. We hadn't dug up a war yet. At that time, the US Kandahar garrison didn't even know what ISAF was. Two US airmen once tried to arrest me, getting back onto our old Hercules. They didn't recognise my British uniform or rank and didn't recognise my ISAF credentials either. I told them to fuck off and kept walking. Nothing happened. Had I done that in 2011, I'd have been shot.

As we descended into Kandahar on that late December morning in 2011, ISAF was a very different beast. Ten years on since those bombs had dropped onto the roof of the TLS, Kandahar airfield had become not just ISAF's biggest base but the biggest and most expensive base NATO had ever controlled in its near seventy year history.

My first inkling came of regime change came when the Marine C-130 began a steady, straight descent. In the old days, we'd corkscrewed in, in a tight spiral, levelling out at the last second, in a choreographed dance to minimise ground threat. In 2011, the implied threat was still there. What had changed was that Kandahar airfield was now so large that a big plane like a C-130 had enough secure air-space to make a flat, controlled descent secure within the vast camp perimeter.

Craning to look through a porthole, all I could see was mile after mile of squat, beige coloured buildings and hangars. We were still eight hundred feet up, yet were already inside the fence line. Even the runway was bigger. The Americans had lengthened it to allow massive inter-continental transports to land, and had then built a whole series of taxiways alongside it for good measure.

Everywhere I looked, I could see aircraft. Literally hundreds of helicopters, neatly lined up, including dozens of the US Marines' new toy, a half-plane, half helicopter of a beast called an Osprey. Queues everywhere of huge jet transports, small jet transports, fighter jets, executive jets, C-130s, propeller driven reconnaissance aircraft and that latest invention, drone planes with no pilots at all. The place was an aircraft spotter's nirvana. There were so many aircraft waiting to unload that we sat for fifteen minutes, propellers spinning, before the back ramp opened up.

Kabul had been near freezing. It's seven thousand feet up, in the mountains. The south is a very different landscape. It's a lot lower in elevation for a start. Kandahar sits on a rather fertile plain, watered by a series of rivers, but surrounded by desert, which slowly encroaches year by year. December in Kandahar is really quite lovely: clean, crisp days, pretty much always sunny, with temperatures up to 20 degrees centigrade. December can get blinking cold at night, but my first 2011 glimpse of KAF was of a runway bathed in brilliant sunlight.

As a very gallant marine helped me down the rear ramp, I was quite disoriented. Last time I had been in KAF, on a different tour five years earlier, landing in the only plane in town, we'd stopped right by the old civilian terminal, and just ambled over to the TLS at our own pace, past a few tents. In 2011, KAF was proving a very different place.

The ramp just throbbed with activity. Everywhere, planes, civilian and military, were disgorging lines of American soldiers, Helicopters whizzed overhead—gunships, big Chinook transports, tiny reconnaissance birds. Forklift trucks dodged between planes, carrying huge pallets of equipment. As we walked, two F-16 fighter planes took off, just yards behind us, after-burners roaring. The scream of jet engines and the stink of aircraft gasoline were disorienting. We double-timed across the flight line as another C-130, engines whirring, moved in behind us. KAF was a place in a hurry.

KAF now played permanent host to nearly 400 aircraft, from across the coalition. That's not including the thousands of other transiting aircraft, flying in and out right around the clock. KAF had become the busiest single runway airport in the world. Some 6,000 flight rotations, every week of the year. KAF, at its height, was busier than Gatwick Airport. All of it dedicated to fighting, and winning, a war.

ISAF, and the US in particular, had gone into the south in a big, big way. Kandahar had become the hub of all that activity. Permanently housing 400 aircraft was just the beginning of the story.

In 2004, I'd gone for a drive around Kandahar city for fun. In 2011, that same journey, done in the same way, would have more or less guaranteed trouble. As ISAF had moved into the south, so war had arrived. By 2011, Ashraf Ghani's prophesy had come true. ISAF was deeply in the mire, fighting Maiwand all over again. All those planes were supporting the fight in what had become a vicious and nasty turf war, with KAF at the eye of the storm.

On all sides, every inch around the runway was covered in huge aircraft hangers. The cacophony of planes landing and taking off never stopped. It went on 24 hours a day. Entire fighter wings were based at Kandahar—in 2011, American, British, Belgian and French fighter planes all flew combat patrols from KAF. The UAE joined the party a year later: dozens upon dozens of fighter aircraft, thousands of bombs and missiles.

KAF had become the headquarters for the entire ISAF regional command in the south. By 2011, it was becoming an ever more exclusively American operation. An entire US army division was tied up in Kandahar. Added to the American effort were sizeable contingents of troops from Holland, Britain, Australia, France, Romania, Slovakia, Bulgaria, Albania, Denmark, the Baltic States and Germany. Canada, which had just ended its mission to Afghanistan, was still clearing up. KAF was as colourful a rainbow coalition as the D-Day landings. KAF played host to some 18,000 military personnel alone.

Alongside all that military firepower and personnel lived tens of thousands of contractor staff, who kept the lights on and performed all the maintenance functions a modern army needs. Nobody ever really knew how many contractors actually lived on KAF. Besides all those western contractors scurried an army of third country nationals—those TCNs—who invisibly emptied the bins, mopped the floors, did the laundry and performed all the myriad of unpalatable but vital tasks that a large town needed. There were actually more contractors than military, even by the official count.

Officially, in late 2011, the camp population was 32,000. That's correct— 32,000 souls. Officially. Unofficially, it was reckoned that there was also anything between 5 and 8 thousand folks living 'off-grid'. Nobody ever formally counted. In any case, 32,000 or 40,000, KAF was a pretty big city, all dedicated to one purpose: fighting a war.

All those folks needed homes to live in, places to work, and places to eat and goof off in. Roads to get about, transport to get them there, equipment and supplies to sustain them. KAF was no temporary tented encampment. It was a 21st Century Sparta city-state.

The scale of it all is quite mind-blowing. Just keeping the place running, the maintenance budget alone, cost NATO six billion dollars a year. Afghanistan took one quarter of NATO's budget. KAF took one quarter of that all by itself. Kandahar Airfield was a city that had grown up like mushrooms spreading under a tree. As more troops had been deployed, so more land had been consumed to build the miles and miles of maintenance yards, offices, storage hangers and buildings they needed. The old Soviet airbase had long ago been bulldozed under and now housed a myriad of accommodation blocks.

The Soviet-era open sewage system, which had been located well outside of camp, now formed an odious traffic roundabout right in the middle of the new city. Every day, columns of traffic navigated their way around the sludge. Called the 'poo pond', a circular couple of open acres of bubbling human excrement, it was one of KAF's few tourist attractions. Visitors would genuinely ask to have their pictures taken there. DHL, the international civilian freight company, had a large compound right next to that steaming mass of human shit. Remarkable enough that DHL even had an office in Kandahar, it must have been a dreadful posting. The stink made you gag, just passing by. In the summer heat, the lake of shit bubbled and oozed putrefaction.

The story went that a soldier had once bet his colleagues he could swim across the poo pond morass. He had immediately been medevacked home with a variety of indescribable contracted diseases. Depending on the teller of the tale, the nationality of the soldier changed, so apocryphal and universal had the story become. The US air force newsletter regularly carried updates on the state of the poo pond and the mighty scale of its content, applying statistical shit analysis to attempt to decipher the true numbers of folks in camp. 40,000 people produce a lot of crap. The poo pond landmark became so legendary that the PX started selling picture postcards of it, as well as T-Shirts emblazoned:

'Kandahar poo-pond, where the fishing is radio-active.'

The north side of the airport, which had been fields until 2007, was now a mess of hangers, bunkers, bomb storage and barbed wire. KAF never had much in the way of paving, but it did boast a levelled perimeter road. It was nearly thirteen miles long.

Out of all that industry, all that expenditure, all that effort, less than 100 Afghans had full-time jobs in KAF. Our 40,000 strong community looked inward. At best, only a couple of thousand folk had a job that entailed leaving KAF. Of those, only hundreds would do anything more than visit the immediate couple of miles around the perimeter.

KAF was, for the hundreds of thousands who came and went in the never-ending rotations, little more than a dusty and hot prison camp. KAF was a camp whose main purpose was to sustain itself. The bigger it got, the more troops, contractors and stuff it needed to survive. KAF ate itself, just to keep being there.

That activity had but one purpose: to support the yet more tens of thousands of soldiers and contractors who lived in their own small camps, all over the South. All of that effort required an endless stream of supplies, orders, people and coordination. The scale of it all was mind-blowing. War in Kandahar was not cheap, in any sense.

KAF was the Klondike meets Mad Max meets The Alamo.

FIDO

The Parachute Regiment has a military acronym to cover those situations where the world lies in pieces and you just stop and wonder what the heck to do; FIDO. Fuck it, drive on.

Arriving in Kandahar Airfield was a FIDO moment. My sole parting wisdom from Eric had been to pass me the name of a US major, with whom I was to be working, and instructions to; 'find him when you get there.' There were 40,000 people in Kandahar: and no phone book.

That was it. No joining instructions, no taskings, nothing else. In my short time in Kabul, nobody on the military side of POTF had shown the slightest bit of interest in talking to me. I'd been just another annoying civilian. Particularly annoying, in my case, as a female with a decidedly un-combat-like dress sense. Hey, in for a penny. FIDO.

As I got off that plane, I didn't even know where I would be sleeping. Kandahar was going to be a complete come-as-you-are party. I'd known the job was going to be a self-starter. I hadn't quite expected it to be a build-your-own-bedroom gig as well.

We were shepherded into the old Taliban Last Stand building. The old regional headquarters had now well and truly moved on. The operation was just too big to contain it all. The TLS now served many different functions, including being a rudimentary arrivals hall. Our pallet of bags was deposited outside, under a mural of the Afghan flag, decorated by a painting of three alien stick figures, dressed as soldiers. The rubric above read; 'Welcome to Kandahar Airfield.'

The other arrivals on my flight gradually thinned out, as folks came to welcome them, until I was left completely alone. As I sat there, with my two cases beside me, my new body armour and helmet at my feet, I wondered just what the heck I had got myself into. FIDO.

In Kabul, by chance I'd met another civilian female. One of the redeeming features of ISAF was the ease with which people just talked to each other. Perhaps it was the ever-present underlying immediacy of life there. She'd sympathised with my news that I was going to Kandahar. The place enjoyed an undisputed and unrivalled reputation as the most dangerous destination in the entire country. In an act of sisterhood, she'd passed me the e-mail of another female civilian she knew who worked in Kandahar. In turn, I'd e-mailed her friend, and she'd passed me a phone number to call if I had any difficulties on arrival.

Sitting in that cold, empty arrivals hall with nowhere to go to seemed just one of those moments. So I phoned my as yet un-met female friend, Steffi. This stranger, who I'd never met, told me not to worry, she'd send somebody to get me. In one of those random connections of chance, Steffi was to become not just my saviour that day, but one of my closest friends in life. Somehow, despite it all, female solidarity had won through. I was in Kandahar—and the adventure was about to begin.

My anxious wait ended with the arrival of my saviour. An impossibly petite, very pretty brunette, wearing an American uniform, and uncomfortably trailing a rifle almost as tall as she was. Maria was a corporal in the US Air Force. Her job was supervising a small Afghan work crew, who performed minor odd jobs around camp. The guys were a hangover from earlier, friendlier days in Kandahar and who quietly continued to exist under the radar.

She welcomed me with a wonderful, toothy smile. My suitcases were quickly gathered up by her Afghan companion. Named Ahmed, he was a swarthy six-foot Pashtun, complete with shawl and cut-down wellington boots. He greeted me profusely in quite good English, while at the same time rather lasciviously taking me in.

Much later, he told me the only time he had ever seen women in the flesh outside his family compound was when he came into camp. Any Pashtun female over the age of puberty is completely enveloped in public by a billowing blue burka. I asked Ahmed much later what he would have done had he seen an Afghan woman dressed like me in the street. He innocently replied he would have assumed I was a prostitute. When he saw my shock, he quickly covered up his error by re-assuring me that, as a foreigner and an unbeliever, Afghans would have made allowances for me and assumed I was mad.

The rest of the team were sitting in the back of a battered pick-up, outside the terminal. I have always found Afghans quite charming company and Ahmed and his gang of cutthroats were no exception. Dressed in their grubby long tunics, waistcoats and baggy trousers, sporting a variety of turbans and long beards, they made a fantastic pirate crew.

Seeing Maria, Ahmed and I, they all jumped out and began an agitated squabble over who should load my bags into the truck. Eventually, the six of them agreed a truce, whereby they all had at least one hand on each case. Much lifting, groaning and good natured squabbling followed, while my cases alternately were hoisted high, then dropped as somebody let go of their end, all accompanied by peals of laughter and covert glances in my general direction. The conclusion of this Sisyphean labour was greeted by much smiling and hand-shaking all round, before they all piled back into the bed of the truck, while Maria and I got into the cab.

The boys seemed quite happy to be driven around by a woman. Behind us, I could see legs and arms precariously hanging off the sides, as an animated discussion raged between them.

'They'll be arguing about which one of them should marry you,' said Maria cheerfully. 'You'll get an invitation quite soon. Don't worry, they do it to all the western women.'

Single women are a rarity in Afghan society. On my previous trips, I had always been in the company of men, whom the Afghans would automatically assume were my protectors. This time around, on my own, I would grow used to the constant questions about where my husband was and who was looking after my children.

I bought a cheap ring, which I called my Kandahar wedding ring, to ward off the most persistent suitors. In Afghan Islamic society, a woman is protected and generally to be revered. However, a woman is very much under the leadership of the male line. Very few women pursue independent lives. It's impossible for a woman to even open a bank account in her own name without a male guardian's approval. A woman's role is centred round family—running the home and raising children. At the same time, women are separated from men, outside of immediate family, because of the temptation they are perceived to represent to a male's sexual nature; thus, the all-enveloping clothing. The clothing is to protect a woman's modesty, and, it is believed, to allow her to converse with a man as an equal, without the burden of sexual awareness. Afghan society is very much torn over women's place and role. The Madonna virgin/ whore duality of perceived femininity is very much alive, as it still is in western society. In Kandahar, the most conservative part of the country, it's a common sight to see men riding inside saloon cars while burka-clad women sit in the open trunk at the rear.

While some of the marriage advances were unwelcome, most were actually done out of sympathy. Pashtun men just could not understand how a single woman could survive without a male protector. The Holy Prophet himself had married several times to provide protection to widows who would otherwise have perished in a male-oriented society. On the flip side of the coin, Ahmed and his crew would happily sit in the back of the pick-up, while Maria drove them around. I asked Ahmed about that once. He told me:

'Inside KAF, things are different. I live by your rules.' Perhaps ominously, he added, 'it will not always be that way. When KAF is returned to Afghanistan…'

His voice trailed off then, and he gave me a little shrug. The rules might be different when that day came—but he knew he would then also be out of a job.

Maria was single. She was twenty-two, in the Air Force for just over a year. She was a reservist, a part-time soldier, who had volunteered to come to Afghanistan. Maria had grown up on the projects in Detroit, a Hispanic American of mixed origin. She'd never known her father and had given birth to two baby boys when she was eighteen, whose father had also deserted the nest. The air force had given her a lifeline, and volunteering for Afghanistan had given her a full-time job for the first time in her life. While Maria spent nine months in Kandahar, her children were being cared for by their grandmother.

She was in primary school when the Twin Towers came down. Maria had only a hazy memory of the day. In that regard, she was unremarkable, for the generation of 2011 was a very different one from the one that I had been part of ten years earlier. The war had moved on, so had the soldiers. For Maria, the Afghan mission was more economic security than eternal struggle for freedom.

She was an unlikely soldier. The rifle she carried was more dead weight than lethal weapon. Maria never cleaned it in all the time I knew her. The military was a last chance for a girl with no qualifications, no prospects and more than a few obligations to aspire to something. Yet, despite the harshness of her upbringing, Maria was charming company. She retained that most attractive of American characteristics—an unbridled optimism about the future. As we drove, she filled me in on her ambitions for a home outside the city, of the new kitchen her operational pay would buy, and the life she hoped for her boys, away from what she described as 'the shithole of KAF'.

I couldn't have made that first day without her. Kandahar airfield was unrecognisable from my previous memories. For a start, we now drove on some actual roads, where before there had only been dirt tracks. Unfinished, with loose tarmac edges and no pavements, they were jammed with fast-moving convoys of huge armoured trucks. We dodged in and out of these monster leviathans, as I wondered at how frightening it all now looked.

As the war had expanded, so the bombs had got bigger, and the soldier's vehicles had got bigger too. The Americans now routinely drove massive armoured lorries, called MRAPs; mine resistant, armour protected. The days when I had happily driven into Kandahar in my white Toyota were long gone.

The concept had been around for decades but the US had taken it to new levels of sophistication and cost. The explosive potential of a bomb going off under a vehicle chassis shoots upwards from the solid earth. If that shockwave hits a flat surface, that surface takes the entire strength of the detonation. Which becomes a straight battle between the power of the bomb's release and the tensile strength of the plate it meets. If the surface is curved, the blast is deflected outwards and upwards, giving the protective plates a huge advantage. I'd seen at first-hand the trial versions, developed by the South Africans, during the Angolan war twenty years earlier. Basically a V-shaped hull had been bolted underneath a raised truck chassis, protecting the crew from blast.

Around 2008, the Taliban had devised roadside bombs that were large enough and powerful enough to beat the armour of any flat-bodied vehicle then in military service. The military, in its never-ending desire to classify everything, rather disparagingly called these increasingly sophisticated and clever devices IEDs, or improvised explosive devices. They may have been made of old water jugs and fertiliser, but the results were anything but improvised.

After an urgent review, the Americans, at great cost, had issued contracts to several different companies for the adaptation of existing civilian vehicle fleets to meet the new threat. Hundreds of millions of dollars later, Afghanistan saw the deployment of thousands of specially converted trucks, replete with massive V-shaped hulls and thick bulletproof glass.

The Americans had then consigned their old, less protected, troop vehicles to non-tactical use. They gave thousands of these no longer fit for purpose vehicles to their Afghan allies: and expected them to use these cast-offs to fight the same war.

The MRAPs were huge. Basically a large goods vehicle with a lot of armour bolted on, they stood around twenty feet high. The crew are totally encased in a thick casing of armour. The only viewing ports are through slits of thick bulletproof glass, so thick that the world outside is coloured yellow. The single human presence visible from outside is one variant with a revolving turret on the roof. From which you could sometimes see the head of a helmeted soldier, high up in the air, standing behind a large loaded machine-gun.

MRAPs are not people friendly. Nor, with the thick protective glass slits, are they easy to see out of. Weighing in at anything from nine to forty tons, they can make an awful mess—and the crew are unlikely to see or feel anything they hit. A lot of Afghans were killed by unknowing MRAP crews, so much so that ISAF was forced to put all its drivers through aggressive safe driving programs after a number of children were run over.

Mind you, anything was better than the armoured vehicle the British used in Kabul in the early days. It was called a Saxon and was quite genuinely just a big old truck with a metal box welded onto the top half. Inside, the passengers sat looking at the open transmission shaft, while the commander sat half out of the turret, in a vain attempt to guide the driver, who could only see out of the front and his side of the vehicle. The other side was a complete blind spot. You disembarked through a sliding metal door on the side. I remember driving through Kabul, stuck on the inside, and observing a half-inch gap, just big enough for a hand grenade, between the side of the vehicle and the door. Every time we stopped, kids would run up and peer through the open slit to gawp at us inside, as we choked on the fumes from the open engine.

Saxon was one of those dreadful export contracts that the Brits do, for a Middle East potentate, who was after an effective internal security vehicle. The Arabs had taken one look at our offering and, rightly, promptly cancelled the contract on the spot. Saxon was fucking awful. But, as the money had been spent and the crap was just rusting away, so the poor, long-suffering British foot infantry been issued with it and then re-classified as 'mechanized'. Granted, the Saxon had an engine, but put it on anything other than a tarmacked road, the whole kit and caboodle would tip over, as the armour was way too heavy for the chassis and suspension. Mechanized infantry? Mechanized death-trap more like.

I spent the best part of a year in Bosnia with Saxon, trundling around in these metal lawnmowers—and they were utter rubbish. Sending them to Afghanistan was a complete joke that the soldiers that had to use them singularly failed to get. The Brits eventually sold the lot to the Ukrainians, which is very kind of them to present to an ally in need.

MRAPs were different. At a million dollars a pop, they ought to be. The US, always the land of milk, honey and money, had about 13,000 of them in Afghanistan.

KAF was full of MRAPs. All of which drove around at high speed, on narrow roads. Some had huge mine rollers attached to the front, making an articulated vehicle nearly fifty feet long. Your chances of survival were very slim, should you pick an argument with an MRAP. At the IJC, the rule was, quite sensibly, that armoured vehicles should have a dismounted soldier walk in front of the vehicle for safety. KAF didn't have any rules. Everybody was in a hurry.

Maria continually drove off the road as we weaved our way through the endless lines of fast-moving armour. We were like a beetle scurrying between the feet of marching elephants. Each time they passed, our pick-up would be enveloped in a cloud of grey coloured dust. In the back, our stoic Afghan friends looked like grey moon men, as they clutched their shawls around them.

The streets, such as they were, were lined with endless grey concrete T-walls, mile after mile, compound following compound, broken only by a metal gate or another barrier, beside which sat a sullen soldier, guarding whatever lay within.

A few of the original eucalyptus trees I remembered had survived, matted with dust, but most of the forest had been chopped down as the camp had expanded. The original airport manager's home, once painted a jolly blue and white, was now encased in sandbags and thick timbers.

What I remembered as a pleasant, almost rural backwater had become an industrialised city: the colour had been completely drained. KAF was a Tolkien-inspired nightmare. On the edge of the camp, the Americans had built three huge incinerators. They burned day and night, casting huge sooty palls of smoke into the air. The troops called these burners 'the gates of Mordor'.

Pretty much everything that could be burned was burned: including a vast amount of toxic material like plastics and batteries. You had to be careful of getting down-wind of the smoke. The acrid soot would smart your eyes and cause the most horrid coughing fits. KAF stank with the smell of it. I doubt any of the burning was ecologically legal. Lord knows what we gifted the atmosphere, or our health.

The earth in Kandahar is dun—a dull, greyish brown. The buildings the military had erected, mile after mile of them, were also dun; inside and out. With the trees and the vegetation gone, the earth had whipped into a dust, covering everything in the same universal nothingness. The people, the buildings, the trees, the roads, the vehicles—everything was the same depressing shade of ochre brown. The bright desert sun exacerbated the uniformity and blandness.

In my three years there, I never once heard KAF being more pleasantly described than as a shit-hole. KAF was not a place for the creative. There was nothing there to excite the spirit or rejuvenate the soul.

Afghans, of course, know their country is a hard land, just as they have a near child-like love of colour. Afghans are the most wonderful gardeners. The most desolate compound will always have, at its heart, a furious patch of flowers and glorious vegetables. Not so KAF. With a few honourable exceptions, the Americans had turned KAF into a desolate, wind-blown place, dedicated purely to war and death, lacking any spark of humanity. It dulled the human spirit—which was, of course, exactly why the generals had built it that way.

Visually, it was difficult to differentiate one dust-covered compound from another. The American accommodation blocks alone were nearly two miles in length: a never-ending visual litany of shipping containers, concrete walls and dust. Aurally, too, KAF was overwhelming. Fighter jets constantly sprinted down the runway, mere yards away, taking off in a roaring blur of after-burner and testosterone. Combat air patrols fly in pairs. It is impossible to speak and be understood over the roar of jet engines. In KAF, you quickly learned to pause conversation when a fighter took off—and just wait until after the second followed twenty seconds later.

Amongst the flurry of jets, the dust whirlwinds, the umber-coloured sea of containers and huts and the endless churn of enormous robot-like vehicles, scurried a sea of faces, all equally covered in dust. Either clad in uniformed dull greens and browns, or contractor khaki, the humans blended in equally to the ochre of the landscape.

The only colour in evidence was a profusion of incongruous yellow belts. At night, or when visibility was low, one of the plethora of American rules dictated that all personnel should wear reflective yellow belts. The only exception to the yellow belt ruling was the US Marine Corps, who were required to carry a torch instead. Presumably in case they get shot at, in which event they would extinguish their lights and fight. Marines are stubbornly, quixotically and romantically independent to the end.

US soldiers were not allowed to wear any civilian attire; nothing except that which their government had issued them with. The only clothes the Americans permitted, other than camouflage uniform, was issue gym kit. Which was uniformly grey and black. Yellow belts were to always be worn with gym kit, day or night. Amongst the sea of brown, you could always reassuringly spot a splash of incongruous canary yellow, appearing and disappearing in the midst of the host.

Maria and I spent half a day trying to sort out life in KAF. An endless whirl of store buildings, reception rooms, form filling, key collection, briefings and yet more badges. Steffi had extremely kindly organised me a room in what was known as the NATO blocks, which were to become my home for the next three years. They were patterned on the same concrete covered with brick-effect render that I had seen in the IJC.

Located right in the centre of camp, the NATO blocks were much sought after by the wise and despised by the war hungry. The interior of KAF resembled a very large, dust coloured factory complex. It could, had it not been for the drumbeat of the war, been just as easily located in the New Mexico desert. The military had trained its people to fight, and had spent months working up the troops into a training frenzy, before they had deposited them into KAF. Remarkably few would ever leave the camp, with its dreary surroundings and equally dreary rules. It wasn't exactly the Seal Team 6 video game glamour a lot of the young ones had hoped for.

The NATO blocks, with their flushing toilets, showers and sinks, just added to the disappointment. A lot of the male soldiers tried to compensate by sleeping with their weapons, in their sleeping bags, incongruously resting on their mattress covered beds. The litany of complaints against the NATO blocks—that it made the troops soft, that they had no place in a war zone—were endless. The blocks were a legacy of a time when the British had run KAF: and NATO had happily indulged plans to stay in Afghanistan for another thirty years.

In 2011, such sentiment had been replaced with American leadership. American generals may have lived in private compounds, but they were quite sure their men and women needed to be warrior monks. I never understood why life had to be so grim. It was miserable enough just existing in KAF without making life even more unbearable. At one stage, the US commanding general, Bob Abrams, hatched a plan to move everybody out of the NATO blocks and into tents. Leaving the NATO blocks empty but still present. What that would have achieved, except to make everybody even more miserable, eluded me. Luckily, at the last minute, wiser heads prevailed at such hair shirt extremism.

It was easy to spend six months in a tent. I'd done it on several occasions. Actually, I had happily lived in much worse. This time, though, I would be staying for years, and I was very happy to indulge in a little KAF luxury: even if I had to endure the never-ending taunts.

I bought a flower-patterned quilt and sheets at the British exchange, part of a small compound the British called 'Heroes'. Clustered around a small, open-air square, the Brit's place in the sun sported two cafes, a small shop and a gym, off-limits to all except British soldiers. By 2011, the British contingent at KAF had swelled somewhat, from those earlier days of the Harrier jets.

Indeed, the changing of the years had brought a changing of government in the UK. Tony Blair, the liberal interventionist who had initially brought Britain into the war, was long gone, as was his Labour administration. The new British coalition government, headed by a centre-right conservative party, had sold off the entire Harrier fleet, for a cut-down price, to the US Marine Corps. While most British military officers would claim an affinity to the conservatives, it is an ironic truism that conservatives always slash the military, Even as the US was ramping up its war, the UK was radically downsizing its military capability. By 2011, as an island nation, the UK no longer even had any airborne maritime surveillance aircraft. The army was smaller than it had ever been since Napoleon had been a threat. All cuts imposed while the politicians claimed to be fully committed to an overseas war.

With a cloth cut smaller had come reduced British abilities, if not British ambition. Aged Tornado aircraft now flew in place of the Harriers. The Tornadoes, most now thirty years old, struggled to take off from Kandahar. The desert air played havoc with the lift capability and the dust ruined engine intakes. While the US-made F-16s, which the other allies operated, nimbly sprang into the sky, the Tornadoes would clamber flatly off the ground, spewing black smoke and making vast amounts of pained exhaust noise. Even the French Mirage, much to French delight, looked more the part than these wheezy cold war relics.

The British also operated a special forces task force in Kandahar, which attracted a lot of hangers-on and some rather pompously self-important attached personnel, not nearly as special as they thought they were, who conflated a posting to Kandahar with service as James Bond. The scale of the British contribution was infinitely out-matched by the sheer size and scope of the US presence.

The Americans now firmly ran the entire ship—and evaluation of British performance by the US was not good. As one very senior US general told me:

'The British are not nearly as good as they think they are—and told everybody else they were.'

Gone were the days when we could lecture the Americans on counter-insurgency, as we had done in the early days, with tales of South Armagh and Belfast. The British may have thought we had a 'special relationship' with the US but as a US Ambassador put it to me:

'We do have a special relationship with the UK—just as we have a special relationship with Germany, France, Spain and all our other allies.'

While the British have never really gotten over the great alliance of D-Day, our Americans friends are much more circumspect and realistic.

British naivety and arrogance towards our allies had been quite breathtaking throughout the Afghan campaign. I had been once directed to write a press release, to say that, unlike the Americans, we had come to help, not fight, and therefore our troops would not be wearing helmets, but berets. Utter bunkum—all the average Afghan saw was a foreign soldier with a gun. What those soldiers wore on their head as a fashion statement was quite irrelevant.

The British had not done well in Helmand, requiring a vast influx of US Marines, twice the size of the British force, to make real headway. Despite the paucity of their force, the British had insisted on building a large number of isolated bases, strung out like a string of dirty pearls, across Helmand's interior. Each small force would engage in doggedly pursuing local patrolling. Patrolling which invariably would end with some poor sod being shot/ blown up or otherwise wounded. Whereupon the survivors would commit to a scrappy casualty evacuation of the wounded, right back to the patrol base where they had come from. Most of the soldiers in Helmand were barely more than teenagers. The expansion into the south became a never-ending loop of chaos.

The British rotated their troops like the wind. Each in-coming brigade would spend scarcely five months in their isolated bivouacs before, battered, bewildered and bruised, they would head homewards to a country increasingly disenchanted with the entire project.

By 2011, the British were still gamely attempting to hold onto the central part of Helmand, but the Marine Corps and the Americans firmly ran the show in Helmand and dictated the war's tempo.

The British presence in Kandahar, which primarily maintained air and logistic support to their main effort in Helmand, was merely one of many allied compounds, not the leader of the pack. No longer the imperial power of the past, the British purposefully reduced themselves to a sometime sullen bunch, keeping themselves to themselves.

I had arrived in Kandahar with a pile of euros, the de facto currency at the IJC, with its large European contingent. In KAF, the world was decidedly run by the US dollar, although NATO countries continued to run euro accounts for accountancy purposes. Maria and I asked the Brits if they would change a little money for me. Being a British citizen, working for NATO as a NATO employee, it seemed a reasonable request. I was point blank refused. Indeed, it took Maria to buy my quilt for me with her own dollars.

The Americans were different. Any US citizen, regardless of what they did in KAF, had the right to go to the American bank and purchase an 'Eagle Card', which was essentially a debit card that was accepted at all the on-camp concessions. No American had to carry cash, of any sort. The United States looked after its people.

All through my time in KAF, the British played alone by their own rules, moaning quietly about the Americans, but not really doing anything to lead the way. Whereas the Americans would lay on concerts and events for all, after 2011 the British kept their visiting morale shows to British personnel only, hidden on the British compound. One year, Prince Andrew came to visit the UK contingent for Christmas. The British colonel in charge didn't even invite the commanding American major general, nominally his boss, to join the royal party for tea. The Americans, who are scrupulously generous, were not amused.

For all that the NATO headquarters in KAF flew more than a dozen flags, and the IJC nearly fifty, the only country that really mattered, as indeed it did in all of Afghanistan, was the United States. It provided the heart, soul, leadership and spirit of the entire enterprise, all backed up by what seemed like limitless men and women, equipment, weapons and ammunition.

I never came to terms with the incessant battle I fought over the American army's draconian work/ life balance, and I certainly bemoaned the singular lack of irony in their sense of humour, but I will always be in awe of the sacrifice the US military made in Afghanistan. Compared to any other country in the world, my own most definitely included, the US stands head and shoulders above any other for the sheer level of commitment and endeavour deployed. There are many serious questions to be asked about what we actually achieved in Afghanistan, and the manner in which the campaign was fought. But whatever those faults may be, the United States can never be questioned for the number of cards it laid on the playing table. Whether that endeavour was correctly used, or even necessary, is another question entirely.

By 2011, that 'Made In America' stamp was well and truly branded across all of KAF. At first sight, the sheer scale of the enterprise took the breath away. It was quite easy to stand in the middle of that vast military-industrial complex and believe the war was already won. When in fact, the limit of that power extended merely to the fence-line. The trouble with all of that commitment was that, despite looking like one machine, the execution of the task in hand was anything but. Under that omnipotent exterior, operating in KAF was a singularly dysfunctional experience.

Kandahar Airfield was home to the headquarters of the ISAF regional command for the south—called HQ RC-S. This had originally been a Canadian command, which the Americans had later inherited as lead nation. The US provided not just the headquarters staff, but the commanding major-general, who was called a 'two star' by virtue of the number of rank stars he wore on his uniform. This headquarters was responsible for the management of the various army brigades and sub-units spread across all the four southern provinces of Kandahar, Uruzgan, Daikundi and Zabul. That deployment included sizeable NATO army contingents from Holland, Australia, Romania, Bulgaria, Slovakia and Albania. In turn, HQ RC-S answered to another US lieutenant general, a three star, at the IJC.

Simple enough at first sight—except ISAF didn't work like that.

Alongside RC-S, there was an entirely separate special forces chain of command, which answered to another, separate US two star general in Kabul. Not to the RC-S major-general. This special forces command maintained two task forces in KAF. One, which the British were involved in, committed to counter-terrorism, and another, run primarily by troops from the Baltic States, committed to training specialist police units. The accountability between RC-S and these units tended to wax and wane, depending on the strength of personality of the generals running each side of the coin.

Already we have two separate chains of command working over exactly the same piece of geographic turf.

Supporting this ground effort were the air component units based in KAF, which were variously tagged to a central ISAF command and also to separate national commands. Some of which, like the British in Helmand, fell under yet another ground command, RC South-West, or to transport commands, or to providing country-wide combat air support. Again, each of these components was commanded by yet more two star generals, none of whom were in Kandahar. All of which was most definitely not helped by the fact that, mostly speaking, the army doesn't understand, or particularly like, the air force—and vice-versa.

The count of different commanders, all empowered to shoot folks in Kandahar, is now running into double figures.

It gets more complicated:

KAF also hosted a heady mix of agency types, flying a tech heaven of surveillance aircraft and other secret agent stuff. The CIA had a large base in KAF. At one stage, even NASA had a unit in Kandahar. Afghanistan is the most surveilled war in history. Every phone call, radio message and e-mail was monitored, if not by us, then by others. Including the Pakistanis, through whose country ran the telephone exchanges and internet servers for all of Afghanistan. ELINT, or electronic surveillance, was big, big business in Kandahar. Then there were the human intelligence teams, the spies, the handlers and the key leadership managers. Whole compounds full of folks in chinos and khaki shirts, all called 'Dave', doing stuff they couldn't or wouldn't talk about.

Alongside all these agency types sat a large number of private security companies, contracted through their own chain of command to different US sub-units, agencies, aid departments, government authorities, Afghan companies or merely doing their own thing. None of which were accountable to anyone in ISAF, or, more importantly, anybody in Kandahar, for the way they conducted business on a day-to-day basis. Southern Afghanistan was overrun with gangs of armed westerners, all nominally working for somebody or other, none centrally accountable.

The mushy layer in the cake was the NATO headquarters for KAF, called COMKAF. Despite the campaign in the south being a US enterprise, NATO fiercely protected KAF as its own airfield. If only for no other reason than to balance the US chess piece of Bagram airfield, which was an entirely American owned facility. KAF gave NATO a place at the table as a serious player. If America had its own airfield, so would NATO.

Afghanistan was nothing if not a whirlpool of geo-political game playing and posturing. Sometimes, the whole operation resembled little more than a game of strategic international willy-waving.

Confusingly the brigadier, or one star, air force general in command of COMKAF was also called COMKAF. COMKAF—the headquarters—had responsibility for running the camp and the airfield. While, nominally at least, every unit inside Kandahar airfield answered to COMKAF—the man—as a sort of resident camp and building superintendent. COMKAF—the man and the headquarters—was in turn answerable to NATO in Brunssum, the Netherlands, which was quite an enviable position to be in, as it allowed the air force brigadier to give the finger to the US army and RC-S with some degree of impunity.

COMKAF—the man—also ran the US 451st air wing, the Kandahar US air component, in what the military call 'dual-hatting'. For this, he was responsible to the US air force component commander, another two star general. All whilst also keeping the army two star in RC-S happy, as KAF hosted his ground units. COMKAF was a busy man, whilst COMKAF, the headquarters, was a manic buzz of conflicting interests and nationalities.

Kandahar Airfield also hosted the US State department, whose southern branch was led by an ambassador, and whose remit included oversight of all the aid projects in the south, which was nominally coordinated by the US embassy in Kabul. Confusingly, the US ambassador had an office right next to the RC-S two star American general, therefore completely fuzzing the demarcation between military and diplomatic initiatives.

The chicken soup command structure was further complicated by the dear old Afghans. Who had an annoying habit of demanding attention from time to time. Somewhat rudely, they had asked to be involved in ISAF's efforts to re-shape their country.

Sitting on the south-east corner of the camp, the fledgling Afghan air force ran its own air wing. Commanded by an Afghan major general, supported by an American colonel, who answered to yet another general in Kabul. This time head of yet another, separate training command, as well as to ISAF special forces command. Next door to KAF was Camp Hero, home to the Afghan army and yet another major general. This time the Afghan army commander who commanded 205 Corps, the Afghan army unit designated for security in the South, who was advised by another ISAF general, this time an Australian. Who, at least, helpfully worked within RC-S.

While all of these ISAF generals worked for the NATO mission, each was acutely aware that they belonged to their own country's military. ISAF service was borrowed service. Every rotation worked for the common cause with at least a passing glance to check on their future career prospects. Innate nationalism trumped NATO consensus every time, with sometime unpleasant consequences. Nobody was going to go out on a limb for ISAF at the expense of personal advancement.

Each of these national contributions were supported by their own national in-country headquarters, and had their own national chain of command which decided what, where and when they would do their business. Just going outside the wire meant careful consideration of who would go and in what circumstances. Very few of the nations allowed their soldiers to commit to that sort of risk.

It was little wonder that the Americans got fed up of the dog's dinner. They'd issue an order and everybody else would say; 'we'll get back to you.'

Which was why they pretty much ended up doing everything themselves.

Beside all of this military chaos, KAF also operated as a civil terminal, with over seventy civilian flights a week, arriving at the old US built terminal, which sat firmly in the middle of the military camp. The civil terminal was overseen by the Afghan Civil Aviation Authority (ACAA), which had a tie-in to ISAF through a German colonel, based in Kabul, again answering to a completely different chain of command. ACAA nominally controlled the airspace above KAF, while the military provided the facilities to run the airfield, excepting the civil terminal, which had its own Afghan manager. This poor man, who was to become a dear friend, was rarely, if ever, invited to any of the key discussions about how what was nominally his airport was actually run. The airstrip at any one time was a confusing collage of military jets, transports, helicopters, unmarked aircraft, drones and passenger airliners.

To the recipe, add a pinch of spice in the form of yet another Afghan major general who ran the police force charged with protecting KAF, and the provincial governor, on whose land the camp sat.

KAF was a nightmare of inter-tangled networks of command. Some units answered to NATO, some to ISAF, some to special forces, some to the state department, some to the Afghan government and some to the sort of people who populate 'The Bourne Identity'.

Unbelievably, it took until 2011 before all these different and competing agencies met together, once a week, to decide any form of common agenda. KAF wasn't so much one soccer team fighting to score a goal, as eleven different players playing different games with different balls on different fields.

Generals come in many shapes and sizes, but they all share one characteristic—a degree of personal ruthlessness. The military can be a remarkably demanding organisation. Generals do not become generals by being gentle. At the end of the day, a general has not only to exhibit military talent, but the peculiar ability to order men and women into potentially lethal situations—and be prepared to live with the consequences of those decisions for the good of the mission. Generals, at the end of the day, have to order up death. A partial object of good leadership is to mitigate that risk, but it is only mitigation. Generals make decisions that get folks killed, in order to fulfil their mission. No other profession in the world asks the same of its senior leadership.

The men—and it is still pretty much all men—who fill these posts are alpha males. Most are intelligent, reserved and somewhat considered individuals, but with that ruthlessness comes with a high degree of personal ambition and not a little ego. Whilst many of the generals I met became friends, I also met several who I would be delighted to never come across again for the rest of my life. Not to mention a few who were actively loathed by both their staff and their peers.

Generals are used to being listened to and obeyed. Entire staffs are dedicated to following their orders. Afghanistan was an arena to cement reputations and become an even more important general. And to do so within the very limited time span of their one rotation in-country. The upside was a cadre of remarkably driven men. The downside was the impossibility of corralling all that competing talent and delivering all those ambitious plans.

Afghanistan was full of alpha male generals—with no daddy bear to bang heads together. The tragedy of Afghanistan was the lack of an Eisenhower. The effort was there. The political will, at least in the early years, was there. More often than not, though, all that energy was dissipated into personal turf wars. KAF was such a place—a dizzying mix of eddies and whirlpools of competing officers, missions and objectives.

Even when all the generals could fit their egos and agendas into the same room, which wasn't often, individual nations still had to refer back to their own governments for approval. It took forever to get anything done in KAF. Which is why, by 2011, the Americans were thoroughly fed up of coalitions and were making a determined, and not very subtle effort, to run everything by American rules, with American leadership. I could understand it—after all, they pretty much paid for it all.

I lost count of the meetings I went to where one staff officer would say; 'my general's intent is this.' Only to be loudly followed by another contradicting him with; 'my general's intent is that.' While all that energy was being dissipated in inter-service, inter-unit or personal rivalries, the other side was busy reminding us that KAF was not a game. What was going on outside the wire was very real—and often became very personal.

The interior of KAF was a mesmerising tornado of activity, people and equipment—all moving with that intensity of purpose that the military like to project. The whole effort screamed; 'we mean business.' When, much of the time, that effort produced little more than a frantic hamster on a wheel would: running very fast to get absolutely nowhere, beyond just being there on exactly the same spot. The military thrive on constant movement: the 'doing' of things. If you stood back and looked at it all, much of that activity was just mindless thrashing about.

Arrayed against that torrent of military might, just across the barbed wire perimeter fence, we fought against an enemy that often exhibited not much more talent than a man wearing flip-flops on a bicycle. We ranged billions of dollars of hardware against a man who had something even more precious—theologically inspired hatred.

In 2011, despite four years of constant ingress of more troops, more planes, more tanks, more money, Abdul the full-time farmer and part-time Taliban was still reminding us all that we were nowhere near winning: and he was doing so on a daily basis.

BOOM-BANG-A-BANG

KAF was so huge it had its own bus services. All complete with different routes, timetables and luxury coaches, providing a door-to-door service, 24/7. Many of the coaches had German, or even Swiss licence plates. How they had ended up in Kandahar was no doubt a very dodgy Interpol tale of skulduggery in its own right.

The buses became well known as late-night trysting places. Privacy was at a premium in KAF, but 40,000 predominantly young men, and the occasional woman, were still human beings with human instincts, uniform or not. Most of the buses had curtains over the windows, and the drivers, as TCNs, had no say over the behaviour of their passengers. Quite often, at night, in the back window of a passing bus, you'd see a pumping, naked ass ride by. Sex on the late night buses got so out of control, the military police had to provide guards.

The public transport system was made the more memorable by the bus stops. These were made not of wood or glass, but of concrete, reinforced by piles of sandbags. The bus stops doubled as waiting places and as refuge from attack. The bus stops were bomb shelters. Just as KAF could seem to be its own little, often funny, micro-sphere, the world outside had a terrifying way of reminding one that Kandahar was, indeed, rather a dangerous place to live.

That first night in KAF, the war came to visit.

It started with three distant rumbles. Explosions are not as they sound in the movies. In real life they have more of a bass rumble. The earth around Kandahar is a close-packed clay and sand. The ground itself will absorb the sound waves of an explosion. The noise hits in two waves. First there is the 'boom' of the immediate explosion, then a higher-pitched follow-on sonic wave, the 'bang'. My Afghan friends called every explosion 'boom-bangs', so solidified were the sonic effects of their delivery in their consciousness.

Being shelled is a surreal experience. A soldier's natural reaction, reinforced in training, is to react. When I was young, we had the mantra instilled into us from the first week:

'Dash, down, crawl, observe, sights, fire'. Do SOMETHING to regain the initiative.

Being shelled is the opposite. There is nothing to do but pray it doesn't hit you.

The army neatly divides lumps of metal flying at you at high speed into two types of lethal agents: direct and indirect fire. Both are designed to kill. The division refers to the method of their delivery.

Direct fire arrives in a straight line; I see you, I fire a gun at you and the bullet travels in a straight line from A to B. Indirect fire arrives in a parabola, over a longer distance, and it is unlikely that I can see you. Indirect fire is generally classed as a mortar, shell or missile. With direct fire, there is a chance you can see the enemy before he sees you. With direct fire you can move, manoeuvre, fire back directly. Do SOMETHING. With indirect fire, the most you can immediately do is duck.

We got an awful lot of indirect fire in KAF.

KAF had a drill for indirect fire. The idea was to fall on your face, tuck your hands under your body, and close your eyes. Then, you just lay there and prayed. After two minutes, if nothing beside you had gone 'boom-bang', and you were still intact to act, you were then required to make your way in an orderly fashion to a shelter or other hardened structure.

Not really the most martial of responses. There is no code of honour in just lying there and waiting for something to happen. Grown men, trained warriors, all armed to the teeth, would just flop down, grab their balls, lie in the dirt and pray. The entire apparatus of war, the billions of dollars of hardware and the tens of thousands of people who serviced them, would just stop and wait. And do nothing.

The cause? Abdul on his bicycle had planted an improvised missile in a field and fired it at KAF. Pennies worth of weaponry trumped billions. Afghanistan was littered with millions of old weapons and munitions. We lay there in the mud because a thirty-year old Chinese or Russian rocket worth little more than scrap had been fired in our general direction.

It was ridiculously simple. The fields around KAF supported farm after farm of irrigated crops, such as grapes and pomegranates. Kandahar lacked trees to make supports for the plants, so the Afghans rather cleverly engineered the problem by digging channels in the ground and laying the vines against the sides of the trenches, in neatly dug V-shapes. V-shapes which then, rather conveniently, provided a myriad of pre-made firing-steps.

Our enemy merely laid an old missile against the irrigation channel, pointed it in our general direction, organised some sort of homemade timing device, and rode off. Sometime later, this innocuous piece of pipe would spring into life and a warhead would fly in our direction. KAF was such a huge target, it was quite hard to miss. The Afghans had had plenty of practise: during the Soviet invasion many of the old boys around KAF had spent their youth doing exactly the same as their sons were now doing to us. Many of these unguided rockets actually did miss, but they came is such numbers that the hit rate was depressingly high.

Against this, ISAF arrayed billions of dollars worth of surveillance drones, observation balloons, ground sensors, locating radars, cameras and ground patrols. Yet how do you secure a base with a perimeter fence long enough to run into double figures, out to the accepted rocket range of nearly eight kilometres? However much hardware ISAF threw at the issue, Abdul always found a way—simply because he was a resourceful Afghan. Plant the piece of pipe, ride away on your bicycle, invisible alongside all the other thousands of Afghans who lived there. And just wait.

The simple truth of dropping to the floor, what the military call an 'IA', or immediate action, was that the only intervention that would save you was luck. The incremental and unnerving truth of those attacks was that, each and every time one exploded, you rode your luck. Sooner or later, one was going to go off next to you.

It was the constant rolling of the dice that took a toll, no matter how hardened and superficially tough one was. You just never knew when it would be your turn. Right through my three years in Kandahar, until very nearly the end, I heard that dull thud nearly every day. From 2011 through 2013, averaged out, KAF endured at least one attack every day.

My own personal record, in 2012, was sixteen separate rocket attacks in one day. Sixteen motherfucking times in one day, we all lay there for two minutes, then made our way to a shelter, where we sweated and waited for an all clear. Not sixteen missiles, much more than that: constant volleys of fire, sixteen times. Sixteen motherfucking times when I just sat there and asked the other side: 'could you give this a motherfucking break?' Reacting to a rocket attack was a fulltime job in itself.

Right towards the end, the attacks stopped. Somebody had had the bright idea of putting a surveillance balloon directly above the camp. The bad guys were scared of the balloons and their all-seeing cameras. Last six months I was there, we hardly had an attack at all. Why the fuck nobody had put the fucking balloon up there beforehand, I'll never know.

Soldiers in the smaller bases laughed at those inside KAF. They faced a different, more immediate threat. Inside KAF it was the inability to do anything but lie and wait that caused a more insidious and malignant issue: folks were killed by those rockets. The threat was very real. Courage comes in many forms. The physical courage to charge a machine gun nest under fire is one. The courage to endure daily rocket attacks, whilst unable to do anything about it, is entirely another.

I saw many brave men quiver under the threat of this invisible threat. One second, a swaggering soldier, all uniformed and gunned up, the next lying in the dirt, praying for home. I also saw several who asked to be sent home. The insidiousness of it eventually plays havoc, regardless. To this day, I cannot bear firework displays.

All those mortars, shells and missiles were universally classed as 'rockets'. Living with the constant 'boom' of their detonations became a source of perverse pride amongst KAF residents. The gym did a roaring trade in branded t-shirts: 'Kandahar—where only a rocket attack stops a workout.' It was superficial bravado.

KAF had an early warning system, called the 'giant voice'. Essentially a public address system, it consisted of an array of enormous loudspeakers, set up across the entire camp. These were linked to direction-locating radar that was supposed to be able to pick up the trajectory of an in-coming missile. Giant voice was supposed to give the residents of KAF three to five seconds warning of an imminent attack. Not where the missile was destined to land, just that at least one missile was on its way. Five seconds, maximum, to hit the ground, grab your nuts and pray…

Starting with a warbling alarm, very reminiscent of the sirens I remembered from civil defence, during the 1960's, it would be followed by a rather disembodied female voice calmly stating, in the same monotone as you would order dinner; 'rocket attack… rocket attack…'

That warning, as short as it was, was not guaranteed. Quite often, the parabola of the in-coming missile was too shallow to be picked up by radar. You'd hear the '*crummp*' of incoming, then the rather plaintive sirens would start a delayed apology. Giant voice didn't start all over KAF at the same time. It ran in increments. The sirens would ripple across camp, as ever-increasing echoes, all repeating the same alarm: 'rocket attack, rocket attack, rocket attack', pealing away into the distance.

After a while, you became de-sensitised to the impacts. It was impossible to maintain the same excited frisson of adrenalin. A rocket exploding was an immediate combat indicator of how long a person had been in KAF. Under three months, folks would follow the drill, lying on the ground like beached whales. After a while, you just sat there, or stood there, or ignored it all entirely. There were just too many attacks, and too much chancing to luck involved to do otherwise. No matter how many times the authorities tried to tighten up on procedures, those of us who lived there knew the whole game was a matter of chance.

The Americans liked to dress the entire event up. Their rules stated that if a soldier had been 'engaged' by the enemy, to the extent that their lives had been put in danger, then that soldier could apply for what was known as a 'combat action' patch; a badge to be worn on the uniform. It was a kind of 'I was in the shit' affirmation. Combat action badges were quite big *juju* for the American military. The generals, however, recognised that awarding a combat action award *en masse* to the tens of thousands within KAF would defeat the purpose of the elitism of the badge, so the criteria became one of distance. It had to be a near-miss, or a hit, with a rocket to qualify. Measuring tapes were applied.

KAF always maintained a special reputation as being in the shit. Lots of folks actively avoided a posting there, some came to see for themselves. I know of one visiting sergeant-major who optimistically put in for a combat action award, on the dubious basis of a single rocket landing within one hundred yards of his office tour: and who was quite devastated when his self-penned request was knocked back. The stupid SOB took the news badly: he went out onto the runway to pace out the distance, marking the yards with an elongated step. Too close and you could die, too far away and no prize. Being rocketed in KAF was indeed a game of snakes and ladders.

There were many close calls with rockets. On one occasion, at five in the morning, the Pizza Hut franchise took a direct blast, spraying packets of dough and tomato sauce for hundreds of yards. As funny as it seemed at the time, had the explosion occurred later in the day, the place would have been packed with soldiers.

On another, a rocket hit the concrete runway and skipped back into the air. Nearby, two Kenyan workers were standing by a re-fuelling truck. One hit the ground, the other stayed standing. The man on the ground opened his eyes to see his colleague's head lying next to him. The missile had decapitated his standing partner, before impacting into the back of a truck. That incident happened less than one hundred metres from me. I didn't even think about claiming a badge. Live in KAF: learn to roll the dice.

That first night, as I lay in bed, three explosions followed in close succession. Giant voice began its eerie call across the camp. The constant background noise of KAF—vehicle noise, planes taking off, people talking—evaporated to be replaced by an eerie silence. I wasn't yet used to life in Kandahar, and I anxiously sought out my body armour and helmet.

Looking out my window, I could see parachute flares gently swinging across the night sky, like airborne lanterns. Then the air was rent with what sounded like a chainsaw being rippled across a log. It was the Apache helicopter gunships. In the darkness, the sky lit up with a sudden stream of light, as the tracers sought their targets on the ground. Just as soon as the light appeared, it would disappear, to be followed a second later by the sound of the bullet's rip, seeking out their targets.

KAF was a busy place alright: it was right in the middle of a hornet's nest.

Just down the road, fifteen minutes drive away, were some of the most fought-over districts in the entire war; Panjwai, Arghandab, Maiwand, Shah Wali Kot. The military rather laconically described the conflict as 'asymmetric', meaning it had no defined front-line, no organised foe. Well, I could have told them where the frontline was: right outside my front door.

In other wars, a huge base like KAF would have been hundreds of miles from the front. In Afghanistan, it was different. Inside the wire we lived an alternate universe. Yet, the boundary between that life and the terrain we sought to conquer was only as thick as a strand of barbed wire on the perimeter. KAF was, in many respects, its own frontline. Just being there was to be in the heart of the maelstrom.

Everybody was armed in KAF. It quickly became quite normal to have coffee with a group of men carrying loaded assault rifles. The very presence of guns was the KAF norm. Even inside the wire, the threat was such, on a huge, supposedly safe base, to militate the presence of tens of thousands of loaded automatic small arms. The place was just alive with guns and bullets.

The only person who it seemed didn't have a weapon was me. NATO rules stated that its staff members had to be unarmed. The person who wrote that ruling had obviously never been to Kandahar. Everybody, at least on our side, was armed. Even the sixty-year old lady pensioner who taught English at the base school was armed, with a pistol the size of her leg. She planned to use it, too, if she had to. The entire camp lived in a perpetual fear of not being armed enough.

Outside the wire, troops died, on a daily basis, from bombs and bullets. Inside the wire, we were rocketed on a daily basis. Every person in there carried a weapon and at least one magazine of bullets. Every day, you listened to fighter jets take off, to a background cacophony of explosions and gunshots. Even on a quiet day, the firing ranges kept on going, as soldiers zeroed in their weapons for the busy days.

There was no relief, no relenting of the constant pressure of war. Work was about war. Conversation was about war. Play was about war. Sleep was rest before war. Life itself was war. In the midst of it all, the constant arrival of the medevac helicopters would remind us of the human cost, while the Taliban provided a staccato punctuation of rocket fire to keep us all from forgetting.

How had it come to this? Why were these tens of thousands, sitting on a dusty, half-forgotten airfield, on the edge of a dusty, half-forgotten desert? What had happened to bring the world's focus to this marginal land? Who are these soldiers that fought here?

THE STEENBERGER GENERATION

I spoke to Private First Class Steenberger most days, for nearly a year. I never heard him swear once, which is a real rarity for a culture that uses the 'f'-word as punctuation. He was unfailingly polite, calling me, 'Miss Abi' and 'Ma'am'. He used to wonder what I was doing in Afghanistan, in civilian clothes, not carrying a gun. Despite my best efforts to explain my mission, it all remained a confusing cloud.

His job was repetitive and simple. He conscientiously applied himself to it. Steenberger sat with his loaded assault rifle at the security entrance to the headquarters building for regional command south, the big military headquarters co-located within Kandahar airfield. His job was to check that the myriad of visitors and passing staff had a valid ID badge and that they took no electronic devices beyond his gate. Nothing more complicated than hour after hour of storing mobile phones and matching flimsy, plastic photographic badges with their wearers.

For this, his country paid him twenty-four thousand dollars a year. For risking his life in Afghanistan, he was granted about three hundred and fifty extra dollars a month in hazardous duty pay. Steenberger liked the money that came from being in Afghanistan. He planned to buy a pick-up when he got home.

When he left Afghanistan, Steenberger would earn an Afghanistan campaign medal, and, quite possibly, an achievement medal, simply for being the best badge checker he could be. A colonel, or maybe even a general, would pin those to his chest, earnestly shake his hand, pose for a photograph, murmur a few words of thanks, and then move on to the next soldier, in a never-ending conveyor-belt of congratulations and 'thank-you for your service'.

The irony is that Steenberger would never see an Afghan, nor Afghanistan: beyond the small patch of dirt he stood on and the few avaricious concession holders within the base, hawking him Pakistani machine-made carpets and trinkets that passed as handmade Afghan artefacts. The only outward sign that he was, in fact, in Afghanistan, and not some other dusty, god-forsaken, desert base was that he carried an M16 assault rifle everywhere he went: and that that rifle was loaded with fifteen 5.56mm bullets.

In coming to Afghanistan, Steenberger had been granted the power to legally kill, and the means to do so, without ever actually getting to see any of the people he had been legally empowered to shoot at.

In this, he was unremarkable. At the height of the NATO Mission in Afghanistan, there were some one hundred and sixty thousand foreign soldiers engaged in fighting the war. Such are the logistics of modern warfare in a landlocked country thousands of miles away that a minimum of ninety-nine soldiers were required to sustain just one in the field. Very, very few soldiers who came to Afghanistan ever actually met an Afghan. The numbers who fired a bullet were even fewer.

Steenberger came from Arcadia, Carroll County, Iowa. His grandparents were refugees from Europe. His father's side from northern Scandinavia, his mother's from Denmark. Brought together by the conclusion of a cataclysmic war, they had sought safety and refuge in a new world. Two distinct families, cleaved from their homeland through man's inhumanity, chaotic accident and a genuine desire for work, brought together in America's heartland.

What little industry as still existed in Arcadia offered the young Steenberger little promise. His parents had bought and owned a general store. Walmart and the inter-state had brought that to its knees. The meagre income the family business provided offered little for the second son of five children.

Steenberger had done what generations before had done. He applied to join the Army. He had grown up with the Stars and Stripes, steeped in the idealist image of an America that promised wealth to all, but which offered little potential fulfilment if he had stayed in rural Iowa. He was proud to go. Steenberger is a member of the post-9/11 generation. Joining the Army in these days reflects a young man's pride with a special sheen.

The army proved Steenberger's salvation. Work, self-identity and honour, all rolled into one. His mother wears her 'Army Mother' lapel pin with pride. His schoolmates had all clapped his back, as he got on the Greyhound, to go to basic training: that day, Steenberger was somebody important.

He told me that Arcadia is famous as the town with the highest elevation in all of Iowa. At just under 1500 feet above sea level, in a pancake flat vista of grassland, Arcadia is positively Iowa Himalayan in stature. That was pretty much it for Arcadia; it has no famous university, no renowned cultural heritage, zero architecturally invaluable monuments. Arcadia is really just a street of homes, on a highway, on a pimple: the last census figures established that 485 souls lived there on the mountaintop.

Being at the summit of that Iowa hillock is all that Steenberger could claim for his heritage, yet he proudly did so, with an obstinate set in his jaw. Arcadia is the keystone of who he was. He came from somewhere—Arcadia, Iowa, the highest town in the state. He hoped that one day, if he served with honour, they might name a street after him.

He became a proud soldier—who, as he told me, answered to the 4th Infantry Division, the President of the United States and God, in that order.

Life for Steenberger is grounded in simple absolutes.

When I first met him, he was 19 years old. He was happily over weight, snug in his uniform, a man who loved his tacos. The Army helped him keep off the weight, but he had never come to enjoy the early morning physical training. Of average height and average build, he has average features, except for his glasses, which were Buddy Holly retro in a sea of uniformity. History will probably not record Steenberger, the soldier. His martial feats will most likely not be mentioned in same breath as Ulysses or Hercules. His memory will not echo through eternity. He is, in most ways, an unlikely soldier.

Yet, for all his ordinariness, he is, in one sense, truly extraordinary. He is one of a generation of Americans, who have signed to serve their country in uniform at a moment of great duress. As much as society eulogises the generation that stormed ashore in Normandy, this generation is just as unique.

What makes them different is that they are all volunteers. Nobody made Steenberger join the army. No yellow draft paper was carefully slipped under his front door. He chose to go. He chose to serve. And he chose to serve knowing that he would, most likely, end up fighting in a war far from the gentle slopes of Arcadia. Of course, economic necessity presaged his decision to raise his right hand and dutifully repeat the oath of loyalty. Yet, just as he volunteered to serve, so he could volunteer to leave. He actively chose not to. The army offered him more than just a pay cheque. The army made Steenberger.

The dichotomy of military service is that young men, and increasingly young women, long for the crucible of combat. Its romantic clarion call is deeply embedded, not just in society but in our DNA as human beings. Soldiers, as strange as it may sound, long to go to war. It is the test of who they are, and the answer to all the questions they hold; can they pull the trigger? How will they react under fire? What is it like to shoot somebody?

As much as succeeding generations of young Americans have uncomplainingly put on the green, there have been few generations that have queued so eagerly to serve on foreign shores. Yes, the Minutemen fought a foreign power. Yes, Dixie's trumpet and Lincoln's obduracy called for brother to make a stand against brother. But both of those conflicts, which define the very character of the United States, were fought on home territory, against enemies that shared the same values and cultural identity.

This war that we have declared is unique. It is fought against a transformative enemy, unlike any other: an enemy that Steenberger and the people of the liberal west struggle to comprehend, even after thirteen years of fighting against them.

For all its flaws, this generation of Americans truly do believe they live in a free society, and that the act of bringing down the Twin Towers on Manhattan Island represents a grave and serious threat to the very existence of that democratic society. American concepts of freedom are as tightly straight jacketed to that self-belief as any other rigid system of human inter-action.

Americans are quite genuinely convinced they live in the best country in the world, in absolute freedom. It is a belief system that is inculcated with the same rigorous enthusiasm as Soviet Russia espoused. The values are radically different: the lessons of belonging and integrating are not.

For an American, being an American is seen as the summit of human ambition. The genius of the program is to weld together disparate millions into one, colossal whole. No matter what colour, creed or religion, the motherland will embrace all: as long as you believe in the flag, the country and the system. It is so unlike Europe, a hodgepodge of quaint tradition and individual identity. Travelling across America is to see a homogeny. The same flag, the same love of country.

The upside has been the creation of the most powerful country the world has ever seen: powerful economically, creatively and spiritually. The downside is a failure to see any other way to exist.

America is, and always will be, an incredibly generous nation. It is the child who got the amazing Christmas present, but who still wants everybody at the party to share it. The trouble is, not everybody does. The human condition has evolved many other philosophies for living. Afghanistan is one of those societies.

The dichotomy of the individual human experience is that it is pluralist in nature. The right to decide one's own destiny is not unique to American aspiration: it is universal.

America's biggest failing throughout this war has been to fail to understand that not everybody wants to be like them or admire them: or even to tolerate their existence. It's not a discussion, or a debate, or an opinion that can somehow be overcome in time.

The people we fight want those of us in the liberal west dead, or subjugated. And our way of life completely, utterly and irretrievably erased. They will not stop until they achieve their aim.

That realisation has proven too shocking for the west. We have sleepwalked to the edge of the precipice. It calls into question the very foundations of everything we believe in. Which is why 9/11 changed everything.

It's difficult now, looking back, to remember exactly the horror of that dreadful day in 2001. While the images, of those colossal towers falling, will remain forever in the cerebellum of every single person who saw the news that day, what has been forgotten is what went before. 9/11 wasn't just about those planes flying into two very tall buildings. It was the rude awakening from a dream turned into a nightmare.

Nineteen months before, the world had engaged in a global celebration of a new millennium. From Pacific atolls to the plains of Afghanistan and the arctic tundra of Alaska, humankind had joined in the affirmation of our species. As the turning of the second great thousand years of human development, since a Christian saviour is assumed to have died for us all, gave way to a new beginning.

Regardless of faith, or the measuring of the days, we had all recognised the turning of the page as the conclusion of an epoch. This time, we all believed, we would not make the same mistakes of the past. No more wars, no more pestilence, no more hatred. Ten years before, the Berlin Wall had fallen. In Europe, successive countries had fallen under the spell of liberal democracy. The Western world was at peace, for the first time in generations. The Good Friday agreement had ended the troubles in Northern Ireland. The Dayton Accords had brought the Balkan wars to an end. A great allied coalition had driven the dictator Saddam Hussein from Kuwait.

American involvement had been key in those closures. America, as the beacon and torch of freedom, had irresistibly swept the board. We basked in what was to be a brief, but golden period of prosperity and happiness. America led the world.

Earlier that decade, I had sat in a rough brick hut in an Afghan refugee camp. Alongside a desolate family, clad in all the clothes they owned, we watched the community's communal black and white television. Beaming in from Pakistan, they looked on raptly at a grainy, poorly dubbed, fabulously incongruous chapter of 'Dynasty'. As Joan Collins had sashayed down her marble staircase, a wide-eyed, bearded mujahideen warrior had turned to me and incredulously, but eagerly, asked; 'does everybody in America live in a mansion?'

The United States, and all it offered, was the dream. Liberal democracy, it seemed, was the answer. Even on a remote hillside in northern Afghanistan. Everybody wanted to be an American.

On December 31st, 1999, we watched the celebrations in Times Square and the fireworks over Sydney Harbour, as 2,000 doves of peace were released in Bethlehem. President Clinton, the great and genial communicator, and leader of the free world, spoke on the steps of the Lincoln memorial, where America's greatest orator of recent times had once proclaimed a vision for an oppressed people:

'As we marvel at the changes of the last hundred years, we dream of what changes the next hundred and the next thousand will bring.... it is the eternal destiny of America to remain forever young, always reaching beyond... So we Americans must not fear change. Instead, let us welcome it, embrace it, and create it.

The great story of the 20th century is the triumph of freedom and free people, a story told in the drama of new immigrants, the struggles for equal rights, the victories over totalitarianism, the stunning advances in economic well-being, in culture, in health, in space and telecommunications, and in building a world in which more than half the people live under governments of their own choosing for the first time in all history... So as we ring in this new year, in a new century, in a new millennium, we must, now and always, echo Dr. King in the words of the old American hymn: 'Let freedom ring.'[5]

Freedom, as defined by western liberal democracy, was surely, we believed, the highest ideal of the human condition. Where self-expression can reach an apotheosis of contentment. By 2000, the west had truly never had it so good. Freedom: the power or right to act, speak, or think as one wants: a way of life where one is not imprisoned or enslaved.

---

[5] Quote from President Clinton's speech, 31st December, 1999.

We were complacent. We forgot that there was a significant part of the world that hadn't bought into the dream we all so avidly celebrated: a part of the world which viewed our prosperity and self-assumed righteousness with hatred and suspicion. Where the acquisition of worldly wealth did not bring happiness, merely weakness. Where every answer to every question that had ever been asked could be found in the words of a book based on events 1400 years ago.

In April 2001, I flew British Airways to New York. I walked onto the plane, five minutes before departure, with no security checks at all. As we neared Manhattan Island, the pilot asked me to join him on the flight deck. I sat right behind him, in the cockpit, as the World Trade Centre, Wall Street and the whole capitalist colossus passed by our port wing. I will never again sit in the cockpit of a commercial airliner over New York City.

September 11th 2001 wasn't just a colossal act of violence. It was the end of the dream.

A previous generation marked the summer of '63 as the last innocence, the final months before a charismatic and invulnerable president was shot. The summer of 2001 was even more epochal. Our new millennium, from that day to this, has been marked with conflict, disaster and war. Our dream ended before it had even fully begun.

Even in the immediate days after, as New York lay covered in a pall of dust and the twisted wreckage of that awful event, the mood had not yet crystallised into revenge. The actor George Clooney organized a national telethon, to raise money for the families of the victims. The event was live, and the great and good of Hollywood and the entertainment world came to help. Kurt Russell and Jack Nicholson manned the phones, while artists such as Stevie Wonder, Faith Hill, Bruce Springsteen, Sting and that old New York stager Billy Joel sang songs of love, loss and regret. Before a simple set of lit candles, Mohammad Ali, flanked by Will Smith, pleaded for reconciliation with Islam. It was an evocation of a mood that was not to last.

The country—and the world—sought leadership. George Robertson, the ebullient Scottish NATO secretary general, brought an invocation of Chapter 5 from the allies to the door of the White House: an attack on one is an attack on all. For a moment, the free world was united. The debate could go either way: people were scared and wanted solutions and answers.

President Bush, at the decisive moment, when the future of the millennia stood in the balance, chose war. He had a myriad of choices he could have made. Reason was defeated by the simple judgment of fear in the moment. It is a decision that is as profound, but surely not as well thought through, as Roosevelt's declaration of war against imperial Japan.

Consider this; we are now engaged in the longest war our modern liberal democracies have ever known. It is a conflict that has lasted more than twice as long as the Second World War. It is a conflict without end, that will last until either our way of life, or radical Islam itself, is extinguished. President Obama may have declared that war in Iraq is over. He may also have declared that 'combat operations' in Afghanistan are over.

The trouble is, nobody has asked the other side. There is no peace treaty. No convention, no understanding, no evolution.

We in the West have done our best to carry on, to accommodate the changes in our lives that war has brought: the intrusions on our civil liberties, the searches, the monitoring, the rising fear of attack. Fourteen years on, we can see that the Twin Towers, as terrible as it was, was not quite the presage of a new dark age. The world has staggered on, regardless. Nonetheless, we who are old enough to remember the world as it was know it will never be the same again.

Steenberger isn't old enough to really remember the world before the towers fell. What it was like to live in a world where we knew we had won because what we believed in was right.

I asked him once why we were in Kandahar. He told me we were there to help the Afghan people. In a little over a decade, his generation of warrior had forgotten that we actually came to Afghanistan to get the guys who had brought the towers down. Invading Afghanistan had little to do with helping Afghanistan. The part about changing a nation state was a by-product, a residual memory of that pre-9/11 time, when we knew we were right: Bosnia, Bulgaria, Poland, a re-unified Germany, Romania, the Baltic States, the former Soviet republics. All of those countries had readily embraced democracy.

Surely the countries we invaded post-9/11 would want the same? The tragedy is that we never asked them: we just assumed we would want what we were peddling. In the peddling process, we forgot why we had come there in the first place. Even when the war started to go badly, we continued to delude ourselves. As Donald Rumsfeld, US secretary of defence, said of the complete chaos after the fall of Baghdad to American arms:

'Freedom's untidy, and free people are free to make mistakes and commit crimes and do bad things. They're also free to live their lives and do wonderful things. And that's what's going to happen here.'[6]

We actively advocated for chaos, in the naive hope it would, somehow, someway, all turn out right. When it didn't, we just threw more soldiers, tanks and guns at the problem. We should have asked: 'What do these people *really* want?'

I would guarantee you, had we asked, that the reply would not have been more fighting.

Steenberger chose to serve because he believed his sacrifice was required to defend Arcadia, the United States and how his family chose to live their lives. That decision was design, ending up in Kandahar was accidental. Trust in a nation and a flag, and the need to defend it, drove a generation of young Americans like Steenberger to choose to spend their youth fighting. What he didn't sign up for was the re-engineering of another sovereign country.

Is it worth the sacrifice? Is it worth the thousands of young Steenbergers,

---

[6] Rumsfeld quote from Pentagon briefing, 2003

who now populate the countless myriad of burial plots across the United States? Is it worth the tens of thousands who, saved by the carapace of a knight's weight of armour plate, will now limp on prosthetic legs or snatch to grasp a cup with metal fingers for the rest of their mortal days?

Equally, was it worth the suffering and deaths of the hundreds of thousands who lived in those far off lands we were to invade, occupy and partially destroy? Was it worth the foment of hatred our actions have raised, creating a whirlpool of dissent and anger across the Islamic world that has yet to reach even a partial crescendo of resolution?

Steenberger did what was required of him, with honour and duty satisfied. He has his medals, as do all the other soldiers. We aren't going back. Our enemies, though, have never left.

As ISAF's mission came to an end in December 2014, I asked a US general what he thought would happen now. He replied; 'whatever the solution is, it will be an Afghan solution'. Like Pontius Pilate, we have washed our hands of the problem, in the fervent, but naive, thought that it will somehow disappear. It will not.

Radical Islam is rooted in ignorance and poverty. These are issues that, for all the billions we spent on fighting a war in Afghanistan, we have never truly addressed. In 2001, we invaded Afghanistan with an unspoken promise to save it. For fourteen years, we sent generations of Steenbergers with equally fervently spoken promises to change Afghanistan. At the end of 2014, we sent those troops home with none of our promises fulfilled.

What we, as the West, are fighting against is an enemy we cannot quantify or define. In the past, we have fought against ideas. Nazi Germany represented an ideology. It was, however, an idea wrapped up in a country. As hateful as National Socialism was, it had a physical home. A country has borders, a government, infrastructure, institutions and systems. These are all big-ticket items, which, in a war, we can identify and destroy.

In the West, we define our concept of war from the 17th century, in the terms of what is known as the Treaty of Westphalia. Following a disastrous series of central European squabbles over succession, the great powers mandated that sovereign powers would only directly interfere in the affairs of others via a formal declaration of war. The key principle of Westphalia mandates that until that decisive moment occurs, no one country has authority to directly interdict the affairs of another. In effect, the Treaty sets out a series of cause and effect steps that formalise the process of mutual destruction. Every war we have fought, until our very recent past, has been presaged by that notion.

It was only the end of the Cold War, with the West's apparent victory by relatively bloodless means that gave rise to the hubris of liberal interventionism, principally for humanitarian reasons. Bosnia was the key example. A doctrine of 'something must be done' justified what we did, in the name of the greater good.

Such a conceit can only be sustained by the contention that the West is always right—and that our enemies are invested enough to accept the decision we make on their behalf and express a wish to enter into a dialogue. It is the same conceit, albeit dressed in a different language, which our nineteenth century forefathers would have recognised in the expansion of empire and western governmental principles. Such liberal intervention relies on one key attribute—that the people we are intervening to help actually want our assistance and recognise our interference as such. Provided the other side plays by our rules, we can define the conflict—and justify it legally.

The case for intervention in Bosnia and Kosovo, the germination events for this new form of radical imperialism, were justified in terms of suppressing regional conflict on the doorsteps of Europe. The active intervention in another state's internal affairs broke Westphalia, but it was justified as the lesser of two evils: continued war or outside interference to bring about peace.

Afghanistan is different. No Afghan was involved in the twin towers. The Islamic Emirate of Afghanistan may have been a hateful and violent brute that brought misery and despair: but it didn't cause 9/11. All Afghanistan did was host Bin Laden and some of the architecture of the Al-Qaeda movement.

After 9/11, the Americans told the Taliban, not directly, but through interlocutors, to hand them over. The Taliban expressed their sorrow at events in New York, but politely refused. The Americans—and its key coalition allies—then invaded: without a declaration of war. The purpose was not just to capture or kill Bin Laden, but the overthrow of the regime that had defied them.

President Bush tried—and failed—to get the United Nations to sanction military action in Afghanistan. The UN did condemn what it called an act of terrorism: but 9/11 was never defined as an act of war. Nor did any UN resolution passed at the time ever specifically justify and invasion of Afghanistan. Even in US domestic legislation, Bush was forced to acquire a war powers resolution to authorise military action with legislative oversight. He was never empowered to declare war: otherwise he would have become a constitutional dictator. In the heat of the moment, the world conveniently forgot that the invasion of Afghanistan was actually illegal.

Does that matter? In one sense, the gunslinger in Bush would have been very happy that revenge was being taken: and damn the method and means of delivery. 'Either you are with us, or you are with the terrorists', as Bush famously declared to a joint session of congress on September 20th, 2001.

On the other, it matters very much. We ceded the high ground, the very systems that we had put in place as a civilised society, to manage our affairs and secure our own rights to self-destiny. We signalled to the rest of the world that western liberalism applied to us: but not to them. Many parts of the world celebrated the fall of the towers. Our invasion just confirmed that act was justified.

America went from being the world's trusted policeman to just another player on the block. The Arab spring, and the chaos that has resulted, has its roots in our ill-thought out actions: likewise, Russian interference in other sovereign nations. We invaded two national states, Iraq and Afghanistan, merely because two airliners flew into two tall buildings. The history books will call it all complete madness.

Of course, there have been terrorist movements before Al-Qaeda. Yet, according to Westphalian terms of war, we have never declared war on them. Baader-Meinhof, the Stern Gang, Provisional IRA, Mau Mau—all of these movements have merely been described as either criminal gangs or insurgent movements. Indeed, the West has a whole treaty, the Montreal Sabotage Treaty, which sets out a clearly defined cause and effect for dealing with acts of terrorism.

The whole idea of a 'war on terror' is a nonsense.

What happened after 9/11, by invading two sovereign nation states without declaration of war, has re-written the rules of international conflict, as we have lived them for three hundred years.

It is this that makes the attack on the Twin Towers so difficult to quantify. The US was not attacked by another country. 9/11 was not a Pearl Harbour moment. An act of great criminality, definitely, but an act of war, as Westphalian sovereignty would assume? No, it was not: Bin Laden and Al-Qaeda was not a country. Al-Qaeda and radical Islam is something else entirely.

The military would describe Al-Qaeda as a 'non-state actor'. Which is, in itself, rather a broad church. Non-state actors can, by definition, be anything or anybody who influences international relations. 'Live aid' was a benign non-state actor.

In itself, the term, when applied to Al-Qaeda, is a dichotomy. There is no 'acting' involved. There is no pretence here, no illusion. Nor is our enemy merely a participant. Al-Qaeda, as a movement, is but one of many that share a common belief: the absolute and rigid faith in the word of the Holy Quran, as spoken by the Holy Prophet himself, direct from the mouth of God.

The *Shahada*, the sentence that every novitiate to Islam must utter three times before embracing the faith, that there is no god but God and Muhammad is the foremost prophet of Islam, is universal. What we know now as radical Islam is founded upon a theological argument that human development, in thought and reasoning, stopped the day the word of God was given to the Prophet. Those words, framed in the society of 7th century CE Arabia, provide all the answers every human requires, from that day, forever more.

We, basking in the predominantly Judeo-Christian traditions of the West, have no cause to condemn those beliefs. It is roughly thirteen hundred years since the Prophet walked the earth as a man. Thirteen hundred years after Christ lived, Christians were burning people at the stake and beheading our enemies. The development of Christianity is as blood-soaked as Islam.

The difference between us now lies in the enlightenment. Where profound thinkers such as Darwin proposed that the world was not made in seven days, and that we may just have evolved from animals. Where Hume, Voltaire, Spinoza, Jefferson and Franklin spoke of the rights of man and in inexorable and undeniable advance of science as an explanation for the failings of the human condition. Islam has only just begun that voyage of self-examination.

Just as the Church was truly threatened by such towering colossi as da Vinci, so those religious conservatives within Islam are threatened by the advancement of human self-examination and interrogation.

What makes radical Islam so abhorrent is its pre-occupation with expression in violence as a self-cleansing instrument. Which is, perhaps, an exposition of the defining difference between Islam and Christianity. The Holy Prophet was a very human man—a warrior and a ruler, as well as the receptacle for the word of God. He achieved his early devotees as much through conquest and annihilation as true devotion. The legend of Christ's life is centred within a complete lack of violence, except in that shown towards him: but, crucially, not by him.

Those defining traditions can still be seen in the justification of the wars that both radical Islam and the liberal West have conducted after 9/11. We in the West frame our responses as defensive in nature, forced by events on the ground. Whereas our enemies are fuelled by the same violent desire for conquest and subjugation as the Holy Prophet himself showed on his triumphant return to Mecca from the wilderness.

Islamic extremism is, indeed, 'non-state', in that it occupies no kingdom, except, perhaps, in its own eyes, that of God himself. However, the assumption in our description is that radical Islam exists as a whole, something definable, with an organisation, a hierarchy, personality and substance. Al Qaeda is none of those things.

We are not fighting a tangible entity. Not a person, a tribe, an army, a state or country. We are fighting a loose philosophy with no borders, literal or philosophic. Radical Islam requires only an individual's self-belief. Anybody, anywhere, anytime can become a warrior of God. It is an idea that has merely one end; the destruction of all that we hold dear. Its fuel is hatred of all that the West and liberal democracy has created over the millennia. Victory will not be defined by the creation of a caliphate, or a pan-Islamic state. Its participants are too fractured for that.

No, victory will be achieved by the imposition of the word of Allah, as prescribed by the literal word of God, contained within the holy Quran. The Prophet's revelations need no augmentation, no debate, no assistance and no country. The holy book contains all that life itself requires—and those who oppose its dictums must die, and the institutions that support them must be razed to the ground. Radical Islam is an act of creation.

What we have achieved with our invasions is an amplification of that evil. In the science fiction classic 'The Forbidden Planet', a human-crewed spaceship land on an alien world with an ancient culture that is completely alien to them: for it is premised on manipulation of the mind. The crew experience a rising sense of unease. They sense a hidden enemy, so they deploy all their weaponry against a foe that they can barely see, but which is killing them, one by one. It is only at the end that they realise their foe is a projection of their mental id, their dark side, which can defeat every weapon they throw at it. Indeed, the monster feeds off the kinetic energy. As the crew's hatred and fear grows, so the monster grows too.

Our wars on terror are our 'Forbidden Planet'. We did not create the monster, but we have breathed life into it. The more we apply our conventional weaponry, so the monster continues to grow, as it senses our growing fear and desperation in our inability to control events. Our wars have provided the evidence that we represent pestilence and evil. The idea has now become reality.

Against that, we have arrayed thousands of Steenbergers. He is our champion. He is an everyman who has answered the fight. More than anything else, he is part of a country, a definable entity. Unlike his opponent, Steenberger wears a uniform adorned with a flag.

The trouble is that the idea he fights for, that of liberal democracy, is, by definition, itself a debate. Our way of life is quantified by the pursuit of individual freedoms and happiness. Liberalism is defined by difference, democracy by the right to choose. It is written into the constitution of the United States. We champion the right to argue, to dissent, to debate, to choose an alternative.

Steenberger takes for granted the right to live his life as he chooses. It includes the assumed right to choose the manner of one's death. While Steenberger entered into a contract to join the army, there is no circumstance in which he would choose to become a suicide bomber. His contract did not include a clause confirming instant death. That very assumption dilutes our mission and our cause.

The enemy we face offers no such debate. To die for radical Islam is a glorious death, an invocation to sacrifice that we cannot ever match. We are paper and our enemies carry scissors.

We frame conflict through a procession of formalised ritual. As defined by the Treaty of Westphalia, we have sought to impose control where, by the nature and chaos of war, none prevails. Our enemies recognise none of that premise. Our definitions of war, its phases, its meaning, its definition, its outcomes, are alien. We presume that when war ends, peace and reconciliation will follow. Our enemies presume that the war will never end.

Steenberger was called to serve when four airliners crashed into the symbols of our freedom. It was a heinous act of treacherous barbarism. It was also a statement of intent, as unsubtle as a gorilla beating its chest. Was it a declaration of war? No—because in our enemies mind, that battle started a millennia ago, when a small group of believers rode out of Medina to conquer their homeland.

What nobody asked on September 11 was exactly WHY the planes flew that day. Why not September 12th? Or 10th? Or any other date? Very little that Osama bin Laden did was ever left to chance. And in the midst of our mourning and anger that day, nobody realised that Osama had very much planned that atrocity to happen on that very day: and for good reason. September the 11th had great significance for him, as it still does for any scholar of Islam and its hitherto thwarted struggle to become the dominant cultural totem for civilisation.

The reason why is all down to a Polish king and the biggest cavalry charge in history.

VENI, VIDI, DEUS VICIT

John III Sobieski is almost unheard of in the United States: but he is revered in his home country of Poland, and in much of Eastern Europe. He ruled the Polish-Lithuanian commonwealth during much of the later part of the 17th century. Contemporary paintings show a large, robustly healthy man, with a seriously impressive set of whiskers.

John Sobieski cut his teeth in a series of endless campaigns against the Swedes and Russian states, before he, and his fellow Christian kings and rulers, turned their eyes eastwards to a much more serious threat.

By the 1670's the Muslim Ottoman Empire has made serious in-roads into mainland Europe. King John himself fought against them as far north as Lviv, now in western Ukraine. The Balkans, from Serbia south, all fell under the thrall of an expansionist Muslim empire, intent on establishing a caliphate against the unbelievers.

The Christian kings woke up the threat almost too late. Christendom itself was still riven with the fall-out of the reformation, with pogroms being waged between the Roman Catholic and Protestant faiths.

John Sobieski saw what was coming: he had been Polish ambassador in Constantinople, and had come to intimately understand the prowess of Ottoman military capability. In 1683, he instigated a pact with Leopold, the ruler of the Holy Roman Empire, as a start of an alliance that was to become the Holy League, blessed by Pope Innocent XI and charged with saving Christendom from Islam.

The Ottomans, commanded by Kara Mustafa Pasha, were nearing the end of a 150 year-long campaign to conquer Europe. They had seen phenomenal success. What is now southern Ukraine had been conquered just ten years earlier. In 1683, Kara Mustapha Pasha set forth with 150,000 men to take Vienna, the gateway to the West.

Emperor Leopold fled westwards, leaving a garrison of just 15,000 men to defend the city's walls. King John raised the banners of the Holy League, and was joined by Charles of Lorraine at the head of a motley collection of Saxon and Bavarian allies.

Together, though, the combined Christian army could muster only 65-70,000 men. By June, Mustapha Pasha had taken Belgrade. By mid-July, Vienna itself had been enveloped by Muslim siege walls. The impoverished garrison mustered a spirited defence, but could only hope to delay the Muslim horde.

The defenders were fatalistically fortified by the news that the invading Ottomans had laid waste to their previous conquests, slaughtering all those they had captured. They knew this siege could only end one of two ways: defeat meant death.

The Viennese held a significant advantage in artillery, which forced Mustapha Pasha to dig long trench lines towards the city walls, in order to lay mines that would collapse the city walls from beneath. Months passed in developing the complicated engineering mosaic.

Incredibly, the allies failed to take advantage of the delay, and instead fell to bickering over who would pay for the war. It took the Pope's personal guarantee of Vatican funding to cement the alliance. But it was not until September 1683 that the allies finally arrived at Vienna.

They found the city in a sorry state. Ottoman mines had successfully destroyed a portion of the outer walls. The defenders had engaged in a subterranean cat and mouse campaign, digging their own tunnels to interdict the Ottoman's own endeavours. A vicious hand-to-hand campaign, conducted deep underground, had delayed Mustapha Pasha: but the end was finally, and inevitably, nigh.

Vienna was within Mustapha Pasha's grasp. With the fall of Vienna, crossroads to Western Europe, the dream of a Muslim caliphate, stretching from Mecca to the gates of Christian Rome itself was within sight.

The allies voted King John Sobieski to lead the final campaign. Not least because he commanded the elite and deadly Polish heavy cavalry, known for their winged helmets. There would be no second chance for victory. The fate of a continent hung on the balance of one single day's combat.

On September 11th, 1683, with Mustapha Pasha leading what he assumed would be the final assault on Vienna's walls, King John committed the allies to the field. Vastly out-numbered the allies, Mustapha Pasha made the cardinal error of continuing with the assault on the city, while simultaneously fighting off King John's relief column. His over confidence in dividing his force evened the numbers defender and assaulting allies each faced.

The Ottomans made some progress against the weakened Viennese walls. Not enough, though, to overcome the remaining ramparts: the city defenders managed to defuse most of the attacker's mines. The close-fought battle before the walls soaked up most of Mustapha Pasha's elite Janissary troops.

Until late afternoon, the battle hung in the balance. The Ottomans had the benefit of entrenched positions and detailed knowledge of the ground. By six in the evening, as the sun hung low on the autumn sky, King John III Sobieski sensed the critical moment had come.

He committed his cavalry: 18,000 strong. In a stirring moment of glory,

Sobieski led them slowly, at walk, in line abreast, from a sheltering treeline. At their head, King John himself, followed by 3,000 heavy lancers: the Polish winged hussars. Gradually, the lines formed, and began their inexorable attack. Walk, trot, canter, gallop: the horde descended on the exhausted Muslim lines.

King John's cavalry broke the Ottoman lines. A rout began, as Muslim soldiers fled for their lives, thwarted assault turning into an orgy of destruction and death. Mustapha Pasha lost anything between 20 – 40,000 men in one day.

On the evening of September 11th, a Christian officer, Margrave Ludwig of Baden, became the first officer to enter Vienna since the siege began. And all of Christian Europe gave thanks that the scourge of Ottoman Islam had been lifted.

King John III Sobieski wrote to his family of his victory, paraphrasing Julius Caesar's famous victory oration:

'Veni, vidi, Deus vicit.' I came, I saw, God conquered.

That December, Mustapha Pasha was ritually strangled by his own men. The war went on for another sixteen years, but by the turn of the century, the Ottomans had ceded all of Hungary and Transylvania. The Battle of Vienna marked the high tide of Islamic conquest in Europe. It was the end of the beginning: but not the beginning of the end. Osama bin Laden saw to that: which is why those planes flew into those towers on that chosen date of September 11th, 2001.

A heinous crime signalled an unspoken, but very clear, affirmation to the Muslim world that the next round in an eternal struggle had been re-kindled.

The war for civilisation itself had been re-started.

Nobody in the west realised. In the middle of our revulsion, distress and anger, nobody, including the President of the United States of America, even asked the question: why September the 11th?

President Bush declared a war—a war on terror. As if Islamic extremism had a patent on such. The attack on the tower was not an act of war. It was an act of gross criminality—nothing short of mass murder. But it was not an act of war.

It was a declaration of imminent oblivion. There will be no peace to come. From the very start of this never-ending conflict, we have viewed its nature through the prism of what we understand, not what our enemies understand.

We took the bait that Osama proffered: to engage our armies in conquest on a field of Osama's own choosing. To fight an irregular war of terror where our technology and civilisation would be hopelessly outclassed and made irrelevant.

Imagine how different this war could have been had we pursued the perpetrators as part of a criminal conspiracy of twisted hate, not as our declared wartime enemies.

There would be no Guantanamo Bay—those captured could have been tried under international criminal law, not left to moulder in a legal limbo, undefined and unwanted by any state. There would have been no invasion of

Iraq, or, quite probably, of Afghanistan.

A firm international pretext to pursue through the ends of justice those accused of conspiracy to murder, most definitely. Perhaps most importantly, we could have pursued our aim of vengeance and retribution against those truly guilty of murder, without suborning our original intent into a never-ending battle of invasion, occupation and regime change. Which was then metamorphosed into a fluid mission end-state, to define a re-established statehood.

Did Steenberger appreciate any of this? In truth, very probably not. Like his forebears, he followed his orders to go to Afghanistan. He cared little for political nuance. When the towers fell, he was six years old. He told me he remembered his mother making him watch the television, urging him to remember the moment. While he has a dim recollection of the collective revulsion we all felt at this heinous act, he has no concept of the outrage, the sense of a collective end of innocence, that that day brought.

This war has gone on for so long that those fighting it have forgotten why we started it in the first place. Our enemies have not. If anything, our actions over the past thirteen years have strengthened their resolve, their sense of aggrieved righteousness. Paper meets scissors.

That effort, to mount a vast campaign in a land-locked, dirt-poor Asian country against the wrong enemy nearly broke our military. The truth is that of all the effort we so freely spent in Afghanistan, our footprint there was, at best, ephemeral. The vast majority of the troops we sent there, and the money we spent, was consumed just by being there.

The 4th Infantry Division, of which Steenberger was a part, had nearly thirty thousand personnel under command, across the South of Afghanistan, for nearly a year. By the time they went home, Steenberger included, mere hundreds would have directly impacted with an Afghan. For the remainder, their tour would have been a litany of never-ending days of staff work, administration and logistics.

Afghanistan, its rich history, its tapestry of ethnicity and tribal diversity, would be merely a pinprick in their rear-view mirror, lost in the dust, forever: an adventure in the sand, nothing more. We never really understood what we had created.

We went to Afghanistan to fight Al-Qaeda. As the invasion happened, they melted away. The edifice we could identify, the ramshackle Taliban regime, fell apart of its own accord. The remnants then met, across the border, in Pakistan, in Quetta and Peshawar, and united with a common aim: to fight the invaders and remove us from Afghan soil.

By 2009, we had killed thousands, but the enemy kept on coming. We called our new foe the Taliban, gifting homogeneous identity to what was little more than a common hatred of the fact that we were there, on their soil. There is no such thing as the Taliban movement. We merely describe a sum of many disparate parts.

How charitable would you feel if thousands of Afghan soldiers came down your high street, with their tanks and guns, telling you how to live? In large part, we made our own enemies, by being there, and by interfering in their lives. Our enemies were, for the most part, bandits and thieves, engaged in their own local larceny. We interrupted the local crime lord, and encouraged others to hate our very presence by blowing up large parts of the countryside and killing too many. All caused by the simple fact that we came with our guns and we stayed with our guns.

When we got to Afghanistan, we re-invented our enemy. Al-Qaeda quickly faded across the frontier to Pakistan and other third-party states, such as Sudan. In our frustration, we turned our armies to fight the Taliban. Which had merely been a reluctant host to the real enemy. The Taliban have never perpetrated a single act of terror against the west. They fight to regain what they lost with our invasion, and, more importantly, against Afghanistan's invaders: our soldiers, airmen and sailors. The Taliban are not our enemies in this struggle of ideology.

For the longest time, our engagement in Afghanistan was justified by the falsehood that we were fighting the Taliban in Afghanistan so we didn't have to fight them on our own shores. And while we dedicated our vast effort in Afghanistan to fighting the wrong foe, we ignored the insidious growth of a snake more vicious than any we have yet seen, but which is directly spawned from the same venom that Osama launched on September 11th.

It is a truth we have reluctantly acknowledged late in the campaign. In 2014, very quietly, ISAF ordered that punitive strikes against the Taliban be quietly dropped. Which is, of course, the sadness of the whole adventure. Had we not so badly skewed our own campaign against a false chimera, Afghanistan's future could have been so much more.

In 2001, as the invasion of Afghanistan unfolded, President Bush, broadcasting from the White House, told the world:

'The oppressed people of Afghanistan will know the generosity of America and our allies'.

In 2005, at the start of his second term, President Bush again told the massed US legislature, during his State of the Union address that:

'The attack on freedom in our world has reaffirmed our confidence in freedom's power to change the world. We're all part of a great venture: to extend the promise of freedom in our country, to renew the values that sustain our liberty and to spread the peace that freedom brings.'

As President Obama took office, in his inaugural address in January 2009, he re-affirmed again that promise to all nations, including Afghanistan:

'To the people of poor nations, we pledge to work alongside you to make your farms flourish and let clean waters flow; to nourish starved bodies and feed hungry minds.'

Both men were inspirational in their remarks. Both men laid out what we should have done: fought an idea with an idea. We should have fostered an Islamic enlightenment, or at least the roots for that discussion. By criminalizing the act of 9/11, we could have kick-started that debate.

We didn't: what we did was send hundreds of thousands of soldiers and hundreds of thousands of guns to kill hundreds of thousands of people who were never, in any way, shape or form, connected to what happened in New

York that terrible day.
   And then we got bored—and looked the other way.

THE 325TH

I was late for work on my first day. Perhaps not surprisingly, I slept in. Three weeks of planes, camp beds, broken nights, briefings and a night of listening to rockets landing was not the most conventional of introductions to a new career.

I was supposed to go find the 325th psychological operations company. They were part of the divisional headquarters, and the regional equivalent of the CJPOTF, except they were all military. The idea was that they worked directly in support of the fighting troops, while my unit did stuff at the strategic level. I never really understood, even after three years in the suck, just exactly how the two units were supposed to dovetail, but there it was. They were to be my surrogate in KAF, and I had to go see them.

Walking across camp, to find my new office, I twisted my ankle. Kandahar is predominantly made up of desert and mountains. There is a lot of rock in the place. Bizarrely, NATO paid a lot of taxpayer's money to have a lot more of it.

Everywhere, across Afghanistan, in every ISAF base, bare rock and sand was covered in what the military called 'aggregate'. In essence, aggregate was big rocks that had been broken into smaller rocks. Ridiculous as it seems, NATO paid millions to have piles of these little rocks pummelled from bigger rocks and then spread over all the other rocks.

The official reason for all this intense spreading of rocks was that it prevented the build-up of swirling dust devils. The actuality was fields and fields of grey rock piles, scattered haphazardly across the landscape. The short-term sense of uniformity must have been pleasing to some sergeant major. There were truly times when I could not understand the military. Soldiers went short of vital radios and body armour, yet NATO seemed to have endless funds for making stones from other stones.

This enterprise was ridiculously, but genuinely, big business. KAF even had its own factory producing the stuff—a huge complex of winches, conveyor belts and enormous, steam-driven hammers, constantly crunching big rocks into NATO-sized small rocks. Armies of trucks would pick up the result and unload mountains of the stuff, to be rollered and scooped into an even covering of rock-upon-rock by the uncomplaining army of Filipino and African TCNs.

The factories were all Afghan-owned, and a few folks I'll introduce later got very rich making piles of rocks from rocks for us. Eventually, vehicles and people moving over the rocks would produce bare spots and channels, so NATO would order new rocks, to be laid on top of the old rocks. We created our own layers of strata, on top of the old strata. Nobody could walk properly on the stuff. We'd all slip and slide our way over the rubble, boots prematurely wearing away.

Next to the rock factory, KAF also had two cement factories, owned by the same guys, producing endless piles of concrete barriers. Rocks and cement, rocks and cement; a barren military experiment in exterior design.

By the end, there were so many unused concrete T-wall barriers that the military dug a big pit and buried them, cemetery row upon cemetery row, under layer of layer of unused aggregate. In years to come, they will be dug up as the coalition's own Afghan terracotta warriors.

The result of all that rock-breaking endeavour was an uneven and constantly shifting moonscape. That first day out, literally a hundred yards from my room, I had turned my ankle on the stuff. Not the best beginning to the adventure.

Hobbling onwards, I knew where I had to go; headquarters, Regional Command South, or HQ RC-S, the brain trust for commanding the war in Kandahar. In late 2011, its location was remarkably obvious.

The US had recently taken over lead nation status in Kandahar from Canada, which had, in turn, rather bitchily shared the job with the Dutch and the British since 2007. The Canadians had made as decent a fist of the job of expanding into the south as a small army could reasonably be expected to do. Even at their peak, Canada could only deploy a taskforce of a little over 2,500 troops. The Americans would bring 20,000 and still struggle.

Like the British, Canada had come to Kandahar thinking that the South would welcome their tanks and guns in the true spirit of liberal intervention. Like the British, they had ended up being mired in serious, full-on conflict with a tenacious enemy. The result had been a stalemate, where both sides had effectively cancelled each other out. The Canadians, armed with, amongst other items, main battle tanks, had won their tactical engagements, with great expenditure of ammunition and whole districts laid waste. They had, however, brought barely enough troops to continue the assault, let alone hold the ground they gained.

Every rotation, a new battle group would sally forth, westward down Highway 1 from Kandahar, win a temporary victory in Panjwai and Maiwand, before running out of steam and returning to Kandahar. The local population, who had initially garlanded the marching troops with flowers and gifts, rapidly grew tired of the chaos and destruction. The Taliban, many of whom actually lived in Maiwand, would go back to their fields until the next rotation arrived.

The whole operation became as depressingly familiar as the turn of the seasons or the ebb and flow of the tide. The remainder of that tour would then be spent just keeping the whole isolated string of ISAF bases across the South maintained and supplied.

It all looked terribly dramatic on the evening news, with convoys of vitally-needed ammunition straggled across the desert landscape, racing to one cut-off outpost after another, but it really didn't achieve anything other than to just keeping on being there. All that enormous effort was being expended just to keep a few hundred soldiers in the ass-end of a country that, at least in Panjwai, didn't want them there at all in the first place.

The surge had put paid to that. America poured resources, people and machines into Kandahar. Canada, meanwhile, had sustained 158 casualties in Afghanistan, the biggest sacrifice the country had made since Korea. Both the Canadian population and the army were exhausted by the effort. Poignantly, most of those losses had come from the campaign in Kandahar.

The first deaths had happened right outside Kandahar airfield. A Canadian ground patrol, out on a training exercise, had been strafed by an airborne US Warthog A-10. The boys hadn't even been in a contact: they got shot up in a drill. The A-10 is a fearsome flying cannon, basically a Gatling gun with wings. The Warthog now holds the dubious distinction of being the aircraft that has caused more friendly casualties than any other in the course of the war. Four had been killed that day, at a place called Karnak Farm.

Canadian-American relations had not been good. By 2010, the pressure had taken its toll. Canada's parliament voted to end their engagement in Afghanistan. By the time I arrived, Canada was all but gone.

Their small headquarters buildings still remained. A small bunch of Conex containers, surrounding one of the few leafy glades left within KAF. In the centre, a small brick wall, inset with several rough concrete squares. Those squares had once held marble squares, on which were inscribed the names of the Canadian fallen. When Canada handed over to the Americans, they took their flags and their war memorial with them.

HQ RC-S was now big business.

America does not do small headquarters. The Canadian oasis was now rapidly being surrounded by bright, shiny white two-storey containers, which were all linked together by an aerial walkway of steel stairs and connecting bridges.

The new owners proudly proclaimed their identity with one of the biggest flags I have ever seen. The thing was literally fifty feet across. You could see it from one end of KAF to the other. In more European, coalition-sensitive days, each nation had flown its own standard in a discrete, proud-but-not-in-your-face- proud kind of way. That all changed in 2011. America was here, and, in the eyes of the new custodians, America's finest too.

So there it was, a kind of flag phallus, announcing who now owned KAF turf: the 82nd Airborne Division.

Their symbol was a red circle, inscribed with the letters 'AA': All-American.

Above the circle, a single word: 'Airborne'.

Paratroopers. Man, the word evokes strange emotions. I have been a paratroop officer, and have led paratroopers in combat. So I know of what I speak.

The job of a paratrooper is to drop behind enemy lines, carrying only the equipment on his, and the very occasional her, back. The aim? To hold the objective until relieved or killed. It is the military equivalent of saying 'fuck you' to the biggest guy in the playground and slugging it out until somebody drops.

The training breeds a rather proud individual. An elite soldier who is physically tougher, more confident and more individualistic than most. The downside comes in the conceited way in which paratroopers regard the rest of the military team. The rugged individuality that allows a sane person to jump out of the back of a perfectly serviceable aircraft with one hundred and seventy pounds strapped to their back is equally dismissive of those who don't choose to do the same.

In the British army, non-airborne soldiers are called 'crap hats': for the simple reason that paratroopers have to earn the right to wear a red beret, which is only ever referred to as a beret, by under-going an intense and extremely physical selection process. Therefore anybody who has not passed the course wears a 'hat', which is obviously 'crap'. In the American army, non-paratroopers are more politely called 'straight legs', as only paratroopers can blouse, or tuck, their formal uniform trousers into their boots.

In either service, the inference is the same: real soldiers go airborne, the rest only aspire to be as good.

When my airborne boys and I were training up to go to Iraq, our host 'hat' unit kindly asked the lads to join them for a karaoke evening. My paratroopers *en masse* invaded the stage and screamed out Tina Turner's 'simply the best, better than all the rest' to an understandably sullen home audience. My boys thought it hilarious, whilst I quietly found the nearest fire exit, just as the first beer glasses flew....

Every paratrooper is inordinately proud of their 'wings', the badge that marks them as having passed the airborne challenge. In the British army, it is known as 'the blue badge of courage'. The whole credo encourages esprit de corps, rather useful for a specific mission of malleting the enemy. More problematically, the near homo-erotic macho club was less well-suited to the delicate issue of low-level counter-insurgency.

While the 82nd did have several female qualified paratroopers, all of whom were resigned to headquarters supporting roles, the 82nd is as John Wayne, big dick, Popeye-muscled as it comes. The big boys were in town—and they brought their 50-foot flag to prove it. The trouble was that KAF didn't have a big enough flag-pole to carry it. So the airborne had stuck together a pile of containers and hung their emblem off the side, where the whole effect drizzled away into a wrinkled version of a decorator's sheet covering. It was kind of an allegory for all that went on there. Good intent, mixed results.

The flag, though, was only the start of it. The 82nd employed spray-painting crews, armed with stencils, who marauded through KAF as a camouflaged Banksy. Marking endless rows of concrete barriers with the divisional shield and their divisional saying: 'all the way!'

A uniquely American call and response mating ritual, soldiers would routinely greet each other with the catechism; 'airborne!' Then reply; 'all the way!' To European ears, it sounded ridiculous, but the Americans were wildly proud of it all and would repeat their homily at the drop of a hat. The start of briefings, phone calls, e-mails, passing encounters, at sports games: just everywhere.

'Airborne!' 'All the way!'

They never got fed up of it. Probably fun if one was in the club. Desperately annoying for those of us who were not. In my perverse way, I took great delight in replying to the perpetual call of 'Airborne!' with a polite; 'do you might if I only go halfway today? I'm wearing heels.' The resultant confusion was mightily pleasing to me, particularly when I took to adding Mork and Mindy clenched fist salutes to my left ear; 'nanu, nanu!' It was all fair sport, in that classic British Monty Python style, but the Americans failed to get the joke.

I reached my nadir when I briefed a very be-starred American general. My first PowerPoint slide read; 'Osama bin laden and my part in his downfall.' Complete with comedy photo of British TV icon Kenny Everett, dressed as an outlandish General Patton pastiche. The Brits in the audience seemed highly amused. The Americans just gently coughed and looked at their shoes. I'd grown up with Robert Altman's MASH. In Afghanistan I often wondered where the fun had gone. The place was otherwise mad enough for it.

On my first day out of the traps, I confused my own 82nd future mightily at the outer perimeter to the headquarters. Not content with being slap-in-the-middle of thousands of armed soldiers, behind miles of concrete and more armaments than several African countries collectively owned, HQ RC-S had its own security perimeter. Comprising of a large fence, lots of barbed wire and several heavily-armed, dark sunglass-wearing, tobacco-chewing, 'airborne!' chanting heavies.

Their paratrooper combat tour wet dreams had most probably not consisted of twelve months of drudgery checking badges and saluting senior officers. My first day outfit of a green polo neck, tartan waistcoat, red suede boots and matching scarf was their first combat indicator that here lay more interesting waters. Add to that a very strange accent and my recently acquired limp, and I was but bait on a hook. A large, out-raised hand brought my determined progress to a halt. My interrogation began with a quizzical; 'y'all ain't from round here, are you?'

Followed by a flat refusal to recognise my newly-minted NATO badge, with its funky red security cleared border. My credentials might have been good enough to get me into the really, really big headquarters in Kabul, but this was 82nd Airborne territory: God's country. I didn't have the special 82nd Airborne badge.

Looking at all the other too-busy-to-talk staff officers rushing in and out, I would need an orange badge, with a big airborne shield on the back. Yet again, close but no cigar. If the war in Afghanistan had merely been scored by who owned the right collection of badges, ISAF would have roundly confounded the Taliban, first round out. After a testy five minutes, it was obvious I wasn't going anywhere.

Somewhere in that maze of white containers, behind the fifty-foot 'AA' flag, I was supposed to have a desk, a chair, a computer and a job. I had NATO top secret clearance, I was standing right outside the place I needed to go to, with the suede boots to match. But I didn't have the right orange badge. And the sergeant in charge was bigger than me. And he had a gun: and friends with guns. I went back to my room.

I did have a mobile phone. One of the wonders of the war was that pretty much all of Afghanistan was now covered by a phone service. There were several providers, but the one we all used was Roshan, which became so popular that an Afghan phone itself became known as a roshan. It actually worked a lot better than the military communications network.

We were all soundly warned that the Pakistani intelligence services listened to every call. The Americans listened to everything too. Careers—and lives—could be on the line with the blabbermouths. All through my time there, I'd see frustrated staff officers try the important red bat-phone on the desk. Then watch as they sat and listened to a series of beeps and pips, as they realised the phones didn't actually work. Five frustrated minutes later, they'd go for a short walk outside, clutching their old reliable roshan.

Every headquarters had rows of harassed officers milling around, desperately trying to make their intent known through daft codes that would defeat the pesky Pakistanis:

'That thing we talked about on Tuesday? Well, it may work if the thing that rhymes with sick comes through with the thing that rhymes with dick...'

I called Eric in Kabul. He might be at the other end of the country, but it was the only number I had. Eric had been in country a bit longer than me. As he had told me: 'it's a marathon, not a sprint'. He promised to call some-one whose name rhymed with prick and get back to me. He didn't get an answer. Eric then tried the military phones to Kandahar, which didn't work either. He called me back to tell me to relax for the day while they worked the problem from the other end of the country with a very long screwdriver.

Several hours later, he called back to say the phones to the headquarters didn't work from Kabul. No shit, Sherlock. He'd tried roshan, but mobile phones were banned in the headquarters, so that hadn't worked either. He'd then sent an e mail to the 325th to try and contact me directly, but he could only send it by the NATO IT system, and RC-S worked on a totally separate US system, so he wasn't sure if it had been received or not. He'd not had a reply. We were part of the most technologically sophisticated war machine that had ever raised its battle standard. And neither the phones, nor the mail system, worked.

Aaaah, Afghanistan.... Watch an average war movie and the military is this seamless, efficient, war-waging, willy-waving colossus that is just itching to fuck up your day. It's the lone survivor, American sniper, super-hero killer in the shadows that you can't escape. The reality is day after day of frustrating, boring clusters of inane, nullifying, dispiriting chaos, occasionally tempered by the mindless insanity of nothingness.

Even the exciting bits—the bombs, the rockets, the gunshots are just auditory punctuation. You really never, ever see who is shooting at you, or what they are shooting at you with. War is a series of distant bangs, with the occasional plume of smoke. Even that isn't like a movie mega napalm, black smoke killer explosion. It's more like the wheezy exhalation of a first-time puffer trying to make smoke rings.

War is not so much the colour part of the Wizard of Oz as reel upon reel of the black and white bit that everybody skips over. You can't skip over army bureaucracy. It's just there, like Harry Potter's blanket of invisibility. It just smothers you in an enormous mindfuck, until you either submit, or make up slides of Kenny Everett to remind yourself that you are not a number.

BOARDWALK BLUES

As so often happened in Kandahar, there was nothing to do. I went for a walk.

If KAF could be defined as a series of unremitting concrete walls and shipping containers, it did have an exception, one green space: and a rather bizarre one at that. Even by KAF standards, where everything was bizarre.

Right in the middle of the madness was KAF's own Central Park, one place where the tens of thousands of inmates of the asylum could at least pretend to be normal. Everybody who ever came through KAF knew it; and everybody visited it, at least once, even if only to stand and gawp. We all knew it as The Boardwalk.

I have capitalised The Boardwalk for a reason. The Boardwalk deserves the respect. I went there every day of my thousands days in KAF: most days, on more than one occasion. I hugged it close, as the only place where I could remind myself I was still human. It was the only place where the endless tick-tock of military BS and crushing uniformity could be temporarily suspended.

When I think of The Boardwalk, I think of happy days. It was the beating heart, the bell weather and the cream.

Physically, it wasn't much. Made of wood, The Boardwalk was a rectangular, wooden, covered walkway, enclosing a patch of dirt about the size of two soccer pitches. On the outside of the rectangle, dozens of shipping containers, with one end cut out, faced inwards, which were filled with a wild spectrum of makeshift shops. The Boardwalk was Kandahar's shopping mall. Constructed of little more than scrap, with the build quality of scrap, at its peak there were more than sixty different stores. I remember them all.

Like any self-respecting mall, The Boardwalk had it covered. Several container shops sold Afghan carpets and trinkets. You could pick up everything from samurai swords to scorpions, sealed in silicon moulds. Somehow, Lord only knows, one store had got a hold of a quantity of Saddam-era Iraqi dinars, which it peddled in ornate display cases. In a country known for its conservative mores, one double-sized, glass-fronted emporium sold women's clothes, including belly-dancing outfits in lurid man-made fabric.

The Boardwalk had four jewellery stores, selling everything from simple rings to pure Afghan confections of gilt and semi-precious stones, all made to order. At one stage, there was even a two-storey sporting goods store, where soldiers could buy golf clubs and the latest Nike Air training shoes. Under-pinning the whole absurd venture were the restaurants: full service, sit-down restaurants.

One, Mama Mia's, produced cardboard pizzas and overdone pasta. On Friday nights, the place was taken over as home of The Boardwalk salsa party. A few dozen women would dance with a never-ending line of suitors, while hundreds of men stood in an eroticised circle and gawped.

The other was a genuine TGI Fridays, complete with bar and rock 'n' roll memorabilia. The menu was exactly the same as the stateside version; buffalo wings, cheeseburgers, mozzarella sticks, enchiladas. You name it, TGI's did it, all to a throbbing rock soundtrack. Every night, another bunch of homesick soldiers would celebrate a team birthday, leaving, arrival, end of week or just a simple 'fuck it' moment with a TGI's cake, replete in sparklers and lit candles.

The Germans had one of their mad soldier PX's, where they made millions of dollars selling surplus army equipment to uniformed soldiers who already owned several suitcases of camouflage, but who wanted an exact copy of a Delta Force sniper's camouflage smock. The store had a designer T-shirt concession, with books of images of tanks, guns and planes that could be ironed on to order, complete with any message you wanted. 'Taliban extermination crew'? You got it. 'Kandahar Killer Team Bravo'? Not a problem. Any size, any colour, all produced within 24 hours.

For those with a leather fetish, there was a tailor which produced hand made, hand fitted pistol holsters, or real fur coats for your loved one back in the World. DVDs? Name your title. There were supermarket-sized emporiums serving up the latest rips from China, complete with Mandarin sub-titles. In a camp the size of a large town, the boardwalk had its own cycle shop, selling mountain and road versions, with camouflage panniers as extras. A tobacco store offered Pakistani coughers in fake Marlboro wrappers. Harley Davidson had an outlet for an individually designed piece of the American dream.

One whole side of the rectangle, about 100 metres long, was a smorgasbord of take-out stores. Every American fast-food fantasy was catered for. From pizza to foot-long hotdogs and ice-cream sundaes. The stores all had flat screen TVs, flashing lights and pumping rock music. The racket was incredible. It was like eating inside Studio 57.

There were two hairdressers, a beauty parlour, a telephone bank, an internet café, an Indian restaurant, an off-licence (which used to sell beer, until the Americans put paid to alcohol), a bank with two ATMs, a handbag shop, two clothing alteration stores, four picture framers, a Kentucky fried chicken and several cafes.

At its absolute, absolute peak, the Boardwalk had just under 70 shops. The last one, to cap it all, was the Indian restaurant, complete with a bloke in a turban to welcome you. The Boardwalk got so big, it had its own staff, just to look after it. Three Romanian soldiers spent their entire combat tour supervising a shopping centre.

As with everything in KAF, the Boardwalk was a dispiriting dun colour. Except for one glorious flight of fancy. The Boardwalk had an all-weather football pitch. Made of plastic grass, it never lost its green hue, even in the midst of the worst dust storms. Next to the soccer pitch, there was a concrete hockey pitch and a basketball court. Circling the whole, running just inside the circumference of the wooden boardwalk, was a pink asphalt running track. Measuring exactly four hundred metres, it was my default setting at the end of the day.

Walking round KAF after dark was dangerous, particularly for females. The Boardwalk was well-lit and full of people with guns. The Boardwalk was safe for women. Every night, I'd go for at least a walk around the pink running track, lap after lap, mile after mile. Same routine, every time.

I'd start in the north-east corner, by emptying a bottle of water on the mangy plant that struggled for life there. Planted by the Afghan store-holders, it never really thrived, being either ignored or forgotten by countless rotations. I'd water it every night I was there, but when I went on leave it would perish. On my return, I'd despair at its health and carefully nurture the weed back to life before I'd take off again for the World, only to repeat the cycle when I got back.

I'd take off round the track, for as long as it was fun, every night. By the time I left, I reckoned I'd done over five thousand miles on the damn thing. I loved to run at night.

At night, the place came to life. The dirt and the grime would disappear into the shadows and the lights and the music would call the troops from far and wide. The one thing Kandahar had in abundance was sun, and during the summer it would still be 25 degrees C at midnight. We partied there as much as alcohol-free nights would allow, in every way that was legal, and a couple that were not.

At one end, troops would be swaying in a salsa lesson. Next to them, a roller disco, complete with '70's cheese music and a disco ball. Folks in uniform would sling their assault rifles over their backs, swap their boots for wheels and spin round in circles to a Bee Gees' falsetto. Behind them, all the razzamatazz of an American football game, with streamers, flags and hotdogs: next to that, a hotly contested basketball tournament. The size and noise of it all, with its flashing lights, music and crowds of thousands, just milling, chatting and smiling was a complete counterpoint to the awfulness of war.

Look down, the party was in full swing. Look up, and you could see the parachute flares, swinging down, just outside the wire, while every now and again the silent, blinking lights of a drone flew overhead. Every twenty minutes the music would be drowned out by a hectic roar of a fighter jet, taking off just two hundred metres away. Conversation and the music would just disappear, as we'd stick our fingers in our ears, while the spectacular firework of an F-16 at full afterburner would cartwheel up into the night sky.

The cacophony of noise was offset by a babel of languages—English, Pashto, Romanian, Dutch, French, too many others to mention—and the complex smells of fast food and coffee.

If you wanted it, you could enjoy a little pharmaceutical pick-me-up. The air round the barber's shop was always redolent with some very mellow weed. KAF had its own military police, but they weren't real cops. They'd tool around in their 4X4's, looking tough, eagle-eyed for seatbelt violations, but they had no nose for actual police work. They'd walk right by the contractors enjoying a very sweet doobie and think they were exotic Turkish cigarillos.

The Boardwalk had an open-air stage. Once a month or so, we'd get a visiting act, who came to entertain the troops. And what names! Robin Williams played The Boardwalk, as did Toby Keith, Hooters' road-show and the Dallas Cowboys' cheerleaders. Lance Armstrong gave out copy yellow jerseys there, before his fall from grace.

The Brits did one show, which began with the Regimental Sergeant Major issuing an opening advisory:

'Sirs, ma'ams, ladies, gentlemen, this is an adult show, so if you don't like swearing, fuck off now.'

As the RSM exited stage left, he was followed on by four very nubile young female dancers, barely wearing some very saucy scraps of clothing. They skipped on-stage amidst a fog of thrash metal chords and coloured smoke. Dressed in very skimpy red basques, riding crops and red silk horns, they took turns in whipping each other in a simulated BDSM frenzy. The sex-starved squaddies in the crowd went absolutely berserk.

The show ended with the senior British officer carolling on stage to the prompts of a comic with a guitar. Both of whom then led a very enthusiastic Royal Marine contingent in a chorus of:

'I'm the only gay Eskimo in the gay Eskimo village.'

The American general in-charge had been invited as a matter of courtesy. As soon as the dancers came on, I saw him quietly disappear before somebody posted a Facebook image that would get him into trouble.

The final encore, by a very competent Queen tribute band, was a thrash-a-long with the memorable chorus of 'don't tell me what to fucking do'. Several hundred over-excited troops, me amongst them, pogoed madly in the mosh pit. The obvious dichotomy of thrashing around in uniform while carrying a loaded rifle passed mentally way out of sight with the simple human joy of just dancing. Man, if you could have bottled up the energy that night, we'd have won the whole fucking war in a day.

The Brits weren't invited back.

Towards the end, the wild shows died out, as the Americans got more in charge and more Puritan in nature. They sucked the last vestiges of fun out of it all. The last show I went to started with the US flag being borne on stage by three soldiers, while 'America the Beautiful' played over the camp tannoy. The parade was followed by a barber-shop quartet, in Andy Williams polo necks, singing wholesome, patriotic American homeland songs.

It was shit. I left during the national anthem, my teeth cloying with the saccharine sweetness of it all.

But, in its day, The Boardwalk was rocking.

I loved the democracy of it all. Everywhere you went in KAF, you had to have your damn badge, with its concentration camp coloured borders and caste structure. The whole place wasn't so much one big joined-up endeavour as little microcosms of BS, all with their own complicated entry codes and etiquette.

The Boardwalk was different. The Americans even put up signs saying; 'no hat, no salute'. Which was as close as the military came to saying take the day off. Third country national worker bees sat right next to senior officers. Everybody got to enjoy the same cheesecake and coffee, provided you had the dollars to pay for it. The Boardwalk was capitalism in action, and it was as close as the war came to being back home. The generals and the sergeant majors hated it.

I never understood the visceral reaction the place evoked from those nominally in charge. The only reason I lasted three years there was because of The Boardwalk. The work was fun at times, and undoubtedly important, but Kandahar was way too tough a gig to last without the steam release valve of The Boardwalk.

Generals and sergeant majors had their own private accommodation suites and meeting places. The top men in charge even had their own chef. I kept hearing the same litany that eating a chilli cheese dog was going to make a soldier soft. With a couple of honourable exceptions who understood the morale boost of the place, every senior officer I came across avoided The Boardwalk like the plague and treated it as an effluent and disease-ridden pit of sin.

It's no co-incidence that my departure from KAF chimed almost exactly with the 4th Infantry Division's all-out push to demolish the whole thing in mid-2014. I took pictures of the bulldozers tearing down Mama Mia's and TGI's, reduced to little more than piles of broken bricks and shards of splintered glass.

My soul was invested in those places. I had laughed, danced, cried and feasted in them. Each broken building was filled with the ghostly outline of old brothers and sisters with whom I had broken bread, lived and, in some cases, died. Tearing down The Boardwalk broke my heart. Until that moment, I hadn't really believed America would abandon Afghanistan. In truth, it hadn't needed to happen. In late 2014, the camp still had over 20,000 people caged inside it.

KAF always had its fair share of suicides. Every soldier there had the loaded means to commit the dreadful act, right by their sides, every day and night. The Boardwalk wasn't perfect, but it was as good as it got for the tens of thousands stuck in the ass end of nowhere. The Boardwalk saved lives and preserved sanities, mine included.

I pleaded with every general I knew to reprieve the place, and I did win it a brief extension, but, in the end, the military aesthetes won out, and the light dimmed in KAF with the ploughing of the bulldozer's blades.

When I think on happy times in KAF, I think almost exclusively on The Boardwalk.

A shitty wooden walkway, with shitty shipping container shops: but, aaah, the fun of it all. The Friday night salsa, the near beers, the ice cream, the fun runs, the laughter and the friends. It was just a pile of scrap, but it meant everything to me.

I miss it.

UNRAVELLING THE BALL OF STRING

At the end of March 2010, on Afghan soil itself, Obama told US troops:
'If I thought for a minute that America's vital interests were not served, were not at stake here in Afghanistan, I would order all of you home right away.'[7]

Yet, on June 22nd, 2011, the tide had turned. In an address to the American people specifically outlining conduct of the war in Afghanistan, President Obama declared a new objective:

'The goal that we seek is achievable, and can be expressed simply: No safe haven from which al Qaeda or its affiliates can launch attacks against our homeland or our allies. We won't try to make Afghanistan a perfect place. We will not police its streets or patrol its mountains indefinitely. That is the responsibility of the Afghan government, which must step up its ability to protect its people, and move from an economy shaped by war to one that can sustain a lasting peace. What we can do, and will do, is build a partnership with the Afghan people that endures—one that ensures that we will be able to continue targeting terrorists and supporting a sovereign Afghan government.'[8]

Between 2010 and 2011, we had gone from broad-brush stroke statements about freedom and vitality to an admission that our lofty aims were beyond our reach.

Three years later, by the summer of 2014, over three quarters of the coalition troops were gone. By the end of 2014, ISAF itself ceased to exist. What regular troops remained were confined to camp, clearing up and taking down what had, just a couple of years earlier, been regarded as absolutely vital to US—and world—interests.

By 2014, my friend the American general was saying any solution would be an Afghan solution. The present plan is that all US and NATO troops will be gone by the end of 2016. Even the enduring partnership proposed in 2011

---

[7] Speech delivered at Bagram Airbase

[8] Broadcast speech from the White House

has ended. It is as if we have suddenly given up. To the Afghans, to whom we have promised so much, and reneged on so much, we leave a legacy that is, at best, bewildering and, at worst, a betrayal of all that we once held to be sacred.

That key period, where we gave up on Afghanistan, came with the ending of the first decade of war, in the summer of 2011. What happened in those crucial months?

History is less about events, but their effect on the people who make those momentous decisions. We have a touching faith in those we elect to lead us. That somehow, someway, they have a shining insight into the world that others do not possess: a kind of Heineken leader.

Our leaders are not. They are as human as the rest of us. Mostly, they are intelligent, hard working, ambitious individuals who strive to do their best. But they are not super-human. Certainly, the offices they hold come with multi-storied trappings: the convoys of darkened limousines, the flashing lights, the bodyguards. But the decisions are as human as the ones that you and I make on a daily basis, with as many fuck-ups and disasters as any other human endeavour.

Where we, as a species, get it right can be read in those serendipitous coming-togetherness of the right mix of personality and people that pepper the great pages of history: Wellington, the Prince of Orange and Blucher against Napoleon, Grouchy and Ney. Churchill, Stalin and Roosevelt against Hitler, Tojo and Mussolini.

Every now and again, more by accident than design, chaos theory bangs the right neutrons together to make epic history. Since 2001, the West has not been so lucky. By 2011, personality and reality had hit home—and hit home hard for Afghanistan.

The big changes began right at the top, with the changing of the guard in the White House. Obama's election and taking of office, at the beginning of 2009, marked the end of the beginning in the course of the Afghan conflict. Elected to bring hope and change, here was a man on a mission to make history. Obama wanted make everything bright, shiny and new. Instead, he inherited two wars and a climatic economic collapse. None of which were of his making, but which have come to define his tenure in office.

By 2009, the awful economic reality of the great home buying crash of 2007 could no longer be ignored. Between 2008 and mid-2009, US GDP alone fell by over 4%. The US government committed 1500 BILLION dollars to buy out insolvent banks and kick-start the American economy. The figures, particularly to an incredulous US public, were staggering. Even for the US, the effects were near ruinous.

Not so staggeringly costly, though, when compared to cost of the War On Terror. By 2009, according to the US think-tank *'Homeland Security Research'*, the US alone is estimated to have spent over 2,300 BILLION dollars on war, very nearly 500 billion dollars in 2009 alone. The cost of the War On Terror remains to this day an estimated figure. The real dollar cost will undoubtedly be much higher. What is indisputable is that fighting this war has cost more than saving the world's economy has done. It is conflict Keynes. The more we spend, the more war rages on.

The American people will always be an optimistic people. The entire country is premised on re-invention and new beginnings. However, that optimism has always been presaged by confidence in the economic munificence of the homeland. By 2009, that confidence had been well and truly shaken. For the first time since the awful days of the late 1970's America's economic pre-eminence had suddenly become a cause of national doubt. America was fighting a war AND the country was heading into the dumpster.

The country chose to elect a President who chafed to fundamentally change America. In many ways, President Obama's personal ambitions and social agenda rival that of Lyndon Johnson. In many ways, his ambitions have been stymied by the same challenge that LBJ faced; the ruinous cost of war.

Obama has always held to a program of sincere societal engineering: although his health care reforms may be the one and only flagship piece of legislation that has passed into law. Had the struggle to pass it not been so titanic, and world events not so overwhelmed his ambition, healthcare would undoubtedly have been just the start.

Social change costs money. In 2009, the money had run out. How tempting it was to wind down that 500 billion dollar annual war cost. The thought was undoubtedly there. Obama's foreign affairs experience on taking office was decidedly limited, specifically to a short term on the senate foreign affairs committee. He knew little about the military, even less about the culture.

The meandering course of the war in Afghanistan should have been an immediate priority for the in-coming administration. It wasn't.

How tragic it is that Obama has always failed to realize his historic legacy is assured in just getting to the White House. No matter what else he does, nothing will ever triumph that.

Obama did commission a new study (Lord knows, by 2009, there had been many) on the course of the war, which kicked the can down the road a little. He was blind-sided by the very process of winning office. An in-coming US president has an enormous burden to overcome, in just getting the government he (and, hopefully, one day, she) wants.

Day 1, all the old team pack up and walk out. The new guy has over 2,000 officials to appoint, just to keep the wheels of government spinning. In the same way as the military rotation system screwed Afghanistan, so the US election cycle screwed Afghanistan's chances in early 2011. The new team was just too occupied finding the White House stationery cupboard to really apply logic and thought to fighting the war: unfortunately just at the time when Afghanistan really looked like it could be completely lost.

The trouble was, of course, that by 2009, the West had doubled down so many times that winding down the war easily was impossible. Plus, despite all the false starts, real and evident change was incrementally beginning to happen. An Afghan army was beginning to finally appear in a coherent form, roads had been built and schools had re-opened. All of it had appeared in a mad spray of a pebble-dash, inherently wasteful manner, but the evidence was incontrovertibly there. What the military urged was one last push over the top: one last effort to win.

By 2009, taking advantage of a new President, as yet unsure of his footing on the war, but still determined to be seen as a strong commander-in-chief, the generals won the argument and, on top of a slow, incremental yearly increase in troop numbers, the President authorized a 'surge' of more 21,000 troops for Afghanistan, in support of a new counter-insurgency theorem.

Without any real empirical evidence that any of this new and costly approach was applicable or wanted by the Afghan people, buzzwords such as 'government in a box', 'anaconda strategy', 'courageous restraint' and 'money is a bullet' suddenly acquired a new and fervent urgency.

Amongst the coalition, listening sceptically to a US emphasis on spending to overwhelm, reluctance to buy into the whole concept was palpable. While the Germans, a major ISAF contributor, had steadily almost doubled their contribution since 2002, they still resolutely refused to allow their soldiers to become engaged in combat operations in the south.

Looking back, it is easy to see the near desperation of the new administration to get something—anything—tangible from the entire Afghan adventure.

Certainly, at that time, there had been no terrorist attacks on the US mainland since 2001. However, there had been several in coalition countries. If the declared object was to protect America, spending 500 billion dollars a year on a far-off central Asian state made crazy operational and fiscal sense to a homeland facing food stamps and economic meltdown. The folks that voted for Obama wanted change—jobs, prosperity—not wars.

Somewhere along the line, the very purpose of the Afghan mission had become clouded. As much as getting Bin Laden had been a poorly thought out, if not illegal, reason for invading, it had at least made sense on a visceral level. Re-building Afghanistan as some sort of Switzerland in Asia did not.

Much of the blame was not American purpose, but American desire to please a rainbow coalition: and a desperate lack of attention to detail, in what had always been seen as a secondary campaign to the Iraq adventure. Until 2009, Iraq sucked not just the air, but the light, out of any debate on the 'war against terror' in Afghanistan, where it had all begun. In truth, nobody was really interested in Afghanistan as anything other than an annex to Iraq.

In 2004, serving with the British army in Afghanistan, as part of my duties, I had to send weekly status theatre reports back to the UK's Permanent Joint Headquarters, which oversaw both operations. My one-page report came right at the back, in a separate annex, to the weekly, book-sized effort that represented the Iraqi side of affairs. After a couple of months, it was clear nobody actually read my efforts. One week, I put down: 'NSTR'—nothing significant to report. I got back a short, but testy, note to say that a junior staff officer always had something to report. The week after, I didn't submit a report at all. Nobody replied. For the next two months, I didn't report a thing. Still nobody replied.

The only game in town was Iraq. Afghanistan just fell off the radar.

Nobody was interested.

Despite being the place where it all began, and—strangely enough—it looks likely to end, Afghanistan was always the poor relation.

The historic devil is, again, in the detail. History is not made up so much of great people making great decisions with great vision, as ordinary folks doing their best to rub along in doing the best they can in the circumstances. With the big background movement of geo-strategic tectonic plates came two of those six-pence spin moments, at the start of the second decade of war.

That first defining moment came in the form of COMISAF: the man who led ISAF as its commanding general.

COMISAF has become one of those poisoned chalices of command. It ought to have been the apogee of command, but the sad reality is that it has become the career graveyard of the majority of those Americans who have held the post. Of seven US generals, four—McKiernan, McChrystal, Petraeus and Allen—have seen their appointments end in personal and career failure.

The first, General David McKiernan, was fired in 2009, after less than a year in post, by the in-coming Obama administration. The reasons, even to the US administration, were confusing. US Secretary of Defense, Robert Gates, couldn't properly explain it, as he outlined his reasoning at the Pentagon press briefing to announce his decision:

'Nothing went wrong, there was nothing specific,' said Gates. *'There probably is no more critical ingredient than that—than leadership. And again, along with all the other changes, it's time now.'*[9]

Something of a whisky tango foxtrot—WTF—moment for David McKiernan, who had just laid out a fifteen to thirty year, Afghan-centric plan, combining military with civil, economic and political development. He had thought he was onto a winner. Previous COMISAFs had mostly come from the coalition, and none had had the gravitas, or the necessary military commitment, to bring the whole effort together.

We'd all talked counter-insurgency, but the truth was that the Afghan mission had become a pleasant, and relatively peaceful, way to grind out six months in a funky country. We'd all indulged in a lot of combat tourism—and done a helluva lot of partying.

A German parliamentary report at the time revealed that, in one year, the 3,500 German troops stationed in Mazar-E Sharif had drunk 1.7 million pints of beer and 90,000 bottles of wine, all by themselves. That frankly bonkers statistic had formed part of an urgent operational review alleging that a large minority of deployed German soldiers was too fat to fight. Steely-eyed warriors we were not.

Meanwhile, the other side had regrouped, re-armed and come back: in force. While the ISAF bars were still going night and day, seven years on from invasion, the Germans regarded four miles down the road from their Kunduz camp as enemy territory.

---

[9] US DoD briefing

Something had to change.

McKiernan's bad luck came in his timing. Obama was a president on a mission and he wanted that 500 billion annual war chest for other stuff. Fifteen years, minimum, of economic spendthrift on a far-off war was not on the agenda in the White House.

McKiernan might have stood more chance had he had the political smarts to align his plan to Obama's projected eight year term. If he had given the president an option to end combat operations by the close of 2016, his tenure might have had a very different outcome.

During Obama's time, the sync between military and political planning has always been in doubt. Obama is a professor and an introvert. He likes debate, thought, analysis and intellectual discussion. Informally, the army call their president 'Spock'. The military likes streamlined schedules and defined objectives. This president likes debate, even when there is no debate. The Pentagon and a democratic law professor are unlikely bedfellows.

McKiernan's replacement mirrored an intense struggle within the Pentagon itself over the conduct of the war. The US military has long been designed to fight a conventional war and it has struggled to justify tactics designed to deliver against massed Soviet tank armies while deployed in the backstreets of Kandahar and Fallujah. The argument was simple, the conclusions were anything but: is it more effective to defeat a cunning and un-identifiable enemy by overwhelming force, or to become equally as cunning and un-identifiable? The followers of big guns and big tanks had mired themselves in the quicksand of Iraq.

The United States military can be a brutal employer. It drives its generals hard—and disposes of them in equally objective circumstances. McKiernan's named replacement was a surprise, though: nobody, outside of a select circle of Pentagon insiders, had heard of him. In a remarkable vault to the top, General Stanley McChrystal was about to personify all that was right—and wrong—about the Afghan conflict.

The rocket fuel that propelled McChrystal's trajectory to the top was to be the *protégé* of the war's most famous general: David Petraeus.

Petraeus had become the darling of the Pentagon for his perceived success in Iraq. First, as commander of the 101st Airborne, then, later, as overall theatre commander, he had pursued a strategy perceived as fist in a velvet glove. He is also a shameless opportunist, who had taken full advantage of good luck, good timing and good media management.

His most lauded achievement in Iraq was known as 'the Anbar rising', where the restive local Anbar Province tribes had decided to stop fighting the Americans and fight the insurgency instead. America had provided the know-how and the money, but it was undoubtedly personal politics, face-to-face negotiation and careful manipulation of local dynamics that had won the day. The rising also just so happened to coincide with a change of heart by the local tribes, who were thoroughly fed up of all the fighting.

As Napoleon enquired of all the recommendations for promotion of his generals:

'I know he is a good commander—but is he lucky?'

A multi-storied and nuanced campaign plan may not seen too unique to any civilian CEO of a large company—but it was revelatory to a US military used to just getting out a bigger stick to win the day.

Petraeus had been hailed by 'Time' magazine as its 'person of the year' for 2007. He was a veritable rock star of a general, more feted than any since Westmoreland in Vietnam. EVERYBODY wanted a piece of the Petraeus action. Petraeus was the thinking man's general, who had mixed together theory, diplomacy, hand-shakes, money and guns into a potent mix of go-get-'em American can-do. The guy was seen as a Jedi master. He'd arrived in Iraq at just the right time to mine a potent mix of tribal antipathy and Iraqi war-weariness, to fuse that discontent into a US-supported, Iraqi-led movement to end the war. Had he tried the same game just a year earlier, he'd have been given the middle finger.

Petraeus had seized his opportunity with both hands. That success had been garlanded with international recognition and certain sense of relief that, finally, the Iraq adventure was nearing the exit sign. By 2009, Petraeus' reputation, rank and image had been buffed to a Caesar-like lustre: and the stars, medals and ribbons soon followed, along with a new counter-insurgency manual, complete with Petraeus' own signature as key author. Petraeus was promoted to command the US CENTCOM regional command, whose geographic bailiwick included US operations in Afghanistan, under McKiernan's command.

Which was unfortunate for McKiernan, as he and Petraeus had a long-standing personal antipathy to each other, stemming from their mutual time in Iraq, where McKiernan had been Petraeus' boss. The worm had truly turned now, and Petraeus regarded McKiernan as slow to uptake his new concepts of counter-insurgency.

Two four star generals butted heads against each other, but only one had the media glitz to access the President's ear. It was all done terribly politely, as generals tend to be to each other: but the net effect was deadly.

Obama, almost desperate to cut the cost of the war, clung to Petraeus as a saviour—and accepted his advice to hire the then little-known McChrystal, in favour of McKiernan.

Petraeus was offering a very different form of snake-oil from McKiernan. In essence, the argument was less about tactics and more about a wider debate of exactly how America saw its role in Afghanistan.

McKiernan believed in the 'Pottery Barn' concept of nation-building. Named after the well-known US home-ware store, and first coined by former Secretary of State Colin Powell, it referred to the in-store policy of paying for all breakages. Powell, and McKiernan, believed that if you invaded a country you owned it, its problems and the moral duty to stick it all back together. If not as good as new, then at least in one piece. The policy had worked well enough in the Bush years, when the political will was there: and the money was too.

McKiernan had also spent a great deal of effort in cultivating good relationships with the rest of the rainbow coalition that made up ISAF. He happily accommodated the various bizarre national caveats on doing any actual fighting, in order to keep the whole thing trundling on for what he hoped would be the generational presence he saw Afghanistan requiring to recover from thirty years of war.

In many ways, his actions were the result of his career experiences. McKiernan had spent nearly a decade working in the Balkans, the apogee of liberal intervention, alongside the Europeans. An enterprise deemed a successful blueprint operation for nation-building.

Obama's team saw it all rather differently. He'd been elected with the slogan 'yes, we can': and as sure as eggs are eggs that wasn't going to mean an open-ended imperial engagement overseas. Bosnia mark 2 was suddenly off the roadmap. In this assessment, Obama openly acknowledged his own family history under oppressive British rule in Kenya—and his suspicion of the military as unsophisticated thinkers. Obama is no fan of liberal intervention, or of men in green suits offering expensive but opaque solutions.

Interventionism was replaced by a ruthless assessment of national interest. The money being spent on re-building Afghanistan was needed to re-build the American economy: and a wildly popular president didn't need the media drag of endless body bags being brought home to sully his reputation. Obama saw Petraeus as clear and level-headed in his interpretation of events: kill the bad guys, create the space for Afghan governance, pay the Afghans to build their own army—and let them do their own dying.

Just as long as none of this happened on US soil: protect the homeland. It was exactly as Roberts had done after Maiwand. The US wasn't going to be in Afghanistan for thirty years, not while Obama was president. Afghan could kill Afghan, just as long as they weren't killing Americans: either in Afghanistan, or in the US. The Pottery Barn policy got ripped up. The china would be self-mended: maybe with American-supplied glue, but definitely *not* by Americans. Nobody wanted the merchandise anymore.

Obama wanted results, money saved, and the troops brought home. And all done by the time he was to face re-election in 2012. The time-scale for deliverable results was *waaaay* outside McKiernan's expectations. The shit was about to travel downhill, fast, and McKiernan was the one in the way.

Petraeus, on the other hand, was the guy who had, apparently, single-handedly 'saved' Iraq. That made him a guy worth talking to about saving Afghanistan. Petraeus didn't want McKiernan. He wanted McKiernan out—and he got the Chairman of the Joint Chiefs, Admiral Mike Mullen, to back him.

So McKiernan was history: and Stanley McChrystal was in.

Not with Obama's active approval. The president had barely heard of McChrystal. He just went with the flow. Remarkably, Obama intended appointing a man to lead his administration's efforts in a theatre of war that would define his presidency—and to lead a coalition of fifty nations—without having even interviewed him first.

He'd briefly shook McChrystal's hand, at a meeting full of generals in glitzy dress uniforms, right at the start of his presidency, but it is doubtful if he remembered him. It's a sign of just how desperate the war had become that this president, who prides himself on his personal empathy and intellectual rigor, could be so rapidly persuaded by the Pentagon. He simply went with Petraeus, Mullen and Secretary of Defence Robert Gates.

What Obama wanted was political and military extrication, with hopefully at least some honour, out of the morass. He grasped at the first straw he was offered. Harry Truman, FDR, or even LBJ, never committed the same error. What Obama was to get in McChrystal was less an Eisenhower, more a Maxwell Taylor: who was to become be the wrong general for the wrong war.

McKiernan, on the other hand, was understandably pissed. At his retirement ceremony in Fort Myers, Virginia, attended by Robert Gates, the man who had fired him, McKiernan described his dismissal:

'If you had asked me 30 days ago if I would be here today at my retirement ceremony, I probably would have said no, maybe in a bit stronger terms. Make no mistake—I was dismayed, disappointed, and more than a little embarrassed.'

McKiernan had grounds for complaint. Many years later, Gates himself would write a less than complimentary critique of his time working for Obama as secretary for defence. In his memoir, he stated that the president was never really focused, or even interested, in Afghanistan. Certainly, Obama's decision in removing McKiernan after only a year in post was extremely unusual. It smacked of determination for change. All he got was more of the same.

Ironically, McChrystal's proposed counter-insurgency policy actually mirrored much of what McKiernan had been saying. What McChrystal was smart enough to do was not to frame his request in terms of a fifteen-year plan.

Swamping the streets of third world countries with heavily-armed and equipped western soldiers has limited success in controlling security: purely achieved by weight of numbers. However, those very soldiers also tend to, unsurprisingly, breed local discontent, as well as forming a large number of obvious targets themselves. Double-down most often leads to double losses. The cost of such open-ended operations are ruinous: in lives and treasure.

On the other hand, low-key, low numbers of specialist troops might, with careful target selection and rigorous intelligence, manage to stifle the command and control networks of the enemy without alienating the local population. Even with additional economic assistance to the local communities, the cost projections, both financial and human, were perceived as markedly less, and therefore much more attractive to the politicians.

The trouble was that to reach that state of low-key economic, political and military co-operation requires some form of central government and overall security umbrella, otherwise the entire dynamic is unwinnable.

The war, in the military's eyes, would need a short-term escalation—one last push. It would also need a joined-up civil-military co-operative plan, which the military intended to own, all by themselves. The military's plan was fatally flawed. The stated objectives were hopelessly over-ambitious. The very framework to make any of this happen just didn't exist.

More troops might just provide increased short-term local security—but then what? Keep them there forever while the army played at statecraft, civil security and governance? Who was going to play mayor, police chief, judge, teacher, doctor, or any of the other myriad positions a modern society requires? The military? The whole concept was a self-perpetuating beast.

The big trouble with the McChrystal plan was its very US-centric measures for success. The previous successes—in Bosnia and Iraq—had occurred in relatively advanced societies, whose descent into war had been relatively short. There was a surfeit of suitably qualified professionals: all they needed was to be given jobs and a salary.

Afghanistan had been at war for thirty years. Anyone with any brains had long since been killed or emigrated. There was nobody left with the skills the country needed. The new team glossed over Afghanistan's past. In the shiny, hopeful game-plan, all those coalition troops would just march on through the centre of town, to be replaced by a home-grown Afghan solution that would somehow magically be sourced all by itself: McChrystal's magic beans were all that would be needed.

All those extra coalition troops would drive out the Taliban, and the space behind would be filled by thousands of grateful Afghans just suddenly embracing democracy and putting on their own show. Stanley would plant his bean sprouts, and, by morning, there would be a fully-grown beanstalk to climb.

It was about as realistic as Judy Garland and Mickey Rooney borrowing the barn to stage a sensational summer stock musical.

For all its supposed innovation, we were back to the supposition that all anybody needed was just to see America in action. Why would anybody then want to be anything else?

What were Petraeus and McChrystal selling? In essence, a souped-up version of the types of operation Lord Roberts had successfully managed during the Maiwand campaign and the Boer War.

In broad stroke terms, Roberts got in, achieved limited military success through ruthless annihilation of opposition, secured subordinate political succession, and then left well alone. In this, Roberts was well-served by his relationship with Lord Lytton, his political boss in India. That relationship allowed Great Britain to succour the development of a useful Afghan ally and leader, in Rahman Khan, with whom to leave Afghanistan to Afghans.

The Petraeus, and, by osmosis, the McChrystal doctrine called for political and diplomatic dovetailing. The tragedy of it all was that, in Afghanistan, the actors, either on the US or Afghan side, weren't going to play the same game. They weren't even playing on the same field.

There is little that is original and new in Petraeus' thesis on counter-insurgency warfare. His genius, though, was to coalesce the thoughts of several key strategic thinkers and historic mystics, such as TE Lawrence.

Then catch the perfect wave. With a president who wanted out, Petraeus rode that crest all the way into shore. In that the plan firmly put national self-interest—US self-interest—front and centre. US troops out, Afghans in, everybody home for tea and medals.

It looked good on paper. But what Petraeus and McChrystal forgot to do, deliberately or otherwise, was to ask the coalition partners: and, more critically, the Afghans. Nobody bothered to ask the allies what they wanted. Or whether they were willing to put up with the inevitable increase in violence all those extra troops were going to bring.

As CENTCOM commander, Petraeus sowed the seeds of failure before the ship had even left dock. Through that eternal American optimism that hard work and a belief in democracy would somehow win the day. His other big problem was to be his surrogate executor. Stanley McChrystal was not a universally popular general: nor, fatally, for both men, was he a subtle one.

McChrystal's public image was a carefully honed *mélange* of warrior monk meets grad school professor: the kind of killer who would dispatch his enemy with one clinical and thoughtfully executed masterstroke of kinetic violence.

McChrystal was undoubtedly completely committed to his craft. His career reads as one of those Sgt. Rock short stories. Airborne, ranger, special forces, he did the lot.

I first saw him on TV, striding out onto the world stage as spokesperson for US forces during the invasion of Iraq. Stan gave good TV: short, clipped, military speak answers, casually dismissive of the assembled media horde.

The only thing he publicly lacked was humour—of any kind. Check out his official ISAF publicity photo from his time in command: he looks angry enough to punch the photographer.

Interestingly, he was about as much a rebel in uniform as it is possible to get. Throughout his military career, McChrystal was protected by his superiors from the full consequences of his constant gaffes. Which repeatedly involved drink and a big mouth. McChrystal spent quite a bit of effort burnishing his rebel-with-a-cause image.

The pay-off for his bosses was in his laser focus on the task in hand—and the constant churn of positive results. McChrystal was a Marmite general: it was his good fortune and good timing that in 2009 the Pentagon liked the taste of the spread.

Where Stan had really hit the afterburners was in running the secret war in Iraq and Afghanistan, as head of the Joint Special Operations Command. As a lieutenant general, he had the moxie to considerably expand the remit of special forces—and he seized his opportunity with both hands, feet and all his teeth. McChrystal was bad-ass. He and his boys killed an awful lot and I mean thousands—of mostly bad people, notably Abu Al-Zarqawi, the head of Al-Qaeda in Iraq. In fact, he made the art of killing an industrial process, vertically and horizontally tying in intelligence and research with the more traditional spec ops image of big men dressed in black kicking in doors.

Back in the US, at a time when Iraq was truly in the dumpster of disaster, McChrystal's relative success in malleting bad guys was welcome news indeed at a beleaguered White House. Bush loved him for his Texan-style simplicity in getting results and Rumsfeld, the lover of lean, loved him for doing it without thousands of expensive troops.

All that dealing of death was laudable in the circumstances and was equally creditable purely in terms of military effectiveness. It is questionable, however, as to whether that type of 'Call Of Duty' campaign is an ideal qualification for the sort of subtle, strategic direction that running the war in Afghanistan would require. McChrystal cut corners in JSOC. The end justified the means. His kind of kinetic, direct leadership was fine, indeed, exemplary, in leading special forces troops.

Could Sgt. Rock down, test and adjust to the bigger game? The first misgivings about his style of leadership surfaced at the end of his tenure with JSOC.

Firstly, in falsely writing up former US football star Pat Tillman, for a silver star. Tillman was a hero back home for giving up a multi-starred—and lucrative—career in football for life as an army ranger. He was killed in Afghanistan by his fellow rangers, in one of those confusing, 360 degree firefights that defined Afghan conflict. He wasn't the first to be killed by his own side, but Tillman's status involved a cover-up of the circumstances by the Pentagon, with McChrystal singing off on a falsified medal citation for a prestigious silver star, stating that Tillman had died heroically in the face of enemy fire.

When the story broke in the US media, McChrystal compounded his error by urgently asking the White House not to comment: as if a story like that could ever have been swept under the carpet. He was never publicly punished for his malfeasance, which suggests that others in the senior chain of command at least tacitly agreed with his course of action.

To the very end of the Afghan campaign, the waiting lounge at Bagram Airfield was called the Tillman Lounge. Complete with a framed photo of Pat Tillman, about as square-jawed and all-American as they come, and his original, McChrystal signed citation. Not the revised story. To the last, the military refused to recognize the truth. To paraphrase John Ford:

'If it's a choice between truth and legend, print the legend.'

The second charge against McChrystal was more serious. In late 2007, the Senate Armed Services Committee raised misgivings about the possibility of his appointment to four-star general level, as word of US personnel torturing Iraqi prisoners at Abu Ghraib broke. McChrystal's men were heavily implicated in the allegations, and over thirty were disciplined for their actions. McChrystal was proven to have barred the Red Cross from one of his task force's detention facility, with the alleged assumption that he knew the international law of armed conflict was being broken there. As their commander, who had either condoned it or not exercised sufficient oversight to prevent it, he escaped direct censure: but he had to put his fourth star on ice for a bit until the dust had settled.

Four-star generals are as much politicians as military men. Quite often, the most effective ones are adept at actually taking no direct action at all. That's why four-star generals have hundreds of staff officers working for them: to do the difficult stuff. Less is more at that level.

McChrystal was quite the opposite, in personality and career record. He made his name by creating the image of personally holding the reins. It was a high-rope act that took considerable panache, and not a little skill, to carry off, but it was always best suited to the special forces arena.

By its very nature and name special ops are staffed by special people. They've had to go through a more demanding recruitment process than your average Joe, tend to be a little brighter, are certainly much more driven, and are usually rather individualistic people with a strong (often over-bearing) sense of self-worth. Exactly the same personality profile as McChrystal.

Had McChrystal stayed in that arena, he would have remained a star, albeit one with a considerably lower public profile than he was to acquire as commander of ISAF. In retrospect, it's hard to think of a command opportunity less suited to his particular skill set than head of the ISAF coalition. He just couldn't keep his hands off, problematically at exactly the times he should have said and done nothing.

His command issues stemmed largely from the fact that he was now required to lead a disparate conglomerate of a force, which had a majority share of un-bellicose national contributors, commanding a majority of troops who didn't share his snake-eating determination and drive. McChrystal was the exception to human endeavour, not the norm. He had real trouble in compromising to bring the horde along with him.

McChrystal was undoubtedly an extremely effective counter-terrorism commander. That is undisputable, even if his ethics in getting results are occasionally questionable. The trouble with appointing all that storied death-dealing ability was that Afghanistan was no longer about killing people.

Counter-terrorism was now counter-insurgency. Politics and diplomacy counted for just as much as men in green with guns. The arena had moved into shades of grey.

Petraeus, as head of CENTCOM, had a problem to solve. He and McChrystal had worked well together in Iraq. Petraeus had set out his store in a similar, but markedly different, public profile from McChrystal. He had also been promoted above the level of operational commanding general to running an entire region: running Afghanistan alone was a step backwards.

As overall commander in Iraq, the spec ops boys under McChrystal had had a vital, but sub-ordinate, role to Petraeus' vision. Petraeus hadn't served in Afghanistan. His war had been Iraq. He must have been concerned at his lack of understanding of the campaign. McChrystal, on the other hand, had been minutely involved in the campaign there.

There can be little doubt that the great hope was that the two would repeat their double-act in Afghanistan. Petraeus needed McChrystal to fulfil his vision. But McChrystal was not Petraeus re-imagined. The double-act wasn't to be. McChrystal just didn't do shades of grey—and nobody spotted it. In fact, he would have loathed the very concept. Had President Obama interviewed and vetted him, as one might reasonably expect, then the administration might have prevented the disaster that was to come.

Inexplicably, Obama didn't.

He did meet McChrystal, right before Stan got on the plane for Kabul. The meeting, in the Oval Office, lasted all of ten minutes, and was mostly about getting the photos right for another grip and grin press release. McChrystal, who had gone to the White House with his pitch speech honed to perfection, was ushered out the door before he had had a chance to get beyond 'hello'.

History is less about events, and more about the people who make the events. The very human, flawed individuals whom fate, design and chance have placed in those positions. Every one of the characters in this tale is a talented man.

It's the mix that matters more: and this mix was decidedly off. McChrystal was appointed in June 2009—and hit the ground running. Assembling a diverse, idiosyncratic and odd-ball team of spec ops characters as his command team, he quickly put in place revised rules of engagement for NATO troops, emphasising minimizing of civilian casualties. He and his team then set off on a fact-finding mission, all over the country, to find out exactly what was going on. Stan wasn't encouraged by the results.

While much of the north and west retained their traditional distance from the worst of the fighting, over in the east, the Americans had got themselves into a hard fight in the remote valleys and mountains along the Pakistani border. In truth, had they read their history books, they would have realised that the east was bisected by the old Durand line, which nobody, particularly the local residents, recognised.

Pashtun lived on both sides of the disputed zone of control, and considered themselves an independent entity—Pashtunistan—free of control from either Kabul or Islamabad. Nobody had ever effectively controlled the east. A sensible ruler, like Rahman Khan, had played off local tribal leaders and been content to exercise a limited control from a distance: let sleeping dogs lie. The distinctly forward-leaning American intervention had not gone well.

In the south, the situation was even bleaker: largely down to ISAF's own incompetence. No single European nation had the political or military will and capability to mount individual command, such as the Americans had in the east.

The American's pre-occupation with the east had let their visibility over progress in the south slip. Despite nominally being in charge, McKiernan's famous tolerance for other nations had allowed strategic campaign management to fall into a dismal series of national squabbles. An uneasy compromise between the Canadians, Dutch and British had resulted in a rolling command. With all the predictable failings of varied experience, national culture and political interference from three nation states with very different opinions of martial prowess, capability and function.

The Dutch, in particular, faced an uphill battle in maintaining home country support for a military adventure that was now a long way from the benign peace support intervention that had been billed.

All three nations had bitten off far more than the treasury-controlled force they had deployed could chew. Critically short of men, machines, helicopters and planes, the casualty count was fast becoming a national disgrace for each country's leaders and generals.

The incipient saviour had come in the form of the US Marine Corps. Fresh from their famous battles in Fallujah and the most restive parts of Iraq, the Corps was eager for more. As part of President Obama's initial agreement to increase US troop levels, the Marines wanted their own piece of the glory. The trouble was, they didn't want to share, or even work, with anybody else to get it.

There were so many coalition troops in-theatre that Afghanistan was getting crowded. The Marine Corp's new deployment fell right between the cracks of McKiernan's firing and McChrystal's arrival. The former was distracted by news of his imminent demise and didn't do enough to influence the eventual deployment. The latter was faced with a *fait accompli*.

The Marines decided, pretty much by themselves, that they wanted to go to Helmand Province, albeit right next door to Kandahar: but not Kandahar.

Kandahar city is Afghanistan's second city. Kandahar was the modern Afghanistan's first capital. Kandahar is important. Helmand is not. It's a predominantly rural backwater. Everybody knew that, from the Afghan president to the Marines themselves.

Why did the Corps go to Helmand?

The Dutch, who were running Kandahar, didn't want the Marines there. The Marines were up for a fight, and the Dutch general, Mart de Kruif, who was currently running RC-S, was not at all keen on thousands of US marines hard charging into downtown Kandahar city: despite the obvious fact that the city sat on a knife-edge, with a significant portion of the million or so local population re-advocating support for the Taliban.

Kandahar was the birthplace of the movement, home to most of its leaders, and the de facto capital of the movement when it was in power. What happens in Kandahar really, really matters to the rest of Afghanistan. It carries strategic weight far above its mere location or size. The Dutch military experience was heavily influenced by their long track record in peace-keeping. They had invested a lot of effort in what they saw as civil-military liaison and aid projects. De Kruif's mantra was: 'shape, clear, hold, build'.

His troops had barely got past the 'shape' part—and they didn't want several thousand US Marines blowing everybody up. The rise in hard fighting in the south was causing severe soul-searching in both the Hague and RC-S.

The US Marines are the self-styled American 911 service. If a nail needed hammered, the Marines were very happy to be the biggest hammer in town.

The two cultures were diametrically different. The Dutch were deluding themselves that they had, together with the Canadian component, anything like the weight of numbers to seriously tip the balance. They were equally sure they didn't want any more Marine Corps-inspired fighting on their doorstep.

On the other hand, the British, who were running Helmand, were seriously in trouble. Far from being the imperial power of old, the British were up to their necks in fighting they could neither win nor even control.

Helmand is Afghanistan's biggest province by geographic size—some 20,000 square miles. Incredibly, the British were trying to conduct operations to control the whole Province with only three full battalions of infantry: no more than 1800 soldiers. The entire force didn't hit the 9,000 mark until the summer—and that was fully 100% bigger than the original brigade-sized force that had been sent there three years earlier.

Perhaps more importantly than a simple number count, and an issue that caused numerous questions in the British House of Parliament, the 2009 deployment had only brought a little over 20 helicopters, which was itself, a vast increase on the original deployment. The British simply lacked the ability to move their chess pieces where they were needed. What frontline troops that could be mustered were badly pinned down in dusty hamlets. The Brits had wilfully surrendered any form of battlefield manoeuvrability. They were achieving little more than a grinding, fixed battle of attrition.

It became a regular occurrence for headquarters elements to form ad hoc reinforcement companies of cooks and clerks. The dyke was broken and Peter had run out of fingers. Three years of endless—and very violent—cordon and search sweeps, what was euphemistically known as 'mowing the grass', had produced little: except resurgent hatred for foreign soldiers.

The US Marines had deployed a small force to Helmand in 2008. Helmand wasn't altogether unfamiliar. The Brits needed help, and the Marines knew they would get a fight. The Corps could establish its own patch, far from any oversight by the US Army: or any peacenik ISAF Dutch general in far-off Kandahar. The word at the time was that the Marines were so punchy and independent, they had formed their own coalition, all by themselves.

The Marines got their way—and went straight into the hornet's nest. They got the fight—and the casualties—they had been after. The trouble with all that Helmand action was that Helmand was not particularly important: and particularly not that important to Stanley McChrystal. His new policy was premised on protecting the people by living with the people. Which meant the biggest city in the south:

Kandahar. Not Helmand.

The biggest component of the initial surge went to entirely the wrong place: simply for reasons of individual service interest and national argument over command and control.

The Brits were quietly delighted the US was coming to the rescue. The Corps was to come to replace the British in the most-hotly contested and casualty-strewn areas of Helmand. The Dutch were pleased their carefully planned softly-softly civil engagements were not going to be interrupted.

The Taliban was delighted because they had an awful lot of new—and inexperienced—foreigners to shoot at, on ground that suited them. The Marines were delighted because they got to blow a lot of stuff up, entirely on their own terms. Helmand became their own private war, with the Brits playing a winning junior partner. McChrystal was furious—but he could do nothing about it.

More or less straight off the bat, US Marines and coalition troops launched another one of those great find, fix and strike missions across Helmand. Called 'Operation Khanjar', or 'Strike of the Sword', thousands of troops were airlifted to dusty towns around Garmsir. A district the British had tried and failed to secure on several occasions. The offensive had mixed results, with the overall conclusion being that the insurgents had merely melted away into other provinces. Yet again, despite the arrival of the surge, the coalition lacked enough troops to hold the towns long enough for some form of ISAF-approved concept of effective governance to take root. Despite some localized success in the town centre, any success in a wider sense dribbled away into the dust.

McChrystal hit the buffers, in the same way as all his predecessors had.

Afghanistan was just too complex, too war-devastated, too broken, for a quick, easy fix: and the same could be said of ISAF itself. At that time, operations in Helmand were still, at least nominally, controlled from Kandahar by what was essentially a brigade headquarters, set up for purely military operations, not a complex and swiftly-changing civil counter-insurgency operation.

In truth, progress in the south had been scandalously tethered to purely military operations. Little had been done to encourage the civil population to look with favour on ISAF. Nor had any key infrastructure projects taken root.

RC-S's role, which should have been to provide overall tactical direction to the campaign, had self-limited itself to coordinating air assets and a regional reserve.

The initial ISAF expansion into the south had become entrenched into a vicious tit-for-tat shooting match which neither side had the capacity to win: and which only succeeded in destroying much of what little was left of the region's shattered infrastructure. More criminally, until 2007, nobody had even seriously thought of trying to build an Afghan army or police force to replace all those ISAF troops. What force existed in 2009 was barely credible: lacking numbers, education, experience, weapons and equipment.

With his initial surge of troops now deployed into yet more small and strategically insignificant fire-fights, Afghanistan was looking like yet more of the same: new commander and new policy notwithstanding. McChrystal took a long look at his centre of gravity: Kandahar.

He was instantly not a happy man.

McChrystal and Dutch General Mart de Kruif came from different planets. Although De Kruif had graduated from the US Army War College, his operational experience had been a single six month tour of Bosnia in 2001: an operation which was then decidedly more about building schools than doing any fighting. McChrystal, on the other hand, had just come from years of killing bad guys.

McChrystal had no hire and fire authority. He could direct De Kruif, but he had to deal with him. The Dutch government decided who was in charge. The Dutch, Canadians and British had their own sweet deal to share command.

De Kruif and McChrystal spoke completely different languages, even if they actually shared many of the same goals. In late 2009, De Kruif travelled to Washington, to explain progress in the south to the US press corps. In his prepared remarks, he explained his take on the all-in McChrystal policy:

'Back in the Netherlands, I made the case that doing counterinsurgency is a little bit

like being pregnant. You are or you are not, but you can't do just a little bit counterinsurgency.'

The assembled hacks just looked at each other: 'dude, did this Dutch guy just compare war to making babies?'

De Kruif was firmly of the 'it takes time to bake a cake' school of thought. He was all for ten years of being in the shit: McChrystal knew he only had ten months before his president would come looking for results.

Both are intelligent enough men. Both saw the war in the same light: neutralise the bad guys, bring in governance and an Afghan security force to police it all. The difference was as much about national culture and personality as tactics. America is a country in a hurry. The Netherlands has always been a patient negotiator: it's been invaded too many times to be otherwise. The two were never going to make it work.

What McChrystal did do was try to change the operational culture. He was appalled at the amount of coffee drinking and deep thinking when folks were dying.

The Dutch HQ in Kandahar had a very lovely café, complete with parasols and deckchairs. I often visited, before it got closed down. I loved the quietness of it. It gave me a welcome opportunity to sit quietly and think. My job is creative writing. I need space and time to formulate the words.

Which was really where the Europeans were coming from: taking time to think the problem through, letting things germinate. Fighting the war was the day job, not a life vocation. A little like the entire European experiment itself: cohesion and compromise trumps divisive vigour. The alternative had been near destruction. Mainland Europe has never forgotten the lessons of the 20th century.

America is totally different. The American dream is one of constant toil, a Puritan work ethic, of success from adversity. No compromises, no dilution. Particularly when its soldiers are dying.

De Kruif, for all his thoughtfulness, failed to grasp the intensity and immediacy of the situation.

At the end of the day, the war on terror wasn't really owned by the Europeans. Sure, we had all gone along in a spirit of mutual support: but the twin towers weren't in Europe. For all that Europe wanted to help, 9/11 wasn't the national crisis that it was in America: and Europe didn't feel the same spirit of righteous aggression. That came from across the Atlantic.

There were comparatively few real idiots in command in Afghanistan: and enough decent folks around to make up for the shortcomings of those that were. The Europeans just saw the world through a different prism from the Americans, who wanted it all done yesterday.

It seems ridiculous now, but, excepting the Americans, all the NATO nations had maintained a limited alcohol policy of two cans of beer per soldier, per night. All that booze around all those guns sounds like a recipe for disaster: except ISAF troops, apart from the Americans, locked their guns up when on base.

The policy was a matter of national culture. Europeans are traditionally gun-shy. As a British police officer, I was rather proud to patrol unarmed. During my military tours of Afghanistan, in the early days of ISAF, my weapons spent more time in the armoury than they did on my person. I took the guns out when I left the base—and locked them up when I returned. Even when I was visiting another location, every weapon had to be securely unloaded and stowed away on a locked gun rack.

McChrystal's Command Sergeant Major, Michael Hall, another special forces hard-charger, took one look at the KAF restaurants, cafes and bars, the hordes of unarmed soldiers, the availability of alcohol: and decided he had seen Sodom and Gomorrah on earth. To the Americans, this was crazy stuff. Equally crazy to CSM Hall were the nightly booze parties and barbeques being held right in the middle of KAF. The parties then were legendary. It was possible to, and I can attest to this, start drinking at sundown, and just keep on going until dawn.

Stuff still got done, kind of, and morale was pretty high, despite being in the asshole of the universe. But it was far, far away from the warrior monk existence that Stanley McChrystal, or CSM Hall, lived.

The trouble was that when he told the coalition nations in KAF to cut it out, they collectively gave him the finger. Not a great moment for the new commander, who was fast discovering the limits of his writ. The American outlets were summarily shut—the Harley Davidson store and the Pizza Hut:

McChrystal was overall US forces commander. He had the power of Grayskull. He had no power over the rest. All the soldiers did was go to the Dutch, British, Canadian and German stores instead. It was a nonsensical battle to expend political capital on.

My opinion? The cafes and bars were a useful morale tool for the troops coming in from the field. The boys in the shit came into KAF for a little relaxation. The cafes gave them a taste of the world they had forgotten, a chance to be at least semi-normal. If normal means sitting in the dust, in uniform, carrying a gun, while drinking a milkshake.

However, the whole Sunday afternoon culture *had* gone too far. The two can booze rule was badly abused. Friday's were a complete day off for everybody. Afghanistan was not Bosnia. It was not a literate country, with established governmental apparatus and developed infrastructure. It was a fucking disaster zone. Too many officers were content to live inside the wire, slurp their coffees, watch the rotation egg timer run down, and get out of dodge with a medal.

Which is where I agree with McChrystal. Whatever his faults, he genuinely seemed to care about Afghanistan. As, frankly, had McKiernan. It's the kind of beguiling enchantment that just creeps up on you. One day, you'd wake up and Afghanistan would have you by the balls. McChrystal drank the Afghan cool-aid: same as all of us who stayed. I'd have liked to have worked with him then: he believed.

McChrystal tried to shake it up. He established the whole IJC concept, where a three-star general ran the war, leaving COMISAF to do his real job of working at a strategic military-political level. He did his best to empower the regional commands to own their areas. He did preach the mantra of working with the Afghans, understanding, mentoring and helping train them.

The trouble is, not enough people shared his enthusiasm. A lot of soldiers are in the military for the simple reason that it is a well-paid job, with an inbuilt sense of belonging. Military service has a kind of cosiness to it: they hadn't signed up to die in Afghanistan. Not everybody can be special forces, or have that special forces motivation.

McChrystal ran every day, slept four hours a night, ate once every 24 hours. At least, his press profile said he did. What is most definitely undeniable is his laser focus, damn the consequences, lead, follow or get off the road determination to get his way—and only his way. He might have been right in most of it, but it was way too much for the normal folks. He just had this special light around him, which confused the hell out of people. Nobody could keep up. He got it wrong.

The fun-o-meter had hit an outrageous Spinal Tap 11. Stuff was way off any normal register. A more considered commander might have changed the equation by ordering all his troops to carry a loaded weapon at all times. He'd have got away with that, on security grounds. Every other commander would then have realised the stupidity of having alcohol-laden troops next to guns with bullets: it might also have brought the job right back into focus too. The whole booze thing would have just died a natural death. Had anything tragic happened, McChrystal would have had the perfect partner to blame.

That sort of lateral thinking wasn't in his playbook, though. He just went for broke, ramming speed. In radically dialling the fun meter down to below zero, he made an enemy of the very troops he needed to buy in to the whole deal. It was a stupid fight to take head-on.

McChrystal further pissed off the team with his new rules of engagement.

Most of his troops were barely out of their teens. Many had just completed a mere four months of training before they found themselves curled up on an Afghan mountain-side being shot at. McChrystal urged them to clearly identify the shooter before shooting back. He called it 'courageous restraint'. When you were the one being shot at, courageous restraint seemed like more complete madness from on-high.

Air support was severely curtailed. In the past, a man with a gun running into a compound had been excuse enough to drop a bomb on the compound. No longer: ISAF had killed an awful lot of civilians that way. McChrystal wanted the Afghans to like ISAF, not fear them.

Trouble was, none of that highfaluting general stuff meant dick when your best pal just got shot, the dust is flying all around and you just wanna kill somebody before they kill you.

Most of the kids—and I mean kids—doing the fighting had never left the States, let alone visited South Asia. They may as well have been walking on the moon. The whole Afghan vibe was *waaaay* beyond anything they had ever known, and the sensory overload really blew the lid off many of them.

What they did know was what they had been taught in training: that the American army is the biggest and best in the world, and they were the biggest bad-asses on the block. Firing their guns was what it was all about. Why else would you want to be a soldier?

One of the most popular T-shirts sold on KAF said it all. On the front was a picture of a grizzled gunner, firing off a belt from his machine gun. The accompanying quote read:

'While you try all that peace stuff, I'll cover you.' Peace sucks. Pray for war.

The troops were extremely pissed off. All their training, particularly the Americans, emphasized winning the firefight, not hiding. The troops wanted to take some names and drop the frames. McChrystal became the one not just stopping them, but disciplining them for doing what they thought they were there to do: get some rounds down-range.

In truth, with a different personality in charge, the necessary change could have happened, just in a longer, and more persuasive, time scale. McChrystal, though, wasn't one for waiting or negotiating. He belonged to the 'pick your window, you're leaving' school of management.

Within months, the entire coalition enterprise was in foment, a state of mind which stretched all the way back to the national capitals. Folks back home were asking some pretty serious questions as the body bags mounted. Take a look at the media from the time. There's practically nothing about the bigger picture, about how Afghanistan was trying to change, and what it could possibly become, with the right effort and commitment. It is all shaky shots of scared soldiers, taking fire from multiple locations, shouted orders, bangs and bullets flying. Complete confusion.

We all wondered: just what the fuck are we doing here?

McChrystal's solution? Americanise the shit out of the war. If the allies wanted to drink coffee, let them. He wanted his people, who he could directly command, in the top spots, with Americans, who wanted to fight his way, out on the ground.

So he came up with a new plan, barely three months after arriving. He wanted more soldiers: a lot more soldiers. At least 40,000 more, to be precise—and that was just the bid for the United States commitment alone.

It was SUCH a traditional American military response: get a bigger hammer out. It was yet another Afghan WTF for Obama. He had appointed this snake-eating warrior who he'd been told didn't just think outside the box, he had made his own. And here he was a couple of months after getting to Afghanistan, coming back for the one thing he had been put in the job to avoid: escalating the war.

It must have been doubly a surprise—because Obama had, incredibly, hardly spoken to the man leading all those American soldiers. During his first 100 days in command, McChrystal had had only that one brief face-to-face Oval Office meeting with his commander-in-chief. That was it: no video conference calls, nothing. He was out there on the tightrope, calling the shots, all by himself.

Bush had had weekly video calls with his key commanders in the field. Obama chose to read second-hand memos from Admiral Mullen or Robert

Gates instead. He didn't even read the un-doctored weekly summaries that McChrystal had penned.

Underneath that snake-eyed exterior, McChrystal is as human as the rest of us. The pressure he was under was extraordinary. Inside his command bubble, he was a rock god, loved and extolled by his chosen team of warriors. He just couldn't sell it to the rest of the coalition—and his boss didn't seem to have his back either. We all want to be wanted and valued. Here he was, at the very peak of his powers, living the command dream he had nurtured since his days at West Point: and nobody seemed interested.

So he did what we would all do in the circumstances. He made a shout out for a little attention. Not just for himself—for all those young boys and girls he ordered into battle every day. Stanley really cared: he put it all out there, thinking that he'd get the same attention that he had always got from his military peers. The tragedy is that he didn't see the new game he was playing was no longer governed by his brand of simple soldier's honesty.

When I was young, I was fascinated by fire. My grandmother had a real coal fire. One day, while she was watching, I put my hand into the flame. I burned my hand, and my mother was scandalized that my grandmother hadn't tried to stop me. Her reply was simple enough; 'had I stopped her, she wouldn't have learned that fire is dangerous.' True enough, I never forgot the lesson.

McChrystal was different: he just kept on putting his hand in the fire. He just couldn't help but be attracted to the flames.

Not only did he blind-side the president with his new plan, he then told the world, via CBS's '60 Minutes', that he had only spoken to the president once since taking office. He carried on with his press self-immolation by later bluntly stating that Afghanistan could become 'Chaosistan'—and that that was one potential solution to the problem he was considering letting happen. Before openly criticizing the vice-president's view that Afghanistan didn't need more troops.

He was now off the reservation. McChrystal just couldn't stop himself. His big mouth just ran away with him.

The White House was furious. Honest or not, the inference was clear: the commander-in-chief didn't have his hand on the tiller. McChrystal found the big presidential shepherd's crook round his neck, being called to a one-on-one with Obama, on board Air Force 1, while the plane sat on the tarmac in Copenhagen, Denmark. McChrystal was clearly told, in polite presidential terms, to shut the fuck up and concentrate on being a general: not a media commentator on his boss's performance.

Obama must have wondered just who he could trust. All those guys in the fancy uniforms, with all the badges and medals, had told him back at the start of the year the original surge was all they needed: a small increase in the force, a new commander with a new deck of playing cards, and the war was there for the taking. Next thing, like Oliver Twist, the man they had said would sort it all out was back again with his camouflage begging bowl held out: and was happily telling the world that the boss was being all Mr. Bumble. You can't really blame the president for asking: just who does the military think is in fucking charge?

A more sensitive man would have realised the ice underneath was now getting rather thin. McChrystal, though, just kept on batting the same old ball stroke.

What else was happening in Afghanistan would prove to be to be an even bigger berg: and the beginning of the end for Stanley.

The old Afghans rather annoyingly wanted a say in how their own country was being run. Specifically, in summer 2009, a say in just who was going to be the country's president. Right in the middle of the most vicious summer of fighting of the entire campaign, it was time to hold a national election. When I look back in the rear-view mirror at the Afghan campaign, there are moments when all I can say is: 'was this for real?' You could just not make this shit up. The election of 2009 is one of the most surreal. In truth, the fact that it had to take place at all was a coalition own-goal that was entirely of our own making.

Once the invasion was over, we had tried to turn the country around. Indeed, those early, halcyon days of ISAF, before we went into the south, were mostly happy and content ones for Afghanistan. Granted, we hadn't done as much as we had promised—but comparatively few folks were getting shot. Back in the UK, people forget that there was an operation before Helmand: and a blinking good one at that.

The man we pinned our hopes to lead the new Afghanistan was Hamid Karzai. Like all Afghan leaders of the modern state, he is a Pashtun. He is a pretty educated guy and he has been around the houses. He got his masters in politics and international relations from a prestigious school in India, while his family was a strong supporter of the late king, Zahir Shah. He is a strong Afghan nationalist, who had worked hard to persuade the Americans to support the various mujahideen factions against the Soviet invasion of 1979. During Taliban days, he was first offered an ambassadorship, but then rejected the regime once he saw that they were as bad as the chaos that had preceded them. His papa was killed in Quetta, by suspected Taliban sympathisers. A tragic event that only reinforced his desire to see the end of the Islamic Emirate.

When 9/11 came around, Karzai was only one of several potential allies courted by the CIA. He entered the country from the south, heading towards his home of Uruzgan and the stronghold of his Popolzai tribe, to the north of Kandahar. Helped by US special forces and their directed air strikes, he travelled towards Kandahar, entering the city to wide acclaim in December.

Once the dust had settled on the initial overthrow of the Taliban, Karzai was put forward as a candidate for provisional leader by a special council, which convened in Bonn, Germany. Karzai wasn't suddenly touted as the coming man, he just happened to be the best of a bad lot: the only name everybody could agree on.

Afghanistan was split in two. The north was held by the Northern Alliance, a confederation of the northern minorities, which had been the sole hold-out in the civil war against the Taliban. The southern tribes, predominantly Pashtun, were dominated by Karzai and his loose confederation of supporters. Many of whom had settled in refugee camps around Quetta, Pakistan for the duration of the Taliban regime. Despite sharing a heritage as Afghanistan's liberators, the two sides, from north and south, did not get on. A group from the west represented what was seen as predominantly Iranian views, while a fourth group of long-time *émigrés* represented the deposed king, Zahir Shah. Nothing is ever simple in Afghan politics.

Fatally for his own chances of a triumphant return, which were at the time surprisingly high, King Zahir Shah, an old man living in comfortable exile, declined to attend in person. Although the Northern Alliance opposed him, had the king attended, he might well have reached a quorum. The Northern Alliance faction itself was split. Headed by another former Afghan head of state, Burhanuddin Rabbani, who also didn't attend the conference. Rabbani sent a surrogate, Yunis Qanuni, instead. In his absence, Rabbani swiftly became yesterday's news. The king was out, for the same reason, as was a non-Pashtun Uzbek from the north that the king's faction vainly proposed.

The only guy left standing in the ring was Karzai, simply as the best known figure who had managed to least offend the most amount of people. Critically, Karzai could also count on the weight of the Americans. Who everybody knew had the casting vote as the only ones at the table with the money and the power to rescue the devastated country.

Karzai was elected head of an interim administration, which was followed in the following year by a transitional administration, with Karzai again, as interim president: a position he had cleverly manipulated his way into with flattery and intense greasing of palms.

The West was happy. In Karzai, we thought we had a partner who was fluent in English and looked western enough to appear in the many grip and grin photo ops he tolerated over the years. He was Western media inoffensive while Afghan-interesting, with his funky hats and cloaks. Karzai received a weekly bag of money from his CIA handlers to keep him on-side and pliant.

His administration was happy enough to sign off on the first ISAF status of forces agreement, giving carte blanche for all those western troops and our well-meaning development programs.

Everybody was happy.

If Roberts had been around, he would have been deeply disturbed. We were getting in deeper, to the point of no return: not extricating ourselves to wave a long screwdriver from afar, as the Afghans sorted out their own country.

As a consensus candidate, Karzai's control over the country was minimal, at best. He relied on a complex web of grace and favour, just to stay in office. He was even to appoint an old Northern Alliance leader, Mohammad Fahim, known as 'Marshal' Fahim in honour of his military experience as a mujahideen, as vice-president. Remarkable—as Fahim had once jailed Karzai for supposedly spying on former President Burhanuddin Rabbani. Afghan politics remained as opaque as ever: friends became enemies, and back to friends again, over night.

We in the West muddled on optimistically and insisted on creating an Afghan constitution. It suited our concept of rule of law, executive and legislative power. The Afghan concept of governance was more:

'I'm in charge, disagree and I'll kill you, unless you manage to kill me first.'

NOBODY in Afghanistan EVER gave up power. A position of power was an excuse to enrich yourself, your family, and your tribe. Why would you want to give that up?

Nonetheless, the Americans championed a new system of democratic rule, supported by democratic elections. The new constitution named the regime as the government of the Islamic Republic of Afghanistan. It would be supported by a bi-cameral system of upper and lower legislative houses—essentially senators and congressmen. These representatives would be elected nationally. The president would also be elected, in a separate vote

The whole concept was completely alien to the Afghans. Voting? What is that? The village elders told the people what to do, the tribal chiefs told the village elders. It had always been thus. Biggest stick on the block wins.

The whole document was a re-written version of the US constitution, right down to the 24th amendment, term-limiting the president to two elected tenures in office.

In the heady days of 2003, it all seemed like a jolly good idea. Even to the Afghans, who cannily noted that signing it would lead to billions of dollars of aid being released. Which is why they supported Karzai to our faces, and then blithely ignored him.

The first elections, in 2004, were deemed a relative success. Karzai breezed into office, helped by his Afghan allies. In those days, Afghans had a patent sense of optimism about the future. I well remember wandering the streets of Kabul on that first election day, at the end of 2004. Lines of excited men and women waited to cast their votes, happily smiling and shaking my hand. The atmosphere was festive, the future bright and the violence had yet to happen. All was good in the world.

By 2009, the US-inspired constitution came back to bite the coalition in the ass. Right in the middle of the worst summer season of fighting thus far, while McChrystal was urgently requesting tons more troops, the constitution dictated a new election for president. And this time, Johnny Afghan had no intention of playing by the rules.

The entire thing was a fix, from beginning to end. To the Afghans, it was one big joke. As Wali Karzai, the president's half-brother said at the time:

'We already have a president, why would we need another?'

Despite the Afghan's reputation for being lazy and disorganised, the fraud they perpetrated during the election was epic, and ridiculously well-organised. Hundreds of phantom ballot stations were invented in places where the government had absolutely no writ at all. Ballot papers, millions of them, were filled in before the election had even begun. Voters were paid to vote over and over again, filing their voting card for a pre-chosen candidate.

The candidate field itself was madness. 32 registered hopefuls named in a ballot paper the size of a restaurant menu. 80% of the population couldn't read or write. Helpful election officials filled in the card for the illiterate, then filled in a few more, just for good measure.

Even with rampant fraud, Karzai only just slunk over the 50% threshold needed for a clear win. His main opponent, Abdullah Abdullah, who claimed loyalty from the old Northern Alliance, had managed over a quarter of the vote. The West, appalled by the blatant and vast scale of the fraud, ordered an investigation. The initial report indicated fraud in anything from 76 – 94% of the ballot boxes inspected. The inspecting body was an Afghan institution. Even they found rampant fault.

A good friend of mine was Karzai's 2009 agent in Kandahar. He spent the month before the election supervising a team diligently filling in voting papers for Karzai. On election day itself, he supervised the destruction of all the official papers, replacing them with the pre-made items, completed by an industrial assembly-line of specially hired workers. The story was my friend's favourite dinner anecdote. To a substantial proportion of Afghans, the election was all one big joke.

In the end, over a million of Karzai's votes were declared invalid, fully one third of all those cast in his favour. By that measure, the election now needed to be re-run. Karzai's share had fallen below the 50% threshold for a win.

ISAF was firmly in the hole. With the only working transport infrastructure in the country, McChrystal had supervised the transport of election materials. With the fighting raging and troop plans being deliberated, nobody wanted ISAF, in the frame for the biggest fuck-up in the war's history, to make more negative headlines back home. With the elections came increased violence: a 50% increase, month on month. ISAF struggled to hold the line. The whole event was a disaster.

After eight years of reporting steady progress, all the elections had delivered was a report card that North Korea would be proud of. The spring was duly coiled up again for a second round, and Karzai planned to be even more devious.

The diplomats entered the fray. America put immense pressure on Abdullah Abdullah and Karzai to call off a second round. There were simply more important things to be doing. Abdullah caved, and Karzai was back in. Abdullah was not a happy bunny, saying:

'*A government that is appointed by an illegitimate commission, a commission that has tainted its own legitimacy, cannot bring the rule of law to the country, it cannot fight the corruption.*'

The US suddenly woke up to the fact that Karzai didn't smell of roses. He had turned out to be a pretty devious snake in the grass. We'd gone to war to help found democracy: and the Afghan president in whom we had pinned all our hopes was just another tin-pot dictator. What price freedom now?

It was over, though. The second round was cancelled, the voting boxes returned to sender. Job done—except somebody had to carry the can for the whole mess. And the diplomats weren't going to be the sacrificial lambs.

In 2009 the US ambassador in Afghanistan was Karl Eikenberry. He was, remarkably, a retired US army lieutenant general: a very unusual background for a senior diplomatic posting. In his military career, he'd been the US general who had overseen the initial ISAF engagement in the South. Obama had appointed him ambassador to Afghanistan as one of the earliest acts of his administration.

Like everybody who got burned in Afghanistan, Eikenberry had his own ideas on winning the war. Which would have been fine and dandy, except was no longer in charge militarily. Eikenberry didn't like McChrystal: or his ideas.

Stanley had put a lot of effort into courting President Karzai, meeting with him on a weekly basis. Eikenberry was excluded by Karzai from some of those meetings. Karzai was extremely good at divide and conquer. Eikenberry felt Stan the Man and his cuckoo counter-insurgency campaign undermined the State Department's supposed lead on Afghan development and undermined him personally. Military egos, former and serving, clashed.

Eikenberry had built up his empire well. He had led the charge on expanding the Kabul Embassy, almost quadrupling the number of staff. The State boys were churning out very impressive stats and plans, for increased engagement and increased aid. All backed by a steady drumbeat of improving circumstances.

Then McChrystal had presented his plan for expansion: without consulting Eikenberry. Stan cut the ground from under State. He'd been telling everybody the grand plan was going well, and here was McChrystal saying the war was lost if he didn't get even more soldiers. The pictures painted didn't match.

Ambassador Eikenberry was furious. He started secretly back-briefing the White House on McChrystal, in extremely unflattering and critical terms. At a time when Obama didn't speak to McChrystal, when his review had arrived as a game-changing shocker, the administration's man in Kabul was now telling the president the military and their plans were a crock of crap: and the ambassador had the background, as a retired general himself, to justify his fears.

Eikenberry had called bluff on the military's expansion of the war. Eikenberry asked some of the questions that needed to be asked: what part would the Afghans fulfil? Where were all the civilian experts coming from to fill the void, once the soldiers had finished fighting? How much was all this going to cost? And how many decades was it going to take?

Eikenberry's memos publicly arrived from under the rock courtesy of WikiLeaks. The 'New York Times' got a hold of them. Suddenly, the US public got a whiff of the boxing gloves flying around at the top: and they decided the US president was fiddling while Rome burned. Eikenberry, though, wasn't the only diplomat trying to stir the brew.

Dick Holbrooke, an old stager who had won fame for organizing the ethnic partition of Bosnia, was back in the big time, as US special envoy to Pakistan and Afghanistan. Obama had seen him as a pair of extra ears on the ground, but Holbrooke carried a considerable ego around in his well-travelled suitcases. He used his tenure to advance a self-serving strategy to have himself appointed as overall campaign czar. All he did was piss off Karzai,

McChrystal, Eikenberry and the coalition allies; pretty much everybody that could be pissed off.

The trouble was Holbrooke had a direct line to the White House, and Hilary Clinton, as secretary of state. He championed what became known as the 'Af-Pak conspiracy', rightly calling time on the illusion that Pakistan had nothing to do with the insurgency. In truth, the Pakistanis hosted, supplied and funded a whole host of Taliban-inspired groupings. Trouble was, all that was kind of embarrassing to acknowledge, as the US funded much of Pakistan's military: and the Pakistanis had the bomb.

Holbrooke then called for peace talks between all sides, including the Taliban. Which was the same game-plan he had led in Bosnia. No doubt planned with Holbrooke in charge this time too. This time, though, GIs were dying every day. In Bosnia, the US had scarcely been engaged. By 2009, the coffins were all too obvious in the heartlands of America. Holbrooke wanted to talk to the same Taliban who were killing American sons and daughters: it was all way too radical. The plan could never fly.

The ideas kept on coming from a fertile mind. Holbrooke was dying. He finally succumbed to a tear in his heart in 2010. It was as if he wanted it all out there before the end. The trouble was it was too much information and half-formed plans, with no formed conclusions: and most of what did surface ran contrary to everything else the president was getting.

Everybody in the game had some good ideas and some nutty ideas. What the whole adventure lacked was somebody, anybody, with the power to cherry-pick and decide. What Afghanistan got instead was a bunch of big-dicked egos pursuing their own personal agendas in a mass fratricide of collegiate *hara-kiri*.

The entire US team, military and governance, was biting each other's hands off. The war looked unwinnable and Karzai was back in power after an openly corrupted vote. After seven years of scattering American treasure around like confetti.

You have to feel for Obama. Here was a law professor, used to deliberating absolutes. He could argue and argue about interpretations, but the law is grounded in absolutes. Theft, murder, rape: as crimes, they all have specific definitions. The foundations of the law debate are concrete.

In Afghanistan nothing was definite. Nobody really knew who was in charge, what we were fighting for, what we had won and lost, how much had been spent. The only definite was the number of coffins coming home. He'd come late to the game, with no background or grounding in just how we had got to this stage. An in-experienced president, he'd appointed all these top-notch folks to find ground truth: and they had all struck fool's gold.

In the back of Obama's mind was one word: Vietnam. It was all coming worrying back into focus. He felt just like JFK:

'The sons of bitches with all the fruit salad just sat there nodding, saying it would work.' [10]

---

[10] 'President Kennedy: Profile of Power' Richard Reeves

JFK had been railing against the Joint Chiefs, over the Bay of Pigs, but now it all seemed just so damned prescient, including Kennedy's own summary of his actions:

'All my life, I have known better than to depend on the experts. How could have I been so stupid?'[11]

Obama was done listening. He would go with his gut: which is what had got him into the White House in the first place.

In the October, McChrystal had his big chance to put his case to the president, right there in the White House. The whole fucking shooting match turned out for that one: VP Biden, through Gates and Clinton, right across all the generals. Stan got up with his maps and PowerPoints and went through his options.

Everything from 11,000 extra bodies, right up to 85,000. The more troops, the more his Afghanistan map got filled with optimistic blue spots: blue spots being the bit he reckoned we could 'secure'. What was secure? Nobody asked the question, or had an answer. Nor did they ask why so many troops were going to be sent to Helmand, fully 20,000 in the big plan. That was the Marine Corps again. They'd join the fight, as long as they were guaranteed their own piece of turf.

McChrystal hadn't read his boss right. Stan talked through his full house of big-COIN: clearing, holding, building, all the mantra. Obama didn't get it.

He wanted Al-Qaeda destroyed, not the chimera of a re-invented Afghanistan. Obama asked Stan why most of his troops were going to the south. Al-Qaeda was supposedly hiding out in the east. Why not send the reinforcements there instead? Stan was trumped. He hung his head for a several, long, poignant seconds. And then inexplicably launched into a description about defending the people. The Marines had out-gunned Stan: they had already decided they were going into the south to finish what they had started, damn the army. Through inter-service loyalty, McChrystal declined to tell the one man in the room with the power to stop the madness that his hand had already been quietly forced. Obama didn't know enough about how the services worked to smell the rat. Eisenhower would have.

Damned if I do, damned if I don't. There were no easy solutions for an embattled president. Yet this was the guy who, as a young senator, had called the Iraq war:

'A dumb war, a rash war. A war based not on reason but on passion, not on principle but on politics.'[12]

He'd done that pretty much on his own, right into the teeth of the nationalist gale. Love him or loathe him, the man had principles then. What he did next, in 2009, pleased nobody.

McChrystal's press offensive hadn't left him with much choice but to agree with a new request for troops. Nor did he want to be seen to micro-manage

---

[11] As above

[12] Chicago speech, 2002

what Stan was doing in the field. Johnson had paid the price for that. The other choice, refusal to support the troops, was domestic political suicide.

Whatever his misgivings, he had to be seen to back the military.

In December 2009, he announced that Stanley could have 33,000 more troops. Right in the middle of what Stan had asked for. Compromise time. NATO piled in with a modest supplement, to keep the Americans happy.

Obama, though, made it clear this wasn't a blank cheque. It would be the last one signed. US troops would now number 100,000. That was it, bust, end of story, do not pass go, do not collect £200. Do not come back begging for more.

Those troops would also be coming home pretty quickly: by the summer of 2012. And the whole shooting match would be over by the end of 2014. By then, Stanley had to be in a position to let the Afghans run their own war and their own country: governance, security, economy, the lot. He gave the army some more soldiers, but on a time-limited loan basis only.

All the Taliban had to do now was wait us out. The compromise was imminent disaster announced. We now had neither the strength nor the will to win.

'Shape, clear, hold, build' was gone. Instead Obama outlined a new, three-stage strategy: ' fight, talk, build'. All that euro-centric chatting over coffee about eventual outcome was yesterday. Hurry it up, get it done, move on.

Very quietly, but assuredly, Obama let it be known that any more fuck-ups would be owned by the generals: not the president.

If he'd paid more attention to what the military was actually doing in Afghanistan, he might have chosen a different course. Especially what was going on in Kandahar. A new British commanding general, Nick Carter, was actually starting to create the first properly joined up strategy.

What Carter did, off his own bat, was to put the Afghans first. Before any coalition military zeal to get into the shit, he actually asked them what they wanted. He did it with a specially-selected team that had lived and breathed Afghanistan for months before even getting on the plane.

'You're kidding me?' You ask. 'This isn't revelatory, it's basic,' I hear you say. To you and me, it most definitely is. To the military, believe it or not, this was remarkable. Which says it all about just how screwed up the whole operation was in the south.

Until the UK's 6 Infantry Division headquarters came over with Carter, the whole strategic direction of the enterprise had been run off some notes on the back of a fag packet. 6 Div HQ didn't actually have any troops. It had been set up specifically as a mobile headquarters: and Afghanistan was its focus.

Carter's first 'eureka!' moment came in recognizing Kandahar as the centre of gravity for the south. While he couldn't do much about the US Marine deployment to Helmand, he made sure the next tranche of in-coming US troops were deployed in the key province.

Secondly, he worked to build on De Kruif's work in securing governance and economic development in the city itself.

Scandalously, mains electricity for a city of one million barely worked an hour a day. Recognising that the big re-development, of re-building an entire transmission network, would be outwith his tenure or scope of operations, he nonetheless arranged for a US-aid sponsored and coalition supplied diesel generator park to begin construction. The Shur Andam plant wouldn't start production until early 2011, but the initiative impressed the Kandaharis. For once, ISAF wasn't just offering bombs and bullets. And the work being planned looked further forward than the duration of one rotation.

Carter spent a long time researching local relationships. He mapped out the complex tribal networks that dominate Pashtun society: and made an ally of Karzai's half-brother, Ahmed Wali Karzai. The Afghan president's Popolzai tribe carried a lot of sway in the south. In Kandahar, Wali Karzai was the MAN.

Brother Karzai came with a mixed and decidedly whiffy heritage—many allegations of drug running, extortion and torture lay behind him. For the first time, though, Carter recognized that getting your hands grubby in Afghanistan is par for the course. EVERYBODY in Afghanistan has a chequered past. It's part of survival.

Carter was prepared to do business to get results, and he recognized Wali Karzai's potential for advancement of the mission. As he wryly remarked of his new ally:

'*My sense is that he's either a candidate for an Oscar, or he's the most maligned man in Afghanistan.*'[13]

What Karzai and Carter created together was a provincial council, comprising of all the local tribal leaders and Kandahar movers and shakers. Here, finally, was a forum for talking, for expression of opinion, and, potentially, a decision-making body capable of persuading and leading the local populace. That council would outlast Carter—and Wali Karzai, who would to be assassinated eighteen months later in his bathroom, killed by his own bodyguard.

Something permanent remained, even if stepping up to the plate in Afghanistan comes with a definite lifespan. Nobody retires from Afghan public life: you get deposed or killed.

It sounds ridiculous now, particularly to anybody who didn't serve there, that it was such a revelation to simply ask the Afghans what they wanted, and to empower them to go get it. It is an indication of just how hermetically sealed ISAF had become from the people it had ostensibly come to save. The war went on inside the mega-bases, in PowerPoint diagrams and briefing notes. Or survived in the conceit that what we were offering was automatically what Afghanistan would want, just because our way of life seemed good to us: 'let them eat cake.'

Carter put Afghan security forces front and centre in securing the city. We'd all paid lip service to the idea of an Afghan lead. Rotation after rotation had looked and wondered at the be-draggled platoons of Afghan renegades they had nominally to shepherd: Afghan soldiers and police with their scarves, make-up, flowers and drug use.

---

[13] 2010 remarks to journalists during press briefing

They didn't get that these kids were the dregs of the refugee camps. They hadn't had the luxury of an upbringing in a stable country. They'd joined the army as an act of survival—and been flung onto the front lines as their reward.

I lost count of the amount of so-called joint meetings I attended, where Afghan officers would come in with their ISAF mentors. We'd all stand around the map table and politely begin to talk tactics. Gradually, the advisors would start to dominate the discussions, all held in English. The Afghans would slowly withdraw. Half an hour later and the advisors would be ripping each other to shreds, while over in the corner, the Afghans would gather round the tea urn and just watch and wonder.

Carter was different.

The Afghan security forces were less than five years old. Their mentors were the product of decades of expensive education at the best military schools the West could offer. How on earth could the Afghans compete? For all the Afghan's enthusiasm, it was pitting a university against a primary school.

What Carter did was encourage the Afghan police, a much-maligned institution, to start to take charge of security in the city. ISAF and the Afghan army then took care of security in the out-lying districts, which acted as funnels for the Taliban to secrete themselves in the main areas of population. The effect was to keep the fighting from the densely populated city and out into the fields. Creating at least the impression of a force-field, what the military called a ring of steel, around the places where people actually lived.

He picked up a guy called Abdul Raziq, who ran a border police battalion, made up of his own tribe of Achakzai, to lead the fight, Afghan style. Raziq was about to start on his own ride to glory. He became a leader I was to get to know quite well, so I'll save his story.

For now, what Carter did was classic imperial action. Deploying an effective local militia to sort a local problem.

Raziq's Achakzai were the natural tribal enemies of the Noorzai of Panjwai District, who sided with the Taliban. Raziq and his boys ruthlessly ran through the Panjwai and the local Noorzai like a saltwater enema. Achieving in days an element of local control that the Canadians had failed to do in years.

All this re-orientation of force was coupled with a rigorous examination of the lethal force being deployed. Carter recognized that just killing folks solved nothing, except perpetuating the cycle of violence to get more folks killed: many of them entirely innocent. For the first time, soldiers on the ground had to get higher authority to shoot. It was all in line with McChrystal's intent. Not everybody was happy.

Carter's directive didn't make him popular at all with his US sub-ordinates. Here was a foreigner telling the US Army to put the guns away and start thinking. US Brigadier Daniel Bolger served under Carter and bluntly described his impression of his boss; *'he's not the type of general I'd put in charge of anything.'*[14]

---

[14] 'Why We Lost', Daniel Bolger

In retirement, Bolger wrote a hagiographic eulogy to US Forces, entitled; 'Death Ground; today's American infantry in battle.' The title really sums up how Bolger would have fought the war, given a chance. Carter made sure he didn't.

Carter's intervention in trying to control the amount of lead flying around cut right across the grain of what the military call mission command: the ability of a commander on the ground to directly control events. It's both a sign of how desperate ISAF's position had become and an inherent lack of trust in the troops deployed that the proposal was even considered.

Too many folks coming to Afghanistan regarded the place as a free-fire zone to have some fun. Carter was right to put the dictum in place, but it is a sad indictment of the training and quality of the troops he had under command that he had to do so. What he did, with McChrystal's support, in the teeth of regular US military opposition, was truly groundbreaking for ISAF. It was the first time Afghan and ISAF forces started to talk to each other, on day-to-day tactical matters, with a game plan to carry into the following year.

Carter didn't have it easy, though. Like a lot of his British contemporaries, struggling for recognition from the their American partners, he took to wearing American-style 2 star rank slides as well as his British rank. I always thought that smacked of a lack of presence. It just looked fucking silly. Folks either know you're the boss, or they don't.

Roberts, and my grandfather, would have recognised and approved the plan. Carter's plan was classic imperial policing. Let the locals look after the locals. Concentrate on the big stuff. Walk lightly but carry a big stick. Be liberal with your money to your friends—and mallet the rest. Most of all, recognize what you can change and dismiss the dreamers and their dreams.

The new wave didn't last. Carter's boss, Stan the Man, was about to make his own historical footnote. The war was about to shift on its axis: and Carter's initiatives would mostly die the day he and his headquarters went home. The milk in the command personality dynamic was about to go from sour to curdled.

In April 2010, Stanley and his staff took off for Europe, on one of those 'shore up the home front' visits he often made to European capitals. A naked attempt to talk up the war and plead for more resources: so far, so good. Except, and it is a HUGE 'except', his media advisor, Duncan Boothby, invited 'Rolling Stone' magazine along.

Boothby was a former TV producer, who had wangled a civilian gig with the military. He loved finding new ways for his boss to express himself—and McChrystal loved putting his hand into the fire.

COMISAF had been told by Obama to stop feeding the papers, so Boothby put up 'Rolling Stone', the quintessential hippie music mag, as an alternative. The writer, Michael Hastings, would tag along on the trip to do a personality profile. The White House would be pissed, but it couldn't say the boss had broken the ban. It was all classic McChrystal risk-tease. It could have worked, had Boothby had the smarts to keep Hastings in his hotel room and staged the access. He didn't. He handed out a VIP, access all areas pass.

Journalists are not the enemy, nor are they your best friend. They just write the best stuff they can in the best way they know how.

Boothby gave Hastings a ringside seat to the crazy house. What did Boothby expect was going to happen? To the outside world, his boss and his mad world of death and destruction was bat-shit crazy. The trip was media gold.

McChrystal and his boys were exhausted. They'd been fighting the Afghan war, the White House war, the Pentagon war and the ISAF war, just to get the ship turned the right way. They were all spec ops boys, who just didn't do ordinary. What the fuck is ordinary? Barbeques and ballgames? These boys are out of the farm. Permanently. The army made them that way: and encouraged them to stay there. What else was the point of being special?

McChrystal and his boys hit Europe hard: from the bottom of a hi-ball glass. And right through it all, Hastings wrote it down: McChrystal falling down drunk, flipping the bird to an in-coming VP call, his senior officers chatting up foreign hookers. Hastings must have known this was a smash. The guy he was writing about was a fucking four star general, but his show was 'Animal House'.

Tired though he was, McChrystal showed the child still lived in the man. All those questions about his maturity and fitness for command came crashing through the ceiling like the 500 pound bomb drops he authorized every day.

The dichotomy was obvious. Here was McChrystal cast as Dr. Strangelove's General Ripper. Except this time, it was all true.

The spark that set the roof on fire was McChrystal alleging that the president was 'intimidated and uncomfortable' on meeting him. He could be excused getting drunk, even insulting his fellow generals. The civilian side was off-limits. The president was the elected commander-in-chief of the United States. Not just another boss. He flipped the bird to the whole system, the whole country that had made him. Nobody was that big, so special, to fly that high and survive.

The story surfaced in late June 2010: and the shit hit the fan. Boothby got the bullet in short order, as he deserved, for sheer stupidity. McChrystal was ordered to the White House. McChrystal had his sympathisers. Folks around the military all recognized the form: a bunch of SOF jerks getting wasted and laid, right before they went back to work. The military encouraged the culture.

Except: this was exactly what Stan the Man had jumped down everybody's throat about. He'd closed all the bars, ended all the fun. Here he was, the Trappist warrior monk, doing just what he'd ordered all of us not to do. All while he was on active duty, commanding over 100,000 troops.

If there was ever an example of ' do what I say, not what I do', this was it. The guy acted as big an idiot as MacArthur had been when he had publicly asked to nuke North Korea. As a leader and as a man, McChrystal failed to reach the mark required. He was supposed to be a four star general, not some dumb frat-school brat.

Obama didn't hesitate. The Oval Office meet between the two, on 24th

June 2010, was not so much a dressing down as a goodbye. General Stanley McChrystal became the first general since MacArthur to be publicly fired by the commander-in-chief.

He could have no complaints. He had stuck his hand in the fire, and the fire bit back.

Stan was just too much, too quickly, too soon. He had the right ideas, the right moxie, the right rep. He just couldn't help but self-destruct. The blame isn't all his, though.

The guy had fought a righteous war for seven long years straight command duty. I went to Kandahar for a mere three years straight and came out thinking I'd been on a full spin cycle: my mind was candy-floss. And I wasn't running a war.

What Stanley needed was guidance and support. He got hung out to dry, by his superiors and his media advisors. The White House appointed a guy to do it all—and didn't realize they had got a genius with a spanner, but who lacked the full tool-kit to build a house.

A lot of what Stan preached—the emphasis on minimizing casualties, the emphasis on governance, security and aid development—would come to pass. Eventually.

What his firing did, though, was to presage the end. It was the first of those two great tectonic shifts that signalled the closing of an epic chapter. The White House and the president went from a position of reluctant trust in the generals to one of outright scepticism. The whole Afghan project went into the dumpster.

Stan's second-in-command, a Brit general called Nick Parker, took over. The British Ministry of Defence unwisely started crowing to the media that one of their own now commanded a coalition theatre for the first time since the Second World War. Which was pretty forward leaning, as the entire affair had come about by ill design, rather than competence, and uncomfortably reminded the Americans of their own screw-up.

Obama had his first Pontius Pilate moment. He looked at his generals, and reminded them that he had warned them: any more fuck-ups and you will own this. McChrystal had been Petraeus' man. McChrystal was history. Petraeus would now own the whole X-rated drama.

Petraeus had to accept a virtual demotion, from commanding general of Central Command, down a rung to a theatre commander, a position he had been promoted from when he had left Iraq. He wasn't given much option. Obama summoned him to the White House and just told him straight. Pentagon snakes and ladders: 'it's your mess. You clear it up.'

Petraeus gallantly stated that he served at the president's pleasure, but the whole concept of big counter-insurgency was a busted flush. Petraeus had already had his one moment, his Warhol fifteen minutes. In Afghanistan, he brought out the old Iraq playbook again, but it was a different time, a different place and a different dynamic. He was exhausted before he even got there.

He made bad decisions, career-changing mistakes: like screwing another journalist visitor given exclusive access to the inner circle while he was in command. Paula Broadwell was pretty hot, all long legs, glossy hair and willing to do whatever it took. He got away with his in-theatre personal relaxation therapy for a bit, and came back as director of the CIA, but the world found out soon enough. He resigned from the CIA in disgrace. It currently looks like he may face criminal charges for giving Broadwell access to official secrets. The press will salivate over that: a four star's pillow talk is definitely worth a few column inches.

The COMISAF black spot hit him just as hard. Morality, not competence, did for them both. The American general staff were three for nought: McKiernan, McChrystal, Petraeus. Afghanistan just ate them up and spat them out.

All of them made a lot of money after Afghanistan. They are still out there, advising and strategizing. War was good to them: but they will be forever tarnished heroes.

Nick Carter went back, as deputy commander ISAF, for Petraeus' replacement, US Marine general John Allen. He then made Chief of the British General Staff. He has just set up the UK's first joined-up information operations brigade.

John Allen, a decent man and a considered commander, got caught up in the Petraeus' manure pile. As the investigation mounted into Petraeus' convoluted personal life, Allen was found to have written e-mails to one of the women involved in the Broadwell debacle. No charges were ever raised, but the timing could not be worse. Allen was up for nomination as Supreme Allied Commander Europe. He decided to retire early instead. COMISAF? Four in a row for nought.

Afghanistan was the morality tale that just kept on giving. The second, and final, death-knell to the adventure came in the form of a 5.56 mm bullet.

Fired by a US Navy SEAL on May 2nd, 2011, it killed the monster for good. Osama bin Laden, the architect of it all, was dead. That night, President Obama addressed the nation:

'The American people did not choose this fight. It came to our shores, and started with the senseless slaughter of our citizens. After nearly ten years of service, struggle, and sacrifice, we know well the costs of war. These efforts weigh on me every time I, as Commander-in-Chief, have to sign a letter to a family that has lost a loved one, or look into the eyes of a service member who's been gravely wounded. So Americans understand the costs of war. Yet as a country, we will never tolerate our security being threatened, nor stand idly by when our people have been killed. We will be relentless in defense of our citizens and our friends and allies. We will be true to the values that make us who we are. And on nights like this one, we can say to those families who have lost loved ones to al-Qaeda's terror: justice has been done.'[15]

That very day, interest in the war in Afghanistan ended. What was the point of keeping going?

The military had proven themselves to be as human as the rest of us, but

---

[15] White House broadcast

when the chips were finally down, they had rubbed out the bogeyman. He deserved to die. What else was there still to fight?

The irony of OBL's long-overdue departure was that, after all the billions spent and the hundreds of thousands of troops sent to Afghanistan, it had all come down to good intelligence and a small team of dedicated operators. Not divisions of 19 year-old soldiers from Iowa.

Did it still matter in the cold light of day that Afghanistan remained a basket case? No.

Who cared in Iowa? They cared enough to elect a president. And presidents tend not to get elected when American boys and girls are dying in far-off lands in wars that nobody really understands. Sure, America would keep on fighting: 9/11 was too totemic an event for it to ever be otherwise. But now, the fight would be done covertly, in the shadows—where it didn't upset the American public.

Bush tried to paint 9/11 in the same light as Pearl Harbor. The War on Terror was to be another total war. It wasn't. The only folks consumed by the war were the warriors we sent there. Less than 1% of the population paid the price of thirteen years of war. Back home, nobody really cared. Life went on as usual. The war was just a flickering image on a television screen.

By the end, the generations of Steenbergers had forgotten why we had gone there in the first place. Obama just called the ball long after closing time had been and gone.

Tough luck, if you happened to be an Afghan. They'd get a couple of years to take over the ballgame. But there it was. The Bin Laden operation proved there was another way—and it shut the book on the madness. The boys would all come home.

By the time I arrived back in KAF in 2011, the train was still chugging up the hill. The hamster wheel was still spinning. The army liked it that way. For a soldier, war is good. It's the playing field. But, in truth, it was over. The enthusiasm had gone. The A Team was now the D list and going south.

It hadn't happened with any real degree of planning or purpose. The whole ball of string had just unravelled: by a very human series of accidents of character and personality. By 2011, all folks wanted to do was end the thing: and not be the last one to get killed. As Obama said:

'We won't try to make Afghanistan a perfect place. We will not police its streets or patrol its mountains indefinitely. That is the responsibility of the Afghan government.'[16]

The war had come full circle: time for somebody else to do the dying.

---

[16] June 2011 broadcast

DAY TWO: FIDO

I was up early, stooging around RC-S like a lost hooker hunting for a date. I found my prey: an important looking colonel, with an array of flashy badges and a big portfolio of paper under his arm. He looked like a guy with the moxie to subvert to my cause.

I might not have had a uniform, a rank, a badge or a gun: but I did have a push-up bra and a low cut T-shirt. Both of which were in full evidence that bright, sunny December morning. The boys in Kandahar were a pretty traditional bunch. It was hard to make your mark as a woman if you played by modern rules. More often than not, the old playbook worked better.

My colonel listened attentively to my sorry tale; and common sense prevailed. We sailed past the glowering sergeant of yesterday, with his gun and gum. Salutes were exchanged. I publicly smiled sweetly and quietly gave him the finger. I was in.

I only had a badge that said 'visitor, must be escorted'. Inside, past sergeant angry and his boys, folks were too busy to really care. I waved my protector good-bye and went exploring.

The 325th were hidden away at the back of the hustle and bustle. It was how they liked it. Amongst all the flashy white containers, they lived in a plywood shack. The Americans had a habit of building with little more than sheets of chipboard, paper shingle and a load of nails. For a country that lavished money so easily, their camps were often little better than refugee reception centres.

The place had been there so long, the wood was stained black with sweat, dirt, smoke and spilt coffee. It stank. Inside was so dark, I thought I'd walked into a hillbilly's moonshine bar.

The 325th was a reservist unit, called out of mothballs for the war. By 2011, even the United States Army, the biggest dog with the biggest bite on the whole global block, had run out of juju. For a long time, the regulars had held the line. Then, the regulars had thinned, to be replaced by individual augmentees from the reserve. Then, the regulars had just run out of folks to send. The early arrivals had done three, four tours, between Iraq and Afghanistan. Too many forgot what their wives and kids looked like. Too many had taken too many chances: they just said 'fuck it', en masse, and walked.

By 2011, entire reserve units were the norm, not the exception. Bricklayers, farmers, cops, accountants, they'd all got to wear the uniform at the weekends, earned a little extra cash. Now, their country needed them.

To an outsider, the United States can seem like a nation permanently preparing for war. The extent of military organisation—the regular army, navy, air force, marines, coastguard, their matching reserve units and the unique national guard—stretches across every seam of the fabric of the country. The entire British Army will probably soon be under 100,000, regulars and reserve together. The US Marine Corps on its own is well over twice as large.

That military colossus forges a national consensus, where defence of the homeland is key. The whole defence edifice receives a level of unquestioning respect that is quite alien to Europe—and remained alien to the functioning of ISAF in Afghanistan.

It would be pretty much unheard of for any of the other coalition nations to deploy a reserve unit en masse. Creditable though that service can be, there is no way full-time experience and capability can be created on one week-end a month and a two week annual camp.

The Americans thought otherwise. The whole concept of citizen service is embedded in the national DNA: an internal struggle for survival, fighting within the borders of the United States to establish governance and legitimacy of the rule of law. The country is not so much one unified nation as an unruly family group of disparate cousins all living under one roof, being knocked together by pride in the family name.

Every national guard unit—and there are an incredible fully complemented 28 brigade guard combat teams—served in Afghanistan. Over 300,000 ordinary citizens from the state's militia were mobilised over the course of the campaign.

They were quite a dissimilar bunch. At one stage, KAF saw the entire Guam National Guard arrive. They were lovely, happy Pacific islanders, characterised by their universally short stature. One female driver I travelled with was so short she had to use blocks to reach the pedals of her MRAP. They wore a palm tree badge and danced in hula skirts on their days off. I was amazed that Guam had a unit in American service. I think KAF blew their minds. It was such a long way away from the ocean.

The 325th wasn't a guard unit. They were, however, all reservists. They came out of Tennessee, which was always self-evident by the number of tobacco-chewers. You could spot them by the revolting half-empty plastic bottles they kept by their desks to regularly spit into.

I liked the boys: they were generally pretty respectful to me. Trouble was, very few of them had actually ever worked in the media, journalism or anything actually related to what they were now being asked to do. The 325th was an all-airborne bunch, and they seemed to be as enamoured of being paratroopers as being creative media types. That led to a continued aggression in their product. It was all fighting, guns, uniforms and more fighting.

The plywood shack was their company headquarters. The unit had small teams embedded across the other major bases in the south, the idea being they would provide local support to operations there, all coordinated by Kandahar. It was the next step down from what I was doing as part of the Kabul POTF. Which also, theoretically, had a say in what the 325th did by coordinating everybody's output.

Trouble was, the 325th didn't see it that way. Their boss, quite genuinely called Major Slaughter, saw his command chain as being the 82nd Airborne, the president and God.

I got to meet him, that second day. To my mind, he was only a major, which is actually the first rank in the army where you get to exercise any kind of independent control. Sort of lower middle management. I had a load of what I thought were bright ideas to re-invigorate and re-invent the relationship between the POTF and RC-S. In my hubris, I saw the both of us as equals. Slaughter had other ideas. He was a decent enough guy, but, to him, I worked for a distant unit that wasn't going to write his report and which had no input on what he was doing.

As part of his duties, he was required to write a weekly report to the POTF, which he only sometimes did. For the simple reason that there were American generals in Kabul, who might read the POTF report. Most of the time, though, he ignored the POTF. Which was going to be difficult for me, as the POTF's anointed KAF ambassador.

Just passing the word around to the right people was going to be a nightmare. Nominally, everybody was supposed to use NATO infrastructure. In reality, that only happened in the really big headquarters. Downstream, every country brought their own gear.

The American system, called CENTRIX, tapped straight into their defence mainframes back in the US. They were ridiculously protective about anybody accessing what was seen as US-eyes only information. I got the whole national security angle, but ISAF was supposed to be a coalition. I never understood why they couldn't just put a firewall in place, to separate US functionality from that being used in Afghanistan.

IT wasn't an issue for just the Americans. The Brits, the French, the Germans, all had their own separate systems: none of which interacted with any of the others. NATO was supposed to gave commonality of parts, weapons and doctrine. Somebody forgot to add computers: and, in today's army, you can't order a sandwich without computers. The NATO system was just one of many that staff officers were supposed to keep tags on. It wasn't uncommon for mid-level officers to have 6 computer screens on their desks, all monitoring different information streams. None of the various e-mail systems spoke to the other.

Further down the feeding chain, the guys who actually did the work would only have their own, national system. So the information flow was always second-hand and limited. Each nation maintained its own databases of statistics and country information. You'd have to hunt for a tit-bit on one system, then switch to the other to develop an idea. Passing that information around meant laborious copy and paste across security scrubbers, or just multiple duplications of manual typing of the same report.

Getting stuff done took forever. I learned that if I put a request up to an American unit, I'd have to allow a lead-time of two or three days for them just to read the email. They were too occupied taking care of their own US information stream to check the NATO systems.

What the POTF did, and I executed on their behalf, wasn't exactly top of the agenda for Clift. He couldn't even communicate properly with them. He answered to the 82nd, not some NATO conglomerate 300 hundred miles away.

Computers caused the nightmare that led to my next big road bump. I'd sneaked into the HQ, and found the right guy to talk to. Major Slaughter even had a desk I could use. Albeit, it was in a corridor, right next to the Afghan interpreters hooch, which was an indication of just how un-important I was to the 325th. But I did, at least, have a nominal home. Now, I couldn't use the computers.

Getting into the HQ on a daily basis would require me to get an 82nd airborne badge, which Slaughter said he could sponsor. He couldn't help with the IT. Getting access to a computer that might remotely lead to something that could be called work would require US security clearance by CENTCOM headquarters in Florida.

The 325th used American CENTRIX computers: and I was a foreigner. I did have UK and NATO clearances, all done and dusted, which had been enough to get me unlimited access to the IJC, but the US didn't recognise those. Despite the fact that we all nominally worked for the same organisation. To get to use American computers, I would have to be vetted all over again by America: a process that would take weeks. Was this a NATO coalition or not?

I was mighty pissed:

'Just how am I supposed to do my job?" I asked.

'Be an American,' replied the security sergeant.

So that was it for the second day. I went back to my room and phoned Eric to tell him the good news. He told me he'd get the long screwdriver out again. I went to The Boardwalk, ate ice-cream and did nothing, all over again.

ISAF was as much its own enemy as the Taliban ever became. The whole place made life a complete dank morass, just to get anything done. It sucked all the juice from you, for no result.

FIDO.

AN AFGHAN FAMILY

Eric came back to me the next day with a solution: work from your room. 'You're kidding?' was my obvious response. 'Nope', came the reply.

Eric agreed the IT thing was silly. He went to see the US colonel who ran things in Kabul. The Kabul colonel agreed the IT thing was silly. The Kabul colonel phoned Slaughter. Slaughter agreed with the Kabul colonel that the IT thing was silly and spoke to his own KAF colonel. The KAF colonel agreed with Slaughter and the Kabul colonel that the IT thing was silly and spoke to the security sergeant, known as the S2. The S2 agreed with the KAF colonel and Slaughter and the Kabul colonel that it was silly.

Everybody thought it was silly. Then the S2 got out the big book of US army rules, which said it was not silly.

I was barred from the HQ, and the computers, until I had US Central Command clearance.

I gave them my UK and NATO clearances, but the Americans didn't understand the British terminology. I got a UK S2 to write, explaining the differences—and confirming I was cleared for NATO Top Secret. The US S2 said it made no odds. NATO Top Secret wasn't in his CENTCOM book of US army spells. I was still barred.

I felt like a pariah—which was rather worrying. I'd come down to Kandahar to embed with the Americans. To produce anything meaningful, I had to have some sort of computer access. Without it, I just couldn't do my job: and I was still in my three-month probation. No access could mean no job. I had given up everything to get to Kandahar. This was not looking good.

I wasn't alone, though, down there in Kandahar.

Out there in the suck, all on their own, POTF employed a team of locals, my team, who did the actual newsgathering part of the story. The maddeningly annoying restrictions that were placed on my movements meant that my best real expression of what life was like out there, in the real Afghanistan, came through my conversations and mail with these guys.

They are the real, unspoken heroes of this piece. As much as we in KAF had the odd rocket to deal with, these guys walked and talked the game, out there in the real world. I envied them.

Everybody knew they worked for us. They had press cards, identifying them as journalists working for 'Sada-e Azadi', the Voice of Freedom, ISAF's newspaper. Their only defence, come the day, was their ability to talk their way out of trouble. All of them showed a near suicidal bravery in collecting stories for us.

I had two guys in Kandahar Province, one in Zabul and one in Uruzgan. A little later, I was to work with two locals in Helmand and one in Farah, over in the west.

It's a sign of just how fucked up Afghanistan's economy had become that each of them ended up working for us. One of my guys, Asker, was a highly talented doctor. He had attended basic surgical school and had been a practising GP for years. A doctor in Afghanistan could expect to earn about $200 a month: ISAF paid him $1000. His only qualification was for our job was fluency in English, for which we paid him five times as much as he would have got for his eight years of med school. ISAF didn't just turn the economy on its head, it twisted it up and chewed the edges.

There's no competition. I would have made exactly the same decision Asker made. Anybody would. He worked for us and forgot about being a doctor: a skill Afghanistan was, and is, critically short of.

All my boys were required to be fluent in English. That fact alone dictated that they came from good families, who could afford the ruinous cost of higher education in Afghanistan. POTF couldn't have functioned without them. But we did steal away some of Afghanistan's brightest and best to work for us. When they should have been working for their country.

It was a source of constant shame to me that I didn't get to see them more. The whole unit got together twice a year in Kabul, but, otherwise, the only time I got to see the faces of the team in the outlying provinces of Zabul or Uruzgan was by patchy video Skype conversation.

The distance between us made for a difficult management equation. On the one hand, I had taskings that needed to be filled. On the other, my actual knowledge of conditions on the ground was filtered by the ever-optimistic summaries I read from ISAF's ever-productive internal reporting cycle. One thing ISAF never lacked was more shiny reports. Yet I was acutely aware that every time I asked the boys to go get a story, it could be the last time they ever left home. I needed their input. I had to be ruthless. I never stopped worrying about them or the potential consequences of what I asked them to do.

Jawwad, my guy up in Uruzgan, was near suicidal in his zeal to report the news. He once sent me a series of photos, in real time, of a suicide bomber who had attacked a bank in Tarin Kowt, the provincial capital. Jawwad had been standing outside the bank with a group of ANP, Afghan National Police officers, when the suicide bomber struck. The ANP had been suspicious of the advancing man, dressed in sacrificial white, with a suspicious lump under his shalwar kameez. The police had cut him down in a hail of bullets. Jawwad had captured the effects of every bullet fired, in a graphic series of photographs. The final frame was of an ANP officer standing beside his victim, one foot on his lifeless head. The bomber's dead fingers still curled around the pressel switch of his live device.

Jawwad sent me the entire series with the pride of a young lion that had just made his first kill. Bravery, and male pride, dominated his life. Jawwad was a valiant Afghan who would never do what I would have done in the same circumstances: run.

The incident made one line in ISAF's daily summary. No ISAF soldiers had been involved, no western witnesses could recount the day. It meant a damn sight more to those ANP guys. I made sure the photos were circulated amongst the senior command. I got Jawwad a certificate for his bravery.

Afghans love paper certificates. It seemed a small price to give for what they did on a daily basis.

My man in Kandahar city, Feroz, was blown up on six different occasions during my time working with him. He survived each blast, but would resignedly shake his head each time. He knew he lived on borrowed time.

Feroz had dreams. A handsome young fella, he studied English at Kandahar University. When we first started working together, he wore western clothes: jeans, a leather jacket, with an early-Elvis mop of curly, black hair. Later, as the security situation worsened, he adopted shalwar kameez, as all the young men of Kandahar did. When the Taliban had originally left, all the men shaved their beards and wore T-shirts. That hadn't lasted long. Eleven years on from our razzle-dazzle entrance, clothes were back to the way they had always been. He worked with us to earn money to buy a house. He lived with his family, but was desperate to start his own life. He had bought a plot of land in a good area, but the down payments crippled him. ISAF was his way out. He was incredulous when he learned I had been to America: that was his dream. Like all young Afghans, he was very internet savvy. He had the latest iPhone, an iPad and a laptop. The internet was how young Kandaharis learned.

What Feroz longed for, as any young, straight, hormonal man would, was for the touch of a woman. Until he came to work with me, he'd never been alone with any female, save his mother and sister. He used to write the most lovelorn poetry, and send me photos of young Asian women he would like to meet. It was all very sweet. I am sure nature will help in the essentials, if he does ever marry. For now, women remain for him, as we are for most Afghans, a species apart.

I'd speak to all my boys, every day, by phone. And I'd try to Skype them as often as I could: but I couldn't see them regularly, or they me. I was sealed into KAF with all the other tens of thousands. When I did go out, I was generally surrounded by a platoon of heavily-armed soldiers. The Kandahar boys would come to see me at KAF, and later on I got to regularly meet them at the governor's place in town, but the Americans wouldn't allow them on base. Despite the fact that they all had ISAF ID cards and had been formally cleared.

We'd meet at the search area, by the main gate. I had to have a soldier with me with a gun, hovering never more than six feet away. The boys were uncomfortable: too many eyes monitored the gates of KAF. If they had been spotted speaking to a western woman, it could mean death for them.

I hated the way I had to work. How could I possibly work effectively with our staff when I could never get to meet them? How could I ever REALLY get to understand the dynamics of everyday life when all I ever saw of the place was mediated by the presence of men in uniform? It made me guilty to stay relatively safe inside KAF. I resolved to get out as often as I could, by any means I could.

My boys became my Kandahar family. I protected them by covertly refusing to carry out Kabul's more exotic requests. Five miles outside the main cities was enemy territory. I'd get asked to send the boys to the out-lying districts to 'take the temperature'. If they'd gone, the boys wouldn't have come back. There was no point in asking, they would have just refused, or not gone, or lied about going. They were brave but they weren't mad. We'd just make it up from what we had.

I didn't lie about it. I told Kabul the stuff was from the city. They used it anyway. It was all we had.

I became an expert in translating pidgin English. The boy's spoken English wasn't bad, but the writing was a language all of its own. Mind you, it was better than my Pashto. In any case, the stuff we wrote had a certain style to it: as long as you mentioned 'victory', 'glorious heroes' and 'Islamic Republic of Afghanistan' at least twice in each article, nobody seemed to really care that much.

It was simply too dangerous to do any real reporting: and it wouldn't have made copy even if it we had. 'Sada E Azadi', our newspaper, presented a relentlessly up-beat and positive picture of Afghan progress. In purely news terms, it was as realistic as reading 'The Beano'.

In any case, I didn't even have a computer I could use. Every day, I went over to the 325th, and RC-S. I wandered the corridors, introduced myself to all the usual suspects—the intelligence guys, the press affairs office, the operations people—but nothing moved on. CENTCOM refused me access. My British security clearances were not enough. Major Slaughter went to his boss, a Colonel Kaiser.

Major Slaughter met the Kaiser. The chain of command was worthy of Brecht. Nothing doing. I was still out. I filled the time by sending the boys out, and by writing general, anodyne pieces on Afghan history and culture. Nothing, though, was rocking the world.

I tried helping the 325th with their product. Their job was supporting the operational troops on the ground, and they saw their role as very much military in orientation. They would produce thousands of flyers, which would be released from a helicopter, fluttering across the Afghan landscape, in advance of coalition troops mounting cordon and sweep operations.

The campaign leaflets were all very 'Apocalypse Now': 'American soldiers are coming to protect you. Stay in your homes until it is safe to come out.'

Wording, which I pointed out, was something of a contradiction in terms in itself. Americans were coming to save them, but it was too dangerous to go out when they were there?

I was lone voice in the wilderness. The 325th just loved that stuff, as did Kaiser, who was one of those 'hoo-rah' warriors.

Actually, 'hoo-rah' is what the marines say. The army say; 'hoo-ah'. The army liked to be different from marines. They all said it in a kind of church call-and-response yell to any verbal instruction. 'Hoo-ah' or 'rah' actually meant something. 'Hoo-ah' is a TLA for 'heard, understood, acknowledged'.

Conversations with American military were peppered with these frat-boy jock aphorisms. It was almost a form of communal re-assurance: 'Airborne!' 'All the way!' 'Hoo-ah!' Drove you nuts after a while. It was just so damn repetitive: and meant nothing, beyond a mutual slap on the back.

Marines said 'hoo-rah', so everybody would know they were not low-life dirty army. Marines washed every now and again. The air force did something else, another derivation of HUA, which I can't remember now. In any case, the whole male mating nonsense makes me nearly lose the will to live.

'Hoo-ah' became more than a verb. It was a state of mind. To be 'hoo-ah' meant a jock who got the system, led from the front and played by the rules. The kind of guy who didn't drop the soap in the shower and would chug a beer while he repaired your car: the sort of man that made America. Kaiser was 'hoo-ah' 82nd Airborne, right down to the parachute silk that he hung from the ceiling of his office.

Which meant that the 325th would produce tons of posters with pictures of big, tall John Wayne paratroopers with gleamingly white teeth and immaculately ironed uniforms coming to save Afghanistan. Just as long as the folks who lived there stayed inside until it was safe to open the door.

The 325th did their creative business via a 'murder board'. Which was, of itself, in the context of an artistic and journalistic decision in the midst of the madness of war, something of an unfortunate co-incidence of term.

Each tasking would elicit three or four drafts, which would then be voted on by the headquarters staff in the 'murder board'. Kaiser would chair, as each draft would pop up on a PowerPoint. The ones with loads of guns and big American flags would raise the rafters: 'hu-ah!' 'airborne!' and the odd whistling of Wagner's 'Ride of the Valkyries'. Everybody knew 'Apocalypse Now' inside out. There would be lots of back-slapping and 'go USA!' chants for the ones with sufficient military pep. Mostly the ones with lots of guns and helicopters and sexy army stuff.

The boys had a brief to illustrate that Americans were going home and Afghans were taking over.

An early effort showed seven soldiers in a row. On the right, reading in the Islamic way, was a fully-equipped ISAF soldier. All radio antenna, phallic rifle, body armour, cool camouflage, Marlboro man type of hero. Moving left, the next five changed out a piece of equipment: different helmet, different rifle, and so on. Until the figure on the left was an Afghan soldier: with no radio, no body armour, ratty boots, darker skin and an old AK-47.

Kaiser got very excited: 'airborne!' 'hu-ah!' The crowd joined in, with much high-fiving and general exultation.

I didn't get it. All I saw was a poster with seven soldiers. I posed the question: how could a poster of seven soldiers mean that the war is over? Which was met with much rolling of the eyes. Dumb female: how could she not get it? They pointed out sequentially the bits of gear that changed: the ammunition pouches, the helmet, the gun.

I still didn't get it: whatever way I looked at it, it was still just seven soldiers with guns, all standing in a row. They didn't even smile, for goodness sake.

Kaiser told me they were soldiers. Smiling was not required. He then pointed out that the guy on the left, the Afghan soldier, was the point of the whole poster. The Afghan soldier was the way ahead.

I looked at the poster again: and pointed out that, if that was the case, how come the Afghan guy was carrying a crappy old gun and gear, while our guy was all 'Starship Troopers', 21st century gleaming with a huge 'Terminator' machine-gun? Didn't that say something about the capability of the forces the locals were being asked to rely on? In any case, to me, the subliminal message of hand-over to Afghan forces was really just more guys with guns. Regardless of uniform, the poster said there would be more fighting: seven men with guns, all in a row. Afghans had just had thirty years of that. Was this all we could promise? More of the same?

I was suddenly about as welcome as a fart under a newly-wed's duvet.

One of the illustrators, a relatively sensitive corporal called Tod, offered to buy me a coffee. We went outside as the crescendo of 'airborne!' raised the rafters.

'Miss Abi, you gotta get with the colonel's program,' he told me. 'We're the 82nd. We're heartbreakers and name takers. We don't do hugs and cuddles.' I opened my mouth to answer him. He cut me off: 'why don't we just wait out here until the murder board is over?'

Everybody had bought into the idea that the Afghan people were our core audience. Heck, we spent billions trying to do just that. Every pamphlet ever produced by ISAF had those words in bold on page 1.

The 82nd bought into the concept: they were just incapable of seeing their delivery in any other terms than the purpose for which they had been formed: violent insertion behind enemy lines. Persuasion, in their eyes, meant just presenting a bigger hammer than the other guy had.

I'm not saying Team Kaiser wasn't dedicated or professionally motivated in executing their work: far from it. They worked sixteen hours a day, every day they were there. Kaiser and his boys were supporting the mission in the way they saw the world: through a soldier's eyes. The only perspective that was ever offered, every message, every metric, every action was predicated on a military schedule.

The trouble was the people we sought to support were not soldiers. They were just average Joes with the same aspirations, dreams and fears as the rest of us: eat, sleep, work, earn a little money to goof off, raise a family and die in your own bed. As a species love, not war, defines happiness in the human existence: unless, of course, you are a soldier.

War, and fighting, is then the profession. Beating the insurgency was the battle that would define success. Which is what we sent to Afghanistan: soldiers to fight a war, in whatever arena they were assigned to.

As a cop, the areas I patrolled that had I most trouble with were the estates that suffered from poverty, a lack of education and a lack of opportunity. The folks there felt disenfranchised. Nobody cared. Down the road, in the posh bit of my beat, people went to work, owned their homes and took pride in their community. In the estates violence thrived: because existence was all about survival. Down the road, all was peaceful. The community there had something to lose. Stability reigned, characterised by a lack of crime and violence.

Economics and education brought about opportunity and investment— intellectually, emotionally and physically—in the community. The wealthy part of my beat rejected violence because they had more to lose. They were invested in success and the maintenance of success.

ISAF didn't offer investment.

From 2006 onwards, when ISAF moved into the south, what we offered the average Afghan was just more soldiers with more guns and more fighting. After 30 years of that, we brought more of the same. The 325th just added to the woes by advertising that very fact.

Nobody on the Afghan side bought into the project. There was no ownership. We sat on our side of the fence and asked why they didn't get it. They sat on their side of the fence and said: 'enough!'

I was doing what I could to provide a different perspective. I was dealing at the wrong level. Slaughter was lower mid-level management. He took direction from above: and I didn't have the connections at that level. Connections that were certainly not going to improve if I couldn't even access a computer.

I persevered with the madness for another three weeks. Nothing changed. Kabul was getting frustrated. I knew my jacket was on a shaky nail when they suggested I move back up to the POTF in IJC and work from there. How would that have worked? I was, at least, in Kandahar, the operational area my post was supposed to cover. I'd built up a good relationship with my team on the ground. I was producing decent material, which was making publication. Albeit, I lived a hobo existence, flitting between The Boardwalk and my room, but I was in the game. Moving to Kabul would be completely non-productive.

My frustration was palpable: I was employed by NATO, the fucking organisation that was supposed to be running the war. I wasn't an attached asset, or a deployed asset. I belonged to *NATO*. The 82nd worked for NATO.

If all this harping on about badges and security clearances is wearing, let me put it in perspective: I was there to write favourable stories about NATO and ISAF, in support of the strategic aim of favourably influencing and changing Afghan perceptions and behaviours towards the strategic aim. This stuff was important.

Yet the bullshit factor had piled the turds so high, I was about as useful as a soldier in the field without a weapon. The quartermaster was refusing to pass the ammunition, just as the enemy were running through the barbed wire.

McChrystal had faced many of the same problems as I now did, where national identity trumped the collective effort. He had directed that every soldier deployed wore a badge on their uniforms, which clearly stated: ISAF, in English and Pashto.

Every American in Kandahar wore that ISAF badge. We were all supposed to be on the same team. Except, I palpably wasn't.

I went back to the S2 sergeant, with the 325th sergeant major in tow. I had another letter from the theatre security officer explaining that I wasn't a spy. My clearances were more than enough to be given computer access. I was part of ISAF and good to go. The local S2 just looked at it and said:

'This is the 82nd Airborne. You're not in the 82nd.'

I'd had enough. I just pointed at his sleeve, at his ISAF badge, and asked him:

'See that badge? What does it say?'

The S2 looked down at his ISAF badge, and looked back at me with anger in his eyes. 'I work for the president of the United States of America,' he snarled. Then he lost it, marching towards me, with his fists up:

'And if you want to fucking take this further, let's step outside, missy.'

Last time somebody had wanted to punch me, I'd been a cop. I had the training. I went into a fighting stance and stood my ground. Fuck you, dickhead.

The sergeant major could see what was coming. And none of it was good. Neither of us was backing down. He intervened and bundled me out of the door, as the S2 shouted at my back:

'Keep that civilian the fuck out of my battle-space, sergeant major.'

Well, that cut the cardboard up into little pieces for me. I'd had quite enough of the US Army in general and the 82nd Airborne in particular. I drew the line at being threatened with physical assault merely for asking questions that needed to be asked.

The 325th were apologetic, but there was nothing they could do. The 82nd big book of security spells had cast its magic. In the British army, some sensible old head would have said; 'I have a cunning plan.' The Americans didn't work like that.

I told Slaughter I wasn't putting up with this, and was considering my options for a complaint. Part of me wished I'd decked the guy, but then there would have been an investigation, and a Brit civilian would always be outgunned by an 82nd internal inquiry into one of its own.

I reckoned my best course was to leave RC-S with honour, so I packed my things and left. I'd been working from my room for three weeks. I could manage a little longer. Mind you, the future looked pretty bleak that night. I was still in my three-month probation. If I couldn't do the job, they could get rid of me with no strings attached. I was fucking angry.

That dumb-ass sergeant had actively tried to whack me, a civilian female, for no other reason than the fact that I had challenged his monolithic stupidity and his big dick airborne masculinity. That said, I needed options: fast.

Everybody else thought they did too—and ran for cover. Slaughter phoned Kabul, to tell them there had been an incident. As usual, wires got crossed.

Some major told somebody at the POTF I'd been in a fight with a soldier. Eric phoned me, thinking I'd levelled a general. I calmed him down, told him it had been handbags at dawn.

Which, in truth, was all it was: wounded pride. I threw it back at him. It wasn't my fault the security clearance thing was screwed. Eric was pretty short. He wasn't in Kandahar. It was up to me to sort it or I'd be recalled to Kabul.

Life could be tough for a contractor if you crossed the military. The safest bet for longevity was to just glide along as the grey man. Do nothing, say nothing, see nothing. The system didn't reward independent thought or action; and, without a uniform, you had no protection whatsoever.

Steffi saved me. My first day benefactor, who had sorted out my accommodation, rode to my rescue.

We lived in the same blocks, right across from each other. Most nights, we'd meet on the steps. Steffi liked a smoke, so we'd sit and shoot the shit.

Steffi is German, from Hamburg. She has a northerner's grittiness. By the time I arrived, Steffi had already put a year under her belt, with the Canucks.

Steffi ran The Boardwalk. She had more contact with Afghans than pretty much anybody else on the entire camp. She escorted the shop keepers onto camp in the morning, made sure they kept roughly on the right side of the camp regulations, and escorted them out again at the end of the day. Steffi was made for that job. She ruled with a rod of iron, but she loved her Afghans, for their humour and their schoolboy pranks.

Steffi had loved working with the Canadians. They'd worked hard and enjoyed a party too. The Boardwalk had been a place of joy then. The general had even supervised the weekly BBQ, handing out steaks and ribs to his boys. Steffi organised it all. She was the mistress of fun.

The Americans had changed everything. The Canadians would negotiate, bend a little with the wind, work as a coalition. Once the Americans arrived, everything had to be done their way and nobody else's. Steffi was forever getting into scrapes with the new authority. The American army doesn't do negotiation. Like me, she was bruised by the in-your-face aggressiveness of it all. It was just so damned unnecessary.

Steffi worked out of COMKAF, the headquarters that ran the camp. She listened to my problem and had an instant solution:

'Screw the 82nd,' she said. 'There's plenty of room in my office. Come work in COMKAF.'

She was as good as her word. Next day, I went to see her in COMKAF, the NATO headquarters. Forget all the security bullshit of RC-S.

COMKAF didn't even have a door. You just walked right in. Steffi took me to see the COMKAF S2 security people. I presented my NATO credentials. Within 20 minutes, I had IT secret clearance, a desk, a computer, e mail accounts and access to all the free coffee and sugary snacks I could handle. THIS was how the war should be run. I had found my team.

SPINNING UP THE WHEELS

COMKAF was a mongrel beast, a coat of many colours. Like the IJC in Kabul, the NATO headquarters was made up of a veritable smorgasbord of rainbow nations. Its job was to run the entirety of KAF and its 40,000 inmates, control the airfield with its 6,000 flights a week and look after the security of the base out to a distance of about 8 kilometres all round.

Unlike every other top-heavy headquarters in the place, COMKAF performed all of that multiplicity of function with a little over 100 bodies. COMKAF would have liked a lot more folks. It permanently ran at about 40% under-manning.

Kandahar airfield was NATO's big iron in the fire, the step-up for Europe to play alongside the Americans, who jealously guarded their own airfield up at Bagram. The trouble was that Kandahar was seen as a hardship posting by most of the rainbow alliance. Anybody with a choice chose to stay up in Kabul, or the north, or the west. In fact, any damn place but KAF.

KAF was dangerous. It was hot and dirty. COMKAF was hard work too. Pretty much everybody in the place did more than one job. Nope, COMKAF was not the place to glide out a quick Afghan adventure.

What made COMKAF different from everybody else on KAF was that it was run—and staffed—by the air force. Which is, of itself, a very, very different beast from the army.

Flying and maintaining a multi-million dollar fighter jet takes brains. Assaulting a foxhole with a rifle and a grenade takes brawn. The academic requirements for even the lowest air force rank are higher than the army equivalent. The service ethos is different too. In the army, it's all salute, turn to right and carry out the orders as given. Which is what you need when you are sending your boys up the hill into the face of machine gun fire. In the air force, if you gave the same order, your boys would most likely say; 'you first, boss...'

Working with the air force was just much more of a collegiate, democratic experience: and one where life could be a bit more pleasant too. A big US air force base generally has a golf course. An army base has a rifle range and an assault course.

As you may have gathered, I'm more of an air force kind of person: particularly at my advanced age of fifty. I've had quite enough of being ordered about and living in a hole in the ground, thank-you very much. So COMKAF was my kind of town. In all my time there, I never heard anybody say 'hoo-rah', or 'hoo-ha' or any kind of 'hoo' at all.

COMKAF was based in the Taliban's Last Stand, the old airport maintenance hanger, where hold out Arab fanatics had made a futile statement with their lives during the initial invasion. The Americans had dropped a large bomb on their heads in payment for their temerity. Inside, the old arches were still scarred with soot from the explosion. Built like an old vaulted bazaar, the honeycomb interior had long been sub-divided into office space by the application of much plywood and off-cuts of wood. COMKAF the headquarters looked like the interior of your grandfather's garden shed. Nobody had an outside view.

Inside was a subterranean cave network of hand-drawn signs on makeshift doors and secret corridors to equally secret cubby-holes. It was fun to just disappear down a plywood-lined rabbit hole, to find some strange person you had never met, doing some job you had never known in some office you had never visited, beavering away in the innards of the beast.

After ten years of rotations, the graffiti was stacked high, right up to the tops of the vaults themselves. Names, units, dates, events, most long forgotten, lined the walls like hieroglyphs. On the roof, the Americans had laid a wooden walkway, leading to an open deck, which had a spectacular view of the runway and the surrounding countryside. All the way out to the city, hidden behind a mountain ridge to the north. In true military fashion, the platform was called the TOD: the tactical observation deck.

We used it mostly to goof off. At nights, we'd have take-out pizza and near-beers delivered (KAF was that kind of place), and sit up there on deckchairs. While the boys smoked big stogies, we watched all the strange and secret planes we weren't supposed to look at come and go. At night, KAF was our very own Area 57; 'is it a bird, a plane or a secret thing?'

Then there were the rows of unmarked executive jets. Every general, every ambassador, every head of program had access to one. The sort of Learjets that Elvis charged around in. We'd take bets on which one had the most important passenger, the top VVIP.

In a different time and a different place, doing interesting things to interesting people in Africa, I'd flown over the jungle in my own playboy bird. My Learjet had been donated to the cause by Bon Jovi. The chairs, in hand-tooled leather, were engraved with the band names. The desks were in-laid with a map of the band's US tour dates.

I got stuck in a crack in the asshole, a town called Huambo, Angola. Two guys called Hank, with a home postal code from Langley, Virginia, taught me to play five-card stud while we waited. Huambo was hit hard by artillery and air attacks. We waited out the night with a bottle of Jack, three tumblers, a greasy billfold and a cassette of Johnny Cash at Folsom. We played as the explosions rained outside. I drew a dead man's hand, a pair of black aces and eights. The hand Wild Bill held the night he got shot by Black Jack McCall. Just as an almighty thump made us hit the deck.

Next morning, we went outside. In the concrete driveway of our hiding hole, the tail fins of a five hundred pound dumb bomb stuck up from the ground, mashed in like Road Runner's Coyote. Had it gone off, I wouldn't be writing these words. True story that.

Learjets were fun to fly in, even if you couldn't properly stand up. KAF had tons of them. We took bets on how many had witnessed the mile-high club in action.

The COMKAF building kept it real. It was a genuine Afghan construction, with a real history behind it. The bomb strike had weakened the building, to the stage that bits of the roof kept falling in. The drill when we got rocketed was to get under the nearest desk. Not because the rocket could get you: COMKAF's plaster walls were two feet thick. The bricks would absorb the power of the explosion. It was just that a direct hit was reckoned to bring down the ancient roof on top of you. The Taliban might not get us with a rocket, but the masonry certainly would.

Steffi had arranged for me to get a desk in her little part of the world. She worked in the personnel office. Part of the function of the people department of COMKAF included making folks happy, which fell under what the military called morale and welfare, or MWR. The military had to give everything an acronym, even the smiley parts.

In short, Steffi ran The Boardwalk and all the recreational facilities on camp. Want to play football? You had to go see Steffi to book the pitch. Want to use the PA system for a presentation? You had to go see Steffi to book it. She worked alongside Maria, who had welcomed me to KAF with her lovely gang of Afghan reprobates, and under the direction of the head of MWR, who was generally an American officer. These guys were career air force morale and welfare troops. The American air force was so big that it offered a specialisation in making people happy.

It seemed a pretty good way to me to spend thirty years in uniform. One of the MWR guys I met there had studied at Walt Disney's university and was in charge of the US air force's Las Vegas recreational hotel. Yep, the US air force really does have its own hotels.

Blow me down with a feather. The most glam event I ever saw in my thirty odd years hanging around the British Army was a truly pants BBQ on a beach in Cyprus. The top attraction we rustled up was a truck inner tyre that somebody hitched up to an assault boat as a high-speed float. We all got roaring drunk. The boys knocked lumps out of each other and then set fire to all the plastic chairs because we were so bored with the whole thing. Somebody stuck the airborne debacle on You Tube and we all got banned from ever going back. Now, if we had been offered Vegas. Then again, maybe not.

Nope, when the US does a thing, it really does a thing.

Steffi had tons of money to play with. The Boardwalk vendors all gave over 10% of their takings from the troops to her as a sort of happy tax on the fun. The Boardwalk made a LOT of money. By 2011, the fund had over three million dollars in it. Steffi couldn't spend it faster than the funds kept pouring in. The Boardwalk sold an awful lot of ice cream, coffee and Pakistani junk.

If you wanted some play stuff, all you had to do was write up a proposal, take it to Steffi, and she'd present it to a committee made up of representatives of all the nations on KAF. There was so much money to spend anything half-decent got funded. Everything from board games to roller discos and sun umbrellas all got paid for. And when I say roller disco, I mean mirror balls and flashing lights, plus free skates for everybody.

By 2011, there was so much money coming in that Steffi had to think of creative ways to get rid of it all. Giving free internet access to everybody on KAF helped a bit, to the tune of about a half a million, but that didn't even make a dent.

Every week, the troops would have a 'fun run', at the ungodly hour of 0500 on a Friday. The MWR fund paid for sponsored t-shirts to be printed up, made to the design of the unit that was running that week's event. These would then be sold to each runner for $20 bucks a pop, money that would then be given to a charity of the unit's choice. The MWR fund paid for the T-shirts to be printed in Dubai and flown into KAF. Tens of thousands of T-shirts were flown across thousands of miles to give to soldiers who had paid for them in the first place by buying crap on The Boardwalk. The rules were such that you couldn't just give the money to charity in the first instance—so all the creative accountancy translated into a cupboard full of daft T-shirts and a lot of expended aviation fuel. It was a mental way to money launder. KAF never made any sense, even to those of us who loved it.

The money had to be spent. At the end, the millions (and there were literally millions) that were left over were sent back to NATO HQ in Europe. Where they no doubt paid for the generals who never deployed anywhere to have a new sauna built at their fancy pants place in Belgium. No matter the madness, while we still could, we agreed it was better spent on the boys and girls who were actually in the suck, as fucked-up as the disbursement actually was.

Steffi's job meant Steffi knew everybody. I'm not talking about the top bosses and all those other movers and shakers. I mean the guys who actually ran KAF and really got business completed. In every company, there are the managing directors and the department bosses. But the folks that really get stuff done are the nice ladies who know where the extra toilet rolls are and the car park guys who keep a space by the front door for you. Steffi knew those sorts of people.

Which was how she'd sorted out a desk for me, in her office. She'd just quietly spoken to the sergeant in IT and the corporal in security and all the other munchkins that the bosses never knew the names of. She'd helped them all get stuff to make life more bearable. In turn, her kindness to me made my life—and my job—not just bearable, but practically possible.

Getting into COMKAF meant I could get hooked into the juice. Instead of

Eric making mobile phone call oblique allusions to the thing that rhymed with dick, he'd call and say he'd sent me mail on the NATO SECRET e-mail: an e mail system I finally had access to. Hoo-rah.

Christmas came with a rush. Being thousands of miles away from home, everybody put an extra effort to making it special. I had no family back home. KAF was my family. That family feeling was never closer than at Christmas.

Across KAF, the Americans built a series of wooden chapels. They were a remarkable affirmation of spirituality. Made out of the compulsory plywood, each was primitive in the extreme. The chapels were among the first structures built on the base. The main one, the Fraise chapel, was built in 2005 to commemorate US army corporal David Fraise, from New Orleans, a handsome African-American who had been killed in 2004 by a roadside bomb. He left behind a wife and a six-month old son. David was one of the first to be killed in Kandahar. He was 24 years old.

It is a fitting memory to his sacrifice that hundreds of thousands found succour in the chapel that bore his name. The church was non-denominational. It went 24/7, open all hours. Scarce was the day that I didn't visit and sit and think and give thanks. Inside, it was just another wooden shack, with a homemade cross tacked to the rafters. The windows were plastic sheet, hand-coloured with permanent marker.

The stark simplicity of it all brought God very close indeed. At Christmas, a wonderfully incongruous Christmas tree, all tinselled and fairy-lit brought a little humanity.

The Fraise had a collection of musical instruments soldiers could use, free of charge, anytime. It was a delight to go in there and hear a gospel choir rehearse, or an individual soldier picking out a Bach minuet.

The 82nd had a pretty mean jazz trio too, which would play in Echoes steakhouse every Sunday night. I'd go listen to them every week. At the end of their tour, they gave me a live CD recording of their last performance, for me to remember them by. They were lovely young men. Their replacements, 3rd Infantry Division, had a really good brass band, including a huge tuba covered with their divisional badge. They marched around camp on their Christmas, playing wonderful carols for us all.

Sergeant majors cut their soldiers a little slack at Christmas. In the midst of the stultifying mix of camouflage, you'd see the odd bright green elf hat, or a Santa beard. Strangers would wish each other 'Merry Christmas', with an earnestness that I have never found in the world. We all knew we could very easily die over there.

I spent every Christmas of my three years there in KAF itself: they remain the most profound festive events of my life. That first year, Steffi invited me to join her at a contractor's compound. Maria was going with one of the private security guys, who worked for a Canadian security company called Tundra.

They lived in a series of containers, right down at the end of the runway. On Christmas Eve, on a freezing cold night, we stood round an empty oil drum filled with burning logs, and sang carols together as F-16s took off less than 50 metres away.

It was a magical night as all of us, stuck in the ass-end of nowhere, found human comfort in just being with another soul. Sometimes, Kandahar rose above the morass to be as profound a life-affirming moment as would ever have seemed possible.

Then, suddenly, it was Maria's turn to go home. Just as you got to know somebody, they left. We'd taken to buying a hoagie and driving out to the wire in her truck to have lunch. We both appreciated the peace and quiet. We had become close. We said our tearful good-byes. She rolled up her rusty M-16 into a travelling case and got on her freedom bird. Maria was the first of hundreds I knew who briefly stopped in and then departed.

After a while, I stopped being their friend. The emotional investment became too much. KAF was my home, not a place to be endured. The long-term ones, like Steffi and me, lived on a different emotional plane. Sure, we'd exchange e-mail addresses with the military, sometimes we'd even get a note six months later, but my life there had a different rhythm. I learned to protect my spirit. The constant wrench of departing friends was too much to bear otherwise.

After my run-in with the 325th, I reckoned I'd hide out in COMKAF under the radar. I beavered away writing my articles and pressing the boys for product.

Under Terry, they'd got pretty lazy and considered producing one radio story a week to be sufficient graft for their thousands bucks a month. My grannie could have created double that—and she never worked in journalism. The boys got used to a barrage of early morning requests for product, even if their early morning telephone voice had a suspicious 'just woken' drawl timbre.

Despite my best intent, I didn't manage to be the grey man for long.

It was my fashion sense that got me back into bother. KAF was a beige-lover's paradise. In all my time there, I refused to compromise. To be a civilian female was rare enough. To be a civilian female in high heels and a variety of outlandish and vibrant high fashion statements made me a very rare peacock indeed.

Military men are a pretty old-fashioned lot: particularly over gender role separation. Women are expected to stay at home and mind the kids. And the many wives I have met are generally a pretty stoic lot. You have to be to accept the constant moves and the separation. It's almost impossible for a military wife to have a career, except one supporting their men.

On operations, the men would wistfully justify their time in the sand as one of protecting the homeland: specifically their womenfolk and children. As a very obvious female, in their environment, reminded a lot of them of home, and their own families. Many military wives have told me they are jealous of my experiences. I got to see their menfolk doing their job, as raw as it came, while they only got to stay at home.

I was forever being given keep-sakes by the soldiers: badges, coins, free coffee. There wasn't a day that went by without some car pulling up beside me containing a hopeful young man offering to give me a lift.

The vast majority of these invitations were not sexual. I am fifty. Most of the guys in KAF were just kids. I could have been their grandmother. I just reminded them of home. Afghanistan was an easy place to be lonely. Despite all the activity, very few really enjoyed being there. Speaking to me offered the soldiers a chance to be human, to talk to a female, to admit their loneliness and weakness amidst a sea of testosterone and masculine ardour.

We few civilian females were part counsellor, part Madonna. We represented an actual, live, manifestation of their fantasies. The boys all had their girlie calendars. They all cracked one off: frequently. Carrying a gun, wearing a uniform and being in a war zone only amplified their sex drive.

Winter in Kandahar is an annual lifesaver. In Kandahar winter brings the rains. In a good year, the more rain, the better. Nine months of the year, Kandahar is roastingly, ridiculously hot. Those three months of moisture are the difference between a decent crop and starvation.

In KAF, winter meant mud. The earth was so hard-packed that rain would just lie on the surface, forming a glutinous concrete that stubbornly clung to any and every surface. Large parts of the camp became swimming pools. In building KAF, nobody had considered that the base itself lay on the flood plain of the Arghandab River, the main tributary for the entire province. In places, the flooding could reach eight feet in depth.

That winter, the boys on the ground floor of the NATO blocks woke up to see their belongings floating out the door. The whole place flooded, under a foot of water. We spent weeks walking across camp on duckboards. The place turned into Flanders Field.

On one of those horrendous, stormy KAF mornings, an American major and a French colonel had taken pity on my struggling figure, gamely plodding in the mud to my office. They had stopped to offer me a lift. When I gratefully alighted outside COMKAF, the Frenchman, a pilot, had given me a tie pin miniature of his jet: a Super Étendard. The American major, not be outdone, had whipped off his uniform ball-cap, and presented it with a great flourish.

I took to wearing the cap for fun. After all, it had been a gift from my knight protector. It quickly accumulated a veritable collection of unit badges, peace signs and other daft, but colourful accessories. The men would just give me stuff; I'd get stopped by some lonely jock and I'd acquire another badge. It kinda fit my look, and I took to wearing my cap pretty much every day.

Steffi had acquired a new boss. The last Canadians had departed and the Americans were taking over. They replaced her boss, a major, with an American lieutenant colonel.

Ask most British officers with experience of the American military and they would, if they were being honest, say that a British officer has the skills of the next most senior American officer. That situation was exacerbated in the top trump environment of Afghanistan. If a rival country appointed a general to a position, every other nation would up their game and post an office of the same rank. The place was awash with senior officers with the main administrative duty of ensuring their pencils were suitably sharpened.

Steffi and her small team of three were now under the command of an over-promoted and under-employed lieutenant colonel.

He came looking for stuff to do: and found an issue to meddle in with one look at my gift of a camouflage cap. The cap had a US major's rank badge on it amongst the other memorabilia and he didn't like it one bit. The lieutenant colonel lodged a formal complaint with his boss: a British full colonel, the deputy commander who ran all the support functions on KAF, affectionately known as 'chief, bogs and drains'.

That daft major's cap ended my self-imposed exile and propelled me into the 'A' team.

Next day, I sat at my desk, as usual, when the deputy commander, KAF, Jedi master, bogs and drains, came by to find out why a civilian female and her funny hat was causing the Americans to go into meltdown.

SEX IN THE SHITTY

Everybody was at it in KAF.

The place was an enormous fuck-fest. Think about it. Put 40,000 healthy men and women together and you're gonna get sex: in every shape, form and combination you can think of. The generals tried to tune it out, and the sergeant majors got very vexed by it. But everybody was at it, every chance they got.

As a chick, it was an easy place to be popular. Even the plainest wallflower left sitting at the end of the tea dance became Brigitte Bardot in KAF. The odds were in our favour. Out of the 40K in camp, at best there were a couple of thousand women.

Just walking across camp became an adventure in sexual politics. The girls in uniform were, to an extent, insulated by the fact they were wore unisex baggy camouflage. The few women who could wear ordinary civilian clothes were numbered in the dozens. Natural female curves on display just shook the place to its foundations. We were rare beasts indeed—and correspondingly the object of endless innuendo, overt stares and unsolicited attention.

The girls had their pick of a bill of very exotic fare. KAF was full of the sort of romantic heroes that you'd only ever read about in novels. That square-jawed, six foot commando with the physique of Michelangelo's David? They were two a penny. The place just oozed big, muscled special forces boys. They knew exactly how to take advantage of being the top of the tree.

The SF lads all had force exemption: in other words they could come and go as they pleased, with no checks on them at all. The Brit SAS lads were all pretty obvious with their long hair, beards and their garish collection of 'Mountain Hardware' macho gear.

The big unspoken KAF secret was their bar. In the midst of the draconian American regular army 'no fun allowed' rules, the Brits brought their own booze onto base; and ran a pretty raucous weekly event, to which they invited every standing and breathing female they could get their hands on.

The SF boys had a pretty active groupie section, which would run through each rotation as a milkmaid tends her herd. The blades hung around The Boardwalk, where they'd invite any likely lass over to see them in hush-hush land. They'd even send a mini-bus to go pick the girls up.

The SF bar could get pretty wild. Usually it was all contained in their compound. The fact that they had their own, separate chain of command meant they were pretty immune from the predatory KAF US military police.

Every now and then it would get out of hand. Like the time the MPs came across a drunk—and totally naked—male contractor wandering through the middle of camp. He'd been at the SF bar and pissed off one of the boys. They'd roughed him up a bit and nicked all his clothes, before turning him loose. The contractor got shipped home next day and the SF boys got a bit of a finger wagging.

The SF boys and the camp cops always had a fraught relationship. One time, the blades went off on a no-notice job. As they boarded their helo, one of them remembered a forgotten, and vital, piece of kit. With five minutes to spare, and the birds on the pad spinning up, a trooper hared across camp in his 4X4 to go get the vital equipment.

In KAF, the cops were all American: and they imposed US road rules and regulations. Which were all a bit unfathomable to the rest of us, who were given no choice but to go along. In point of fact, KAF never produced a formal highway code. But the cops were mostly national guard highway patrol officers back in the US, so they just defaulted to what they knew and made the rest of us suffer.

One of their rules was that vehicles had to come to a firm stop for three seconds at all pedestrian crossings, whether or not anybody wanted to cross or not. Most of the roads in KAF were ruler-straight, you could see people walking a mile away. Nonetheless, in the ass end of nowhere, with nothing about, wherever there was a crossing, cars had to stop for the mandated three seconds. And the cops really did take a stopwatch to measure the three seconds. Lots of friends of mine were done for stopping for less than the obligatory three-second orgasm. Three tickets would see your licence and ID badge impounded, regardless of rank. The traffic police wielded considerable power.

The SAS lad was in an understandable bit of a hurry. One junction, he didn't stop for the mandated three seconds and got pulled. In his haste, he got out of the cab of his car to protest. Which was another US-inspired no-no. In true US-police fashion, the cops jumped out, weapons pulled, and ordered the SF lad to lie down in the road, arms out, legs crossed. The SAS lad told them to fuck off, he was busy. Next thing, all three were rolling around on the ground. Result? The cops jailed the SF lad.

The quick reaction team on the pan sat and waited, and sat and waited. Their mission got scrubbed because the US highway patrol refused to release their prize from custody. KAF could be crazy-land sometimes.

But the SAS were the rock gods of the place and they knew it. No camp authority could change the nights out. A couple of my BFFs had a succession of sexual adventures that will give them bragging rights for years to come.

My favourite special forces team was the French outfit. They knew how to party. Their compound had a bar with a stage and a pole. The boys would get filled up on the 'special punch', strip off and just go for it. You'd walk in and two naked men would be simulating gay sex on stage, with a hundred others, all stripped to the waist, eagerly cheering them on. My finest moment came when I got fed up with the constant Euro-disco thrash. I persuaded them to stick on my '70's iPod mix. A hundred half-naked, very ripped jocks and me all went mad to 'YMCA'. Arm actions and all.

Soldiers have always been inveterate shaggers. It's one of those macho rites of passage that come with the uniform and the gun. I've travelled a bit with the army: and seen the caveman complex at first hand.

A posting to Kenya came with a long and intimately disturbing lecture from the regimental doctor on the perils of going with the local prostitutes. Graphic photographs of weeping penises, huge, disgusting genital warts and herpes underscored the stark, very real fact that 90% of the girls had AIDS. A visit to the local brothel carried a severe and terminal health warning.

My entire battalion sat stony-faced in Nanyuki as we digested the lesson. That night, I watched the officer's mess heading out the gate behind the commanding officer, as they all trooped off to the local brothel. As one company commander put it: 'might as well find out what all the fuss is about.'

The top of the KAF tree wasn't immune from the shenanigans either.

Brigadier General Jeffrey Sinclair, decorated paratrooper of the 82nd Airborne, was number two bossman in RC-S. According to a later transcript, he described his command as:

'I'm a general, I'll do whatever the fuck I want.'[17]

He didn't get to do whatever the fuck he wanted for too long, as he ended up in court.

I'd see him, cutting about KAF in his blacked-out limo. The 82nd were fond of their toys, and the generals had a convoy of SUVs, all sirens and flashing lights. The boss men had a special team of paratroopers to get them about from high-powered meeting to high-powered meeting. On KAF, everybody else had to hit the kerb as they swooped by, much like the Soviet politburo with their Zils in the reserved central lane.

Sinclair sported a ludicrous Mohawk haircut that made his thin face look even more drawn. A lot of the Yanks went for the whitewall sides, leaving just a tuft of hair up top. It was OK on the young ones. By the time you reached Sinclair's age, it was a bit sad. He'd come over to COMKAF a fair bit, with his crew of loyal supporters and note-takers in tow. One of them was a pretty young female captain that Sinclair had specifically requested for his personal staff.

His young assistant did a bit more than just take written notes. She was helping the general with some extra-curricular sporting activity that was definitely not in the rulebook.

---

[17] Transcript of trial documents, US DoD

Sinclair had been having his wicked way with her for quite some time. As his trial papers would reveal, Jeffrey Sinclair had carried out a rigorous personal campaign of conquest with five female officers. Across the States, Germany, Iraq and Afghanistan.

The top dog, Jim Huggins, knew Sinclair well. He didn't know that the guy was the kind of dirty old raincoat wearing perv who hung around parks after dark. As a military prosecutor would reveal, the locations for his alleged sexual liaisons—including charges of rape—involved sex:

'In a parking lot, in his office in Afghanistan with the door open, on an exposed balcony at a hotel and on a plane.'[18]

The guy was apparently an avid reader of porn, including soliciting photographs and videos from his female officers to help while away those stressful hours alone in Kandahar.

He'd probably have got away with his grooming of young, impressionable junior officers. Had he not had the temerity to double-down in Kandahar: with more than one supplicant getting on her knees for a forced Kandahar office Lewinsky.

His female aide got a bit upset over Jeffrey's two-timing. She'd been writing him lewd mail, offering to do whatever her master commanded. She'd then read Jeffrey's personal e-mails and realised she was just the hors d'oeuvres. Jim Huggins had been quietly sitting in his office when said captain busted in and spilled the beans. According to the scuttlebutt at the time, she'd pulled her weapon and threatened to kill herself unless something was done. I've no idea if that is true: because the whole thing was hushed up, big time and sharpish.

Jeffrey got whisked away next morning by executive jet. He got stuck on administrative duties while the army prosecution organised a case against him. It took forever. Courts martial require an officer of two ranks above the accused to preside. That would mean a general sitting in judgement of another general.

General officers are a bit like the Davos Club. Once you're in, you never speak ill of your fellows outside the circle. Convict or acquit, sitting on Sinclair's trial would be a poisoned chalice.

In the end, Sinclair was convicted: once he'd done a plea bargain. He got off with the assault and sodomy charge he faced. He pled guilty to inappropriate liaisons with two female officers, possessing pornography and conduct unbecoming an officer. He was demoted to lieutenant colonel and fined $20,000 dollars. Sinclair then retired from the army on a stipend of just over $6,000 dollars a month. If he'd done all of that in civilian life, he'd probably have got jail.

Sinclair wasn't the first general to get caught with his trousers down. Canada's top man in Kandahar, Brigadier Daniel Menard, had been sent home for the same sort of sexual shenanigans, back in 2010. He'd added to his list of woes by negligently discharging his rifle on base. Menard then retired

---

[18] Transcript of trial documents, US DoD

from the army, and came back to Afghan as head of a private security company called 'GardaWorld'. Whereupon he promptly got himself jailed by the Afghans for non-compliance of regulations. Normal jogging for the sort of character Afghanistan tended to produce.

Back in KAF, the slightest mention of Sinclair's name was met by embarrassed coughing and nervous shuffles. The army likes to think of itself as a team of warrior monks defending freedom. Like the 'Night's Watch', they 'Game of Thrones' their way to glory. Sinclair got rubbed out of history: he didn't fit the image, or the legend. Unfortunately, his kind of abuse of power was all too common.

KAF had a highly active prostitution network. If you knew where to look, it was pretty easy to find. Girls and boys, whatever took your fancy.

Out there on The Boardwalk, round the barber's shop, you'd see the same group of third country national's each evening. Nothing much would be said, but the guys and gals would quietly pair off and head to wherever they did their business. The going rate was $50 bucks a pop. The military police were oblivious to the whole racket. They weren't real cops, just soldiers. They didn't have the nose for crime. The MPs were Rottweilers on the easy stuff, like cracking down on not wearing a seatbelt: but the real crime stuff, they had no idea about.

The vice racket came to head, late 2011, when the waste disposal guys found a foetus in the trash. You read that right: some poor female, somewhere on KAF, had disposed of her unwanted, aborted child in the rubbish bin.

KAF always had a seedy side. Pretty much every contract company on KAF kept their own 'comfort girls': usually Thai or Filipino. Ostensibly there as cook or cleaner, they also bestowed extra favours when required.

The most unexpected folks were on the game. Two Kenyans, a girl and a guy, became quite good acquaintants. They served me coffee every day at the Downtown Café, a nice place that also did real fruit, sliced up in a cup. Quite the KAF treat.

They got dismissed in 2014, for serial prostitution. They'd been madam and master of a whole ring of Kenyan labourers selling themselves to the Americans. One client had picked up an STD, which he'd then passed on and had been reported for. Otherwise I doubt they would ever have been caught.

Even those supposedly in charge took part in the whole sordid game. One of the US army senior sergeant majors used to go around The Boardwalk and tell the Afghan vendors which of their female staff he'd like. The shop owners would drive the girls over to COMKAF, where they would indulge the senior warrant. The Afghans would complain, but they knew the sergeant major could have them closed down in seconds few if they refused to provide the flesh.

Whatever floated your boat could be found in KAF. The British mess hall, known everywhere as Cambridge D-FAC, was hosted by a very camp and utterly adorable Thai boy. He had better sculpted eyebrows than me, and immaculate make-up. Maria, as he liked to be known, was very much in love with a terribly tall and very butch French special forces sergeant, who adored

Maria. The two were quite inseparable until Marco had to back to *La Belle France*. Maria never got over being left behind. I'd ask him every day if he had heard from his lover. He'd just roll his eyes and moisten up. KAF was hard on all of us.

One COMKAF chum, an American major called Chris, had an absolute riot. Despite the repeal of 'don't ask, don't tell'—a hideous Clinton compromise that failed to take a stand on either side of the fence—Chris remained fully closeted. Even the US air force, the most lenient of the services, was a difficult environment to be gay. And Chris was most definitely out there. He used to come by my room to try on my shoes. The guy had a better wiggle than I did. Chris spent his weekends as a drag artiste in Vegas, in between his day job.

It could be hard to cosy up to a suitable partner in KAF. Until Chris discovered that Grindr, the gay dating app, worked rather well on the COMKAF supplied free Wi-Fi. We tried it for fun one night on The Boardwalk. Chris' mobile detector lit up like a Christmas tree. He spent the next four months learning the interior of every shower stall on camp. The MO was a late night soak, with a little soapy encounter along the way. Chris really carved up the KAF gay community. It was funny to see him getting ever more exhausted as his tour went on. The guy was getting so much sex, he was living on four hours sleep a night.

The straight team could show some troop to task dedication too: with a bit of voyeurism thrown in for good measure.

Trysting spots were hard to find on a camp as busy as KAF. Out by the wire, there was an old pond, which had once been used as a pitch and putt area in more enlightened, Euro-centric days. In amongst the reeds, a previous KAF rotation had planted a whole slew of targets, painted up as cartoon characters. Nobody had thought to take them down, and the area was left to grow fallow once the US banned good times.

It became a favourite spot for a bit of pick-up flat bed action. All through the night, a succession of troops would drive their duty SUV out to the pond, and get on down in the open back, secure in the knowledge they were apparently all alone.

What they didn't know was that the perimeter was covered by CCTV: and the pond was well and truly within range, back in the base defence centre. The entertainment unknowingly provided by some very enthusiastic and flexible participants could be enlightening. I didn't realise that the human body could bend in quite so many directions. Must be something to do with the youthful vigour of the participants.

Even in the dark mid-winter, and the middle of the KAF flood season, the screwing went on unabated.

COMKAF was blessed for a while with the presence of the Mississippi Twins. They were a pair of ghetto African-American female corporals with the foulest mouths I have ever heard. I like the odd swear word as a useful epithet: but in the midst of their otherwise impenetrable ghetto patois, the only intelligible word I ever heard them utter was 'fuck'.

They ran the printer room in COMKAF: which was closed whenever they were on duty, as they had a habit of just locking the door while they were in the office and pretending they weren't there, to avoid doing any work at all.

Their other remarkable attribute was their capacity for sexual adventure: and all callers were welcome. COMKAF had a few pool cars, which they controlled the keys to, and treated as their own personal fleet. Every night, the two of them would speed off to another front cab assignation.

In 2012, the floods hit KAF hard. The entire southern half of the camp just disappeared under a biblical deluge. The roads there were protected by four foot deep drainage ditches on either side. By late January, the ditches couldn't cope with the vast amount of water. The roads just disappeared. The whole camp was turned into a large, fetid lake of dirt-brown waters that refused to drain away. Each night, the skies would open, each morning fewer and fewer landmarks would remain, as the swirling mass dissolved anything man-made.

The swamp became an ideal hunting ground for the Mississippi Twins. Nobody in their right mind would go over there. Except, Mississippi X2 decided they would. The two of them, together with a willing male participant, headed off into the night, along KAF's main southern highway.

Unfortunately, they forgot the road took a sharp right turn.

They drove straight through the bend. Headfirst into a ditch, which was covered by six feet of water. Luckily, they managed to somehow scramble out the back window of their truck, just as it disappeared into the primordial ooze.

Next morning, the sergeant major couldn't find his vehicle. His truck had somehow disappeared—without a trace. The Mississippi Twins couldn't hide in their closed office for a bit, as they had developed a braying cough and cold that gave away their hitherto successful possum act. We knew what had been going on, but the seniors just couldn't pin it on anyone.

Two weeks later, the sergeant major was amazed to be told the back-end of his truck was now visible in southern KAF, sticking up in the air like a hippo's head in the draining floods.

CID came round and took sworn statements, particularly from the Mississippi Twins, as the custodians of the car booking ledgers. Butter wouldn't have melted. They were positively angelic in their replies. The removal of the sergeant major's wagon went down into KAF history as one of those 'unexplainable events'. Sometimes, finding out the truth was more of a problem than anybody ever needed to know about.

The Mississippi Twins went on to many more sexual successes, before they were sent home early for telling their sergeant major to go fuck himself. When they were told their early dismissal meant they wouldn't get a medal, they told him to go fuck himself all over again.

Discipline was hard to sustain when the command team were going at it like jack rabbits themselves.

One particularly earnest aide to the commanding general, a full American army colonel, was a married man with three kids and a committed Roman Catholic. On Ash Wednesday, he cut about camp with a sooty cross emblazoned on his forehead. Which was all very ostentatiously honourable:

except for the fact that he was engaged in having some very energetic sex with his own deputy. A very pretty, blonde major. Who was herself married with children.

He only got caught because of one of the frequent alerts. The quick reaction force happened to be in the HQ at the time and headed up to the roof to take up sniping positions: only to tumble out on top of said colonel and his moll frantically pulling on bits of underwear. The boys remembered enough squaddie acumen to stand to attention and stare for a bit while the bosses got it together. Wasn't the finest moment for officer-like poise and command. As one of the lads told me afterwards:

'The air force has some great tits.'

The worst moment of in flagrante delicto happened during another tiresome alert. The weakest point in the camp defences was the machine-gun post that guarded the entrance to the civilian terminal. It was the only direct action entry point to KAF that we didn't control. The Afghan police ran the control entry, so it was entirely possible that a determined team, if they got past the Afghan cops, could get onto the runway. The only thing stopping them was an American sentry post, which contained two usually very bored guards and a machine-gun.

Most of the alerts were false alarms: dogs crossing the tripwires, or kids getting in to do a little minor theft or vandalism. This night, though, the alert went on for a bit longer than usual, so the chief of staff decided to go out in his wagon and check on all the guard posts. He was good enough to let the boys know he was coming, just in case an unexpected arrival at a sentry point during an alert got him killed by accident. That night, every-one checked in, except the vital post at the airfield.

The balloon went up. Who knew what was going on? The chief of staff gathered the nearest armed troops and headed off in a couple of packed jeeps to save the day. Visions of swarthy Taliban charging across the runway were in everybody's minds. The bad guys had recently accomplished just such a raid on Camp Bastion, the main British base, and several soldiers and a lot of very expensive aircraft had been lost.

The boys all locked and loaded and crept carefully up on the sentry position. They could see one man behind the machine gun. They hailed him, but he didn't reply. He just rocked slowly from side to side. What was going on? Did the Taliban have him tied up, or were they torturing him? The relief vanguard vaulted the sandbags, weapons raised.

The machine gunner was alive, but kind of crouched over and moaning. He was behind his personal weapon though: which was being frantically fellated by his female battle buddy.

The two were engaging in close combat alright: as they did soon afterwards, in a different way, in front of the sergeant major's desk.

None of us really cared about the sex: but we all surely did about getting killed by the Taliban. We had a lot of ethical discussions about it afterwards. What price a blowjob? Our two sexual stalwarts were sent home. Without passing go, or collecting £200. On separate planes.

A lot of what went on was kinda funny. You could look into most dark corners on KAF late at night and see folks hurriedly doing up buttons and other assorted bits of clothing.

There was a darker side to KAF.

Rape was endemic on camp, both male and female. The number of sexual assaults got so bad that the US drafted in fifty extra military police, just to conduct safety patrols around the living areas. I thought we were quietly immune in the NATO blocks, as we lived slap bang in the middle of camp, in a well-lit and well-populated area. I was wrong.

In late 2012, a Thai cleaning lady was leaving one of the blocks in the early evening. She was held up at gunpoint by two Romanian soldiers and repeatedly raped: within fifteen feet of an accommodation block. The soldiers were identified two days later, after a camp wide sweep. They were sent home for discipline within the Romanian structure. KAF had no civil code of justice. The only punishment that could be exercised was within the individual national military codes. Which, of course, only worked if the individual committing the crime was military, or could even be found within the vast 40,000 camp population. For civilians, the only recourse was to put them on a plane to Dubai.

The problem of sexual assault got so serious that the two star commanding general personally headed up the weekly assault group, tasked to deal with the problem. The man in charge running the war also had to devote a considerable portion of his time to fighting an internal war on sexual attacks. The Americans barred anything that might be considered to have a sexual element. All the girlie magazines were seized and burned. Staff officers were allowed two items of family-related mementoes on their desks, nothing else. And the general in charge personally supervised the clearing of the desks.

As ever with NATO, the writ only ran as far as the US. While the American PX was cleared of magazines as innocent as women's running weekly, simply because they contained images of women in shorts, the other nations carried on regardless. In particular, the UK continued to sell 'Nuts' and all the other boy's mags that, when I was young, would have been considered to be top-shelf pornography. It drove the Americans crazy.

As much as they tried to stamp out the sex, the more it proliferated.

My neighbour, a vulnerable young female with a background of abuse, was attacked in her room by two male airmen she had invited in for tea. Naïve, perhaps, but the NATO blocks had long been co-ed. And in any case, an invitation to hot drinks does not mean invitation to rape, in anybody's language.

The Americans, who now ran pretty much everything on camp, went completely nuts. How could an accommodation block be co-ed and nobody had noticed? The NATO blocks had happily co-existed for years. A lot of civilian staff lived there, several of whom were in long-term, stable relationships. There was a discreet turning of heads to the shenanigans that went on, just as long as it was all kept discreet and consensual. We were all as appalled as the next person over the attacks.

Overnight, the blocks were cleared. Mass migration enforced a general apartheid, with locks being placed on all external doors, block monitors and night-time curfews. Overnight, the atmosphere changed to being back in 6th grade boarding school.

I knew the young girl involved quite well. She was another one of those recruits who had to choose between the trailer park and the service as a way out. She'd long complained to me, often in tears, of the openly contemptuous and misogynist attitudes in her unit. Part of her duties involved limited work along the fence-line. According to her, she and the other lone female in the group had been barred from taking part in the patrols. Their section leader believed women had no place in the military.

It is impossible to avoid this kind of attitude in the military, and was particularly prevalent in KAF. The men there could actively tune out the women, particularly, as in this case, when rank allowed them to do so. I myself went through one particularly trying rotation where the US colonel in charge forbade me from any kind of local inter-action as he believed:

'Having a female along just makes it all too complicated.'

That is an exact quote. It took an angry e-mail to the general to get that one sorted. I may have got out on patrols, but I was forever referred to as an 'ICL' afterwards:

'Ice-cold lesbian.'

Women like myself had long argued that what was needed was not more military police, or generals checking desk contents, but a wholesale education program on gender awareness and acceptance. You could put in place as many rules as you liked, but what was wrong with KAF was the pre-dominant military culture of machismo and aggression. It was the mind-set that needed re-setting, not more rules.

You could hear that misogyny in the morning PT sessions, where the instructor would refer to his class as 'ladies'. Or spur his students on by saying, 'you're running like a girl.' Simple stuff like that just fed into the psyche. Women were somehow not good enough.

Even if the girls were good enough, they were denied the chance to prove it. Although Afghanistan saw the widespread deployment of women in numbers hitherto unseen, the military still barred women from pretty much all front-line positions. Even in a war where there was no front-line, the US army still operated a complete bar on women being in the combat arms of infantry and armour. How on earth could attitudes on women be expected to match the rest of society when the gender-inspired discrimination was being perpetuated by the very organisation itself?

The Americans kept reading out their 'general order number one'. Which included in its voluminous prohibitions a requirement to avoid 'impregnating a soldier'. This order used to really annoy the shit out of the rest of us as the grown-ups amongst us reckoned we could behave as adults without the school lesson. As we weren't Americans in the first place, the whole thing was a maddening nonsense. The Americans, however, were singularly insensitive to any other opinion other than their own, so we all had to listen to it and silently count to ten. It didn't stop any of the crap happening.

One of my female friends decided to hand wash her delicate lingerie and hung it out to dry. The corporate washers ruined everything. The bleaches were too harsh for anything other than the heavy cotton uniforms the soldiers wore. Her underwear quickly disappeared. Then re-appeared the following day, covered in semen.

While most of the men behaved rationally, something in their primeval DNA was encouraged by war and the whole military circus. Women became merely amplified sexual objects for a significant minority.

Females in general were routinely described as 'bitches'. Women in uniform were known as 'combat mattresses'. Once, I verbally intervened when I overheard a group of 3rd infantry division troopers openly planning to rape one of their female colleagues. They surrounded me, while the group leader grabbed his crotch and told me what I needed was; 'a bit of Alabama cock to square you away.'

It wasn't funny. In fact, it was downright scary. They all had guns. I told the chain of command, they mounted an investigation. But, in a camp with an unsupervised population into the tens of thousands, it went nowhere. Civilian women like me were very careful where we walked at night. KAF had too many dark corners. I stuck to my block, or The Boardwalk. It was just too risky otherwise.

I sat in an MRAP, on my way into Kandahar, with a mid-ranking officer, a ranger jock. He was well regarded as a leader and as an officer. He was a big, big man, who spent his days off doing unarmed combat. Halfway into town, he leaned over me and whispered:

'I want you to know you are giving me the biggest hard-on. I want to fuck you right now.'

What could I do? What could any of us women do? A female in Kandahar quickly learned a defence mechanism. None of us were universally treated equally, fairly or respectfully. Every woman I ever met there had a story.

The situation was made worse an ever-increasing eastern European contingent. Many of these countries have a worse gender rights record than the Afghans they purported to be there to help. The worst offenders were the Georgians, who arrived in KAF in 2013. Georgia had contributed a battalion of very average soldiers, all clothed, equipped and paid for by the Americans. The Russian invasion of South Ossetia had forced a re-run of old Cold War politics, one of the fallouts of which had been a Georgian contribution to ISAF.

They had originally been deployed alongside the US Marines in Helmand. To help the troops make their stay easier, the Georgians had deployed with a platoon of 'comfort women': paid prostitutes in uniform.

The Marines quickly tired of them, not just for a lack of professionalism but for an alarming rise in theft on camp. RC-S agreed to take them on, to fill a shortage of troops to do searches on the gates. Which is a mind-numbing and very dull task. Somebody, nonetheless, had to do it.

The Georgians spent their first week in KAF cleaning out the PX. The standing joke became that if you heard the rustle of polythene bags, it was the Georgians heading back with their latest shopping. Like most of the Eastern Europeans, NATO enforced pay scales that were way in advance of what they could expect to earn back home. Indeed, the Romanians held a lottery for Afghan service: the winners got to go. Serving in Afghanistan meant a quadrupling of their salaries.

None of these nations were considered first rank, so they all got the second string tasks. The likelihood was that a posting to Afghanistan would be a relatively safe one, but a profitable one.

The women in KAF really blew the Georgian's minds. Walking around KAF went from mildly irritating stress to full-blown intimidation. The harassment got so bad, the Americans were forced to set up special training. Which made the obvious point that women were not just there for fucking. In anybody else's military, they could do a real job too. The comfort platoon got sent home.

Nobody really trusted the Georgians. The word went out that we shouldn't allow them access to our intelligence. Several of the senior ones were reputed to be KGB agents: and that tit-bit of information came from the Georgian command themselves. *Quis custodies ipsos custodiet?*

In truth, KAF was a social experiment of 40,000 human beings penned into a cage with minimal rules. The fact that most everybody in there had a gun was really the only law and order that existed. As one Australian colleague put it:

'A well-armed society is a well-behaved society.'

Not that having a gun could save you. In 2012, a bunch of US army jocks were playing around in one of the mess halls. One of them took his pistol out and started waving it about. Somehow, he forgot he had one up the chamber and he let loose a round. A contractor, sitting on the other side of the room, was shot in the leg. In the stunned silence, the shooter stood up and walked out: as the contractor bled out on the floor. Officers in the room identified the area the round had come from. Not one soldier there came forward and identified the shooter, and he never turned himself in. The contractor lost a chunk of his leg and will walk with a cane for the rest of his life. Nobody was ever caught or held responsible for it.

To the end, the lack of any real police force, or governance, or justice system, created a 'Lord of the Flies' mentality that was never very far from the surface. KAF could be a very nasty place, if you just scratched the surface.

Me? Well, I kept myself to myself. I had a couple of minor trysts. I wasn't in the army. It was more a way to fill in the long, long periods of boredom than anything serious. Discretion was the name of the game. You try being a nun for three years. Nothing past second base, though. The war kept getting the way.

After one romantic night, my companion *de jour* walked me back to my block. Just as our lips met for a first romantic kiss, two rockets flew right over our heads, no more than fifty feet above us, exploding a mere couple of hundred yards away. Survival was always more important.

Absolutely true story, that. Promise.

BECOMING LORD ROBERTS' VALET

I had only been in my wee cubby-hole in COMKAF for a week or so, so I was rather flustered by the sudden appearance of a British full colonel intent on checking up on my dress sense and my crazy American ball cap of badges. I sensed danger in his visit, but the fact that he was a Brit was a blessed opportunity. I was pretty cautious about not creating any more waves, after my 82nd debacle. So I suppose my mad answer to him makes sense in that light.

'Why are you wearing an American major's rank?' He asked. To which I replied, 'I am Lord Roberts' valet.'

You, like me writing this, are suddenly wondering for my sanity at that moment.

As it happens, I've been a life-long Beatles fan. At that particular moment, I was waist-deep into a highly entertaining, if rather prurient, biography of John Lennon. During those crazy, hazy, hippy days of the mad sixties, London's glitterati all got their wacky military-influenced 'Sergeant Pepper' togs from a second hand army surplus joint called, 'I was Lord Kitchener's Valet'. Think Jimi Hendrix' cavalry jacket from the Isle of Wight festival and you have classic lord Kitchener's gear. The place was pretty legendary back in the day.

Lord Kitchener was the British army's top dog at the turn of the 20th century. It's his face that you see on the classic 'your country needs you' WW1 recruitment poster: an image that was itself the inspiration for the post-ironic Pepper handlebar moustaches and appropriation of military gear. Kitchener's great rival in the army of the day was Lord Roberts, who, you will recall was the hero of the Kandahar campaign in 1879.

With an over-active imagination and a knack for putting together truly inconsequential and boring detail, I thought I had come up with a pretty funny line: fashion-forward, retro, with a little Afghan tilt. Not to mention quite clever: I was Lord Roberts' valet.

My colonel merely looked completely confused and concerned for my sanity. I launched into a long and rather meandering explanation of who Roberts was, who the Beatles were and how rock stars dressed in the sixties. Heady stuff for a slow Monday in COMKAF, I am sure you will agree.

'Highly interesting,' he replied, before adding: 'fashion history notwithstanding, will you be a good sport and just take it off?'

Since a disastrous stint at boarding school, where I absolutely smashed the corporal punishment record for insubordination, I've not been awfully good at doing as I was told. We compromised on retaining the hat, and taking off the rank badge. A badge which I had never really liked anyway. My interrogator seemed amused, so he followed up with:

'And who are you and why are you in my headquarters?'

There followed a long discussion on CJPOTF and my part in its downfall. At the end of which the colonel said:

'You seem much too important to be a valet to anybody. I shall call you Lady Beaver.'

Which was a little forward, but also rather funny. Amidst a sea of American po-faced seriousness, British humour at the nonsense of it all struck a chord with both of us.

As it turned out, COMKAF had a shortage of folks to do information operations. It was the baby brother of headquarters, in a camp full of headquarters. So what I was peddling was suddenly and urgently taken up. We quickly came to an informal contract: COMKAF would support me, my hat and my lifestyle: and in return I'd wire them Afghanistan.

Over the next three years, I would become the go-to gal for pretty much anything to do with life outside of the wire. My boys, out there gathering the news, were to become my eyes and ears onto the world. Everything inside the camp was geared to inside the wire. Yet, as much as we tried to make the place just like home, so Afghanistan kept knocking on the door. Not least by the fact that they were rocketing us pretty much every bloody day.

COMKAF had nobody who was wired into the rhythm of Afghan life. The national holidays, the religious events, how to conduct meetings, Afghan style, the news, the personalities, the significance of tribal culture, who was who, how they inter-acted, the family rivalries. All of it, really, the zeitgeist of Kandahar. I built a unique role for myself, which took years to fully develop, but which, by the end, was a kind of walking one-woman Wikipedia. By the end, I could even tell you why buildings in camp were constructed and when. My official job for CJPOTF became almost part-time labour. But the work I did do for them was immensely enriched by the relationships I cultivated in my other role as COMKAF social secretary and chief gossip collector.

I couldn't have made it happen had I been in uniform. As a civilian, I could talk with impunity to pretty much everybody. Within the wire, nobody felt threatened by me. I had no rank to get in the way. Over time, the Afghans would come to welcome me first: as I became the only face in an ever-changing litany of ISAF advisors that never changed.

As one Afghan general came to tell a visiting US senator: 'Abi is family to us.'

BALES

Robert Bales came into this world on June 30th, 1973. He is the youngest of five brothers. He grew up in a suburb of Cincinnati, Ohio. He attended Norwood High School, where he captained the football team. After graduation, he went on to study economics at the University of Ohio. He worked as a stockbroker for several large financial brokerages. He married and sired two children. On the face of it, a normal life of aspiration and growth.

Just after the 9/11 tragedy, like tens of thousands of other Americans, he enlisted in the US army. He joined the infantry, the tip of the spear. Bales would serve three long tours in Iraq, where he earned the respect of his fellow soldiers for his selfless leadership. He was promoted to staff sergeant. In early 2012, Bales was sent to Afghanistan. As a decorated, trusted and experienced leader, Bales was posted to Panjwai district, Kandahar. He would lead a small team of infanteers protecting special forces troops.

On the night of March 11th, 2012, Robert Bales walked out of his base and shot dead sixteen Afghan civilians. He wounded six others. He went to their homes, kicked in their doors and opened fire. He killed nine children, as young as two, by walking up to them while they slept and shooting them point-blank between the eyes. He then stacked the bodies and set fire to them. He didn't kill his victims in one spree. He killed four, went back to his base for a break, then went out and killed another twelve. Nobody seemed to either see him or hear any of the shots.

Bales then put his weapons down and handed himself in to his colleagues, simply saying:

'Sorry for letting you down, boys.'[19]

I was woken early on the morning of the 11th by an urgent call from Kabul. Confused reports had hit the IJC on what exactly had gone down. What did I have? I called Feroz, who was also up early. Kandahar Governor Toryalai

---

[19] Courts martial transcript, US DoD

Wesa had personally asked for the press to come to the governor's palace. Feroz and his fellow journalists were on their way with the governor to Panjwai.

I went over to COMKAF. The first dribbles of senior commanders were opening up their offices. Nobody knew anything. One US colonel refused to accept my news could be real:

'Americans don't shoot unarmed civilians,' he told me.

Feroz called me back at about ten in the morning. He was in Najiban village, looking at the partly burned bodies of four girls, aged between two and six, and the bodies of several slightly older boys. All of them had been shot between the eyes. They were stacked like cordwood.

Afghans are not sensitive over death. Feroz took pictures of all their faces, their tiny bodies still clad in the clothes they had been wearing their last night alive. The elders of the village were in shock. Zangabad had seen a lot of death, but the burning of the bodies was the greatest crime any of them had seen. In Islam, a body must be cleansed before burial. By burning the bodies, Bales had denied them even that right.

Bales had not just committed mass murder, he had committed a religious hate crime.

As I listened to Feroz' voice crack with emotion, in the background I heard the first shots ring out. Governor Wesa's writ had little influence in Panjwai. He represented authority. Authority that had colluded with the Americans: an America that had killed Afghan children. A full-scale gun battle had broken out.

Feroz sprinted for his car, as the governor's convoy sped off in a cloud of dust. One of the governor's bodyguards was wounded in the brisk fusillade that followed the retreating vehicles. In any case, the cause of the whole tragic event, Robert Bales, had already been secreted away, back to KAF.

Wesa's convoy headed straight for KAF.

Two months earlier, a rogue Afghan soldier had killed four French soldiers, and wounded another sixteen, in a rogue incident. The Afghans had been shocked, and French premiere Nicolas Sarkozy had flatly stated his troops were not going to stay in Afghanistan to be shot at by their own allies. The Afghans had arrested the shooter, Abdul Sabor, and imprisoned him. In July, 2012, he would be sentenced to death by hanging.

Wesa's opinion was simple: Bales should be arrested and imprisoned too. He had committed the same, if not a more heinous, murder, on Afghan soil.

He reckoned without the military technical agreement, which President Karzai had signed in 2003:

'The ISAF and supporting personnel, including associated liaison personnel, will under all circumstances and at all times be subject to the exclusive jurisdiction of their respective national elements in respect of any criminal or disciplinary offences which may be committed by them on the territory of Afghanistan... The ISAF and supporting personnel, including associated liaison personnel, will be immune from personal arrest

or detention.'[20]

When Wesa got to KAF, he was barred from entering. What followed was the stand-off at the OK Corral. Wesa and his bodyguards demanded Bales be handed over to him. The Americans were equally adamant that wasn't going to happen. Weapons were drawn and it all looked rather serious. Inside KAF, we went to escalated threat levels. Bales was quietly flown out to the US. Eighteen months later, he pled guilty to sixteen counts of murder and six counts of assault and attempted murder.

The presiding judge, Colonel Jeffery Nance, asked him:
'What was your reason for killing them?
Bales replied:
'There's not a good reason in this world for why I did the horrible things I did.'[21]

He stated he could not remember many of the details of what he had done that night, including setting the bodies of his victims on fire. He did not deny the evidence that he must have done so. Bales never faced trial. After a series of pre-trial hearings held in secret, he entered a guilty plea, avoiding the death penalty. Bales was sentenced to incarceration for life without parole. As he was prosecuted under the Uniform Code for Military Justice, a general may still reduce the sentence to life with the possibility of parole.

The families of his Afghan victims wanted, indeed expected, the death sentence.

That terrible morning of the shooting, Feroz sent me photos of the dead. The wounds were horrific. I have seen innumerable dead bodies. I have seen innumerable wounds and injuries. This was different. I can still see, to this day, the mutilated faces of those children.

Local Afghans insist that Bales killed more than sixteen. They also say that more than one soldier was involved. As ever with Afghanistan, the true facts, beyond Bale's own admissions, remain murky and impossible to verify. What is true is that Bales was a psychiatric case waiting to explode. He had enlisted in the army after a failed financial career. He and his erstwhile business partner owed $1.4 million in punitive damages to their clients. By the time he came to Panjwai, he had already completed three tours in Iraq. In Afghanistan, he reportedly got drunk regularly and was abusing anabolic steroids. His troops openly talked of his volcanic temper and his aggressively negative opinion of Afghans. Yet nobody saw it coming.

Bales is a product of the war. In ordinary times, his financial meltdown would have been picked up before he signed on. In ordinary times, his behaviour once recruited would have been more rigorously examined. In ordinary times, he would not have been asked to serve four almost back-to-back tours. Bales is a damaged human being. The war caused many such Bales figures to be sent to fight for democracy.

---

[20] Section 1, MTA agreement

[21] Trial transcript, US DoD

In 2010, twelve soldiers from the US 2nd Infantry Division, stationed in Kandahar, were convicted of involvement in the deliberate murder of three Afghans: and then collecting their body parts as souvenirs. They were not alone.

The crimes of a US special forces team in Wardak, which are still under investigation, caused so much Afghan upset that President Karzai himself barred US troops from operating in the province. By the second decade of war, the American army was exhausted. Combat is a gradual attrition of the soul. Every human soul has their breaking point.

In Bales case, the bar was too low to begin with. Yet, as one of Bales' own junior soldiers said at his trial; *'nobody was that crazy.'*[22]

In truth, justice in a war zone is a variable feast, dependent on circumstance and chance. What will happen to Bales?

In March 1971, Lieutenant William Calley, of the US 23rd infantry Division, was found guilty of the pre-meditated murder of 22 Vietnamese civilians. He too was sentenced to life imprisonment. President Nixon went on to pardon him. Calley is today a free man, and has been for over forty years.

In an America that lauds its military and which overwhelmingly views the Afghan conflict as unwinnable, will Bales be quietly set free too?

In Panjwai, the Americans paid $50,000 compensation for each person killed, along with roughly $10,000 for each wounded. Eleven of the dead came from one family. In a country where the median wage is less than $1,000 a year, mass murder made the father of the eleven, Abdul Samad, rich beyond an Afghan's wildest dreams. So much so that he was forced to move. Neighbourhood jealousy made it impossible for him to stay.

Samad came from Panjwai. He had originally moved away because of the war, but returned to Panjwai because he believed the American's message that they would protect him. After the massacre, President Karzai phoned him. Samad told him:

'Either finish us or get rid of the Americans.'[23]

There was comparatively little unrest in Afghanistan over Bales' crimes. The Taliban came from Zangabad. The country was so traumatised by decades of warfare that the over-whelming impression was one of; 'you did it to us, now you know what murder feels like.'

A month later, American soldiers in Bagram sent up to a hundred copies of the holy Quran and other religious texts to be burned. The books had been boxed for disposal from the Parwan detention facility, where the Americans incarcerated thousands of suspect Afghans. The Americans believed the books were being passed amongst the prisoners containing concealed messages.

Whatever the reasoning, Islam, as with any religion, has very prescribed procedures for the disposal of holy and venerated text. American processes

---

[22] Trial transcript, US DoD

[23] As told to my journalists

belied a deep ignorance and an implied disregard and disdain of Afghan cultural and religious beliefs. When the news of the book burning broke, national rioting took place. Americans were killed. Two were shot by a member of the Afghan security forces. Seventeen Afghans were killed, over fifty wounded. ISAF bases across the country were besieged.

General John Allen, ISAF commander, was forced to intervene directly. The commander of a supposedly disciplined and organized army had to directly plead with each and every one of those soldiers sent there to defend freedom. He sent a personal letter to each and every soldier and contractor, including me:

'Now is not the time for revenge for the deaths of two US soldiers killed in Thursday's riots.... resist whatever urge (you) might have to strike back.'

He added:

'There will be moments like this when you're searching for the meaning of this loss. There will be moments like this, when your emotions are governed by anger and a desire to strike back. Now is not the time for revenge, now is the time to look deep inside your souls, remember your mission, remember your discipline, remember who you are.'

There can be precious few moments in history where a commanding general has had to beg for clemency and appreciation of human dignity *from his own soldiers*. His letter was a tacit admission—from the very top—that the discipline of his troops, supposedly the best in the world, could no longer be taken for granted. Allen was a sensitive commander. The words he used belied his own real fears of a bloodbath.

Allen ordered that each and every one of us undergo cultural training seminars on Afghan culture, ethics and Islamic tradition. Ten years after we had invaded, our soldiers were massacring Afghan children, burning Qurans and our most senior generals reduced to imploring our soldiers not to kill anybody else.

War, regardless of reason or execution, must have a moral baseline. In Afghanistan too many lost their compass.

ROAD TO NOWHERE

Whuuump!

It's the displacement of air that causes the atmosphere to shake. Close enough, it's like being thrown deep underwater, really, really quickly. Suddenly, you feel the over-pressure just rip the air from your lungs, as your chest wall compresses.

The windows blew in with the crash. I'd got used to the daily rocket attacks, and the pre-arranged detonation of expired explosives. This was different. The air moved differently, like a solid wall. As the wooden window covers came in, so a ton of dust came down in a cloud from the roof, plus a couple of bricks. The TLS was made of stern stuff, but this explosion was bloody close—and bloody big.

The siren started to warble; 'ground attack... ground attack...' Fuck me. This is for real. Bad guys in the wire. Custer time.

The military all dived for their weapons, to lock and load. The clerk in my office—a 19 year-old female air force corporal—went extremely white and promptly dropped her M-16. The magazine fell off and bullets rolled about the floor. Bloody hell. I stood an immediate chance of having some new recruit shoot me by accident.

I dived for my body armour. Or would have done, if the armour hadn't been in my room, not in my office. Double fuck.

I was surrounded by kids with suddenly very lethal weapons. One itchy trigger away from being slotted by my own side and I was a mere powerless observer without the succour of a half inch of Kevlar.

There was suddenly a lot of yelling and shouting, marked by panicking officers and soldiers all screaming at each other. None of them had patently ever been in a situation like this before. And COMKAF didn't even have a front door you could lock.

I was desperately aware that these kids could be a lot more dangerous than any Taliban. It wasn't as if I could make a break for it. The standard operating procedure was to stay put, if you were in a 'hardened' building like

COMKAF. Any movement outside while the sirens were going was a marker for a possible enemy.

Nope, nothing for it but to sit tight and make sure I stayed well away from the muzzle direction of our young clerk's rifle. She was now very engaged in trying to do up her helmet strap with shaking fingers.

The word gradually filtered down, in fragments and passing comments from harassed staff officers. A massive car bomb had detonated amongst a group of civilian fuel tankers, waiting at the main gate. The follow-on had been a couple of Taliban on motorcycles, who were engaged in a firefight with the local police. None of the bad boys had thus far got past the main gate, but there was obviously a real threat that this attack, as large as it was, was merely a distraction as a pre-cursor to another attack elsewhere on the massively long perimeter.

Every compound had to be searched before an all-clear could be sounded. So we all just sat there and waited. And waited. And waited. Our young clerk got told to go wait in the inner office as she jumped up with her rifle pointing every time anybody came over the office threshold. Some folks could deal with KAF, and some, no matter what their service and training, just found it all too much.

My guy Feroz, madman that he was, was actually not far from KAF, doing another story for me. When he heard the 'c-rummp", he immediately beetled over to see what all the fuzz was about, and started taking photos for me, which he e-mailed via his phone.

I went round to the ops room, called the J-DOC, the joint defence operations centre, where all the brass had convened. All was actually quite calm in there, nobody shouting, but a lot of speculative information was flying around: tower two had seen three men with long, dark packages in their hands moving towards the gate, that sort of thing.

All uncorroborated and fragmentary, but it was obvious that an awful lot of folks had an awful lot of loaded guns and all it would take was one wrong call and the place would be lit up like the 4th of July.

I did my helium hand bit, raising my arm, coughing gently and saying, 'excuse me? I may be able to help...' Cue lots of big men looking quizzically at the female civilian and her phone—neither of which, in normal times, would have been in there.

'I have some near live photos of the scene that I may be able to share with you.'

Cue lots more silence, followed by:

'Ma'am, who are you? And who said you could be in here?'

Quick explanations followed, including minute examination of my legendary pass, which, having a red border, did actually allow me bragging rights to be in there. Then a voice cut through the fog, which carried more authority than the rest:

'Take a look at her intel, captain. We have the time now to use every source.'

The voice belonged to a man with a single star on the front of his uniform.

The general. Around COMKAF, the top dog in the whole show: Brigadier General Scott Dennis, US Air Force.

Scott Dennis is a fighter pilot. He's happily retired now, but, along with making the rank of general, he also has nearly 4,000 hours on an F-16. Which isn't chump change. He isn't the tallest guy in the world, in common with a lot of fighter pilots, but, boy, do you know when he is in a room. We more or less arrived at KAF at the same time. He'd gone to the top of the pile, while I'd been kicking around at the bottom.

Scott was to become my friend. I liked and admired him in equal measure. We had quite a few laughs; but that first day, he was, rightly, all business. People's lives were at stake. And the US military is extremely good at putting the mission first.

Having Feroz on the ground was invaluable. Scott had buttoned all the ISAF assets up, holding in place, until we knew what was going on. Outside, where the explosion happened, was chaos.

From COMKAF, we could see the roiling clouds of black smoke from the gasoline fires. The gate was only just down the road. There were crowds of Afghans running all over. Feroz, my charming, madly brave brother, had gone straight into the middle of it all.

I called and got him to start sending photos of the scene. There wasn't enough bandwidth for video, but it was the only source we had in our bunker of what was going on on the ground. The military kept trying to grab my phone, but I was insistent. Feroz was my asset. Ask me, and I'll task him.

Scott just smiled and let his team do their work. He knew exactly what was going on, but he was a good leader. He had troops that were highly trained, enthusiastic and experienced. Let them do the work, and fine-tune it at the key moments.

The attack was a solo effort. A few hours later, we got stood down. The damage to the camp was non-existent. Outside, some tankers had been wrecked, seven innocent Afghans had been killed and a couple of police officers had been wounded. At least, that was the figure that was released later. In Afghanistan, there was no crime scene investigation. The dead just got shovelled up and the next day, life just went on. The Afghans had seen too much death, and nobody had the expertise, or was willing to take the risk, to properly check anyhow.

The funny thing about suicide bombers is the head. When the vest goes, and the rest of the body eviscerates, something about the physics of the explosion shoots the head right up like a football. It can fly for hundreds of metres. You think you've got all the body bits left over and some woman down the road will come by days later with a head she found in her compound when she'd been putting out her washing.

At the end, as I was leaving, I saw Scott turn to Deputy Commander Bogs and Drains, my hat inquisitor, and ask who I was. I knew I'd done the right thing that day. Scott wanted to know more. Good for me, I thought, but along with the attention would come more work. That mission first thing again. If you offered something useful, the Americans were ruthless at exploiting it.

We'd been extremely lucky. The main fuel tanks for the camp were right next to the site of the explosion, separated by a mere wire fence and a couple of hundred metres of scrub. The fuel bladders had been there for years. They are designed to be a short-term option for an expeditionary stance. Literally huge rubber bags, much like a balloon, that were laid in half-excavated trenches and hooked together with a hose system.

The bags should have been replaced years ago with a hardened structure. But, as with so much in the chaos of KAF, the build had slipped through the rotation cracks. The sunlight had really got to the integrity of the bladders and they were notorious for their constant leaks. One small explosion and the whole lot, tens of thousands of gallons, would have gone up. Nobody had thought to put in a fire-suppression system.

Right after the gate incident, we took a volley of in-coming rockets. One actually hit right on the bladders, but didn't explode. Man, we all counted our lucky rabbit's feet that day.

Then we all had an 'oh, shit' moment, as the realisation of just how exposed KAF really was hit home.

After the bomb, there was a big push to start putting the house in order. KAF sits on a totally flat plain, so it would have been theoretically possible to just drive cross-country, crash the gate, or the wire, and just keep on hammering right into the middle of the base. It was the nightmare scenario for the generals—a suicide attack, right in the middle of the camp.

In truth, once you got past the outer fence there was nothing to stop you. All the roads were built for interior communication: pretty much ruler-straight, with no obstacles. Nobody had even thought about putting in a chicane, or even a pole across the key road junctions.

Which is why one bright spark had come up with the idea of building a moat and a berm, right around the base. Julius Caesar would have approved. There's little that's new in the world of military engineering.

The trouble was that, while NATO had sort of squatter's rights on the base itself, outside the wire, the Afghans were very definitely quite engaged as to who owned what. Several of the big local families all had entrenched interests—and, as I was to experience myself, quite a bit of cash invested. Being next to KAF meant the chance to inter-act with Westerners. Westerners were where the money was at. We were worth hanging with.

With some annoyance, our Afghan friends found out that we were going to built a berm right along the southern perimeter, without so much as an ask from us. The plan wasn't just for a berm. Our construction would have a tarmacked road on top of it, to help our outer patrols get around.

We did a pretty good job of hiding the real purpose of the berm by building that black top. But we all knew what it was there for. The berm would be built on the side where all the fuel blivets lived. The big rubber tanks that held hundreds of thousands of litres of highly flammable jet fuel, diesel and petrol. If they went up, it'd make one hell of a bang. The berm was there to help stop that happening.

The Afghans, specifically the aviation authority and the governor's offices were, understandably, pretty pissed about it all. Not pissed enough to try and stop the development, though. After all, roads were roads, but pissed enough to moan that they had not been consulted.

When KAF had been put together, the civilian air terminal had had an access road that ran along the length of the runway. As the camp had expanded, NATO had just blocked off the road and used it as an interior access. If you came along Highway 4 and tried to turn into the airport, it meant a near cross-country deviation just to catch a flight. Which was yet another example of us not really caring what the Afghans had to put up with. The new road we were building would parallel the old road.

Something obviously had to be done, so COMKAF came up with the compromise that we'd advertise the new road as a 'gift' to Afghanistan to right a previous wrong, with a spur running off to the civil terminal. The whole shebang, about two and a quarter miles long, could be opened by an Afghan delegation as new access way: face-saver all round.

We finished the construction pretty quickly. ISAF was good at that sort of project. The problem came with how to hand it all over. Nobody had a clue how to make it happen. Connections between COMKAF and the Afghan community were, unbelievably, pretty rudimentary. We knew some of the security chiefs, but we had zip connection to the civil government.

Chris, a young Australian air force officer newly attached to the HQ on his first overseas tour, suddenly found himself nominated 'Head of Visits and Protocol'. The general told him to come see me, as the HQ's newly anointed Afghan expert, and so I suddenly found myself roped in for an assist.

I helped Chris with the right invites, by reaching out to my guys in Kandahar. Between us, we managed to rope together the governor and the local district chiefs. The governor, Toryalai Wesa, then reached out to Kabul. Road-building was pretty important stuff in Kandahar. Particularly when that road had been directly built by us. It meant it had been built properly.

Next thing I knew, Feroz let me know that the president's office was sending down a special advisor and a government minister. What had been planned as a low-level grip and grin was suddenly becoming a whole other ballgame.

Chris did what any protocol officer would do. He planned for a full-on VIP engagement, with all the bells and whistles. On the day, he'd arranged for row upon row of fold-up chairs, a speaking platform, flags, a refreshment table, the lot. We planned to set up on the new tarmac, right outside the civilian terminal. I helped him translate a welcome packet and a formal agenda, translated into Dari and Pashto, for everybody. All emblazoned with Afghan, US and NATO flags. We rehearsed the lot: and I got called in to meet the general directly for the first time.

I knew where Brigadier General Scott Dennis lived. His office was the one next to all the flags, same as every other general. Apart from the banners, though, he lived in the same dust-filled cubby-hole the rest of us endured. There was nothing fancy about COMKAF.

Like all US senior ranked fighter pilots, Scott still flew. Twice a week, he'd light up his F-16 and shoot off down the runway in a blaze of flame and unspoken intent. Like a lot of fighter pilots, he has a kind of stocky 'don't fuck with me' swing to his gait. More often than not, he wore his flight overalls in the office. First and foremost, Scott is a warrior.

I said a few pages back that I got to know a few generals well enough to count them as family. Scott was the first.

We didn't instantly fall for each other, though. Together with Chris, we briefed him on the up-coming visit. Scott knew this visit was important: and that the Afghans had to feel this was their road, not another ISAF hand-me-down. He quizzed us hard.

In truth, we were only moving a few hundred years outside the main gate. But, psychologically, it was 'outside the wire'. Folks got awfully nervous about crossing that line. To the stage that, by 2011, ISAF actually had different levels of clearance required to be allowed out of jail. The military had to qualify, with a ton of extra training, to get to go see Afghanistan, the country we had come to save. Nobody ever asked me to do the training. I wasn't that important. I just went outside anyhow.

We got all trussed up in our combat body armour, trauma kits, weapons and ammunition. I was supposed to be in the VIP welcoming committee, but I felt anything like welcoming, in my blue helmet, thirty pounds of Kevlar and a big bag full of bandages and tourniquets.

There had been a lot of debate about what Scott should wear. By US rules, he should have been in his helmet and armour, like the rest of us. I'd argued strongly that that was way too aggressive a stance. To an Afghan, for the American general to welcome his guests dressed in his war gear would portray fear.

Scott sided with me, and had gone for the 'bullet-catcher' option: a covert vest, which he wore under his shirt, and his baseball cap. The vest was for emergencies only. It wouldn't stop a high-velocity round, and it made him look a little chubby, but, to my mind, it was sensible compromise.

The security guys were horrified. So they upped the personal security detail. All round the podiums, there were response teams, snipers posted, MRAPs blocking off all the roads. While Scott had got away with dressing down, the word on the rest of us was clear: no armour, no go. I wasn't overly happy about it, but there were times that, with the Americans, there was no point in pushing it further.

A stern sergeant gave us the usual dire briefs, which the military call 'actions on': what do if we got shot at, rocketed or blown up. Then, off we went, out the gate, into the badlands.

Which was, unsurprisingly enough, exactly the same barren scrubland that we had on our side of the gate. Folks changed, though, the second we left that imaginary protection of our gate. This was outside, different planet time. Everybody walked a little more on their toes. Weapons were gripped a little more intently.

We walked down to the podium Chris had laboured long and hard to set up. The NATO pennant, the stars and stripes and, centremost, the Afghan flag, hung listlessly in the baking heat. The rows of metal chairs glinted in the sunlight. We worried about whether, in the heat, anybody would actually be able to sit on them.

Then we waited: and waited. Kick-off was supposed to be 1000. We'd got there at 0945. Security had been out since 0700. It hit 1030, and still nothing.

Afghans have a different clock. To them, a time and date is a moveable feast. They just march to a different drumbeat. So we just stood there in the heat—and cooked.

About 1115, like that scene where Omar Sharif appears in 'Lawrence of Arabia', we could see a dark disturbance in the miasma of heat striations, off in the distance. It was the Afghans: and they had come in their hundreds. We'd laid out chairs for about thirty, but this was a wandering caravan. All male, as is usual in public life in Afghanistan, the excitement and enthusiasm was palpable. This was truly a big deal.

In the middle of the swirling mass, a small coterie of older, better dressed men, surrounded by extremely large Afghan men, with an equally impressive array of weapons. They all carried assault rifles, with grenade launchers attached. We had some serious firepower out on the ground too. The event had become a gunfighter's convention.

Chris' carefully laid-out chairs just got swept aside in the rush. The crowd just pushed them aside. A crew of flunkies at the back carried a couple of large poles and a long green ribbon, emblazoned with lots of plastic flowers. There was a bloke with a tray of sweets. Whatever plans we had had for a polite western-style handover were obviously not on the Afghan agenda.

Right in front of our reception area, the flunkies strung the ribbon right across the road, between the poles. The group of older men lined up, side by side, behind it, while a really buzzed bunch of assistants, journalists, aides and bodyguards all chattered excitedly.

Scott took his cue and found a spot right at the end of the line of VIPs. I knew most of them by their photograph: Governor Wesa, Major General Sherzai, Major General Hamid and Habibullah Faizi, the manager of the civilian airport. Alongside them, the minister for aviation, Daoud Najafi, and a presidential special advisor, Yousef Pashtun.

Minister Najafi is a brave man. The first post-Taliban aviation minister, Abdul Rahman, had been murdered at Kabul airport in 2002. A mob had literally dragged him off his official aircraft and beat him to death on the runway. They somehow reckoned he had personally delayed their hajj flight to Mecca. Life expectancy in Afghanistan can hang on a very shaky nail. Najafi is a Hazara, something of an oppressed minority in Afghanistan. Hazara have been the punching bags of Afghan hatred for generations. He was indeed a brave man to come to Kandahar, home of the Pashtun.

Habibullah Faizi was the minnow in the group. He is a jovially round man, who sports a series of shiny mohair western suits. In socially conservative Kandahar, he took many risks in dressing as a westerner. Faizi had originally been a primary school teacher. When the Taliban fell, he was one of the first to shave off his beard and get rid of his shalwar kameez, the traditional baggy pyjama suits Pashtun men wear. In the complicated snakes and ladder game of Afghan politics, he went to work for the powerful Sherzai family: as the man who washed the family cars.

His big break had come with the arrival of the Canadians. Faizi has excellent English, including several choice swear words, which he uses in a droll and amusing way, purely for the shock factor. He came to work for us through my line of psyops, assisting the Canadians in putting together posters and leaflets. When the civilian airport came to be handed back, in 2007, Faizi was the man in the right place at the right time to take it on. At the time, he knew nothing about running an airport: and remains refreshingly sanguine about his aviation skill-set. He fought hard for his place at the table, and adroitly used his coalition contacts to build himself an empire. On this day of days, though, he was very much the court jester, not the king.

The main players in the group were Generals Sherzai and Hamid, together with Governor Wesa.

Alongside the absent police chief Abdul Raziq, Hamid and Sherzai were the security triumvirate in Kandahar. In the middle of a war, these three were the real owners of the Kandahar game. And their stories are an allegory for the perverse battle of survival Afghanistan has suffered.

General Abdul Raziq Sherzai is a tall, well-build man in his forties. He runs the Afghan air force component in the south, based in KAF. While the aircraft he possessed didn't fly too much, he did have a potent force of over 1,000 men under his command. Which is a useful marker to have in a country that measures influence by projection of power. The Sherzais had originally made their name during the jihad against the Soviets.

General Sherzai's father, an imposing, white-bearded Gandalf lookalike called Haji Abdul Latif, was a Kandahar guerrilla legend. Haji is an Islamic honorific, to indicate the person has completed the obligatory pilgrimage to Mecca, but it is also an indication of leadership and respect. Abdul Latif was an old man to lead an insurrection. He was in his seventies when he fought the Soviets in Kandahar. Ironically enough, he mortared KAF from exactly the same fields that this generation of insurgents were using to mortar us. His early days are a little murky, but it is certifiable that he was a smuggler and a convicted murderer. All skills that made him an extremely effective underground commander and leader. So much so that he was accorded the title 'Lion of Kandahar'. In Pashto, 'lion' translates as 'Sherzai'. Hence Latif became Sherzai.

After the Soviets withdrew, the Sherzais and their tribe, the Barakzais, successfully engineered a rise to power. Haji Latif was poisoned by his own bodyguards, but his oldest son, Gul Agha Sherzai, stepped up to take over the reins as Kandahar governor.

The Barakzais are one of the most powerful tribes in Afghanistan. Together with the Popolzais, they have traditionally provided all of Afghanistan's leaders. Gul Agha Sherzai is an important figure in the south.

He was Kandahar's governor when Mullah Omar raised the Taliban in Panjwai. Sherzai's private militia were infamous for their depravity. Indeed, rumours have swirled for decades over Gul Agha's personal preferences for pederasty.

The Sherzais were forced to flee for Pakistan, where they saw out the Taliban years with a degree of comfort in Quetta. 9/11 gave them the opportunity to get the throne back again. One US special forces group landed in Uruzgan with future President Karzai, a rival Popolzai, north of Kandahar city. Another group of Afghans and special forces, headed by Gul Agha Sherzai, left Quetta by land to re-take Kandahar from the south.

Sherzai couldn't muster more than a couple of hundred fighters, including his younger brother, the future General Sherzai. Overwhelming US air power stole the day, and a series of devastating strikes saw them quickly make the outskirts of Kandahar, at the airport, within a fortnight.

With Karzai approaching the city from the north, and Sherzai from the south, the remnants of the Taliban government fled.

Sherzai's group split into two, with Gul Agha heading into the city to occupy his old governor's palace. His younger brother, Abdul Raziq, stayed outside the city to take the strategically vital airport.

A small group of Arab fighters, with nowhere else to go, held out in the ruins. The US had conducted a series of pin-point strikes, crippling the runway, but most of the infrastructure had been spared. The Arabs holed up in the old maintenance hanger, made of solid brick, and refused to surrender. In the first week of December, 2001, a bomb through the roof ended their ambitions. That building was to become COMKAF headquarters, the Taliban's last stand.

Sherzai and his militia became the first owners of KAF, alongside their US special forces advisors. The first regular forces, a task force from the US Marines, took possession of the civil terminal, but the rest of it was handed over to Sherzai's control. Which was where he had remained, all these years. He and his men had laboriously helped clear the place of mines. A rapidly-established security company provided an Afghan screen around what quickly became a key US asset. His transport company ran convoys to the mushrooming coalition bases. His catering company set up two vastly profitable hotels for the small army of contractors that arrived with the troops. His construction company set up a concrete factory and a stone-making company and a building firm.

The Sherzai family, and their surrogates and endless cousins, came to own the KAF contracting scene. Possession being nine tenths of the law, the general also came to own huge chunks of real estate around the airport, stemming from a time when there was no government to say 'no'. The family became extremely rich. Just one of their KAF hotels was audited in 2011 to be pulling in three million dollars a year.

When the US tried to set up a nascent air force, there was only one person that could really fill the bill. So Abdul Raziq Sherzai became air force General Abdul Raziq Sherzai. Overnight. His was a political appointment, but an important face-saver.

Immediately after the invasion, older brother Gul Agha and Karzai got straight into a pissing match over who was boss of Kandahar. Karzai, at that stage unsure of the writ of his authority, backed down and Sherzai got his old job back as governor. Sherzai was later forced to step down, and moved to governor of Nangarhar, where he controlled the important northern road corridor to Peshawar. The Nesh crossing-point into Pakistan meant ripe pickings for Sherzai. Gul Agha stood twice as a presidential candidate. He took around 3% of the national vote each time. Not bad for a provincial Pashtun.

Karzai had to deal with Sherzai, if he was to retain the south. General Sherzai and his armed air force militia are an important place-setting in the complex politics of the place.

General Hamid couldn't have been more different. Even if his story is perhaps all the more remarkable. He doesn't look much like your traditional idea of a general. He is remarkably quiet and diffident. Slightly hunched, he sports a scrappy beard that makes him look more unshaven than groomed.

By 2011, Hamid had been fighting for thirty-five years. He had started his career as a paratroop commander in the Afghan communist regime. When Soviet Spetsnaz special forces came to kill Afghan President Hafizullah Amin in December 1979, Hamid was one of those mobilised to fight. He got stood down, despite his protests, and watched as the Soviets completed their invasion with the imposition of a puppet president: Babrak Karmal. Hamid continued to fight on the government side before the eventual disintegration of the country, as the government regime finally fell. When the Taliban took power, he was imprisoned by the regime and only released after elders spoke on his behalf. Suddenly unemployed, he then took a job with the BBC in Kabul, as a translator. Before joining up again with the Afghan army when the coalition looked to reform the state's security apparatus. He has been fighting in the south since 2005, when he commanded the Uruzgan brigade of 205 Hero Corps. By 2011, he had been promoted to major general and corps command.

Hamid had no truck with politics. He had seen enough of that throughout his life. Out of all the Afghans I met, Hamid was the one I always thought least likely to indulge in off-the-books activity. He is remarkably modest about his storied past, or his remarkable adventures. Again, President Karzai appointed him. As a Ghilzai, from the east, Hamid has no power play in the south. He was a useful counter-weight to all the rest of the swirling politics of patronage and graft that dominates society there. I always enjoyed my time with him. He spoke excellent English: and made a point of correcting his interpreters.

Governor Wesa was the relative newcomer. He had gone to school with Karzai, and had actually married into the family. Wesa is an academic, having studied in the Lebanon and the US. He was the founding president of Kandahar University. During the civil war, he had lit out for Canada, where he earned a doctorate in agriculture. He had written his dissertation on the development of the Arghandab valley. His wife, Rangina, is a talented gynaecologist. Karzai had lured him back to Kandahar as governor. Which is a pretty dangerous gig. Wesa survived countless attacks, but I always got the sense he knew he lived on borrowed time. I know, for a fact, that he always kept a suitcase packed. His trouble was he didn't have a powerbase in town.

He owed his position to Karzai, which was fine as long as Wali Karzai, the president's strong-arm brother, had run stuff in town. After Wali Karzai was assassinated in July 2011 by his bodyguards, Wesa was more on his own. He got up to a load of real estate deals, and made himself pretty rich through working with another of Karzai's brothers, Mahmoud, who was director of an elite Kandahar real estate development called Aino Mena.

The one missing card in the deck of Kandahar politics that day was General Raziq, the all-powerful police commander. Raziq was still on his rise to fame in early 2012. He'd got the gig as Kandahar police chief after another assassination. His predecessor, General Mohammad Mujahid, had been blown up by a suicide bomber while sitting in his office. Indeed, the reason Raziq wasn't at the airport that day was because he himself had narrowly avoided death in January, when another suicide bomber had hit his vehicle convoy. Raziq had been seriously wounded, but remained alive.

He is remarkably young to be chief of police, barely into his '30's. Raziq is a small man, very lean. When he started out, he tried to grow a beard that turned out vaguely embarrassing. Mind you, it turned him into a passing Che Guevara. Later, as he matured, his beard got bushier. Now he looks more like Fidel. Raziq is reportedly illiterate, so his rise to power is even more unique. None of his remarkable arc would have been possible without the steadfast support of the US, which has poured resources into funding and training his men. The US loves Raziq.

The simple reason for all that largesse is that Raziq hates the Taliban. With a passion that has led to him reportedly committing atrocities that would turn a strong stomach: including private torture prisons. The accusation got so serious that by 2011 the US had suspended handing over prisoners to him.

Raziq's tribe, the Achakzai, historically fought for control of the border smuggling trade with their arch rivals, the Noorzai. When the Taliban rose to power from Panjwai district, home of the Noorzai, the Achakzai found themselves on the receiving end. So much so that the Taliban hanged Raziq's uncle, Mansour, from the barrel of a tank, before going on to kill his father and other members of his family.

Raziq had sat out the Taliban in Quetta, before he had joined Gul Agha Sherzai's motley crew as a foot soldier. Not many in ISAF were ever aware of his link to the Sherzais. The coalition invasion allowed Raziq and his men to take back control of the Chaman crossing point—and the lucrative cross-border trade rackets. He caught the eye of the coalition by his ferocity in combat and his reliability in fighting. In his twenties, the tribe recognised his success and elected him leader. Raziq was on his way.

First off as battalion commander of the border police in Spin Boldak, down on the favoured home turf along the frontier. When the coalition ran into trouble in the Panjwai, Raziq had been the boy asked by British General Nick Carter to go sort the problem out with the Noorzai. Which Raziq and his men did with relish, backed by US-funded equipment and air power. ISAF just lapped him up, even as they ignored the darker side of the coin. Nick Carter, the British commander in Kandahar in 2010, described him as:

'A pragmatic solution. He is Afghan good-enough.'

An American source of mine was more sanguine:

'If you need a mad dog, he's not a bad one to have.'

Raziq himself confirmed his own point of view:

'I have a clear policy: when the enemies are killing us, we shouldn't be giving them flowers.'[24]

There's no doubt that through ruthless application of force, he brought an element of stability to Kandahar. Just as there is little doubt that he is generally loved and revered by the people. Afghans love a tough guy. When Raziq came back home from Dubai, where he had had surgery following his near-fatal assassination attempt, literally hundreds had mobbed him at his home.

Raziq is a bit of a rock star Robin Hood. And he knew how to cement his popularity. He gifted a lot of infrastructure development: solar street lighting, statues, roundabouts, new roads. All the good stuff that meant giving back to the community.

Those guys, plus Raziq, that stood in a row behind that plastic ribbon with its incongruous coloured flowers, represented the survivors of generations of Afghan struggle. Whatever the rights and wrongs of it all, their stories are a remarkable tale of survival and pragmatic bending in the wind: just as they are all ambitious and ruthless men.

Each and every one of them would not be in the position they now hold if it were not for our invasion and the relentless king-making of ISAF and the coalition. The west made all those men: and their fortunes.

In time, they were all to become more than passing acquaintances. A couple even became good friends.

On this day, as we all listened carefully to an Islamic blessing of our new road, it was another Afghan guest who made the day profound.

Leading the government delegation was a former Kandahar governor, Yousef Pashtun. He came to visit as President Karzai's special advisor on construction. Yousef Pashtun is a Barakzai, and another who came across the border in 2001 with Gul Agha and his band of warriors.

While Gul Agha succeeded in regaining the provincial governorship, he was soon unseated by a clever political play by Karzai. Pashtun, as a fellow Barakzai had been Gul Agha's replacement. Which was a rather thoughtful face-saver. Karzai is a past master at such patronage.

Pashtun is a highly intelligent man. He has a double masters and a bachelor's degree in engineering, town planning and architecture. He speaks six languages. In point of fact, all the Afghan delegates that day are highly intelligent men. Pashtun stood in front of the assembled multitude and gave a

---

[24] Quotes from Wall Street Journal article, 18 Nov 2010

highly impressive speech in fluent English. He told us of his youth in Kandahar, during the time of King Zahir Shah, a golden era of stability for Afghanistan:

'I well remember coming to this airport as a young boy,' he told us. 'In those days, I was travelling with my family to a holiday in the UAE. We boarded an airliner like normal people the world over. War destroyed all of that, but I have never forgotten those days. Standing here today reminds me that we can re-build what we had before. Afghanistan is once more a proud nation.'

I doubt more than a couple of the assembled ISAF troops knew who any of these Afghan gentlemen were.

In the West, we portray Afghans as greedy, incompetent and corrupt. Many are: but, equally, there are many who are the match of anything the West can summon. When I remembered all these men had been through, the suffering and the struggle, I felt privileged to be there with them.

A flunky gave Pashtun and Najafi a pair of scissors each. The two of them cut the gaudy ribbon to declare the road open. And then both held a piece of the ribbon up by hand and gave the scissors to Scott so he could re-cut it too.

It was an inspirational piece of diplomacy.

They made sure we understood this was an Afghan road, in Afghanistan, for Afghans. We might have paid for it, and built it, and they were grateful for it too. But it was still, first and foremost their road, not ours. They cut the ribbon first.

The man with the tray of sweets came round and we all had a toffee. Handshakes and smiles abounded. That day was a happy time.

Lord, I thought, why did we not do more of this stuff?? If we had brought a few more tarmac machines and a few less guns, how different it all could have been.

THE PRISM CHANGES

That night, we got badly rocketed. Salvo after salvo. In-coming rained down.

It started as I ran round The Boardwalk jogging track. Hour after hour of just sitting in a bunker, listening to the Giant Voice and the bangs. Some close by, some so close you could see the flash. Some further away, some just a distant *cruump*! Life and death: just a random lottery. Every now and again a siren warbled: the fire brigade or other emergency service, taking their lives in their hands to go sort out the mess.

Then the tracer started, from the big hill between KAF and the city. Somewhere over there, on the big hill between us and the city, the bad guys had set up a heavy weapon.

Tracer is funny stuff to watch. It begins really slowly, just a lazy pinprick of light in the distance, that just gets faster and faster, the closer it gets. Same as the Millennium Falcon hitting warp speed. The stuff just drips along, and then it's whipping over you in elongated streams of light. Little copper jacketed messages of death.

The day had started well with the road opening. My running that night had developed an ugly purpose. I ran to get over dreadful news, just received.

Khalil Dale was born Ken Dale. He converted to Islam over thirty years ago. Khalil was a slight man, almost owlish, with professorial glasses and a quiet, diffident manner. His physical frailty masked a moral core of steel. Khalil dedicated his life to protecting the innocent and the disenfranchised.

I met him first in Afghanistan, in 1994. Khalil worked for the International Red Cross. He lived next to a massive refugee camp near Mazar E Sharif, the main city in the north. Khalil was one of a very few westerners to brave Afghanistan in those days. The entire country was ruptured by a series of vicious internal wars, fought between various power factions left over from the collapse of the post-Soviet invasion.

We flew up from Kabul to Mazar on a UN plane. The airport was protected by a group of young thugs, waving AK-47s around like batons. They got very excited at our arrival, a disparate group of westerners. Our clothes alone were worth more than they earned in a year. They were obsessed with my video camera, convinced I was a spy. Khalil calmed them down. He was a small man, but he had a way with him that just dissipated a threat. We had travelled across the world to visit this remarkable man and his one-man struggle to provide the Afghan people with a small shred of dignity. During a time when the world scarcely knew where Afghanistan was.

Government bodies call refugees IDPs: internally displaced persons. No blithe phraseology can adequately describe the human squalor that condition creates.

The camp Khalil helped run held over 50,000 people. The lucky ones lived in tents. The unfortunate ones lived in self-made huts, constructed of hand-made mud bricks, thatched with grass. Whole families hiding out in the kind of hole we would balk at keeping livestock in.

We visited in December. It was bitterly, bitterly cold. The struggle these people faced was biblically primitive. Crowds of women stood around the one hand pump well, waiting for the weak rays of the winter sun to defrost the frozen water enough to fill a plastic bucket with a thick coloured ooze.

Children wearing rags, with bare feet, played in the mud: boys using sticks as guns, girls with dolls made of grass and string.

Khalil arranged for me to film inside the Blue Mosque in Mazar. I didn't quite understand at the time what a privilege I was being accorded. The Blue Mosque is one of the most holy shrines in the world for Shia Islam. It is rumoured to contain the remains of Ali ibn Abi Talib, the Holy Prophet's son-in-law and personal assistant, the first convert and, according to Shia Islam, the last of the true caliphs.

As a foreigner and an unbeliever, I was allowed to film the assembled thousands at prayer within the sacred dome. The people of Afghanistan wanted the world to understand they were not primitives. The Imam spoke of the power of the media to spread the word of Afghanistan's suffering. His words implored those who could to share the story of Afghanistan's suffering and to pray to Allah for restitution and peace.

It was a truly profound moment in my life: and I will never forget watching Khalil prostrating himself before God within those hallowed halls.

Khalil was a true Muslim, at one with his faith and his life of sacrifice and poverty, far from his Manchester roots. Khalil was one of those rare human beings who just gave all of himself for others. There was no personal ambition or desire for material worth in his life. He was simply one of those special and extremely rare people who radiate the will of God.

In 2012, he had moved from Afghanistan to work outside Quetta, Pakistan.

He was still working with refugees from Afghanistan. Different geography, different time, the same struggle for human dignity. The same Khalil: doing his best in appalling circumstances. With the same innate kindness, compassion and empathy.

On January 5th, 2012, Khalil was abducted by the Taliban. At the end of April, Quetta police found a plastic bag at the side of a main road. Written in black marker on the bag: Khalil Dale.

Khalil's body was inside the bag. He had been beheaded and his body chopped up to fit the plastic. A note with the bag, addressed to the local police chief, said the body was being returned because a ransom had not been paid.

Khalil had been kidnapped before, in Africa. He was no stranger to danger or war. He knew the risks of working in a place like South Asia. He did it anyway.

Khalil was sixty when he was murdered. He had just found love and was looking to return to Dumfries in Scotland, to retire.

I ran that night to escape the torment of the news. I mourned his passing, the loss of my friend, an extraordinary man. I was in shock at the manner of its happening. I was angry. I ran because I wanted to commit violence: and running was the only physical action I could take. I ran to exhaust my body and my emotions.

Those motherfucking Taliban motherfuckers. I wanted them all dead, every motherfucking last one.

We'd done a good thing that day for Afghanistan with our road. Khalil had done good things all his life. And still they hated us. They'd chopped Khalil up for sport and rained rockets and bullets down on the rest of us.

Well, I hated them right back.

Back in the JDOC, Scott agreed with me. That wonderful military aviation workhorse, the Hercules, begat one very special variant. It mounts a large calibre howitzer and a chain gun. All the plane has to do is lazy eights over a target and whatever is below is toast. It's called Spectre. It's one of the most effective weapons of death ever created.

KAF happened to have one. We heard it take off, saw it bank slowly over to starboard, towards the hill. The hill where the Taliban were firing at us from. The Hercules navigation lights winked away. Then, a stream of light swam from its side. A noise like a chainsaw ripped the air.

Fuck you, asshole.... Eat that, you motherfuckers. The word came through that the point of origin had been neutralised. We knew what that meant: Terry Taliban had been smoked. Fucking good riddance.

The follow-on ground patrol, sent to investigate the firing point, sent back a message that their route was blocked by a couple of suspicious mounds. They suspected a trap.

Scott pulled them back and called in a helicopter gunship. We sat back and watched as several hundreds of thousands of dollars worth of guided missiles blew big holes in the hillside. And we cheered every flash of light and every bang.

I hadn't come around the world to deliberately hate Afghanistan. In my heart I knew that there were still good people around. I'd met some of them that very day. Yet, by 2012, a whole generation of good people had already been killed. Afghanistan is just surrounded by death. It's as much a fact of life there as breathing the air. Stay there long enough and it is inescapable.

Every day, we'd hear the medevac birds come in. The hospital was right next to COMKAF. We'd see the Blackhawk helicopters swoop in, low and fast. The ambulances lined up, the medics standing by, the gurneys prepped. Some poor soul was never going to walk again, or hold their sweetheart. Somebody's life would be changed forever.

Most days, on the same ramp, columns of soldiers would solemnly line up in formation, as taps played and eulogies were offered. The dead were going home.

The daily litany in the briefings was not of killed and wounded. The tragic count was of 'heroes' and 'saves'. It didn't lessen the sacrifice, however the pill was sweetened. The count was relentless.

By June, 2015: 2,316 US military dead. 20,051 wounded. 1,173 contractors killed.

The American tally alone is numbing. Let alone the 26,000 estimated Afghan civilians killed: and nobody kept an accurate count of civilians.

The military tried to turn every heroic return into a celebration of a life. A simple cross, marked with an upturned rifle, boots, helmet and dog tags, would form an informal pulpit. Comrades in arms would step forward and utter a short memoriam. Their fallen bother or sister was the best squad medic, or machine gunner, or scout or leader: each was indispensable. Each had died a warrior and a shining sacrifice for freedom. Each had died for their country and their fellows.

The tributes were as much for us, the living, as the fallen. Regardless of the loss, we had to go on. There were just too many of them. Each young person that left Kandahar inside a flag-covered box was an un-spoken question mark. They were all so young. In another life, they would have been leaving college, having their first true love, getting married, buying their first car or house. The military was uncomfortable with those doubts. I understood the hero part. I owe my own survival in KAF to the sacrifice each and every one of them made.

Yet nobody wanted to ask, what the fuck is all this about?

The army is content to just go where it is told. It convinces itself that whatever it is doing, wherever it is doing it, is in defence of freedom and it is right. Stay in Afghanistan long enough, though, as I did, you had to wonder. Gordon Brown, British prime minister, said that we were fighting the Taliban in Afghanistan so we wouldn't have to fight them in Britain.

The evil fuckers that chopped up Khalil never went to Britain. They just hated him because we, the western soldiers, were in Afghanistan and they thought he was one of us. We shot up a load of men on a mountain who were shooting at us simply because we were in Afghanistan. Everybody was shooting at everybody else. Nothing more complicated than that.

The end result for us was simple too: a row of stolen dreams encased in flag-covered steel coffins.

AIR AFGHAN

After the road opening, I was in demand. As the only female out there, I'd been noticed: by both the Afghans and their ISAF mentors. I'd been sharp enough to get an introduction to them all. I worked the contacts ruthlessly. These guys were gold dust to me.

Sherzai was the easiest to get to. His air wing lived on KAF, right out on the eastern edge. He had a pretty good gig going down there. From a standing start in '09, within two years NATO had built him an impressive hanger complex. In time, the air wing would have its own fire station (and expensively equipped fire brigade), accommodation blocks, parade square, offices and mosque.

It wasn't all gravy. They built him a huge mess hall, which was great to look at. Trouble is, NATO forgot to indent for tables, chairs, plates and cutlery. So the boys ended up sitting on the ground, eating homemade kebabs cooked over an open-fire-pit, same as they had always done. Afghans are used to adapting.

Each of the key Afghan commanders had a colonel from our side looking after him. In Sherzai's case, he had a whole expeditionary air team. Sherzai's key mentor, Colonel Jim Breck, USAF, was a real hard-charger. He was doing his damnedest to get the road show together.

The Afghan air force was split into three air wings—Kabul, Kandahar and Shindand, in the west. Kabul had the headquarters, and the nascent special mission wing, while Shindand did all the pilot training. That left Kandahar as the poor relation: a poor relation with one of the biggest combat areas and the one with the most fighting.

Sherzai was key to bringing the whole thing to life. He was up against it. The trouble was, for all that they had great buildings, nobody had thought to get them some planes. Or any qualified pilots for that matter. A proper ten-year plan for an Afghan air force hadn't been drawn up until 2010. Which was pretty scandalous. By 2011, only 4,000 Afghans wore air force blue.

An air force is a complicated beast. Setting one up from scratch is a logistical and training nightmare.

The Afghans had inherited a small war stock of ex-Russian helicopters. Mostly aged Mi-17 transport helicopters, and a few of the fearsome Mi-35 Hind helicopter gunships. The only fixed wing transport aircraft left flying were four absolutely ancient ex-Russian An-32 cargo planes, fit only for the scrapyard.

Equally critical, no Afghan had graduated from an Afghan military flight school since 1992, when the Najibullah regime had fallen. In Soviet times, Afghanistan's air force was a formidable beast. When I had first hit KAF, early on in the war, the place had been littered with the carcasses of old MiG fighters. Even the Taliban had managed to keep some supersonic fighter jets airborne.

Now, the Afghans had none. They barely had a working helicopter fleet.

In the case of the Kandahar air wing, no working aircraft at all. Sure, driving past the air wing buildings, all looked very efficient and spick and span. The place was kept immaculately. On the pan sat five Mi-17 helicopters, and a big transport aircraft, a C-27A. The headquarters building was a hermetically sealed, air-conditioned hubbub of activity. Trouble was, nothing worked.

The helicopters were fit only for spare parts. Lack of maintenance and anybody trained enough to maintain or fly them had condemned them to sit and rust in the heat.

The C-27A was an even bigger tale of broken dreams.

One of the first decisions ISAF had made was to scrap the old Russian An-32s. They were a deathtrap. The Americans raised a contract, which came to cost $468 million dollars, with Alenia North America. The cash would replace the An-32s with a more modern C-27 aircraft.

Alenia is an Italian-based company, known internationally as Alenia Aermacchi. They make the C-27, essentially a smaller version of the workhorse Hercules C-130. It has a smaller hull, and two engines instead of four, but the loading ramp, cargo bays and cockpit are pretty much the same concept.

The US air force already owned a number of C-27s, which are mostly used in the special forces and coast guard arena. They are rugged, dependable and a good choice for the smaller and less well-maintained airstrips Afghanistan offered. Indeed, the Germans were already using the aircraft in-theatre.

Trouble was, by 2010, everybody used the C-27J variant. For the Afghan contract, Alenia provided C27-A aircraft.

C-27As are the original variant, which had long been superseded. The aircraft they transferred to Afghanistan were re-furbished ex-Italian air force machines, dating from the 1970s.

For $468 million, the Afghans, not unreasonably, thought they were getting new, modern aircraft. They got second-hand rubbish. What was worse was that the procurement contract came without maintenance, or even a spare part, addendum.

The only air-worthy Afghan pilots and mechanics had learned their trade twenty years previously on Russian aircraft. Their ISAF mentors were Americans, with a heavy leavening of eastern European contractors, who were used to Soviet aircraft. Nobody knew how to fly Italian planes. And they came without even a spare set of spark plugs, readable manual or wrench.

The Italian government had an arms export embargo with Afghanistan. When the US turned the aircraft over to Afghan ownership, Alenia was in breach of its home country embargo. Any manufacturer's support was suspended. Nonsense, but that's how lack of due diligence scuppered so many of those early contracts. The C27s flew until they broke down. Then they were abandoned.

KAF had one of the beasts. It had been flown down from Kabul and had then refused to start. The airframe had been towed to the end of the pan and left. By 2012, it was missing a propeller and all the tyres were flat. It never flew again.

The US quietly ended the program in 2014. The aircraft were all sold to Afghan vendors, who re-cycled what they could get. $468 million spent returned $32,000 in scrap fees.

Jim B and his boys were doing what they could. But an air force without planes is a little like a doctor without a stethoscope or a bottle of pills. The Sherzai team was well in place. The general was energetically putting himself about. Access from KAF was pretty easy. All you needed was a car to drive around the perimeter road to their base. I went down to see him pretty regularly.

Sherzai had a huge office, comfortably outfitted with overstuffed sofas and glass coffee tables. The walls were decorated with an endless collection of plaques and certificates from the dozens of rotations that he had seen come and go. Sherzai was always a very genial host. He liked nothing better than to sit and practice his English, fortified by an endless supply of tea and treats, brought in by very pretty chai boys.

Afghans do that funny old-fashioned thing of shoving all the furniture against the walls. We'd sit opposite each other, twenty feet apart, the intervening space filled by an expanse of carpets. And smile and shout over at each other.

I always liked Sherzai. You pretty much got what you saw. He knew he knew very little about planes but he was held in great respect by his boys. Many of whom had been with him for years.

His chief of staff, Azim Azili, had actually been a MiG fighter pilot during the Soviet days. He used to laugh loudly at the irony of now being back in the military air business, flying the same combat missions over his homeland for a different set of imperial masters. Afghans are a race of consummate survivors.

Sherzai always took great pride in wearing a metal American combat infantryman's badge. In the US army, the CIB is a greatly prized award. It is only open to the infantry, and denotes that you have been in close combat with the enemy. The badge is a Kentucky long-rifle, surmounted with oak leaves.

Sherzai had been given one by his special forces handlers, when he and his men had liberated the airport in 2001. He was prouder of that one badge than any other. And he wore so many, there was no room on his uniform. It drove the Americans crazy. They thought it was an insult that an Afghan wore their badge. The CIB was for US infantry only.

To me, it was quite sweet. Despite the way he was treated by his different mentors—and some of them were scandalously abusive to him—Sherzai never stopped being grateful to the US for freeing his country. As he said, without America, his family would still be refugees in Quetta. Not did he forget that America had made him and his family extremely rich. Barely a local contract existed in KAF that didn't have a Sherzai stamp of approval. From the stone factory to the DVD store on the Boardwalk, they all belonged to him and his.

So the air wing and Jim and his boys soldiered on, doing ground training and practise drills. They couldn't even let their mechanics work on the grounded helicopters. They only manuals they had were in Russian. It took a year to translate them into English, and then into Pashto. Until then, it was all personal knowledge and experience.

It could all get pretty comical.

One time, they needed to move a big, container-sized generator. They tried to lift it with a lightweight crane. Their advisors told them the crane couldn't take the weight, but they went ahead anyway. The driver enthusiastically swung the crane out, at right angles to the truck base. He didn't bother putting out the stabilisers. With much yelling and mutual encouragement, somehow the crane lifted the generator about ten feet off the ground. Amidst a grating and screeching of tortured metal, the inevitable happened and whole caboose, crane and all, toppled over.

The driver's compartment got crushed in a maze of broken glass and twisted metal. To our amazement, the operator crawled out from under the wreckage, looking a little dazed and worse for wear. All the watching Afghans started applauding and he found himself being hoisted around on their shoulders as a rock star.

Jim's boys got a big ISAF crane and sorted out the mess. Amazingly enough, the Afghan crane and generator kept on jogging for another few months. A little dented but still functional.

In mid-2011, the air wing took a quantum leap forward with the acquisition of five new Mi-17 helicopters. They were the upgraded V5 version, the main difference being better avionics. The pilot's dash looked like an iPad display. No more dials and analogue meters.

Jim was keen to get his boys flying. He was a command pilot himself. I liked his manner a lot. He just wanted to go flying: and every day that was wasted on admin was a day wasted in the air. He pushed and cajoled his boys to get those Mi-17s into the air, leading by example himself.

Jim took me along with him: Breck, a load of Afghan air force trainees and me, off out over Kandahar. Jim would take the lead bird, showing his charges how to land a helicopter in a dust-out. Up and down we'd go, practising over and over again how to avoid losing situational awareness in the clouds of dirt that each landing threw out.

We'd load up with door machine-guns and boxes and boxes of ammunition. South of KAF, the air force had set up a really exciting range, along a box canyon. The helo would fly low and fast, while I got to bang hundreds of rounds at orange barrels, set out as targets for our guns. It was bloody exciting, whizzing along with all the doors open, blazing away.

Less than three years later, the UK would lose some of its last Afghan fatalities, when a Lynx helicopter crashed in the same spot, killing all five crew members. Their helicopter had been performing the same run, through the same range complex. Survival in Afghanistan was a fine line. Even the rehearsals could be fatal.

I kept my air wing adventures pretty quiet around KAF. Getting to go anywhere could be a nightmare of paperwork. As a NATO civilian, I had to get approval to get on a military bird, and that meant going grovelling to the 325th. They were decent enough to me, but they were a headquarters unit and could get pretty jealous of anybody off freelancing. It was simpler just to mosey up to Sherzai's people and go along with them.

They loved it that I trusted them enough to go flying with them. Most ISAF troops thought the Afghan helos were coffins on rotors, and wouldn't touch them with a bargepole.

I didn't care. I just loved flying. The boys would fit me up with a harness and I'd go sit right on the edge of the open rear door and watch the paddies and compounds whistle by beneath me, only a couple of hundred feet below.

Sometimes, we'd pair up with an ISAF team, mostly doing spot vehicle checks. Highways one and four are pretty big arterial routes that can be seen for miles in the air. They were easy enough to follow. We'd glide along until we saw a suspicious looking vehicle, then just swoop down ahead of it, drop a squad off and wait for them to come into the spider's web. What we called an eagle patrol.

Most local folks were very proud and quite amazed that the guys manning the check-points were Afghan. Most of the trucks we stopped were impossible to do more than a cursory check on. The norm was to pile crap up, way beyond anything stable, tie it off with a piece of string, and just hope for the best. If we'd started digging into the cargo, the whole lot would have tipped over.

What the air wing was doing was important. It proved Afghan capability, in a technically advanced area of operations. Any country can give a guy a gun and say; 'you're now a soldier.' Afghanistan was awash with that.

But pilots? Planes? Helicopters? That spoke of advanced capability. If we were ever to get out of Afghanistan, the air wing would be critical. It gave the Afghans tactical mobility, the means to move people and stuff into an area. Equally crucial for morale, they now had the means to get casualties out and into hospital.

It took ISAF, an advanced military, years to set up and operate an Afghan CASEVAC system: a system that would save tens of thousands of lives. By the time I left, end 2014, the Afghans, in less than five years, had developed a rudimentary capability, both fixed and rotary air, to do the same thing: and from absolutely nothing too.

The Afghan army was just as accommodating to me. Across in Camp Hero, 205 Corps, under the command of Major General Hamid, was rapidly acquiring a reputation as the most effective unit the Afghan army possessed.

Hamid's advisory team was Australian. They lived in KAF's best-kept secret, Camp Baker. In true Aussie style, they had the place equipped with a barbie, volleyball court and KAF's only patch of real, and very green, grass.

Hero was less than a mile from Baker, but getting there involved the usual KAF rigmarole of armoured vehicles and guns. In the old days, I'd walked there.

Early on in the war, the vast collection of leftover Soviet armour that littered southern Afghanistan had all been corralled onto Hero. Ten years later, the tank park still stood: row after row of rusted Russian tanks and armoured personnel carriers. In 2004, it had been safe enough to wander around and take photos. Eight years later, the only approved way into Hero was in our own generation of armour. The irony was not lost on any of us: and in ten years time, I have no doubt the armour we bequeath the Afghans will likewise stand in rows of rust.

Hamid was a genial host. He liked the company. Afghans run a pretty free office environment. As a guest, you can stay as long as the chai is flowing. It's part of the custom and tradition.

The advisors never stayed long enough to adapt to Afghan custom. I'd get shepherded in with my officer of the day. We'd sit and chat for half an hour and my western escort would get itchy feet. The meeting would move on from us, and we'd move more to the periphery, but it was expected that we'd stay and enjoy the hospitality. The western advisors were all for heading off: just as fresh tea was being delivered. It was really rude, but Hamid had been around us for long enough not to take it personally.

We always took a protection team. We'd all be suited up in body armour and helmet, surrounded by armed guards, called 'guardian angels'. The Afghans just sat around in their normal clothes. They were polite enough not raise it as an issue, but several told me privately they knew we didn't trust them. They thought us cowards for bringing so much firepower into the office.

We were allies, but wary allies.

Not that all was well on their side either. If Sherzai found out I was in his camp—and his internal bongo drums were very efficient—he'd appear in seconds few. It took me a while to twig to it. He felt an obligation to protect me, and he and his bodyguards would break off their day's activities to come walk with me. He always welcomed me with a big grin, and, very unusually for an Afghan male to a female, he would hug me. Sherzai was very effusive that way. I took it that he accepted me and was proud to have gained his trust.

Later, both Hamid and Sherzai gave me Afghan medals. I assumed it was for my work, but I also think it was for trusting them and sticking with them.

The Afghan army used to love taking me out on patrol with them. It was a pretty risky thing to do in hindsight, but I never really thought about the danger.

If ISAF went out anywhere, they'd tool along in some numbers, in their up-armoured MRAPs. I'd go with the Afghans in their second-hand Humvees, the very vehicles the Americans refused to use because of their vulnerability to mines and IEDs.

Most of the land around KAF is a big dustbowl, marked by irrigation canals, farms and the odd abandoned industrial complex. Travelling around with the Afghans reminded me of how we, ISAF, had been welcomed in the early days. When the Dutch first came to KAF, they would patrol on bicycles. Absolutely true, that.

The boys would wave, the farmers would wave back, and all seemed pretty calm. Except when the Americans arrived. Then life changed and the atmosphere got quite intense.

I liked to go with the same Afghan guy, Sergeant Mohammadzai. He spoke decent English. He came from the north, and was a native Uzbek. He'd been posted to Kandahar for two years. Like most of the Afghan army, he wasn't from the south. In many ways, the Afghan army was as much an army of occupation in Kandahar as we were.

His family had been forced to flee from Kabul when the Taliban had arrived. Like hundreds of thousands of others, they had returned to find their home destroyed and their land occupied by others. He had enlisted in the army to feed his wife and kids. In all that time, he'd seen his family twice. Afghans just got posted and left in situ until they deserted or were killed. They were careful about what they did. Many of them were the sole breadwinners for their families. They couldn't afford to get hurt or killed.

We'd talk about the West a lot. He was a keen fan of western movies, especially anything involving Schwarzenegger or Stallone. The whole Rambo look was pretty key to the Afghans. The entire patrol would be dolled out in bandanas, mirror aviator shades and more knives and grenades dangling than a gypsy's jewellery. Old Mohammadzai would crack off a quick 'hasta la vista, baby' and the whole crew would just dissolve into laughter.

They were infinitely respectful towards me. They would clean the seat for me, and offer me bottles of water. I was kinda careful about my water intake. Going to the loo in the desert around KAF would have been an event. They weren't used to having women along.

When the Americans came along for the ride, there was an obvious, but un-spoken apartheid. The Afghans would take the lead, with the Yanks a little ways back. Less risk of driving over something that way, if a half-dozen Afghan wagons had led the way.

The leaders would debus and talk, but the troops just eyed each other warily. Our Afghan lads were loaded with a ton of weapons and ammunition. They all loved their gear. Even in daylight, they would cut about with their night-vision goggles on their helmets. They just loved the army toys. There was no escaping that that the stuff they had was either knackered Soviet gear or hand-me-downs. As much as they took perverse pride in their lashed together gear, there would be an unspoken envy of the Yank's Gucci kit.

Sometimes the Americans would be culturally sensitive, other times you could see why sometimes fatal arguments happened.

One time, we met up with a patrol of the 82nd. Mohammadzai and I got out to talk to the American patrol leader. He was a big southerner, who had a big hunk of tobacco wadded into his lower lip. Just as Mohammadzai started to welcome him, the American turned his head to one side and shot out a big stream of tobacco juice. Afghans are quite fastidious in the company of females about their behaviour. The Yank may as well have slapped Mohammadzai. He was mortally offended: and turned to me to apologise or the American.

It wasn't that the American knew he was being deliberately offensive, he was just being a good old boy. He should have known better. Folks got themselves shot for a lot less.

Outside the governor's palace, the road split into quite a tight chicane. If cars were parked by the roadside, as they often were at the governor's place, the road would be too tight for the American's MRAPs, which had a pretty huge wheel-base.

The Afghans tended a lovely flower garden in the road divide. If the Yanks couldn't get past the cars, rather than de-bus outside the gate, they would just drive right over the flower-beds. On more than one occasion, it came to weapons being raised on both sides.

I got into a blazing row with an 82nd sergeant, who proclaimed that:

'The 82nd are God's fucking chosen... who gives a fuck about some flowers.' Well, pretty much every Afghan I ever met did care about the fucking flowers. Every patch of ground in Afghanistan that can bear a plant has one. Even the most downtrodden compound has a bit of carefully tended green. It pissed me that a lot of the Americans didn't see the damage they caused through wilful and un-necessary ignorance.

I cut an incongruous figure on those patrols. NATO rules didn't allow me to be armed. Even the Afghans thought I was nuts. But, in many ways, being bare was my best defence. In those awkward moments when the boys had stopped some truck and the crew on board just stared in disbelief at me in my jeans and blue body armour, Mohammadzai would just laugh and tell them I was his mad daughter. I'd wave back and do a little dance, and everybody would just grin at each other.

It was fucking risky, though. If I'd been injured, the Afghans would have had to rescue me. ISAF didn't even know I was there. The juice, though, was immense. The stuff I was turning in was some of the best product of my life.

My boys and me, between us, just ruled our area. We fucking owned that turf.

Up in Kabul, I became Eric's poster-girl. I was churning out unique copy, right from ground zero, and demonstrating what ISAF viewed as the Holy Grail: definable Afghan progress in taking the war over.

ON THE HAMSTER WHEEL

All that activity had a keen under-current. Folks were going home. The clock was ticking. Whatever was going to be done to win the war had to be done now, and fast and dirty too.

Newly arrived Chairman of the Joint Chiefs, General Martin Dempsey, was Obama's choice to end the war. He hadn't been the first draft pick. Obama had wanted General Jim Cartwright, but he'd fallen out with a Bush hangover: Robert Gates, Secretary of Defence, who Obama had kept in office. So Dempsey found himself promoted from chief of staff to chairman, right into the top spot, barely four months after he had first been appointed to the war cabinet. Once again, people politics came first.

Dempsey had a difficult job. The United States had run out of cash. The piggybank was bare. Dempsey had seen how the 'more and bigger' crew had fared. His boss wanted creativity and a cash refund.

Dempsey set about his job with some zeal. He was later to write an open letter to all his senior commanders in Afghanistan that nothing mattered more than closing bases and saving money. Not the war, or winning it, the balance sheet became number 1.

Jim Huggins and the 82nd were in the line of fire. The endless, expensive tactical battles for local control had to end. Tactics had to become strategy. Not just bringing a lot of firepower to bear. The 82nd's legacy as light infantry really helped them.

The division's 4th brigade, arriving in-country early 2012 under the command of Colonel Brian Mennes, had already implemented a novel and thorough training regime. Before the troops got anywhere near Kandahar, Mennes had over 150 of his junior soldiers complete a four month full-bore course in Pashto. Bizarrely, nobody had thought to do that before.

Mennes insisted on every one of his soldiers completing full culture immersion training. Paratroopers generally speaking can't call on the big guns to go help them when trouble starts. The 82nd could be a pain in the ass with their 'airborne!', 'all the way!' enthusiasm, but I did respect where their brass was coming from. Jim Huggins pushed the envelope.

He had a cool and loose command environment. If you had something to say, he had a forum. Inside the information operations field, I could, as a civilian, have my say. I didn't yet have the access I was later to gain. Which was fair enough. I hadn't yet been there long enough to be mama bear, but folks were interested in what I had to offer.

Particularly in the magazine the POTF ran. Across the South, we fortnightly printed about a half million copies of the thing. 'Sada E Azadi' (Voice of Freedom) cost millions to produce: and it had been something of a potted success. The paper had begun when the Germans had been ISAF's biggest players. Back in the day, it had been the only newspaper printed and nominally distributed across the whole country. On the surface, an important product, all that muscle had only had a limited effect.

The broadsheet format the paper originally used was truly bulky. Each issue took up far too much space on ISAF's small and over-worked fleet of transport planes. Printed in Kabul, piles of papers were just left by the side of various runways across the country. In those first few years after the invasion, ISAF had to do all the work. There was no credible Afghan distribution network.

The concept of the paper, though, was credible. The spine came from the Kabul newsroom, while each regional command had control over the four inner papers: a sort of localised paper within a paper. Handled properly, it could have been a real influencer for change. Pre-mobile phones, Wi-Fi and internet access, the paper was quite often the only contact many parts of the country had with the outside world.

Printed in Dari, Pashto and English, with the different language columns side by side, schools just ate the thing up. In a country with no textbooks or curriculum to speak of, SeA quickly found a place as a teaching tool.

It also quickly gained a reputation as being useful chip paper. Patrolling soldiers would be given great handfuls of the things to supposedly hand out while they were out risking their lives. Not surprisingly, they would walk out of sight of camp and just chuck the lot into the nearest ditch.

Being a German produced paper, SeA used very high quality materials. Just the sort of thing your average Kabul butcher in the street appreciated to roll up the latest off-cut. Kabul's stockhouse district is called, simply enough, Meat Street. Here you could find the raw material bleating and mooing away, and observe the end result being hacked to bits in a bloody orgy. It was quite common to see a cyclist tottering off home with yards of entrails wound round the handlebars.

SeA saved a lot of shop-owner's packaging difficulties and it became a pretty ubiquitous carrier all over Kabul. Which did the German's dinger in. While I could see the frustration, I didn't share the objections. It didn't matter if the paper was being used for packing potatoes or hoofs, it was being seen: and probably more effectively than ISAF's other efforts to achieve the same.

What bugged me was the content, which was universally anodyne. It still is.

A newspaper is a friend who wants to have a good conversation with you. It's why we all have our favourite. The print is a reflection of your thoughts, fears, aspirations and secret delights. Every newspaper owner carefully crafts a product to suit their market.

Newspapers are not there to report the news. They exist to make their owners money. News is a business, with a carefully tailored product for a carefully researched market.

The trouble with the military producing a newspaper is that everybody thinks they are an expert. Information operations attract opinion like the open bonnet of an E-type Jag attracts instant mechanics.

In the military, it's tough to get a quick win. No matter the decision, a general has to watch his intent disappear down a rabbit-hole of staff officers and a paper miasma. There are so many cooks in the broth that the stew is quite often a congealed mess.

Not so with information operations. Every general can be an instant self-appointed genius. I have lost count over the years at how much time senior commanders can devote to changing the colour of the border on a poster, or the position of a comma. Fucking leave it alone, gentlemen!

Do what Rupert Murdoch does. He employs talented and rhino-skinned editors that sleep with their mastheads imprinted on their foreheads. Then he sacks them when he has squeezed out all the juice. I know this because I worked for just such one man: Kelvin McKenzie, who will forever be known as the editor of the infamous 'Sun' newspaper. In two years in his employ, he fired me three times, called me a cunt more than once (and was probably right at least once) and took me on a mad rollercoaster of work-obsessed madness. I loved and loathed him in equal measure, but, by God, I respected his editorial genius. The stuff we produced under his tutelage was absolute magic. Love it or leave it, you couldn't stop looking at it or reading it. He taught me how to sell journalism.

In ISAF, and SeA, nobody sold the product: because nobody figured out who or what we were writing for. Nor did they really care.

Who we wrote for were the faceless colonels in the IJC. They had the approval over the articles: and none of them, in all the time I was there, had any creative ability at all. No doubt fantastic artillerymen, tankers, parachutists and dealers of death. But newspaper editors? Nope. Nothing, though, could convince them that they were not.

The colonels were all trying to impress the generals, who wanted to impress the politicians with a magazine that talked about how wonderful ISAF was and how great the Afghan army was, or was going to be.

One night in downtown Kandahar, with no electricity, no fresh water, beggars in the street and the auditory punctuation of gunfire would have told them it most certainly was not all fucking great.

Instead of creating a conversation that sympathised with the average Joe, what ISAF got was a paper that just turned everybody off. With its relentless stories of Afghan soldiers passing training courses and ISAF soldiers handing out sweets to village kids, it was the printed equivalent of an overdose of Valium.

The Soviets used to produce the same sort of stuff. In my early career, we'd go across the wall into East Berlin, and gather their product up for intelligence. Their papers were near unreadable fantasies. Full of headlines like; 'five year wheat production target exceeded!' Accompanied by a smiling photo of a blonde Aryan lass in a traditional skirt wielding her sickle in a field of perfect corn. It was as believable as Spock's pointy ears. SeA was the same hardcore Vulcan.

By 2012, SeA had transformed into a magazine. It had a talented sub-editor in Kabul, called 'the Viking', mainly because he was a Dane with a big bushy beard. Erik was a cool cat, who just loved playing with words. As do I. I'd send him my stuff, he'd kick it back, I'd kick it back to him, and the end result was a Lennon and McCartney.

Without telling the colonels, we'd start to stick in some controversial stuff, like implicit criticisms of the government. We'd do a piece on refuse collection in Kandahar, which looked innocent enough. But, halfway down, we'd throw in a few lines from a local complaining that the city was a dump. What we wanted to do was create a CONVERSATION.

Sure, ISAF was doing a lot of good stuff that deserved to be advertised. But a whole paper, week after week, was a mighty big shit sandwich to digest.

The 82nd jumped onto the change in tone. They were pissed that they didn't control SeA, as it belonged in Kabul. But then the POTF got a cigar-chewing US paratrooper boss in 2012. He just loved the 82nd and loved that we were changing the gears.

Huggins and his boys needed the juice. In typical airborne fashion, they were about to re-set the game: by giving the war to the Afghans.

The biggest disgrace of all the disgraces we perpetuated in Afghanistan was the dilatory way we failed to create any real kind of Afghan security forces for the first six years we were in the place. Hamid, Sherzai and Raziq were working wonders, all three of them, in building something out of nothing in less time that it took George Washington to put together his Continental Army.

Scott was doing his bit with Sherzai. He started asking him down to COMKAF, to brief on what the air wing was all about. Old Sherzai just ate it up. As is military custom, the room stood up when Sherzai entered. Scott was always careful to let Sherzai assume seniority as a major general to his brigadier. In reality, the staff stood for Scott, as their commanding general, but it said all the right things to Sherzai about respecting an ally.

After the road event, Scott and I developed a good working relationship. Together with Jim, we went on a Sherzai bridge-building exercise.

The Sherzais had done their bit for their countrymen, as all good Muslims must do, under the terms of 'zakat', or alms to the poor. Gul Agha had spent millions building the Baba Wali shrine, up on the Arghandab River. Baba Wali Kandhari was a noted Sufist pir, or saint. The Sherzais, in common with a lot of Pashtun, are Sufists, which is an Islamic doctrine that stresses the mystical and ethereal. Sufists believe strongly in acquiring and developing knowledge from teachers, not just from books.

The extremist Wahhabist doctrine that the Taliban espouses stresses the opposite. To my mind, anything that stood against Taliban extremism is a good thing. Sherzai was therefore a good thing, despite all the flaws: and Scott agreed.

Every year, at Eid, Sherzai gave alms at Baba Wali. In common with all Muslims, he made no fuss about it. I picked up on it and made sure the staff got the word in my briefs: which Sherzai attended. For the first time, Sherzai got some recognition for his family and their status in the eyes of ISAF.

Ironically enough, Baba Wali was the exact spot where Robert's field force had defeated Ayub Khan, back in 1880. Anywhere you went in Afghanistan, you couldn't escape the history. You just had to know where to look.

I put an interest board up outside the COMKAF conference room, all about the air wing and what they were doing. At the time, I was producing about two stories a week on them. Sherzai passed that board every week. He got the message: we were interested.

Jim worked out that Sherzai turned up when I came to visit the air wing. If Jim needed Sherzai to pay attention to something, he'd ask me down and button-hole Sherzai when he showed. I'd write it up, get him into the national magazine.

To my mind, Project Sherzai was influence operations at its best. Sherzai was doing the work. But he had a habit of disappearing off to do family business. By working him into the whole influence piece, he became part of the jigsaw. We just worked the game from behind, as a true mentor should do.

I had the same relationship across at 205 Corps. I wrote up Hamid, got his soldiers into the magazine, stressed their achievements. When I visited, I had soldiers coming up and saying their families had written to them, praising their heroism. Way up in Badakshan or Nangarhar, they had seen their relative fighting for their country in the pages of 'Sada E Azadi'.

Scott asked me to sit on the airport development board. I started going over to the airport, which required special access, to meet with Faizi. His wife is an extraordinary cook, and she'd rustle up the most delicious Afghan dishes. With incredible spices and ingredients, they tasted like real food after the mush we got served in KAF.

Feroz and the boys could get into the civil terminal easily enough. I found the workarounds I needed and built the contacts to make it happen. For four or five months, I built the rhythm, encouraged all the way by Scott and Kaiser, over at RC S.

The 82nd had a joined-up plan to finish off their year: ahead of everybody else, they were going to hand the shooting match over to the Afghans. Jim Huggins was being pretty bold. Up until 2011, ISAF had ruled the roost. Literally everything on the security front was provided, supplied and run by us. Old Johnny Afghan was an also-ran. We paid lip-service to them, but quietly scoffed at their efforts.

One Australian sergeant-major I knew spent an entire year trying to get the Afghan recruits to do the laces up on their boots. They just refused to do it. I pointed out that they had grown up wearing sandals. They didn't know what bootlaces were for. They weren't being slow, or difficult. We were just asking them to behave like westerners when they were actually Afghans.

Hamid, with his Soviet training, got the big picture. He is a consensus leader, who worked hard to bring all his men together. Hamid's mantra was that 205 Corps was not made up of the 14 tribes of Afghanistan. It was made up of another tribe, the family of the army. He had seen enough tribal and ethnic hatred in his life to know that the country needed to find another dynamic: being Afghan.

Unwittingly, he laid the seeds for me to push that very idea forward two years later.

Huggins and the 82nd set their stall out well, by running a series of big operations across the south. Which were, for the first time, planned and led by 205 Corps. The results were patchy. Quite often, the troops involved never even reached the start line, let alone the objective. Huggins was bright enough to see that this was a train set that was running new engines and carriages on newly laid track. It was going to take time to bed in: and there is nothing like driving your own train to get it all right.

Huggins was aided immeasurably by having another light infantryman cover his back, up at the IJC, the headquarters that ran the war. Lieutenant General James Terry had taken over Kandahar from Nick Carter, before getting promoted to run 5 Corps in Germany. Huggins had been Terry's successor. In May 2012, a promoted Terry and 5 Corps HQ came back to Afghanistan as the IJC. Terry knew Kandahar inside out. Huggins was pushing at an open door. Terry knew the clock was ticking: and giving Hamid the lead would be an impressive opening gambit.

This was important stuff. Giving Hamid overall command was unprecedented. Kandahar, and the 82nd, would be leading the way: all the way.

In true style, Huggins didn't make a big song and dance out of it. He was smart. He knew the day would be extremely important to Afghanistan. It was not a time for ISAF triumphalism. Too many civilians had died for that. The war wasn't over. This was not a victory parade. It was the end of the beginning, not the beginning of the end.

On the 1st of July 2012, Afghan defence minister General Abdul Rahim Wardak inspected an Afghan ceremonial guard of honour at Camp Hero. Wardak is a big, burly man who holds considerable clout in Afghanistan as a mujahideen war hero from the time of jihad against the Soviets. Having Wardak take the parade was a considerable feather in 205's cap.

Together with Major General Hamid, flanked by Major General Jim Huggins and Colonel Richard Parker, head of the Australia's 205 Corps advisory team, General Wardak watched as the NATO command flag was lowered and replaced by the command flag of the Islamic Republic of Afghanistan.

With a load of foot-stamping and goose-stepping and over-enthusiastic saluting, it was all done. The band struck up the national anthem. They were so out of tune and rhythm it sounded like a five-year old playing the piano badly. But it was done.

The Afghans were deliriously happy. There were a lot of tears shed. For the first time, they felt their country was coming out of the shadows.

General Hamid must have felt a particular sense of pride as he addressed the assembled troops. After all, he had been there from the beginning:

'It wasn't that long ago that we had no security forces. We started with a small force and today we have over 20,000 soldiers and all the equipment we need—we are ready for this moment.'

There was no ISAF honour guard. In fact, there were hardly any of us at all. This was the Afghan's day. They had earned it. I got to go, along with Feroz and my boys. It was a sign of how valuable what were doing was becoming.

The whole team was humming. We all knew each other's foibles. We knew each other's strengths and weaknesses. Most importantly, we had been there long enough to understand this country we lived in.

Afghanistan was in our blood.

And then, the 82nd all went home. They were nice to me when they left, they even gave me a medal. But everything I had built just stopped the day they left.

It was rotation time. Just as we had momentum, we ruined it all by going right back to square one. A year's worth of knowledge and relationships forgotten.

Day zero. All over again.

CONTRACT CRAZY

Getting gas in KAF was easy. The US army ran two petrol stations: unmanned petrol stations. All you had to do was drive, fill up, and drive off. The place was open 24/7. No attendant, no paperwork, nothing. You just took what you needed.

Originally, the place had been filled with military vehicles. It made sense that they were filled up, every time they went out. By 2011, KAF had changed. There were over 20,000 civilian contractors in the place, nearly 600 different companies, all operating their own business, doing 'something' to support the war effort.

Well, most things had changed. The petrol stations had not. They stayed open, open to everybody. Not everybody was there in service of freedom. The civilian companies were there to make money. The petrol stations were easy cash.

The scam was to take a four by four down to the pump, fill the tank to the brim, drive to a compound, siphon the gas, then drive back for another load. All day, every day, 24/7. The gas would then be decanted and sold on to the local market. Companies got a TCN to do the driving. It was their full-time job.

The US army was paying over 25 dollars a gallon for the stuff. Gas came in by tanker to Karachi, Pakistan, where a significant amount disappeared. It then travelled by tanker up through Pakistan and through Afghanistan in a never-ending stream of traffic. Where up to half would disappear en-route, prey to smugglers and Taliban right-of-way bribes and theft.

KAF alone needed over 250 tankers a DAY, just to keep it going. The scale of the enterprise just to get it to Kandahar was vast. The stuff would finally end up where it needed to be: only to stolen by contract companies and re-sold back to the Afghans. For the people concerned, it was hundred per cent profit margin, all courtesy of the United States taxpayer.

Incredible though it seems, nobody stopped any of this until late 2012, when somebody realised that KAF alone had somehow grown over 6,000 contract vehicles, just for ferrying civilians around. All of which needed gas, all of it paid for by the United States, all of it given away for free. Nobody stopped it because the theft of millions of dollars worth of gasoline was just the tip of the iceberg. The fuel was nothing.

Everything that came into KAF arrived in 20 or 40 foot container loads. There were hundreds of the things lying around. So many that the military took to laying them out like massive Lego bricks in defensive walls.

Although the containers were modern, the logistics management chain was not. Right to the very end, nobody knew what most contained. Beyond the original requisition notes, there was no paperwork. Stuff would arrive, higgledy-piggledy, from Pakistan, at variable times, in variable convoys, requested by a rotation that had long since gone home.

The containers would just be stacked up, un-opened, and left to rust. The border was forever being closed and re-opened. In 2012, it was shut for months on end. Convoys just sat in long queues, while the perishables perished.

Effective logistics management was truly impossible. It was no wonder mountains of gear just got lost, stolen or destroyed. It's more of a wonder that any of it actually arrived on time and in the right place.

In 2013, as the mission wound down, a company contracted to clear KAF hired hundreds of Filipino and Kenyan workers to hunt through the stacks of containers, like locusts hunting corn. They found several Walmart's worth of brand-new gear. Everything from exercise bikes to bed frames to computers to literally thousands of air-conditioners. All still wrapped up in protective plastic.

It wasn't economically worth transporting the stuff back again, so piles and piles of brand new equipment were just moved from their container to vast mounds of condemned but perfectly serviceable gear that the hired labour enthusiastically turned into un-useable scrap. Millions of dollars worth turned to rubbish. That's on top of the stuff that normally got thrown in the trash.

The amount of crap produced by KAF was legendary. Disposing of it could be dangerous work. A whole line of TCNs was employed to try and sort the dangerous stuff out before it hit the incinerators. So much ammunition was simply thrown in the rubbish, they had a special screen put up before the burners to try and protect the workers from exploding ordnance. Visiting the burners required body armour. It was blinking dangerous.

Every time the US rotated, each soldier was entitled to a new mattress. There were thousands of the things, just lying around, waiting to be destroyed or taken away. All of which had had to be transported into Afghanistan in the first place.

Which is where the Sherzai family came in. They had franchises, run by westerners, to transport the waste away. Only as far as outside the gates, but it was off KAF and out of sight. The transport was done for free—and Sherzai had a fleet of over fifty trucks. Then another army of Sherzai employees would pick through the stuff and sell on our rubbish. Worth fortunes to the average, penniless Afghan. Where there's muck, there's brass. ISAF was a very lucrative business, ripe for the picking.

There had always been a very healthy trade in truck-jacking. Up to a third of the stuff that left Karachi never made its destination.

Outside Kandahar there were piles of stolen containers, being sold as desirable homes. Enterprising Afghans, always handy with a blow-torch, ran a brisk line in cutting windows and doors to order. Pretty much every market in southern Afghanistan consisted of rows of coalition-sourced containers.

Over the years, ISAF tried all sorts of security checks to stop their gear being pilfered.

When the locks kept getting picked, and the containers turned up empty at their destination, they tried sealing the doors at Karachi. Even then, the boxes turned up empty, with the locks still intact. The Afghans were using a welding torch to lift the roof off, empty the containers, then solder the top back on again, before passing the container off as full at point of arrival. Utter genius.

Nicking the full ones, inside KAF, was a full-time business too. The trouble was getting them on and off the back of a lorry. A forty-foot container is a heavy load. KAF had two giant lorry-cranes to do the job. They were massive vehicles. The wheels alone were nearly twenty foot high. Driving them around was always an event, requiring a military police escort and lots of flashing lights.

At night, both were locked into a secure compound. Those cranes were a scarce and valuable asset. One night, in mid-2012, the ground crew locked both their precious charges up. And came back in the morning to find they only had one.

The military police spent weeks doing compound searches and taking statements. Despite being in a locked compound in the middle of a camp with over 30,000 souls, a camp which went 24/7, and which was surrounded by several battalions of trained, armed guards and a supposedly secure perimeter, monitored by CCTV and innumerable guard posts, nobody ever saw or heard of the crane again. It just disappeared: into thin air.

The temptation was just too much. ISAF was awash with cash, or the next best thing. Unguarded piles of stuff, just waiting to be lifted by the light-fingered.

Sergeant Jimmy Dennis served in Afghanistan in 2008 and 2009. He worked in Bagram airfield at the distribution yard for Afghan vendors. He was responsible for buying local goods with coalition funds, part of a program to encourage local trade. Jimmy also encouraged himself: to the tune of $250,000 dollars. He took bribes from local vendors, whose goods he then preferred. He sent the cash back to the US in the mail, hiding the notes inside toy trucks sent to his family.

When he came back to Tennessee, he persuaded his pal, James Whitman, owner of a local landscape company, to launder the money. Dennis and his family gave the cash to Whitman, who then sent the Dennis family salary cheques. Jimmy was unfortunate: he got caught. Dennis wasn't the only one. His pal, Ramiro Pena, who served in the same yard, pled guilty to taking $100,000 USD in cash and jewellery bribes.

The sums the two controlled are breath-taking. Between the two relatively junior sergeants, they supervised contracts worth nearly 31 MILLION dollars.

Afghanistan was just awash with money. The wonder of it all is that Dennis and Pena were actually caught at all. In those early days, nobody really cared.

Early on in my time in Kandahar, I went for a cash advance float from accounts. In Kandahar, there was no other way to get money, and the place existed on a dollar economy. I was given a very fat envelope, no questions asked. To my horror, when I counted it out, I had over 8,000 dollars more than I had asked for.

Apart from the moral aspect, I actually thought I was being stung. KAF had a team of special agents that looked out for just this sort of thing. One of them lived opposite me, and I called her in to witness that I was declaring the overage. She was amazed that I had admitted it.

After a sleepless night, I took the cash back. The sergeant in accounts just shrugged and said he hadn't noticed the loss. I was kinda surprised—to me 8,000 dollars is a lot of money. Wordlessly, he opened his safe, and asked me:

'Ever seen a million bucks?'

Which is what he had, in cash, just sitting there as his petty cash spend float. More than your average big bank, just lying there. Nobody cared about 8,000 dollars.

KAF had one civilian bank: a branch of the Kabul Bank.

Kabul Bank is the institution the US uses to facilitate payment of security force and government employees. In 2010, the bank held a billion dollars of US taxpayer's money in deposit, to pay the essential servants of the state.

Chief executive Khaliullah Ferozi didn't quite see it that way and gave away $850 million in unsecured loans to a small coterie of shareholders. Ferozi didn't keep any accounts. The money disappeared. Including loans to Mahmoud Karzai, the president's brother, who now owns the very opulent and recently constructed Aino Mena housing development outside Kandahar.

Tens of millions were smuggled out of the country in plastic bags and airline food trolleys. Much of it ended up in property deals in Dubai. Everybody was at it: Gul Agha Sherzai was stopped with $25 million in cash getting off a plane in Germany. He claimed diplomatic immunity and was released: with his money.

Despite a long winded investigation, only around $70 million of the bank's lost cash has ever been recovered. Yet, despite that fraudulent record, which Ferozi denies vehemently and blames on an erroneous Price Waterhouse audit, the bank continued to be the one-stop in KAF.

In 2012, over 600 companies were based in KAF. That one branch of Kabul Bank was processing $11 million in cash every WEEK. The sums involved, and the scope and scale of the contracts were immense. To this day, much of it remains unaccounted for. Nobody even knows what it was spent on.

The simple truth is that, at any stage of the war, there were more contractors in-country than soldiers. Contractor deaths in-country pretty much match the military too: over 1,600 dead by 2014.

For all that the army brought a ton of stuff and people to the game, Afghanistan was never that expeditionary a conflict. From the earliest days, the war settled into the rhythm of an army of occupation. Occupation requires bases. Bases need buildings, accommodations, latrines, mess halls, motor pools, generators, communications, recreation, refuse collection.

What we built there was a series of army towns, inhabited by a transitory population in uniform. At one time, the army would have done all those maintenance jobs themselves. Not in Afghanistan. It was all contracted out.

The business of keeping all that military-industrial complex functioning became a complete racket. While we built the towns, we never installed a town government. Instead, we licensed out all the support functions in a series of competing, over-lapping and unsupervised contracting regimes that made a lot of folks very wealthy indeed. War in Afghanistan could be a very profitable business.

Top of the tree were the big three; DynCorp, Supreme and KBR (Kellogg, Brown and Root). In general terms, DynCorp were known for providing people, Supreme for raw materials—food, fuel and the like—and KBR for facilities and facilities management.

Between 2002 and 2013, the US state department alone spent $4 billion dollars in Afghanistan. Just under 70% went to DynCorp. They were everywhere: spot a civilian embedded in a military operation, they probably worked for DynCorp. From President Karzai's security detail down to the guys who worked on the Blackhawk maintenance, they were all DynCorp.

The money was pretty good too: a friend of mine, whose job was cleaning helicopters in Kandahar, earned $130,000 a year. His job was pretty important: dust quickly pitted the rotors and glass windows of the birds unless they were kept scrupulously clean. Nonetheless, $130,000 for a cleaning job is pretty good wedge.

DynCorp depends on federal money for its very existence. In 2009, Forbes magazine estimated that over half of the company's annual $3.1 billion annual earnings came from federal military contracts. DynCorp went to considerable lengths to hide some of the program's vaunted effectiveness. Despite federal investigation, over $1 billion dollars worth of investment in Iraqi security forces, administered by DynCorp, remains reportedly unaccounted for. Employees have been accused of serial prostitution, drug taking and child trafficking.

Supreme has an even murkier record. The company, which is Swiss-owned, operated a vast warehouse operation in Helmand. The 290,000 square foot complex is one of the largest buildings in Afghanistan. In total, at ISAF's peak, the company owned over 800,000 square feet of warehousing country-wide. Their Helmand operation, next to the British Camp Bastion, accommodated up to 2,000 staff. The housing modules all boasted private bathrooms. Supreme employees enjoyed perks and salaries far in excess of anything their uniformed clients could ever enjoy.

Since 2005, until recently, Supreme provided every piece of food consumed by ISAF in Afghanistan. The initial five-year contract was worth $4.2 billion.

Supreme also provided much of the fuel, in simply eye-watering quantities, including over 30,000 litres a week to keep KAF running. Supreme operated fuel storage facilities nationally for over 70 million gallons of gasoline.

When the surge into the south happened, in '06-'07, the Americans asked Supreme to up their game. They expected to be charged extra. The bill they got was three times what the US government was reckoning on: an extra $33 million for deliveries alone. The government got involved: and sued Supreme, all while the company was continuing to supply the troops at the front.

What the investigation found was that Supreme was using a Dubai-based subsidiary, Jamal Ali Foods, to act as a middle-man. Supreme would buy goods from their surrogate at an inflated rate and charge the overage to the tax-payer. The margins were ridiculous: on non-alcoholic beer, the profit was pushed from 25 to 125 per cent.

The US government tried to break Supreme's stranglehold, by getting out of the contract, but there was simply nobody else who could stand up the operation in time. Only the winding up of the war stopped Supreme.

In late 2014, after years of litigation, the company paid a total of fines to the US taxpayer of $434 million for proven fraudulent activity.

Supreme made $9.1 billion. The company's owner, Stephen Orenstein, has earned over $1 billion in dividends since the start of the war.

Supreme's chief of operations is former US Lieutenant General Robert Dail. In 2006-08, Dail was the head of the US Defence Logistics Agency, which awards contracts. In 2007, Dail awarded Supreme the DLA's 'new contractor of the year'. Four months after resigning his commission, he took up a post as head of Supreme USA.

The US government action excludes the litigation still on-going in Afghanistan, raised by Afghan sub-contractors. All that fuel and food needed Afghan trucks to get it into country. Haulage companies there are still demanding $23 million in unpaid dues.

The US House of Representatives Oversight Committee looked into Supreme. Representative John Mica was rather scathing:

'This has to be one of the prime poster children for government contracts spun out of control. If we're looking for areas to cut waste, fraud and abuse and rip-offs of the taxpayer, this is the kind of contract that has to be stopped in its tracks.'[25]

Supreme could be pretty intense in getting their cash. In 2012, the Bulgarian president came to see his boys in KAF. Bulgaria provided a company of soldiers for perimeter defence of the base. On landing, while the president went off on his grip and grin, the pilots asked to have the government jet refilled. Supreme, who had the fuel contract, wanted cash up front: $25,000 up front.

The Bulgarians thought that, as NATO members, and a troop contributing nation to boot, that ISAF would bill their government. Not where Supreme was concerned. No money, no fuel. An embarrassing stand-off ensued, only

---

[25] HoR records

solved by the Bulgarian presidential pilot producing his black American Express card. The Bulgarian president got to go home and we got to wonder just how much a presidential pilot would have to earn to be offered a black AmEx.

Between Iraq and Afghanistan, from 2001-2013, around $160 billion was awarded by the US to private contractors. The daddy company of them all is KBR, which has seen contract awards of nearly $45 billion.

KBR started life as Halliburton. During the 1990's CEO Dick Cheney—that Dick Cheney—won the company $2.3 billion in US defence contracts. In 2001, post 9/11, with the same Cheney now as US vice-president, KBR won an open-ended contract of undefined duration and value to provide 'selected services in wartime'. For the next eight years, it won further extensions without a single open competitive tender being offered.

Without KBR, the US would simply have been unable to go to war in either Iraq or Afghanistan. KBR did everything. From buildings right over the spectrum to ammunition supply. In 2009, the Pentagon's top auditor declared that $13 billions worth of work was unaccounted for in Iraq and Afghanistan. Government auditor April Stephenson went on to say that KBR was accountable for 'the vast majority' of the alleged fraud. The trouble is that, without KBR, the war is simply not possible. Some companies are too big to fail.

Underneath the top-soil lay hundreds of small companies, all beavering away on their pet projects. KAF had a whole area, 'contractor central', where they lived. A shantytown of concrete barriers and 'acquired' shipping containers, it was a notorious place to visit after dark. The trouble was that nobody really knew who was doing what, or indeed who was actually in KAF.

Officially, a company had to have work on KAF to have a compound on KAF. Unbelievably, though, until 2013, anybody could just rock up onto KAF and declare 'open for business'. KAF had no entry or exit law. Two private airlines, Aerotech and DFS, ran daily private charters to Dubai. $600, return, saw you transported in an old Airbus back to and from the world. There were so many contractors on KAF that seats were forever at a premium.

All you had to do to get into KAF—bear in mind this is transport between two international countries—was buy a ticket. Neither airline checked that you had any credentials or identity documents to get into KAF. All you had to do was check-in at Dubai and get off at the other end. KAF was a military airbase, governed by the military technical agreement. It may, technically, have been Afghan soil, but nobody bothered to check. You just got off the plane and disappeared.

KAF was the Klondike. Each US unit held its own internal budget for contracted services. If you were, say, an internet provider, you'd just turn up in KAF and wander around until you found a contracting officer who needed internet. They'd write you up a letter as a sponsoring agent and, suddenly, you'd be an official KAF agency. The US devolved local contract authority to a really low level of authority: generally a sergeant. Those guys were pretty popular.

Every night of the week, some company would hold a barbie, with shrimp and near-beer. I'd get invited quite a lot, as did all the civilian females: for obvious reasons. And, lo and behold, the same contracting sergeants would appear at every do. The gifts came thick and fast too. Carpets, iPhones, laptops, watches, all were available. As were the TCN females, nominally employed as cooks and cleaners.

KAF had no land management. All you had to do was find a spare piece of dirt and set up a compound. Or, sub-rent a piece from somebody already there. Nobody really cared all that much: and none of the soldiers ever stayed long enough to find out.

Labour was easy. Just go back to Dubai and any number of people traffickers could take you to the docks. A whole society of economic migrants from any number of poor countries lived there, just waiting for work. All that you needed to do was buy them a one-way ticket to KAF, stick them in a shipping container turned dormitory and you're all set. Some of the living conditions these poor sods had to endure were horrific. Piled like cordwood in bunks five or six high, twenty or thirty would be rammed into containers that held four US troops. Every day, we would walk around work crews of TCNs doing all the crappy jobs that kept us in our gilded cages.

The road sweeps, the rubbish collectors, the cleaners, the domestic staff, the cooks, the labourers. All of them came from Africa or the sub-continent.

The whole sordid mess just chugged along while times were good. When the war started to wind down, it went bad. Companies were cut overnight, their TCN staff abandoned, often without paperwork.

KAF had a whole homeless community of workers that had somehow been left behind. They lived in the bomb shelters, and wandered the camp during the day, looking for work. One Kenyan woman broke into our block so she could use the shower. She had been on the run for two weeks. Her employer had lit out with all her identity documents. She was stateless as well as homeless.

Matters came to a head when the KAF police found a minibus full of lost workers. They had been living out of the van for months. COMKAF did a camp-wide sweep. The military police found hundreds living rough. Nobody wanted to claim them. Their companies were long gone. Their national embassies refused to pay for them. The proposed solution was for the troop's welfare fund to pay for tickets to fly them to Dubai, where they could claim asylum.

While General Sherzai wasn't directly implicated in any of this, his family definitely was.

His son, Farid, ran a very successful 'hotel', right outside KAF, that employed hundreds of TCN cleaners. His company was fronted by western staff, managing the contract on his behalf. Years later, I found out from a good friend of mine that Farid was wanted by the CIA for smuggling, grand theft and people smuggling. The egg broke when one of Farid's western staff was arrested for stealing classified armour plating. He confessed, but was banned from KAF for life and stuck on a plane to Dubai.

Which was the nub of all of it. KAF had no applicable laws. No matter what you did there, all that could happen was to be put on a plane out of there. KAF truly was the Klondike meets Mad Max. None of this frenetic and vast expenditure benefited ordinary Afghans in any way, shape or form.

Supreme would import food to its Helmand operation to feed its warehouse staff, guarded by Supreme security staff. Food which was then cooked by Supreme chefs to feed Supreme security and warehouse staff that needed to be there to bring the food in the first place. It was a never-ending circle of 'we're here because we're here'. All of which was maintained and paid for by the US taxpayer.

In the early days, I spent time in a town called Maimana, in the northwest, where the British had a small provincial reconstruction team. We bought all our fresh food locally and got the rest from ration packs. We cooked on an old army portable stove, basically a few gas burners on a trailer rig. The food was prepared by an attached army chef. It was basic, but nobody starved.

By 2006, suddenly everybody had acquired the right to have ice-cream with dinner. The private contractors just lifted the base subsistence line to luxury level: all of which required more haulage, more storage, more preparation. All at more cost. As the big bases upped the ante, so the smaller bases wanted the same. All at more cost.

The contract world was a self-generating monster. It was in everybody's interest to just keep the war trundling onwards. The place was awash with illicit cash. The soldiers never stayed long enough to even see it. So the companies got richer and the politicians trumpeted the money as being spent on Afghan reconstruction.

No Afghan ever saw any more than a tiny percentage of the money that went straight back to the contractors. All that cash was actually doing was feeding a military-industrial monster.

A NEW FUTURE

Question: what are the basics a government needs to provide its people? I don't mean a welfare state and all that other mother jazz. I mean the basics, the real biscuit, that will get you from day to day. Answer? Comes down to three things: roads, water and electricity.

Sure, there's other stuff that would be nice to have. If you want your country to have a future, stuff like security, schools and banks would be pretty high on the list. But for the get-out-of-bed, live-your-life signs that a country is functioning, you can't beat roads, water and electricity.

Roads get you from A to B. They allow you to go see your neighbours, take your goods to town, and your purchases home. They allow governance to get at you. Stuff like police and town officials. Normal life.

First thing the English did after they beat the rebellious Scots highlanders in 1745 was to build a network of roads across the mountainous interior. They then built a series of forts on top of those roads, right at the strategic breakwaters. Roads didn't just allow the English to move troops to trouble spots—although they did plenty of that too. The mere sight of a blacktop, going right through rebel territory, reminded folks the war was over and government had arrived. Feared or not, the English made their mark. And those roads are still in use today, two hundred and seventy years later.

Afghanistan, its mountains and impenetrable clan culture bear more than a passing resemblance to the Scottish highlands and their culture. Roads play the same role in Afghanistan as they did in Scotland.

Since 2001 the West has funded an awful lot of road building. Around $4 billion worth of construction, two thirds of that vast sum from the US. From the very beginning, ISAF recognised the importance of the project. *'Wherever the road ends, that where the Taliban starts,'* said US Lieutenant General, later Ambassador, Karl Eikenberry in 2006.

The most important road in Afghanistan is the much-vaunted ring road, right around the country. It's vast, over 2,200 kilometres in length. More than two thirds of Afghanistan's population live within 50 kilometres of that road.

It's been around for a long time.

Nikita Khrushchev, Soviet Premier in the 1950s and early '60's, bequeathed the initial funding for construction. The most important legacy project from those days is the Salang Tunnel, which cuts through the Hindu Kush, connecting Kabul with the northern territories in an impressive series of covered roadways and tunnels. The US wasn't to be outdone either. In the '60's America built the important Kabul-Kandahar leg of the ring road, and levelled the spur out from Kandahar down to Spin Boldak on the border.

Even the Taliban regime recognised the importance of a road network. During their inglorious period at the helm, they repaired over 200 kilometres of the ring road, and paved 40 kilometres of the route to the border from Kandahar.

When we arrived, we went road mad. The initial USAID infrastructure survey, completed in 2001, estimated that only 50 kilometres of decent paved road remained across the country. Building roads was a quick win.

Despite initial scepticism from Washington, based primarily on the fact that USAID had never run a road construction program before, the Louis Berger Group (LBG), a New Jersey-based design conglomerate, was contracted in 2002 to upgrade the Kabul – Kandahar highway. The initial cost estimate was $162 million for 480 kilometres of two-lane highway. Two years later, after significant delays, multiple deaths and frequent attacks on the construction crew, LBG turned the road over at a cost of £311 million. Nearly double the initial estimate.

Full costings were never implemented. LBG had sub-contracted to an Indian construction and a South African security firm, which had sub-contracted to local Afghan firms. Afghans that then performed their own local sub-contracting. Everybody factored in a profit. As ever in Afghanistan, large sums of cash changed hands for minimal result, with foreign companies creaming off the mother lode.

LBG got caught. A whistle-blower contacted the US government. Turned out that LBG had both over-billed the US government and paid off the Taliban to let the road be built. The Indian sub-contractor LBG contracted paid off a local Khost Province warlord, Ghulam Arafat, through a ghost company. Which then directly sluiced $161,000 a month to Arafat.

Arafat then paid local insurgents $1 million a year to not attack the road. Which adds up to $932,000 a year commission for Arafat. Not a bad tariff for doing nothing.

The bad guys in question are the Haqqani network, which is one of the most organised and feared of the various insurgent groups. Arafat grew up with the group's founding father, Jalaluddin Haqqani.

LBG got fined over $18 million in criminal liabilities and $50.6 million in civil fines by the US government.

Rather than using local labour, LBG and other international companies had flown in Indian, Turkish and Chinese labourers. The architects didn't even ask local elders for permission to build on their land. They just drove the road right through.

As you might imagine, the locals got mighty pissed off. The result has been a surge in violence along the new highways. In 2012 alone, the Kabul-Kandahar stretch suffered 190 known bomb attacks, as well as 284 shootings.

It's not just the insurgents doing the fighting: local folks just stick on half a uniform and pretend to be police officers. Shakedowns are endemic. The government are in on the game too. In 2012, Afghan Minister for Public Works, Najibullah Ozhand, told the BBC that his staff at the Salang Tunnel was taking £3,000 dollars a day in bribes.

None of that cash ever found its way into maintenance. Today, the fifty-year old tunnel is a near-death trap. Literally thousands of vehicles pass through the strategic route every day, winter and summer. The tunnel hasn't been repaired in decades. There is barely a kilometre left of asphalted road. All along the precipitous route, wrecked vehicles that have slipped off the open roadway litter the hillside.

Across the country, the roads themselves are literally falling apart. The problem got so bad that in 2012 Minister Ozhand actually suspended all new road construction.

New construction between Gardez and Khost had started disintegrating a mere six months after construction. The 64 mile highway cost over $2 million dollars a mile to build, $128 million in total. Over $40 million was spent on international private security companies providing over-watch for the construction. The construction company had built the road with a mere skim of asphalt. Enough to look pretty in the pictures they presented in exchange for payment, not enough to hold a truck.

Most of the roads just couldn't cope. Around 40% are now worn away, caused by a mix of poor construction and a complete lack of vehicular traffic regulation. Standard bill of fare in Afghanistan is just to load up your truck until the axle breaks. Then you are good to go. There are no rules, no traffic authority. The Kabul to Jalalabad highway, one of the main trade arteries in the country, is just one big divot of tyre-tracks.

Then, there are the bombs. In the second half of 2013, just one Afghan army battalion defused 200 IEDs on their twelve-mile stretch of highway one. There's one crater in Gardez that is twenty-five feet deep.

Afghanistan has no road repair or maintenance at all. We put all our cash into building an impressive statistic, none into preserving it. Although USAID did put $53 million into operational maintenance between 2007 and 2012, it then cut all funding. In 2014, USAID said that it was still working towards establishing a sustainable road repair and maintenance body.

Some of the projects planned got ridiculously stupid. Andrew Natsios, the USAID Afghan program administrator in 2005, was a big alternative livelihoods nut. The sort of well-meaning charity stuff that generates basket weaving and traditional sculpture carving programs.

Natsios had recently been to the Bolivian rain forest, where he had seen local tribes-people beavering away on cobblestone roads. The Americans were always obsessing over Bolivia. Afghanistan produces the world's finest drugs, which is pretty much all it has in common with Bolivia. Except that the US is deeply mired into both countries.

I lost count of how many times I was asked to do articles drawing parallels between the Afghan and Bolivian experience. I always demurred, suggesting Bosnia might be a better example. Which always got knocked back because of the religiously inspired struggle in the Balkans. Which seemed to me to be a pretty good parallel between the West and our Islamic fanatics. I never could get that idea to stick, though.

Natsios—and this tale is quite genuine—decided to bring the rain forest to Afghanistan and recruited a bunch of Bolivian cobblestone experts. He flew them into Helmand, pan pipes and all. A Washington for-profit development firm called Chemonics was given a contract, worth $166 million in 2007, to promote this sort of rubbish.

The Afghans wanted asphalt and gravel. Instead they got eleven Bolivians who spent months training up forty-six bemused Afghans in the art of putting stones into symmetrical patterns.

Several months later, a full one-sixth of a mile of cobbles was put together on the outskirts of Lashkar Gah, Helmand's provincial capital. US ambassador Rod Neumann flew in and made a lot of noise about ancient Roman technology providing the answer to Afghanistan's future. It made for a lot of optimistic column inches in the US media. The Afghan stonemasons had enough of rolling stones around and promptly deserted.

Chemonics quietly dropped the whole thing and spent the money on other things that the Afghans could live without, like a women's centre and an internet cafe.

All that madness means that 85% of the new roads we constructed are now judged to be of poor quality. Which, fourteen years earlier and $4 billion richer, is pretty much the same percentage statistic we inherited in 2001. There's just a lot more terrible tarmac out there now.

Kandahar is essentially a desert, with a fertile bit maintained by the Arghandab and Helmand river basin. The Americans had been pretty smart in the south, back in the '50's, when they had built KAF. Right across the fertile region, they built a complex and highly effective series of irrigation canals. At its peak, it must have rivalled the Dutch experience.

The endeavour was fed by two enormous dams. One in Kandahar, across the Arghandab, to the north of Kandahar city, called Dahla dam. And one in Helmand, Kajaki Dam, which the Yanks cleverly designed as a dual-purpose hydro-electric facility.

Dahla is a remarkable project. Fly over it and the difference it produces is vivid. To the north is all desert scrubland. To the south, under the sluice gates, is a green paradise. That one project, built in 1952, was designed to provide water for a huge 36,000 hectares. Even thirty years of war hasn't completely destroyed its effectiveness. Although the canals have mostly long silted up, and the dam itself is seriously in need of repair, downstream some 20,000 hectares of cultivated land still receive the precious water it delivers. Which is pretty impressive for a region that is perpetually in drought.

When Canada ran the war, they put a lot of money into renovating the

Dahla project: about $50 million dollars worth of commitment. A Canadian company, SNC-Lavalin, got the contract. It took them three years to dredge a mere 8 canals. They got fired and were replaced by the Central Asian Development Group. The money assigned all got spent on the tributary canals. Not on the dam itself. So, while the water flowed a little easier, the capacity of the aged dam itself was left un-changed.

As a security guarantee, about $10 million of the proposed $50 million was given to private security companies. The main beneficiary was Watan Risk Management. Watan also ran security for every convoy between Kabul and Kandahar, under a depraved commander known locally as 'the butcher'. The company is run by two of president Karzai's cousins—Rashid and Ahmed Popal. Until his death, the whole was rumoured to be under the control of Wali Karzai, the influential Karzai half-brother that General Nick Carter cosied up to. Both Popals are convicted drug smugglers and strongly rumoured to have worked for the Taliban. In 2010, the competing private security concerns had a Mexican stand-off at their headquarters in Kandahar city. Weapons got raised and folks nearly died. Two Canadian advisors got the next plane out of the country.

The same year, the US debarred Watan for corruption and drug-smuggling. After Wali Karzai was killed, his brother, the president, wound up their operation into a new, state-sponsored organisation.

The Canadians suspended the program. After burning through $50 million, the dam hadn't been touched and the canals were left to silt up again. By 2014, 30% of the renovated canals were assessed by the US Corps of Engineers to be inoperable.

The Americans, again, stepped into the breach. The new idea was to raise the dam's height by eight meters. Total capacity would rise from 300 hundred million cubic metres to 484 million metres.

The new project would cost $308 million dollars, of which the Afghans would be expected to provide $38 million and the US taxpayer the rest. Critically, a new pipeline would be added, to provide clean drinking water to Kandahar city. The project was split into two phases. The first would build new sluice gates and overflow tunnels. The main construction, to raise the dam's height, would complete phase two.

To date, nearly three years on from the Canadians withdrawal, phase one is not yet complete. The construction is now run by a Turkish company, 77 Turkish Construction and Trading Company. Over $70 million dollars have been spent so far on this version of the re-vamp. The project still has no completion date. That's $120 million bucks total and nearly ten years work for an unfinished return.

Lord knows, Kandahar city could do with the water. The place is home to nearly 700,000 folks. To feed that demand, Kandahar theoretically has 15 wells. Except, only 9 of them actually work. Even at full capacity, the wells can only produce enough water for a third of the population. An antiquated pumping system then reaches a mere 20% of the population.

The system is deeply, and structurally, broken. As US Dr Ed Majano, a US army Corps of Engineer water expert, described in a 2012 Pentagon report:

'If there is a fuel shortage or an electrical outage, the pumps stop working and the system loses pressure. This situation allows contaminants to infiltrate the system—a situation made worse by a distribution system in which an estimated 70 percent of the pipes leak, and the complete lack of a wastewater collection system, which almost guarantees sewage and other contaminants will get into an unpressurized potable water distribution network.'

What the city urgently needs is a feeder from Dahla: which may or may not ever be built. And a citywide standpipe system: which is currently not even being considered. And a wastewater facility: for which there is no funding.

Well, that lack of capacity is not strictly correct. Kandahar did have a highly effective groundwater extraction and bottling plant. And no less than three waste water plants. They were in KAF. We built them for our own troops.

Everybody on KAF drank bottled water. There was no other source. Until 2012, the lot was shipped into the country. It was pretty horrible stuff too, mostly desalinated liquid from the UAE.

Funnily enough, Kandahar Province has quite a lot of the stuff. It's just that it is way underground. About a half-kilometre underground.

In 2012, NATO's logistic agency, NSPA, commissioned the construction of KAF's own water extraction plant. Using our old friend Supreme as contracting agent, they drilled two boreholes 500 metres into the bedrock. They cut right into Afghanistan's main deep aquifer, which stretches all the way up to Kabul.

Utilising state-of-the-art European technology, NATO then built a hugely impressive bottling plant. The whole rig was based on the same set-up that Perrier uses. Staffed by mostly Kenyan workers, situated in an over-pressured and sealed warehouse, the plant produced an astounding 23,400,000 litres of fresh drinking water every year of its short production life.

Most of KAF was pretty jerry-rigged. Visiting the water plant was different: it was a glimpse into an industrial future. NATO remained very coy about how much it all cost, but the rumour at the time was $75 million dollars.

The plant didn't last long. It got closed down at the end of 2014. After enough water had been extracted to supply the remaining garrison for five years. Instead of gifting the mothballed complex—and the technology is unique for Afghanistan—it was quietly sold off to a local metal dealer. It's never produced another bottle of water since.

Same MO applies to the waste-water plants.

The poo-pond was the impetus for construction. The US magazine 'Stars and Stripes' got fixated on the whole odious mess: and ran a regular blog on the shit level. NATO jumped into the breach and built a very impressive-looking sewage treatment plant. When the Americans arrived, they built another, right next door. And then began a second one on the north side of the airport.

Trouble is, the NATO plant came with the wrong sized filters. It looked good, but it never worked. The US plants got bulldozed. All that was left was a big concrete hole that got covered over. All that money spent, and no Afghan ever saw any of it.

Except for the KAF water. Branded as 'Quench2O', the stuff came in nifty little half litre-sized bottles. Patrols never left without at least a half-dozen cases. All over KAF, there were huge piles of 'Quench2O' plastic bottles, all internally distributed. The plastic bottles themselves were not so easily disposed of. There were so many discarded, they clogged the storm drains all around the camp.

Until 2013, KAF had a very willing company of Slovak engineers. They were burly men who willingly obliged in cleaning up their comrade's mess. When they left, there was nobody left to do the necessary outside the wire. All around KAF are piles of empty plastic bottles, our Kandahar water legacy.

The other great water project in the south, at Kajaki, has an even less-storied history.

Again built in the 1950's by the Americans, USAID provided two turbine generators in the 1970's, which, together, should provide about 33MW of electricity. Remarkably, the dam continued to produce electricity all through the Soviet and civil wars. However, the downstream transmission lines were badly vandalised.

It took the Taliban to try and sort out the power supply. They actually re-built the transmission lines all the way to Lashkar Gah and Kandahar city. Albeit, they used inferior cables, so that the turbines could never work at full capacity, but they did work. The Taliban also contracted the Chinese to provide a third turbine, agreed to cost a very reasonable $3.5 million dollars.

Remember that figure when you get to the end of this tale.

The Americans then bombed all that progress during the invasion. Once again, the lights went out in 2001.

Kajaki became one of those prestige re-development projects that were in vogue in the early years. Louis Berger Group (LBG) was again contracted to repair the plant. They, in turn, sub-contracted it to a German company, Voith-Siemens. VS turned in a contract bid for $20 million dollars. Already war economics was providing a very healthy inflation rate.

USAID wasn't impressed and went back to the Chinese contractors the Taliban had used: China Machine-Building International Corporation (CMIC).

Kajaki didn't really need a third turbine. The spillways had never been finished, so a lot of the water just ran away unused. Both of the original turbines were desperately in need of repair. Even in the good days, the dam only produced 24Mw of the capacity 33Mw. Repair would have been the simpler option.

LBG kept on with viability studies. There was very little ISAF presence in those days, and the work progressed fairly freely. Then, having spent $15 million with no work completed, the British arrived in 2006. The British paratroopers brought a lot of violence with them. The last road trip by LBG was in May 2006. After that, it was just too dangerous. LBG pulled out.

The British found themselves besieged: and taking casualties. Multiple legacy mines, laid by the Soviets, caused multiple casualties. Kajaki Dam still wasn't producing.

LBG tried again, in 2007, to reach the dam. Three employees got killed in a well-planned and executed ambush. The British mounted a series of tit-for-tat battles and tactical operations. Kajaki became one of those totems of progress that neither side would abandon.

What had been initiated as a simple re-construction project became a matter of international pride.

A new turbine was delivered to Karachi, from China, together with a bunch of installation engineers from CMIC. Somehow, the bits ended up being sent to Kabul, not Kandahar. It cost another $7.5 million to get them to Kandahar.

The project had taken so long to get the moving parts together that the original British paratroopers had left, rested, and then come back for another tour.

The trouble was that the turbine might be in Kandahar, but the 900 tonnes of concrete and aggregate it needed to sit on was not. Concrete mix has a very short shelf-life in the Afghan heat. There was simply not enough truck capacity to transport the aggregate and the turbine, nor could the roads take the load. USAID had sub-contracted repairs to Route 611, but the Taliban had driven the contractors off. Another $5 million was spent for no return working the logistics planning.

The British elected to take the turbine. The concrete could wait. In what was billed the biggest logistical move by the British army since the Second World War, the new turbine was transported cross-country to Kajaki. The paratroopers didn't have the numbers to fully secure the road. Nonetheless, the operation was a success. Finally, the new turbine was where it should be.

Then, the CMIC Chinese engineers lit out. They said they had received Taliban kidnap threats. Nobody was left who knew how to put the boxes full of parts together. In any case, nobody had brought up the cement. The thing couldn't have been built anyway.

By the end of 2009, the two existing turbines had finally been repaired. The crews and parts had been expensively air-lifted in. It was too dangerous any other way. It was too dangerous to repair the transmission lines. Now the power couldn't go anywhere.

USAID was spending a million a month to guard the wooden boxes containing the turbine parts. They just sat there, rotting in the sun.

Their security company, US Protections and Investigations, hired locals to do the actual work. They provided a lot less workers, vehicles and expenses than they invoiced for. In 2009, Delmar and Barbara Spier, the husband and wife co-owners of P&I, were convicted of fraud and forced to repay $3 million. USAID cancelled the project until further notice.

The whole turbine deal should never have happened. Kajaki just became one of those big-ticket items that fixated the powerbrokers.

At a time when Helmand was falling apart, the British should never have spent six months obsessing over getting it there. It just became a 'win-win' for

16 Air Assault Brigade, who were looking for a success in their six-month tour of glory to show the Americans. The project became a vanity item after the pasting they had sustained first time around. As brigade commander Mark Carleton-Smith told his officers:

'Gentlemen... The Americans are coming! We risk being put in the corner, sidelined and forgotten. The Americans think we're wet and present only problems. I am not here to listen to how a mission is not possible. I want you all to take on board that it is our job to carry out the tasks we are set—not go on about how we can't do things. I want a complete refocus on finding solutions not problems.'[26]

The parts to repair the existing turbines had been kicking around Lashkar Gah for years. But that sort of incremental progress didn't light up the headlines back home. You can't blame the Taliban either. They weren't actually against improving Kajaki. They had proved that. They were just against ISAF doing it. As their spokesperson said in 2011:

'We will never let the Americans do anything here, whether installing the turbines or any other project... The Americans have their own aims behind every project... This is why we say that no U.S. projects are acceptable.'[27]

In point of fact, despite pretty much controlling all the districts south of Kajaki, such as the infamous Sangin, the Taliban very rarely attacked the transmission lines.

After all that effort, the power was still only on for an hour a day in Kandahar city. 2009 saw the arrival of Stan McChrystal and the whole COIN-dinista movement. Together with British General Nick Carter.

Carter took one look at the whole Kajaki mess and came up with the 'Kandahar bridging project'. The military would step in and provide power.

Over the heads of USAID and the US Ambassador Karl Eikenberry, Carter accessed the US military's own private funds, called the Commander's Emergency Response Fund (CERP).

By 2008, the US military was directly spending $488 million a year on aid projects: work that would traditionally be done by civilian agencies. McChrystal didn't just Americanise the shit of the war, he took over the whole re-construction stuff too.

Carter's plan was for a massive provision of diesel generators. The military could easily daisy-chain a few of their container-sized generators. The trouble is that diesel costs a lot of money: to buy and to transport. But the park could be brought on-line quickly.

Longevity was never a concern: the military only ever stayed a year tops. Making it work always took precedence, keeping it going would be somebody else's problem. By 2015, the two diesel farms would cost over $200 million.

Shur Andam diesel park provided 10Mw of power. It opened at the beginning of 2011. Eikenberry gritted his teeth and came to the opening

---

[26] 'Desperate Glory', Sam Kiley

[27] 'Watershed of Waste', Global Post

ceremony. Shur Andam was followed by another 10Mw park, at Bagh E Pol. Together, the two parks doubled the amount of electricity available to Kandahar city.

Kandahar Governor Toryali Wesa wasn't a happy bunny. He told me:

'Nobody was thinking of something permanent. Everybody was talking just of short-term, quick impact projects. We were told we had to take it or leave it. This was their money and they spent it the way they wanted.'

Not surprisingly, power brought business. Shur Andam business park saw over 60 companies open, everything from packaging to ice-cream plants. Not surprisingly, insurgent attacks went down. People had jobs and stuff to buy. A happy man doesn't make for much of a guerrilla.

Which was fine as long as the US was footing the bill for all that diesel. In 2013, the plants were estimated to cost $100 million to run. Except, the Americans were going home. They told the Afghans the funding for diesel would end in September 2015. The Afghan power company, DABS, makes about $150 million a year across the whole country. Running the Kandahar plants alone would cost two-thirds of its entire revenue. It is the end for the diesel parks. Afghanistan simply cannot afford them.

Shur Andam was only a bridging plan. So we're back to Kajaki again. In 2011, USAID assigned another $75 million to finally bringing the new turbine on-line. It is part of a bigger $266 million contract that now resided with Black & Veatch.

The work was due to start in 2013. Black and Veatch got pulled for slow progress, so the project was again sub-contracted. This time to GFA consulting. The latest estimate is that the whole thing will cost $300 million to complete.

The US Afghan inspector general, John Sopko, has questioned whether it is worth it. Nobody knows when, or indeed even if, it will ever be finished. In the meantime, the turbine boxes are still where the British left them.

Roads, water, electricity. Afghanistan is still waiting.

CANDY STRIPE MADNESS

Just as real and substantive security progress was being achieved, it came time for Jim Huggins and his paratroopers to go home.

As always with Afghanistan, just as good stuff was really gaining momentum, ISAF rotated out its folks. Roberts would have been appalled. How on earth could you fight a war with a completely new team every year?

On 2nd September 2012, a sad-looking Huggins said goodbye to Kandahar. The new guys took over: in the shape of the 3rd Infantry Division, commanded by Major General Robert 'Abe' Abrams.

Abrams was, and still is, a man in a hurry. His family name is US military royalty. His father, Creighton Abrams, was the four-star general who took over command in Vietnam from the ill-fated William Westmoreland. Creighton Abrams made his career name during World War 2, serving under General Patton, who called Abrams the 'world champion' of tank commanders. Creighton went all the way to Chief of Staff of the Army, before a heavy cigar habit led to cancer that killed him in 1974. Abrams senior had six children: three sons and three daughters. The daughters all married into the army. The three sons all became generals. The US Army named its main battle tank, the M1A1, the Abrams, after Creighton.

Abe Abrams is not just the son of one of the US Army's most famous post-war officers. He is the youngest son. His path was more or less set for him when he was born. His ruthless ambition, as the baby boy with something to prove, shines throughout his entire life. By the time he reached Kandahar, at the head of the 3rd Infantry Division, he had done well. His entire career had been a carefully orchestrated rise to prominence, ticking all the correct command and executive boxes, from ranger school to a master's degree in strategic studies from the War College.

Interestingly, which affected the way he led operations in Kandahar, pretty much everything he achieved had been in tanks. He is an undoubted master of the heavy end of the spectrum. If the US ever needs a guy to go blow Russia up, Robert 'Abe' Abrams would be in the first draft pick.

The Afghans were sad to see the 82nd go. I often wondered what they REALLY thought of us, coming and going. Unlike ISAF, they just kept on keeping on. We'd turn up, all full of vim and vigor, and think they were lazy, not doing 18 hour days, seven days a week, for our short twelve months 'in-country'.

Thing we always forgot is that they didn't get to take leave overseas, or head off back to normality after twelve months. This place was home. They didn't do a year and head off to a promoted post. They couldn't leave. Afghanistan's war was their life.

At the hand-over, General Hamid, unusually, was invited to speak. I knew from private conversation that he always worried about the handovers. It was a moveable feast as to whom he got as his new 'mentor'. Could he work with them? Would they understand him? Sometimes, you won, sometimes you lost: change of command was an Afghan lottery.

He got up to speak, in that characteristically humble and modest way of his. His words, though, spoke of his sadness at parting:

'These... past divisions that were assigned to RC-S, we never, ever thought for a second that they were our partners. We always sensed that they were our brothers. I felt that the 82nd was literally a part of 205th corps. I never felt that they were anything but Afghan forces.'

For a military flag hand-over, this was lachrymose stuff indeed. Jim Huggins stuck his chin out and swatted at grit in his eye:

'I came here as a student of Afghanistan, and I leave a student of Afghanistan. My team and I may never fully understand this country's amazing culture, religion and social dynamics, but we will always appreciate, and, most importantly, respect them. And with our Afghan partners we have formed a bond that cannot be broken.'

Huggins spoke as a general who had realised the limits of ISAF abilities, and acknowledged that Afghanistan would accept ISAF on its terms, but never be conquered by ISAF. The 82nd had done Kandahar a solid turn, placing Afghan forces into the lead, being humble, and letting Hamid and guys learn on the job, while being there to back them up when they were needed.

3ID was a different beast.

The 82nd were all light and mobile, ready to improvise. 3ID was heavy infantry, a blunt instrument of armoured soldiers, trained and organised to fight Russian divisions on the plains of Europe. Their brigades were called 'Raider', 'Spartans' and 'Sledgehammer'. During WW2, they had suffered more casualties in a single day than any other US division. Audie Murphy was part of 3ID. Their verbal refrain was 'Rock of the Marne', named after a particularly bloody engagement during World War 1: a conflict that earned the division their first two medal of honours.

I met them in Bosnia, where 3ID was engaged in peacekeeping. All through their tour, despite a pretty normal environment, they had insisted on keeping their helmets and body armour on, their rifles loaded. In Abrams, 3ID had a perfect foil for all that aggression.

He was a tank man: a lots of metal, lots of noise, lots of destruction, kind of fella. The 82nd had a paratrooper's natural sense of superiority. 3ID were non-airborne, but had a non-airborne sense of aggrieved vulnerability that they were just as good as the vaunted paratroopers. Abrams encouraged that sense of aggression and elitism. In the military, it's an easy leadership win. Harder to persuade the guys to prove they are the best by their actions, not just the badge they wear. 3ID came to Kandahar all fired up to steamroller the bad guys.

Abrams backed that intent up with his opening speech, the day he got his hands on the command pennant:

'We believe in this mission. It will be done; by the Rock of the Marne.'

Those of us in the audience who had been there a while, and would still be there for a while, shivered. 3ID were gonna throw that Marne rock into what had been quite a calm pool, where stuff was being done, without a great deal of fuss. And those self-generated waves would come close to ruining all that the 82nd had done.

In COMKAF, we saw the change the first week 3ID were in charge. Abrams commissioned teams of guys to go out and re-paint KAF in 3ID colours. The division symbol is a blue candy-stripe within a square. That damn sign cropped up on any flat surface everywhere. Anything remotely Airborne was removed, painted over or defaced. The helicopter waiting area, which had been branded 'Lobo Air' for years, was promptly re-badged 'Marne Air', all in divisional blue and white.

One hapless left-over 82nd officer, tasked with continuity of hand-over, made the fatal mistake of starting his morning brief to the 3ID staff with: 'Airborne, general!' Silence followed. It was the last brief that officer made in Kandahar.

Next up, 3ID started putting up 'orders of the day', including instruction on that precious United Nations square acre of The Boardwalk. Amongst other madness, runners were now to move counter-clockwise on the running track, walkers clockwise. The micro-management became very intense, very quickly. 3ID patently didn't get it that KAF was still, in 2012, very much a NATO base. There were over a dozen different national contingents on the place. KAF itself was a NATO command.

The 82nd had been quite content to work on their main task, winning the war. They'd happily left COMKAF to run the war inside the wire. Scott had done a pretty good job of welding all that conflict of interest, culture and language into one working part.

3ID weren't happy. Abrams saw a bit of the puzzle that he didn't own: he wanted it back. COMKAF and Abrams were to spend a whole year playing cat and mouse over stuff that most two star generals would just leave alone. COMKAF itself became a bone that just festered with 3ID.

For Scott, the bell had tolled. Barely six weeks after 3ID arrived, he had his hand-over.

Just before he left, he gave me my NATO medal. I liked this particular award: because everybody got one. Anybody in NATO who served in

Afghanistan was awarded it. Several countries, including the UK, didn't officially allow their soldiers to wear the NATO medal, but everybody was entitled to a parade to get one. I always thought it petty to order troops to accept the NATO medal as a 'keepsake' only. It's the only medal I have earned, and I have several rows from several countries, that I actually got on the battlefield, direct from the guy who was my boss. It means a lot to me that Scott Dennis, my friend, gave it to me.

Scott was going to retire after Kandahar, so he was pretty relaxed about 3ID and their paint teams, but he knew the war was going to change. He advised me to help advise the new guys, but we both knew the wheels were coming off the truck.

He took one last flight in his F-16, right before he left. It would be his last combat flight ever. We drove out to see him off. He taxied out to the slipway, where he stopped for clearance. We sat there, in the blazing heat, as he did pilot stuff and the ground crew did that cool thing with the ping-pong paddles. At the last second, Scott turned in the cockpit towards us. We could tell he was smiling under his Darth Vader flight mask. Then he did that funky chopped salute that Maverick did, right towards us, and hit his afterburners.

I cried as he disappeared down the runway in a confluence of roaring flame and the smell of combusted jet fuel. There were times when the movie romance of KAF just got too much.

We got rocketed the day of the medal parade. It was an apt scene setter. About forty of us lined up in the fire station hanger for rehearsal. Christopher, a kind and funny command sergeant major, called us all to attention.

I'd dressed for the occasion in heels, jeans, a black polo neck, waistcoat and baker's boy cap. I thought it was rather sombre and fitting: I hadn't counted on having to march. My marching made Danny La Rue look butch. Christopher laughed and told me to stand at the back, out of the way.

Scott came by with his command team and gave a rather good rendition of his stump speech about being 'one team'. I'd given him comments to help frame it, but being the subject, at that time, in that place, knowing he would soon no longer be there, had me crying again.

By the time Scott got to me, there was only one medal left. In my heels, I was about six inches taller than him. Christopher gave him the medal, and he looked for somewhere to pin it, the usual place being the left breast. God made me bigger in the chest than most, and the polo neck wasn't helping. Scott went a little red, which I didn't notice, and he tried to hand it to me.

'No, boss, I want you to pin it on, like all the rest!' I exclaimed.

Folks all turned round at this point. Christopher couldn't contain himself. He started giggling uncontrollably. With trembling fingers, Scott started to pin it on, but he stuck me right in the boob with the rather long pin.

'Oww!' I cried, at which point the whole parade dissolved.

Scott was, by now, thoroughly confused, but I demanded a picture, same as everybody else. His face is a peach. Still makes me laugh now, to think of it. Afterwards, we joked about it: and he hugged me and kissed my cheek. Which is unheard of in the US military. The rules forbid anything that could smack of sexual contact. Every Yank in the place just audibly inhaled.

That simple gesture meant more to me than all the rest put together. I fucking loved working for that man.

Scott held one last big old clambake for everybody, down at Liberty Hall, which had a large open space with a firepit. Christopher put on some cool rap music and we all line-danced into the night as the sunset refracted into the dusty twilight. It was our last big get-together. Not just for this rotation, but for KAF. After that, we never again came together in such numbers.

We had one last headquarters photograph. Scott invited everybody, from the office staff to the firefighters to the force protection boys. Hundreds of us lined up beside the toys of war: Hercules, F-16s, Reaper drones, MRAPs. The whole shebang. It is an awesome snapshot of the sheer effort and commitment KAF still enjoyed.

Folks were moving on up north too. In the POTF, Eric declared he'd had enough. I'd only been up to Kabul a couple of times, so I didn't have much to do with the inter-office politics. In any case, I was having a ball down in Kandahar.

It was game over for Eric, though. In total, he'd pushed out around three years, in two separate stints. He was fried. There always comes a point in dear old Afghan, where somebody will wish you 'good morning', and you'll reply; 'what's fucking good about it?' Eric was at that stage. He asked me up north to talk over the future. I knew I was doing pretty well. My stuff was good.

I'd had a few issues recently, though. Erik the Viking had popped smoke and headed back to the world. His replacement was a Pakistani fella called Omar. Quite how a Pakistani ended up with NATO secret clearance, which we all had to have, is beyond me: as it was to quite a few other folks. Anyhow, he'd ended up in Erik's shoes. And was taking some pretty wild editorial decisions.

I was still going out, risking my neck to get good stuff. I'd fire up some piece about Raziq, Hamid or Sherzai, or a piece on Wesa that I'd done myself. It would just disappear, never to be seen again. I repeatedly asked Eric, but he didn't have editorial control.

I'd been up to Kabul once before, and had it out in public. Omar had shouted me down, saying Raziq and Sherzai were 'bandits and thieves'. We'd got pretty intense about it. He said he'd grown up in Pakistan with these guys and was determined that none of them would get in the paper.

I didn't see that as Omar's decision. Nobody was clean in Afghanistan: and these two were key players in the ISAF game. We made them both and we needed them both. Both were seen as pretty legendary around town too. The impasse was getting embarrassing around RC-S. The 82nd were going out of their way to help and weren't seeing the end result. I saw what we were doing as supporting the guys doing the bleeding on the ground. Omar saw it as his personal fiefdom.

His latest decision had been to end the regional inserts. From now on, everything was to be pitched nationally. The concept had already gone horribly wrong when he had put a picture of a dancing Hazara girl on the front cover. Women do not get to dance in Pashtun southern culture. The whole edition had been impounded as pornography by Raziq and burned. I wanted it sorted.

Getting to Kabul was interesting. We got rocketed all morning. I'd got the air terminal at 0600, but I didn't arrive in Kabul, an hour's flight away, until late afternoon. In and out of the shelter all day, I was exhausted by the time I got there.

I walked into the POTF compound to be confronted by a paddling pool, full of apples, and the staff running around, soaking wet, in sun shorts and flip-flops. They'd taken the day off for a 'team-building' exercise. They'd organised a treasure-hunt, which involved ducking for apples in the paddling pool and rushing around to find hidden chocolates. Well, I wasn't fucking impressed. I'd spent the day ducking shrapnel and they were playing at being fucking infants.

KAIA-N was always a kind of Walter Mitty place. It very rarely got attacked. Mostly, it was day after day of staff work and PowerPoint in an office, broken up with coffee. Lots of folk getting massive in the gym, very little to do with war. Most nights, the civilian staff went out on the piss.

I suppose I was getting smoked by Kandahar. I'd been constantly in-theatre for eighteen months and I was beginning to run a little ragged. I wasn't in the best of moods to meet Eric.

He had a serious offer, though. He wanted me to take over the section after he left. The POTF was going downhill and he wanted a safe pair of hands. Eric and I hadn't always seen eye-to-eye, but he cared. I respected his work ethic, and his patience in walking the corridors.

The POTF was going downhill. The Americans had pulled their command element. The Romanians had stepped in. No doubt some folks will get pissed at this comment, but the Romanians weren't up to the job.

The only nations who really got stuff done are what is known as the ABC-A group: America, Britain, Canada and Australia. We were collectively seen as the only players who brought serious military might, the will to use it and, crucially, fluency in English. English is the default international language of the military.

The Romanians were only just coming out of the Soviet nightmare. They were autocrats. Influence operations is all about the creative debate. Say something out of line in the old Romania, you'd end up in the gulag. The Romanians weren't used to dealing with the media, or what we were trying to do in psyops.

When the Yanks ran the place, they had the chops to go straight to COMISAF, plant a size 12 in the in-tray, and get stuff done. The Romanians, with their cheap cotton uniforms, cardboard boots and leather holster action, were quaint but outside the loop. They just didn't have the juice.

Down in KAF, I had the general's ear, my contribution was appreciated and I was having a ton of fun. Up in the POTF, promotion meant being an office cog, under a Romanian colonel straight from a '70's movie. All Mexican bandit moustache and an Afghan-bad case of BO and halitosis that would kill an elephant at twenty paces. There was no more money in it either. Didn't seem like much of a deal to me.

However, and Eric was right in this, our section needed representation. Somebody had to fight the good fight. Nobody else in the section had the military and civilian leadership CV I mustered. Best of a bad lot, but I couldn't do it from Kandahar. Too long a screwdriver. I said I wanted to talk it through with the media director, the military officer who nominally controlled our product.

I got ushered in to meet an extremely young American female reservist major. She'd never deployed before, nor ever worked in psyops. I buttonholed her over Omar. She replied that she delegated all editorial decisions to him. Fucking excuse me?

The entire output had been handed to one Pakistani fella with a grudge. We tossed concepts, like editorial integrity, around for an hour or two, but we just didn't connect. In truth, I didn't connect with many of the Kabul team. They saw us field people as the wildlings. To them, we probably were. The only time they saw us was when we cycled through KAIA on our way somewhere.

We'd come barging in to their nice, clean air-conditioned offices with our body armour, dust and bad attitude. We were used to making it up on the hoof. I'd created my entire operation all by myself. It was easy to be disdainful of their weekly diary meetings and paper-clipped files.

The Yank colonel from the previous year had loved the field boys. He was gone now. Fuck it. I'd stick with Kandahar.

Eric proved to be quite prescient. He told me that the POTF would likely cut my program and keep the core Kabul team. Unlike the Americans, who had loved the FMTs, the Romanian guy was all about empire-building at headquarters.

Hey, I'd taken my chances just coming to Afghanistan. I took my chances every day down in Kandahar. I came for the juice, the adventure, not the monotony. It's how I had always lived my life.

I stayed for my friends: and for Kandahar. I loved the place. I was in the shit and I was proud of being a field-bunny. I turned Eric down. Somebody else took his job. Then, the people I had stayed for left too. I won a pyrrhic victory, very Afghan in the making. I became the last woman standing.

Down in Kandahar, Abrams came to Scott's handover of command. He slouched in his chair and scowled throughout the whole thing. I have the photos to prove it. Scott was pretty cool. He even waved at me from the stage.

I'll admit I was pretty set against his replacement, Brigadier General John Dolan. Scott introduced me to him, right before the start of proceedings. John was a good twelve inches taller than Scott, with a Bart Simpson buzz cut. Scott is handsome, but Dolan is Charlton Heston good-looking. He had that bear paw kind of handshake that left me with a couple of broken bones. Scott told John I would be his 'go-to gal' for all things Afghan. Which was kind of him. After all the speeches, I said one last farewell, and Scott was gone.

The US has an admirable tradition of the out-going guy disappearing sharpish, so the new guy can bed in. I was really upset at Scott leaving and determined I wasn't going to like John. Nonetheless, the man was my boss, and needed my help. I grabbed him and introduced him to the Afghans he needed to meet: Hamid and Sherzai.

John said something in his opening remarks that made me prick up my ears. Normally, these are anodyne stuff about 'achieving the mission', 'one team', 'God Bless the USA' sort of stuff.

John was different. He said everybody would be treated the same, with no bias or prejudice. As a civilian female, I really related to that sentiment.

In time, John would become a really good friend: and a commander and a man I admire.

In the interim 3ID started doing dumb stuff.

The 82nd had expanded a whole series of local radio stations across Kandahar and Uruzgan. These broadcast kits, called a 'radio in a box', or RIAB, had everything an aspiring DJ could want. Together with a low-powered transmitter, capable of ranges out to about 15 miles, they came with microphone, CD player and mixing desk.

The 82nd had been pretty flexible about the program. In some areas, they'd been given to the district chief, or a local security chief. In some areas, they'd kept the stations on an ISAF base, and run a competition to find the best local DJ. Some real stars had come out of the process. In Tarin Kowt, provincial capital of Uruzgan, one of my guys, Jawwad, had quickly got himself into the loop and broadcast a pretty lively talk show most afternoons. He had a lot of fans—and not a lot of folks knew he also worked for us. An ideal, and friendly, mouth-piece.

We had a RIAB in COMKAF, which had a bigger than average reception circumference, as the transmission aerial was right up high on the roof. Our station was run by the local interpreters, who just loved the gig. They'd do all sorts of mad poetry competitions and some funky folk tunes. I'd provide them with POTF radio adverts for the breaks, together with some training. It was exactly the kind of locally grown product that, with a little coordination, was turning out to be a really useful product. Everybody had a radio in Kandahar. The output was genuinely local product, made by locals, for locals.

The RIABs were a win-win. They were good adverts for us, and a potent weapon for the local ISAF commander, who could use the radio station as a real value-added weapon of effect. Want to get the local police chief to tell the people what his priorities were? Get him on the box. Want to spread educational material on animal husbandry and vaccination? Get it on the box.

It was cool stuff. As Kelvin McKenzie taught me: all news is local.

3ID took one look at the program: and promptly shut it down.

Not that they told anybody. First I heard of it was a COMKAF sergeant coming in to tell me that 3ID were in the headquarters and wanted to see me.

I walked over to the station, to find an unsmiling 3ID staff sergeant and a young corporal.

'Who runs this?' I was brusquely asked.

'These guys do,' I replied, pointing at our local staff.

'Do they know this equipment is United States army property?'

'I am sure they do,' I replied. 'If you look at the top of the box, it says so,' as I pointed to the rather obvious government stamp on the lid. The staff sergeant didn't seem to find this very funny, and handed me a piece of paper:

'This is a notice to say we are impounding our equipment and will be back tomorrow to take it.'

And with that, he turned on his heel and left, leaving me, who, by rights, had nothing to do with the station, just standing there.

COMKAF had an integral information operations cell, nominally in charge of the station, which had rather fallen into decay. As ever, operational functionality depended on the occupant being interested. The current owner, a Romanian, was not interested in much except buying stuff in the PX.

So I went direct to John instead. At the end of the day, it was his radio station. He listened patiently. The running of his information cell was so poor that, until I raised the issue, I don't think he actually knew he had a radio station. He listened to my arguments about utility, longevity and practicality. He then thought for a bit: and, probably sensibly, decided that it was better to fight another day.

At that moment, 3ID were kicking up a fuss that their helicopters had to answer to a NATO flight control and operations centre, not a US army gig. A small radio station was a battle that had no politically good outcome. I know he wanted to fight for the station, but he was a junior one star from the air force, and his nemesis was an army two star with an illustrious name. Only one winner in that battle of the steers.

Next day, with no warning, the 3ID team came by with a pair of cable snippers and just yanked the thing out of the wall. The COMKAF radio station had been on-air for nearly six years. It stopped broadcasting literally mid-sentence.

Some of the sub-units out on the ground made a big play for their stations. Abrams compromised to the extent that he demanded that those who made a strong case had to hand it over to the police. I have no idea why the police got top notice. One staff officer got rudely cut down to size when he had the temerity to suggest that a district governor, who had owned his station for a couple of years, be allowed to continue to keep the station.

Abrams told him, in no uncertain terms, that it was to be taken from the governor and given to the police chief, who answered to the governor. It was fucking stupid, but Abrams didn't entertain debate.

Jawwad lost his broadcast and his station. The vast majority of the RIABs were just unhooked and brought back to KAF. A resource that had taken years to develop just disappeared: and was not replaced.

A year later, Paul LaCamera, Abram's erudite replacement, was keen to know what had happened to the radio stations. Nobody could find them. 3ID had stuck them into a storeroom: and they had just disappeared. Over 30 complete radio stations, all gone. Nobody knew what had happened. I was the only one who was still there that remembered the history. Somebody got rich, stealing or selling them.

I had a pretty close relationship with Huggins' team. After the cool way COMKAF had treated me, I wanted more. I was the best part of a year in, and, more importantly, I remembered stuff that had happened before 3ID had got off the plane.

I wrote to Abrams. I told him all about the POTF, what it did, what I did, and what we could offer. About a fortnight later, I got a note from a lieutenant colonel telling me that 'Marne 6 acknowledges your mail'.

That was it, one line. Nothing more. I had no idea what 'Marne 6' was, or what 'mail' he was talking about. So I asked him. The reply was one line: 'the CG.' And that was it, frankly, for the rest of the year. No follow-up, nothing. I was being told; 'who the fuck do you think you are? Don't have the temerity to bother the general.'

I never got to meet Abrams. But I did get to meet several of his staff. And none of those meetings were pleasant.

The Afghans, too, closed up shop. Jim Breck's replacement, over at the air wing, got the cold shoulder from Sherzai, early doors. Jim was a big, bold man who impressed by his 'take it or leave it' mentality. The Afghans liked and respected him for his workarounds and ability to bend.

His replacement was a much more buttoned up, military rules kind of guy. He and Sherzai just hated each other. Sherzai suddenly became unavailable. The Americans would go over to his office and Sherzai would just have left. I knew more about where he was than his advisors did.

I got the picture. Suddenly, I was old school too. I'd only seen one rotation. Our Afghan friends had seen dozens. We all down, tested and adjusted to wait out the year.

Pretty early on, John decided to change the gears. Every commander has their own quirks, how they like a staff to work. Scott had been more big tent, big picture. John was keen on statistics. He widened the command briefs to include a lot of PowerPoint stuff on predicted trends for stuff like passenger transport expectations. In that sense, he was acknowledging that we were now moving into more constrained times.

The Americans were starting to wind the war down, and a lot of troops would be leaving. John needed to get a handle on that. Scott had had the freedom of knowing the war was going full-tilt and whatever he needed could be sourced. Scott also got on well with the 82nd, who had left COMKAF well alone to do their stuff. 3ID was not the 82nd.

John encouraged all the national contingents to come together, as well as representatives from the considerable contractor community. I got an elevated role, to present a kind of 'zeitgeist' picture on what was happening outside the wire. As John acknowledged, beyond the weather brief, my piece was the only input the headquarters had to the rest of Afghanistan.

It was a lot of extra work for me, and nothing to do with what I was paid to do, but I took the deal. The way he got me in the loop was pretty clever management.

I'd got into a pissing match with the American security lieutenant. For some time, I'd been doing a weekly roll-up of key news items, which I sent out on the unclassified, open source NATO system. It was a useful tool. The product went to all the key component commanders, and all the different national commands. The distribution list was pretty long and I spent a fair bit of effort in drawing it all together. The work even went to the joint intelligence centre in Kabul. I had earned a bit of a name for my analysis, and I could see some of it informing the debate that John Allen, COMISAF, got in his daily brief.

The lieutenant got upset that I sent the mail out in an open group mail shot. He said that using folk's e-mail addresses on an open source system ran contrary to regulations. To me, that sounded pretty stupid, as the mail addresses were open source and unclassified. The lieutenant pulled out a big book of rules to justify his decision. Turned out, it was an American book of rules. I then got the NATO book out, which had no such prohibition. Didn't even mention the issue. I pointed out that COMKAF was a NATO headquarters, not a US joint. The lieutenant lost his rag, reported me to the deputy commander and removed my computer rights. Which was fucking stupid.

I lost my dinger and left a message with John's executive assistant that I would no longer be providing COMKAF with any information, as his security lieutenant was being a dick and had cut me off. The turf war ended with me and the security guy having a robust conversation over US rules vs. NATO, involving a lot of words prefaced with the letter 'f'.

John was in a difficult position. The NATO staff, and the various coalition elements, backed my position. We'd all had enough of the USA waving its big stick about. At the same time, he had to back his lieutenant over a civilian female. I was equally obdurate. I wasn't backing down. John wanted both our input.

JD did his Solomon bit. He had me in for a chat. I knew it was serious because he had asked his deputy to sit in as a witness. John cleverly offered me an enhanced position in his HQ, as his go-to-gal for all things Afghan. Including a weekly one-on-one chat with him. Gold dust for me, as it gave me an elevated access to the top tier. The quid pro quo was that I would stop doing the newsletter. Which, actually, wasn't that big an issue, as it was extra work for me. Deal.

John is a smart leader. He knew he could have just shut me down: as he could equally have shut down his junior officer. He worked it so we both left the battlefield a little bruised but unbowed.

I couldn't resist sending one more e-mail, telling everybody that this would be the last one. The lieutenant was furious. John's deputy told me JD had quietly laughed.

I continued to personally send John stuff on his unclassified, but neither of us told the lieutenant, who left six weeks later, together with his ego, presumably to go attend anger management classes.

John got his pound of flesh. The requests started coming thick and fast from his office. I didn't mind in the least. I loved being in the team. And those weekly chats became pretty key stuff.

In addition to my one-on-one, I got asked to join the weekly chat with General Sherzai. I was already on the airport management committee. It was all good access, and I think John got a lot out of it too.

For the first time, RC-S sent their chief of staff to the meetings. He was a real, died-in-the-wool divisional guy, all starched uniform and salutes sort of G.I. Joe.

I got asked to do a kind of roll-up for everybody of where we stood in the big picture, and what the year would bring. I pointed out the 82nd's really big success in handing over to 205 Corps, and how that had changed the way the campaign would be conducted. I then looked forward to 2013/14, which would bring a national presidential election.

Not unreasonably, I then stated that 3ID's 2012 year lacked a similarly momentous event. This year, in my opinion, was all about consolidating previous success and setting up the conditions for the change of government the following year. Nothing glamorous: but a whole load of necessary spadework. It was what I'd been told by Sherzai, Hamid and Raziq. They needed time to breathe and develop.

The 3ID team were not happy. In fact, they were raging. They were going to win the war by themselves. The Chief of Staff actually broke his pencil listening to me. Afterwards, he came up to me and spat:

'You talk too fucking much.'

Which is where 3ID and the 82nd differed. I may not always have been right, but I was a different voice. I knew my subject, I'd done the time and COMKAF respected that opinion enough to give me a platform, as had the 82nd.

3ID came with their own agenda, which had been decided before they had arrived in Kandahar. They were going to be the team that would win the conflict in their year. I'd heard this before, and seen each team spike up the violence, fight another series on inconclusive tactical battles, then declare victory and head home with their medals. It quickly became apparent that this year was gonna be one of those where you just hunkered down and waited until they left.

Thing was 3ID had come with the bath and the kitchen sink. The 82nd had had a kind of lean and mean HQ staff, which fitted comfortably into the old Canadian container camp.

3ID brought hundreds. There simply wasn't enough room for all their headquarters people. In thirty years, in eight different wars, I have never seen a divisional headquarters as big as the 3ID team. It was just as well that the new headquarters building had finally been finished: all $40 million of it. To be fair to 3ID, they hadn't ordered the thing, but they did take ownership of a city block-sized series of hangers and compounds. Their divisional headquarters was bigger than the headquarters of the British field ARMY.

All those extra staff needed work: and stuff like COMKAF's radio station suddenly became very important. A presence was demanded at RC-S to explain why COMKAF had been broadcasting without 3ID approval.

I got volunteered to represent COMKAF, so I trooped over there for a meeting of what was called the 'influence activities cell'. Chaired by the same lieutenant colonel who had tersely acknowledged my missive to Abrams.

Basically, all over the south, each large base had a small team of guys doing information stuff, on a micro-tactical level. The idea was the divisional team coordinated this. Pretty much all Americans, a few Romanians made up the numbers, relegated to sorting out the communications. Which could be, as you might expect in a war, rather patchy.

I walked in to said colonel screaming at his Romanian signaller 'why can't I speak to fucking Qalat?' The staff, about thirty-odd, just sat and looked at their shoes. As each detail reported in, the colonel sat there and muttered to his deputy:

'They aren't doing the fucking mission. What the fuck is wrong with them?'

It was a relentlessly bullying and oppressive environment. He turned to me and asked if I was the person who dealt with the COMKAF radio station. I told him I wasn't, but I was part of the POTF and had come to see what the issue was as an associated part of COMKAF. The colonel looked at me, then told me:

'Go tell that fucking air force one star that 3ID run this war.'

Bizarrely, for a so-called influence expert, he then asked me what the POTF did. When I explained all about the paper, the radio, my guys, the surveys, all of it, he went even more red-faced and demanded to know why I, and the POTF, weren't under his command. I told him it was because the POTF was a strategic asset under command of the IJC. I told him none of his ask was gonna happen and that he had better start amending the way he spoke about me, my job and about John. Brigadier Dolan was a general officer, not some underling.

I may as well have thrown up on his lounge carpet. He told me that he was ordering me to stop all activity until he had cleared my presence in Kandahar.

Somehow, he had got wind of the fact that I spoke regularly to the governor, Raziq, Sherzai and Hamid. He flat out told me that he was forbidding me from conducting any engagement with any Afghan without written permission from him first. He raged about my relationships with the Afghan leadership. These had long presaged his recent arrival, but he didn't want anybody seeing the Afghans without his authority.

I told him that I couldn't do that, and it wasn't his call to make in the first place. These guys were my friends. We actually liked and respected each other. Which wasn't the required response. He stood up and yelled:

'You need to fucking understand who runs Kandahar. One word from me and General Abrams will have you put in handcuffs and put on the first plane out of here.'

Which was quite enough for me. Not only had he, a junior officer, publicly denigrated COMKAF's commanding general, he was directly threatening a civilian who had no management or leadership responsibility to him. I walked out.

I reported what had happened to the POTF and to COMKAF. Both of them told me to ignore the noise and keep on doing my job. It was a ridiculous threat. I never directly heard from that colonel again, but he carried on his one-man obsession with rubbing me out.

Although my stuff wasn't directly broadcast around RC-S, I did have a 'code share' with the American set-up. I sent them all my stuff. They sent me theirs. Everybody was happy. Double the output all round.

Two weeks after my meet, I got a quick text message from Ahmed, who ran the American divisional psyops radio station. He'd been ordered to sever all contact with me. He was sorry, but his job was on the line. For the rest of the year, I only sent my stuff to Kabul, and RC-S resolutely refused to run anything from the POTF, nor allow me access to any of their assets. It was the most ridiculous willy-waving.

The info ops guys were terrified of getting on the wrong side of the colonel. One of their functions was to gather what the military call 'atmospherics'. In the old days, these had been gathered in a more or less scientific way, by going out amongst the population and conducting surveys and such. Sometimes, combat conditions got in the way. So some weeks were a nil return. That was life in AFG.

Not for the 3ID info cell. Nil returns meant another blistering series of expletives. So folks just started making it up.

In Qalat, the provincial capital of Zabul, to the north east of Kandahar, started sending in stuff like:

'A man said he was pleased with ISAF soldier's restraint.'

Unbelievably, all this 'evidence' would get gathered up into a big old PowerPoint pie chart and passed off as improving relations across the South.

The troops in Qalat weren't lying. That would be against the service code. They were, however, fraying the edges of a truthful tale. I had a good friend in Qalat, an ex-special forces operator, who clued me in on what was going down.

The info ops guys there were feeling the heat, and were so short-staffed they didn't have time to get the usual metrics. They were asking anybody who classed as an Afghan to contribute. In the case of the man with the favourable view of ISAF, turned out he was the base cleaner! Hardly likely to diss the folks who paid his wages. Something of a hard top-spin to the story. 3ID might be a hard-charging outfit, but they were chronically short of top-drawer operators.

By 2012, a lot of the A-team had had their fill of constant deployments and got out. Their replacements were now off somewhere else. Afghanistan had stopped being the instant promotion-winner it had once been. Operations in Qalat were being run by a finance colonel. Probably not the best pre-qualification to run a main operating base. My friend got seriously alarmed at what he saw going on. He bugged out for somewhere safer. He didn't feel safe there anymore.

Just as state department diplomat Anne Smedinghoff arrived. She was 25 years old. On April 8th, she left the Qalat ISAF base on foot to go to an adjacent school to hand out books and pens. On the way, she and four other

Americans were killed by an explosion.

The first reports came out that the team had been hit by a vehicle borne IED. Then, that she had been taken out by a suicide bomber. The story kept changing. According to my SF buddy, the gate guards had failed to notice a pile of wood that had been left by the main gate 48 hours earlier. Nobody came to check it. When the US team left on foot, itself an unusual procedure, the woodpile exploded. Afghanistan was not a place for amateurs.

None of that fitted the 3ID narrative, which was one of martial success and achievement. Except, across the south, the year was proving to be that year of gradual expansion and improvement I had talked about. Nothing was quite proving to be the game-changer 3ID thirsted for. Abrams knew this was his year to shine. He wanted success. His press and public information office were relentlessly flogged to find worthy press releases. Abrams himself took a leaf out of Petraeus' game book. He wasn't exactly media shy.

The press courtship hit its peak with Obama's second inauguration, in January 2013. On a night of nights, the new president is swept from celebratory ball to celebratory ball. One of which is the commander-in-chief ball, for servicemen and women. Not unreasonably, given the number of US service-people in Afghanistan, the service chiefs wanted a live contribution from Afghanistan. The first call went out to RC-E, but they dropped out of the game early on. Abrams stepped in with alacrity.

Time differences to Washington meant a 0400 commitment from Kandahar. A full court press went out, and the headquarters staff was ordered to attend en-masse. In military-land, that sort of three-line whip means a ton of rehearsals and preparation. Which meant a sleepless night for a load of staff. Except, the live feed only had enough lighting for a small part of the front rank.

On the night, as briefed, the president turned to a monitor, and delivered his prepared remarks to 'Abe' and 3ID. An obviously star-struck Abrams ran forward, introduced himself, and then held the mike as he ran down a line of four senior enlisted soldiers, who all uttered two sentences each. The whole farrago finished with a loud 'Rock of the Marne!' from the assembled hundreds. None of whom could be seen.

Obama looks slightly confused by the whole thing, but gamely went back on point to his prepared remarks about troop sacrifice etc.

The whole event was a notable coup for Abrams. Not only had he been seen by the president and the nation, but he'd been anointed as Afghanistan's media star by the joint chiefs, over an appearance by John Allen, COMISAF, or even James Terry, the man who ran the IJC. Abrams knew his appearance made him hot property. Divisional commanders do not normally get to make the headlines. He wanted a follow-up.

Events down in Panjwai District, right next to where Bales had killed all those kids, proved fertile opportunity. Panjwai was one of those places, when it came to fighting the war, where the pedal truly hit the metal. From the first arrival of Canadian troops in 2006, the place had been a thorn in the side for every succeeding rotation. The northern part is quite lush, being irrigated by the Arghandab and Helmand river basins, the rest is mostly desert. It is a complicated Rubik's Cube of inter-changing irrigation canals, vegetation, farms and mud hut villages and compounds. It is classic Afghan terrain that created the confused battles so beloved of breathless video journalists.

Panjwai is the terrain that Burrows covered with his fateful brigade before his momentous encounter at Maiwand. Panjwai is also where the whole Taliban movement began. In the early 1990's Mullah Omar was little more than a locally famous cleric. His rise to notoriety began the day he organised thirty local men to free two girls who were being imprisoned and sexually abused by the local governor. Ironically enough, Gul Agha Sherzai, older brother to General Sherzai, was the provincial governor at that time.

The rest is history. From the day of the invasion onwards, Panjwai was always an extremely dangerous place for coalition soldiers.

Much of that enmity spans from the tribal make-up of the place. Panjwai is the heartland of the Noorzai. Together with the Achakzai, the two tribes traditionally controlled all the smuggling and cross-trading around Spin Boldak and the southern Durand Line. SB is the district that bridges the main trading route, through the border town of Chaman, between Afghanistan and Pakistan.

When Afghanistan fell apart, the Noorzai naturally enough aligned behind the Taliban and Mullah Omar. He had started his movement on their doorstep. They earned the eternal enmity of the Achakzai, and its young and ferocious leader, Abdul Raziq. The Noorzai had displaced their rivals in the trade wars.

By the time ISAF moved into the south in a big way, Raziq was well entrenched and on his way to the top. When the Canadians, and later Nick Carter, asked him to clear out the Panjwai Taliban—read Noorzai—it was truly game on. Raziq and his men performed an enema on the place, reportedly killing men, women and children alike.

Raziq's sidekick in those days, down in Spin Boldak, was a large, heavyset man called Sultan Mohammad, also Achakzai. Mohammad acted as chief of police for SB, while Raziq ran the border police. The two are actually rumoured to be cousins, which, given the Afghan trend for inter-marrying potential rival families is entirely possible. Once Raziq made provincial chief of police, Sultan Mohammad helped out with all the difficult jobs: first in Maiwand, then moving to Panjwai as chief of police.

The other thing about Panjwai is that it sits across Highway 1, the main ring road right round Afghanistan. Pretty much everything heading west out of Kandahar towards Herat has to go down that road: and through Panjwai. The Canadians built a new road from the middle of the district, right into the western edge of Kandahar city. A lot of trade happened down that road.

Raziq may be chief of police, but he hasn't lost that smuggler's appetite for trade. In fact, he's a pretty canny dealer. He has made himself an extremely rich man in the process. The kickbacks he earns by creaming the take at the Chaman crossing point is rumoured to be 44-6 MILLION a MONTH.

Sultan Mohammad may have been Raziq's guy in Panjwai, but Panjwai wasn't an easy gig for Sultan Mohammad. He may have come from Panjwai, but he was Achakzai, and the events of 2006 didn't exactly warm the average Panjwai Noorzai memory banks.

Mohammad was onto plums in the short term. He could mount local initiatives, and his men were quite well known for their shake-downs, but he couldn't muster that vital resource for effective counter-insurgency: the approval, or at least tacit acceptance, of the local populace. The Taliban gave Mohammad an ideal excuse to rake over the coals one more time.

The local Taliban military commander, Mullah Noor Mahmad, over-reached by demanding that an influential elder, Hajji Abdul Wuwood, hand over two of his sons, in retribution for Wuwood calling out two of Mahmad's younger fighters over a beating they had inflicted on a villager.

Wuwood and his eight sons gave Mahmad the finger, and called on Sultan Mohammad, who was related to Wuwood by marriage, to lend a hand. About the same time, US special forces killed Abdullah Wakil, the Taliban's shadow governor for Panjwai.

Alongside the official government apparatus, the Taliban operated another administration, as part of their information operations plan to show the people they had never really left. In a province like Panjwai, where security was tenuous at best, the Taliban operated everything from their own police to courts to jails. They were cannily effective at dealing out instant justice, quite in contrast with the creaking and often invisible official government.

Wakil had been around for over a year. He knew the score, and was supported by a substantial team. When US SoF took him out—deservedly so, as he had organised the suicide bombing of several legitimate government officials—his removal created a vacuum.

Sultan Mohammad saw his chance.

Aided by Wuwood, and encouraged by US SoF, he raised a detachment of Afghan local police. This was a program that had been Petraeus' brainchild. In its simplest terms, it was the Minutemen of 1776 come to life. Local guys just grabbed their AKs and started patrolling their own neighbourhoods. Nominally, the US agreed some form of uniform and equipment, but, mostly, the aid came in the form of a cash payment, to make up for all that patrolling away from the fields where the crops grew. How much of the payment made to Sultan Mohammad actually reached the troops is a moot point. The key result was a formation of local guys fighting what ISAF saw as the enemy.

Sultan Mohammad had some real success. By the end of April, US troops in Zangabad were reporting that they were only being shot at 'about once a week'. Afghan police casualties dropped from roughly ten medevacs a month to about two.

By spring 2013, 3ID were working towards the end of their tour. As I had predicted, their year had been one of incrementally increasing Afghan-led security cordon-sweep-clear operations. All useful stuff for an Afghan army still coming to terms with its nascent ability to manage complicated movement of troops and equipment. It was crawl to walk time.

The Australians, who managed Afghan Army mentoring, were really pushing the Afghans to approach their operational planning the same way as ISAF. Rather than the more traditional Afghan way of a cross-legged chat over endless cups of tea. They'd pushed the Afghans to use the dreaded PowerPoint. which is so ubiquitous in the American army that it will cease to function if Microsoft ever pulls the licence.

Briefs over at 205 Corps were unwittingly hilarious. The Afghans, with their in-built desire to please, would produce their usual 12 year-old's version of what they thought their Western advisors wanted to hear.

Operational charts, which usually came with very serious map symbols, would, in an Afghan PowerPoint hedonistic trip, be covered with little flying helicopters and audio punctuation of gunfire and explosions. The authors had discovered every button and effect they could press, all at one time.

After one operations brief, which had me stuffing my handkerchief in my mouth to stifle my giggles, the logistics guy stood up. Normally, this is big juju, and goes on for quite a bit. Understandably: the army is all equipment and one-use items, like bullets. Logistics takes a LOT of coordination to bring it all together. Our Afghan man just stood up and pronounced:

'We will all be very well fed and we will all be very happy.'

And promptly sat down again, to lots of appreciative nodding from his Afghan colleagues. And burst blood vessels from their ISAF mentors. 'Are you fucking kidding me?' hissed the major next to me. You know what? They probably would all be OK. They'd just go into a village, grab a goat, butcher it and all have a cook-out. Afghans are a supremely happy bunch: and I love them for their simplicity.

Some folks would have been happy enough that they had actually started dealing with tasks as a staff. How they presented the material was always going to influenced by local culture and education.

None of this incremental change stuff was giving 3ID the war-winner Abrams wanted. Every hard-charger that came in wanted a 'big win' at the end of their year. It took a truly strategic leader to be content with incremental progress.

Abrams had a family name to live up to.

I'm not saying the guy had no talent, far from it. I just know that, by this stage, the staff officers I spoke to were getting mighty fed up being the vehicle to push their boss to his third star. Sultan Mohammad and his little ALP venture gave them the break they were looking for to please the boss.

Mid-March Abrams took a video link briefing to the assembled Pentagon press corps back in Washington. Not every commander in Afghanistan was keen to personally appear in the spotlight, but Abrams was hot and very keen after his inauguration pitch. Right at the end of his prepared remarks, which were military dry lists of achievements, he zoned in on Panjwai and Sultan Mohammad and his ALP. The conclusions he drew lifted a local family alliance right up there into strategic movement:

'*This is absolutely the first time that we have seen this sort of an uprising, where the people have said, 'enough is enough'...It's an incredible sight to see now. You go into a place, a village where we've had countless firefights, vicious fighting, you know, expended a lot of blood and treasure, and today you go there, and there's 300 Afghan flags from every mud hut and qalat in the village. It's inspirational.*'[28]

Which was putting something of a top-spin on it, to say the least. It was the choice of the word 'uprising' that grabbed the press by the nuts. Petraeus had made his reputation in Iraq, 2006-7, by claiming to be the author of the famed 'Anbar rising'. Here was Abrams, in 2013, claiming exactly the same words. At a time when, in an exact mirror of Iraq, the surge was coming to an end. To a team of journalists, ever hungry for something to take from the endless Pentagon fire-side chats, this looked like was history being re-run. The 'Anbar rising' had been credited as the key event that had allowed the Iraq war to be brought to a close. Now an American major-general was saying the same stuff was happening in Kandahar Province.

I'm not sure that Abrams understood the full implications of what he was claiming, or understood exactly what was actually happening. At one stage, a journalist asked him exactly where the rising was happening. Abrams falters, looks off-camera, and gets a whispered prompt; 'Zangabad.' Which he then repeats. Maybe it was lack of rehearsal, but he must surely have known how is comments would be received.

Predictably enough, his statement generated mega column inches. The 'New York Times' called it:

'The most significant popular turning against the Islamist insurgents in recent years.'[29]

Everybody in Kabul got very excited too. In truth, so did I. I expended a lot of effort in keeping tabs on what was happening around the dear green place and this one had taken me by surprise: as it did my boys in the field. We all knew about Sultan Mohammad, but my guys' analysis was that this was yet another round of Raziq extending his remit through his surrogates.

Since had made provincial chief of police, Raziq had made quite a few similar appointments. Raziq is a tough guy, and he has a singular approach to law enforcement that has not been free of tactics that would make a strong man blanche. Was this truly a strategic turning point? Or was ISAF once again grasping at straws?

To their great credit, my boys took a turn over to Zangabad to find out. Panjwai is a dangerous place for even a local Kandahari to visit. Sultan Mohammad was only too happy to host them, and took them out on patrol with him around Zangabad.

His local police detachment was a swarthy-looking bunch of coves. A couple of them had Afghan flag armbands, but the rest were the usual shalwar kameez wearing, turbaned and bearded men you normally see in rural Afghanistan. Including Sultan Mohammad himself. The difference was that they were all armed to the teeth with a motley collection of obviously well

---

[28] Pentagon transcript

[29] NYT, March 2013

used small arms and a couple of rocket propelled grenade launchers.

I showed the video we took to a couple of our targeting guys afterwards. They said that Sultan and his men was exactly the sort of group they were continually hunting for. In other words, Sultan and his boys looked exactly the same as the Taliban. The 'Panjwai rising' truly was a war between neighbours.

Patrolling consisted of stopping a few locals on motorbikes and having a chat. Sultan was in great form, doing the usual expansive Afghan chest beating about his local successes. Afghans are natural media stars.

I'd asked Feroz to get me some photos of the flags flying. The main drag in Zangabad was smothered in Afghan national flags, which flew from pretty much every shop.

We chatted about the photos afterwards, and I commented that the flags seemed to be a real expression of patriotism. Feroz' reply was illuminating. He told me that the flags were flying at Sultan Mohammad's insistence. In return for his police 'protection', every shopkeeper was now paying a 10% revenue 'tax'. If you paid up, you got to fly a flag. It helped the collectors identify non-payers.

In other words, the most obvious outward sign of the so-called 'rising' was nothing more than a local extortion/ protection racket. Dig a little deeper and the plot swirls even more.

Prior to being chief of police in Panjwai, Sultan Mohammad had been chief of police in Maiwand, immediately to the west. He'd been put there by Raziq.

Maiwand is one of the most productive poppy-growing areas in the country. The revenue there is worth a fortune. Raziq reportedly remains deeply implicated in that trade, as Mohammad was also rumoured to be. The difficulty lies in getting the stuff from Maiwand to market. The processed opium has to travel east to Kandahar city, and then to the border at Spin Boldak, before disappearing into Pakistan.

Raziq controlled the border crossing. By his own admission, he retains close contact with former Taliban regime members in Pakistan. By 2013, the US had helped put him into running Kandahar city. One of his first appointments was to put Sultan Mohammad into Maiwand.

The one sticking point in the poppy delivery chain was Panjwai: he didn't control the highway between the fields of Maiwand and the city. Panjwai was stuffed with the Taliban's surrogate, the Noorzai. The Noorzai and Raziq hated each other. Raziq needed to open up the Panjwai delivery route. Reliable Sultan Mohammad got swapped into Panjwai: and the 'help' he then gave to his cousin Noor Wuwood in controlling the key villages in the north of the district opened up the artery.

Raziq is an extremely smart businessman. Afghans always have another agenda. Nothing is ever quite what it seems in Afghanistan. Abrams then turned his ire onto another Afghan target.

He went for dinner with Governor Wesa. The governor absolutely hated the Sherzais. Wesa never quite got over the charge that he had sat out the *jihad* in Canada. Unlike the Sherzais, he didn't have an actual power base in

Kandahar, beyond his family relationship with President Karzai. Once Wali Karzai was assassinated, Kandahar suffered from a dangerous power vacuum.

Gul Agha Sherzai, on the other hand, as a former two-time governor and head of the powerful and extremely wealthy Barakzai, regarded himself as the anointed key player in Kandahar affairs. The guy ran twice as a presidential candidate. Gul Agha Sherzai is a big fish in the Kandahar pool.

Both Wesa and Sherzai had been clashing dramatically over land ownership and development. The Sherzais had squatter's rights over considerable chunks of land that they had either re-gained as family land, or taken as war spoils, as the first group to enter Kandahar after the invasion. Wesa and the Sherzais were continually getting into it over title deeds, particularly over plots around the airport where the Sherzais had built their lucrative business and hotel empire.

Wesa himself was rumoured to have made around $30 million in real estate deals, particularly around the exclusive Aino Mena estate and the Shur Andam business park to the east of the city. Wesa was later to find himself in hot water after a tax demand letter he issued was sent quietly to the president. Wesa had demanded in writing, quite publicly, that all land- owners pay the provincial government a land tariff. A not unreasonable demand, except that Wesa had helpfully included account details for payment. A pay-in account that happened to be Wesa's own personal account number.

Wesa speaks good English and is well used to dealing with North Americans. I always found him to be quite charming. So did General Abrams: and rather persuasive in providing 'proof' that General Sherzai was criminally complicit in extortion and fraud.

Abrams came back to KAF fired up that General Sherzai must go. Which I, and many others, pointed out would be an absolute disaster. General Sherzai was the younger brother of one of the most powerful and well-known men and clan leaders in the entire country. He was also an Afghan government appointee. As head of the Afghan air wing, he held a crucial role as a leader and placeholder for Barakzai business interests around the strategic hub of KAF. Around KAF, the guy is a bit of a legend. General Sherzai was part of complex Kandahar political checks and balances. After all, Sherzai had been personally appointed by President Karzai himself. Diplomatically, ISAF forcing his removal would be extremely embarrassing for the Afghans, not to mention quite possibly illegal.

Nobody is perfect in Afghanistan, but, in my opinion, General Sherzai is less personally engaged than others. As one senior ISAF figure told me, the intelligence services would be keen to speak to members of his family, but the general himself was careful to keep his military and family activities quite separate.

I personally liked Sherzai: and I could see his men adored him. I always thought he was doing his best in difficult circumstances. And the air wing was actually finally beginning to produce some real results. In my opinion, we would have been seen as duplicitous on the one hand in supporting Raziq, who had a much darker personal record, in favour of removing Sherzai. We would have introduced a game changer in the delicate power balance between the tribes.

Abrams made an awful lot of noise about ditching Sherzai, much to the horror of everybody else. Kenneth Wilsbach, the major general who ran the air component for Afghanistan, flew his F-16 down to sort it out. I liked Kenneth enormously, and respected his intelligence. Together with John, the case was made for Sherzai.

The end result was stasis. Nothing changed on the surface. The long-term casualty, though, was COMKAF's independence. Abrams was furious that the air force had ganged up against him. Proposals were floated to put COMKAF under operational command of RC-S, rather than NATO itself. Abrams got his way. John Dolan was to be the last independent NATO commander of KAF. After that, COMKAF got rolled up into the RC-S empire.

Abrams lit out before the rest of his division on July 8th, handing over to Major General Paul LaCamera of the 4th Infantry Division, who got an early baptism. Abrams did pretty well out of his stint in Kandahar. He got an early draft pick to go to the Pentagon as the military aide to the secretary of defence. It was clear he was moving on to better things.

The 'Panjwai rising' bit died a death the day after Abrams left. Raziq is still ruling the roost, but all the talk of a major strategic shift in the US media just fizzled. It gave Abrams the right boost at the right time, though. Abrams is now, a bare two years later, about to get his fourth star, as head of US force command.

When he left Kandahar, most of Abram's staff still had another month to fill. Abrams departed as he had arrived. His final words, from his last speech, on the day he left:

'Rock of the Marne.'

NEW CHAPTERS

By 2012, the writing was on the wall for the whole Afghan venture. The new guy, the 4th Infantry Division, was a full brigade of bodies short on the previous year: the first inkling we had that Obama really meant business.

Business in KAF continued to boom. We were the clearing-house for everything in the south. The pan was as full as ever of aircraft, bodies and stuff. What we couldn't see was that, for the first time, the majority of the aircraft were out-going. For the first time, the vehicle maintenance yards were full of gear being steam-cleaned for transport back to the US, not back to the field.

KAF had always been a showpiece stop over for US government visits. You could always tell when some VVIP was in town. Whole roads would be shut. Lots of military police would tote their assault rifles high. Inter-sections would melt down, as diverted traffic was sent in circles. Even the lowest-ranked senator seemed to warrant vast convoys of blacked-out SUVs and outriders of flashing lights.

KAF was so vast that just driving round the perimeter took over an hour. Inside our carefully protected perimeter, with all that activity and sense of military order, it was easy to forget that we were still losing this war. Spaced-out US delegations would arrive after a fourteen-hour flight, straight into the dazzling forty-degree heat. An armoured limo would drive them at speed to an air-conditioned headquarters where impressively verbose staff officers would list endless PowerPoints of jargon and slides. All marked with brightly coloured arrows and upward bell curves pointing towards success.

In the afternoon, the various senators would go off to meet carefully selected soldiers from their home states. Sergeant majors would carefully brief the victims beforehand not to complain, to get with the message:

'Yes, sir, we're winning. Proud to serve, sir.'

So many came to visit that the tour around the gear became as well organised as a Disney ride: staff officers called it 'petting the helicopters'.

The US State Department had a pretty big compound in KAF. Originally, the diplomats had kept a presence downtown, at the provincial reconstruction team's headquarters. This was always a pretty popular visit, as the PRT compound had a swimming pool. Staff officers would head off for meetings with a document case and a towel.

Eikenberry's empire building had included an optimistic plan to establish US consulates all over Afghanistan, including Kandahar. Herat, in the west, got one, which was based in an old high-rise hotel. That made a pretty easy target for attack, so it wasn't the most popular of postings. Kandahar's never materialised, so, once PRT operations closed down, State moved into KAF. It was a breach of normal protocol, to have civilian diplomats co-located with the army, but KAF was really the only safe place to be.

The move meant increased meddling in projects that had previously been military territory. In 2012, that meant the airport.

Old Faizi, the manager, had become a garrulous and fun chum to be around. While he didn't have any money to turn the old airport terminal into anything more than a stunning museum to 1950s aviation romance, he had put together some really lovely gardens. Which boasted a working fountain, several songbirds and, of all things, a petting zoo. Complete with two tame deer (named, by me, as Bambi and Thumper) and a couple of peacocks.

I used to love going over there. We'd take coffee out in the fragrant rose garden. Faizi had a permanent US military advisor, some of whom were really good and some who were dreadful. But I was the only one who stayed.

For most folks on KAF, the airport was enemy territory. The Afghan police airport protection team—and there was full company of them—were all armed and loaded for bear. It just spooked most folks. Even the US advisor drove over there in an armour-plated SUV, which was parked ass end first at the exit. All set for a quick getaway.

State was paying for the ubiquitous DynCorp to set up and run improved airport security. Faizi had acquired a load of expensive scanners and electronic passport readers. Trouble was, the place wasn't wired for electricity. Nor, given the issues with Shur Andam transmission, did he actually have any electrical power. The stuff just sat in boxes, waiting for inspiration. The usual Afghan shuffle: one step forward, one step back.

State and COMKAF were indulging in a bit of a turf war, over who owned what. The airport was run by the military, but State saw the civil terminal as re-development, so they wanted a say too. John Dolan, as new COMKAF commanding general, walked straight into it.

JD was a different personality from Scott. John is a more private man than Scott. He was never fond of the show business part, being the public face of KAF. Both are exceptional men, but John took a bit more persuading to do the grip and grin stuff.

Scott had authorised the re-surfacing of the taxiways around the civil terminal. As ever with ISAF, it took so long to actually re-tarmac a half-mile of runway that he had left before it was finished. The new apron was actually a pretty useful development. As with the road, we hadn't planned it as civil progress. The work was designed to help our own fighter jets get to their hangars.

Happy confluence meant we could both benefit. Again, we hadn't asked the Afghans if we could build the thing. But they were keen to make the most of it. Faizi was trying hard to get new business: and the apron was a good news story for him.

John was in the pocket for the big day. Which Faizi and Wesa were determined to be as high profile as the road opening had been the year before.

JD wasn't overly keen on the whole issue. But when Faizi invited Minister Najafi, the Afghan aviation chief, back down again, he had no real choice but to follow Scott's lead from the year before and get set to glad hand. Then State found out the minister was coming, and demanded that they had an ambassador attend too. Afghanistan got like that. So many big dick personalities and competing agencies that everybody had to have a piece of the pie when it needed cutting.

The Americans passed word over to COMKAF that they would be sending a fella called James Warlick. After Dick Holbrooke had died, Hillary Clinton had tempted an old chum, Marc Grossman, to take over the helm as special representative for Pakistan and Afghanistan. James Warlick was Grossman's deputy. Warlick had never been to Afghanistan before. A career diplomat, most of his experience had been in Europe. However, he had served as principal advisor to the disastrous Paul Bremer regime, right at the start of the Iraq fiasco. To a lot of Americans, Iraq and Afghanistan are the same piece of the puzzle.

JD was still pretty new in post. As I'd met all the Afghans before, I got elevated to social secretary. Faizi had the paint crews out prior to our arrival. The terminal stank of turpentine. This was going to be another important day for my friend, the former school teacher. He was hyped, hopping about from foot to foot.

Najafi was on time too. He remembered me and complimented me on the coverage we had given the road opening. John is a pretty big, purposefully erect officer. He towered over the two Afghans as they exchanged chit-chat. I was happy, though. When we were all talking, good stuff usually happened.

Then Warlick turned up. He'd been on one of those whirlwind tours of the south. He blew in on a big helicopter, with a couple of gunships as escort. State had a convoy of black SUVs waiting on him. The US projects power like nobody else. The whole get-up, from the flashing lights to the big, bulked-up private security detail and the plethora of aviator sunglasses was pure Hollywood.

Warlick marched in at the head of a phalanx of acolytes. There were dozens of them, all either talking into sleeve microphones or on mobile satellite phones. His security guys aggressively chewed gum as they boxed the room and scanned all of us from top to toe.

I couldn't get over how young his State team were. He was supported by a staff of under-graduates. None of them could have been more than twenty-five. They looked like a school trip out. The staff all wore the obligatory State department overseas expeditionary Brook Brothers hiking boots, chinos and sensible outdoor jacket.

Warlick isn't a big man. He didn't smile much either. He greeted the Afghans perfunctorily. The ambassador was on a tight timeline. He had an hour window, then he was due off on the next leg of whatever important stuff he usually did. His staff worked endlessly to finesse his travel details. The non-stop phone calls were all tee'ing up the next engagement.

Trouble was, Faizi had also invited governor Wesa.

Faizi and Wesa were having a bit of a spat. One of the governor's folks had tried to leave the country with a half million in cash in his suitcase. Faizi had tried to impound the dough and reported the governor to Kabul: Wesa was understandably pissed. He'd agreed to Faizi's invitation, as important folks were coming, but he was going to make his mark by being fashionably late.

The Afghans present all made the usual obligatory helpful remarks. Their meetings are not like ours. Everybody gets a say. It takes hours, going round in a circle, while every invited guest gets a chance to talk about being professional and working in a modern way.

Warlick was getting more and more agitated as the minutes ticked on.

We always confused the process of movement with progress. We were transfixed with meeting schedules. Afghans would happily sit for hours. It was all part of the hospitality culture. To work profitably there, you just had to accept it. The two systems were butting up against each other and the tension in the room was rising.

Still, Wesa hadn't turned up. Even Faizi ran out of platitudes. To fill the gap, in near desperation, he asked if any of his other visitors had any questions. I felt for Faizi. I felt for Najafi.

I piped up, introducing myself and 'Sada E Azadi'. I'd been busy taking pictures, to turn the meeting into another article. I needed a comment, so this seemed as good a time as any. I asked Warlick if he had any comment to make on progress in Kandahar's civil aviation sector.

Warlick looked up and me and replied:

'No.'

That was it. One word, nothing else. He may as well have publicly farted in my face. He just didn't get what he'd done. I knew all the Afghans personally. They were my friends. As a female, I held a special place of respect. They remembered what I had done for them. Everybody just looked at each other. Warlick looked at his watch.

Najafi broke the silence. He explained at length how Kandahar was prospering, how ISAF and the government were working together. All the usual bollocks and platitudes these occasions demanded. He did his best to smooth over the cracks.

Warlick seemed exasperated. 'I've got a question myself,' he said.' Can anybody tell me why Kandahar airport is important?'

All the Afghan hands again closely examined their shoes. While the State Department kids put in more loud phone calls to confirm that the ambassador was running unavoidably late. The fun balloon had been well and truly popped.

Faizi adjourned the meeting. He announced lunch. We all trooped out, while Najafi kept the principals in Faizi's office for a heart-to-heart.

The worm was beginning to turn with the Afghans. In the past, Wesa had had to accept stuff like the Shur Andam plant as a take-it-or-leave it option. After all, despite his misgivings, we'd promised we'd stay for thirty years. Now, post-Obama surge, they all knew we'd be gone in two years. They wanted some assurances on how the fuck they were going to keep the whole thing together once we cut and ran.

Lunch got cut short, as Wesa finally blew in with his own heavily armed team and a ton of journalists. Security guard eyed up security guard as they all eyed up firing angles. God, there was a lot of posing with guns in Afghanistan.

Then, we were off for the pink ribbon-cut. Faizi danced about as the court jester on the edges, while Wesa studiously ignored him. Warlick and Najafi took centre stage, flanked by Wesa and JD. Everybody got their own personal pair of scissors. Each time they cut the ribbon, the press corps said they wanted one more take. In the end, we ran out of decent-sized bits of ribbon to cut and re-cut. There were little bits of pink nylon flying all over the place.

The important folk all made quick speeches about togetherness and marching into a bright future for Afghanistan. Trouble was, Faizi had set the flags up on the old, broken tarmac. Not the new bit we had paid for. The visual message was at odds with the words.

JD was furious. When they had met privately, Faizi had presented Warlick with a list as long as your arm of stuff he wanted done at the terminal. Warlick had turned and asked:

'Your opinion, general.'

Airport development wasn't COMKAF's bill of sale. He didn't own development. If anything, it was State's ballgame. John got hammered on something he couldn't deliver by somebody who didn't know why any of it was important.

The way it had panned out pissed me off, as I'd been the one who had pushed JD into representing COMKAF. Not as much as it pissed John off, though.

And with that, Warlick and his teen-agers were off, in a blizzard of flashing lights and spinning helicopters. We never saw him again.

In our culture, Faizi would have worked the field before the ball got played. In our world, he'd have had forty-five minutes with the principals to ink it. After he'd got the details all sorted first. In his world, he expected to sit around all day drinking tea, while everybody worked the issue in a communal think-tank. Afghan culture devolves decision-making to the whole. It's a meritocracy. Different strokes and different agendas spoiled the day.

Everybody there had wanted to do the right thing. We just didn't understand each other enough to make it all happen. The personal politics of it all ruined the moment. The airport spent the next year languishing in the shit bin. John wouldn't be burned twice.

Faizi's only big success that year was in attracting Pakistan airlines to run a shuttle to Kandahar from Quetta. Wesa and he made up enough to co-sign the agreement in front of a big international media crowd.

The very first in-coming flight got rocketed as it landed. 40 invited business- men, movers and shakers all, looked out the port windows to see several explosions erupt a mere couple of hundred yards away. There followed a short delay, as the crew scrambled to get the heck out of Dodge. It was the quickest turn-around in aviation history: and quite the welcoming committee.

The service got cancelled six weeks later.

What aircraft that did land were barely air-worthy. One Ariana flight, the in-house Afghan airline, on final descent, had a real close call. They had lowered the under-carriage and one of the wheels had fallen off. It went bouncing down the runway, narrowly missing a taxiing F-16.

Outside the terminal, three aircraft sat gently rusting away. They had landed OK, but were so knackered they had never taken off again. They'd just been towed to one side and left. Faizi had a plan to convert them into cafes.

Times were changing too for all those private security heroes. Besides all the military and their guns, Afghanistan was still awash with security contractors and their guns too. Behind all the guns stood ISAF. We brought all the foreign soldiers. But we also empowered the security contractors to protect the stuff all those foreign soldiers needed.

From 2001 onwards, two competing families, the Karzais and the Sherzais, had fought hard for ISAF's favour in the south. At one point, ISAF even rented KAF itself from the Sherzais. Ahmed Wali Karzai and Gul Agha Sherzai made hundreds of millions of dollars in contract fees from ISAF. The place was just awash with private militias.

Watan Risk Management? The biggest security contractor in the south. Run by Karzai cousins. Asia Security Company? Another powerful security contractor. Run by a third Karzai cousin. The Kandahar Strike Force? The CIA's paramilitary proxy. Run by Ahmed Wali Karzai. The Kandahar national security directorate? Afghanistan's own security service. Run by General Gul Ali: an ally and former sub-ordinate of Gul Agha Sherzai. The KAF security force? Run by Abdul Sherzai, brother to Gul Agha Sherzai. The situation was so out of control that, in 2010, General Nick Carter publicly stated that private security companies operated in a 'culture of impunity'.

Alongside the home-grown companies, there were dozens of international firms. In 2013, some estimates put their number at over 40,000 bodies in-country. In 2010, 52 different security companies were formally registered for work in Afghanistan. By some estimates, Kandahar alone had another 22 working off the books.

If you had a contract supporting ISAF, then your work was covered by the terms of immunity from prosecution the military enjoyed. Except, the foreign companies had no code of uniform justice: or a proper training and recruitment program. I lost count of the number of severely touched idiots I met running free with very big guns. Afghanistan just seemed to attract them. A large number were former vets who couldn't settle and came back for the pay cheque—which could be very generous. An equally large number talked up a short career as a reservist chef and just strapped on an assault rifle.

In '03, my boys and I landed at Kabul on our way back from a long op. We were driving our wagons off the back ramp of our RAF Herc, when a bearded goon in a leather jacket came running up, pointing his rifle at us. He started shouting at us in a very strong American accent, which we couldn't understand as the plane engines were still running. I chose to ignore him, but you couldn't miss the dozen or so equally-clad guys behind him.

We all lined up, weapons at the ready. My twelve paratroopers in uniform facing twelve blokes in khaki and sunglasses. It didn't look good. I grabbed what looked like the oldest guy and asked him what the fuck he was playing at. He told me they were pulling security for President Karzai, who was shortly due to pick up a plane right where we were standing.

I told him I didn't see any plane waiting—which was true, as our Herc filled the taxiway. I didn't see any president either. In any case, we were the ones formally mandated to save Afghanistan. Not some adrenalised Rambo parody. I was the guy in uniform, not him. We exchanged a few more choice words, which ended up with a severe eyeball to eyeball, only saved by the guys telling me we were good to go.

The goons came from the infamous Blackwater company, which got such a bad rep for indiscriminately opening fire on civilians that they had to change their name just to keep on working. I later found out the guy I inter-acted with had been fired. He'd been pulling the president's detail when he threw an Afghan to the ground for approaching the president. Turned out the guy thrown on the floor had been the minister for energy.

By 2011, even Karzai had had enough of security companies.

He set up a nationalised institution, called the Afghan Public Protection Force (APPF), to replace all the homemade outfits with one Afghan-led organisation. In part, his sudden motivation may have stemmed from the assassination of half-brother Wali Karzai, who ran the majority of ISAF security contracts in the south. After he was gone, the scene got a lot more fragmented. Karzai family income wasn't what it had once been.

APPF was a pretty impressive scam. Essentially split into a revenue raiser and a nationalised employment scheme, it purported to turn the impressively funded security game into an Afghan revenue stream. By early 2013, the scheme had amassed $90 million in reserves.

Private security companies had to place a considerable six-figure marker (which I doubt will ever be seen again) with the Ministry of Interior, followed by an annual registration fee, just to get a license. All foreign owned weapons were supposed to be turned in for inspection. I knew several reputable operators who handed in well-maintained, modern M4 assault rifles: and got handed back an old, rusty AK47 in return. The ministry then hired all the security guards. And controlled their salaries.

The APPF were supposed to run all convoy security, and provide key static point guards for infrastructure. The main ISAF supplier, Supreme, hated the idea. They had their own, chosen contractors: who were strongly rumoured to have paid off the bad guys en-route to let their trucks through. ISAF never really worried about how the stuff got to the big bases, as long as it got there on time.

The game created a sort of wacky races stand-off. With unlicensed convoys pulling a cannonball run at night, and the local APPF commanders taking fees to add-on a few extra trucks at the end of the officially mandated convoys.

The APPF didn't originally have their own gear. The various police outfits in Afghanistan, of which there were at least five, all had different sponsors. Each had their own different uniforms and vehicles. Which made for a complicated target picture. Who was a cop and who was a bad guy?

The APPF picked up a load of surplus stuff belonging to all five agencies: from a wacky digital uniform to unmarked former police vehicles. And some big old 12.7 mm anti-aircraft guns, which they mounted on the back of flatbed Ford Rangers. The APPF was Mad Max on wheels.

The Afghans set up APPF in the south without telling anybody. Then turned up at KAF in a whirlwind of heavily-armed, but unmarked Ford Rangers. They started setting up their own checkpoints, which agitated the Bulgarians on the wire. Once again, the quick reaction force got called out and we had another gunfight at the OK corral stand-off.

It really is a wonder that more people didn't get killed in Afghanistan. We got the word back in COMKAF that lots of armed Afghans in a new camouflage were at the gates. Nobody knew who they were.

Completely by chance, I was writing the APPF up. I'd snuck out on one of my private trips with some private security boys I knew earlier in the week and gone to visit them in their new, shiny camp on Highway 1. Just as I had with Scott and the big IED, I was in the right place at the right time. I had the photos and the explanation. John called off the attack dogs. Afterwards, the base deputy commander told me that I had stopped a fire-fight breaking out. If I hadn't been around, then there would have been blood spilled.

The airport *debacle* was promptly forgotten. Whatever doubts JD had about letting me into the inner circle were dissipated. It was just luck and timing, really. But I am proud of that moment. After a year and half of assiduously assimilating my area of operations, my knowledge had saved lives.

Not everybody thought of my contribution in the same light, though.

The Brits ran a special forces task force in KAF that they kept pretty super-secret-squirrel. The brass in Kabul didn't agree: and I got instructed to go make contact and advertise what they were up to.

At the time, ISAF counter-terror night ops were becoming really unpopular with President Karzai. There were a huge amount of complaints, most justified, that civilians were being killed in the crossfire. The Afghans wanted oversight. The whole issue was de-railing relations between Kabul and Washington.

My job was to find something to write up that was good news. The order came straight from COMISAF.

The SF contingent were easy to spot. Unlike everybody else, they wore their own combination of self-assigned uniform. The rig was 1970's secret agent combat porn. Lots of big side-burns and pistols shoved in the back of belts stuff.

The blades, the strike teams, were pretty decent lads, easy to talk to. But the outfit had mushroomed support bodies. Who loved themselves disproportionately to their talent or selection.

In the old days, I had a chum who fancied himself as a bit of a ladies man. He came from a decent enough line regiment, but, just to up the action, he bought himself an SAS beret. In every military town, there's a set of women who go on the prowl for a soldier. They know exactly who is who in the hierarchy. My pal would leave the beret on his bed and set off on the prowl. He'd get the chick back to his room and leave her to find the headgear:

'Oh, I am sorry... Shouldn't leave that lying around. You won't tell anybody will you? Rather hush-hush and all that....'

That guy had an impressive hit rate. In KAF, everybody attached the SF took on the same mystique.

It took a contact in Kabul to get me the name of the task force press guy. Which must have been a pretty easy gig as they were in the crapper for not doing any press at all.

The hero in question reluctantly agreed, by e-mail, to meet with me. We missed each other by a couple of hours, as the chosen day coincided with my KAF record of sixteen rocket attacks in one afternoon. I wasn't in a great mood by the time we finally hooked up. Even so the chat when we did meet was remarkable:

'Hi, I'm Abi, from the POTF,' I said, by way of introduction.

'I can't tell you my name,' my interlocutor replied.

'Really? Well, who do you work for?' I replied.

'I can't tell you that either,' he answered. This wasn't going well.

'Well, what do you do here?' I tried again.

'I can't tell you that,' he re-joined.

'Well, if you can't tell me your name, who you work for or what you do, why are we meeting?'

'I can't tell you.'

No point in hanging around, I thought, and called it a day. As my new friend walked away, he turned back, and as a portentous after-thought, announced: 'I'm SAS.'

Well, by now I was thoroughly pissed off. I'd risked my neck by going outside on a busy day of metal rain to meet this bloke, who'd offered me nothing. I also knew that most, if not all, of the SF lads were actually reservists.

'Really,' I replied. 'So what do you do for a living during the week?' And that, not surprisingly, was as close as I ever got to covering the UK taskforce.

They needed my help a year later, though, when their prison hit the headlines.

By presidential decree, coalition forces were barred from keeping Afghans in detention. In KAF, that got a bit embarrassing. Worries over General Raziq's reported predilection for applying car battery electrodes and other sundry interrogation toys meant that the US applied a temporary ban on handing over detainees for human rights reasons.

Raziq was our champion. So, while the Americans gave him a quick 101 in why torture was not a good idea, the Brits were in the uncomfortable position of providing long-term lock-up for up to 25 sundry Afghan bad-guys. The Brits locked some of them for over 6 months without sentence or trial, according to the press reports. Which must have been an interesting experience.

When Karzai found out, he went ballistic. By 2014, relations between Karzai and the US were at the 'I hate you,' 'I hate you more' level of literacy. Karzai leaked the whole affair to the media, which whipped up a maelstrom of ISAF conspiracy theories.

KAF had to host a very high-level delegation from Kabul and all the bad boys were promptly returned to sender. The prison's days were over.

When a building got ' de-scoped', as the military called demolition, the troops usually only took the stuff above ground. They would leave the poured-concrete foundation, which was known as a 'lily-pad'. In the prison's case, the US engineers came by with a ton of jackhammers and a big old bulldozer. Under a security umbrella, they lifted every shred of the place, foundation and all, right out of the ground. You'd never know we had even had a prison.

SOAK

John Dolan and I became pretty good chums. I liked and respected the man enormously. He was one of those re-assuring presences to have around. I always felt we were in safe hands when he was in town. He always defended me against 3ID.

His aviator call sign was Soak. A call sign is a pretty big deal in pilot-land. Yet, right until near the end, he stayed really reticent to talk about it.

JD was big into his barbeques. He had a fire-pit built out back of the base operations centre, where we'd go sit and enjoy the sunset. We'd get Supreme to send over cake, cokes and some dead stuff to cremate. My job was putting together the music. Soak was a bit of a country nut, so we'd all gather for a cookout and watch the jets take off while Tammy Wynette serenaded us about her man.

Some of my happiest memories of the whole three years are of the team gathered around that fire-pit.

Soak and the boys all loved a big stogie. He actually had a humidor in his office. We'd all look deep into the flames, what the military call 'Ranger TV'. The boys would puff away and shoot the shit. I was part of the team and I loved them all.

We were a fun bunch. John's executive team had somehow escaped the military orthodox net and were a couple of goof-balls. The two of them were both B-52 bomber pilots, but also science-fiction nuts. The office was full of Battlestar Galactica posters. We'd spend hours quoting Star Wars dialogue to each other in fake Yoda voices.

The boys had these florescent violet gum shields they'd stick in their mouths. They'd turn the lights off, wait for the next office visitor, and frighten the shit out of them by screaming from the darkness with their vivid purple teeth.

John always stayed above the high jinks. At heart, he is a bit of an introvert. He never let the mask of command slip, until his last week.

We got together for one last barbie. He'd flown his last F-16 flight that day.

At his rank and age, it would be the last combat mission he would ever fly. During his tour, he'd amassed an impressive 200 missions. I gave him a T-shirt, with general's stars and a picture of an F-16, marked 200.

As we laughed about the madness of the last year, I pushed him one last time. Why was he called Soak? Heck, I'd just shelled out for a T-shirt. He owed me. He looked over at me and smiled, before putting his feet up on the fire-pit and leaning back.

He'd been flying in a four-stick flight of F-16s from South Korea, back to Hawaii. Somewhere over the Pacific, they'd hit a huge tropical storm, right at the spot they were due to do a mid-air refuel. As John's bird had lined up to take on the tanker hose, the pilot had lost control and the back of the tanker had dipped suddenly, right into his F-16. The force of the collision sheared off his wing and John found himself in a flat spin, out of control, 20,000 feet up, in the middle of a hurricane. The tanker was OK, it was a big plane, but JD was in the shit.

John told his remarkable story in that unemotional, deadpan way of his, doing that pilot thing of using his hands to describe how the planes hit, dive-bombing his watch... 'see, I came in on his six like this...' I was enthralled. Then JD just stopped and puffed on his cigar a bit, while I pounded him for answers. What happened next? The SOB was a natural born story-teller. He just laughed and took up the tale.

He'd punched out and drifted down, dangling under his parachute. The winds took him miles away. He lost sight of all the other planes. He spent eleven minutes in the air, watching the ocean get closer and closer. He was thousands of miles from land, equally thousands of miles from help. He hit the water, dragged himself into his life raft and spent the next eighteen hours being smashed from pillar to post by mountainous seas.

The Japanese launched a twin propeller engine rescue seaplane to come get him. They found him through his locator beacon, but the waves swamped one engine as they dragged a nearly unconscious John on board. The pilot waited until he hit a trough and judged it just right to get the bird aloft and back to safety. A one shot to glory deal.

'Wow,' I told him. 'That is some pilot story.'

'No,' replied John. 'The Japanese pilot has the story, not me.'

That's the kind of man General John Dolan is. And why he became Soak forever more.

INSIDE SHOOTER

Daniel Kavuliak was thirty-five when he came to Kandahar. He was a sergeant in the Slovakian army. The 11th Mechanised Battalion, to which he belonged, is the first full-time, professional unit that Slovakia has ever possessed.

Daniel joined the Slovak army in 2002, less than ten years after the country's creation and independence. Before coming to Kandahar, he had served as part of the UN peacekeeping force in Cyprus. He married Lucia in 2007. Together, the two of them had high hopes of a family. Lucia worked in a supermarket. The young couple had a home in Turzovka. Their wedding photos show a couple very much in love. They went to Croatia on holiday in 2012. The holiday photos show a couple holding hands under a lovely sunset. Their hopes and dreams all lay before them. It was to be the last time the couple ever took a holiday.

Lamber Khan came from Jalalabad, in east Afghanistan. He joined the Afghan National Army in 2008. He was posted to Kandahar, where he formed part of 205 Corps, based across the road from KAF, at Camp Hero.

On 09th July 2012, Daniel Kavuliak found himself in KAF. Slovakia had been part of ISAF operations in KAF since the very beginning of the big push into the south in '06/ 07. In addition to a headquarters element, they provided a force protection company, a very effective contingent of combat engineers and a special forces component. The Slovakian commitment was a highly regarded member of the team.

The Slovaks lived right by my accommodation. Like all the liberated former Soviet countries, they were super-proud of their new status as NATO members. At night, they played traditional folk songs and held very competitive arm-wrestling competitions. They were a happy-go-lucky bunch. I liked them enormously.

Kavuliak arrived as part of a new rotation. On 9th July 2013, the new guys had literally got off the plane. Straight into a searing 45 degree heat and a very unfamiliar combat arena. KAF at any time was a mind-blower. In July it is a scorching pit.

Every new unit had a breaking-in period. That first day, Daniel Kavuliak drew his weapon and put on his body armour. Number 1 priority; orientation, a tour around the dear and dusty old place. As part of the force protection element for KAF, Kavuliak would be guarding us. He needed to know ASAP what he would be guarding.

While ISAF guarded most of KAF, the southeast corner was an Afghan responsibility. A quarter-mile stretch of perimeter marked the edge of General Sherzai's air wing. 205 Corps manned a number of guard towers along that part of the perimeter.

The eastern edge of the camp butted onto highway four, the main drag up to Kandahar city. The Brit Tornado fighter wing had the northeast corner. From there, heading south, a chicane in the perimeter road led past the concrete and aggregate factories, down to what had been the old entrance in Soviet times. A battered MiG on a plinth still heralded entrance to KAF. A sharp right angle back west then led the road past the entrance slip, through the Afghan air wing, and on to the southern ISAF hangers.

On 09th July, Lamber Khan drew guard duty at KAF. He was posted to one of the guard towers in the southeast corner, near the road junction to the outside world, right next to the air wing. His arcs covered highway 4 and the main entrance with the MIG. For some reason, he drew guard duty alone, which was against normal practise. He was armed with an old Soviet-era PKM belt-fed machine gun: and a belt of 120 bullets.

Around lunchtime, Kavuliak and eleven comrades from the command team filled a civilian minibus and set off on their initial familiarisation tour of the camp. There was nothing unusual about the day, nor their transport. The tour was strictly inside the wire. We all drove around in 'white fleet': rented civilian vehicles.

Nor was there anything unusual in the route. The perimeter road was the easy way to get about. I often went that way myself, past the Afghan part of camp, on my way to the British part of the world. The Afghans all knew me from my years of visiting. They would wave from their guard posts as I drove by.

On 9th July, I was in my office in COMKAF, about a half mile from where Lamber Khan was pulling his duty. John Dolan was up in his F-16, keeping us all safe from above: normal combat air patrol. Usual day in the suck, nothing doing but dust and sun. The world was turning, folks busy doing the normal staff niff naff and trivia.

The Slovaks stopped their tour at the main gate for a closer look. As our force protection team, this was key terrain for them. Gates and entrances had to be carefully watched. From above, in his guard tower, Lamber Khan carefully watched the Slovaks stop, get out and do their planning.

For some time, Khan had secretly been in touch with the Taliban. Lamber Khan picked up his PKM, aimed at Daniel Kavuliak and opened fire. A PKM on automatic fires 750 7.62 mm rounds a minute. The first burst tore into Kavuliak. He stood no chance. The first burst killed him instantly.

Khan had 120 rounds. He hit five other Slovaks in a concentrated mad minute of spraying machine gun fire. The Slovaks fired back. Khan was in an entrenched position, with superior firepower. The Slovaks had their small arms, but only enough ammunition for personal protection. They were in a minibus, not an MRAP. Khan continued firing.

The Slovaks managed to get their wounded onto the minibus. The driver, despite being hit himself, weaved westwards, back towards ISAF territory. Somehow, he managed to drive the bullet-ridden vehicle, with his bleeding, dead and dying comrades on board. They had been in KAF less than six hours.

General Sherzai was in his office, a couple of hundred yards away. His security detail could see the guard post. They saw the fall of shot, the little dust devils of sand bursting, where the Slovaks return fire hit Khan's guard post. Sherzai and his bodyguards charged Khan's guard post. The man that Abrams had wanted to get rid of led the response to stop the rogue shooter.

Khan's 120 rounds didn't last long. The air wing team stormed his guard post, firing back.

In COMKAF, we heard the fusillade of rounds go off. Kavuliak fell just down the road. I was outside, taking a break, when the sounds of the long bursts erupted.

It was one of those moments when you just knew bad shit was going down: and going down close by. The whole place just took a big inhalation of breath. Suddenly, it all went very quiet. The only sound was the crack of automatic gunfire, then a pause, them more rounds, different sound. Not the deep bark of a machine gun, single rounds, but plenty of them, smaller calibre too, higher pitch. Whatever was going on was a furious exchange.

We waited.

The Slovak minibus drove straight for the Role 3 NATO hospital, right next to COMKAF, the main clearing-house for casualties from all over the south. Better fitted out than most hospitals stateside, it was exactly the right call.

Daniel Kavuliak was dead.

Two fellow Slovaks had been severely injured—in the head and body. Four others had been wounded. The Slovaks were understandably in shock.

Milan Kuder, one of Kavuliak's comrades in the minibus, later stated Khan had fired on them from less than 30 metres away. The Slovaks stood no chance. They could count themselves lucky that, with 120 bullets, Khan was obviously a terrible shot.

Company commander Miroslav Stanik was particularly fortunate. He carried a knife on his belt, a memory of his time in Iraq. The boys always laughed at him for it. One of Khan's rounds had hit the blade, deflecting the killer round and saving Stanik's life.

The balloon went up in KAF. Giant Voice warbled the dreaded message: 'Ground attack...ground attack...'

Folks dived for their body armour. Staff officers drew their pistols and took cover behind their desks.

Up in the air, John's plane got put in a holding pattern. He flew lazy 8's over KAF, desperately waiting for news.

The British mobilised their quick reaction force and sealed off the area. That particular British RAF rotation was fortunate to be led by a really sharp cookie. He had spent a lot of time sharpening defensive protection measures. The Brits were the fastest off the mark: and showed admirable restraint. There were a lot of Afghans running around with guns that afternoon who can count themselves lucky they were not shot.

As ever, the facts came in slowly. We got word that there were multiple casualties at the Role 3.

The usual arrivals came in by air. This time, the casualties drove themselves right to the front door. Not only did the hospital stabilise the two severely injured soldiers, at the same time the doctors and nurses mounted their own force protection measures. They applied drips and blood plasma as they were locking and loading their own weapons.

At the time, none of us knew Lamber Khan was a lone shooter. Most of the folks in KAF were rear area troops. They hadn't expected to be in close combat. Those few hours that we all sat and waited were a time for deep reflection.

I'd been through a fair few of these alerts. Most of the time, I seriously thought that I stood more chance of being shot by my own side than the enemy. On one occasion, a Marine had even levelled his loaded weapon at me, finger on the trigger: which had been fucking scary.

This day, though, was different. Folks I knew and trusted as commanders were making sure their helmet straps were properly done up. This time, part of the KAF family had perished. Daniel and his fellow Slovaks might not have been with us for long, but they were part of our brethren.

KAF took it personally.

We got stood down late afternoon after several sweaty hours of manning sangar positions. General Sherzai's people had captured Lamber Khan alive. I had no doubt he had a couple of black eyes, but he was in custody. He was extremely lucky one of his own got to him first.

John spent 17 helpless hours in the sky, re-fuelling mid-air as he waited for the chance to get back to his command. There was no way he could have predicted what had unfolded: but like the rest of us, he was angry.

For some time, there had been concerns about the air wing. Just the previous week, I'd sat in a meeting where we had discussed putting in protective fire positions between us and the Afghans. We had worried at the example it would set, at a time when the air wing was making real progress. Yet, at no time had we even thought of closing off the road around the camp.

Why would we?

What had transpired wasn't Sherzai's fault. He had led the charge to get the shooter. Khan was an army guy, not air force. He fell under the command of another Afghan general, Gul Ali, who was responsible for outer base security.

Still, serious questions needed to be answered as to why he had a belt-fed weapon: more importantly, why was he on guard duty alone that day? And why a soldier with five years service had turned that day to a cold-hearted killer.

Khan was taken into custody at Camp Hero. His gaoler, a senior Afghan sergeant-major. We waited to see what the Afghans would do. Previous form was clear: Khan would face the death sentence. And none of us were terribly upset about that either.

Daniel Kavuliak was the first Slovak soldier to die in Afghanistan. The news hit the country hard. Next day, a delegation personally led by Slovak Prime Minister Robert Fico and Defence Minister Martin Glváč flew to KAF to take Daniel's remains home.

John led the COMKAF funeral cortege.

It was a sombre moment for us all. Many of us had driven that perimeter road, passed that very spot where Daniel died. KAF was a game of numbers. It could have been any one of us. Just as any one of us would gladly have taken out that fucker Lamber Khan if we could have saved Daniel Kavuliak.

Prime Minister Pico thanked John for the solemnity that we attributed to Daniel's leaving. We hadn't had the time to get to know him, but he was a brother departing. We honoured that. Pico then asked John how many men he needed to augment the Slovakian contingent. Khan had changed nothing.

Tough country, Slovakia.

Over in Camp Hero, Lamber Khan was a little the worse for wear following interrogation. He said he had shot Daniel and the Slovaks in protest at ISAF bombings of his home village in Nangarhar Province.

His gaoler, who also came from Nangarhar, filled out a form to release Khan into his custody to attend camp hospital for treatment to his superficial injuries. While the pair sat waiting for a medic, aided by his gaoler, Khan slipped his restraints and the two lit out for Pakistan.

The Taliban run a professional media operation. Their website, 'Shahamat', or 'Voice of Jihad', is just as good as anything ISAF managed to put together. It is a darn sight more interesting for the average Afghan reader than anything the POTF ever did.

The website is based in Dubai, but the work is produced by a corps of journalists living a bit closer to home. Home being Kandahar. I'd been reading the site for some time: and they had one tell that I had got pretty effective at reading. Generally speaking, I could tell when we were going to get a spike in rocket attacks around KAF. The rain arriving usually coincided with a team infiltrating from Pakistan. When the bad guys meant to do some serious damage, they rather effectively tied it in with the media set-up at 'Shahamat'.

Their journalists were classically trained. When the stuff they were reporting was gleaned from the local lads, they'd write in the third person. Such as 'reports indicate that…'

When they had a team inserted, the language would change. The wording would read with much more immediacy and purpose. Such as: 'Mujahideen heroes destroyed three enemy tanks.'

It took a lot of analysing, but after a bit I got to be quite good at predicting when the spikes would come. When the language changed, it meant there was either a reporter or somebody with direct access to one on the ground. That meant thought had gone into exploiting the mission, so we had better pay attention.

At that time, nobody else was working on this combat indicator. Other folks read 'Shahamat'. I think most of their web hits came from our intelligence community. But nobody was thinking about the language they used. I'd tried raising it with colonel idiot at 3ID, but he hadn't bothered to pick up the phone.

That work was why I had been invited to the meeting the week before Daniel got shot, about force protection. The wording on the site at that time indicated to me that something was being planned.

The week before Daniel arrived, I had picked up the language tip. The bad guys were in town. Something was brewing. None of us could have predicted Lamber Khan, but the awfulness that we had missed something was still there.

Lamber Khan and his buddy couldn't have made it on their own. The local team helped them get out. Once Lamber Khan and his accomplice made it across the border both men were quickly picked up by 'Shahamat'. They put them on TV, conducting an open press conference from Pakistan.

Khan, a thin-faced, sallow individual with a scrappy beard, didn't speak much. Most of the talking was done by a media spokesperson, face hidden by a scarf, sitting next to him. The video, all thirty-five minutes long, invoking the will of Allah and death to the West every minute, was the usual slick and professional production I'd come to expect.

Khan was presented with a ceremonial turban and a truly gross heart-shaped garland of plastic flowers. His assembled Taliban handlers formed a circle around the jubilant pair of traitors and fired off celebratory rounds of gunfire.

They dressed the video up with pictures of Bales' atrocity as justification for Khan's actions. It was a direct slap in the face for us: and it fucking hurt.

Back at COMKAF, I sent the link to JD and the command team. It was a difficult time. Trust—that vital commodity between allies—had been broken.

The security boys sent out photos of Lamber Khan, in case he was daft enough to come back. I don't know if they ever got him. I hope they did, though. The fucker deserves to die for what he did.

Yes, that incident got to me too. For some time, I'd been a bit of a lone voice in the wilderness, pleading the case for Sherzai, Faizi and the Afghans. John already felt burned by Faizi over the Warlick thing. Sherzai never recovered from the Khan incident. John now had no choice but to raise the drawbridge. We knew Sherzai's men hadn't done the deed. We knew he had tried to stop it and that his men had arrested the shooter. But enough was enough.

Daniel wasn't the first killed by our allies that year. By the July, he was the sixth ISAF soldier to be shot by a member of the Afghan security forces in a supposed 'safe' area that year.

The fences went up between us and the air wing. The road got blocked off and we looked at each other with suspicion over the top of a very thick and high wall of aggregate-filled bastions. After the July shootings, I only went back a couple of times to the air wing. And then, I needed a full close protection detail. I never got to fly with them again.

To visit us before the July shootings, Sherzai had just driven round the camp road. Post-Khan, he had to go through the main entry-exit gate. That meant an outside trip for him. For which he needed his own private security detail. Sherzai was a prized target for the other side. His guards had to de-bus and hand-in their weapons. It was demeaning. On one occasion, the guards tried to body-search Sherzai himself. An Afghan major-general, who had been the one to liberate the airport itself twelve years earlier, found himself detained at the gate by a suspicious Bulgarian junior soldier half his age. Sherzai just stopped coming to see us. Who could really blame him?

Two months earlier, 450 soldiers from the 1st Battalion, the Royal Regiment of Scotland, The Royal Scots Borderers, had marched through Edinburgh to mark their homecoming from Helmand. They should have marched with Captain Walter Barrie. Walter had risen through the ranks to get his commission. All the way up from private soldier to captain, quite an achievement. In his forties when his battalion was called to go to Afghanistan, Barrie could have sat the tour out. As family's officer, the link between the wives and the men, he had more than enough to do. Walter, being the man he was, volunteered for one last tour with his lads.

Captain Barrie ended up training the Afghan army in Forward Operating Base Shawqat, Helmand.

He loved football and was a formidable player. To Walter's mind, a good game of footie was the way to build bonds between trainer and recruit.

On Remembrance Sunday, 2012, Walter asked Mohammad Ashraf, who was supposed to be on guard duty, to join the game. The story gets a little confused at this point, but the most repeated version is that Walter, competitive sportsman and all, tackled Ashraf once too often. Ashraf walked off the pitch, picked up his rifle, turned, and shot Walter in the head. Ashraf then ran off, and was, in turn, shot and killed by two other Scots soldiers after a furious shoot-out.

Walter died where he lay, on a dusty football pitch in the ass-end of nowhere in the middle of Helmand. He was married with a teenage son. Captain Walter Barrie had been a soldier for twenty-five loyal years.

The Royal Scots Borderers are great soldiers. They had kept me safe through Desert Storm and a couple of other adventures. Their brigade commander in Helmand, himself a Royal Scot, has been a chum since university, over thirty years ago. Bob Bruce is a sensitive, talented and charismatic general. Before he left on that tour, we had met up at a hotel in Scotland. We had talked a lot about trying to relate to Afghan culture and how best to change the country through development, not by shooting. Bob had made all his officers read up on psychological warfare before they had departed. It's a mark of the kind of leader he is.

Both of us knew Walter well. Bob had spent a considerable portion of his career with him. Walter had been Regimental Sergeant-Major when Bob had commanded the Royal Scots. I sent a quiet, private note to Bob when the news broke. As ever, he sent me a dignified, succinct reply:

'We must just keep buggering on.'

There wasn't much more that either of us could say. Even in his evident shock, Bob was absolutely right: we must just keep buggering on. It was what soldiers did. Until somebody told us we could all stop.

From 2013 onwards, every time we met an Afghan, we had to have at least two fully-armed soldiers, all kitted out in body armour and helmet, alongside us. We called them 'guardian angels'. Afghans had to be unarmed. Even people we had known for years.

My own understanding had been worn thin too. By 2013, there were no good guys left. Too many of my friends had died. I am not a hateful person, but even now I feel hatred when I think on the people I cared about who were taken.

The Afghans too were suffering. By 2013, the UN estimated that 14,000 civilians had been killed by the endless fighting. Too many had died and were continuing to die. The dream had ended.

In 2005, a very senior member of the British government had told me: 'There is something worth fighting for in Afghanistan. We must make this work.'

By 2013, I had lost sight of exactly what it was that we were trying to achieve. The generals were desperately parading statistics of roads built and schools opened to justify it all. It was all bollocks.

None of it was worth the candle anymore. Afghanistan had stopped being a noble venture. A majority of us wanted to go home: and nobody wanted to be the last one to die.

THREE BECOMES FOUR

On July 8th 2013, the day before Daniel Kavuliak died, 'Abe' Abrams headed off for his general's jet and a bright future in the Pentagon.

I wasn't invited to the hand-over. I was persona non grata. As was the lieutenant colonel who had so rudely ended my relationship with RC-S. A month earlier, his entire staff had rebelled and written a letter of complaint against him. So close to the end of tour, Abrams had spared his blushes and got him an early transfer. A disciplinary measure against a mid-ranking career officer was messy stuff.

I found out about it in the gym. My relationship with 3ID had got so desperate that the head of the psyops unit, with whom I had to keep at least a nodding relationship, was forced to meet me over the free weights. That way, our encounters could be kept on the 'accidental' level.

While we both breathed a deep sigh of relief—and a little righteous indignation that the colonel had got off scot-free—the legacy was appalling. Part of our nemesis' final brief had been to recommend force retention levels for the in-coming division.

Influence operations had already been cut, from around 130 82nd to roughly 70 soldiers for 3ID. Basically, all the headquarters and non-productive elements had been chopped. Core capability had been retained. We were still broadcasting, still pumping out leaflets, papers, surveys and all that good stuff influence operations were supposed to sustain. What the good colonel proposed—and had been approved by Abrams—was a cut from 70 to 12.

12 in formation operations people out of a headquarters of 600, with a division-sized area of operations. At a time when troops were withdrawing and the battle-space needed to be filled with something else, 3ID left a rump of 12 people.

It was the end of the entire production arm. The printing presses remained, the stuff was all there (minus the mysteriously disappeared portable radio stations). There was just nobody left to make it work.

As the troops left, 4ID were left with no means to explain the withdrawal, nor the means to answer the arguments the vacuum left behind. Influence is supposed to be the first in and the last out: that's formal NATO and US doctrine.

It was a criminal omission. And a game-changing handicap for 4ID and its commander: Major General Paul LaCamera. Paul is a very different man from Abe. While Abrams was all Patton, LaCamera is Eisenhower.

Of all the generals I met in Afghanistan over the years, LaCamera is the one I was most impressed by in command there. He is also one of the most modest men I have ever met: a quality not most often evident in a general. Paul was to become a friend and a very supportive colleague and commander. But while I liked and admired him as a man, it is his innate leadership and achievement as CG in Kandahar that seal the deal for me.

Paul couldn't have been more different, in military terms, from Abrams. His opening remarks, at that change of command, clearly set out his stall:

'It's humbling to be in front of this group of warriors and the proud people of Afghanistan. It is also good to be back in Afghanistan among Afghan and coalition friends... it is a relationship that that has help to shape and define me as a military leader and a citizen of my own country.'[30]

No 'Rock of the Marne' stuff. Just an honest admission he was now in different waters and had a lot to learn, but that he had come to help.

Paul is an army ranger. It's his proudest achievement as a soldier. He has won a lot of awards and medals, but the one event he always talked about was humping his ass over the hills and swamps of Georgia and Florida to win his prized ranger tab. Interestingly, despite the Rangers' long and illustrious past of male-only achievement, Paul was all for female integration. Provided women could reach the required standard. It is just how he views his troops: best person for the job. You could be a giraffe or a Martian. He didn't care, long as you matched or exceeded expectation.

Since graduating from West Point in 1985, he has spent the majority of his command career in the special forces arena, including as commanding officer of the 75th Ranger Regiment. Then as director of operations for Special Operations Command: with Stan McChrystal at the helm. He stayed on there as deputy commanding general after Stan went to AFG, before a stint at the 25th Infantry Division set him up for command of the 4th and Kandahar.

By the time he came to KAF, he was still a relatively junior two star general, but his background was all counter-insurgency. He cut his teeth on the operations in Grenada and Haiti, not Desert Storm, where Abrams started.

Paul's world was all shades of grey, intelligence-led, nimble, light, effective and rapier-sharp application of force. He is also a keen student of history and economics. Exactly, in fact, the sort of leader McChrystal was. A bit funky and off-base too: Paul's favourite movie is 'Talladega Nights'. He can quote you the script.

The first thing Paul wanted was an accurate and timely summary on

---

[30] US DoD transcript

Kandahar. Not just the usual military stuff on what troops were where and doing what. He wanted to know what tribe lived where, who was important to know, how people made a living and what drove them. He wanted to know how much a loaf of bread cost. It drove his staff nuts.

Abrams wanted to know how loud the bang was, Paul wanted to know what made the bang.

The regular army wasn't set up for that. Even after thirteen years of war. In the Rangers and spec ops, the command structure was fundamentally fairly flat. McChrystal's biggest achievement as a commander had been to create synergy and equality of effort. The regular army is strictly hierarchical.

The military is fond of the term 'troops to task'. Using the right spanner for the right job. In spec ops, they asked if a spanner was the right tool: and if it needed to be unscrewed in the first place. To thrive in that environment is to be a staff officer who is not afraid to speak your mind, and to know when to shut up and apply the effort to the group consensus.

The second part is quite familiar to the regular army. What the general says is what the army does. 4ID weren't used to the first part of the conversation beforehand.

Paul could be quite ruthless. I told him that once; and he replied that he thought I was being harsh. I told him it depended on the context. He routinely had to balance risk and reward, with his soldier's lives being the bet. Most people would freeze when making that decision. What I admired about Paul was not his decisiveness: all successful generals have that quality. It was that I always felt he first wanted to inform his decisions with every perspective he could muster. Including ones he might not like or agree with. The guy just cared. Not only for his troops, for Afghanistan and its people too.

He'd spent enough time there, right from the beginning. He'd been with the Rangers as they toured through Tora Bora, hunting for Osama. In spec ops, he'd cycled through Iraq and Afghanistan with the regularity that most folks have in choosing Florida for their annual holiday.

3ID's manning cuts just hobbled him from the get-go. 12 influence operations folks didn't stand a chance of gathering the information he needed. The word got back to me that he was casting for answers, the questions coming in an un-remitting stream. Who is this? Why is he important? Who lives in this village?

The rotation system struck him down. 3ID were not the best at updating the in-house Wiki. NATO had a pretty cool database, but the machine needed feeding. A lot of the entries had not been updated since the 82nd days.

John kept telling me that a lot of the stuff I was feeding him was the answer to a lot of the stuff Paul was after. But I was really, really wary. I was in the groove, doing my time, watching the cheques go in the bank, secure with my private network of chums, Afghan and ISAF.

John thought it would be useful for me to go meet Paul. He offered to set the gig up. I turned him down.

JD spotted early on that Paul's staff were struggling. It wasn't entirely their fault. They'd done the usual recce visits and the stateside training scenarios.

Nothing, though, could replace on the ground experience. Which was the one thing they didn't have in the locker.

The military like to think on war as sports. With rules, regulations, uniforms, a recognised pitch and four quarters of play. Which, of course, assumes the enemy wants to play the other team: and by the same rules and regulations. THAT type of war, the Americans could understand: because they knew they were the Miami Dolphins, the New England Patriots and the San Francisco '49'ers, all rolled up into one. They'd never lose.

In Afghanistan, there were no rules, no regulations, no starting whistle and no time-outs. The other side didn't just want not play the game, they didn't recognise the game. I lost count of the times an exasperated staff officer would ask:

'Why don't the Afghans appreciate we are dying here for them?'

The simple answer, which always went down like the barman calling 'time, gentlemen, please', is that an awful lot of Afghans, particularly after eleven years of being bombed and watching foreign soldiers pad down their high street, didn't want the Americans there at all: let alone dying for them. Because all that dying brought a lot more death to everybody else round about.

They knew that, at its heart, the Americans weren't really there to die for them, but because some nut-jobs had flown a couple of planes into a big building they would never see in a country they would never visit, striking at a system that was as real to them as Mars is to us.

UPPING THE ANTE

What really swung the scales for me was Soak coming by, unable to contain his laughter. Apparently a marine officer had been briefing Paul on RC-SW, over in Helmand. He'd punched up a slide headed 'economic development', with no specifics underneath. The marine officer had jokingly said:
'I'll skip that, general… nobody's interested in the economy.'
Paul replied:
'Well, I'm interested, colonel, do continue.'
The marine had nothing. He'd come to the birthday party without a present. There followed one of those embarrassing moments where said colonel mentally dug a career grave, laid in it and watched the dirt fall around him. Folks just coughed quietly and looked at the ceiling as the silence boomed around the room. The 4ID staff took the note—and thanked the Lord that they were not wearing marine boots.

John was right: this was a team I could do business with. JD had been just as beaten up by 3ID as I had been: but generals never speak ill of other generals, it's a closed cabal. So he couldn't really let rip to me on what had happened. I'd seen and heard enough myself, though. Soak was giving me the nod that, this time, it would be OK.

What made Paul different was the quality of his mind. He didn't give a shit what uniform you wore, or what rank, or what you'd done in the past. He wanted your ideas: and he was quite ruthless in using talent. He was equally ruthless in cutting you from the herd if you didn't deliver. It didn't actually matter if you disagreed with him. I often did. What he wanted was the debate.

Although an army is constituted of many moving parts, the entire organisation conforms to a rigid hierarchy. Officers have set functions, as do non-commissioned officers: officers write policy and set direction, NCO's execute it. Policy and direction is promulgated by written operational orders, which also follow a set –and very rigid—format. Every officer—including me once—was sent to staff officer school to learn how to write staff orders.

I'd hated the experience. Every nuance of creativity was ruthlessly eliminated. The formatting, the headings, the font, the spacing, the style, just everything was all rigidly linear.

That was fine for getting the most people to the right place at roughly the right time and moving in the right direction towards the right target. The army wasn't bad at contingencies either: they were part of the format too. As the old military aphorism went:

'No plan survives contact with the enemy.'

What made Paul different was that he'd change the plan before it had even been written, let alone issued.

His staff would work up an op order—and these were quite often the size of a small book—and Paul would just throw in a new spanner-shaped curve ball. He was working in Afghanistan, not fighting the 3rd Soviet Shock Army: and he was absolutely right in his command style for the Kandahar time and space.

What he did was not so much change the objectives, or the broad-brush strokes, as just finesse stuff, right down to the last moment. He saw Afghanistan as a nuanced series of shades. He came from special forces, where he was surrounded by the kind of agile thinkers that could accommodate his mind.

4ID was a different organism. The senior command team had been hand-picked by Paul. They rubbed against each other with just the right amount of ego and friction to spark thought. They'd all grown up in the system together to fight and make up: and there were plenty of fights and some very large egos. Downstream, though, RC-S and 4ID was just too big and too cumbersome to down, test and adjust.

3ID had started the imperial rush for big HQs. They'd brought fucking hundreds. The headquarters personnel alone could have staffed an entire infantry battalion. 82nd and 10th mountain before them had been all light infantry, kind of lean and mean, but the straight leg infantry had brought the bath, the sink, the bidet and a full set of towels.

The place just fed off itself, like a cannibal continually eating a self re-generating limb. All that false energy re-produced miles and miles of PowerPoint slides and self-created friction, but it was all froth. They even had a Google 'knowledge cell' of extremely highly paid contractors, whatever that was supposed to do. It was like expecting a vanilla ice cream and getting a vast, extremely sweetened sundae with a plastic monkey and umbrella.

All the majority did was report on each other: masses of data in and masses of data out.

So many folks were engaged in producing the statistics stuff that nobody had time for any conclusions. The whole thing just looked in on itself: and it was a party the Afghans were never invited to. The decision process was conducted, led and produced by American officers looking at the problem in an American way with American solutions.

Which usually involved blowing stuff up or spending tons of money on stuff nobody really wanted. Trouble was, the problem was Afghan in origin and would be Afghan in solution. Not American.

3ID, who had kicked off the navel-gazing, would probably have been the bunch to go to if the US had wanted to nuke Kandahar. Bob Abrams was the boy for that: he just loved the sound of bang. But credible change had been mighty thin on the ground when they had carried the baton.

Abrams had cut and run early, on to better things, and all that spinning of the wheel had got him an extra star. His kind of big hand, small map had worked in conning the beltway, but in Kandahar, the place had become a self-licking lollipop.

Paul tried to change it up. He wanted agility, nuanced thought and direction. He was the kind of guy who'd ask the private soldier who brought in the coffee what he thought. The private would invariably reply; 'I think whatever you think, general'. Which always got a laugh.

But I always thought Paul felt frustrated by the lack of argument and genuine dissection. He wanted to know everything he could, in advance. He didn't want consensus kiss-ass. At the end of the day, somebody had to make the decision, and I respected the fact that the buck stopped with him.

The difference I think I brought was that I thought it was my responsibility to give him options and honest thought: not management speak. That included saying on occasion; 'I don't know the answer to that'. In all my time in Kandahar, I never heard anybody else admit that. His staff officers always had one eye on their evaluation reports: bad news or no news could be a career benching.

I am most definitely no genius and I didn't have a magic potion: but I had lived the dream for two years, straight, by the time he arrived. Which was more than anybody else. I just knew shit. I had earned my spurs—and I lived outside the bubble. I remain an opinionated and driven pain-in-the-ass on the verge of Asperger's about my subject. I had been around the army for long enough to know that the good times came with a commander that allowed me the room to breathe. I always thought of myself as a kind of guerrilla information stream.

I didn't read much secret stuff, or much of anything that ISAF produced, except to fact check. What I did do was read everything I could find on the net, from newsfeeds to Twitter and Facebook. I kept a diary of all my meetings—and a dossier of conclusions—all correlated to events. It was a big book of stuff unique to me and the time and the place. After two years, I knew everybody, where they came from, their motivations, their links to the other main players, what stuff had gone down—all the juicy gossip. I called it journalism.

The military had their human terrain mapping wonks and their intelligence gathering, but they never tied it all together. What I had discovered, mostly by trial and error, was that I could predict, with a fair degree of certainty, the sort of mood music that was driving public opinion and key decision-making.

What made it all possible was the simple fact that I regarded Kandahar as my home: I lived there. Nobody in the military could match me: because they came and went like the wind. Just when they started to catch me up, they'd rotate out.

The army could never replicate the process. It's in the culture. The military is all about two-year postings: onwards and upwards. The result is a cadre of officers who confuse command ability with specialist knowledge. Sure, they've 'led' soldiers in a variety of situations: but the system creates jack-of-all-trades, master of none.

At one stage in my army career in information operations, my unit had been led by a naval captain: who had previously specialised in aircraft carrier operations. Defence cuts meant the British navy had no aircraft carriers left, so he'd ended up as my boss instead. He was a complete knob: worse than useless.

He knew nothing about influence—but he was the kind of thruster who needed to have everything run past him. My year with him was miserable. I spent my time as a journalism kindergarten teacher: akin to walking around with a ball and chain on both legs. I'll never forget the time a general asked him:

'What exactly is news?'

He stroked his imaginary philosopher's beard and replied:

'News is as news does....'

I may as well have replied seagulls likes bananas and stripey socks, but only on Mondays. What was more appalling is that his be-starred audience just nodded sagely and wandered off. Blind leading the fucking blind.

I'd picked up the template for my KAF activity from my time in the police. I never forgot the time we had a new detective come in to our shift to ask for our help. He had a number of outstanding cases of burglary. Each crime had a similar MO: a knife had been taken from a drawer and left on the kitchen counter. One of my colleagues had been a beat cop on the same ward for twenty years. Chris just wrote down the detective's name and number and went out on patrol. Two hours later, he came in with a slightly bruised bloke in a tracksuit.

'Tell the detective I have his man,' said Chris. He just knew everybody and everything that happened in his area. He owned that ground. He personally knew the guy who did it. He'd arrested him years before for the same stuff. Chris just loved his job and didn't want to do anything else. Police culture respected that, and he was left alone, as a constable. In his lane, you couldn't get better than Chris. In his lane, he was a genius.

The army never leaves anybody alone. They just create more types like my navy captains, who fall back on bluff, bluster and BS to cover for a lack of technical capability: and then move them on every two years before the evidence catches up with them. I wouldn't dream of trying to fly a fighter jet. Why did the army keep insisting on sending nuclear missile guys and ship driving jockeys to drive my lane?

Despite a career spanning decades in media management, I was once passed over to be military spokesperson for Bosnia. The reason given was I would have to be locally promoted to lieutenant colonel and I didn't have the command time expected for such a post. I wasn't go to fucking lead an airborne battalion, I was going to spout crap to journalists in as intelligent a manner I could muster for as long as possible without giving any secrets away. It was a job I'd done for years. To me, the rank was immaterial. It was the job that mattered.

To the army, though, regulations were everything. The general in charge wrote, personally asking for me. The rules won out. They gave the job to a nursing corps colonel whose sole command experience had been running a hospital and who had never been in front of a camera in her life. She spent her tour writing urgent notes to army HQ about the state of her pets back home.

In the peacetime army, officers get moved on every twenty-four months. In Kandahar, the process was accelerated. Even with the Americans, who stayed longer than most, they'd pack up every nine months. Most of the Europeans came and went every four months. They'd just about find the toilet and the pencil cupboard then they'd go home with a couple of medals and the pretence of a job well done.

With my police and journalism experience, sheer longevity and a large quantity of 'FIDO', I'd created, almost by accident, a resource that the generals now wanted. I didn't want to do anything else, nor was I overly interested in anything else. I LOVED my gig. I didn't get out of my lane either. What did I know about commanding tanks and planes? Nothing. But I did know my subject—and I took pride in that. Folks came to respect that, I think.

Nothing I did was truly radical: but it was a different voice. Army service is all about uniformity. It's a rare staff officer that brings sour fruit: nobody wants to be the lookout on The Titanic. It's bad for career prospects. Making predictions is also bad. What if it goes wrong?

I did both: pretty much mostly on a hunch too. My hit rate got to be pretty good, but, equally, I didn't mind that much if I got it wrong. What I did was use that experience to lessen the odds next time around. The longer I stayed, the better I got. I didn't have any skin in the game. ISAF wasn't going to promote me and I am old enough to have lost a lot of that ego that went hand-in-hand with aspiring army officers.

John reckoned I had something to offer the mission. He didn't give up. What he did was suggest I meet Patrick Kidd, the RC-S deputy commanding general. PK is a Brit.

PK is one of those officers who just wanted to get stuff done—and he didn't stand on ceremony or protocol. By the time he arrived in KAF, I was two years down the line—and a rather 3ID bruised tomato.

John told me PK was a decent egg, but I was very wary of getting into another pissing contest with RC-S. Yet John was another one of those guys I really respected. If he said I had something to offer that would be listened to, I trusted him. He was also decent enough to say he'd mediate my meet.

PK was in charge of all things Afghan. By the time 4ID arrived, the war was on the back slope. Folks were going home, and in big numbers. Paul's priority, which came direct from the White House, was to cut numbers, close bases, minimise US casualties and save money. It was the end of the road for the big adventure. PK got the rubber duck.

Patrick was a bit of an anomaly, even for a mongrel like ISAF. A tall man, like all tall men, he stoops slightly, in his effort to listen and not appear overpowering. PK is a past master at that endearing British senior officer habit of appearing to be merely an interested amateur: when the reality is a razor-sharp mind. He remained to the end, despite my constant questioning, extremely self-deprecating about his personal achievements: which were considerable.

Patrick had started his career in the British Royal Tank Regiment, which he had commanded during the invasion of Iraq.

The Royal Tank Regiment was born on Flanders battlefield, in the mud of the First World War. The cavalry found that war's new-fangled machines, which Winston Churchill called 'tanks', far too un-glamorous. So the Royal Tank Regiment was formed as a mix of machine-gunners (the original armament) and mechanics.

By the time Iraq came about, the RTR had lost most of its tanks and been re-born as chemical warfare specialists. They'd been given some groovy six-wheeled armoured personnel carriers (APCs), which were a damn sight more comfortable than anything the infantry had to ride about in.

None of us were really that keen on chemical warfare, what is now called chemical, biological, radiological and nuclear warfare, but known to my generation as nuclear, biological and chemical (NBC). We hated it for the simple reason that NBC involved wearing ghastly charcoal lined suits, a rubber gas mask and naff rubber wellingtons with an unfeasibly complicated lacing system. The get-up was a BDSM (that is not a military term, although wouldn't it be fun if it were?) fetishist delight and a personal sweat-box of nightmarish proportions.

The worst part was the drill for shitting, which involved depositing the dirty deed into a polythene bag, then rubbing dirt, called Fuller's earth, into your arse to mop up any stray droplets that might otherwise kill you. As this involved peering into your ass crack to check for strays, anatomically rather straining, the army used the 'buddy-buddy' system. Which involved a well chosen, and soon to be very intimate, friend. Their job involved holding a bag somewhere within the jobby exit arc to catch the specimen and then apply the purifying Fuller's dirt up your anus with a paper pad.

There are clubs in Soho that offer the same experience. The army whimsically describes the whole drill as; 'blot, bang, rub.'

How we found the bad boy gasses and liquids in the first place involved the farcical process of waving a piece of coloured paper in the air. Which, we were told, was designed to change colour when it came into contact with a nerve paper or other agent. The kit came with a helpful colour chart, like a Dulux paint sample, to illustrate the desired colour and its origin: sarin, mustard gas, whatever took your fancy for your living room wall.

Needless to say, word of NBC training always brought groans and deep sighs.

Which is why my paratroopers were, for once, quite enthused at hearing the tank regiment boys in their fancy black overalls were coming down to visit us and demonstrate their bright, shiny new six-wheeled vehicles and their much-feted new NBC capability. Anything that kept me from examining my radio operator's piles and pink cheeks at close quarters was to be encouraged, so I was as delighted as my boys to go along. We turned up on time and looked on jealously as the brand-new RTR wagons piled up, in a near-silent wheeze of purring engine and air brakes.

The boys got even more excited when the hatches opened and a couple of black-overalled tankies appeared.

'Christ, it's the fucking Waffen-SS,' said my colour sergeant.

The boys always got a bit moist at Gucci kit, but the boys in black spoiled it when they were asked if their whizz-bang armour could 'fly'. What the boys meant was whether it was air-portable or not. To a paratrooper, anything of any use can, and therefore should, be dropped from an airplane. Anything else was hat-land, irrelevant, and not worthy of consideration.

7 Regiment, Royal Horse Artillery, won grudging airborne respect, as they used light guns that were eminently capable of being dropped by pallet from a charlie-130.

Likewise, The Household Cavalry had an airborne squadron that used air portable light tanks called Scimitar, and, in the dim and distant past, a variant called Scorpion. The Scorpions had been withdrawn when somebody discovered the ammunition they used produced toxic fumes in the turret when the gun was fired. Quite why nobody had checked that before they were built is another one of those military WTFs.

The Scimitar is rarely dropped by airborne pallet nowadays. Mostly since a Scimitar parachute bundle failed to open over the British army's main training area, Salisbury Plain. The tank had steamed in from a great height, making an impact crater the size of a house, right in the middle of one of England's most pristine wilderness environments. What was left of the recovered tank resembled a hub cap.

From that day forth, exercises 'assumed' the light tanks had been air-dropped, and they mysteriously appeared already on the ground in support of the Toms. Much to the disappointment of the Regiment, who were all desperate for a repeat performance of the pile-in from 1500 feet.

The NBC tankie thoroughly disappointed his audience by assuring them that his armoured car was too heavy to be dropped by air. Audience interest went instantly from low to zero. If it wasn't airborne, it was nothing. If he'd asked me first, I'd have told him to lie.

The tankie sensed the change in the atmosphere and, attempting to save the day, announced that his wonder car would now capture a suspicious device and neutralise it. He pointed out an issue water bottle, lying on the ground about fifty metres away, as the object his boys would now take care of.

My paratroopers got excited as the armoured truck moved off. They were all expecting some sort of death ray, or a big mechanical hammer to grind the threat to dust.

The big truck trundled over the water bottle and rocked to a stop. From the bottom back end, a black rubber glove appeared, encasing a very human hand. The black glove gingerly picked up the water bottle and put it in a stowage bin, before the whole kit and caboodle drove off.

'Having recovered the suspicious device, our specialist team will now examine it from within the safety of their vehicle, thus identifying and neutralising the threat to ground troops,' our tankie pompously pronounced.

My boys just looked at him. 'Boss, that's fucking gash,' opined my sergeant. 'My missus does that to my dog's turds with a pair of her fucking washing-up mitts.'

Nothing could save the lesson. We hosted the display team to tea and toast, but they couldn't get away from airborne-land quick enough.

Nonetheless, when Bush and co. incorporated decided Saddam must fall, Patrick and his black rubber glove men got the nod to be on point. His men had the unenviable task of hunting down the supposed weapons of mass destruction. Armed with stiflingly hot decontamination suits and lots of replacement gloves, they had hunted through the ruins of Saddam's various weapons stockpiles and factories.

Nobody knew then that there were no weapons: which made the threat seem very real. PK was awarded the Order of the British Empire for his leadership: no mean feat in its own right.

After the war, he and his family emigrated to Australia and Patrick joined the Australian army. Late entry foreign officers usually end their careers at their transferred rank. Patrick shone and had been promoted to brigadier. His posting to RC-S was to be his last foreign adventure before retirement.

What PK got in Kandahar was a brief to deal with the mentoring of the Afghan security forces, police and army. The Australian army had migrated its key effort, from leading operations in Uruzgan, down to Kandahar Province, expanding its role in partnering what was, in late 2012, still very much a fledgling force.

By the time of his arrival, I'd spent a lot of effort and time in advising and helping the mentoring team, so I knew how difficult his job was going to be.

The biggest journey Patrick faced was in recognising the limitations of what he could actually achieve. Afghan forces were not the Australian army. They didn't do saluting and shoe polishing: yet most of them had more war-fighting experience than their mentors could ever acquire. What they didn't have was the ability to fight as a joined-up 21st century force—and getting to anywhere near that stage had already broken many good men.

On the other side of the clock-face, the American's key effort was on disengaging. The egg timer was running out of sand. Paul's distinctly realistic brief to PK was brutally simple:

'Do what you can as quickly as you can.'

JD set up a meet between us. John was a regular visitor to RC-S and he was a keen observer of what he regarded as a bit of a strategic drift. Paul was asking lots and lots of very relevant questions. His staff was not delivering. They had the troop movements and all the other daily military BS down pat.

The staff just didn't have a handle on what made Kandahar tick.

Paul wanted a fast-moving, fleet of foot, team of name-takers and heart-breakers. What he'd got was a regular heavy infantry headquarters that fell back on the old decision-making cycle: the general would tell the colonel, who told the major, who told the captain, who would tell the lieutenant, and then the process would laboriously go back up the other way. And there were hundreds of them who all wanted their fingerprints on the document.

The end result was a mishmash of what the collective staff thought Paul wanted to hear, not what he actually wanted; which was accurate, up-to-date and original, unvarnished thinking. The regular army boys just gave him good news in military-speak. Which was, frankly, mostly bollocks. You just had to look out the window at the number of medevac helicopters landing every day to see that all was not well in the real world.

I picked my ground carefully. Obviously PK, as deputy commander, wasn't going to come meet me. Generals don't hunt out consultants, however appealing I thought I might be. Then again, I was determined I wasn't going to be another supplicant waiting in line outside his office. I suggested we meet on the boardwalk for coffee. To his credit, PK was up for the challenge. I don't think an American would have agreed, their culture was much more rigid. But PK was British, and he understood the staging on an intellectual level.

I got to Downtown Cafe, ahead of schedule, and ordered up the warm beverages: my first commitment to our relationship. I saw him coming from way off. The Boardwalk may have been a no salute area, but general officers were a rarity. He parted the waves of troops like Moses. As he got closer, I noticed he only wore Australian rank: he eschewed sewing on additional American ranks. Unlike many coalition, especially British, senior officers, who developed a fetish for adding stars and other crap wherever they had a spare collar or cuff.

Patrick let his command presence do the talking. I liked that in him: PK was always very modest about his rank, and his boys liked him all the more for it.

Handshakes done, I gave him the usual brief on CJPOTF. As usual, he hadn't heard of the unit. Par for the course, and the usual indicator of just how marginal all that effort and expense was. What interested PK much more was my take on the Kandahar vibe: and my assessment of the key Afghan players.

We talked at length about Hamid, Sherzai and Raziq. I sensed early on that I would be foolish to sugar coat the pill. Not all the news was bad, of course, but PK was just one of dozens of mentors that had passed through RC-S, all promising great things. PK was sharp enough to know that he needed the inside track if he was ever to build up any kind of game-changing weight in the short time he had in the chair.

The chat was agreeable—but I was resigned to it being just another brain-pick, 'thanks for the info' kind of brief I was used to doing in my sleep.

PK wanted more. He had ambitions beyond just being a pal to Hamid and the rest of the Afghan cast. He'd studied Nick Carter's efforts, back in '10, working with Wali Karzai, to set up the Kandahar council. He understood that 'mowing the grass', military style, just led to more grass growing more quickly.

He had high ambitions: to really try and change the battlefield perception of the Afghan government and the whole nascent Afghan security force. That battlefield really was the Afghan people.

The bugbear at the back of the room was the presidential election—which was coming like a steam train down the track. Whatever remained after the end of 2014 was going to an Afghan effort: and that meant carrying the Afghan people to the point where they cared enough about the regime to want to perpetuate what we had spent so much money setting up.

PK and Paul both realised that the Afghan people were scared: scared of the future, scared of a return of the Taliban, scared for their jobs, scared for their families, scared of the fighting and scared that we were all going home. And the last part was indubitably true. The whole country was in the grip of a mass soul-searching hysteria.

None of us could change the decision to call it a day. What we could do, perhaps, was aim to build a consensus of popular support for the Afghan institutions that were going to have to carry on the fight. PK posed the question: how can we help get this country behind their own future?

He was that kind of man, the type that was capable of just blue-sky'ing the majorly important questions. Not the minor stuff, like moving map symbols about, counting bullets or mounting another 'big push'. This stuff was REALLY crucial: and nobody, not the 10th, the 82nd, and definitely not the 3rd, had ever asked the big question. And if they ever had, they had definitely not asked me. What else could we do to end the fighting? Killing folks never solved anything. We HAD to do more.

PK was the man I had been waiting for. And the moment was right. All that I had learned, my whole career, all that time in Kandahar, it came together in that meet. I sensed PK was offering me a real chance to contribute, on a strategic level: if I was up for it. Still, I wanted backup. PK wasn't *the* man: I wanted to meet Paul. I wanted to see the commanding general. PK said he'd set it up.

Fuck. My bluff had been called. FIDO.

AIMING FOR THE SUN

I got the invite the next day from Paul LaCamera's office: an evening with the CG. No agenda items, just drop over. I liked the way the offer was framed. It was an encouraging start.

John gave me a heads-up that he thought Paul would be after answers to cultural stuff he had been railing for answers over. 'It's the sort of stuff you brief us on every week,' he advised.

After all the badging nonsense I had suffered through the years, I took some satisfaction at being able to tell the headquarters security guys I was going to see Paul. That fact helped a few of them sit up in their chairs.

That day was the first time I met my pal Steenberger. Normally, he would call through to the person a visitor was going to visit, just to confirm the date. Saying I was off to meet the commanding general sent him into a tailspin. He just point blank didn't know who to call. He was too scared to call Paul's office direct.

In the end, Steenberger decided to personally escort me. Then he got cold feet when we went upstairs to the general's corridor. 'Too much brass in there for me, miss Abi,' he muttered, before releasing me on my own recognisance, leaving me to my devices.

Paul's patch was indeed rather swish. No flags, for a change, just an enormous four-leafed clover picture, the divisional emblem, some rather nice leather sofas and a terribly clean-cut and smart executive staff: who were actually expecting me.

Those big, purpose-built headquarters were always more like visiting a large insurance company than a lean and mean army outfit. Apart from the fact that most everybody was in camouflage, the place was the same big, open-plan vista of partitioned cubbyholes that you'd get in any call-centre. The executive floor was just the same too.

Paul was running late—no surprise there. What was surprising was a very pretty female clerk ushering me to a sofa and presenting me with a copy of the divisional magazine and a coffee while I waited. John Wayne never had to deal with this in the 'Green Berets'. I felt like I was going to the dentists, not to see a general.

Even the hard-charging Marines, over in Helmand, had one of these purpose built warehouse headquarter buildings constructed for them. It cost $25 million. Inside, it occupied a footprint of 64,000 square feet of office space. Nearly $3 million was spent on IT and another half-million on audio-visual equipment. The Marines would probably have been happier in a slit-trench, but the building fever was on. In the end, the drawdown came quicker than they could finish and occupy the building. To this day, it sits empty, furniture still neatly stacked inside, packed in its original protective plastic sheeting. Around $30 million wasted. At least RC-S got lived in.

Paul arrived with the usual coterie of armed guards and staff officer flunkies. In my heels, I was taller than him, but he is solidly built, like a middle-weight boxer. On his left arm, in pride of place was his 'ranger' patch. On his right his divisional patch. The two proudest command peaks of his military career.

I liked him straight from the off. He has an open, welcoming manner, suffused with just enough modesty to reveal the man within the general's uniform. He knew exactly who I was and laid it out right from the off, in that seemingly-innocent, inquiring way he has:

'I'm told I should speak to you about some of the stuff I need to know. Is that right?' he asked. 'Depends on the questions you have, general,' I replied.

I had a rule about not calling anybody 'sir', or 'ma'am'. I wasn't in the army, but first meetings needed an element of formality. And something about Paul demanded the respect.

We went into his office at six thirty in the evening. We didn't re-appear until nine. Just me and him, for two and a half hours straight jaw-crunching. Every now and again, a staff officer would knock and pop his head round the door to remind him he had other meetings. Paul would just nod and ask them to wait: it was his call, after all. He could have kept them waiting all night if he wanted to. He was in charge.

Instead, he wanted to spend time talking to me. It was immensely flattering, after the year I had just had with 3ID. The breadth of his mind was remarkable. We went everywhere, from the Durand line, to Lord Roberts, to Karzai's state of mind, to the price of rice and petrol in the markets and my read on the Kandahar Afghan leadership. He wanted to know if his female soldiers should wear headscarves. We even riffed on the possible winner of 'Afghan Idol', the very staid Afghan version of 'American Idol', which was nonetheless culturally significant at the time for employing a female host. That had sparked off a whole social media debate, which Paul wanted to know about.

A lot of the military leadership in Afghanistan was only interested in military stuff: numbers of troops, how many working tanks they had, how many bullets fired, that sort of thing. Paul knew all that stuff inside out. What made him different was he wanted to know the un-quantifiable, the un-identifiable and the esoteric too.

What difference did knowing stuff like the price of fuel in Kandahar make?

The only power available most days was by generator. In July, it was 45-50 degrees during the day. Anybody with any status needed air conditioning, particularly in the city. That took power, which needed fuel for your generator. If folks couldn't afford air conditioning, they got restless. Restless people in the city meant trouble. Power meant industry. Industry meant jobs, goods produced, and the means to pay for the goods. Pricey fuel meant job cuts, increased goods prices, less available income, unemployment. Unhappy, unemployed folks make ideal insurgents.

Paul was interested in the price of fuel. Hallelujah. That meet was a Damascene moment for me. He finished by giving me a list of his key lieutenants he wanted me to meet and a couple of jobs he wanted done. Suddenly, I was back in the team, green-lit for go.

I took my chance. For some time, I had been writing an informal daily blog of events in Afghanistan and international shaping policy for the COMKAF folks. Next day, with something of a nervous tick, I 'cc'd Paul. He wrote back with a one-liner:

'Enjoyed that. Keep it coming.'

Rotations in Kandahar always happened during the height of summer. It was a difficult time for new troops to acclimatise to the heat and dust. Summer was the height of the fighting season. The war in Afghanistan always has a cyclical, seasonal rhythm. A large proportion of the insurgents we fought were local lads who enjoyed a bit of sport, shooting at the foreigners. Truth is, very few were hard-core. Most were smugglers, thieves or unemployed kids enticed by the thought of a wage. The Taliban paid quite well, often the only living wage going. It was a steep learning curve for the new boys. Un-blooded and inexperienced, the first month of the new rotation always brought death.

4ID's arrival had been marked by Lamber Khan's contribution. That had happened the very day after 4ID had taken charge. All over KAF, folks were busy excavating new fighting positions. Sandbag filling became a full-time occupation.

My first contribution to the new cause was a reveal and analysis of the 'Shahamat' Lamber Khan video. Together with an analysis of the Taliban's up-coming campaign plan. Which, given that I didn't have access to anything super-secret, was, if I may modestly say, punching rather above my weight.

The clue was in the title. 'Shahamat' announced the big summer enemy plan as 'Operation Khaibar'. Those guys never did anything by chance.

Khaibar was the name of a battle that the Holy Prophet won against the Jews in the year 629 CE. What was interesting was how he had won the day.

The Jews had out-numbered the Muslims by 5 to 1. They had formed a confederation of allied tribes and surrounded themselves with walled forts, protected by high walls and defended by ranged weapons. The Muslims won by speed of attack. Surprising out-lying Jewish forts one-by-one, overcoming their overall lack of numbers by local concentration of force and surprise. The final battle had been marked by the near-suicidal courage of Ali, the Prophet's son-in-law, who became the last true caliph in the Shia tradition.

The Taliban are overwhelmingly Sunni. By using 'Operation Khaibar', they invoked a pan-Islam call to arms through recalling a significant Islamic victory inspired by a pre-dominantly Shia hero. The victory at Khaibar was so memorable that the battle has its own reference in the Holy Quran:

'Allah has promised you abundant spoils that you will capture, and He has hastened for you this...'

The Taliban liked a morality tale. Their psyops set-up remains one of their more impressive achievements. Imagine the effect of telling this tale on a bunch of illiterate recruits. Everything you need to teach about how they fought is there in that one story.

Which is actually how the campaign in 2013 started to roll out. Isolated, pre-dominantly Afghan, outposts were being swarmed by hundreds of fighters, before a relief force could arrive. ISAF air assets didn't routinely coordinate coverage of Afghan positions. Afghan security force morale was becoming insidiously terminal: up in Uruzgan and Daikundi provinces, far from help, Afghan soldiers and police officers were refusing to go on patrol. They knew that if they were hit or ambushed, nobody would come get them.

Later that year, in one such incident, it took 205 Corps three days to mount a relief effort to one far-flung fort in Daikundi. The defenders were long dead by the time they arrived.

Understanding your enemy's intent is key to beating him. Get inside his decision loop. I'm not claiming to be the only person in ISAF who came up with this stuff: but I was the first to get this to the decision-makers.

So I was off to the races again. Paul didn't always write back to my missives. Some of them were a bit controversial, op-ed pieces on US geo-political strategy. In the post-Petraeus scandal days, generals were becoming very careful about what they committed to e-mail. The US military regarded any formal communications as a public record.

I'd often get a follow-up from some officer I had never heard of about something I'd written. Within a couple of months, my stuff ended up in Kabul, being read by a three-star general at the IJC and COMISAF's intelligence cell. It was Paul who started that. He recognised that I was a different voice.

John and Patrick were delighted for me. Soak told me I would have a long and happy relationship with RC-S. Patrick took me on a long office-hop, round his fellow deputy commanders: Brigadiers Jim Rainey, the manoeuvre guy who ran all the war assets, and John Thompson, the support, logistics chief. Then, it was off to meet the US ambassador, Edward Alford, who proved to be a clubbable, affable fellow. I was never quite sure what Edward and the State folks actually did, but the coffee was always fresh.

I got to re-set all my Afghan contacts. Suddenly, meeting Sherzai, Hamid and the rest was no longer a cloak and dagger affair. My presence was actively considered.

Late summer 2013 personal summary? Fucking brilliant, top of the tree 'tastic. I just churned through the days.

Paul didn't ask me along for the fun of it. 4ID was going to have a tough, demanding tour. 82nd had set the playing field, 3ID had minded the shop, but 4ID had the twin tasks of drawing-down the hundreds of bases we had dotted all over the south, right in tandem with negotiating the next Afghan presidential election.

Karzai couldn't stand in this one. He was constitutionally barred. 2014 would mark the end of ISAF combat operations, all our troops going home and a brand-new government would be bedding-in. All while the war ramped up.

Once again, ISAF had given itself one helluva load without any real strategic fore-sight. It was going to be one bumpy ride for 4ID.

THE CLASS OF 2012

Just as it was all going so swimmingly well, up on the old COMKAF calendar came the news that Soak was going home. End of tour time: again.

I had lost count of the amount of people I had welcomed, bonded with and mourned their departure. I had been there so long, I was welcoming the same faces back again for another tour. A few for their third tour. They had been home, recovered and come back. All while I continued to grind it out.

I was fraying at the edges, even if I wouldn't admit it. The relentless grind of KAF just got to you after a bit. It wasn't just the dirt and the primitive life we lived, nor the endless military bullshit and nonsense. Nor even the constantly changing sea of faces. It was the lack of continuity.

As much as I put my shoulder to the burden and pushed the boulder up the hill, I just knew that the next rotation would mean starting the grind all over again from scratch. The new guys never remembered the stuff that had been done before. We just re-learned the same lessons every year. As much as folks valued my contribution as the continuity asset, I knew how the Afghans felt. They had seen dozens come and go.

I'd seen so many rocket attacks, shootings and random acts of violence, I knew that all the body armour in the world couldn't save you if your number was up. Like the Afghans, I was displaying a shocking lack of concern about my personal safety. All us old-timers did. When a rocket hit, we didn't bother to even duck. Direct gunfire might get our attention, but we learned to know when it was merely close and fucking terminally close. It's all in the sound of the rounds in-coming. Out-going we didn't worry about. That sounds totally different. In any case, it was going the other way and goodnight Charlie if it got you.

The new guys would run around practising all their ever more elaborate drills and we'd just sit back and say:

'It won't make any difference. If God wants you dead, you'll be dead.'

I stopped wearing body armour. It was fucking heavy, hot and killed my back. I took a cushion to sit on for those interminable hours trawling around in an MRAP.

The war was getting old, you know what I mean? How long had I been in-country? All fucking day.

In any case, after a bit you just learned a combat sixth sense.

Going into a village, you knew if something was going to happen: no sounds, no kids, no animals about. Bad shit waiting.

Always keep moving: movement is life. Never leave your back open. Put a wall behind you.

Make sure somebody with a weapon has a clear 360, all the time, every time you take a meeting. Look for two alternate exits, cover them all. Don't shake hands unless he offers first. Don't engage in long eye contact. Watch his hands and his eyes, always his hands and his eyes.

Don't walk on broken ground. Look for dips and depressions. Don't touch anything shiny or inviting. Hug a wall, don't lean on it. Don't stand in the open. Never get left alone. Work out your next step in advance. Keep turning, check your arcs. Don't laser in, watch the big picture. Keep your gear within arms reach.

The combat skill-set became normal. If it didn't, you could die. It's not a normal way to live.

I just got cynical. The war did that to you. You just woke up one day with that mad, bat-shit crazy stare that said you had been there too long, seen too much. The conundrum was that the more terse I got, the more openly opinionated and cynical I became about the operation, the more the new guys lapped it up. I spoke to one high-level British delegation and told them that sending our troops to Helmand was the equivalent of invading Scotland and sending your forces to Skye, not Glasgow, where the people lived. They just nodded.

By now, I had a dog-and-pony show brief on Kandahar: what you needed to know, who you needed to know, the history, the dumb stuff we did, that sort of thing. Every week, I'd do two or three of those briefs to all sorts of different folks: from new units to visiting government ministers.

The POTF cut back its field crews. Everybody else headed for Kabul, as part of the big drawdown. I stayed in Kandahar. I got 'promoted' to running the whole of the south, southwest and the west; because there was nobody else left. On top of the blogs, the visits, the meetings, the briefs, I ran the psyops output for half the country.

My work day started at 0630 and finished at 2300. All I did was live, eat, breathe, sleep and shit the war. I got so juiced by the spinning wheel, I stopped taking leave. I just stayed in Kandahar.

Some days were so fucking exciting. Travelling with a general or an ambassador is not travelling like a normal person. It's all blacked-out limos and whirring helicopters. Crew chiefs would open doors and snap off salutes as I followed in the wake of an important person. We'd swoop in on a Blackhawk, door gunners swivelling in their seats, jump off onto a speeding convoy of paratroopers, bristling with guns, to meet a room full of swarthy, bearded Afghans.

Adrenalin, adrenalin, adrenalin. All the time. Every day. When it wasn't there, when the day passed like molasses, you prayed for the next hit. Bring it on.

Paul's helicopter had all this fancy communications stuff on board. We would hover over some dustbowl and speak to anybody we wanted on the ground, like fireflies over a pond. We flew with the doors open, inches away from the roaring slipstream, listening to the pilot's grooving their clipped pilot speak.

One time, after flying over Kandahar with Paul, and looking down at the city from 300 feet at two hundred fifty miles an hour, I wrote to him that there were some days where life was never so fantastic.

To anybody else, I was in the shithole of Afghanistan, in the middle of a vicious civil war, risking my life. To me, I had never found life so exciting. Some nights, I'd lay down on The Boardwalk football pitch, look up at the stars and truly thank God for putting me there. I was in the vortex, spinning madly, burning life up. I fucking loved war.

Soak leaving was the five-minute to closing bell. I was really angry at him for going. The team had never been stronger. Once again the dumb military system was going to break it all up again.

Steffi left too. The girl who had helped me the day I arrived. She was burned. Truly exhausted. We'd had a sticky patch, brought on by KAF tensions, but we had bonded strongly after the tears, as the only continuity item in the place. The military came and went: but we had stayed.

Now, the team was breaking up. I spoke to JD about her contribution. He wrote her up for a commendation, which he gave her on the roof of the old Taliban's Last Stand, as the sun went done and the F-16s took off behind us.

We cried and hugged and then she was gone too.

Ken Wilsbach, John's boss who had helped save Sherzai, brought John's replacement down for his familiarisation visit. Ken was leaving too. Another good, strong leader for the off.

Man, I was sick of them all going. Time to up for another new one....

Brigadier Michael Fantini and John Dolan have been life-long buddies. Michael joined the military a year after JD. They transitioned through 3,000 hours in F-16s together. Their careers have mirrored each other. As John left KAF, Michael took over. John asked me to give Michael my dog-and-pony brief. He asked me to hug Michael close. Just as I had done when John had replaced Scott, I was upset. John told me not to worry. I was forever bugging Soak about the Afghans. JD told me I'd be pushing at an open door about that with call sign Fanman Fantini.

I needn't have worried. Michael was to become the American general I became most close to in all my time in KAF. He is a thoughtful, considered, highly intelligent man: a fantastic, consensus leader. Out of all of them, he cared the most about the Afghans. Politics is in Michael's blood.

We didn't know it at the time, but Michael was to be the last COMKAF. He would leave a wonderful legacy, even if he inherited a bit of a shit sandwich.

The Abrams' legacy had bit back from the grave. After the tussle between RC-S and COMKAF, Abrams moved to have COMKAF, the NATO headquarters, placed under RC-S, effectively ending its independence. By the time Mike Fantini arrived, RC-S had taken over.

COMKAF was mostly about logistics: movement of people, aircraft and maintenance of the resources needed to keep the place going. RC-S already had its own logistics general. Brigadier General John Thompson was no shrinking violet. Logistics is the unsung hero. Forgotten until it's not there. It's also a black and white art: you either have the stuff, in place, on time in sufficient quantities, or you don't. You need to shout to make it so. Logistics generals tend to be black and white people. Thompson was like that.

Before the big change, the dividing line had been the wire: outside the wire, RC-S, inside the wire, COMKAF. Thompson and Dolan had already crossed swords before the transfer of authority to RC-S happened. The US army had brought its own inspection teams, which were cracking open coalition facilities without asking. Much to coalition annoyance, headed up by John Dolan. The argument had been good entertainment as long as COMKAF had the authority to give RC-S the finger.

Now COMKAF would be working for RC-S. Michael lost the power of Grayskull before he even got the throne. Fanman would have to work out who was going to do what. Two brigadiers with the same remit, but Michael would be an air force general in an army-led camp.

Michael's job would have been easier if he'd kept his planes. When JD arrived, there were scores of fighter aircraft around.

During Soak's year, the UAE had deployed an F-16 wing. Their planes were way in advance of the American ones, all brand-new, with a cockpit that looked like a PlayStation console.

The UAE boys had just turned up with their birds. When John asked them where they intended keeping them all, their colonel had waved at his aides, who had struggled forward with a big metal chest. The colonel opened it, to reveal row upon row of new, shiny $100 billfolds. There were millions in there. 'Will this cover it?' The colonel had smiled.

The UAE built the best camp in KAF. It was the only one with tarmacked roads. Food was served by liveried waiters: and guests always left with a gift of a watch or an iPad. The UAE pilots were unfailingly polite, absolute gentlemen. They arrived in time to watch the American planes leave.

By the time Michael hit KAF, the drawdown meant the bolts were coming undone. He'd done all the work-up training to fly F-16s in Kandahar, but his fighter wing was being withdrawn to Kabul mere days after he would arrive.

No planes to command and a sub-ordinate command to the army. Michael would need all his diplomatic skills.

John had his handover in the same hanger that Scott had used. Despite all that had happened, Sherzai, Hamid and Faizi came to his ceremony. We met before the main event for cake. All the RC-S crew came too: and were very nice about the stuff I had been writing.

We had a minor panic as the protocol officer didn't know who everybody was, so I had to do a quick assist to shuffle the cards around. I helped JD write his speech for the big day. Sherzai gave JD an Afghan Kuchi woman's traditional dress, as a present for his wife. I took one last photograph of us all together before we stepped out onto the stage. I don't remember a lot about that event. I was on the edge of tears for all of it.

Just like Scott before him, JD had protected me. I was pretty cut up about his departure. When it was over, I watched John say goodbye to his staff, who all lined up for a handshake. I got grabbed to take a photo of some other dignitary. When I turned back, JD was gone. I never saw Soak again.

The 2012 class had graduated. Mind you, only John and I were left from that time. End of an era: again. All my friends had left: again.

Michael proved to be as good a leader as John had promised. He kept up my relationship with COMKAF. If anything, it expanded. Michael worked out a role with Thompson and RC-S, where Thompson would run the war, while Michael would effectively manage the run-down of KAF, as drawdown approached.

It was a massive job. Within twelve months, COMKAF had to put in place and execute a plan to return the camp to the pristine state it had been before we had inflicted twelve years of occupation, plus get rid of over 30,000 people. Half of whom were not military and didn't have to take orders.

We had an obligation to turn the place over to the Afghans in some sort of working order. If Kandahar had a future, it would need a working airport. In late 2013, ISAF ran everything. The Afghans would have to learn how to run an international airport in less than twelve months.

Back in the world, all these generals had wives who organised the social side. A service wife is a vital adjunct to an officer's game card. She takes care of the dinner parties, the barbies, the civilian interface that is just as important as the uniform side. The generals can relax around the wives. There's no rank involved. In Kandahar, the generals didn't have that. I became a sort of unpaid platonic substitute-wife social secretary.

After Lamber Khan, Afghan relations had gone into stasis. Afghanistan has the same sort of festivities we do: Eid, Nowruz, or Persian New Year, that sort of thing. Plus, they weren't immune to our side of the fence, such as Christmas. The Afghans we dealt with are all intelligent men. That sort of joint cultural interface could be used to re-kindle the relations that had been soured by the shooting. We just needed a face-saving excuse to get everybody together to talk.

Michael embraced the concept. We got Faizi and Sherzai over for tea: and Michael went to visit them. Which happened just in time. Relations were so bad at the air wing that when the out-going chief American advisor left, Sherzai turned up late for the flag ceremony and was refused an opportunity to make a speech.

Michael was brilliant at smoothing feathers. Even the daft stuff.

Afghan New Year is a time of renewal, coinciding with the arrival of spring, around March time. The main sketch is that Afghans plant thousands of trees. They are superb gardeners and inveterate plant lovers.

The plan was to have Sherzai and Faizi over for tree-planting at COMKAF, which was a pretty plant-free place. The two of them loved getting the invite. We organised a ceremonial shovel, but next thing we knew, they were down on their knees, kneading the earth by hand. Michael, true trooper that he is, got down and dirty with them.

Our bit was pretty pony, just a couple of weeds in a pot, but Faizi invited us over to the civil terminal to reciprocate. We went over with Edward Alford, the US ambassador, to give it some diplomatic heft.

Faizi had organised a full honour guard, a complete platoon of Afghan police, with AK-47s shouldered. We'd gone force protection-lite, just one long weapon and a few pistols. There were looks of concern all round and a couple of white faces on our side. 'Don't worry,' Faizi conspiratorially whispered to me. 'I took the bullets off them before you arrived.'

After a flag ceremony and a truly execrable rendition of 'America the beautiful' played by an atonal police band, Faizi led the platform party to a huge pile of trees. We'd given the Afghans one tree each to plant. Faizi had brought a fucking forest.

I just loved them that day. We'd showed the Afghans a glimmer of human hospitality and, in return, Faizi had rolled out the whole orchestra, brass section and all.

As the local boss, Faizi had a couple of locals digging post-holes for him. They must have been gravediggers in a previous life, because they went at it like gophers on heat. Poor old Michael and Edward had no such help.

All the diggers had the same amount of trees: literally dozens of trees each.

Amidst much Afghan amusement, Faizi and his graveyard henchmen shot off in a frenzy of organised activity. The sweat lashed off Michael and Edward trying to keep up. Neither of them are young men. They were distinctly lathered by the time they finished. Their efforts were covered from every conceivable angle by a large and very excited Afghan press corps. To their credit, in between the wheezing, Michael and Edward managed some very convincing smiles for the camera. It was worth the sacrifice.

We routinely took local atmospherics from locals in Kandahar. Usually, at that stage of the war, we didn't do too well.

The following week, we got a rare positive return from a group of local drivers. They had seen a regional newspaper article about an American general planting trees in Kandahar. The general was Michael, at our airport event. The drivers were impressed that an American understood and cared enough about Afghanistan to join in with local traditions. They had never seen that before.

Our tree planting wasn't traditional military activity, but it was surely a lot more positive effect than shooting people.

This time, this rotation, Faizi did his homework properly. We talked through what he needed in advance, in a constructive way. Then we took it to Michael. Fanman re-started the airport handover committee. Faizi was back in the game again.

Michael's essential humanity and decency never shone brighter than my last Christmas in Kandahar. Fanman's wife sent over a huge box for him. Inside were dozens of Christmas stockings she had made from his old flight suits. Ann is a military surgeon. Like all military wives, she knew the pain of separation, and what Christmas meant to us all.

Michael went round the whole headquarters, handing out his own Christmas cheer. The stockings were a wonderful touch, typical of the man and his family.

On the big day, the Romanians came round with a guitar and serenaded us. Michael took time off to gather us in the corridor outside his office. We all linked arms and sang badly off-key. I videoed it all on my iPhone. Even now, you can see we are all just the right side of tears. We shared solidarity of purpose, and the affection soldiers all enjoy in moments and places of great stress. Behind the smiles, you can see our minds are torn between the here and now and those we have all left behind.

I loved Michael for taking that moment to share it all with us. Of all my generals, he is the one who was the kindest and the most compassionate. It is a rare gift in a man.

PK AND THE LION

PK came back calling, once he knew that Paul and I had got along. He'd actually stuck his head around the corner before that first meeting to wish me luck. PK was always very modest about his leadership skills, but he is a past master at putting the right people to the right task. He describes it as 'facilitating'. I describe it as inspirational.

What came after was equally inspired. At Paul's behest, PK didn't think that we were doing enough to change the information warfare aspect of the job. The dictionary definition, of altering and changing attitudes and behaviours in the target audience, just wasn't matching either Paul or Patrick's ambition.

PK had this habit of innocuously inviting you for coffee: and then socking you between the eyes for answers. We'd got in the habit of meeting for an off-line latte on The Boardwalk. One day he just asked me, in that sly, but weighted, way he had when what he was after was important:

'If you had your way, what you do to really change the way the Afghans think about us leaving?'

We weren't doing well by late 2013. Election fever had hit Afghanistan: and the issue of whether we should stay or go was the whipping boy for creating votes amongst the candidates. We were an easy hit. The bases were beginning to close *en masse*. Development money, once an endless stream, was being shut off. The economy was in the dumpster. Obama and Karzai were having very public and very obvious rifts. Karzai was openly saying that he wished the coalition had never come to Afghanistan.

We were going home, that was set and un-changeable. What PK and Paul both shared was the foresight to try and leave something tangible behind us.

I had never forgotten General Hamid telling me that he didn't see different tribes and ethnicities, he only saw Afghans. Part of my background was marketing: corporate branding. IMHO, ISAF's brand management was simply terrible. We just didn't have one. Nor did we have a single coherent message.

What did we need? Try this:

You're stuck in some lonesome, god-forsaken town and you're looking for something to eat. There are lots of choices available. Some look appealing, some downright scary. In the midst, you spot the golden arches. McDonald's.

Whether you go there or not, you automatically associate with the iconography. At the very least you'll consider it. It's automatic: because of the branding. You know what the arches mean. McDonald's brings forth three key human emotions with the name: familiarity, consistency and a need to belong. Together, they bring desirability.

We all know the McDonald's menu. It's ubiquitous, wherever you are in the world. The recipe is the same, the ingredients the same, the taste the same. We are intimately familiar with it. We also know the stuff is safe, edible and tasty. McDonald's is consistent.

Most importantly, we all feel we have a share in it. McDonald's cleverly buys into the concept of family. Ronald McDonald, 'I'm lovin' it', the family meal. McDonald's does nothing by chance. You can be in any McDonald's, anywhere in the world, eat any menu item and you will feel the same sense of satisfaction: because the associated emotions that branding and product induce are universal human needs.

The same principles apply to any successful brand. The accessible universality of Coca-Cola, Starbucks, Heinz, Kellogg's, Budweiser *et al* encourage us to buy into the dream.

Nationalism plays the same card. The emotions an American feels when he or she proudly flies the Stars and Stripes in their front yard are exactly the same as when they buy a McDonalds: familiarity, consistency and belonging. The system keeps Americans safe: and the flag is an expression at their pride in membership and shared ownership of a piece of the dream.

Afghans, on the other hand, have known little but chaos, war, disease and disturbance. Life is a struggle for existence. The country remains fractured.

I return to the notion that those basic human needs that McDonalds personify are universal. Afghans want the same things we do: a safe haven to bring up kids and family, a job to fill the days, money to spend on nice things, week-ends to goof off.

Of course there are bad folks in Afghanistan. There are bad folks in every society. What makes our society different is that the pressure of organised society, of the vast majority that belong, negates the effect of the few idiots. Afghanistan doesn't have that unifying spirit. They don't believe in the project because the project we delivered doesn't believe in them. For twelve years, we have either lectured Afghanistan or promulgated esoteric concepts that Afghanistan didn't understand.

The POTF's product was labelled 'Sada E Azadi'. The' Voice of Freedom'. What did that mean to the average Afghan? Nothing. You can't own freedom. Freedom for what? War? Chaos?

Afghans want to belong with the same urgency we do: to be part of something bigger than themselves. To feel that familiarity, consistency and belonging we all take for granted. A country is nothing more than a collection of disparate parts that believe in a whole.

You can market a country, same as you can market a cheeseburger. Just ask Goebbels. I saw the war through a different prism from the soldiers. To me, the biggest challenge facing Afghanistan is not the insurgency. It is that the country will hold together.

In 2014, we were going and the country would have a brand new president and government, all in the same year. Folks were scared. Last time around, when the Soviets left, the place had fallen apart within four years. They had watched ethnicity, tribal history and local warlords divide and conquer the country into factions.

The real difference we should have been making was to encourage the coalescing of the whole into a proper sense of country: of belonging and ownership.

What I came up with was as simple a concept as 'Drink Milk'. The result bought into the sense of nascent Afghan pride and countered Afghan fears of not owning a future: 'Our Afghanistan.'

That was it: one line, a simple branding concept. Simple on the surface, complex in its delivery.

Every product we made would have the same strap-line: 'Our Afghanistan.' Every product we produced would carry the same imagery: the Afghan flag.

We would entice folks to believe they had a share in the adventure.

Hardly a 'Eureka!' moment, I hear you saying. Yet, it was, in that time and place. Everybody was out there doing their own thing: the police, the army, the governor, ISAF, RC-S, the US.

Every-one was exhorting the people to do something: don't pick up suspicious objects, support the soldiers, pay your taxes. Lectures, lectures, lectures. Collectively, we had created a series of outside agencies hectoring ordinary citizens without offering a reward or a reason why.

I mocked up some images for Patrick: an Afghan woman picking grapes. General Hamid saluting. A city official typing at a computer. A police officer directing traffic. A child flying a kite. A shopkeeper stacking tins on a shelf.

Every image surmounted by an Afghan flag, next to 'Our Afghanistan':
Project OA.

It didn't matter who you were, what you did, or how you did it. The message was the same. We are all in this together, and the fight is worth it: familiarity, consistency, belonging.

PK got it, straight off the bat. He had that kind of mind. What I was looking for would take a strategic change of mind-set from a lot of working parts that all had different priorities. None of which had any inherent reason to listen to a mad Scots-woman and her mad ideas.

'Our Afghanistan' was going to be a tall order to sell. PK was the man who made it happen. Without his star behind it all, the OA idea would have stayed just that: an idea.

He took me up to Paul to brief him in on the concept. I needed a wheeze to grab his imagination. KAF had a donut shop. I ordered up eight: two blue, with coconut icing, two plain blue, two pink and two pink with coconut icing.

Paul liked donuts, same as the next man. When I opened the box and offered him the choice, he went straight for the blue one with the coconut. He was a man, and a general, so the pink was out, straight off. But he went for the one with added sprinkles too. An out and out alpha male choice. Before he'd picked his bun, I'd shown him a piece of folded paper, on which I'd written down my bet on which one he would pick. I unfolded it and showed him my choice: 'blue with sprinkles.'

I'd sold Paul by offering him a choice that played to his internal preferences. I'd done it consciously and in advance. The point I was making was that I could, by simple application of human psychology and analysis of personal need, easily entice him to choose what I was selling.

With the 'Our Afghanistan' program, I could likewise sell our information messaging. The donut thing was a bit obvious and corny, but I had got his attention.

The program wasn't a message in its own right. It was a branding mechanism. What OA would do was promote desire.

Once we had the audience hooked, we could sell any message we wanted. Same as Heinz sells baked beans. It's the same stuff in each can, all you do is change the ingredients slightly: same message. It's the brand name that keeps you going back for the new stuff in the new sauce. You trust Heinz.

In military terms, I was promulgating a better delivery system for munitions. To increase the range of artillery pieces, you added a super-charge to the shell. OA would be the super-charge, the existing delivery mechanisms, the body of the shell.

If this stuff grabs you, check out the annex: I've stuck the whole proposal on there. It's the same document I presented to Paul that day.

Pink and blue donuts and McDonald's branding strategy was pretty unusual fare for a two star army general, but Paul bought into the whole cuckoo idea straight off.

The next bit proved a bit of a step too far, too quickly. I reckoned we needed a Ronald McDonald. He fills a vital part of the McDonald's brand. He is the conduit for sales message, dressed up in a family-friendly character.

I'd used the same principle in Bosnia, a decade earlier. I was serving there with a Scottish regiment, which had a stag's head emblem as a cap-badge, surmounting a St Andrew's cross. What the Jocks called a 'crucified moose'.

We were having difficulty getting the regiment recognised as friends, not enemies. Exactly the same drama of unfamiliarity and suspicion we were having in Afghanistan.

I came up with a cartoon character called 'Hector', which looked rather like a teenage Bambi: a young deer that echoed the stag's head in the Jock's cap-badge. I was deliberately looking for image-association. My Hector then became our poster-deer for our messaging. I had posters, pin badges, flags, even string puppets, all made up of Hector. The kids just loved him: get the kids, as Hitler said, and you have the country.

Counter-IED was a big priority for us. Bosnia was littered with unexploded munitions. Hector appeared on billboards, with a big pile of unexploded and dangerous mines behind him, with a bubble coming out of his mouth: 'this is dangerous. Tell Hector's friends where they are.'

I got an anonymous help-line set up, with a recorded message from Hector. And advertised it as: 'Tell Hector'. Lo and behold, folks started phoning in intelligence. Weapon hand-ins increased. The kids started recognising the soldiers as friends of Hector. We got less threats, more acceptance.

I wanted to add the same mascot concept to the OA program.

Kabul had once had a zoo, with two lions as prize exhibits. Lions are Afghanistan's national animals. They represent everything the country wants to say about itself: strength, independence, nobility, fearsome.

The Kabul zoo lions, a male and female, were called Marjan and Chucha. They survived starvation during the civil war. When the Taliban took Kabul, they tried to kill them with hand-grenades, wounding the female, Chucha. When one intrepid Taliban soul went into the cage to finish her off, Marjan mauled him badly, protecting his mate. Both animals survived right into the liberation. I reckoned they were the perfect tale of Afghan hardiness, survival and redemption. I bought two soft toys on Amazon and made outfits for them.

From an old T-shirt, I cut and sowed a miniature traditional pakhol man's hat for Marjan. He had a medal for bravery too, made from an ear-ring, held on by a home-made ribbon, coloured red, black and green: the Afghan national flag colours. For my Chucha, I made a miniature headscarf, again coloured in the Afghan national colours. Modest, yet patriotic.

Marjan and Chucha breathed life into the OA program. Same as Ronald did for McDonald's. Same as Hector had done for The Highlanders.

Paul didn't quite get the cuddly toys. He was a bit reticent to talk homemade fashion for fake fur lion puppets. I consoled my self that at least he could see I was serious.

PK had me come over again, the next morning, for the general's breakfast: after he had asked me to 'go easy' on my toy lions. He wasn't against my enthusiasm, just reminding me my audience would be rough and ready soldiers.

They were all there: Jim Rainey, John Thompson, Paul and Patrick, plus the key full bird colonels. Every day, they met to discuss key events in the AO. That day, they shared breakfast with pink and blue donuts, me, my mad ideas and two stuffed miniature lions, which I had brought along anyway. Stubborn old me. Shucks.

It was one of those events where everybody just took their cue from the CG:

'What do you think, colonel?'

'I think whatever you think, general.'

Despite some animated Spock eyebrow action over the lions, I passed. Thanks to PK and Paul. I had the equivalent of royal assent. Green-lit for go. The colonels fucking hated it.

Paul had had them burning the regular army oil overtime, to keep up with his special forces thinking. Now, he'd invited some mad female with a strange accent and some homemade puppets to make over the Afghan program. I may as well have presented typhoid.

PK killed the objections. He just told the bird colonels to get over themselves and get with the idea. When he was around, it was all gravy, but the off-line with the junior staff was memorable. All I had was the power of persuasion. And the ultimate conversation-ender:

'No? No worries. I'll just got tell the major-general....'

Worked every time, but it took a lot of sensitivity, cajoling and begging. I could only use Paul's name in extremis. If I'd been in green, I could have just ordered them. My patience for the military and their fucking rank-ranged egos was wearing more than a little thin.

In the midst of all this strategic messaging, social secretary, mass briefing stuff I was doing, it was easy to forget that I was actually employed by the POTF, up in Kabul. Even though the work for them was strictly the day job, I was still running half the country's output.

In the midst of the happy KAF times, I had taken my eye off the ball politically. Which was quite easy to do. In all my 1,000 days in Kandahar, I only had one visitor, for two days, from Kabul. I went up there just four times. In truth, to them, I was little more than an in-tray e-mail address. Anybody I had personally known was long gone in the rotation blizzard.

Even the redoubtable characters I had started with had disappeared. We had gone from twelve hardy souls in the section to four by February 2014. Of the four left, I was the only one left still operating from the field. The others had long since moved their operation back to the compound in Kabul. My champion, Eric, was long forgotten. Nobody was left with the management ability or the smarts to fight my corner.

In March, just as the 'Our Afghanistan' project was winding up, I got a fastball summons to Kabul. Omar and I were still going at it hammer and tongs, so I was actually looking forward to getting into the weeds up there as I left on the Herc for KAIA.

I had a major issue on my hands: or, more accurately, as I shall explain, I didn't have an issue at all.

'Sada E Azadi', our paper, was supposed to publish 40,000 copies in Kandahar each issue. The entire printing and distribution service had long been handed out to the Afghans. The process was nominally controlled by a young lieutenant, from up in Kabul.

Some time earlier, I had negotiated a deal with Faizi to get SeA sent to the airport. He had agreed to put piles of the thing in the waiting areas, and his staff would put one in the seat pockets of every in-coming airliner that they cleaned and serviced. A pretty good deal for us, given that the paper was supposed to be for movers and shakers. The deal meant everybody coming in and out of Kandahar would see the paper.

Trouble was, Faizi hadn't seen a copy in months. I had agitated with the local distributor, and with Kabul, but nothing was being done. The paper never arrived.

I got a list of all the points the paper was supposed to be distributed to: about 150 different locations. Some of them, like the governor's palace, I could check myself. Others, in the out-lying districts, my boys did for me, at not inconsiderable risk.

Without exception, the paper had either not been delivered, or in insufficient quantities, or badly published.

The deal was that the outer cover was supposed to be high-quality gloss, A4 paper bound into A5 by doubling over. The few copies I had rounded up were all printed on really cheap paper. Most with the text squint on the page, not stapled in the spine, or stapled in the wrong place. The majority of the copies I could find were months out of date.

It was obvious to me that we were being ripped off: and nobody was checking. The paper cost $4 million a year. That was just the cost of printing and distribution, let alone the invisible costs of all the staff and resource that went into making the content. We were just throwing money out the window.

It wasn't the first time I had complained. When Eric had been around, he'd tried to work the problem. But the military boys rotated so often that what happened downstream always got lost in the mix. One new guy would start to get on top of it, then he'd be gone, and any checks we had started just got forgotten.

The Afghans knew we never stayed; and exploited it ruthlessly. Yet again, playing at Don Quixote, I wanted to go tilt at windmills with the new ones. Trying to supervise national programs from an office in Kabul was a waste of time. You needed to be on the ground to do that. Which is where I felt I came in.

I was also extremely concerned about the content.

The IJC had a new general, Mark Milley, who from somewhere had come up with the instruction to turn the paper into a primary school reader. The concept had always been that we would be high-end, for folks who wielded influence. SeA had always been designed as a newspaper, not a textbook. Milley turned the whole thing on its head.

We'd already cut the content from 16 stories to 12 per issue to save money, as well as losing the regional inserts. Now, to fit Milley's frankly bizarre concept, we were to reduce to 8 stories so the centre pages could be used for basic reading and writing comprehension papers.

The idea was that the SeA pages would be complemented by verbal lessons to back-reference the written text, which the POTF would broadcast on its own radio station.

Millcy's plan might have worked if everybody had heard of the program, had access to a current issue of the paper, a radio, a pen and paper and listened at the right time. Which was one heck of a lot of assumptions for Afghanistan.

First off, as I'd found out, nobody in Kandahar was getting the paper. Second of all, the POTF radio station wasn't broadcast in Kandahar: and hadn't been for years since the Americans had started doing their own thing. Nobody raised any of that with Milley. I'm not sure anybody in Kabul even knew.

Our flagship product was now going to be a mere 8 stories per fortnightly edition, with some kid's school stuff that, at best, required a considerable degree of coordination to exploit. In Kandahar, none of it would never be seen or heard of at all.

The whole thing was a fucking mess, with Milley's plan being the cherry on the cake. It was typical, though, of the non-stop bright ideas that came out of IJC and the POTF. Nobody down-stream ever got consulted. We'd just get these edicts that had been issued from the coffee-shops of Kabul.

It's a mark of how little anybody thought of Milley's plan that the day after he rotated out, the POTF cut the program without telling anybody: right in the middle of the course. No fucker was listening to it.

I got to Kabul late—we got rocketed again en route—but just in time for a new Romanian colonel I had never met to tell the four FMTs left that the entire program was being cut. I'd been summoned to Kabul in order to be fired. Not asked about how it was all going. From July, the FMTs would be no more.

Everybody was packing up. If Eric had been there, there would have been a scheme to keep somebody in the key bases, which were to stay for another year or two. But, without him, the PowerPoint graphs led relentlessly downward to zero.

You couldn't argue with the result; that was a decision that had ultimately been made, for better or worse, in the White House. Nobody was listening to me. But I did have something to say about Our Afghanistan, the paper and what I had been doing in Kandahar.

To be fair, I was told the colonel would listen to my pitch. Then he got called away. I went back to Kandahar unheard.

By that stage, a colonel didn't really mean that much to me: middle management. Down in Kandahar, we were all first name buddies. After all the OA stuff, I was working at a lot higher level.

Life was different in Kabul. I had to work to two different systems. In KAF, I worked alongside a two-star general in the middle of a war. In Kabul, folks were bending the knee to a colonel in between long lunches and sessions in the gym.

The new POTF commander was heavily exercised about researching the previous chiefs, so he could have a wall of fame of everybody who had run the shop. With his smiling face at the top of the pile: different priorities, different culture, different vibe altogether.

The POTF was paying my wages. It was made very clear to me that whatever I was doing for RC-S wasn't what they were signing the cheques for. They didn't give a rats about any of the cream. They had to make budget cuts. To protect the Kabul core, the regions were to go. Which meant me.

As much as they didn't know me, I didn't have much respect for them either. Nobody had even been to see what I had been up to in three years of graft. A more politic person would probably have grovelled a bit. But I have always been a suicidally stubborn soul, particularly where my work was concerned. Fuck 'em. I'd make this work another way.

Back in Kandahar, the POTF quickly disappeared into the jet stream.

There was just too much to do. I went to see Paul and mentioned the whole Romanian sacking piece. RC-S told me they would support the project: and me. In any case, COMISAF himself had been to visit and was now on board.

Joseph Dunford, a four star US marine, was in the COMISAF hot seat. He'd taken over from John Allen. Two marines in a row: two commanders who recognised that we couldn't just kill everybody. We had to do better.

Although Dunford had earned the title 'Fighting Joe' for his command time in Iraq, from 2005 onwards he had served pretty much exclusively in joint plans and operations. He is a thinking man's general. Crucially, he was open to left-field ideas involving stuffed toys.

I'd been in Kabul when Dunford came down to Kandahar. Paul was brave enough—and he earned my eternal respect for it—that he got his staff to present the OA idea to COMISAF. Dunford is a busy man. What I had presented to LaCamera had gained enough traction that Paul put his trust in the project to promote it to COMISAF. Which was pretty ballsy. I wasn't even one of his troops.

Until Soak had proposed meeting with Paul, he'd never even heard of me. Here he was, a matter of weeks later, pinning his information operations policy on my briefing paper, over and above everything else his own hand-picked staff had come up with. Not many blokes would have had the stones to make that call. Regardless of how good my idea was.

I was pretty pissed somebody else had done the brief. But, in the great game of army politics, in retrospect, 4ID staffers needed to own the idea to make it work. As a make-up and hug, I got a fastball from PK to come meet Carter Malkasian.

Malkasian was Dunford's key policy advisor: a position he had earned by toughing it out in Garmsir district, Helmand, for two years, as US State's man in paradise. He'd been late in getting to Afghanistan. An academic by trade, Carter could have happily sat out the war up in the puzzle palace of the Embassy, with its swimming pool and meditation garden.

Instead, he'd asked for a combat posting with the marines, who were kicking in the door around Helmand. Unconsciously or not, he'd built a role for himself emulating the example of the kind of guys my grandfather hung out with on the North-West Frontier. Malkasian lived as the old colonial officers had done. Carter had gone out of his way to walk amongst the people. Listening to their problems, solving the ones he could, apologising for the ones he couldn't. Dispensing wisdom, decisions and money.

Most of all, Carter stayed in Garmsir for two years. That was what made the difference. Human beings like familiarity. It takes time to build trust. You can bring all the guns you want to the party, it means dick if there is no trust.

Carter came back as Dunford's muse. I always admired that about the Americans. They didn't always get it right, but they had a facility for listening to different voices that many of the allies, my own country included, never had. Carter wasn't a diplomat or a soldier. Dunford brought him back on a contract because he offered something different. For most countries, including the UK, war is a closed and incestuous shop that always proposes the same answers from the same faces and names.

Dunford was a busy guy, running the war. If PK could get Carter on-side, he would be a key tool in not letting the idea wither on the vine.

Patrick hosted the meet. Carter being in town was so super-secret-squirrel I didn't get advance warning. I pitched up without my pet lions: and I was pissed when finally I got into RC-S.

Yet again, the fucking badge rules had changed. Three years in and I now needed another badge with a blue, or black, or striped or rainbow-patterned something that I didn't have in my full deck of badges. It was a 4ID thing. Like all the new arrivals, they brought their own badges. Fine for them, they only stayed for one rotation, but impossible if you lived there, to keep up with the never-ending bullshit of it all. I'd stood in the sun for a full half-hour while private dip-shit with the big gun had phoned the world to figure out what to do with the gobby female who said she had an urgent happening with the general. Fuck… the army killed me.

PK got it in the neck, when I finally turned up with serious sunburn from all the stooging around to get in. It was hard enough just existing in Kandahar without the military crap. It was the bullshit way they looked down on anybody that didn't wear uniform. Guaranteed to ruin your day.

Carter just smiled. He is a slightly-built man and very mild-mannered. But smart too. He listened politely. Then asked his security detail what they thought. The boys with the beards and the guns waded in. I had done the brief often enough that I fielded the balls out of the park.

Carter may not have got the whole piece, but he picked up the innuendo enough to know I was a believer. Just like him. Time in Afghan just gives you this weird internal light, like those kids in the breakfast cereal adverts of my youth. You'll never be the same again. I was gonna make this thing fly: and Carter promised he would make sure COMISAF stayed tuned.

Couldn't have asked for more. After he left, PK got the carrot cake out to celebrate. We both have a sweet tooth. The man had taken a real Hail Mary on me, but now the pieces were in place.

Let's play….

DAYS OF WINE AND ROSES

It was time to give something back. For all the years we had been in KAF, and all the hundreds of millions we had spent, we had done nix for the local people who lived nearby. In any direction, you could step a couple of hundred yards from the wire and be back a thousand years. For thirteen years, the locals had watched our planes fly over their heads and our vehicles rumble through their streets, but their lives were the same, poverty-ridden struggle that they ever were.

When the Canadians were in town, it had been different. They had run a program called 'Afghan first'. Any casual labour to be done on KAF had been done by locally recruited folks. Historically, that was where Ahmed and his Afghan rascals, who had picked me up that first day at the airport, had come from. Somehow, they had survived as a COMKAF anachronism, but the Americans had got rid of everybody else.

The most successful local venture we ran was the KAF marketplace. Once a week, about a hundred or so vendors got to come onto KAF and sell a mad variety of local produce. You could buy everything from a sniper scope to a scorpion sealed in amber. The bazaar was an important revenue source for local businesses. You could order up a carpet from a sample and, three weeks later, it would arrive, freshly woven. The bazaar was much more than just a sales opportunity. We encouraged an entire supply chain and professional business practise.

The Canucks built a school to go along with the market. Every Saturday, the stall owners would bring their young sons with them, and we'd educate them for free for a morning. Teaching at the school was a lot of fun. The Afghan boys were wild with excitement: and we would spoil them silly with pencil sets, notepads and toys. For many of them, the COMKAF school will be the only education any of them will get. Perhaps more importantly, it proved to them that westerners were not just one-eyed ogres who drove around in noisy armoured trucks. We were human too.

Christopher, the COMKAF sergeant major, a huge tank of an African-

American, willingly ran himself ragged giving crowds of squealing youngsters piggy-backs. The school was one of those few places we created where the war was immaterial.

In 2013, despite my protests, COMKAF had closed the bazaar, and with it, the school. Soak had little choice. The closure came after the Lamber Khan shooting. Khan may have felt aggrieved at us, but he also cost the livelihood of a hundred vendors. And their children their education. As the last vendor left, amidst a sea of hugs and tears, he drew his finger across his throat. It was the end for his business. We had done our best, issuing certificates of gratitude to them all, but it was a bitter day.

The Afghans never brought their daughters to the school, despite our requests. At first sight, it seemed to many that the women were being deliberately excluded. That isn't quite right. The bazaar was full of western men. A couple of the volunteer teachers were western male soldiers. The Afghans were protecting their daughter's honour. To their mind, it would have been off-the-scale inappropriate for their female off-spring to be in the company of western, and un-related, men.

Women have a shitty deal in Afghanistan. I well remember travelling in Kunduz province, to see a man ploughing his field with the same kind of hand-plough and oxen set-up that has been used for two thousand years. About fifty yards in front of him, his daughter walked along the same line the plough would follow. She walked there because the field had not been cleared of mines. His daughter was a living, walking counter-IED mine-detector. Her life was worth less than the oxen.

Around KAF, you could see female human scarecrows, picking over the detritus that lay in layers around the entrance to KAF. Years of convoys, soldiers and a changing perimeter had stacked up piles and piles of rubbish, excrement and pools of green, stagnant effluent. A whole gypsy community had sprung up around KAF, feeding off the stuff we threw away.

Women and children would pick through the rubbish, looking for the odd bauble they could sell, re-cycle or re-shape. Oblivious to the comings and goings of international military operations, they would scarcely glance in our direction as they fought a never-ending battle for simple survival. It was impossible to drive past that dreadful example of human tragedy and not want to do something about it.

For a long time, I had harboured the notion of building a park for women, where they could, for a moment, sit amongst their peers in a tolerable environment.

Women in Kandahar are fundamentally excluded from normal society. You'll see the odd woman out and about in the city, curtained from the world by the all-enveloping burka. They are walking human shuttlecocks. What freedom does exist happens within the walls of the family compound. Only inside can they show self-expression. Even there, the price can be high.

In 2013, two teenage Pashtun girls, Noor Basra and Noor Shesa, aged 15 and 16, went outside to their garden. It started to rain. They danced, goofed around and jumped for joy at being caught in the deluge, as any normal teenager might. They made the mistake of filming themselves on their mobile phone. Their father found out about the footage and arranged for the girls, and their mother, to be murdered for dishonouring the family.

In that strictly segregated society, women are routinely barred from enjoying life. Including simple pleasures such as the company of other women.

In the early days, up in Kabul, we in ISAF had been appalled at the lack of drinking water available to the huge influx of refugees. They had built vast shanty camps on the outskirts of the city, made of mud bricks. The women walked for miles to the nearest source of water, taking half a day to trudge there and back with a couple of precious buckets of liquid.

In our ignorance, we decided to do something about it. We spent a fortune drilling and installing fresh water pumps within easy walking distance of the townships. Within a month, they had all been vandalised: by the Afghan refugees themselves. They went back to their long distance iterations with the buckets. Why would they destroy the one development project we had been able to deliver?

For the simple reason that we had destroyed their day out. Women's freedoms were so closely controlled that the excuse to go and get water was the only chance they had to get outside. The wells we dug ruined their day. Their male husbands and guardians demanded they quickly return home from their chores. We had, inadvertently, taken away their only chance to talk to another female. The long walk to water was their only chance to socialise. We let the new wells wither.

A new woman's park was my KAF solution. Where women could gather in privacy. In Kandahar city, there were a couple. Behind high and solid walls, women could unrobe and enjoy a picnic, or put their children on a swing. Around KAF, there was nothing. I wanted to build them one. It took two years to make it happen.

The biggest issues were land and money. Around KAF, nobody was quite sure who owned what. I thought of going to Sherzai first. To be fair, he did immediately volunteer an acre when I asked. We just couldn't prove that he owned the land. At the time, Sherzai was under a huge amount of pressure from Governor Wesa. He was organising surprise police raids on all Sherzai's property to put pressure on him to give up some of his land empire. I couldn't get funding without a definitive lease, so Sherzai was out.

It was Faizi who came to the rescue. My regular lunches and coffees at the airport paid off. He wrote up a formal release to give us title over two acres of prime real estate, right next to the terminal.

With that in hand, it was off to find the money. None of the usual donors were interested in helping: a women's park didn't fit any of the holes we had to put pieces into. However, COMKAF did have a welfare fund. The one that paid for all the free T-shirts and free internet for us.

It took a lot of work, but I found that COMKAF, the general, had a discretionary portion of the fund he could use for local development projects. In the dim and distant, the Canucks had used it to build a few gravel roads for local villages. Soak was interested, but he left before we could get the matter tied up. To raise the money required would need the agreement of the NATO partners: and that would be a long process. I needed to get the proposal costed and planned before I could go ask anybody for money.

Luckily, COMKAF had another old stager on board, in the shape of a retired British airborne engineer officer: Andy Bratt. Andy is old school. He cut about camp in a safari jacket and an old Gurkha hat, with the band and the bit turned up at the side. Andy was, remarkably, 64 years old in 2014 and still doing the business on operations. As a younger man, he had led his engineer platoon through the mud of the Falklands War. Andy was tough as nails and grumpy to boot. But underneath the exterior, Andy was as kind and gentle a man as you could wish for. He just got embarrassed expressing it.

When I approached him about the project, he got straight on board. Together, we went over to the airport, without any protection or the usual bollocks. Andy did that engineering thing with pieces of string, pacing out the perimeter of the proposed compound, while I drove him mad with my ideas of rose-trellises and fountains.

We needed a town planner to draw the thing now we had the plot and the engineer. RC-S had one. There was so much construction going on that the planning cell never truly wound up. Amazingly enough for us, the guy in RC-S had spent the majority of his career designing theme parks for companies like Disney. He did a fine job of translating my wild visions into practical architectural drawings that a construction company could actually use.

We priced the whole deal at $150,000. Which was chicken feed in Afghanistan. It took eighteen months of patient negotiating, plotting and politics, to bring it to life. What really brought the pimple to a head was the sober reality that we really were leaving. Everybody just woke up to the fact that all we were really leaving behind was dust. Our departure just changed the dynamic. Everybody got on board, after months of frustration. The NATO support staff alone raised nearly $600 with a whip-round.

Mike Fantini signed the deal off in April 2014. The gesture was typical of the man. He signed right up to the limit he could personally authorise. I owe him.

Altogether, we raised $160,000. The deal, and I insisted on it, was that an Afghan company did the construction. The internationals could take their inflated profit margins somewhere else.

The plans were great. We would have a sixty-foot pond, with fountains at either end, ablutions with running water, gazebos and rose gardens. The money didn't stretch far enough to buying swings and other play park stuff, but I had allowed for a soft area, with bark flooring. If I could raise more money, the toys could be added, post-construction. Faizi went at it like a man possessed. Every time Andy and I went over to check on construction, he'd be out in the middle of the field, hand-planting more saplings.

I then wanted to field-test the 'Our Afghanistan' concept. I knew it would work, I'd been there long enough to just sense the zeitgeist in the air, but I needed demonstrable proof: what the military call MOE, measure of effectiveness.

Kandahar has long been famous as a centre of the creative arts. The city has some remarkably beautiful and wonderfully meditative and peaceful shrines. The most famous is probably the mausoleum of Ahmad Shah Durrani, Afghanistan's first emperor. He is buried in a fragrant and fabulously ornate tomb, clad in blue and white tiles. Every day, a queue of penitent pilgrims visits a grove of trees in front of the shrine. The trees are reported to have curative powers, particularly for toothache.

Durrani guards one of the most precious artefacts in all of Islam. Shah Durrani brought the cloak of the Holy Prophet himself to Kandahar, a gift from the Emir of Bokhara. It is carefully stored, away from public gaze. The same family have guarded it for 250 years. The icon is only brought out for the legitimate rulers of Afghanistan. The last time it was seen in public was when Mullah Omar took power, wrapping himself in the cloak and declaring himself 'Commander of the Faithful'. Every day, a patient queue of men from across the Islamic world removes their sandals and passes by the ornate catafalque, touching the case containing Durrani's brass helmet.

That artistic tradition carries on to this day. Kandahar has always been the creative lodestone of Afghanistan. One of Kandahar's most famous sons from this generation is an incredibly talented street artist called Durukshan. He is Kandahar's Banksy. His art is quite remarkable.

We have bequeathed Afghanistan a sad legacy of a veritable ocean of concrete walls. Every building of status is surrounded by never-ending lines of protective walls and bastions. It is a depressing and never-ending diorama. Durukshan was doing his best to change the dynamic. Sometimes with official permission, more often without, he was out there, turning the walls of grey into bright flights of fancy. With his spray cans and his febrile imagination, he was on a one-man mission to turn Kandahar back into a place of joy.

He painted anything that came into his head. Like all good art, he was re-defining the culture of the time. Just like Pollack, Lichtenstein or Warhol, he caught the moment, to elicit a visceral reaction from his audience. Durukshan's art melded traditional Islamic imagery, of dreaming spires and distant sunsets, with contemporaneous themes. Right in the middle of a stunning vista, he would place a broken body, or a child crying. His art was an evocation of pain and hope combined, suffused fear and hope.

In 2014, Afghanistan was obsessed with election fever. Not who was running for office, but a very active discussion on what democracy meant to the new generation. The old power base in Afghanistan, the warlords and tribal chiefs who dictated what would happen to the masses, were growing old. This new generation all had mobile phones, access to the internet. They yearned for change.

They had seen westerners in their country for fourteen years. While we were not universally respected, or even liked, we were a different dynamic. We had changed perceptions. Fear grows from ignorance. The new generation of urban elite are Afghanistan's future; and they wanted more than to be told what and how to think by their elders. They had seen us.

On his own, Durukshan had come up with an image of a dove of peace, holding a ballot paper in its beak. Next to the stylised image of a bird in flight, he had written one word: 'Vote.'

Not in Dari or Pashto: in English. Durukshan is multi-lingual. He firmly believes that Afghanistan's future is in the League of Nations. English is the *de facto* international language. He used an English word deliberately, to suggest modernity, innovation and progress.

I wanted to find out what 'Our Afghanistan' meant to the average Afghan. I wanted to meet Durukshan.

Faizi hosted the meeting at the airport. I explained the concept to Durukshan, but I was careful not to show him any imagery. I asked him what 'Our Afghanistan' meant to him. Would he put his express his thoughts for me? Durukshan loved the idea. He was sketching thoughts even as he left. A week later, he sent me the results. He'd spray-painted his imagined image onto a big T-wall, downtown, right opposite police headquarters.

What he came up with was a clenched fist, garlanded by an unbroken circle of birds. The fist was not clenched with knuckles foremost. That was too aggressive. The fist was out-turned, palm uppermost, in the black power symbol of my youth. It is an image that signifies solidarity, strength, defiance and resolution of purpose. The surrounding garland of doves was individually named: with the names of each of the tribes of Afghanistan. All fourteen of them, in an unbroken ring. The circle is an image as old as civilisation itself: unity, protection, all-inclusive, never-ending. The doves and the circle spoke of peace and reconciliation.

That was what 'Our Afghanistan' meant to Durukshan. As much as I had come up with the concept, Durukshan breathed life into its meaning.

Poor old Paul had to put up with me doing my history of art dissection of the imagery. He was always tolerant of my flights of fancy. But I was onto something: Durukshan's image had been picked up around town. Copies were appearing all over. Kids were making the reverse fist symbol in the streets. I wanted to build on the success.

I didn't want to present an idea to the Afghans. We had forever forced stuff on them. I wanted the idea to grow organically. 'Our Afghanistan' should develop its own, personal connotations, not be dictated by us. I needed somewhere that the key Afghan leadership could access the imagery. To see it as something inspirational, not just graffiti, however clever the art was.

The civil airport was the nexus. Right next to the park site, Faizi had an entry control point, a heavily-guarded security check-post that was surrounded by dozens of concrete T-walls. A pretty depressing place to begin and end your journey to the world, surrounded by guns and high, grey walls. However, everybody that was anybody used the airport; and drove past that control point on their way in and out. I could fuse my two great projects together. Perfect.

I gave Durukushan $1,000 dollars of my own money to turn the control point around. Trying to get money out of ISAF for art would have been a never-ending road to stress and antipathy. We'd spend millions on guns and stuff, but nothing on nurturing the human soul. Hardly surprising; we put soldiers in charge. I wanted to jump-start the project. If you want something done, best do it yourself.

Faizi loved the idea. He gave Durukshan a dozen T-walls, a forty-foot canvas to work with. Right on the entry-way. Every air passenger coming and going to Kandahar would have to stop right next to the mural. Durukshan went to it with a vengeance. He surpassed himself.

He re-used the by now ubiquitous clenched fist, this time with an Afghan flag behind it, but still with the tribal names. Next to it, he stylised images of what he thought the new Afghanistan was capable of. He drew Afghan cricketers (by now in the first tier of international teams), an aircraft taking off, with a man and a woman together waving an Afghan flag, looking at a bright sunrise. He went a bit paint-crazy and added a full 'welcome' and 'goodbye' mural too. Durukshan just loved the project.

$1,000 bucks was a lot of money for me. I was personally financing work stuff. As much as I believed in the idea, folks thought I was nuts. I shelled out for a commemorative OA bench in the women's park, which we'd christened 'Paradise Park'. Afghanistan was getting personally expensive: but I just loved the place. Kandahar had become my life.

I asked all the generals if they would like to contribute. If I got $100 bucks from each of them, we could do over some more T-walls. The only one to reply was Mike Fantini. He ante'd up, which is entirely typical of the man.

When Fanman saw the results, he loved it. We were trying hard to improve the airport. Despite the years of ISAF screwing around, this year we were changing the dynamic. Together with 'Paradise Park', the place was visibly changing.

Mike came over to give Durukshan a certificate. We just ambled over there, no protection, just Faizi, Dukshan, Feroz, Mike and me. No guns, no drama, right into the big, bad outside world beyond the wire. Mike would have been a big scalp. It was typically brave of him: and showed the lengths he was willing to go to treat the Afghans as true partners.

I let the mural percolate for a couple of weeks, until I was sure the governor had been through a couple of times. The airport entrance was the place to advertise our wares. The mural was so damn big, so powerfully expressed, that you couldn't miss taking it in, even if only on a subliminal level.

PK and me beavered away on spreading the message. More than anything, I wanted the Afghans to own the words, to own the concept, to buy into the psychology behind it. The stated aim was simple:

'To promote Afghan national unity and pride in order to foster benign acceptance of the rule of law and the pillars of state.'

I'd written the words, but I couldn't force our audience to believe. The Afghan government was going to be in charge from the end of 2014. We had promulgated our own rule of law, with all our bombs and guns, but those times were over. The country's only chance for survival was to hold together. Regardless of who was going to be in charge, ordinary folks had to have faith that it was all going to be OK.

The guys with the juice, the money and the people to make the project happen were the Afghan army and the police.

3ID had gutted RC-S's capacity to produce information operations product. The POTF were off in their own orbit somewhere, drinking coffee and congratulating each other. This one would only work if we could organically grow the seed at ground level.

By 2014, quite a lot of effort had gone into helping the Afghans work their own media efforts. I'd had a hand in assisting the army, having trained a fair few 205 Corps officers in media production the year before. Another off-the-books project I took on without the POTF's knowledge.

PK took to adding me to his never-ending round of visits to the senior Afghan leadership. He worked at an impressive rate of knots. As a general, he had the star power to get the helicopters and vehicles lined up. My days would be spent in a blizzard of high-speed convoys and dizzying helicopter rides to visit some Afghan commander in another run-down building somewhere in Kandahar.

We developed an impressive double-act. PK would do the usual introductions, then I'd haul out the lions and the posters and the photos of Durukshan's work: which was the key. Most everybody of influence had seen the mural when they had travelled.

I knew a lot of those guys already. I'd been there long enough. But what sold OA was the fact that I had paid for the mural myself. Afghans put a heavy weight on trust. If I was willing to personally invest a year's average Afghan salary in this, I was worth listening to. Even if the ulterior motive was how they could get their hands on some of the money too.

205 Corps was on board. The police were on board. Persuading them wasn't that hard: they loved the idea. None of it would have been possible without PK backing me up to the hilt. If I'd wanted to stop at the security forces, that would have been it. I wanted more.

We'd done enough of that sort of stuff for the previous twelve years. We still were. The POF owned some sixty billboards around Kandahar. Out on patrol, I'd see the same, tired images. ISAF soldiers, Afghan soldiers, ISAF and Afghan soldiers: everything military-focussed. Our newspaper was full of army stuff, or dull cultural pieces about ancient castles built by Alexander the Great. Didn't they see that that was just another piece about another invading conqueror?

Life should be a celebration. Experiences should be fabulous. Optimism should be owned by all of us. We all share that basic human desire to be happy.

I borrowed one of Nick Carter's initiatives. Back in '10, he'd set up the Provincial Council, which was still meeting regularly. I wanted to give the project to the Afghans to run. We would be gone in a year. It had to be their idea, and their will, for the concept that Durukshan had profoundly expressed to work. I wanted to set up an Information Operations Coordination Committee. I wanted every government department, every local interest group to have a say. Together, we would move the project forward, or it would die.

The RC-S staff got round the project. We'd had a sticky patch where they had to get used to this mad civilian and her mad ideas getting straight access to the CG. When I left Paul's office, I'd get mail, asking:

'What did you and the general talk about?'

I always replied, 'ask him'. If Paul had wanted to share the discussion, I was sure he'd have told them. Paul and I talked about a ton of stuff. As somebody outside the command chain, he used me as a sounding board for lots of wild stuff. And we talked about family, home and what we'd do after the war. Generals are as human as the rest of us. Those chats helped give me the perceived gravitas to break orbit.

It took a lot of coordination. Feroz became quite inspirational in bringing it all together. He'd become quite a key actor in Kandahar's journalistic community. On 10th April 2014, two and half years planning came to a head.

We were all due to meet at the governor's palace: the governor, the heads of the security services, all the district governors and the heads of all the government departments. I'd jumped on board Carter's Provincial Council meeting. Once a month, everybody came together to talk, from all over the province. I planned to make my presentation the same day.

Another 0500 start for me. I didn't have a general with me this time, so it was back to MRAP convoy time. PK had wished me luck, but this was my show this time. Training reins had been removed.

A 30 minute taxi journey to Kandahar city became a back-breaking four hours in the back of an armoured truck, wedged next to the ass of the top gunner above. Every time he swivelled his turret around, he accidentally kicked me in the face. I took two cushions, but I was in clip order by the time we finally got there.

The wagons were pretty full of RC-S staffers. Word had got around that this project was pet CG stuff. Everybody and their dog sent a representative. I'd sold the generals, done the spadework with the Afghan security boys, but this day would be the one: if it worked, the Provincial Council would buy into the idea. If not, it would die. There and then. I'd have to make the pitch: and I had one chance to get it right. The wolves had gathered for the spectacle.

I made a special effort to get dressed for the occasion. I'd have to speak publicly, so how I presented was important. Particularly presenting as a female in public.

Like a lot of the old timers, I always eschewed a head scarf. I wore my usual hat, a big baker's boy cap, with a lime green scarf draped over my shoulders, over a full sleeve skin coloured undershirt and a long T-shirt dress over that, plus jeans and my usual heels. I reckoned I cut the right mix of modesty and professionalism.

Being a female in authority in Afghanistan is always a difficult tightrope. Pashtun Afghan men are not used to women speaking their mind. In fact, they are not used to women speaking in public at all. The educated elite was always very gracious towards me, but outside of that closed circle, daily life was always an issue.

I'd had an unfortunate run-in the previous month. PK had grabbed me to go downtown for a meeting with General Raziq. I'd come straight from a breakfast meeting with Paul and I wasn't expecting to go anywhere. It was Sunday, a special day for me.

I'd worn a long, full length patterned skirt, with a mid-sleeved T-shirt, emblazoned with a gold cross, spelling the word 'love'. Although I had my ubiquitous hat, my *décolletage* was in evidence. Hey, I was on KAF. I'd dress as I pleased. I enjoyed Paul's company and I liked to look as nice as KAF would allow. I was off to church after breakfast.

Next thing I knew, PK led me to a spinning Black Hawk. We were late for our meet. I had no time to change, despite my protests. Walking to the helo, the down draught caught my skirt and I did a full 'Seven Year Itch'. Up, right over my head. The crew suddenly got very interested in their passenger. As I struggled to regain my modesty, cameras were suddenly much in evidence. I ended up hobbling on board, holding my skirt between my legs.

In town, Raziq blew us off, as was his wont by 2014. He wouldn't have dared do that a year earlier. We were leaving, so interest in keeping us sweet was rapidly diminishing. PK took us to an ANP training place instead. When I appeared, the whole place just stopped, stock still. The Afghans had never seen anything like it. As usual, they ran around asking for photos. I didn't mind the snaps, long as they didn't touch me. They had a bad habit of groping. That day, the queue turned into a near-riot. I had to run for the vehicles. The Afghan base commander was not amused.

After that trip, I got word that there had been a complaint about my dress from PK's interpreter. I was used to it by now. No matter what you did as a female, there would be a complaint. And KAF wasn't exactly a bed of gender equality itself. It was just another layer of complexity to daily dealings.

PK had put me in a difficult position that day. This time, going to do my brief, I thought I had nailed the look: sophisticated, but chic. I've travelled all over the Islamic world. In Tehran or Damascus, I'd have got compliments.

The Kandahar governor's place is rather lovely. Think Afghanistan and you'll most probably think mud huts and dust. True, Afghanistan has a lot of that. It is one of the poorest countries in the world. Afghanistan also has a wonderful architectural heritage, in the true Islamic style. The governor's palace is one of those classically designed buildings. Outside, you step over open sewers. Inside the compound, there are large, beautifully tended rose gardens, water features, manicured lawns and cool cloisters of arched columns.

The main committee room is a magnificent pine-panelled colossus, over sixty feet long, with a vast table to match that can seat forty. At one end, an impressive photograph of President Karzai looked down on proceedings. Beside each seat, there was a switchable pa microphone, bottles of water and trays of boiled sweets.

I ran straight into a full house. Election fever was in the air again. Every swinging dick in Kandahar had pitched in for the love fest. RC-S had an embed with the governor's office. Jack lived and breathed the space, wearing shalwar kameez and growing a big old bushy beard. He showed me to a chair at the end of the boardroom table, with Feroz right next to me to whisper the bits of language I missed.

All the usual suspects were in evidence: Raziq, the army colonels, the district governors, the head of hajj, even somebody from the women's affairs department. Apart from her, I was the only chick in the place. Some of them, I already knew, others just stared at me in that accusing but disarming Afghan way. Afghans have different concepts of rudeness from us: they will stare and stare, as a child would stare at an adult in our society. They don't mean any offence, it's just the way they operate. Disconcerting, nonetheless, as I prepped for my big moment.

Only a half hour late, which was something of a record for an Afghan meeting, Governor Wesa breezed in from his private offices. He waved down at me, which was re-assuring. I'd been remembered. After brief introductions, he mentioned me by name, and welcomed me to the committee.

Which was my signal for the off. Out came Pashtun translations of the initial proposal, plus my toy lions, which really got some arched eyebrow action. I genuinely don't think they'd seen anything like that before. Off I went, with the old record playing. I knew the script by heart now. After a twenty-minute speech, Wesa thanked me, stood up and walked out. Promptly followed by everybody else.

One of the ISAF boys came up and said:

'Great speech, Abi, but our meeting is scheduled for next door.'

Fuck me sideways. I'd done my pitch to the whole committee, when the ISAF planners had only meant me to do an introductory 'hello' and then break off for a sidebar. Wesa had scooted off because he was expecting the imminent arrival of a team of ministers from Kabul. He was in trouble again for one of his money-making schemes. Right on cue, an impressive convoy of blacked out SUVs sped through the gates.

Trouble was, nobody had told me the plan. I hadn't organised the details. That was RC-S's area. Hey, FIDO. You know what? By accident, I'd actually hit just the right levers. The fact that the governor had sat and stoically endured my furry lions had, unwittingly, put the top dog seal of approval over the whole shebang.

The sidebar was a bit of an anti-climax. About twenty of us, ten ISAF and ten Afghans, sat in an open circle. Rather than a normal discussion, we went clockwise round the group for individual comment. The Afghans did their usual solemn statements about being professional and working together. The ISAF staffers all echoed the same sentiments. We spent an hour just agreeing with each other that we agreed we all needed to work together. Everybody left with the proposals, and a firm commitment to meet again in ten days time.

Which was, in Afghan terms, a real result. To get any kind of an agreement in Afghanistan was a real step forward. Afghan projects always go slowly. The only way they succeed is if everybody buys in. Each participant has an opinion—and a right to express it. It's a bit like being in the European Union. We, on the ISAF side, had made life particularly difficult by turning up with so many hangers on. Less folks at the table, less buy-ins needed. For the first meet, I'd done the political thing and brought the kitchen sink and the bath, but I wanted to go lean and mean with the next one. I wanted the numbers whittled. There were just too many damn egos to deal with. I wrote an encouraging note to Paul, which he liked. I was then fucking annoyed to find one of the RC-S staffers writing a negative appraisal of the same event.

They looked at it from the US perspective of time scale. For an entire day travelling and sitting around the governor's pad, we had come away with a firm Afghan agreement to form a committee to discuss an idea. That was all. For a regular army staffer, that was negligible progress. To me, it was remarkable.

It all came down to the rotation thing again. The Afghans had been up and down this particular pole on many occasions before. They would come on board, I was sure of it, but only at their pace.

What had swung the day was a dear Afghan friend of mine reminding the other participants that, in the old days, the Canucks had run a similar committee. Like the Canucks, he stressed that my idea was to give the concept to the committee to run. I was all about brand ownership: to use the McDonald's analogy again, I wanted to franchise the project.

The Afghans had pointedly asked me why they should trust me. Was I worth the effort? I told them they should because I lived in Kandahar, had done for years, and had no intention of leaving. Yet again, my length of tenure counted. When Feroz told them I had invested my own money in the deal, they were sold.

If we'd come to them with another ISAF instruction, they would have turned us down flat. It's why I had called the project 'Our Afghanistan'. Not 'Your Afghanistan'. I wanted that communal buy-in.

Paul gave me the room to run with it. PK did the assist in culling the excess traffic. The planning cell got cut to one RC-S liaison officer. I now owned the idea, pass or fail.

I got hit with another clothing complaint, this time from the police spokesperson. He was a pervy wee shit who had followed me around like a salivating sheepdog all day. PK whacked me with the details over coffee. I was pretty gypped and said so. We had to do a wee reset after that meeting. I wasn't giving in but PK was a general. Sometimes the trains can't help but hit head on. In the interim, I conceded enough to swap out my skinny jeans for a boot-cut pair. Apparently, the sight of the outline of my calves had been the issue. Go figure.

The boys at 205 Corps hit the mother lode by adopting the idea, all on their own. They were pushing hard for election security awareness. They had the job of looking after each of the polling stations. Brigadier Shah, the Chief of Staff for 205, was a pretty sharp cookie. We'd thrashed the concept through and he had bought in, hook, line and sinker.

The voting process involved dipping a digit in a permanent ink, to signify a vote had been cast. It was a powerful image of participation in the democratic process. Entirely of their own accord, 205 ran up these huge billboards of an Afghan soldier and an Afghan civilian, standing together with their inked fingers up, all under the billboard banner of 'Our Afghanistan'.

It was the brand that brought the image to life. Uniform and gun be damned, both people, the soldier and the civilian, were just Afghans. Everything I had been hoping for coalesced in that one image: togetherness, ownership, belonging, familiarity, shared endeavour. The Afghans got what I was after in one easy swoop. It wasn't the photo that joined the message at the hip, it was the slogan and the flag. 205 had devised, produced and distributed it all, with no help at all from us. Paul, PK and I were delighted. We were gathering speed.

Not so within ISAF. Out of the blue, I got a note from the POTF commander, the first in six months. The last time we had spoken direct, I had sent him an urgent e-mail security update about a bombing incident. I'd got a terse one-liner back, saying that he was too important to be bothered with and the name of a subordinate to work it through. This time, he was writing in rather a falsely friendly manner, asking for information on 'Our Afghanistan'. COMISAF had been over and had asked about the project that one of the POTF folks had come up with in the south. POTF had some catch-up to do. Carter had been as good as his word.

I wasn't impressed. I'd been in KAF for over 900 days and nobody had shown the slightest bit of interest in anything I had done. I had been twice nominated for a NATO meritorious service medal by the RC-S generals, which had gone up to the POTF for ratification as my chain of command. I'd just found out that the commander there had unilaterally quashed the noms: without even consulting or telling me. The POTF could only put in for one nod a year, and my nomination had been cut in favour of a Kabul-based hero. Even though my two nods, on two successive years, had been signed off by flag rank officers. I know we are supposed to do the job for the sake of the job, but I'd been pretty fucking chuffed to get one nomination, let alone two. So find out I had been quietly dropped both times without telling me had really pissed me off.

This latest letter was the icing on the busted flush. Nonetheless, I still worked for the POTF, even if my days were all 'OA' and RC-S. The POTF wanted the paperwork, so they could take the project on as part of their operations. I went to RC-S and passed on the news. They were not impressed either. RC-S had put a lot of effort into making the experiment in the south fly, and they had no intention of letting go to an outfit in Kabul they had no ties to.

I was stuck in the middle, between a Romanian colonel who I had never heard of and a bunch of guys who had adopted me as one of their own. To whom I owed the success of the whole project. There were times I wished I had been like everybody else and just kept my mouth shut, done my job, watched the days turn and banked the money. Playing on the high wire was not so much an issue of Afghan failure. The real battle was in fighting all the military egos and ISAF bull.

I tried to do a Clinton and find the third way. I put the Romanian colonel in touch with the RC-S colonel who was looking after the deal. Let them fight it out. The Romanian wasn't amused. I got a note reminding me that he signed my pay cheques. Which didn't amuse me much either. I had been out in the boonies fighting my war for nearly three years, with no assistance or even interest from him at all, at any time. He'd only been there for six months of the struggle. Fuck you.

In any case, remember, last time we had met, he'd told me he was cutting my job. I figured I didn't owe him a pay cheque anymore. He was colonel number five in Kabul, to my one tour in Kandahar. I just ran out of patience with all the crap.

I got word that there may be a compromise position. Instead of cutting the entire FMT section, the POTF would retain two positions. By this stage, there were three of us left. The other two had long since abandoned the field and had been long-distance dialling their locals from the POTF. That had allowed them to build up relationships in Kabul that I just didn't have. I knew nobody there.

On the other hand, I was the most senior hand left standing, with the most service. I had my MSM nods and sheaf of other written commendations and awards that they could not match. I produced more by myself than they did put together. Leaving nothing to chance, Paul, PK and Fanman all wrote me glowing recommendations for my retention. COMISAF supported the OA program. That was a lot of star power on my side. I followed up the blizzard of paper with an interview that I know I knocked out of the park. I hung up the phone feeling pretty confident.

I didn't get the gig. I came last of three.

The Kabul team stuck together. I would be going home, the last FMT left in the field. Well, fuck you then, Mr. Romania. Find your own proposal. That was the last time we spoke, directly or indirectly.

The POTF then tried to rubbish OA as something they had tried before and which didn't work. Wrong.

Once the army billboards turned up, the floodgates opened. By the next meeting downtown, the police and the health department had joined the rush.

The police used the program to advertise road safety, and the health boys used the logo and slogan to top their malaria awareness flyers. Everywhere you looked, Kandahar carried 'Our Afghanistan' posters.

Paul took me downtown for the next big meeting, and personally introduced me by name. Which, I have to admit, was a pretty cool moment for me. I stood, did a quick curtsey, blushed and sat down. Governor Wesa said some lovely words, about welcoming me into the heart of the Kandahar family. And all the big, bluff, bearded boys that would frighten a strong man in daylight all turned and smiled at me. Wesa invited Paul and Raziq and me to join him for tea in his private office. We sat and talked through the next phase, how we could expand the whole concept.

It was one of those 'pinch me, I'm dreaming' moments. After three years of plugging away, here I was with the provincial governor, an American and an Afghan general, all asking my opinion to better work my program. My, oh my. Some days, you just never forget. I floated out of that office for my helter-skelter flight back with Paul in his personal whirly-bird.

Fanman was to add to the personal sense of achievement by giving me a fastball to go to his office. He wasn't there when I arrived. His aide asked me wait in his office, as he would be coming by with an important visitor he wanted me to brief. Around the corner, I saw Fanman coming, alongside Ken Wilsbach, the Air Asset Commanding General, on his last trip south before leaving. No biggie, I thought, I'd briefed him before. The brief wasn't for him: behind Ken was the US Secretary of State for the Air Force, Deborah Lee. I was going to be one-on-one briefing a member of the US cabinet.

Secretary Lee was lovely, and very good at picking my jaw up from the floor. 'I've been told you are somebody I should speak to,' she said, by way of introduction.

Deborah was new in office, on an Afghan fact-finder. She had a wide gamut of questions, everything you could want to ask for an Afghan 101. I remained respectful, but honest. She is a sharp lady. Very polite, but I reckoned honesty was the best policy here. As Ken Wilsbach left, he turned to me and said:

'Thanks, Abi. We asked you to do this as you can say the things we believe in but can't say out loud.'

Deborah Lee wasn't the last senior government member I spoke to either. I had earned my spurs.

Which was the paradox of the time. The unit I was nominally working for had cut me as superfluous. Down in the place I actually lived, I was now the default go-to for background. Every week, I was in seeing the generals, or doing another one of my briefs. Alongside running the whole 'OA' project and supervising the building of the women's park.

You try keeping your morale up in that schizoid environment. I just loved what I was doing: and I truly believe we were on the cusp then of something very important indeed. At the same time, as the personal achievements mounted up, I was getting e-mails asking me to hand my gear back in.

I wasn't the only one being asked to wind it up. When PK had first arrived, Paul had asked him to do what he could in the time left. The sands were running thin for us all.

Across KAF, work crews were trashing the place, pulling down all the clapboard buildings that we had called home for a dozen years or more. The camp was disappearing around our eyes. The concrete walls were still there, but the buildings inside the walls were gone. The roads were empty, the war machines were all leaving. You couldn't paper over the cracks anymore. Even in place as vast and busy as KAF, life had suddenly gone quiet.

When The Boardwalk came down, I knew it was all over. In 2013, 3ID had tried to rip it up, but Soak had withstood the rush. By 2014, the war's end was no longer on the far horizon. Anything non-essential had to go.

The PX went first. All the good stuff—the magazine store, the clothing lines, the computers and the cameras all came off the shelves. What was left was what the US called 'expeditionary': socks, underwear, a few simple food stuffs.

Then The Boardwalk shops went. After years of working for us, the Afghan stores were given three days to close down. To add insult to injury, their contract required them to raze their shops to the ground. At first, you could ignore the holes in the superstructure. There were seventy stores, after all. The restaurants and the big stores got culled: TGI's, the pizza place, Downtown café, the Indian take-out place, the German PX. The Americans took a bulldozer to them all. They had been built out of steel girders. It took weeks to blowtorch them apart.

Every day, I went to work past piles of bricks, broken glass and shards of mortar. The Afghan storekeepers had become friends. They stood in the midst of the destruction of their livelihoods and just looked at me with sad eyes. What could I tell them? KAF still had over 25,000 people inside. I went to the powers that be and told them killing The Boardwalk would destroy morale. We had enough suicides as it was. Did they want to make life in KAF unendurable? 'Yes,' was the reply. 'If we take down The Boardwalk and make it miserable, then maybe we'll manage to encourage the contractors to go home.' The push was on to cut, cut, cut.

Getting rid of a few shops didn't make any sense to me. I took it personally. After so long in KAF, that dusty wooden square was my home. I felt like I was being robbed. The military didn't see it, they came and went, but I had real, emotional roots in the place. My home was being destroyed, right from underneath me.

Bizarrely, as fast as buildings were coming down, construction was still on-going. It took so long to get a contract approved in KAF that some building projects were only just coming on-line, at the same time as were destroying everything else we could.

COMKAF itself was a case in point. The old Taliban's Last Stand got pensioned off. It took over a year to build a sterile, unlovely and unloved concrete block next door. We shuttered the romantic old warren and moved to a block that would itself only last for months before the entire headquarters as an entity would cease to exist. NATO was leaving too. We spent over $10 million on a building we used for less than six months.

KAF plumbing and wiring continued apace. In the good old days, some bright spark had thought that mains electricity and sewerage would be a good idea. Millions had been agreed for construction of an underground cable and water-piping network round the camp. That contract couldn't be turned off. Pledges had been made. Inside compounds, buildings were being flattened, as the road outside was being dug up to receive cables that would never be connected to anything. More millions wasted.

The British Imperial War Museum came to visit with a film crew. They were recording the last, great days of the adventure before it all disappeared. I did an interview for them, showing them around the TLS, pointing out the decades worth of graffiti, where the bombs had hit, the bullet strikes. We ended up on the roof, on the old TOD deck. I pointed out all the hangers, who had been where. The rather pompous Army escort officer told the cameraman to junk the footage, as it was sensitive. 'What does it matter?' I told him. In less than six months, it would all be gone. Forever.

4ID were getting set to go home too. Another year was coming to an end. You could se the momentum changing again. It was always the same. First third, learning the job, second third, real stuff got done, last third, folks just looked forward to going home. Patrols got questioned: was the risk really necessary? The tempo just began to slacken.

The next team came in for their recce. A cavalry bunch, they arrived with blue Stetson cowboy hats and yellow neckerchiefs. The army is such a dressing-up box.

The Afghans outside didn't see any of that decline. 'OA' kept growing more legs and wings. The education department were next on board. They organised a poetry competition, to be run for school-age kids across the whole province. Literally thousands of students were invited to write a few stanzas on the theme of 'Our Afghanistan'. For our part, I got PK to arrange for some microwave ovens as prizes, plus certificates for all participants.

That might all sound a bit bizarre, but poetry is precious in Afghanistan. In the south, there is a long and glorious legacy of wordsmithing. Some of it is raunchy stuff indeed: *'your breasts are the size of pomegranates'* is one memorable line. Every summer, all over the south, poetry competitions were ferociously contested. Poetry reading is the Pashtun equivalent of 'The Voice'. The winners become real stars.

Our prizes, microwave ovens are seen as massive juju. In a land where cooking is paced to the heat of an open fire, the scientific ability to shower food with electronically produced waves is the height of technical sophistication. A microwave is a real status symbol. Our prizes had juice.

Afghans just adore certificates. Any Afghan of note will plaster their office walls with pieces of paper. The more florid and baroque the better, particularly if it comes from an international organisation.

We pitched the gig just right. The poetry competition was going to be a real winner: and the whole idea came from the Afghans themselves. Which was, for me, the real achievement. They just got the idea, and bought the whole deal.

Paul and PK were really pleased. I was quietly delighted too. The Afghans put the cherry on the cake by assigning Deputy Governor Abdul Patyal to run the 'OA' committee. The provincial executive got right behind my idea too.

Abdul Qadim Patyal was something of a celebrity in Kandahar. He had been a visiting poetry fellow at Kandahar University. When the Taliban had come to power, the writing of poetry was deemed un-Islamic. Patyal carried on with writing anyway; and was imprisoned for his beliefs. His art was published across south Asia. His words from that time still carry the mark of the struggle for freedom. And his contempt for the Taliban:

'The rush of the devils have started again
And they are counted as devils
But they are more professional than the original devils in this work
They have the ability to commit fraud in their work
They count themselves the most professional

They count themselves the servants of the galaxy
But the real true love is the hug of the sun.'

When the Taliban fell, Patyal became the head of culture for Kandahar Province. Under his watch, artists like Durukshan had flourished. Governor Wesa then appointed him deputy governor. Patyal knew he was taking a massive risk. Deputy governor made him a prime target.

He was a gentle man in life. In a country where officials tend to look like rough and tough versions of Gandalf, Patyal was an aesthete. Always immaculately turned out, clean shaven, with long, delicate fingers, he looked more like a concert pianist. Patyal was the ideal candidate to lead the OA project. Under his tutelage, and with his authority, the committee flourished. Instead of leading the conversation, I sat back and let the Afghans take the reins themselves.

Everybody had an idea they wanted to pitch. The sports department wanted to run a football tournament. All they asked for was strips for the winning teams as prizes. I agreed: we'd get them run up in the national colours, with 'Our Afghanistan' across the front. If I couldn't get the money from ISAF, I'd pay for them myself.

The women's department wanted help with a meeting room at the governor's palace, where they could meet to discuss women's issues. Patyal agreed to that one too, to be called the 'Our Afghanistan women's space'.

The poetry competition was to be extended north to include Uruzgan province: a development that Dr Patyal was particularly pleased with. The army and police carried on with their stuff too, developing leaflets and flyers using the OA theme on operations.

In short, for the first time in years, Afghan leaders were actively taking charge of an ISAF-inspired project. Governor Wesa invited me into his private quarters for tea. He was delighted. He told me that, while he respected ISAF, we had always told him what was going to happen, how it was going to happen and how Afghans would benefit.

'We were never involved, dear Abi,' he told me, with a regretful shake of his head. 'You came with all this money but did what you wanted. In Kandahar, we have many professional people who could have done this work. Yet, we were never asked.' From the beginning, he had demanded that the OA program be published in Pashto, and the projects derived from Afghan interest. Which was all absolutely fine by Paul, Patrick and me. Who wants to do all the work? Afghanistan is their country. Who are we to tell them how to run their lives?

Security stuff meant I couldn't always get downtown. ISAF had closed all the bases in the city. Just getting to the governor's place meant a four hour journey by road, picking up security escorts, being briefed, doing all the necessary checks. It was exhausting. But so, so satisfying.

As delighted as I was by the progress, I knew I was lying. I had asked them to believe in me because I had said Kandahar was my home and I was staying. They had believed me. The project was working. Everything we had hoped for was coming to pass. I had the sword of Damocles hanging over me.

ISAF was demanding I leave. Right at the moment of success, my unit wanted rid of me. Paul and Patrick protested the notion. As did Fanman. They wrote to Joe Anderson, the three-star general who now ran the IJC, the second most important general in the whole operation. They told me not to worry. RC-S wanted me to stay. The program was working, and the Americans wanted it to carry over to the next rotation. I would be the only mission memory, one more for the Gipper. It would have been my fourth annual rotation.

One last time at one last meeting, Patyal shook my hand, a rare thing indeed for a Pashtun male to a female foreigner, and thanked me for bringing this together. We now had a Kandahar Information Committee. Every department had put forward a representative. They would meet every fortnight. Of course, it was all very stilted and long-winded. But stuff was happening.

The committee was making the news. I was interviewed by several local papers. Patyal and I did a grip and grin press conference. Patyal wore an immaculately ironed, pristine white shalwar kameez. He had such gentle features, almost feminine, with big, round, expressive eyes. Classically handsome, very similar to Jude Law, I liked him very much. We spoke at length about Kandahar's future. He walked me to the gate of the governor's palace, and waved me off. I turned to wave, as he stood, a lone figure in the midst of a glorious rose garden. It was the last time I saw him.

When I got back to KAF, my leaving orders had been cut. Despite all the letters and the phone calls, despite a bevy of US and Australian generals who actively wanted me to stay, they were over-ruled by the Romanian colonel at the POTF. The manning plot had been set in stone. The mission was not about increasing Afghan capacity anymore. It was about cutting jobs, closing bases and sending folks home.

The POTF had looked at my project: and dismissed it as un-workable. Nobody ever came to Kandahar to see what we had been doing. Nobody even phoned. There was no room at the inn for me. I was devastated. Three years work, three years risk, in the most dangerous part of the country, counted for nothing. We were on the cusp of delivering the project, a project that COMISAF, Joe Dunford, himself had signed off. The foundations for the women's park were being laid. The murals were finished. All on my own, everything I had ever dreamed of was actually happening.

I wrote to Dunford direct. One last grasp for glory. I had nothing to lose. He may be a four-star general, running the war, but this was important. He wrote me a lovely note back again, and told me he'd look at it.

Paul asked me over to his office. He asked me what I wanted to do. I told him I wanted to stay and see it through. Paul wrote, there and then, to Joe Anderson, his boss, at the IJC. The two are old friends. Paul took over 4ID from Anderson. Paul used personal political capital to fight for me, a mere contractor. Not as a favour, but because he believed in what we were doing, and my part in it. That's the kind of man, and the kind of leader, he is. Anderson replied that he had handed it on to the personnel and finance boys.

Paul could do no more.

LaCamera told me he wanted to give me something. He offered me the choice of a 4ID engraved knife, or a 4ID pen set. I'm a writer. I took the pen. We sat and talked until he could put off the staff no more. The war still needed to be fought. We hugged one last time, he thanked me for my service, and I was gone. It's the last time I saw him.

The finance guy wrote back with the inevitable. Yes, the project was important, but NATO had to cut the personnel bill. Regardless of the support or the success of the work, I had to go. And then it was my turn to go to the inevitable leaving dos. I had been to dozens through the years. I couldn't believe that now it was my turn.

I did one last brief to all the colonels. I couldn't finish it. I broke down. Most folks were desperate to leave KAF. I was desperate to stay. Colonels looked at their shoes a bit, then shuffled out. Lots of contingent guys came up and gave me gifts, citations, mementoes, plaques, commemorative coins, the whole nine yards. People were lovely: but I was empty and numb. I didn't want to go home.

Paul and PK took me out for dinner. Two generals took an evening off from running the war to say goodbye to a nobody. I gave them both a copy each of Churchill's memoirs of his time on the North-West Frontier. PK gave me a huge toy lion, in recognition of Marjan and Chucha. I have no idea where he got it from. It was a wonderful gesture.

My second last day, PK invited me to an Australian medal ceremony. Lines of young faces proudly smiled as PK gave them tray after tray of medals. Kandahar could be a terrible, violent place, but it also made an awful lot of young men and women. A whole generation grew up there. And proved themselves the equal of any generation before them. No matter who you were, no matter how short a stay, Kandahar left a branding mark on us all.

PK gave a very stirring speech, pure Napoleon. I had never seen that side of him, the public commander. Lord, he was good. And, right at the end, he asked me to stand, and said a few words about 'Our Afghanistan' and what I had achieved. A whole Australian rotation had to stand and listen to stories about toy lions and daft logos. I made a fool of myself and cried: again.

The bad guys sent me a leaving present too, in the form of one last ground attack. I was on Skype to home when the Giant Voice warble kicked off:

'Ground attack, ground attack....'

My corridor was full of young ones, new in-country. I could hear the nervous discussions in the corridor. Nobody knew what to do. The immediacy of war kicked right in. I excused myself from the video phone, went out and organised a long and a short weapon on each exit, made sure everybody was in armour, called the ops room for an update and came back and carried right on talking, wearing my own helmet and body armour.

I was going home in a couple of days. Man, that stuff got fucking old fucking quickly. The people I was speaking to back in the world had a real-life inside track to the madness. They sat there with their tongues on the ground. For me, all the action was just normal jogging. I'd been there so long, bad guys in the wire was just another day in the suck.

The Role 3 hospital invited me over to help celebrate the anniversary of the creation of the navy corpsman. Corpsmen are the field medics who patch the wounded up. Mary Beth Neill, the ballsy colonel who ran the whole shebang, met me at the gate. She told me I was the guest of honour. On my last few hours in KAF, they had not forgotten me.

I always liked going over to the hospital. The medics kept a pristine meditation garden, with lovely wind chimes and carefully tended flowerbeds. It was a quiet corner amidst the madness. Somewhere that humanity was never forgotten.

The evening was a formal one. Hundreds of guests lined up for a buffet dinner. I sat next to Mary Beth as her corpsmen enacted a series of play-lets, recreating the ages of the corpsman. From the early days of rigged sail ships, though Vietnam to now, each three-minute segment ended with one of the amateur actors being shot and tended to. Accompanied by blood-curdling screams and a bucket of raspberry coloured liquid doubling for the real thing.

Beth is a ballsy lady. She is a dentist by profession. When the Georgian battalion arrived, they brought six hundred sets of Soviet-era teeth. Replete with enough steel fillings to resemble rows of James Bond Jaws look-alikes. When they found out that ISAF offered free in-theatre dental care, Mary Beth's chair was rarely empty. They queued around the block to get Stalin's mercury taken out.

Mary Beth and I ended the evening with a mad half hour of hip-hop line dancing. We twerked and shook with the eighteen year-olds, to a soundtrack I didn't understand but which fit the moment. I danced to stave off the despair.

Last night was my official turn to say 'good-bye'. Fanman had organised a big old cook-out behind the base operations centre. We met in the same spot where I had toasted Scott Dennis and Soak had told me of his name-earning, near-death flight years earlier. I had helped build the damned place: and now it would host my epitaph.

Over one hundred people came. As did Faizi, Fanman and Patrick. General Sherzai came with whole staff. That wasted me. He'd braved the nonsense security checks we made him go through to come see me off. My leaving do, nobody important, I had three generals say nice things about me.

PK said some more words, so did Faizi and Sherzai. Fanman did a lovely speech about 'Our Afghanistan' and what it had meant. Faizi gave me a nice certificate, as did Fanman, along with another medal. Sherzai topped the lot by presenting me with a pure silk carpet the size of my living room. It was so heavy I couldn't hold it. Most of the troops there that night had never heard of Faizi or General Sherzai. I did a wee speech, talking them up. They deserved it. I managed a thank-you to my brother Fanman. He had been my guardian and protector for a year.

Then it came PK's turn. Without him, the whole 'Our Afghanistan' project would have been nothing. I had some words written down. It just got too much. I just ran out of fuel. The words dried in my throat. I just stood and looked at him.

The years of work, the joy, the laughter, the pain, the loss, the despair, the boredom, the madness, the whole shooting rocket to the skies just came crashing in. I mumbled some words about service, thanking all of them for being there, for what they were doing for freedom. And then it was done.

They all headed off, back to their jobs. KAF never truly slept. The war was still going on. My moment was over. The limb had been severed.

I walked back to my room alone.

ANJA

Anja Neidringhaus was one of the world's best photo-journalists. In a glittering career, she was, amongst a slew of accolades, part of a Pulitzer-prize winning team that covered the Iraq war.

I first met Ana during the awful Balkan wars of the 1990s. What made her different was the quiet way she went about photographing the victims of the war. The rest of us were all busy fighting over the war porn: the UN stuff, machines of war, the bang-bang that made a lot of careers, my own included.

Ana would go off on her own, shooting something kooky. She just had a different way of seeing the mundane in an extraordinary way. Her pictures are a study in contrast, suffused with a hint of humour: a soldier, dressed in a bright red Santa Claus outfit, surrounded by a sea of ochre camouflage. A burned out tank being used as a playground by a swarm of kids. In the worst of circumstances, she always found a way to show humanity's struggle. As a person, she just loved life. She went from the Balkans to shooting international tennis championships. I just loved her sensitivity. Her talent was phenomenal.

She was in Afghanistan from the beginning. Often in the company of another redoubtable female journalist, Kathy Gannon. Unlike most of us, Kathy had stuck with Afghanistan through it all. Even in Taliban times. She never covered her hair either. It was just her thing. I just love sassy women who do it their way.

Both Kathy and Anja built a formidable reputation by working on their own, away from the pack. They did embeds, like the rest of us, but then they'd just shoot off and do their own thing from the other side, out in the badlands. There are probably no other journalists alive who could match the two of them for the sheer length of time they had devoted to covering Afghanistan.

In April 2014, they cut away from the rest to get the skinny on the election. I knew Kathy was in town when she appeared in the middle of a shoot-out at Raziq's place. His police guards cut down a couple of suicide bombers trying to get into Raziq's compound. Feroz was there: right in the background was Kathy, just snapping away.

Anja and Kathy hooked up a couple of weeks later to head over to Khost Province to cover election papers being delivered. They went with the Afghan police, in a civilian vehicle. No protection team, nothing. Just them trusting in the Afghans. Kathy was 60 and Anja 48, two women out there in the boonies doing it their way. Nobody else was out in the regions. It was just too damn dangerous.

After the election stuff had been delivered, Anja got into the left rear seat of her car. Kathy got into the seat beside her. They were being watched by a local police commander, called Naqibullah. He walked up to a colleague, took his AK-47 from him, and walked up to the left side of the car where the two journalists were sitting, waiting to leave.

Shouting' Allah U Akbar', Naqibullah opened up on full automatic into the car. Anja was closest and took the brunt of the fire. Her body protected Kathy. Even so Gannon was hit six times, in the body and arm. Anja was mortally wounded. Despite a madcap drive to hospital, she died en-route.

The world lost a precious spirit.

Kathy underwent months of re-constructive surgery. Naqibullah was disarmed, arrested and sentenced to death. He said in his defence that he had been avenging the death of family members from a NATO air strike.

The Taliban had warned that all westerners were now targets. Nobody could be counted as safe anymore.

I took Anja's death hard. The violent and senseless manner of her passing was another body blow, after so many others. Stay in Afghanistan, then your number came up. So many friends dead, so many talented people just slaughtered for no discernable reason.

I went to The Boardwalk running track and ran. I ran for miles, until I could physically run no more. The usual crowd were out enjoying the five-dollar lattes. The music was blasting. The 'Kandahar Chokers' cigar-lovers club were furiously puffing away. Suddenly, I fucking hated them all. For their complacency and self-satisfied air of superiority. What the fuck did they know? They came for six months, strutted around inside KAF and thought they'd 'done' Afghanistan.

Anja had been trying to tell the world for decades that Afghanistan was more than just a medal destination for endless rotations of soldiers.

Durukshan was putting the finishing touches to the 'Our Afghanistan' mural. I asked him to dedicate it to Anja Neidringhaus. Durukshan knew what had happened. Completely off his own bat, he added two birds of peace next to her name. I like it that everybody that enters or leaves Kandahar will read her name.

She shot a single frame downtown, at one of the newly opened parks. It is of a father on a scooter. Perilously perched with him are no less than five children. One, his daughter, is smiling excitedly at the camera. She is going to the park with her papa. Her father has one arm out, fist stuffed with a wad of Afghanis. He is passing the entry fee to an anonymous outstretched palm. Consciously, Anja evokes the classic 'Creation of Adam', by Michelangelo. The opening of the park was, indeed, an act of creation for the new

Afghanistan. Parks were banned under the Taliban. Fun was banned, enjoyment was banned. Life was banned. Life is different now in Afghanistan. her photo shows that re-birth. It is its own act of creation.

That image is my favourite. Anja just encompassed in one frame everything you needed to know about how Afghans were struggling to survive and thrive in a half-formed state of chaos.

It is funny, touching and perfectly composed. Just as, in life, the woman was too.

LAST POST

I got up early, to go see the sunrise. Last chance for a vitamin D shot: 0500 morale booster. The dear old place was much quieter, now the planes and most of the soldiers had gone. Kandahar, Kandahar.... How was I going to replace it all? Every step had a memory: where I had twisted my ankle on that first day, the troughs where the water had gathered to flood the NATO blocks, they gym where I had learned Zumba, the bunker where I sheltered.

And The Boardwalk: where all the good times had happened. I stood on the stage where Toby Keith had sung of bombing A-rabs, with 5,000 screaming GI's roaring their approval. Where the British dancing girls had whipped themselves and their audience into a frenzy. The war memorial was still there, with its totem poles and signs, pointing the way home: the way I now had to travel.

I went to the Green Bean, where my regular barista Oliver was still on duty, bleary-eyed from another all-nighter. Past the empty plinths where once had stood KAF's emporiums of cheap wares. There wasn't much left. The wrecking crews had done their jobs well. Still, I remembered who had owned what, where Steffi and I had laughed and cried.

The guys from the Green Bean all came out to say good-bye. Most of them had been there longer than me. I felt the tears start at the back of my eyes. So many people came and went like the wind, most were just forgotten in the maelstrom. Yet they remembered me. I thought I was cried out: a fortnight of open wounds, never-ending farewells, dinners and handshakes had left me numb. The Green Bean boys opened up the barely healing scab all over. We hugged and shared a last joke. They gave me my large latte and weird yellow cake thing for free.

The early morning running crew was slowly growing. The old running track was back in business. On the football pitch, some young marines were doing wrestling moves on each other. I heard the peals of laughter. My time had arrived to hand over the torch. I suddenly felt old. KAF had stripped the years from me. The place had made me feel thirty. It couldn't last: I was suddenly fifty again. The adrenalin shots were limited. I was the run flat tyre that had just hit the biggest pothole going.

24 hours ago, I had been part of the team, valued and admired. Now, I was just another middle-aged chick, lost at sea. The sun slowly rose across the horizon. I felt its heat on my back. How I had come to love the warmth. Forty degrees? Just wonderful, thank-you very much.

I took it for granted the sun would be there, every day. In Scotland, I ran outside every time the bright, golden orb made an appearance, in case it disappeared. In KAF, it was just there, every day. My skin glowed with health. Now, this would be my last sunrise.

I sat there for as long as I could. I didn't want to go. I loved this fly-blown, distant shit-hole.

My old friend Andy, who had paced the park dimensions with me, came to sit with me. He knew how much I was hurting. He just sat beside me, saying nothing. Until he looked at his watch and gently said:

'Abi, it's time. You have to go.'

I burst into tears. The dam just broke, as it is breaking again as I write these words. I had fought, argued, cajoled, bitched and moaned about the system, the Americans, the army, the place, the whole fucked up mess of a place. But it was my HOME. I didn't just live in Kandahar. KAF had nurtured me and protected me. Everywhere I went, people waved at me. Folks came to find me, to ask me for stuff. My brain was picked, my knowledge put to good use, my skills demanded.

In return, I had fussed over them all. Those men and women there were my family. I had loved them all with the passion of a mother. I had mourned the loss of every life and prayed that each and every one of those precious souls would go home with all their fingers and toes intact.

I was the space shuttle on permanent re-entry. My heat shield was warping. I had wrapped myself so tightly around the vine I had become part of the tree. For all that, I wept. Not casual tears: deep-seated tears of loss. Andy embraced me, leaned my head on his shoulders, and let me smear mascara and snot all over his clean white shirt. He knew. He would be 65 in a couple of months, NATO retirement age, when he too would be forcibly discarded. He shared my tears, in his own discreet way. I cried for both of us.

He did his man thing, and took my hand to lead me to his truck. If he hadn't been there, I would have just sat there and watched the plane take off without me. I would have become another KAF homeless person, wandering in the twilight. I didn't have it in me to freely unplug. Andy had to do it for me.

Andy threw my battered gold cases into the flatbed, heavy with the weight of Sherzai's carpet and PK's lion. I gave him my room key, to look after, until I came back. We both knew inside that was not going to happen, but I couldn't give up the dream. I couldn't articulate that this was the end. It hurt too much. I was still part of ISAF for another week, until my contract ran out. I told myself I was just going on another leave, same as before. I wasn't cut. I still had a home.

The departure terminal was full of the usual contractor flotsam. Andy and I joined the happy queue of departees. I half-heard the usual calls:

'Where you headed, man? 'Home to Tennessee.... Me and Jack Daniels have a relationship to start up...'

I was already home. My feet stood on the land I wanted to be part of. Going back to the world scared me. I didn't belong there. I belonged here, in KAF, where my family was just getting ready to go to work.

I looked round for Michael. He had gone with his senior staff to the steps of the big bird of freedom, to see them off. Would he come to mine? I wanted to ask him if he had heard anything. Was there still hope I could stay? He didn't show. There was nothing left for him to say—and KAF still needed commanding. I was gone, but the curtains still needed to be pulled back for today's one act play.

Andy hugged me one last time. He told me I was wonderful, what I had done was important, and I was leaving a legacy. He had to go, work was calling. I watched him walk away, with his bandy-legged stride, off to do something meaningful: as I had done until this day of days. He was all khaki safari jacket and Gurkha hat, an English eccentric in a sea of conformity. I miss him so.

His words meant a lot, but I knew my legacy was as permanent as a love wish written in the sand. The in-coming tide would wipe them away. My legacy would wither the day I left, and would be gone in an instant when the last soldier I had known rotated home. Nobody ever stayed. Nobody ever remembered.

I was in a few of the fading group photos of the COMKAF command group. My image would hang on the wall for another couple of months. Maybe a new troop would ask:

'Who's the chick with the feather boa?'

Somebody might reply, 'oh, she worked here for a bit', or something equally anodyne. And everybody would go back to work. Most likely, nobody would ever look, and the pictures would go unnoticed, next to all the other unnoticed pictures. in any case, the whole place was scheduled for closure in a couple of months. My picture would end up in a builder's skip, along with all the others.

KAF, though, will be in my heart forever. You can't take that away. None of you, nor any of the fuckers who ended the program before it had really got going. For a moment there, me, PK, Michael and Paul did stuff that could have changed the war, and re-written the history books. Those men will forever be my brothers. We were a moment, you know... a real, bona fide, American idol, star wattage, spotlight on glory, motherfucking moment.

Now it was gone.

The old aerotech airline boys gave me my usual seat up front. They knew I was going for good, but nobody mentioned it. It was the embarrassing truth none of us could confront. As the door closed, they awkwardly shook my hand and wished me a pleasant flight.

We taxied down past all the empty revetments. I knew them all. The ones where the French had shown me their Mirages, the one where NASA had their secret planes that we weren't allowed to talk about. The British special forces place. All of them were empty now. Nothing left but grey concrete. Everybody had gone home.

The only place with life was the civilian terminal. I imagined old Faizi out back with his songbirds, measuring the distance between his freshly planted trees, over where my park was being built. It stretched down to Durukshan's mural with my name: and Ana's and Michael's. Maybe Faizi would remember me.

Finally, down past the Afghan Air Wing, where the helicopters sat in an arrow straight line. They flew every day now. Somewhere in there, old Sherzai would be having tea—and laughing. Behind it, Camp Hero. Hamid would be hosting tea again, in his quiet, modest way.

We turned onto the runway for the last time, and rocked gently to a halt. We waited while I was granted one last KAF salute. Two RAF Tornados sat on the pan, right in front of my window: their wings heavy with camera pods and missiles. I scrambled in my handbag to find my iPad, to film their take-off, as the engines wound up, bright orange flames bursting out of the exhausts. I thought of John and Scott and Michael, my old bosses, whom I had loved and admired. I had watched them in their jets, on exactly the same spot.

The pilots hit the afterburner: first one, then the other. They started slow, as the noise built and the flames grew. Then, from nothing, they just exploded down the runway, one behind the other. I watched their exhaust glitter, then fade, as they flew off towards the horizon. The Tornados, too, would be gone within a couple of months.

The tears came again, swift and fast. We gathered speed down the runway. I felt the bump as we went over the old join in the tarmac that the Americans had put in to extend the runway. As we took off, I saw the empty hole, all that was left of Tundra's compound, where I had spent my first Christmas. Then, it was gone. KAF was behind me. Below, the green fields gave way to ochre desert. My adventure was over. KAF had gone, disappeared into the jet trail.

I booked into the Grand Hyatt in Dubai, and tried to tell myself this was just another leave. I tried hard to enjoy the splendour of my surroundings. I had a beer, and people watched. They were just shadows. The wealth meant nothing. I wanted to be back in KAF.

I went up to my room early. I took PK's lion out of my case, and sat him on the bed next to me. I talked to him, a stupid, stuffed animal, as if it were PK and Michael and Paul and all my other chums, right there in the room with me. I took a picture of me there, no make-up, hugging a child's toy, chugging a couple of Budweisers. I sent it to them all, back in KAF: my eyes are bright red. My smile is false. I tried, for them at least, to be happy:

'Having a drink for all of you!'

I was supposedly going home—but I had left my home behind. The boys sent me encouraging replies. 'Go, girl!' 'Have one for me!' It made no difference.

My war was over: and I will never be the same again.

LAST ENCORE

I hated being in the World. It was fucking freezing. I came back to the UK in the height of summer. In Kandahar, it had been nearly fifty degrees. In the UK, I went out wrapped up in a cardigan and an anorak.

I went through all the usual veteran stuff.

A woman in front of me in the supermarket queue complained that her cut flowers had wilted. I wanted to ram the fucking stems down her throat. People were dying in Kandahar. All she could do was moan about plants??

My neighbours set up a paddling pool for the local kids in the communal gardens around my home. I went crazy at the noise. I couldn't deal with the commotion. In Kandahar, folks running about signalled stuff was going down. I couldn't deal with the constant fight or flight twitches.

I obsessively cleaned all the time. Everything had to be perfect. Towels had to be lined up on rails, clothes perfectly pressed. I scrubbed my body in a daily bath, rubbing at imaginary dirt, physically trying to get Kandahar off my skin.

Three weeks into being in the World, I snapped. I bought a big and very fast sports car. I went off to the end of the Scottish Western Isles. Any further away, I'd have parked in the Atlantic. I holed up in a cottage in the ass-end of nowhere while I put myself back together. I started writing, but every second word was 'fuck'. Now it's every fourth. I am getting better. I wasn't writing a book then, more a self-immolation of fury and rage.

Michael and Patrick both dropped me concerned e-mails. They too were winding up their tours. Patrick left first, then Michael. Both gone by end-August. Everybody I cared about had left. I had nothing to hang onto. No news from home.

COMKAF itself got shuttered. The big, fancy headquarters that had taken three years to get built had stayed open for a mere six months. The building, split new, millions spent, got padlocked and abandoned.

Three months into purgatory, of being home, dear old Sherzai wrote to me. He missed me. I welled up just hearing from him. We Skyped and he asked if I would be interested in coming back to visit with him and his family. Sherzai brought me home.

I took off for Dubai. Sherzai's son, Farid, hosted me in a swanky hotel and we toured around his business empire. I'd known the family were worth a few bob, but the extent of their riches popped into perspective. They owned a significant portion of one of Dubai's most exclusive residential retreats. The Sherzais were seriously blinged: in real gold.

I was invited back to Kandahar. The deal was to help the general get his family history into order, maybe turn it into a book for him and his. I jumped at the chance. Home beckoned.

I was genuinely excited to be landing at KAF again. We flew in on Ariana, the old scary airways. The flight was only half-full. I was the only Westerner, and the only female, on board. The crew sat us on our own, up at the front, while twenty pairs of eyes behind us stroked their collective beards and wondered just who the heck I was.

KAF was deserted. I couldn't believe how quiet it all was. As we taxied in to the civilian terminal, I craned my eyes out of the window, looking for the old hubbub. There was nothing. No aircraft, no people, no movement. What buildings and hangers that remained were either empty or shuttered. When we disembarked, I could hear birds chirruping. KAF was deserted. Six months earlier, you couldn't have moved for combat aircraft. Now, everybody had gone.

Faizi was still at the airport. We met in a blizzard of hugs and smiles. It was wonderful to see him again. He had prepared the most delicious lunch. As ever, his wife had gone to town on the cooking. We sat in his office and talked of old times.

Since I had left, the airport committee had been dissolved, through lack of interest. When Michael and the whole of COMKAF left, commitment in the airfield had gone with them. Faizi was on his own. He'd taken on more responsibility, but was even more bitter about the legacy. 'They are leaving us nothing, Abi,' he told me. ' I have begged and begged to get our people trained, but they still won't let my staff into the control tower.'

Despite Michael's best efforts, the private contractors had gone on their merry way. Their contract was due to run out in less than six months. Afghans would then be asked to run an Afghan air hub, but nothing—not a single thing—had been done to train them for that moment.

Faizi was even more bitter about the British legacy:

'We went over to Bastion to see what the British had left,' he told me. 'We went up into the tower. They stripped everything. They left nothing we could use. The radars, the control screens, the fuel trucks, everything… all gone. All you left were some golf carts and three walkie-talkie radios. That is all your country left me to run an airport.'

I liked and admired Faizi. He still wore his old western business suit. He had worked with the West for ten years, and had tried hard to like us in return. His disappointment was palpable.

Outside, he was still planting trees like crazy. Bambi and Thumper were still in their cage and the songbirds were in full lilt. We walked around the site for Paradise Park. The foundations were being put in. I could see where the water-course would be, where the gazebos would sit. It had taken three years of my life to breathe life into this.

Faizi led me down to the main gate. The 'Our Afghanistan' frieze was still there. The paint was beginning to peel in the corners, but the whole was still in one piece. I read my name aloud, and Michael's and Durukshan and Feroz, and dear Ana's. All of us had contributed to this.

Sherzai put me up in his hotel. Six months earlier, four hundred people had lived here. Now, nothing but tumbleweed occupied the compound. Six private security contractors and engineers lived in one container block. They were vainly trying to finish off the Kajaki dam hydro-electric project. Five years after the British Army had delivered the turbines in their boxes to the site, they were still lying there, gradually rusting away into the Kajaki dirt.

I was the only other hotel occupant. It was scary quiet. Nothing worked. The food, such as it was, was inedible. I got appalling food poisoning on the second day. I couldn't choose which end to eject from.

Sherzai remained his usual loveable self. Filling myself with Imodium, I struggled over to meet him. We hugged and laughed over lunch, while I did my best to keep from vomiting my glass of water. His office was even more crammed with certificates and plaques. Before, the whole display had seemed an expression of his commitment and drive. Now, at the fag-end of the adventure, the place was a mausoleum. He wanted me to collate it all for him. He knew the end was coming. He wanted a record of his time with the Americans, for his children.

I stayed for a bit. I went over to see Faizi at the airport. He talked enthusiastically of building his hotel, and a new terminal. We met with his American advisor: another new face I didn't know. Faizi said she never came over to see him. He lamented the passing of the old days. 'Now, nobody comes to see me,' he mourned.

The new American was suspicious of me. She told me she was scared to be in the airport. She'd volunteered for the Af-Pak program to help her promotion prospects. She hadn't counted on being alone in an Afghan airport. She didn't trust the Afghans and wanted to go home to her cats. I had arranged extra funding for the park, to buy swings for the kids, but I would need ISAF help to get the stuff shipped. I asked if I could get badged to go into KAF. She told me she'd get back to me but I never heard from her again.

An old friend of mine, still within KAF, phoned me. She had stayed, part of the security team. She told me the American army ran everything now. All they did was rip stuff down. Nobody left the wire to go anywhere. Nobody wanted to be the last one to die.

I did smuggle myself into KAF one last time, on my old ISAF badge, which was still in date. I went in with the private security guys who shared the compound with us. The Georgian and Bulgarian gate guards were gone. In their place, bored Americans barely registered us before waving our vehicle through. They didn't get out of their armour-plated hut to speak to us.

Inside, KAF was bare. The place was littered with concrete pads, the foundation where once buildings had stood. What remained—piles of wood, mattresses, boxes, twisted metal, hundreds of empty containers—sat in abandoned piles. Barely a human could be seen. The Boardwalk wooden structure still stood, alone, forlorn, with an empty lattice of roadways around it. The silence was eerie. KAF was over. Everybody had left.

It was truly depressing. Suddenly, I didn't want to be there anymore. Sherzai understood. To the end, he remained my friend. We embraced awkwardly. We both knew this was the final goodbye. I had come back, but the machine that had supported me and which I had represented had abandoned them. I think he hoped I could have got the Americans engaged, one last time, like it was before, when Paul, Patrick, Michael, John and Scott were around.

I didn't have the juice anymore. There was nothing I could do. The machine had expelled me. Nobody inside KAF cared.

Faizi drove me into the airport, past the layers of enthusiastic police guards. Curious Afghans took our pictures and stood staring. I went into the female search area, where a robustly-framed female put me through the usual Afghan search ritual of intimate moves best kept to the bedroom. She had put her make-up on with a trowel. Her rouged cheeks glowing with pink ardour.

She smiled at me and asked:

'Afghanistan, good?'

'Yes', I wanted to say, 'this country has been very good to me.' I couldn't. I had never wanted to leave first time around. I felt ashamed that I was doing it all over again.

We had promised these people we would always be their rock. We had told them there was no more important struggle in the world than the battle they faced to re-build their country. We had brought soldiers and guns and planes and bombs. We had brought an awful lot of fighting and death. Then, we got bored of Afghanistan.

Change was neither quick enough, nor had the Afghans shown us sufficient gratitude. The leader we had appointed to be our patsy Afghan president had shown far too much independent thought. Thirteen years on, the West had not been able to tie the whole package up with a bow and gift itself a neat victory. We just up and walked.

War is inherently messy: messy in its inception, its conduct and its aftermath. We forgot that.

My last departure was just as conflicted. I felt torn between an unspoken obligation to stay with these people who had accepted me, and a relentless emotional exhaustion with the never-ending struggle of it all. There was the struggle against Afghanistan's enemies, to be sure. But that hadn't defeated me. What conquered me was the struggle to fight our own system. ISAF had exhausted me. There had just been too many rotations, too many made ideas, too much military BS.

At the end of the day, I realised Afghanistan was not truly my homeland. I had fought, cajoled, persuaded and dreamed for it. But I could get out. I had a passport that allowed me to travel. An Afghan passport without a visa will take you to Iran, Dubai and Pakistan. Nowhere else. I was lucky. I could go anywhere.

1,000 days before, I had returned as part of a great expedition. I believed Afghanistan was worth fighting for. Had God not spared me, I would have given my life for the dream. 1,000 days later, Afghanistan had drained me, to the last dregs.

As we boarded our Ariana flight to the world, the steward winked and gave me his phone number. We took off in darkness. I skulked away from Kandahar, lost and destitute.

I had nothing left to give.

WATCHING FROM AFAR

On May 24th 2015, Eric Robinson, a forty year-old resident of Eagar, Arizona, was shot dead by law enforcement officers after a protracted gun battle. He was the 453rd person killed by US police since the start of 2015.

UK casualties incurred in Afghanistan, for the period of October 2001 to mid-2014, some 13 years of combat operations, stands at 453 dead. That number includes non-combat deaths, accidental shootings and suicides.

It took very nearly thirteen years of full-on war to kill the same number of heavily armed, well-protected and trained British soldiers as American civilian police officers killed in less than six months.

Michael Brown was a big lad. Aged 18 at the time of his death, he stood at 6'4" tall, weighing in at a very comfortable 295 pounds. He lived in Ferguson, Missouri: a town with a pre-dominantly African-American population. Brown was an African-American.

Late on the morning of August 9th, 2014, he stole a box of cigars from a local store. Responding to the call, Officer Darren Wilson of the Ferguson Police Department sped to the scene. Wilson is also a big man. Aged 28 at the time, he stands 6'4" tall, weighing in at an athletic 210 pounds. Wilson caught up with Brown and a friend minutes later. An altercation resulted, where Wilson and Brown ended up wrestling with each other. Wilson's service pistol was drawn and he fired a reported two rounds, one of which wounded Brown in the thumb. Brown ran off, away from Wilson, but pursued by the officer on foot. About 150 feet further down the road, roughly the length of a football field, Wilson caught up with Brown. Accounts differ, but the general opinion is that Brown turned on Wilson.

Wilson fired his service weapon another ten times. At least six of those rounds hit Brown, including an instantly fatal one through Brown's right eye. The bullets were later estimated to have been fired from no further than three feet away. Audio analysis of a sound recording made at the time estimated that six rounds were fired, followed by a pause, then a further four rounds.

Brown was killed by a fusillade of shots, at close range: for the crime of stealing a box of cigars. A crowd gathered at the scene, which quickly turned ugly. At least twenty other police cars raced to the scene, accompanied by a heavily armed SWAT team.

A grand jury acquitted Wilson of any crime. The court opined that Wilson was justified in fearing for his life.

In his own evidence, Wilson, the same size as Brown, and in considerably better shape, stated that in wrestling with Brown he 'felt like a 5-year-old holding onto Hulk Hogan.' He went to say that he had considered reaching for his mace spray, or his baton, which were next to his pistol on his issue belt, but that he could not reach them. He drew his pistol instead. Brown was unarmed. Wilson's only injury was a bruise on his face.

Brown's high-profile death proved a catalyst for revealing a series of police killings of African-American citizens that has caused months of national rioting directed towards fear and loathing of a pre-dominantly white police force.

A civil policing force has increasingly come to resemble an occupation: uniformed, armed and trained to act as an army.

The two functions are mutually exclusive. An army exists to protect the people from outside enemies. A police service exists to protect the people from themselves. When the police become an army, the enemy becomes the people themselves.

In 1989, the US congress authorized the instigation of Program 1033. Initially designed to prosecute the Reagan-era 'War on Drugs', 1033 formalised the transfer of military grade weapons and equipment to civil law enforcement agencies. In the 1990's, the program's aim was extended to include counter-terrorism activities. Post- 2001, the creation of the department of homeland security vastly increased the remit of the program: as did the creation of vast weapon programs and investment to fight the War on Terror.

Since 1997, through 2014, $5.1 BILLIONS worth of war-grade material have been transferred from the armed forces to civilian police officers. In 2013 alone, nearly half a billion dollars of gear was gifted. The scale of the transfers are staggering: 79,288 assault rifles, 11,959 bayonets, 205 grenade launchers. And more than 600 MRAPs, the massive armoured vehicles designed to protect the occupants from directed, kinetic roadside bombs.

Over 8,000 policing agencies across the US are licensed to receive the equipment. Agencies simply apply to the Government's defence logistic agency for formal recognition. Each state has its own coordinator to assist the process. All the police have to do is make up a wish list of what they want from a vast discounted list of war stocks.

San Diego Unified School District, a California collective of over 200 secondary educational schools—applied for, and got, an MRAP all of its own. The district employs its own on-campus policing service. It's stated aim, according to its own website, is to:

'Spend more quality time in developing positive interpersonal relationships with those in our schools and in our community. Personnel engage in daily contact with students, teachers, staff, and members of the community to help promote a positive

learning environment with the schools, and to build ever-growing cooperative partnerships among the schools and the surrounding communities.'

Whether that community outreach required a sixteen-ton, fourteen-foot high armoured truck is a moot point with the school board. The police force mocked up the MRAP in a 'search and rescue' paint job, complete with red-cross markings. The police chief, Ruben Littlejohn, went to great pains to point out the animal had changed its spots:

'There will be medical supplies in the vehicle. There will be teddy bears in the vehicle. There will be trauma kits in the vehicle in the event any student is injured, and our officers are trained to give first aid and CPR.'[31]

He didn't say if the teddy bears would come with body armour as well. The student board didn't buy it. The police had to hand it back. As local parent Andy Hinds pointed out in a local op-ed:

'Why does my kid's elementary school need a tank?'

Not so in Ohio, where the state university campus police acquired an MRAP to use while policing state football games. The force went on say they would remove the gun turret before deploying the MRAP on campus.

In 2008, the Sheriff of Clayton County, Georgia described the War on Drugs as:

'I liken it to the Vietnam War... Hit and miss, there is no clear win — we don't know if we're gaining ground or not. What we want to do is we want to change our strategy. We want to make this more like a Normandy invasion.'[32]

Sergeant Glen French, the commander of a SWAT team in Sterling Heights, Michigan described life on the streets:

'We trainers have spent the past decade trying to ingrain in our students the concept that the American police officer works a battlefield every day he patrols his sector... That is why commanders and tactical trainers stress the fact that even on the most uneventful portion of your tour, you can be subjected to combat at a moment's notice... Why shouldn't officers utilize the same technologies, weapon systems, and tactics that our military comrades do? We should, and we will.'[33]

In 2010, Sterling Heights, where French works, was rated as one of the top 100 cities (above 100,000 residents) in America to raise a family. The city's own website declares Sterling Heights to be the safest city in Michigan state to live.

French's language is interesting. He talks of sectors, battlefields, commanders, tours, weapon systems and tactics. Officers are described as 'he'. In short, it's one big phallus of testosterone-powered warrior philosophy.

Police shootings in the United States have now reached epidemic proportions, particularly towards ethnic minorities. The propensity for police

---

[31] NPR broadcast, September 2014

[32] Huffington Post, August 2013

[33] Huffington Post, August 2013

officers to reach for their handguns first is enshrined in training. A recent police executive research forum survey of 281 police agencies found that the average recruit received 58 hours of firearms training, plus 49 hours of defensive tactical training, but only 8 hours of de-escalation training.

It's a national policing culture of fear. As one Seattle police officer told the 'New York Times':

'Last week, there was a guy in a car who wouldn't show me his hands. I pulled my gun out and stuck it right in his nose, and I go, "Show me your hands now!" That's de-escalation.'[34]

I'd call that terrifying: from every perspective. The War On Terror is now on America's own streets, right at home.

The root cause of this paranoia is 9/11. The net effect of that one event, terrible though it was, has been a fundamental change in the way we see risk. Around every corner, there now lurks a shadowy terrorist. If you doubt me, go enter any large public building, or go get on an airplane. What the twin towers did was mobilise our fears, to the stage now where we live, as a society, on an edge of advanced paranoia. Every traffic accident draws speculation: is the driver a terrorist? Every Muslim is now a suspect, every backpack is a potential bomb.

To counter our fears, our democracies have passed ever more draconian legislation that further erodes our liberties. Phone records, e-mail trails, bio scans for passports and driving licences. Vast databases of information, anonymously trawled from a population both terrified and ignorant of the intrusions their elected officials propagate to supposedly 'protect' liberty.

In the midst of all this noise is the silent conversation that has never taken place. Why did Osama hate us so much that he wished for our destruction? Why does ISIS want to establish a 7th century caliphate? What is so abhorrent about all we hold dear to a significant portion of the planet? What is so repellent about democracy? Once we have had that discussion, what exactly we intend to do about it?

Bombing Syria and Iraq proves nothing. Just as the invasion of Iraq and Afghanistan have fundamentally failed. If there is one lesson of the past fourteen years of conflict, it is that war on its own solves nothing.

In the interim, Europe is being overwhelmed by a tsunami of terrified victims fleeing the wars we created. Amongst the displaced diaspora are some of the greatest Islamic thinkers and philosophers of this generation. The very people that the world needs to challenge this hateful spread of a diseased and warped parasite of one of the world's great philosophical religions.

In 1933, Albert Einstein eloquently gave voice to the fears of a different time, faced with the same existential struggle for fundamental freedom. At the Royal Albert Hall, he addressed an audience of 10,000 to plead for the preservation of the human quest for knowledge and self-development against the motivation of a twisted system that wanted to return freedom of thought to

---

[34] NYT, June 2015

the dark ages:

'Resist the powers which threaten to suppress intellectual and individual freedom,' he stated.

Einstein was right. All the beheadings, the destruction of two thousand years of physical history, the enslavement, the rapes and the murders are but dumb expression of a philosophy of hate. We can't defeat an idea with a bomb from the sky. Radical Islam speaks to the dispossessed and disenfranchised. It offers safe haven to a section of society that does not belong.

That was what 'Our Afghanistan' was really about. Spreading the umbrella of belonging across everybody. Sharing ownership of the dream. ISIS and all the rest are offering the same panacea, only at the cost of your human soul.

The way to win this war is not through bombs and bullets. It is to encourage a debate, a new enlightenment, authored by Islamic scholars and thinkers taking ownership of their own concepts of sovereignty and individual right of self-expression. As Einstein said that day in response to the monster of national socialism:

'It is only men who are free who create the inventions and intellectual works which to us moderns make life worthwhile.'

We in the West must admit that our campaign in Afghanistan to date was largely a failure. In the south, those crucibles of conflict are now largely lost. Musa Qala, Sangin, Nawzad, Maiwand, Arghandab are all now either wholly or partially controlled by the Taliban. In terms of defeating the Taliban, our soldiers fought and died for nothing. We spent money in a river that was largely wasted and only enriched the military-industrial complex.

As British troops departed Southern Afghanistan for the last time, at the end of 2014, General Nick Carter gave his opinion on the Afghan legacy when he was asked was it all worth it:

'We have made a big difference, no doubt about it. Afghanistan is now a country moving in the right direction. And let's not forget the lack of terrorist attacks stemming from the region. None have occurred in the last eight years and that is a tribute to the way the country has been developed. Sure, there are still violent incidents, as we've seen recently, but you have to judge progress in Afghanistan over a long period of time.'[35]

Yes, Afghanistan is moving in the right direction. Only, largely because of the actions of Afghans themselves: despite us, not because of us. It is nonsense to say that there have been no 'terrorist' incidents. There is scarcely a day that goes by in Pakistan or Afghanistan that does not see death and mayhem pass. What he means, I think, is that there have been no terrorist incidents in the UK. There have, however, been plenty elsewhere in Europe and the US, all inspired by our actions since 2001. We are qualifying victory to suit our own definitions.

So what of those achievements? What exactly are they? General Carter goes on to quantify them:

'70,000 kilometres of roads, a sophisticated media system and eight million kids in

---

[35] 'Soldier' magazine interview

schools, of whom 40 per cent are girls. This has led to a civil society which in turn creates even more progress hence last year's presidential elections where... around eight million voted.[36]

Is that it? Really? After fourteen years of war, an operation that is still ongoing, the Afghan army is losing more soldiers than it can replace. Over 4,000 have been killed this year alone. Not a definition of a civil society I can recognise.

As for the schools, over 1,100 are now known to have never opened at all. The $1 billion that the US spent on trying to build a national education system has been largely wasted. The figure of eight million kids? Nobody really knows where that figure came from. The Afghan Ministry of Education openly admits counting kids as being in education for three years after they were last heard of. I know from first-hand experience touring round Panjwai that most of the schoolhouses we built now lie empty. The Taliban scared away the teachers. Everything else was stolen: doors, window frames, desks, chairs. Everything. All that is left is peeling concrete walls.

The truth is that, had we merely left the Afghans to sort out their own country, they would very probably have built a ton of roads and a media network themselves. Even the Taliban managed to build roads. That is natural human development and endeavour in action. Had the country not been convulsed by war, who knows what could have been achieved?

What Carter omits is the 26,000 civilians dead and the 29,000 that have been wounded by the constant fighting that we perpetuated.

Towards the end, the military cycled through as many young soldiers as it could. The Brits called it 'blooding' the new generation. They would come and go for four weeks at a time, long enough to earn a medal, long enough to feel the sun on their faces, inside the camps we built. For too many, Afghanistan was a military play-park. Too few came to learn about the rich and intricate country they had come to nominally help. Nick Carter took that lesson home:

'I decided (in 2009) to exercise command through Afghans. It meant taking risks to inspire them, and to give them the confidence to take over from us.'[37]

Which is where, finally, we are beginning to righten the ship again. The early days of ISAF were generally good days. Now that we have sent the majority of the soldiers home, the residue that remain are achieving the sort of long-term support Afghanistan needs, by training, advising and assisting, not fighting.

Would that it had always been thus. The sadness of it all is that our war in Afghanistan has not left the world a safer place. It is an infinitely more dangerous one.

What happened to my brothers, the real heroes of this tale?

POTF Eric went back to San Francisco, where he works for a power

---

[36] 'Soldier' magazine interview

[37] 'Soldier' magazine interview

utility. I went to see him there. He was bored with life. He missed the war.

COMKAF Steffi moved to the Caribbean, where she goes snorkelling in the sun every day with her beau.

Andy Bratt, who helped measure out the women's park, was forcibly retired not long after I left. Otherwise, he would probably still be there. He was a big fan of Afghan handicrafts. I am sure his Brighton flat echoes with Kandahar.

My first day saviour Maria met the love of her life in KAF. When she got home, she bore him a fine son. She left the air force and now lives a happy life of domesticity in Michigan.

Abrams got his fourth star, which will make him happy. He is now head of US Force Command. Same as Mark Milley, who is now the four-star US Chief of Staff of the Army. Jo Dunford went all the way to nomination for Chairman of the Joint Chiefs. Jim Huggins got his third star and works in leadership development.

Scott Dennis went on to retire from the air force and founded a very successful private consultancy practice.

John Dolan has made lieutenant general. I am happy for him. He is an outstanding leader. He currently commands all US forces in Japan. I'm gonna go visit him someday.

Patrick Kidd retired and now works as a senior consultant for an international management group. Good luck to him. We talk often. He will always be my brother.

Michael Fantini went back to Washington, where he now runs the Pentagon policy desk for the Middle East. Just the right job for Fanman. He is a consummate political general, much in Colin Powell mode. I miss him.

Paul LaCamera went back to run his division. In all his time in Afghanistan, he never gave a single press interview or conference. When he handed over divisional command, a TV crew finally cornered him. When he was asked what he would remember most about his time in command, he said it would be the awfulness of breaking the news to the families of his fallen soldiers. Paul is an extraordinary man, a fine general, humble and modest to the end. He is now back in Iraq, still fighting the war.

Governor Wesa hung on until long after the last bell had rung, before he was replaced. He is lucky to still be alive. The week after my last conference in his palace, the building got hit in a complex attack. Over twenty were killed in a vicious gun battle.

General Raziq is still there. He is an embattled chief of police nowadays. As American support has waned, so has his star. He has made several media interviews in which he has made his personal eulogy. He knows he a marked man. His second in command, Matiullah Khan, a man I personally liked, but with a dark past, was killed earlier this year. The same shadow hangs over Raziq.

General Hamid moved north. This year has been a hanging on by the fingertips operation for the Afghan security forces. In the spring, it looked like the strategic city of Kunduz, in the north, would fall. Hamid took command of

203 Corps there, to stabilize operations. The old stager is still on-point, fighting another campaign, nearly forty years since his first on home soil.

General Sherzai still runs the air wing. His brother is waiting on a government appointment. The family is in something of a transition now. General Sherzai's health has not been good of late. We keep in touch, but he knows the winds of change are coming.

Faizi got promoted to run several airports across the south. He sends me photos of the park at the airport from time to time. It looks good now. The fountains are all finished, the walls are up. Our trees are blooming and the petting zoo thrives. Faizi still wears western clothes, still swears like a trooper, and still dreams of a better Afghanistan.

My brother Feroz graduated with a master's degree in English from Kandahar University. He became a youth ambassador for Afghanistan and is now a regular on television in Pakistan and Afghanistan, speaking of reconciliation and progress. I pray for his safety: he is the future.

The POTF is still there. Another Romanian is still in charge. The paper is still supposedly being printed.

ISAF no longer exists. Neither do any of the bases. By the end of this year, KAF will likely be gone too. All that is left are memories and dust.

On 2nd November 2014, my friend Deputy Governor Abdul Patyal went to Kandahar University to lecture on Pashtun poetry. The 'Our Afghanistan' committee was still going, and Patyal was actively promoting the project on his Twitter feed.

He left his personal protection team outside the classroom, so as not to disturb the students. As he stood to read his verses in class, an unknown gunman leaned in through the window shot him multiple times. He died shortly afterwards.

The OA committee would wind up soon after. Nobody else wanted to take the risk.

Too many have died in this war. Too many good and noble spirits are gone.

My fervent hope for Afghanistan is that it will find another way. Right before he was murdered, that very same day, Deputy Governor Abdul Patyal made one last tweet. I can think of no finer last words to this lengthy note from Kandahar:

'Let's completely drain the hatred from our blood. In one human-istan, let's celebrate love with love.'

APPENDIXES

WHY I LOVE AMERICA

I do love America. I may have railed at the military sometimes, but I will forever be in awe of all that it stands for. There is no nobler statement of the human condition than the right to personal liberty, freedom of expression and the pursuit of happiness.

After I left KAF, I went to work for the European Union. I was shocked at the level of anti-American sentiment I found there. To my generation, the United States is the ultimate guardian of our freedoms.

When each of my American brothers and sisters left KAF, I wrote each of them a private letter, expressing what I feel for their country, told through the prism of my life experiences. This is the last letter I sent to Paul LaCamera, the day I left. It is my testament of thanks for an extraordinary adventure, and my pride at having been an invited part of the American dream:

My first real memory is of the United States.

I remember being woken from sleep by my father, in the middle of the night. He took my by the hand, down to the living room, where our black and white television was showing some snowy, static-ridden pictures. He quietly explained to me that a man was about to land on the moon. He told me it was very risky, and it might not work, but two men were thousands of miles away, about to attempt something that no-one had ever done before. He wanted me to watch it, as I would remember it for the rest of my life.

The next day, I asked my father what the moon was. So, that evening, he took me out to our small back garden, and pointed at a ghostly globe, floating high in the sky. He told me it was even further away than my grandmother's house, which was the biggest journey I had ever taken. I asked him if the men on the moon were going to be OK. So we held hands, and waved to Neil and Buzz, and prayed they would come home safe....

My family is part American. My grandfather came from strongly working class stock. During the Great Depression, Scotland offered little opportunity for steel workers, shipyard welders or railway mechanics, the stock-in-trade of the Millar family. So, my grandfather's brother emigrated.

He went to Virginia, where the war swiftly caught up with him. Uncle Jimmy joined the US Air Force. He was a waist-gunner sergeant in a B-17 and flew 53 missions over Germany before being sent home. He was very, very lucky. Uncle Jimmy never spoke about what he saw, beyond to say he wasn't the hero, all he did was survive.

He had a son, Jack, who looked like the Golden Bear, Jack Nicklaus. He was 6'4", wads of blond hair, tanned and very lean. He married Milly, a classic American beauty.

They came to visit us in Scotland, when I was about 10. I'd never met an American before—but I did have David Cassidy and Donny Osmond on my bedroom wall. I was most obsessed by American teeth. In Britain, we all had squint teeth. Although we had socialised medicine and dental care was free, cosmetic dentistry was unheard of. All my grandparents lost their teeth at an early age. My grannie used to take her teeth out to clean them. When she got older, she used to lose her dentures, and we would be dispatched to find them.

Jack and Milly arrived like movie stars. They both wore plaid suits, Jack with a yellow jumper. In my country, brown was seen as an adventurous colour for a man. When he met me, he picked me up in his arms and smiled straight at me. I told him he had teeth like Donnie Osmond. Jack was a little confused, but he continued to smile indulgently. Neither of my parents were demonstrative people. Jack and Milly kept holding my hand, hugging me.

I loved it. I loved them, and wanted them to be my parents. I just loved America.

They brought my brother and I such amazing gifts. We both got an American flag—the tag said: 'Made with Pride in the USA.'

Jack gave us a baseball bat, a ball and a glove. Neither of us had ever seen baseball, or understood anything about it. We had a game called 'rounders', which girls played, and is a little similar to baseball. When Jack explained the rules, my brother walked off. He wasn't going to play a girl's game. So Jack explained it to me. I was too small to swing the bat, but I treasured his stories, of how he learned the game at school, and how the girls all got to be glamorous cheerleaders.

When Jack and Milly left, I was quite distraught. America had gone home.

A year later, my parents sent me away to boarding school. They say that the British Empire was built on the playing fields of its public schools. The experience was designed to toughen you up—sleeping in dormitories, cold showers, draughty corridors, corporal punishment if you misbehaved. To this day, I have never understood why they sent me away, and the entire experience was thoroughly, thoroughly miserable.

On a Saturday night, we were allowed to watch television from six until ten. We all crowded round the set to watch the staples of terrible British 1970's light entertainment. The night was magical to me. Most weekends, the TV showed a Hollywood movie until seven. The film started broadcast about five-thirty. We were allowed to tune in from six. I spent my childhood imagining first acts.

We watched a veritable feast of American classics. Usually a Western, I grew up watching the last act of John Wayne's battles against the fearsome Comanche. How I longed to be Maureen O'Hara, helping my man on the old frontier. It's no exaggeration to say I learned my sense of right and wrong, of service to your country from watching those old films.

At nine, we got a US cop drama. The teachers closely monitored these for violence. For some reason, Kojak was forbidden. I can't explain how groundbreaking these shows were to my generation. Police officers in my country were unarmed, wore blue tunics, and were usually WW11 veterans, with grey hair. Not in the US.

Starsky and Hutch were my favourites. David Soul was just, well, yummy. David Cassidy bit the dust. One of the first records I ever bought was 'Don't Give Up On Us, Baby'. I adored the way they drove a cool car, wore really funky clothes, spoke in street slang, and just riffed off each other. Our cops never had gut hunches, or were given 24 hours to solve a case. All they did was chase us from the park.

Starsky and Hutch ate peanut butter and jelly sandwiches a lot. We didn't have peanut butter in the UK, unheard of, and 'jelly' to us was what you would call 'jello', a dessert. So I tried to make my own peanut butter and jelly sandwich, by spreading a piece of bread with salted butter, then sticking some of my father's salted peanuts in the butter and adding strawberry jello. It looked REALLY odd, and tasted terrible. My father laughed at me, but, in my imagination, David Soul ate these, so I was happy.

Later, I was to fall in love with 'Dallas', 'Hill Street Blues' and 'Petrocelli'. Everything just seemed so much more alive and glamorous—and so BIG. Everything was big in America—the hair, the teeth, the lapels on the suits, the houses and the cars... I so wanted to exchange my own drab country and live with my Uncle Jack.

When I joined the army, I got posted to Berlin. Part of my job, which I took terribly seriously, was to go through Check Point Charlie and tour around the East, counting all the Russian war stocks we could see. It was a bone job that nobody else wanted, but, to me, it was real spy stuff. We had a terribly posh black Range Rover to drive, with a British flag on the front, and we all wore our dress uniforms, to impress the East Germans.

We had nothing on the US. The MP's at Charlie wore their green uniforms, with trousers bloused into their black boots, with white laces. I remember they had highly polished helmets, with "MP" across the front, and white gloves. When we passed, they saluted in that US flat hand way—just like Big John had done in 'The Sands of Iwo Jima'. They had an M-60 tank, the one with the big searchlight on the front, pointing straight at the Soviet side. It was as raw an expression of super-power strength as you could get.

Although the Brits had 3 battalions in Berlin, our only shop contained one row of dog-eared newspapers and out of date sweets. On special days, we got to go to the US PX. There was stuff in there I had never seen before, mostly strange food—Oreos, popcorn, Hershey bars. What I remember the most was that it was just never-ending. There was just so much stuff.

In the UK, we had a restaurant chain, called 'Wimpys', which was a greasy spoon kind of place. The food was rough and ready, but it had waitress service, you sat at a table and ate off china plates (usually cracked), with a knife and a fork.

At the PX fast-food outlets, your food arrived in a cardboard box, down a chute, pretty much as soon as you ordered it. That was such a thrill, we re-ordered, just to see the box whizz down to us. And what food! The sugar and salt rush was ridiculous. We didn't have hamburgers in Scotland, we had pork shaped into what we called "flat sausage". I sat in my first McDonalds, with a groovy smile, eating with my fingers for the first time, and stuffed myself with all the unhealthy, empty calories I could get my hands on.

It wasn't until 1988 that I got to visit the US for the first time. I was working for a TV company and they sent me to do a couple of stories there, to do with US law and order. The sense of palpable excitement as I boarded the silver "American Airlines" jet is something I will never forget. Instead of a proper 'good morning, ladies and gentlemen', the pilot opened his announcement with; 'how'ya all doin' back there, folks?' I was convinced papa Walton was at the stick.

We flew into Detroit, after hours and hours of being over land. It was the first time I got a sense of just how big the land mass of North America really is.

We had very few black people in Scotland at that time, so Detroit was a revelation. My only reference point was my love of Motown. I'd spent my youth watching The Temptations and The Supremes do their wonderful dance routines, in their wonderful costumes, awkwardly attempting to ape their slick routines across my parent's living room. The first time I saw the Jackson 5 do 'Rockin' Robin', I just sat there, completely mesmerised. Off I trotted through Motor City and worshipped at the home of Motown. Literally. It was hallowed ground to me. Dirty, run down, but completely authentic. I stood where Marvin and Smokey had stood, in awe that I had finally made it to America.

We were doing a comparison between Scottish and US policing. At that time in the UK, a new imported American crime theory of 'the broken window' was becoming fashionable, along with 'zero tolerance' areas. Detroit, although not nearly as bad as it is now, seemed like Ground Zero to go see what it was all about.

So I got to meet the real Starsky and Hutch, in the form of Officer Savage, of the Michigan State Troopers. I have never seen so many guns on one person. He was a SWAT officer, so he had pistols, shot-guns, assault rifles and sniper rifles in his patrol car. I sat in the back as he took me round some of the tough neighbourhoods of Detroit. He was under strict orders to look after me. Just as well. I was petrified. He got out to do a traffic stop and told me: 'stay in the car and keep the doors locked. If anything happens, hit this button on the dash—and there's a back-up piece in the glove compartment.'

How I prayed. At the end of the shift, I swaggered in to the shift room with the air of a veteran. I had survived a day in Detroit.

Then came the Gulf War. I went to cover the war. My country sent 30,000 troops. It was my first really big war, and a huge under-taking for the UK. I flew in a C-130, to Al-Jubail, in Saudi Arabia, where the British movement folks met us, in a small tent, by the side of the runway. I'd never been in the desert before. My senses were overcome by the smells, the light and the heat.

The UK effort was a mere appetiser to the USA going to war. Day after day, one a minute, 24/7, an airliner from the States would land and disgorge thousands upon thousands of men—and a few women. That one runway contained more aircraft than the entire RAF possessed. Row upon row of attack helicopters (we had none at that time), Chinooks (the UK had a sum total of 3) and fighter jets, just like the ones Maverick flew.

Then there was the camp. We lived in tents. The US flew in specially designed pods, like trailers, that slotted together to form living and office accommodation. Everything we had just seemed so inadequate.

The internet hadn't been invented. We were lucky if we got a letter a fortnight. Navigation was done by dead reckoning, map and compass, or the stars. There was one GPS in the entire British armoured division. My grandfather, who fought in the desert, under Montgomery, would have fit straight in.

The US had it all.

GPS was a military system then. Down to company level, all your vehicles had it. You also had funky uniforms. We worked with the US Marines. They had different uniforms for day and night. We didn't even have desert uniforms, we all ran around in green stuff. To get a US Marine desert night-fighting smock was military-Gucci nirvana. That, and a US camp bed. We didn't have any issued. We slept on the ground. That aluminium folding bed was stolen, acquired, bartered and traded for anything we owned. The US army must have lost tens of thousands of those to us hard-up Brits.

At the end of the war, I got to go into Kuwait City, to help the press cover the liberation of the British Embassy. We flew into the airport, which had been taken by the US Marines. On the runway, there was the still-smouldering wreckage of a British Airways 747. I asked some very happy Marines in their Sheridan tank what had happened. Those Iraqis must have left with a scorched earth policy to destroy our Jumbo Jet. The Marines just smiled a little, and said even less. Hey, it's not every day you get to smoke hundreds of millions of dollars worth of aircraft.

After we took back the Embassy, we flew north, over Mutla Ridge, where a retreating Iraqi Division had been caught in the open by US air power. I had never, and I hope I never see again, anything like it. Literally mile after mile of vehicle, burned beyond recognition, bodies reduced to charred flesh. It was industrial warfare at its most lethal.

That was when I got to be in the same room as General Schwarzkopf, when he came in to brief us on the peace ceremony. He really was John Wayne. For a start, he was huge. He wore simple harness webbing that looked like braces on his frame. After a short speech on victory and sacrifice, he swept by us with a practised wave, and was gone. We all stood there, speechless. Ulysses had left the building....

I got to travel to the States a lot after that. Not just the usual places like New York and LA. More than half the individual states. By then I was making real money in TV-land and kept on coming back, three times a year. I hiked through the Grand Canyon, blew it all on red in Vegas, drove the Pacific Coast to Carmel, attempted to play golf in Hilton Head and fell in love with the Smoky Mountains. I had lunch in World Trade Centre, in the basement, in a sports bar, with a load of traders in suits and suspenders, laughing with them as we watched an NBA championship game on TV. How they welcomed me! I often wonder what happened to them.

Later that year, I got to live my dream, as I got a documentary commissioned to cover the Old West. We flew to Colorado and headed north, across the Great Plains, through the Dakotas, Wyoming and Montana. Our guide was a real-life honorary colonel in the 2nd Cavalry. He lived his life as a horse-soldier from the 1870's. We met him in Bismarck. He literally came into the hotel in his blue uniform, with his Colt pistol, to meet us. Nobody else even turned side-ways, but I could hardly speak. It was my youth, watching the 3rd act of Fort Apache, come to re-visit me.

Duke (yes, he really was called that) taught me to ride Western-style, and to fire a Winchester. He took me to a Western store, where I got a real pair of cow-gal boots, a yellow bandana and a really big hat. He showed me how to do-si-do and to grape-vine, and explained what a Dixie cup was for. He told me he only had five bullets in his Colt revolver. In the chamber under the hammer, he kept a five dollar billed, tightly rolled, so he wouldn't shoot his foot off and there would be something to pay for his burial.

We went to Mount Rushmore, the Crazy Horse memorial mountain, Wounded Knee, saw the Oregon Trail and buffalo grazing, before standing at the bottom of the flattop mountain from Close Encounters. Then, we rode Custer's last campaign, on our horses, as he brought to life the Greasy Grass and that last moment of utter madness. We ate in the log cabin that Big John had eaten in, when he was filming Red River, and I sat in his huge rocking chair (at least they said it was his chair) and thought life could not be finer....

The Army asked me to come back full-time after that, so off I went to Bosnia and Kosovo, doing the same IO job again.

The US in the Balkans couldn't get enough of what I did. My section comprised of a staff of two—me and my driver—and I had a wonderful time, driving all over the Balkans, helping out the Ambassador and the 1st ID. I'd travelled a lot in Bosnia, as here, as a journalist, and I knew a lot of folks, again, same as here. It was a fun time.

In 2001, times were quiet. I was in Cyprus, doing IO for the peacetime garrison, bored out of my mind with organising cocktail parties and BBQs for the brigadier. I came up with a scheme to thru-hike The Appalachian Trail. A chum of mine is the author Bill Bryson, who wrote a wonderful book on the AT, a bestseller called 'A Walk In The Woods'. We'd travelled through the Mid-East together, making a film on Lawrence of Arabia. He inspired me to walk the 2,200 miles from Georgia to Maine.

So off I set, with five months of unpaid leave authorised. I climbed Springer Mountain, near Dahlonega, GA, on April 1, 2001. It was the start of the most wonderful summer of my life—an American summer.

Along the way, I met extraordinary folks. Not just the wandering community of gypsies that make up each season of thru-hikers, but just the most open, welcoming and genuine Americans you could ever hope to meet as human beings. On countless occasions, they opened their homes and their hearts to me, the wearied traveller.

And the scenery! Oh, my word, what beautiful country. The trail is largely wooded, so the views are obscured until you climb to altitude. Then, the most stunning vistas God ever created just burst into view. Often time, I'd just burst into tears at the grandeur of it all. A land so big that, even in the 21st Century, no matter which way you looked, there was no sign of man anywhere.

I stood on rattle-snakes, encountered bears, got charged by an elk, scared a ground-hog and watched a beaver make a dam. I got so hill fit, I could walk 40 miles a day and not feel tired. I learned to live on ten pounds of personal equipment, sleeping under stars, on the ground, to the stage where a bed felt uncomfortable.

I summited Mount Katahdin, in Maine, on September 23rd 2001. I'd listened to the towers come down on my small transistor radio, in the wilderness of Maine. I knew my world was about to change. I had my army beret with me, for photos for the boys back home. On my last night in Maine, I went to a bar with my fellow thru-hikers, wearing my beret. I'd checked my mail and my orders had come thru. I was to get back as soon as possible. The bar-keep shouted:

'Hey guys, there's a paratrooper in the house...'

Neither I, nor my friends, bought a beer all night. A week later, I was deployed.

In those days, Afghan really was a quiet, unseen war. All the troops were older, wiser and more circumspect. Plus, the Afghans just loved us. We ripped around in hired 4X4s, wore what we liked, went where we liked, and did what we liked, as long it was in the cause of freedom. The boys looked after me, and I did my IO bit. When we went to a village, I went in and met the elders, took tea, chatted and smiled, while the boys did the hard stuff. We drove all the way from Mazar to Maymana, then back across to Kunduz without firing a shot. The first liberating troops, I will never forget it.

I spent the next five years dotting between Afghan, Bosnia and Iraq. It was mostly fun, but I got tired. In late '07, I was involved in an IED in Kunduz, with the Germans. We got lazy, kept the same patrol routes, and I ended up being medevacked home. I retired and joined the police. I thought it would the same buzz, just allowing me to stay at home, but I got bored. When NATO called, I jumped at this last adventure.

Once here, yet again, the US rode to the rescue. Yours is a country of re-invention, of second chances. Exactly the opportunity you have extended to me here. Lord knows, I can be difficult, stubborn to the point of self-destruction, and completely focussed on my own lane.

However, you have granted me the chance to show you what I can do—and to share that knowledge with others. This time has been the most glorious combat experience of my life, no exceptions. Yes, there have been frustrations. Yes, the mid-level majors and light colonels have gripped me. Yes, I am tired now. But, boy, what a ride!

I have felt enormously privileged to sit and watch and listen to you. Men like you have that solidity I saw on that boarding school television, all those years ago. I have felt safe, accepted and involved in your company. Respected, even. I will never forget those moments.

I didn't want to end this way, in failure. I've cried every night since I heard that my job had been cut, and could not be saved. I feel as if I have let folks down. Forgive me for retreating a bit into myself, for not writing my blogs and doing my updates. It's been a very emotionally trying withdrawal. Yet, I know that, had you had your way, I would still be here. That is a comfort.

I am pleased that Paradise Park will be built. It's been a long journey to get it to the stage where it is ready to go to contract. I am also delighted to see that the 'Our Afghanistan' project has been adopted by our Afghan friends. The last picture I received from my boys downtown was of a professional looking ANA soldier, standing in front of a huge billboard, which boldly advertised the Afghan Army. All surmounted by, 'Our Afghanistan'.

Together with the collage at the airport ECP, I am rather proud of that work. It's just a shame that NATO didn't see it that way. I do wonder how we can ever take credit for much of what has happened here, when it is truly Afghan effort, not ours. How many good ideas have we shot down over the years?

What has been achieved this year, though, has been real and concrete progress. It is because of your leadership, your empathy, compassion and understanding. I am grateful that I was allowed to ride your coattails for part of the ride…

It's at an end now, though. My time here is over. I've not been silly with my money. I've put a bit aside, enough to dream once more, and tick off a bit more of my bucket-list. What will I do? Well, at some stage, I think I'm gonna go back to the US. I've not been there since 2001. If the seasons work, I'll walk another trail, climb some mountains, breathe that clean air and renew my faith in mankind.

You have such an extraordinary country. I have been so blessed to have been allowed to share in that lofty ambition and freedom you are given as your birth-right. I can think of no other place in the World that so allows a person to change, to aspire, to succeed. Thank-you for all that you have given me.

God Bless America.

JOINT INFLUENCE OPERATIONS FUSION CELL PITCH

Definition of Influence Operations: "Military operations that alter or change attitudes and perceptions in the target audience"
Definition of corporate marketing: "Marketing is what you do, branding is what you are"
The fusion cell will join both concepts:
"To promote Afghan national unity and pride in order to foster benign acceptance of the rule of law and the pillars of state"

INTRODUCTION

The international military mission is two-fold:

1. To deny safe haven to Al-Qaeda and other terror organisations
2. To create a viable Afghan state that is a credible actor in assisting regional stability

To achieve this, it is intrinsic that the Afghan people buy into the concept of the Islamic Republic of Afghanistan, its government and security forces, to accept the rule of law and the pillars of state.

It is not necessary that they like us, just that they like the alternative a lot less…

A brand is your promise to your audience. The foundation of the brand is your logo. Packaging messaging and promotional materials—all of which should integrate your logo—communicate your brand. It is the unifying identifier that defines a disparate range of products.

In the retail sector, consistent, strategic branding leads to strong brand equity, creating the added value brought to products or services that allows a supplier to charge a price premium higher for their brand than identical, unbranded products can command *(see enclosure 2)*.

The added value intrinsic to brand equity comes in the form of perceived quality or emotional attachment. This does not happen overnight, it is the result of constant allegorical messaging that produces complementary sense memory and association in the target audience.

In this sphere, our brand is Afghanistan—as one entity.

WHY?

Afghanistan is currently under-going an attitudinal shift. The election process, which marks the first democratic regime change since the formation of the country, also marks the decline of traditional influence-makers; war lords, mullahs and local power brokers.

12 years of relative peace have granted a new generation of Afghan the opportunity to gain exposure to international influence, education and economic improvement. Near total access to media platforms has allowed a free media to promulgate serious discussion of philosophical concepts such as justice, freedom of expression, human rights and life expectations.

Integral to that discussion has been a nascent sense of national "ownership".

As the international presence wanes, the Afghan people are being asked to fill the battle-space, across such diverse areas as economic stewardship, governance, security operations, education and rule of law. It is critical to the future of Afghanistan that this development is fostered within a relatively transparent bubble of security and governance.

Looking to the past, the country disintegrated, following the Soviet intervention, due to a critical lack of effective governance. This led to a splintering of the country into local factions. Whilst part of that break-up was caused by the withdrawal of logistic and financial support by the Soviets, the regime was critically ham-strung by a lack of acceptance and support within the population.

The post-Soviet regime never enjoyed the benign acceptance by the people of the pillars of state and the security forces. A significant section of Afghan society turned to support of the insurgency, which, in turn, drew on that support to present a united front against the regime. The Afghan government was therefore doomed to failure, regardless of tactical military success.

As a developing democratic state, Afghanistan again faces the major challenge of large-scale withdrawal of international resources. The Afghan people have shown remarkable resilience in shouldering the burden of self-determination. However, history gives them cause for concern.

This country has never enjoyed strong, central government. The metrics of geography, poverty, ethnic division and language will probably ensure that is always the case. However, there is strong evidence to suggest that Afghanistan is regaining a sense of national identity, primarily through a relatively free media and increased education and awareness. For example, the national pride in the achievements of Afghanistan's sporting teams and the indignant condemnation of the recent Serena Hotel attack.

The purpose of the joint influence operations fusion cell will be to promulgate inclusive ownership, through awareness and understanding of the work being done by the Afghan Government and security forces, in overcoming those challenges. Thereby, to multiply a sense of pride in national unity and achievement, and winning the trust and acceptance of the Afghan people in the Afghan state.

Put simply, we sell this Afghanistan better than the enemy sells its brand.

WHAT?

Election monitoring has high-lighted three major areas of concern to the Afghan people:

1. Security (freedom of movement, safe and secure environment)
2. Justice (transparent, inclusive, objective)
3. Education (including economic development)

These strands will be gathered under the branding umbrella of:
"Our Afghanistan"

The purpose of marketing tactical achievement in these areas will be to:

1. Deny legitimacy to INS shadow government, thereby removing the oxygen of INS acceptance, including rejection of acts of violence
2. Foster governance by consent
3. Create "ownership" of Afghan national identity
4. Support security operations and rule of law by ensuring community acceptance and involvement

This is NOT about achieving localized effect, either temporally or geographically, although framework operations would occur in both areas. What branding currently exists (Sada-E-Azadi, Bayan) is well-known to be ISAF-owned. This branding concept is entirely Afghan-owned. The concept is further strategic in thought, operating to set the conditions for increased success twelve months from now, in the deep battle-space, post-ISAF mission completion.

See enclosure 1 for sample imagery. Note the similarity in messaging to the themes expressed in the McDonalds imagery in Enclosure 2.

HOW?

Exploitation is achieved by ensuring the horizontal and vertical integration of influence effect during tactical events. In effect, IO operations exist in three phases:

1. Pre-operational planning
2. Execution
3. Post-operational exploitation

In general, mission effect here tends to be horizontally integrated at the tactical level—J3/5 shop, localized leafleting, messaging, followed by post-visits, such as FET engagement. The aim is generally tactically focused to assist in minimizing kinetic response to ISAF/ ANSF troops.

The difference with this approach is that it is intended to pre-set the conditions for success before, during and after events, by strategic level integration of messaging that will pre-form the human landscape.

To refer back to enclosure 2, we are McDonalds. The enemy is a new fast food restaurant that has opened next door, selling the same menu. Our market domination is assisted by the branding association McDonalds has acquired. This is NOT local dynamics—store efficiency, local demographic etc—it is associative brand loyalty that achieves a market effect.

Strategic vs. tactical operations.

Vertical integration comes in two ways:

1. Temporally. By assigning strategic aims that look to shape the market as we see it 12 months from now. The deep battle-space.
2. Physically. By diversity of media platforms and products, in particular mobile and net-enabled technology.

Finally, brand marketing is only effective when depth of market penetration is objectively measured. Target audience analysis (acceptance of institutions, brand recognition and loyalty) are ephemeral qualities that require constant evaluation and a capacity to adjust the campaign narrative.

WHO?

Brand ownership does not just encompass the target audience—it also encompasses the product originators.

The concept would be to partner and advise Afghan agency representatives, on a near one-to-one basis, from the following:

1. ANSF (ANP, ANA)
2. Governance (PGov)

WHERE?

The natural forum would be the Joint Security Co-Ordination Centre, as an adjunct to the discussion. This will ensure tactical inter-operability and strategic co-operability and ownership.

WHEN?

The immediate critical battle-space is about to occur, with the establishment of a new Government. However, the campaign should look forward, to the environment post-2014, when international engagement is minimised. It is then that GIRoA will have to stand on its own two feet, and the time when national will be most tested.

CONCLUSION

Although RC-S and ISAF have introduced many different IO components to the battle, they have never been brand-marketed. Nor, indeed, have they ever been seen as anything other than an adjunct to ISAF operations. In many ways, the target audience has been less the Afghan people and more ISAF general staff officers.

Further, the effort has been hampered by the insistence on maintaining a tactical effect, in general not further than the duration of the current rotation.

I can think of no other ISAF institution that has created such a capacity. This proposal is a legacy project—both in Afghan critical capability and in long-term perceptions of a viable Afghan state. It is a hybrid of corporate and military thinking.

However, if we are to be serious about the long-term success of a post-ISAF Afghanistan, it is a project that I would firmly propose is vital to the future engagement and consensual acceptance by the population of the Afghan government and security forces.

Abi Austen
140327

PHOTOS

Here's the hat that gave the book its title…shorn of the offending rank badge but complete with silver bling!

Kandahar's most-famous artist, Durukshan, getting his certificate from my brother Mike Fantini. Behind them both is the 'Our Afghanistan' mural at the airport, which was the catalyst for the whole OA program.

Doing the initial OA brief at the Kandahar Governor's palace, flanked by my best bud Feroz. He took mad risks for us; I worried about him so. And this is the outfit that earned me a complaint for being too revealing!

Where all the good times happened. This is The Boardwalk. It's nothing much, just some planks of wood in a dustbowl, but it was home to me for the happiest years of my life.

Opening the airport runway. From left to right in the front: Amanullah Faizi, under the US flag, my brother Soak, General John Dolan, Ambassador Warlick, Minister Najafi, and Governor Toryalai Wesa. Behind us you can see Kandahar Airport terminal, quite a wondrous piece of US design.

Just a normal day at KAF. The planes, people, and stuff just never stopped coming and going. The flight-line went like a fair 24/7.

Looking out over the back ramp of an Afghan air force Mi-17. Down below, the typical Kandahar landscape, of scrubland and desert.

Out on the ground in the Arghandab with the Afghan army. Behind me, you can see my two 'guardian angels'. Trust came at a premium in Kandahar. My friend beside me is Sgt Habibullah. We used to go out together a lot. He is still there, still leading, still fighting for Afghanistan.

The sharp end of the stick. These boys are from the ANA, and we are about to do an airborne insertion into the Panjwai.

My favourite photo of 2013. After all the upsets, General Sherzai, right, came to see Soak off, when he left KAF. Here my favourite men are sharing a special moment. I liked it when we all got on.

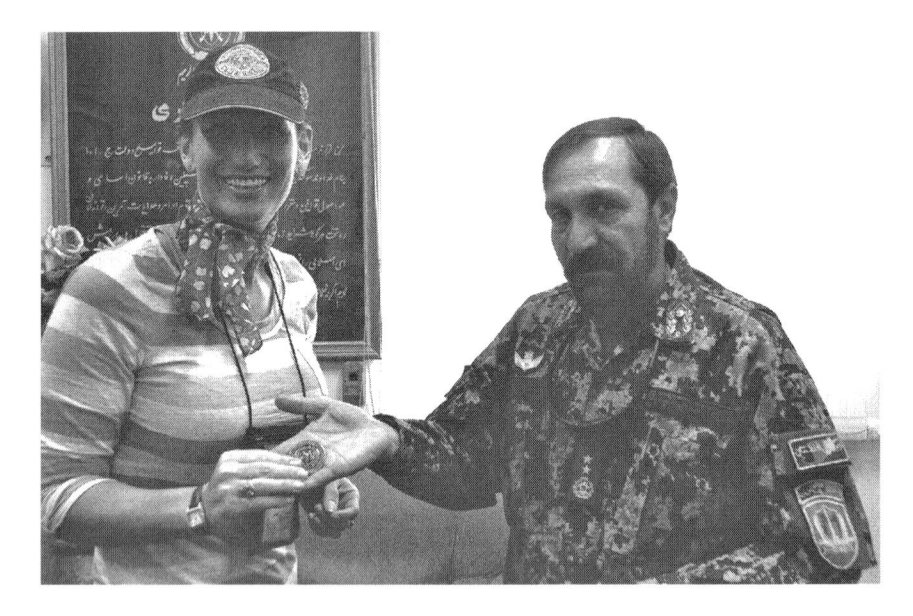

General Hamid, CG of the Afghan 205 Corps, is a humble and undemonstrative man, but a leader with a core of steel. I admired him very much. He is giving me an Afghan medal, of which I am very proud.

My last supper with my two besties. On the left, General Mike Fantini, and on the right General Patrick Kidd. They are brilliant men, exceptional leaders. It was my privilege to serve with them.

The last time General Paul LaCamera, CG 4ID, and I met, right before I left. I admire Paul so much. He is an extraordinary leader and a wonderful friend and brother to me.

My last night, all the generals came to see me off. General Sherzai has just given me this silk carpet, which is so heavy I couldn't carry the damned thing… I loved that man, and his carpet now has pride of place in my orangerie.

AUTHOR'S NOTE

Please check out:

www.lordrobertsvalet.com

for maps, pictures, background and video

Or find
Lord Roberts Valet
on Facebook

ABOUT THE AUTHOR

Abi Austen has been a paratrooper, army officer, police officer, journalist, award-winning documentary-maker, author, diplomat and adventurer.

Lord Roberts' Valet is the story of her three years as a senior advisor in Kandahar, Afghanistan.

She lives in Kyiv, Ukraine, where she is working on another novel.

Printed in Poland
by Amazon Fulfillment
Poland Sp. z o.o., Wrocław